Brooks-Cork Library
Shelton State Community College
DATE DUE

BLACK SUN

NICHOLAS GOODRICK-CLARKE

BLACK SUN

Aryan Cults, Esoteric Nazism and the Politics
of Identity

New York University Press • *New York and London*

NEW YORK UNIVERSITY PRESS
New York and London

© 2002 by Nicholas Goodrick-Clarke
Nicholas Goodrick-Clarke has asserted his right to be identified
as the author of this work.

Library of Congress Cataloging-in-Publication Data
Goodrick-Clarke, Nicholas.
Black sun : Aryan cults, esoteric Nazism and the politics of identity /
Nicholas Goodrick-Clarke.
p. cm.
Includes index.
ISBN 0–8147–3124–4 (cloth : alk. paper)
1. Neo-Nazism.   2. Occultism.   I. Title.
JC481 .G567 2001
320.53'3—dc21   2001004429

New York University Press books are printed on acid-free paper,
and their binding materials are chosen for strength and durability.

Manufactured in the United States of America

10   9   8   7   6   5   4   3   2   1

Contents

All illustrations appear as a group following p. 186.

Introduction

THE RELIGIOUS AND MYTHIC elements of German National Socialism often made the Third Reich resemble a cult in power. The pageantry of
the Nazi rallies and their quasi-liturgical nature were matched by the extraordinary fervor of the huge crowds in attendance. Most participants were
caught up in an intense atmosphere of collective excitement and self-surren-
der. Hitler's undoubted charisma and the assiduous development and cultivation of the *Führerkult* since the earliest years of the movement were crucial
factors in the construction of Nazi religiosity. Huge congregations, banners,
sacred flames, processions, a style of popular and radical preaching, prayers-
and-responses, memorials and funeral marches were all essential props for
the cult of race and nation, the mission of Aryan Germany and victory over
her enemies. The messianic figure of Adolf Hitler, the savior of Germany, tow-
ered over the entire project.

National Socialist ideology was also deeply imbued with ideas drawn from
radical religious imagination. The belief in a Jewish world conspiracy, ostensibly backed by the notorious invention *The Protocols of the Elders of Zion*, provided the image of a demonic enemy. Nazi anti-Semitism was rooted in this
apocalyptic demonology, which blamed the Jews for all ills, including liberalism, communism, the corruption of morals, and the downfall of a traditional
world. The notion of national regeneration was also presented in an apocalyptic spirit: only the destruction of the Jews could guarantee the salvation of
Germany in a racially pure millennium. Alfred Rosenberg, the chief Nazi Party
ideologue, was an early publicist of the *Protocols*, establishing their core status
in Nazi philosophy during the early 1920s. Dietrich Eckart, Hitler's mentor in
Munich, held a gnostic-dualist view of the Jews and their antagonistic role in
German national life. Hitler's own belief in a Jewish world conspiracy remained a life-long conviction, finding terrible fulfillment in the Holocaust.

In an earlier book, *The Occult Roots of Nazism*, I traced these ideas of
racial election, demonology and millennium among Austrian German nationalists prior to the First World War. That study was intended to show how

I

quasi-religious and even occult ideas could bolster German identity in response to the perceived threats of liberalism, laissez-faire capitalism, and the rise of subject nationalities at the beginning of the last century. At this time, large-scale industry, new metropolitan cities, the growth of capitalist finance and organized labor were all perceived as threats by traditional groups. These *völkisch* Ariosophists offered a defensive ideology of "Aryan" German folk identity as a panacea for unwelcome, disruptive challenges to traditional status, custom and political authority. Against the rise of anthropology and eugenics, these sectarians embraced ideas of race and stigmatized the Jews as the supposed agents and beneficiaries of liberalism and modernity. Their occult notions of racial superiority combined with anti-Semitism and millenarian myths of national regeneration to find ultimate expression in the ideology of the National Socialist movement.

Multicultural societies face a similar challenge today. In 1900 the white European races constituted some 35 percent of world population. Owing to declining birthrates among whites in advanced industrial nations, coupled with the explosion of Third World population due to improved medicine, sanitation and increasing industrialization, that figure is now just under 10 percent in global terms. Guest workers, immigrants, ecomomic migrants, refugees and asylum seekers all represent major population flows, bringing the population surplus of developing countries into lands traditionally settled by white races of European descent. These advanced industrial economies are absorbing ever larger levels of immigration, and their political commitment to multiracialism is now an article of faith. Today, the United States and most European nations are facing a demographic shift against their historic native stocks. The resulting issue of white identity recapitulates the dilemma of Austrian Germans fearing a loss of influence in the old Habsburg Empire.

Black Sun examines the survival and revival of "Aryan" racial ideas in response to the challenges of the postwar world. More than half a century after the defeat and disgrace of Nazism and fascism, the far right is again challenging the liberal order of the Western democracies for political space. Radical ideologies are feeding on the threats of economic globalization, affirmative action and Third World immigration. The book explores the farther shores of right-wing extremist ideology. Aryan cults, aristocratic paganism, anti-Semitic demonology, Eastern religion and the occult supply underground beliefs to individuals and groups who fear a loss of status, cultural tradition and identity in the emergent multicultural societies of the United States and Europe.

The scene is set with a historical review of neo-Nazism in the United States and Britain. Here Nazism revived as an extremist response to communism, liberalism and more especially the desegregation of African Americans and colored immigrants. In their quest for a radical counterideology, American and British neo-Nazis championed Hitler and National Socialism against liberalism and the presence of ethnic minorities. Their underground publications eulogize National Socialism as a racial policy to guarantee the global preeminence of the white race for all time. However, despite their overriding concern with colored races, neo-Nazi ideology still identified the Jews as the demonic adversary of the white Aryan peoples. Here the Jews are regarded as the architects of a multiracial world order, which supposedly dissolves all nations, traditions and loyalties, before the final accomplishment of Jewish world conquest.

The survival of anti-Semitism in a modern racist discourse predominantly concerned with opposition to ethnic groups highlights the enduring demonology of Nazism. Like Gnostics cut off from the transcendent deity in a benighted world, American and British neo-Nazis claim that Hitler and Nazism offer the only hope of racial survival to white nations populated with growing ethnic minorities. Anti-Semitism acts as a manichaean dualist heresy dividing the world into forces for good and evil. Millenarian racial cleansing and the demonology of a Jewish world conspiracy are the defining moments of such neo-Nazi religiosity.

From the 1950s to the 1970s, neo-fascist and neo-Nazi groups essentially imitated the past with uniformed cadres, swastika flags and marches. The fringe political parties remained the preserve of fanatics, and recruitment was strictly limited to those who admired fascism or were convinced anti-Semites. Even if German nationalism was transformed into a global ideology of white racism, the historical and political experience of Nazi Germany remained the dominant model for emulation. This historic allegiance was the hallmark of the neo-Nazi cults associated with George Lincoln Rockwell and Colin Jordan, together with their successors and followers in the postwar Anglo-American world. Hostages to the memory of German National Socialism, the Anglo-American neo-Nazis remained trapped in a nostalgic cult of Hitler worship, while universal condemnation of the Third Reich and the Holocaust blocked any prospect of political success.

As in the case of the Ariosophists in the early twentieth century, political isolation in a hostile world committed to liberalism has led many neo-Nazi and neo-fascist groups to embrace occult notions of ancient Aryan wisdom. From the 1970s onward, right-wing extremists began to repackage the old ideology of Aryan racism, elitism and force in new cultic guises involving esotericism and Eastern religions. In Austria and Germany, the former SS man Wilhelm Landig revived the ariosophical mythology of Thule, the supposed polar homeland of the ancient Aryans. He coined the idea of the Black Sun, a substitute swastika and mystical source of energy capable of regenerating the Aryan race. He popularized esoteric ideas current among the pre-Nazi *völkisch* movement and the SS relating to Atlantis, the World Ice Theory, prehistoric floods and secret racial doctrines from Tibet. He also drew attention to Nazi interest in the medieval Cathars and Grail traditions as an alternative Germanic religion of dualist heresy. In Italy the aristocratic elitism and esoteric Aryan-Nordic traditions of Julius Evola inspired a whole generation of postwar neo-fascists. When wanted far-right terrorists fled abroad, they carried Evola's ideas to far-right parties and groups elsewhere in Europe. By the late 1980s this little-known philosopher had become a major political icon of opposition to democracy and liberalism in the West.

Julius Evola's interest in the Indo-Aryan world embraced the exotic world of Hinduism and Tantrism. Following the early lead of James Madole's adoption of Theosophy and Hindu caste hierarchies, neo-Nazi ideology assimilated Eastern themes in the mystical doctrines of Savitri Devi and Miguel Serrano, currently hot tips in the racist underground. Savitri Devi, the French-born Nazi-Hindu prophetess, described Hitler as an avatar of Vishnu and likened Nazism to the cult of Shiva with its emphasis on destruction and new creation. Adopting the Hindu cycle of the ages, she claimed mankind is living in the Kali Yuga (the dismal dark age), which can only be ended by regenerative violence, war and genocide. Miguel Serrano, a retired Chilean diplomat and author, blends exotic oriental religion with his Gnostic-Manichaean doctrine of "Esoteric Hitlerism." Tracing the semi-divine Aryans to extraterrestial origins, Serrano recommends kundalini yoga to repurify "mystical Aryan blood" to its former quality of divine light. His other themes include a Gnostic war against the Jews, the Black Sun, the Hitler avatar and Nazi UFOs in Antarctica. Neo-Nazism has thereby acquired new myths and meanings for a younger generation.

Another revaluation of Nazism resulted from the demonization of Nazism in numerous thrillers and accounts of Nazi occultism published in sensational paperback editions during the 1960s and 1970s. Here Nazism was mystified and romanticized into a neo-Gnostic religion with links to oriental mythology, secret Tibetan doctrines, and demonic inspiration. The effect was to dehistoricize the facts of dictatorship, terror, war and oppression into a mythological tableau. Reality soon followed popular literature. Already in the early 1970s, satanist groups in the United States flirted with Nazi themes as symbolic of the forbidden, dark side of life. These experiments in the shock value of Nazism were superseded in the 1990s by Nazi satanic cults linking anti-Christian paganism to a transgressive praise of Hitler and the Third Reich. In America, Europe and Australia, such "darkside" lodges espouse a vulgar Nietzschean worship of force backed by anti-Christian, elitist and Social Darwinist doctrines.

In the 1980s and 1990s, the far right witnessed a dramatic revival in Europe and America, especially among an alienated white youth and lower-income groups increasingly marginalized by new high-tech industries and the advancing integration of ethnic minorities in their communities. The fast increase of Hispanic and Third World immigration in the United States and corresponding immigration from developing countries into Western Europe has fueled fresh fears of racial inundation. The collapse of the Soviet Union and Yugoslavia has led to further migrations involving Gypsies and East European nationals to Western Europe. Free-trade agreements, the collapse of traditional manufacturing industries and the export of service jobs abroad through computer communications are stimulating racism and hostility toward liberalism.

Globalization is unleashing a massive flow of capital, information, skills and personnel across national borders. The Western world is now rapidly moving through a period of far-reaching structural transformation. Borders are increasingly permeable. Skilled workers, economic migrants, refugees and asylum seekers are migrating in increasing numbers into the advanced industrial countries. The arrival there of increasing numbers of immigrant peoples confronts traditional national culture with unfamiliar customs, norms and religions. At the beginning of our new century, the very idea of the nation-state is hard-pressed by these cultural trends. A century later, liberalism and laissez-faire capitalism are again seen as the motors of unwelcome and threatening change. And once again, extremist nationalist reaction echoes *völkisch* ideas by concentrating on defensive ideologies of race to counter threats to national and cultural identity.

Certain challenged groups turn to racial identity as a last resort. In the United States, the doctrine of Christian Identity mixes motifs of heretical Christian dualism with a vicious theology of anti-Semitism, which regards the Jews as the "spawn of Satan." African Americans, Asians, Hispanics and all other colored peoples are stigmatized as the "mud" races that are now diluting and destroying the Aryan race in its traditional white homelands. Here, Nazi demonology and apocalyptic are freely invoked, together with Hitler worship and Third Reich symbolism, to mobilize violence in support of a white racial state. Other groups mix racism with Nordic pagan religions. The runes are celebrated as magical signs of ancestral heritage and a mystical blood loyalty. In the United States, Britain, Germany and the Scandinavian countries, racial pagan groups ponder runes, magic and the sinister mythology of the Norse gods Wotan, Loki and Fenriswolf. The racial interpretation of these esoteric ideas, cosmology and prophecies betrays these groups' overwhelming anxiety about the future of white identity in multiracial societies.

This book originated as a sequel volume to *The Occult Roots of Nazism* in order to document the survival of occult Nazi themes in the postwar period. As work progressed, however, my perspective broadened considerably. Far from tracing faded fascist mystics and redundant ideas, I found that I was actually having to write a new history of contemporary neo-*völkisch* groups and ideology in America and Europe. It became apparent that this new *völkisch* revival, especially prevalent in the English-speaking world, documents the reaction to the high tide of liberalism and globalization from the 1980s onward.

Just as the original *völkisch* movement arose as a defensive ideology of German identity against modernity in the late nineteenth century, this neo-*völkisch* revival acts as a defensive ideology of white identity against multiculturalism, affirmative action and mass Third World immigration. As these neo-*völkisch* groups elaborate their concerns with identity and ethnicity, many of them are drawn, as were their German predecessors, toward esoteric themes of Aryan origins, secret knowledge and occult heritage. Like the Ariosophists of 1890–1945, the new white-pride movements represent only the most radical response of Western societies that are now having to confront fundamental challenges to their cultural identity. The original *völkisch* movement was the ideological precursor of National Socialism and the Third Reich. The rise of a new *völkisch* movement must therefore give us serious pause. Who knows what sort of politics and societies will emerge by the years 2030–50 from the growing sense of white marginizalization? I am aware that this provocative study of contemporary racist movements may well offend politically correct sensibilities by posing the very questions which liberal elites prefer to ignore or suppress.

The risks of racist religiosity are great. By projecting grievances, fears and anxieties onto the "shadow" figures of other races, religious transcendence is stunted and perverted into the dynamics of exclusion and hatred. Instead of genuine spirituality, there is partiality, separation, restriction. A rigid self-righteousness leads down into the spiritual basement of a primitive dualism, where pseudo-salvation depends on the elimination of the Other. The political projection of religious Manichaeism onto human differences inevitably leads to strife and violence. Whenever human groups are interpreted as absolute categories of good and evil, light and darkness, both the human community and humanity itself are diminished. Such degraded religion never leads to light but only into darkness. My hope is that an understanding of the substitute faiths documented in these pages, together with their causes, can help us avoid the recurrence of past conflagrations.

1

American Neo-Nazism

AN EXOTIC IMPORT from Europe, American neo-Nazism has always transcended American nationalism. American neo-Nazis regard themselves as the brothers of all white men in a global movement of racial nationalism. While they remain fixated on the figure of Adolf Hitler as the lost savior of the Western world, his German nationalist horizons are superseded by their wider vision of a pan-Aryan movement led by the United States as the leading white power of the postwar world. American neo-Nazism traces its roots to the early 1950s, when the anti-communist ideology of the Cold War could find a nostalgic model in Hitler's attempted destruction of the Soviet Union. Neo-Nazism quickly stigmatized liberalism and the American Jews as the aides and abettors of communism in a violent anti-Semitism based on Nazi models. However, it was desegregation and the black civil rights movement of the early 1960s which have provided the enduring political motivation for American racial nationalism. The social enfranchisement of black Americans, forced integration, busing affirmative action and equal opportunities led the American neo-Nazis to cast themselves in a white supremacist role. When large-scale Hispanic and other Third World immigration began in the 1980s, American neo-Nazism regarded itself as the front-line defense of America's survival as a white nation. The changing ethnic composition of the United States is a profound issue, as is the political cohesion of an increasingly diverse multicultural society. The progression of American neo-Nazism from George Lincoln Rockwell in the 1960s to William Pierce in the 2000s illustrates how the religious myths of German National Socialism are brought to bear on dramatic cultural changes in American demography and identity.

The self-styled Führer of the 1960s, George Lincoln Rockwell will always be identified as the founder of the overtly pro-Hitler, postwar Nazi movement in the United States. Rockwell's extravagant praise for Hitler, his violent racism against the Jews and blacks, allied with excess and exhibitionist tactics, have ensured him a lasting place in the folklore of American political extremism. Despairing of his earlier political efforts with old-style far-right groups,

Rockwell founded his American Nazi Party in 1959, adopting a brazen Nazi image complete with swastika flags, stormtroopers and open declarations of his intentions to gas the Jews. He fantasized that he would become president of the United States by 1973 and that he would enjoy the support of a Senate and House of Representatives made up of members of his party. His political program was firmly grounded in a policy of "white survival" which aimed at the wholesale repatriation of all American Negroes to Africa and at the extermination of the Jews, whom he regarded as the architects of racial desegregation, national decline and cultural degeneracy.

A mixture of clowning and provocation characterized all of Rockwell's public appearances. Soon after founding the party, Rockwell and his men regularly picketed the White House with signs that read "Save Ike from the kikes," "The only communist party in the Middle East is in Israel," "Gas red Jewish spies" and "Communism is Jewish." In 1961 Rockwell drove a "Hate Bus" through the South until his party was apprehended at New Orleans. The sides of the vehicle were hung with notices such as "We do hate race-mixing" and "We hate Jew-Communism." Back in Washington, his stormtroopers used to drive a bus around the city bearing the slogan: "Rockwell is right! Who needs niggers?" In Boston and Philadelphia, the party picketed cinemas showing the popular film *Exodus*, which told the story of Jewish immigrants to Israel after World War II, with banners demanding "America for Whites and Gas Chamber for Traitors." Throughout the mid-1960s, Rockwell and his American Nazi Party were involved in numerous protests and disruptions. Charges against stormtroopers ranged from fighting, loitering, vagrancy and assault to desertion, criminal defamation and unlawful possession of firearms.

What makes an American Nazi? Examining Rockwell's life, one finds a mixture of religious conviction and idealism driving a noisy program of anti-Semitism and anti-communism, white supremacy and eugenics. His exhibitionist tactics were very likely influenced by his parental background. George Lincoln Rockwell was born on 9 March 1918 in Bloomington, Illinois, the eldest son of theatrical performers. His father, George Lovejoy "Doc" Rockwell, was a vaudeville comedian of English and Scottish ancestry with a top act on Broadway and well known on radio and in the leading theaters of the country. His mother, born Claire Schade, was a young German-French toe dancer, part of a family dance team. Following his parents' divorce, he spent his childhood staying with his mother in rural Illinois and his father on the Maine coast, where regular house guests included Fred Allen, Benny Goodman and Groucho Marx.[1]

After completing prep school at Hebron Academy, Rockwell attended Brown University in 1938 to study philosophy and sociology. He quickly became politicized against the liberal, egalitarian tenor of social science and his teachers. Later, he became convinced that liberalism was the "pimping little sister" of communism. His grades were poor but he was art editor of the campus magazine, *Sir Brown*. His cartoons ranged from the humorous to comic-book horror with images of violence, destruction and bombings.[2] The prospect of war offered a welcome relief from his studies. Eager for action, high-strung and edgy, Rockwell was swayed by the contemporary buildup of anti-German opinion. By March 1941, he had enlisted in the Naval Air Corps and quickly won his wings. He served as a naval aviator flying anti-submarine missions in the South Atlantic and South Pacific throughout World War II, commanded the naval air support at the battle for Guadalcanal and during the invasion of Guam in August 1944 and was demobbed with the rank of lieutenant commander and several decorations in October 1945.[3]

Meanwhile, he had married a girl he had known as a student at Brown. Rockwell spent the first five years after leaving the navy studying art and then taking a variety of jobs as a commercial photographer, a painter, an advertising executive and a publisher in Maine and New York. He showed some promise as a commercial artist, enrolling at the Pratt Institute in New York. In 1948 he won a $1,000 prize in a national art contest sponsored by the National Society of Illustrators. But war again intervened in his career. In 1950, with the outbreak of the Korean War, Rockwell returned to active duty, training fighter pilots in southern California. His involvement with the Korean conflict bred in him an enduring hatred of communism and a paranoid fear that it would undermine the United States.[4]

It was here that Rockwell first became politically engaged in the campaign to have the military hero General Douglas MacArthur elected president. The anti-communist revelations of Joseph McCarthy also dominated this period, and Rockwell was deeply suspicious of the motives of those who sought to discredit him. An old lady in San Diego involved in the MacArthur campaign showed him some newspapers that she claimed were controlled by Jews and out to smear both men. She introduced him to McCarthy's speeches and Conde McGinley's anti-Semitic newspaper, *Common Sense*, which contained startling revelations of a secret Jewish-communist plot behind the scenes of twentieth-century history. She also encouraged him to attend a speech of the veteran anti-Semite and rabble-rouser Gerald L. K. Smith in Los Angeles. Rockwell was overwhelmed by Smith's emotive exposure of the Jewish conspiracy and bid for world power.[5] Through further reading in the San Diego public library, he became convinced of the existence of a Jewish-communist world conspiracy. Rockwell was staggered by both the seeming magnitude of the conspiracy as well as the official and media silence concerning its existence. Down in the dark book stacks of the San Diego library one autumn day in 1950, Rockwell experienced illumination and political awakening. He had always felt that the world was out of joint, that mischief was afoot, but now he felt he held the key to the past and the present. But how could he fight against this monstrous and universal plot? Given the apparent enormity of the Jewish world conspiracy, Rockwell now wondered why America had gone to war on the side of the communist Soviet Union and opposed "Christian Germany, which never had a single highly placed spy in [America], and no plans for conquering the world." The example of Adolf Hitler and his crusade against world Jewry and communism quickly came to mind. Rockwell believed Hitler had understood the Jewish menace from the outset of his career and that the Jews had involved Britain and America in the conflict for their own interests. Early in 1951, Rockwell found a copy of *Mein Kampf* in a local bookshop, read it and saw the world anew:

> [Here] I found abundant "mental sunshine," which bathed all the gray world suddenly in the clear light of reason and understanding. Word after word, sentence after sentence stabbed into the darkness like thunderclaps and lightningbolts of revelation, tearing and ripping away the cobwebs of more than thirty years of darkness, brilliantly illuminating the mysteries of the heretofore impenetrable murk in a world gone mad. I was transfixed, hypnotized. . . . I wondered at the utter, indescribable genius of it. . . . I realized that National Socialism, the iconoclastic world view of Adolf Hitler, was the doctrine of scientific racial idealism—actually a new religion.[6]

Thus was George Lincoln Rockwell converted to the religion of National Socialism. In later years he would write that "future generations will look upon Adolf Hitler as the White Savior of the twentieth century, and the Fuehrerbunker in Berlin as the Alamo of the White race."[7]

Some eight years were yet to elapse before he became an outspoken Hitlerite at the head of the American Nazi Party. Meanwhile, in November 1952, the navy had assigned him to a base at Keflavik in Iceland, where he spent two years as a F8F Bearcat pilot and achieved the rank of commander. Here he met his second wife, Thora Hallgrimsson, a member of a prominent local family and the niece of Iceland's ambassador to the United States. Rockwell was still engrossed in *Mein Kampf* and took his bride to Berchtesgaden, Germany, for their honeymoon. They made a pilgrimage to Hitler's Eagle's Nest in a mood of reverence and fascination.[8] On returning to civilian life, he decided to enter magazine publishing, hoping to find both a livelihood and a forum for his political ideas. He was also active among right-wing groups, attempted to launch an American Federation of Conservative Organizations and tried to advance by concealing his Nazi hard-core ideology behind a respectable front. But eventually he despaired of this strategy as it failed to attract dedicated racists and anti-Semites.[9]

Prompted by a series of recurrent dreams in the winter of 1957–58 that always ended with his meeting Hitler, he decided to go public against what he perceived as Jewish power in America, with the financial patronage of Harold N. Arrowsmith, a wealthy anti-Semite. At Arlington, Virginia, they formed the National Committee to Free America from Jewish Domination. After a maverick campaign for the governorship of Georgia, Rockwell's first opportunity for confrontation was provided by the U.S. government's military aid in May 1958 for the Chamoun regime in Lebanon, which was unpopular with Lebanese Arabs but enjoyed the support of the Israelis. On 29 July 1958 Rockwell led a picket of the White House, protesting against Jewish influence on the government, and organized simultaneous demonstrations in Atlanta, Georgia and Louisville, Kentucky. Earlier in the year, Rockwell had been involved in the founding of the National States Rights Party, a new anti-Semitic and racist party in Georgia.[10] When a synagogue was blown up in Atlanta on 12 October, the police seized Rockwell's supporters there, and newspapers around the world carried stories implicating Rockwell. Now he and his family were harassed and his home was attacked; Arrowsmith retreated from the glare of the publicity and withdrew his support.[11]

His wife and children soon found the strain too great and returned to Iceland. Deserted by his family and former supporters, Rockwell faced a bleak and solitary future in the early months of 1959. One cold March morning in his house at Arlington, he found himself alone communing with a huge swastika banner and a plaque of Hitler. Following another "religious experience" involving a brief state of universal awareness, he became convinced he had to fulfill Hitler's mission in a total, global victory over the forces of tyranny and oppression. He would henceforth become an overt National Socialist and self-proclaimed devotee of Hitler, abandoning all thought of liaison with conservative groups and respectability. He proudly displayed his Nazi banner, recruited a handful of stormtroopers to whom he issued grayshirt uniforms and swastika armbands, mounted a large illuminated swastika on the roof of his house and founded the American Party, later called the American Nazi Party. Besides the party headquarters at his house at 2507 North Franklin Road in Arlington, Rockwell also maintained a barracks in a run-down farmhouse nearby for his growing detachment of stormtroopers.[12]

Once Rockwell had decided on a flagrant, open avowal of Nazism, his activity was wholly directed toward the provocation of the Jewish enemy and society at large, which he regarded as its passive victim. Besides flaunting their Nazi uniforms and insignia, he and his stormtroopers missed no opportunity to shock and outrage domestic opinion. From 1960 onward, his brash and sensational exploits were designed to achieve maximum press coverage for an otherwise crackpot fringe group that numbered no more than two hundred members at its peak.[13] Surrounded by fluttering Stars and Stripes and swastika flags, Rockwell held speeches before curious crowds and eager reporters advocating a national and then global program of eugenics to purify the Aryan race. He ceaselessly denounced the Jews as representatives of Marxism, unbridled capitalism, racial degeneration and cultural bolshevism and demanded their trial and execution by gassing. Rockwell effectively forced the media to give him publicity by concentrating on the distribution of imflammatory leaflets, creating public incidents and haranguing crowds to provoke violent opposition.[14] The American Nazi Party also pursued a racist policy toward blacks. Rejecting all race mixing and desegregation as Jewish wiles to mongrelize the American racial stock, Rockwell proposed to resettle all American Negroes in a new African state, to be funded by the U.S. government. He even appeared as a guest speaker at a major convention of Black Muslims in Chicago on 25 February 1962, where he told an audience of more than twelve thousand that he considered Elijah Muhammad the Adolf Hitler of the black man. Privately, Rockwell imagined that such a deportation program would be preceded by an imminent race war and the mass slaughter of blacks.[15]

Rockwell's success in achieving notoriety owed much to the growing strength of the contemporary civil rights movement among American blacks, led by Martin Luther King Jr. During the early 1960s, Negroes were becoming more politically aware: protests, marches and the Watts and Harlem riots signaled Negroes' impatience for genuine equality in American society. This was the period of liberal concern for the blacks' predicament, measures for desegregation were undertaken and the busing of white and black children to mixed schools became widespread. All this was anathema to Rockwell, who regarded blacks as a primitive, lethargic race who desired only simple pleasures and a life of irresponsibility. Formerly content as slaves, their problems had begun after their closer involvement with the social and economic life of whites. Rockwell was convinced that Jews had promoted blacks into a hopeless position of alleged equality with whites. Deeply frustrated by their inability to compete in education and for jobs, blacks had become violent and thereby fulfilled Jewish plans for fomenting the breakdown of the traditional order and the advent of communism.[16] By harping on the threat of escalating

Negro riots in conjunction with his rabid anti-Semitism and anti-communism, Rockwell attempted to exploit profound American anxieties about the
apparent disorderliness of the 1960s.

The American Nazi Party engaged in a constant barrage of protests and disruptions at this time.[17] Jewish youths were beaten up, a synagogue was
bombed in Bridgeport, Connecticut, and the word "Jew" was painted on front
doors. In early 1962 Rockwell began planning a massive rally to celebrate
Hitler's birthday in April. During the summer he attended an international
Nazi camp-congress organized by the British neo-Nazi leader Colin Jordan in
Gloucestershire in defiance of a Home Office ban on his entry to Britain. Here
agreement was reached on the founding of a World Union of National Socialists.[18] Following his deportation back to the States, Rockwell picketed the
White House in protest. In September 1962 he awarded one of his captains,
Roy James, a medal for punching Martin Luther King Jr. in the face in Birm-
ingham, Alabama. There were also several disruptive incidents in the House of
Representatives, including that of Robert A. Lloyd, who ran into the proceed-
ings in blackface and a stovepipe hat, shouting "Long live Rockwell" and ask-
ing to be seated as a Missisippi congressman in a parody of Negro speech.[19]
Rockwell himself was charged with disorderly conduct and stood trial in New
York in June 1966. Defended by a Jewish lawyer, Rockwell was acquitted
through the court's upholding of the free speech he would deny to his enemies.

Alongside all this headline-grabbing activity on the American scene, Rockwell was attempting to establish the philosophical credentials of the World
Union of National Socialists (WUNS). The leadership of the WUNS, a federation of some seven national Nazi groups and parties in various countries, including Britain, the United States, Chile, Denmark, France, Argentina and
Australia, was originally vested in Colin Jordan on its establishment in August
1962. However, after Jordan was sent to prison on public order offenses later
that year, this office passed to Rockwell. Through the WUNS, Rockwell was
determined to present the racial idealism of National Socialism as a program
of global Aryan power above the nationalisms of the past to a younger generation of new supporters. Only with such an ideology, he believed, would it be
possible to counter the Jewish world conspiracy and the rising tide of colored
peoples all over the planet. In the spring of 1966, Rockwell commenced publishing a new WUNS periodical entitled *National Socialist World* from his
headquarters at Arlington as a new forum for international Nazi ideology.[20]

Rockwell had appointed as its editor Dr. William Luther Pierce (b. 1933),
a newcomer to the neo-Nazi movement. Pierce was a physicist by profession
who had studied at Rice University and the California Institute of Technology, completed his doctorate at the University of Colorado and then spent

three years teaching at Oregon State University. From the outset, *National Socialist World* cultivated its image and status as the leading international Nazi periodical, with long articles and book reviews ostensibly written for an educated and literate readership and employing high standards of production. The magazine was intended as a quarterly, with each issue having over a hundred pages. The first issue comprised a philosophical appraisal of National Socialism by Colin Jordan and an article by George Lincoln Rockwell on the value of vulgar Nazi propaganda; pride of place was given to a condensed edition of *The Lightning and the Sun* by Savitri Devi, the Hindu-Nordicist whose Hitler cult and philosophy of history has exercised a deep influence on neo-Nazi intellectuals (see chapter 5). Six numbers of the magazine had been published by the winter of 1968, and these included such subjects as Gottfried Feder's twenty-five points of the German Nazi Party, Matt Koehl on Hitler and National Socialist doctrine, and Robert F. Williams on race war in America.[21]

While fostering the historical memory of Hitler and the Third Reich in articles and book reviews, the periodical put much emphasis on the future importance of the United States in the coming global racial struggle. In a long editorial for the summer 1967 number, Pierce drew up the order of battle between "150 million more-or-less Aryan whites, 25 million Negroes and 6 million Jews" in a war of dominance and survival. He claimed that the elemental aspect of the conflict was concealed by the Jewish control of public opinion, finance and education and pessimistically anticipated that disorders would increase for the time being. All Negro arson, murder and insurrection would continue to be attributed to poverty and discrimination, white prejudice and bigotry, police brutality and injustice. Welfare bribes and leniency toward blacks would increase, the need for more tolerance would be preached, while America descended into an inferno. He expected that active National Socialists would soon find themselves outlawed and driven into illegal, underground activities. Nevertheless, Pierce ultimately hoped that "once Aryan America has become racially self-conscious, has organised itself, flexed its muscles, and scented blood, the Jews will follow the Negroes into history's garbage pail in short order."[22]

Recognizing the limitations of a movement entirely devoted to publicity stunts and provocation, Rockwell had begun planning a longer-term strategy for the party involving mass organization and electoral campaigning. On 1 January 1967 the party had been renamed the National Socialist White Peoples' Party (NSWPP), and issues of fund-raising, propaganda writing and membership recruitment were addressed at a party conference in June.[23] But these plans were cut short. On 25 August 1967 Rockwell was shot by a sniper's bullet as he reversed his vehicle out of a parking lot on leaving a laundromat in Arlington. The assassin was John Patler, who had edited the party bulletin, *The Stormtrooper.* He had been associated with the National Renaissance Party and Rockwell's American Nazi Party before leaving to start his own organization, the American National Party, which lasted from 1962 to early 1963. He returned to join Rockwell but eventually became a source of friction due to his unstable character and Marxist leanings. Rockwell finally expelled him from the party in March 1967 for fomenting dissent between fair and dark-skinned members. Patler was tried for murder, found guilty and sentenced to twenty years in prison.[24]

With Rockwell's death, the U.S. Nazi movement found a martyr but soon splintered into several small extremist political groups driven by fanaticism, paranoia and suspicion. The five hundred or so members of the NSWPP split into various factions, with Rockwell's chief lieutenant and formal successor, Matt Koehl, a member of the party since 1963, retaining the party name and headquarters in Arlington and having the largest following. The American Nazi Party title was formally re-adopted by one of the schismatic groups in California that was first led by James Warner, who had been secretary of the parent party in the early 1960s. The other major heirs of Rockwell's party were the National Socialist Liberation Front, the National Socialist Party of America, the National Alliance and the Christian Defense League.

The son of Hungarian immigrants of German descent, Matthias Koehl Jr. was born on 22 January 1935 in Milwaukee, Wisconsin. After studying journalism at the University of Wisconsin, he enlisted in the U.S. Marine Corps, serving two years on active duty. Already as a schoolboy, Matt Koehl was drawn to anti-Semitism, and in New York City he had joined James Madole's National Renaissance Party. In 1957 he helped organize the United White Party in Knoxville, Tennessee. By 1958, he was the national organizer of the National States' Rights Party (NSRP), which agitated against desegregation in the southern states.[25] He joined Rockwell's movement in 1960 and became leader of the Chicago section in 1961. In 1963 he joined Rockwell at party headquarters in Arlington and was appointed corresponding secretary of the WUNS and national secretary of the NSWPP. He also edited and published both the *WUNS Bulletin* and the party's *NS Bulletin.* His attraction to the American Nazi Party was inspired by pride in his own German origins and an admiration for Adolf Hitler bordering on religious adulation. In an early article for *National Socialist World,* Koehl had extolled Hitler as an idealist, a visionary and the creator of a heroic new worldview—someone who had worked for a broad Aryan racial revival beyond the limits of German nationalism, an idea inspired by the pan-Aryan Savitri Devi. His swastika was intended to represent "the mission of the struggle for the victory of Aryan man" and a New Order of racial blood-brotherhood.[26]

In 1968 Koehl proclaimed that "Adolf Hitler *is* National Socialism, just as National Socialism *is* Adolf Hitler" and wrote of Nazi ideology as a creed and a new faith. He dismissed those who thought that American Nazis were fighting for some historical German phenomenon. These critics had not grasped "the Truth which Adolf Hitler revealed to the world nearly 50 years ago. . . . Our goal involves far more than the realization of some superficial political or social scheme. It entails a universal transformation of ideas and things, an upheaval of unprecedented magnitude." Impressed by Hitler's claim that man can live only by higher ideals, Koehl quoted from a lengthy passage of *Mein Kampf* that claimed "the [National Socialist] philosophy of life corresponds to the innermost will of Nature, . . . until at last the best of mankind, having achieved possession of this earth, will have a free path for activity in domains [beyond]."[27]

Koehl's full-blown Hitler cult is even more evident in the New Order, the name adopted by his party after a general reorganization in 1983. According to its literature, New Order has about two hundred full members and four hundred active supporters organized in some forty local branches across eighteen states from California to the East Coast. Regular activities include the celebration of Hitler's birthday and the holding of lectures and seminars to disseminate the Nazi gospel. Matt Koehl's own addresses to domestic U.S. groups and occasional forays to European neo-Nazi gatherings, together with his books *The Future Calls* (1972) and *Faith of the Future* (1995), set forth the "racial idealism" of modern Hitlerism in robust, evangelical prose for all fresh recruits and initiates of the New Order.

Literature currently distributed by the New Order from its headquarters in Milwaukee include small votive pictures of Hitler with the caption "He lives!" Another small card carries the text "Our Creed" in English and an overleaf in German. The self-conscious imitation of Christian liturgy and belief implicit in its blasphemous substitution of Hitler for Jesus Christ comes close to parody:

> We believe in Adolf Hitler,
>> the immortal Leader of our race,
>> singular gift of Providence,
>> greatest figure of all time,
>> alive in our hearts today and forever.
> We believe in his holy Cause,
>> which is the *New Order*,
>> the fulfillment of Aryan destiny

in accordance with the eternal laws of life,
the hope and future of of our kind on earth.
We believe in his Movement,
the true, undivided body of his followers,
which bears the name of his Cause
as the instrument of his will,
consecrated by the blood of heroes and martyrs
—*the only way to world redemption.*

HEIL HITLER!

In his writings and speeches to New Order audiences, Matt Koehl regularly invokes religious mythology and symbolism. These effusions are strongly influenced by the Hindu-Aryan ideas and nature worship of Savitri Devi. His piece entitled "Resurrection," written on the occasion of Hitler's birthday in April 1987, recalled the words of the *Bhagavad-Gita*, that "ancient book of Aryan wisdom and insight," according to Savitri Devi: "Age after age, when justice is crushed, when evil reigns supreme, I come; again am I born on Earth to save the world." Mingling Hindu, pagan and Christian motifs, Koehl ruminated on Nature's eternal message of renewal and resurrection. "Adolf Hitler was born on Earth. He became flesh and blood. He fought, and he died." He claimed that Hitler had to die, that his immolation was a foreordained necessity. The tragic events of 1945 were a cataclysmic precursor of a new world to come. "Hitler lives in our very own hearts and minds.... Our Leader is risen. *He is risen indeed!*"[28]

In a 1991 speech to an assembly of Dutch, Flemish and German members of the New Order held in Europe, Koehl likened the end of the Second World War to the start of a new dispensation. He compared postwar Hitlerism with the progress of early Christianity. This new religion had appeared defeated after Jesus was crucified in A.D. 33 and his disciples were scattered and persecuted. But Calvary signaled the ultimate triumph of Christ in which Christians had complete confidence. In an obscene metaphor, Koehl alludes to the later victory of the faith as the Christian *Endsieg* and asks whether modern Nazis have the same will to triumph. How long the struggle lasts is unimportant, but only an unshakable faith can sustain them. "We can make a start . . . and whether it takes 50 years, 100 years, 500 years or 1,000 years, the important thing is that one day—sooner or later—the cause of Adolf Hitler does indeed prevail on this earth."[29]

Despite his rejection of Christianity as an alien (Semitic) faith, Koehl has expressed New Order doctrine in religious symbols that are unmistakably Christian in origin. He enshrines Hitler as the messiah of Aryan salvation:

"He is our law and guide as Aryans for all time to come. He is our hope, our redemption." He speaks of Hitler's "transfiguration" and the gathering of a "sacred retinue." Koehl's use of redemptive symbolism is often overwhelming: "As the darkness of dying civilization casts its lengthening shadow over a confused and despairing world, the faith of the future will shine forth . . . a resplendent New Order . . . guided and instructed by the immortal personality of the greatest figure ever to walk the face of this earth."[30] It would be harder to find a more fervent expression of Hitler worship than these messianic and apocalyptic outpourings so obviously taken from Christian models.

This sectarian character of the New Order is also implicit in its embattled rejection of the modern liberal world that is equated with unbridled license, moral decline and physical disease. For those who judge Hitler by the standards of his democratic opponents, Koehl asks what kind of world did the victors of 1945 actually give us. What is the cultural and political record of the Allies without Hitler after fifty years? Koehl sees a world of rat-race consumerism, self-fixation, environmental devastation, pollution and race mixing. "They altered the national demography and introduced us to integration, busing, Affirmative Action, minority quotas, sensitivity training, Black History and—the Holocaust. They gave us permissiveness, drugs, MTV and teen suicide. They gave us safe sex and unsafe streets and gun control. They gave us rock 'n roll and rape-counseling centers. They gave us 'alternative lifestyles,' sodomy, AIDS, filth, perversion, chaos, crime, corruption, dumbing down and insanity of every kind."[31] This overwhelming cultural pessimism is mobilized to indict the modern world as the last gasp of an old order following its (temporary) defeat of Hitler and National Socialism.

While Koehl was building a church, another NSWPP faction embraced outright terrorism. Joseph Charles Tommasi (b. 1951), a young leader of the NSWPP in southern California, founded the National Socialist Liberation Front (NSLF) in 1974. Tommasi broke with the "straight" conservative image of American Nazism, grew his hair long and smoked marijuana. Aping the militant left, Tommasi called for an armed guerrilla struggle against the "Jewish power structure" of the United States. One famous NSLF poster read: "The future belongs to the few of us still willing to get our hands dirty." Along the barrel of a cocked gun ran the words "Political terror. It's the only thing they understand." Tommasi denied all interest in law and order. He wanted anarchy and chaos so that the NSLF could attack the "System" and its hated police protectors. NSLF armaments guidelines included magnum shotguns, 45-caliber automatic pistols and semiautomatic military assault rifles. Propaganda pictures showed the twisted wreckage of a bombed-out Bank of America branch, while the cover photograph of the NSLF periodical, *Siege*, showed the ruins of another terrorist target, an image incidentally taken from the radical left-wing Students for a Democratic Society (SDS).[32]

The NSLF's advocacy of armed struggle would not be matched for another decade until the terrorist outrages of The Order or Brüders Schweigen in the mid-1980s. In 1980 James N. Mason (b. 1952), a violent Nazi who had joined Rockwell in the mid-sixties, revived the NSLF (it had lapsed with Tommasi's assassination in 1975) as a forerunner of new militant American white supremacist movements committed to an armed struggle against the so-called Zionist Occupation Government (ZOG), a current far-right epiphet for the U.S. government as a Jewish-controlled puppet regime.[33] Mason relaunched *Siege*, in which he preached violence, racial strife and an all-out war against the hated "System." In his quest for extremist mentors, Mason then became obsessed with Charles Manson (b. 1934), the notorious killer serving life imprisonment for conspiracy in the murders of the actress Sharon Tate and others in 1969. Although Manson had carved a swastika into his own forehead, his politics were vague. However, Mason regarded Manson as the supreme outlaw and adopted the convicted criminal as the spiritual leader of his new Nazi group, the Universal Order (the name came from Manson). Mason's Nazi religion embraced both Hitler and Manson as saviors, thereby combining Koehl's messianic piety with the millenarian violence of Tomassi. In the pages of *Siege*, Mason paid extravagant tribute to Hitler, Tommasi, Manson and Savitri Devi.[34]

Already in the mid-1960s, WUNS had served as a pilot scheme for exporting American neo-Nazism back to Europe. This Euro-American partnership was now followed by another Rockwell heir, the National Socialist Party of America (NSPA), founded in 1970 by Frank Collin, a partly Jewish fascist expelled from the NSWPP due to internal party friction and slurs cast upon his racial ancestry. During the late 1970s, the NSPA achieved massive publicity through violent rallies held in the Jewish district of Skokie near Chicago. The NSPA has frequently been involved in violent incidents involving Klansmen and in an abortive invasion of the Caribbean island of Dominica. In November 1979, members of a local branch were implicated in the killing of five left-wing radicals attending an anti–Klu Klux Klan rally at Greensboro, North Carolina.[35]

The NSPA became important in an international neo-Nazi context as the sponsor and supporter of the offshore German NSDAP Auslands- und Aufbauorganisation (NSDAP-AO). Founded in West Germany in 1973 by the German American neo-Nazi Gerhard (Gary) Lauck, this group moved its operations to the United States following Lauck's expulsion by the Bonn authorities in 1974. Here, Lauck was initially based at the Arlington, Virginia, headquarters of the WUNS (aligned with Matt Koehl's NSWPP) and received financial backing from several U.S. Nazi groups. Later on, the NSDAP-AO joined forces with the NSPA and it now shares their offices at Lincoln, Nebraska. Originally set up in exile from Germany to campaign for the legalization of a National Socialist party in Germany, the scope of the NSDAP-AO has expanded dramatically over the past twenty years to span the globe. The joint publication with the NSPA, a monthly periodical entitled *New Order*, is published in English, German, Swedish, Hungarian, French, Dutch, Spanish, Italian, Portuguese and Danish. The U.S. Commission on Civil Rights has described the NSDAP-AO as "one of the world's most influential neo-Nazi propaganda outfits . . . the biggest supplier of propaganda to neo-Nazis."

The main purpose of Lauck's organization still remains the unhindered provision of support and publications for neo-Nazis in Germany operating under constitutional restrictions. To further this objective, the NSDAP-AO also publishes a German-language journal, *NS Kampfruf,* and produces thousands of leaflets and labels bearing Nazi slogans for illicit distribution in Germany. The organization claims to have many secret members in Germany and had extended its activities to Scandinavia and Austria during the 1980s. In May 1995 Gary Lauck was arrested in Denmark. He was subsequently convicted in Germany on charges of distributing illegal neo-Nazi literature and sentenced to a term of imprisonment. However, his removal barely halted the propaganda activities of his organization, which has effectively absorbed the NSPA. A similar outfit called Liberty Bell Publications is run by George P. Dietz in Reedy, West Virginia. Dietz is a farm broker and a former member of the Hitler Youth who emigrated to the United States in 1957. Besides selling a wide variety of anti-Semitic books and Nazi literature, regalia and replica party badges (made in Taiwan), Liberty Bell publishes its own periodical, *Liberty Bell,* and a neo-Nazi bulletin, *Der Schulungsbrief,* for distribution in Germany.

The other major successor to the NSWPP after Rockwell's death was the National Alliance, led by William Pierce, who formerly edited *National Socialist World.* Thirty years later, Pierce is still the most important neo-Nazi organizer and publisher in the United States. His authorship of *The Turner Diaries,* a cult novel of race war, and his regular radio broadcasts, meetings with top nationalist leaders of European parties and involvement with youth culture and white power music via Resistance Records have more than vindicated his status as the house intellectual of the original American Nazi Party leadership. The National Alliance traces its origins to the National Youth Alliance, founded by Willis Carto of the Liberty Lobby in late 1968 as an outgrowth of a campaign organization, Youth for Wallace, originally associated with Governor George Wallace. The NYA was intended to combat anarchist and left-wing groups on university campuses and increase the receptiveness of students to right-wing ideas. It stood for law and order, and for opposition to black power, hippies and the drug culture. The racist and anti-Semitic policies of the NYA quickly attracted the attention of Pierce and other NSWPP activists. Due to internal strife, the organization had split into two factions by the spring of 1971: one now known as Youth Action and loyal to Carto, and the other led by Pierce, which had become known as the National Alliance by 1974. Pierce quickly built the organization into a new Nazi lobby group through *National Vanguard* (formerly *Attack!*), published from 1970 to 1982 as a tabloid and thereafter published in magazine form. True to the tenor of his racist editorials in the WUNS periodical, Pierce promoted belief in a Jewish conspiracy to destroy the white race through socialism, black power, the banking system and racial mixing.[36]

Pierce established his headquarters in Washington, D.C., and enjoyed extensive domestic contacts with the American far right. *National Vanguard* circulated widely among neo-Nazi groups, and the National Alliance liaised with a number of foreign organizations. John Tyndall, then leader of the National Front in Britain, visited Pierce in 1979, and the Alliance was also in contact with other British groups, including the National Party, a short-lived NF successor group, and the League of St. George. Pierce keeps in regular touch with Tyndall and attended the British National Party annual rally in November 1995.

In the early 1980s, Pierce shunned the burgeoning black population of Washington and purchased a 400-acre retreat behind a high barbed-wire barricade near Hillsboro, a remote village in West Virginia amid the Appalachian Mountains. Here he runs a large bookselling service based on Western culture and pagan tradition (including many Penguin Classics), edits *National Vanguard* with the aid of his staff, and preaches a racist gospel in his own "Cosmotheist Church" within the compound that is emblazoned with a Nordic man-rune representing creation. This aspect of his organization well demonstrates the pan-Aryan religiosity of his mission. In his newsletter, Pierce quotes Savitri Devi regarding the ultimate purpose of evolution as "that mysterious and unfailing wisdom according to which nature lives and creates: the impersonal wisdom of the primeval forest and of the ocean depth and of the spheres in the dark fields of space." Pierce's Cosmotheism sees each race and species assigned a specific role in relation to the Whole. While the Negro is content to idle and the Jew acts as a ferment of decay, the white man is guided by the Divine Spark within him ever upward toward the Creator, who is a living part of his Being.[37] This call to unending evolutionary progress is thus cast in terms of a Platonic doctrine of souls in which the ascent to the Godhead is

restricted to Aryan individuals. Here Cosmotheism reflects Lanz von Liebenfels's prewar Ariosophy.

Pierce's racist imagination is ultimately driven by a crusading zeal to save
the Aryan race by building a territorial enclave of white rule in the Appalachian Mountains. This notion corresponds to ideas current in the Christian Identity movement, which drew its original inspiration from late-nineteenth-century British-Israelism. This loose Christian grouping in England
originally claimed the chosen status of the Anglo-Saxon races as the lost tribes
of Israel (as distinct from the Jews of Judah) but displayed little or no hostility toward the Jews. However, by the 1930s the American followers of British-
Israelism had embraced a fierce anti-Semitic theology that regarded the Jews
as the implacable enemies of the Aryan race in America. Since the 1970s, the
Christian Identity movement has been a loose network comprising, among
others, the Church of Jesus Christ Christian, Aryan Nations; the Church of
Christ; and the New Christian Crusade Church (now superseded by the Christian Defense League) of James Warner, formerly with the NSWPP. Aryan Nations advocates the creation of a territorial sanctuary and eventually a white
sovereign national state in the Pacific Northwest states. The religious sentiments of election, demonology and an inevitable apocalyptic battle between
the Aryans and the Zionist-led forces of darkness color Identity thinking.[38]

Although no supporter of Identity himself, Pierce's own brand of Nazi
racism displays a similar sectarian concern with the embattled white Aryan
elect and a coming Armageddon against the Jewish political establishment.
Pierce's underground right-wing novel, *The Turner Diaries* (1978), presents
an eyewitness account of a future armed struggle of white revolutionaries
against the "System," regarded as an oppressive and corrupt U.S. government
dominated by liberals, Jews, blacks and other minorities—all committed to
anti-racist, egalitarian public policy. In a compelling narrative, the novel describes the activities of a young white patriot, Earl Turner, and his fellow
fighters in the "Organization" in the wake of a government crackdown on the
private possession of firearms. They are further politicized by ever more
forceful measures to achieve complete racial integration. Pursued by the
hated racial-equality police, Turner and his confederates start to fight back
with a campaign of sabotage and assassination. As the struggle escalates, an
all-out race war breaks out across the United States.

The guerrilla tactics of the Organization against the System lead to civil
war following a successful military attack on Los Angeles, racial mutiny in the
local armed forces and large-scale defections to the rebels. Through draconian measures of racial segregation and the forced collection and expulsion of
the colored population, a large white enclave in southern California is estab-

lished as a base for the assault on the rest of the country. Pierce's novel glories in detailed description of mayhem and wholesale destruction as the Organization daily gathers new forces and strikes at other major U.S. cities in a war of attrition against the Jewish-dominated multiracial establishment still entrenched in Washington and New York. Nuclear bombs devastate Miami, Charleston, Detroit and New York. Israel and the Soviet Union are attacked, and the number of dead victims in the United States alone exceeds 60 million. Total savagery and a relapse into barbarianism mark a period of five "dark years" until the final "liberation" of North America in early 1999.

The Turner Diaries describe a white revolution against the alleged political domination of the U.S.A. by Jewry and the ethnic cleansing of blacks, Hispanics and other colored peoples in America. But Pierce's Nazi inspiration is manifest in the numerous references and passages that uncannily recall the Nazi extermination of Jewry during the Second World War. The Organization issues proclamations warning of the dire consequences to anyone who knowingly harbors a Jew or other non-white during the deportations. While the blacks are summarily expelled to System-held territory, the Jews and other half-castes are marched away to their death in a canyon, reminiscent of the 1941 massacre of Ukrainian Jews in the ravine of Babi Yar near Kiev. In order to instill terror and right racial thinking in the civilian population of the California enclave, some 60,000 anti-racists among former leading politicians, lawyers, media and press personnel, teachers and priests are hanged in a single day of lynchings; the victims bear placards reading "I betrayed my race." Female partners of mixed couples are similarly dispatched with the caption, "I defiled my race." The small beginnings and growth of the Organization reflect the rise of the Nazi Party in Weimar Germany, while its inner elite is called the Order (identified as a successor to the SS). The Aryan revolution is seen as a replay of the uncompleted Holocaust in the 1940s, and "the dream of a White world" is finally realized "just 110 years after the birth of the Great One [i.e., Adolf Hitler]."[39]

The white revolution is ultimately global. After nuclear attack, Israel is overrun by the Arabs, and anti-Semitism becomes endemic in the European states and the Soviet Union. The victory of the white Aryan forces in America soon reaches Europe.

> The takeover came in a great, Europe-wide rush in the summer and fall of 1999, as a cleansing hurricane of change swept over the continent, clearing away in a few months the refuse of a millennium or more of alien ideology and a century or more of profound moral and material decadence. The blood flowed ankle-deep in the streets of many of Europe's great cities momentarily,

as the race traitors, the offspring of generations of dysgenic breeding, and hordes of *Gastarbeiter* met a common fate. The great dawn of the New Era broke over the Western world.[40]

The global victory of the Organization is completed with the annihilation of the Chinese in a campaign involving chemical, biological and radiological weapons and the creation of a "Great Eastern Waste" extending 16 million square miles from the Urals to the Pacific, from the Arctic to the Indian Ocean.

Pierce's projection of anti-Semitic and racist Nazi fantasies into a millenarian vision of universal Nazi rule is unique. His paranoid view of liberal, democratic society assumes strong religious overtones in its fervor and apocalyptic release. A foreword, ostensibly written a century hence, describes Earl Turner as being born in 43 BNE (Before New Era) in Los Angeles, a former metropolitan area now occupied by the Aryan communities of Eckartsville and Wesselton (named for Hitler's mentor Dietrich Eckart and Nazi martyr Horst Wessel).[41] Writing of the early beginnings of the white revolution in California, Turner prophesies "we are forging the nucleus of a new society, a whole new civilization, which will rise from the ashes of the old. . . . There is no way a society based on Aryan values and an Aryan outlook can evolve from a society which has succumbed to Jewish spiritual corruption."[42]

The prophetic and religious aura of universal Nazism has brought *The Turner Diaries* an international underground readership. The book circulates widely among American and European neo-Nazi groups as a kind of modern *Mein Kampf*. During the 1980s the novel was sold by the National Front and has had an important influence on the recent development of neo-Nazi terrorism in Britain (see chapter 2).

Pierce's apocalypse soon became manifest in the United States with the formation of a militant racist sect called The Order at Metaline Falls, Washington, in September 1983. Also known as the Brüders Schweigen or Silent Brotherhood, this terrorist group was founded by Robert Jay Mathews (b. 1953), who had a long history of far-right links. His plan was the creation of a small cell with the will and resources to attack and overthrow the "Zionist Occupation Government" (ZOG) of the United States. For this purpose he required funds to buy arms for a guerrilla campaign against the state, which, it was expected, would lead to a mass revolt of the white population. The Order began its operations with large-scale counterfeiting and armed robbery, stealing $3.8 million from a Brinks armored car in Ukiah, California, in July 1984. Other acts of violence included the assassination of Alan Berg, a Jewish radio presenter in Denver known for his outspoken opposition to right-wing groups. Mathews was killed by the FBI in a siege at Whidbey Island, Washington, in December 1984, while the remaining Order members were apprehended in 1985 and 1986.[43]

The inspiration for The Order came directly from *The Turner Diaries*. Mathews told recruits that his organization was based on the fictional inner elite and presented the book to members. There are also many other parallels with the novel, including the use of code names, the production of "hit lists" of racial and ideological enemies, the execution of traitors and the initiation of members through a ritual oath. Members taking the Order oath upon "the green graves of our sires [and] the children in the wombs of our wives" swore "to do whatever is necessary to deliver our people from the Jew and bring total victory to the Aryan race." While Mathews's own religious inclination was pagan Odinist, he also had Christian Identity connections with Aryan Nations while a quarter of The Order's recruits had Identity associations with Aryan Nations and Church of Jesus Christ Christian. David Lane, who drove the getaway car after the Berg murder, was an Identity church member and also founded the 14 Word Press, whose motto has become a mantra for white identity groups across the world ("We must secure the existence of our people and a future for white children").[44]

The Turner Diaries has in turn influenced the Christian Identity movement. In the latter half of the 1980s, Christian Identity groups elaborated varied plans for the secession of a separate Aryan territory, a theme anticipated by Pierce's novel, with the establishment of a white California as the first stage of the revolution.[45] Pierce popularized the idea that the U.S. government is a Jewish-controlled puppet regime, which has now become a staple of far-right racist discourse under the ZOG acronym. The power of the book to motivate far-right terrorism is undiminished. Friends recall that Timothy McVeigh, convicted of the Oklahoma City bombing of April 1995, the largest terrorist atrocity in the history of the United States, repeatedly reread the novel, and it is claimed that he also copied the bomb attack on an FBI office described in its pages down to the smallest details of his delivery and timing.[46]

The swift defeat of The Order led the radical right to formulate more secretive and desperate strategies for a race war. Eschewing all organizational frameworks as too vulnerable to official penetration, many Nazis now advocate terrorist actions by individuals or very small independent cells. Bombs and murder replace nuclear devices and open warfare. William Pierce again supplied fictional inspiration with his second novel, *Hunter* (1989), which describes Oscar Yeager's one-man war against Jews and colored people, especially mixed-race couples. The concept of the "lone wolf" was not new. Misfits and psychopaths in the American Nazi movement such as Joseph G.

Christopher, Joseph Paul Franklin (a.k.a. James Vaughn) and Frank G. Spisak committed serial racial killings in the early 1980s, while John Hinckley, the would-be assassin of President Ronald Reagan, also had Nazi affiliations.[47] While James Mason applauded these murders in the pages of *Siege*, Pierce was outlining a new tactic against the superior military power of the state. *Hunter* suggests that isolated, small-scale and untraceable acts of violence can raise public racial awareness and effectively demoralize and destabilize multiracial society.[48]

Another strand in this thinking was supplied by Richard Kelly Hoskins, a Christian Identity follower, who wrote about "the Phineas Priesthood" based on biblical references in Numbers and Psalms. When the Lord is angered by the Israelites' cohabitation with Moabite women, Phinehas (in the King James spelling), the grandson of Aaron, thrusts his spear through a race-mixing pair of lovers. The Lord is pleased, spares the Israelites from the plague and makes a covenant of "an everlasting priesthood" with the zealous Phinehas (Numbers 25:6–13). The psalm text repeats the story, saying that Phinehas "executed judgment" and the plague was stayed (Psalms 106:30). Hoskins claims that corruption and disease always result when strangers force their way into Christian society, and he identifies a line of "Phineas Priests" who have purged the aliens through history, ranging from King Arthur and Robin Hood to the Ku Klux Klan and the SS.[49] The modern Phineas Priesthood is a cult of lone killers who never link up but carry out independent acts of murder against blacks, Jews, homosexuals, liberals and left-wingers, all perceived as the enemies of the white race.

Louis Beam, another Identity figure with a Texas Klan background, supplied a strategic framework for these acts of individual terrorism. Beam had been involved in The Order and was a leading defendant in the Fort Worth sedition trial (1988) arising from its activities. The FBI shooting of the Weaver family at their home on Ruby Ridge, Idaho, had led to a seminal conference of patriots, far-right groups and Christian Identity followers at Estes Park, Colorado, in October 1992. Here Beam outlined a new blueprint for militant opposition to ZOG in his highly influential essay, "Leaderless Resistance." He was convinced that anti-government resistance with hierarchical command structures was hopeless and suicidal. The cellular model developed by Russian revolutionary communism had an advantage, as the loss of a single cell still left the rest of the structure intact. But such cells required central direction and outside resources that the far right could not afford. Beam concluded that the only rational strategy was "leaderless resistance" or "phantom cells." Single individuals or tiny groups should operate in total isolation from one another, while the need for central direction would be obviated by their common outlook and similar reaction to given situations. He allowed that alternative communications media could reinforce these uniform attitudes, an evident reference to the increasing use of the Internet by far-right and racist groups worldwide.[50]

A Vietnam War veteran with a capacity for passionate oratory, Beam was an important ideological inspiration to the far-right underground of the 1990s. Leaderless resistance offered several attractions to the Nazis who now despaired of mass electoral strategies or armed uprisings. It promised security from enemy infiltration; it avoided the embarrassing question of why the Nazi movement cannot attract a mass following; and it suggested that stealth could succeed where heroism had failed. While avoiding any specific mention of violent acts, Beam's message was clear. With its scattershot of mayhem, sabotage and murder, leaderless resistance would represent an "intelligence nightmare" to government. The strategy has now been adopted by individuals associated with The Order in the United States, Combat 18 in Britain and White Aryan Resistance (Vit Arikst Motstånd, VAM) in Sweden. Acting singly or in small groups, Nazis pick a target, then strike and destroy. The absence of any formal organization makes official reaction hesitant and detection difficult. Timothy McVeigh's passage from the Michigan militia to his "lone wolf" bombing in Oklahoma City suggests a similar tactical progression.

Harold Covington briefly featured as a leader on the American Nazi scene. Following his involvement with the NSPA at the Greensboro massacre, Covington left the United States and traveled to Ireland, Britain and Rhodesia, acquiring an Irish wife and dual citizenship. Back in the States, he succeeded Frank Collin as leader of the NSPA in 1980, and then won 56,000 votes in a primary election as the Republican candidate for the post of state attorney general. In 1981 he founded his own Excalibur Society, which advocated Nazi policies on racial, social and economic issues. Yet he remained close to Sean McGuire, a Klansman with strong IRA sympathies, while penning his own "Mein Kampf." Covington's book The March up Country maps out the Nazi path to power in America. Later, in the summer of 1991, Covington began to plan an international network of Nazi terrorist cells in Europe based on common enemies and linked by modern computer communications. He made contact with the Swedish VAM, whose guerrilla activities extended to Norway and eastern Germany. In 1991–92 he worked closely with the Sargent brothers in setting up Combat 18 in Britain. Through clandestine bulletins, this Nazi militia publishes lists of the private addresses of its enemies who are affiliated with left-wing, green and peace politics, who are then subject to death threats and attacks by individual cell members.[51]

Covington refounded the NSWPP in April 1994 at his Chapel Hill, North Carolina, base. Once again, the NSWPP was for a short while the most active self-proclaimed Nazi party in the States. Under the Orwellian pseudonym of Winston Smith, Covington maintained a prodigious propaganda output with a daily Internet bulletin and a weekly paper, *Resistance*, in loose-leaf format. Domestic and international links were maintained at high volume via e-mail and a website. Loyal to Rockwell's original vision, the new NSWPP was a revolutionary Aryan party that sought to ensure the survival of white people in North America by the creation of a sovereign Aryan Republic. Covington's program was aggressive and inflammatory in seeking to mobilize disgruntled white voters against an administration that enfranchises racial aliens to guarantee its political survival. Covington had issued dire warnings about President Bill Clinton's second term, foreseeing a "terrible time of tyranny, corruption, and collapse into Brazil-style squalor."[52] But, as indicated by his book and terrorist links, Covington actually despaired of mass electoral strategy. In view of worsening racial conditions in America (racial quotas, hate crime laws, media vilification of white identity), he believes it is time for the Nazi movement to accept armed struggle as the next phase of its development.[53] He is no longer fronting the revived NSWPP.

In comparison with native right-wing radical organizations such as the Klu Klux Klan, the Christian Identity movement, Posse Comitatus and the survivalists, American Nazi groups like the NSWPP, the New Order and the National Alliance appear exotic and distinctly un-American. American neo-Nazism has attempted to graft its own religious doctrine rooted in a dualist anti-Semitic demonology onto complex issues of black desegregation and mass Third World immigration, which continue to cause genuine social stress. However, most anti-integration groups such as the White Citizens Councils were very pro-American, were by no means anti-Semitic, and resisted any Nazi association. This critical disjunction between the political circumstances of integration and anti-Semitic ideology helps explain why American neo-Nazism remains a sectarian phenomenon. The success of any neo-Nazi movement beyond its sectarian activities must involve the building of a wider base among alienated sections of white American society. There is some evidence that efforts have been made to carry the message to groups such as skinheads (see chapter 10), the Patriots (see chapter 14), and white prisoners, especially in the South.[54]

However, in certain respects, neo-Nazism commends itself to a tradition of religious fundamentalism in the United States. After Rockwell's flamboyant gospel, Matt Koehl presided over a Nazi church. In their sectarian enclave, American neo-Nazis embrace a prophetic religion in which Hitler is no less than a Christ figure, and Rockwell equates to St. Paul. As Jim Saleam has argued, the neo-Nazis see

> Nazi Germany's twelve years [as Hitler's ministry], the times of revealed faith and miracles. The war was the crucifixion. The swastika was the cross, a talisman against evil. The Nazi chiefs were Hitler's disciples. The Nuremberg trials produced martyrs and forced the faith into the political catacombs. No man spoke Hitler's name for fear of the Jews. However, Rockwell was converted to the new faith and charged with the mission of proselytizing the new doctrine. Whereas Hitler preached only to the Germans, Rockwell would convert all nations.[55]

Saleam goes on to compare Rockwell's assassination as a betrayal by a disciple in the manner of Judas, while Matt Koehl becomes the first pope of a church built on orthodoxy, while he is empowered with the keys of salvation and rites of excommunication from the one true party. There is a indeed a certain structural, if not theological, parallel between the Christian gospel and the racial evangel of neo-Nazism. This prophetic and structural similiarity, especially in view of the millenarianism and the messianic status of Hitler in neo-Nazism, makes this doctrine of racial salvation intelligible to individuals in a culture where Christian fundamentalism has always flourished.

The Nazi heritage of George Lincoln Rockwell can be traced back to the patriotic, pro-German and appeasement groups during the 1930s. Rockwell and his own heirs in America have continued to peddle a similar offering of anti-Semitism and ultranationalism while adding new postwar concerns. The anti-communism of the Cold War era has now been superseded by a suspicion of federal power and a "New World Order." However, the persistent issue is white identity with racial hatred directed toward blacks and other colored populations in order to counter the effects of the civil rights movement and equal-opportunity legislation from the early 1960s up to the present. Second, given the defeat of the Third Reich, the neo-Nazis espouse an intensified anti-Semitism that promises the completion of the Holocaust in a new war against American and international Jewry. Third, and perhaps the hallmark of the Nazi sects, they practice a devotional cult for Adolf Hitler as the savior of a white, Western world. In all Nazi groups, Hitler's birthday is regularly celebrated as the high point of their calendar, a time when Nazi relics are collected and displayed in secret shrines. Both the trappings and the myths of American Nazism reflect the behavior of a persecuted religious sect that prepares for militant action against a fallen world.

2

The British Nazi Underground

THE TOTAL DEFEAT of the Axis powers in 1945 and the confirmation of Nazi atrocities in the concentration camps did not delay for long the reemergence of a fascist tradition in Europe. Following the first postwar gathering of various European neo-fascist and neo-Nazi movements at Rome in March 1950, about a hundred delegates from parties in Germany, Italy, Austria, France, Spain and Sweden assembled in May 1951 at Malmö in southern Sweden. Within a decade, the larger neo-fascist parties in Europe were moving toward a new International, and the National European Party was founded by a convention of Sir Oswald Mosley's Union Movement, the Deutsche Reichspartei, Jeune Europe and the Movimento Sociale Italiano at Venice in March 1962.[1]

The postwar fascist Internationals were generally careful to distance themselves from their wartime legacy and sought to avoid any embarrassing references to Hitler, the SS, Nazism and the Holocaust. Mosley sought to update the politics of his prewar British Union of Fascists with an appeal to European unity, a major plank of the Union Movement's 1948 national election campaign. While commanding considerable loyalty on the British far right, Mosley's strategy invited a challenge from nationalists and unreconstructed fascists. Such caution was completely cast aside for the first time since the war in the spring of 1962 by Colin Jordan, the British neo-Nazi leader who admired Hitler and revived all the Nazi props of brown shirts, breeches and jackboots, swastika armbands, together with the slogans of "Sieg Heil," "Juden 'raus" and the Horst Wessel Song. Together with George Lincoln Rockwell, Savitri Devi, Bruno Lüdtke and others representing Nazi groups in seven countries, he founded the World Union of National Socialists (WUNS) as a self-proclaimed Nazi International in August 1962.

Colin Jordan's British neo-Nazism was a radical reaction to the presence of a colored population. While the American Nazis were protesting the emancipation of a Negro underclass in the United States, the British protest was directed at the rapid growth of colored immigration from the New Commonwealth countries beginning in the late 1950s. Besides this reactive racial nationalism, Jordan was chiefly inspired by a prewar fascist tradition of anti-Semitism and an unalloyed admiration for Hitler and German National Socialism. These ideals have remained the hallmarks of Colin Jordan's political program from the war years up into the 1990s and make him the leading representative of the postwar Hitler cult in Britain. By looking at Colin Jordan's career, important lessons can be learned about today's miltant Nazi underground. Contemporary terrorist groups like Combat 18 and David Myatt's National-Socialist Movement trace their lineage back to Jordan, just as many violent groups in America revere George Lincoln Rockwell. Also, since Colin Jordan's rise to prominence occurred against the background of mass immigration, the British story holds a wider significance for developments in Europe today.

John Colin Campbell Jordan was born in 1923 in Birmingham, England. He attended Warwick School, a prestigious prep school, where he won a scholarship to study history at Cambridge University. He interrupted his studies to volunteer for the Fleet Air Arm but failed his naval pilot's course. Undeterred, he transferred to the Royal Air Force and awaited fresh flying training. He claims that his political ideas were so developed by the end of 1944 that he declared his opposition to the continuation of the war and support for a negotiated peace with Germany. As a member of deferred service personnel, he was then sent to the Royal Army Medical Corps, where he became an educational instructor. On demobilization, he resumed his degree studies at Sidney Sussex College, Cambridge, in 1946. Like other mature servicemen undergraduates, Jordan played an active part in university life, serving on the staff of the university newspaper, *Varsity*, and speaking on the front bench in debates at the Union. He took a second-class degree in 1949.[2]

During his time at the university, Jordan began to contact a number of British nationalist and neo-fascist groups with a view to promoting the cause at Cambridge. He became a member of the anti-Semitic British People's Party (BPP) and was elected to its national council. This party had been founded in the summer of 1939 by John Beckett, who had formerly headed the National Socialist League in 1937–38 with William Joyce, later known as Lord Haw-Haw for his pro-Nazi broadcasts from Berlin during the war; he was subsequently executed as a traitor. Committed to social credit economics, aimed what it saw as the dangers of usury and seeking peace with Germany, the BPP, under the aristocratic patronage of the Duke of Bedford, had managed to survive the war and the internment of British fascists. Jordan also organized the University Nationalist Club and, after leaving Cambridge, he founded the Birmingham Nationalist Club, which he ran until moving to Leeds to take up a teaching post. At this time he became an ardent opponent of communism and published his first book, *Fraudulent Conversion* (1955), which asserted that the Soviet Union was run by Jews despite the apparent anti-Semitism and pro-Arab line of late Stalinism. Jordan argued that the struggle between communism and Zionism was an internal Jewish feud over the best way to achieve world domination.[3]

Foremost among Jordan's contacts at Cambridge and afterwards was Arnold Spencer Leese (1878–1956), an inveterate anti-Semite who had founded the Imperial Fascist League in 1929, a small (two hundred members) party that was the most pro-German and openly anti-Semitic group in England during the 1930s. It had always remained independent of Oswald Mosley's British Union of Fascists. Leese in fact regarded Mosley as an opportunist and argued that his fascism was not based on racial nationalism. Suspicious that Mosley's first wife had Jewish ancestry, Leese called Mosley a "kosher fascist," a Jewish agent planted to discredit the notion of fascism in Britain.[4] Leese had published a pro-Nazi magazine, *The Fascist* (1929–39), and was detained during the war under the 18B regulation against suspected German "fifth columnists." Upon his release he resumed his anti-Semitic publishing at Guildford with his scurrilous periodical *Gothic Ripples* (1945–56).

In his first postwar book, *The Jewish War of Survival* (1945), Leese conceded that the Jews had won a victory with the defeat of Hitler, but he argued that a vigorous policy of anti-Semitism could still break their power. He was again briefly imprisoned in 1947 for giving aid to two fugitive Dutch members of the Waffen-SS. Leese's views were even cruder in the postwar period. He believed that Jews were encouraging colored immigration to dilute Britain's racial stock, so that the Aryan civilization could be destroyed. While he credited the Aryans with creating all of civilization, he saw the Negroes as the most inferior type of human being. Like Hitler, Leese regarded the Jews as an anti-race, an infernal opponent of Aryan mankind. Leese was encouraged by the interest of Jordan, in whom he saw a youthful, intelligent and enthusiastic successor. For his part, Jordan regarded Leese as a major mentor figure, and the two men remained close friends until Leese's death. Leese's widow (who taught her cat to give the Hitler salute) was a staunch supporter of Jordan in his subsequent struggles on the far-right scene. Leese's influence on Jordan was a crucial factor in Jordan's combination of racial populism in reaction to colored immigration and a prewar tradition of anti-Semitism.

Returning to the Midlands to teach in Coventry, Jordan joined the League of Empire Loyalists (LEL), a lobby group founded in 1954 by A. K. Chesterton (1899–1973), a former deputy of Mosley's in the prewar British Union of Fascists. The LEL existed to reverse British policies of decolonization that were then being pursued by the Conservative government. Just as Rockwell had initially tried to find a home in more conventional far-right groups, Jordan was drawn to the LEL for its aggressive defense of white rule in Britain's African colonies. With its noisy rallies and outrageous publicity stunts, the LEL acted as a vehicle for vigorous nationalist protest.[5] Jordan became the Midlands organizer of the LEL but found little scope here for the anti-Semitic and Nazi ideas he shared with Arnold Leese. It was not until the late 1950s, with the emergence of opposition to colored immigration to Britain, that he discovered a domestic issue that held out the prospect of a mass movement on the extreme right.

The postwar shortage of labor in the economies of Western Europe had been met by importing workers from other countries. In Britain's case, they typically came from its colonies or former colonies, especially the West Indies, India and Pakistan. The first group from the West Indies arrived in 1948, and from that year to 1954, some 8,000 to 10,000 immigrants came into Britain each year. In 1954 and 1955, immigration from the West Indies rose to more than 20,000 each year, while that from India and Pakistan rose to about 10,000. A total of 132,000 colored immigrants from the Commonwealth arrived in Britain between 1955 and 1957, of whom 80,000 had come from the West Indies. The newcomers were perceived with some apprehension, especially in those working-class communities where they were expecting to settle. However, because all the major political parties wished to avoid making immigration a political issue, it was forseeable that new political groups would arise to demand immigration control.

The immigration issue was addressed in an inflammatory fashion by the National Labour Party (NLP) and the White Defence League (WDL), which were founded, respectively, by John Edward Bean (b. 1927) and Colin Jordan in 1957 when they left the LEL. In August 1958 race riots broke out in Nottingham, followed in September by similar riots in Notting Hill in West London. Jordan ran the White Defence League from Arnold Leese House at 74 Princedale Road in Notting Hill, which Leese's widow had placed at his disposal. He organized nightly rallies in the streets of this immigrant neighborhood throughout the tense, hot summer of 1958. He also published a local newspaper, *Black and White News*, and a flood of racist pamphlets that provoked strong feelings of resentment against the newcomers.

Colored immigration provided a new angle on old racist and Nazi ideas. In Jordan's view, the great importance of the immigration issue was that it forced people to think in terms of race and thus become more receptive of his primarily anti-Semitic convictions. In 1959, he advocated the cause of Nordic racial unity through the publication of a small periodical, *The Nationalist*. By February 1960, the WDL and NLP had merged as the new British National

Party (BNP) under the motto "For Race and Nation," with Andrew Fountaine, a Norfolk landowner, as president, Mrs. Leese as vice-president, Jordan as national organizer, and John Tyndall, also formerly in the LEL, as a founder member.[6]

The potential for the extreme right in Britain seemed very great in the years 1960 to 1962. In 1960 some 60,000 immigrants from the West Indies, India and Pakistan were added to the population, three times as many as in 1959, and in 1961 the net increase exceeded 100,000 for the first time. It was BNP policy to send all colored immigrants back to their home countries and to impeach the Tory Cabinet and members of the 1945–50 Labour Cabinet for "complicity in the black invasion." Despite its limited funds and small membership (about 350), the BNP's activities were highly sensational and headline grabbing, including demonstrations at London railway terminals to confront immigrants arriving from the ports, two public meetings in Trafalgar Square and demonstrations against the parade of a Jewish Lord Mayor of London and the Anti-Apartheid Movement. In order to expand into the provinces and to attract younger members, a paramilitary organization called Spearhead was started within the party. A summer camp, attended by twenty delegates from European nationalist groups, was held on Fountaine's land in 1961. After a busy schedule of lectures, the participants celebrated their Nordic racial identity with folkish songs and tankards of traditional ale around the campfire.

Despite the runaway success of the immigration issue for racial nationalism, ideological divisions were becoming apparent in the BNP leadership. In February 1962 Bean presented a resolution to its national council that "Jordan's wrongful direction of tactics is placing increasing emphasis on directly associating ourselves with the pre-war era of National Socialist Germany to the neglect of Britain, Europe and the White World struggle of today and the future." Bean and Fountaine clearly saw that Jordan's chief motivation was his admiration for Nazi Germany, whose example he wanted to translate— together with all the paraphernalia of swastikas, uniforms and Hitler cult— into contemporary Britain. In their view, this was a huge political liability as Britain had paid dearly in materiel and human sacrifice in the Second World War. What they wanted was a modern British nationalist movement addressing the issues of the 1960s. Jordan was defeated by a vote of 7 to 5, but he refused to stand down and reminded everyone that he held exclusive right to the use of the Arnold Leese House. The BNP therefore split, with Bean and Fountaine taking the party name, the magazine *Combat* and over 80 percent of the membership. Jordan retained the headquarters, John Tyndall, most of the Spearhead militia group and the Birmingham and West Essex branches of the BNP.[7]

Born in 1934, John Hutchyns Tyndall was the son of a Metropolitan police officer who had emigrated from Ireland as a young man. The family originally came from County Waterford, with a long line of service in the Royal Irish Constabulary. Following National Service in occupied Germany between 1952 and 1954, Tyndall had joined the LEL and became an avid reader of A. K. Chesterton's *Candour* magazine, which was devoted to Jewish conspiracy theory.[8] Tyndall believed that military prowess was an important way of maintaining national awareness against the corrosive forces of liberalism. Secret military training had been Tyndall's penchant ever since he began leading his Spearhead group in the provinces on weekends. The Special Branch had already started to take an interest in Spearhead's activities in July 1961, when policemen found such slogans as "Race War Now" and "Free Eichmann Now" on the wall of an old stables at Culverstone Green in Kent (Eichmann had recently been abducted by Israeli agents from Argentina to face trial in Jerusalem for his part in the Final Solution). Tyndall and his lieutenant, Roland Kerr-Ritchie, were subsequently observed drilling a squad of eighteen men, dressed in the Spearhead uniform of gray shirts, armbands with sunwheel symbol, boots and belts.

Jordan renamed his rump faction the National Socialist Movement (NSM) and, together with John Tyndall and Denis Pirie, began to develop a British neo-Nazi party with all the trappings of Hitlerism. He launched the NSM with an inaugural party on 20 April 1962, Hitler's birthday, featuring a swastika-decorated cake. Great excitement attended a transatlantic telephone call to George Lincoln Rockwell, the leader of the American Nazi Party, to exchange congratulations, "Heil Hitlers" and "Sieg Heils." Jordan made a speech about Britain's "loss and shame" for its role in the Second World War and the defeat of Hitler. However, he ended on an exultant note about the prospects of the NSM: "In Britain—in Britain of all places—the light which Hitler lit is burning, burning brighter, shining out across the waters, across the mountains, across the frontiers. National Socialism is coming back." In May he began editing a new magazine, *The National Socialist* (1962–66), and published the NSM manifesto: "The greatest treasure of the British people—the basis of their greatness in the past, and the only basis for it in the future—is their Aryan, predominantly Nordic blood; and that it is the first duty of the state to protect and improve this Island."[9]

Racial nationalism and the glorification of German National Socialism were distinctive features of Jordan's NSM that repeatedly seized the tabloid headlines in 1962. This year also witnessed a climax in the public concern over immigration, with some 212,000 colored immigrants having entered Britain over the eighteen months before the new Immigration Act was finally passed in July. On 1 July 1962 the NSM held a rally before a crowd of four thousand in Trafalgar Square, at which Jordan declared: "More and more people every day are opening their eyes and coming to see that Hitler was right. They are coming to see that our real enemies, the people we should have fought, were not Hitler and National Socialists of Germany but world Jewry and its associates in this country." John Tyndall fulminated in a similar anti-Semitic diatribe that "in our democratic society, the Jew is like a poisonous maggot feeding off a body in an advanced state of decay."

This open avowal of Nazi sentiments and vicious anti-Semitism quite overshadowed the precipitating factor of colored immigration. The NSM was true to the spirit of Arnold Leese and the interwar Imperial Fascist League. The rally ended in a riot with a huge crowd of Jewish people, Communist Party members and leftist CND (Campaign for Nuclear Disarmament) supporters storming the platform. The NSM would claim that the rally unleashed the racialist strife that summer. Oswald Mosley's Union Movement held rallies during July in protest at colored immigration in Trafalgar Square, Manchester and the East End, which were all met with uproar and disorder. In early August, race riots lasted for three nights in Dudley near Birmingham, and again many arrests were made.

After the BNP split, Tyndall and Jordan continued to foster the paramilitary stormtrooper spirit in the NSM. During April and May 1962, Jordan was regularly watched by detectives as he led the Spearhead squad on military maneuvers involving mock attacks on an old tower at Leith Hill on the North Downs near Dorking in Surrey. Such paramilitary training was an integral part of the NSM ideology based on the rise of the Nazis in Germany during the 1920s, as Jordan and Tyndall were especially attracted to the swashbuckling romance of armed struggle in the event of a national crisis. But the Spearhead maneuvers were also intended to rehearse the prowess, drill and discipline of the British contingent at the Nazi International camp that Jordan planned to host in England in August 1962.

Colin Jordan had two main reasons for holding this international Nazi conference. In the first place, it was important to him to boost the profile and membership of the NSM. At the time of the split with the BNP, he had been left with as few as twenty activists, including John Tyndall, Denis Pirie and Roland Kerr-Ritchie. The Trafalgar Square rally had kept the NSM in the spotlight, but Jordan was aware that he had to attract more members, not least to compete with the BNP, which was now claiming a membership of one thousand active supporters. But Jordan's ambitions were also global. By convening a gathering of foreign groups devoted to racism and anti-Semitism under NSM auspices, he sought to place himself at the head of an international Nazi movement.

When Lincoln Rockwell attended the NSM summer camp at Guiting Wood, Gloucestershire, on 3–7 August 1962, he was probably the most notorious neo-Nazi on the contemporary world scene. His clowning tactics had won him international news coverage in which he could regularly invoke the name of Adolf Hitler, quote *Mein Kampf* and pay tribute to the Nazi crusade against the Jews and all racial inferiors. Rockwell had been banned from entering Britain by the Home Office, so that his clandestine attendance was a further publicity coup for the British leader.[10] At the camp, Jordan was eager to impress his guest of honor with his own credentials for Nazi world leadership. On Sunday morning, Jordan demonstrated the military prowess and efficiency of the British Nazis to his guests by putting the Spearhead unit through its paces. Led by John Tyndall, uniformed NSM members were deployed down the valley and attacked sham strong-points, rushed imaginary enemy concentrations and fought off make-believe counter-attacks, while Jordan, Rockwell, Savitri Devi, ex-SS lieutenant Fred Borth and others watched the maneuvers through field glasses from high ground.[11]

The climax and real business of the camp took place that afternoon and involved all delegates. A new neo-Nazi International called the World Union of National Socialists (WUNS) was set up under the terms of the Cotswold Agreement, whereby Jordan, Rockwell and the leaders of the other foreign National Socialist parties formed a confederation. The major objectives of the WUNS were defined as follows:

1. To form a monolithic, combat-efficient, international political apparatus to combat and utterly destroy the international Jew-Communist and Zionist apparatus of treason and subversion.
2. To protect and promote the Aryan race and its Western Civilization wherever its members may be on the globe, and whatever their nationality may be.
3. To protect private property and free enterprise from Communist class warfare.

Long-term objectives included the "unity of all white people in a National Socialist world order with complete racial apartheid." While much of this would have been quite acceptable to other right-wing and nationalist groups, paragraph 7 of the twenty-five-paragraph codicil formally established the Nazi credentials of the WUNS: "No organization or individual failing to acknowledge the spiritual leadership of Adolf Hitler and the fact that we are National Socialists shall be admitted to membership." Likewise, the long-term objective "to find and accomplish a just and final settlement of the Jewish problem" identified the WUNS as a direct heir of Hitler's plans for a Final Solution. Jordan was elected world Führer and Rockwell his deputy and heir by the twenty-seven delegates, who with their respective parties became founding members of the WUNS.

After the camp broke up in disorder due to an invasion of local villagers, Rockwell was subsequently arrested in London and deported back to the United States.[12] Worse was to follow for the British Nazis. On Friday, 10 August, a dozen Special Branch officers raided and searched the NSM headquarters.[13] The authorities' clampdown on the NSM effectively removed Colin Jordan from the center of WUNS activities at an early stage following its birth. On 16 August, Jordan, Tyndall, Kerr-Ritchie and Pirie were charged under the Public Order Act with organizing and equipping a paramilitary force. Jordan was sentenced to nine months' imprisonment, Tyndall to six and their lieutenants to three each. Leadership of the WUNS now passed to George Lincoln Rockwell and the American Nazi Party. With its radical Nazi and anti-Semitic programme, the WUNS soon succeeded in attracting many members of the Nouvel Ordre Européen (NOE), founded in 1951 in Zurich, into its own ranks. By the beginning of 1964 the WUNS announced that it maintained national sections in France, Germany, Great Britain, Belgium, Denmark, Switzerland, the United States, Argentina, Chile and Australia.

A new split repeated the earlier division between the BNP and the NSM. John Tyndall wanted to develop a British form of national socialism with due emphasis on patriotism, racial pride and contemporary circumstances. He found the overt Hitler worship and meticulous imitation of German Nazism so beloved of Jordan increasingly anachronistic and a political liability. His bitter humiliation over losing his fiancée to Jordan was also an additional factor in the break. In August 1964 Tyndall launched the Greater Britain Movement (GBM) with its own magazine *Spearhead* and some 130 members. Following their acrimonious rupture, both Jordan and Tyndall courted Rockwell for their party to be recognized as the British section of the WUNS. Rockwell instinctively sided with Jordan as he had long advocated brazen Nazism and was suspicious of Tyndall's plan to drop the swastika as a political symbol. The question of how openly one could afford to embrace Nazi iconography has remained a persistent faultline in the future development of the British far right.[14]

Secure in Rockwell's favor, Jordan now developed his credentials as the leading theorist of modern National Socialism in the Anglo-American world. Writing in the inaugural issue of the WUNS *National Socialist World* in 1966,

Jordan offered a "philosophical appraisal" of universal Nazism to an international readership. He argued that National Socialism had survived the defeat of the Third Reich and its subsequent vilification because it was "synonymous with higher man's will to survive, his instinct for health and strength, and his desire for beauty in life." Tracing its origins in Plato's Greece, Roman state service and the feelings of blood kinship among the Nordic tribes, Jordan saw National Socialism as a healthy, organic revolt "against the whole structure of thought of liberalism and democracy, with its cash nexus; its excessive individualism; its view of man as a folkless, interchangeable unit of world population; its spiritual justification in a debased Christianity embracing a sickly 'humanitarianism.'" National Socialism, he claimed, was much more than a political scheme, but rather a worldwide rebirth of the Aryan race and its folk-feeling beyond the confines of nation states.[15]

After their split in 1964, Jordan remained an intransigent Nazi, while Tyndall cloaked his former extremism in British nationalism. Jordan successfully agitated on a racist platform for a Conservative candidate against Patrick Gordon-Walker, Labour's intended foreign secretary, at Smethwick in the 1964 general election. Copying Rockwell's use of demonstrators in monkey suits to get his racist message across, Jordan then ran his own campaign against Gordon-Walker, who again failed to secure a seat in the Leyton by-election of January 1965. The next two years saw terrorism replacing electioneering. Behind the scenes Nazi action commandos drawn from Jordan's NSM, Fountaine's BNP and Tyndall's GBM attacked Jewish properties (thirty-four in the London area alone), destroyed synagogues and mounted a firebomb attack on a Jewish *yeshiva* (seminary) in Stoke Newington, resulting in the death of a student. NSM members were jailed for attacks on synagogues in Clapton, Ilford, Kilburn and Bayswater; Jordan's wife, the French heiress Françoise Dior, was jailed for eighteen months in 1968 for conspiring to burn a synagogue.[16]

Meanwhile, the mainstream nationalists hoped for increased electoral support on the right following a renewed Labour victory in the general election of 1966, and a convergence of Labour and Tory policies on immigration. Frustrated by Rockwell's formal recognition of Jordan in early 1965 as the official British representative of the WUNS, Tyndall regretfully laid his Nazi past aside and decided to build bridges within the radical right. His efforts were rewarded when he and members of the GBM were welcomed into A. K. Chesterton's new coalition of the League of Empire Loyalists, the British National Party and the Racial Preservation Society, which formed the National Front (NF) in February 1967. With his embarrassing and unabashed Nazism, Jordan was intentionally excluded from these negotiations by Chesterton. He therefore played no part in the development of this new nationalist "fourth party" in British politics which enjoyed some significant electoral results in the 1970s in response to successive immigration scares.[17] Jordan remained a man of the Nazi underground.

How large was the NSM? In 1966 the police recorded that there had only been 187 full members in the NSM's history, with several hundred supporters and subscribers to *The National Socialist* (1962–66). But *Searchlight* has claimed that 1,200 were involved at one time or another, with a peak of nearly 700 in 1962.[18] In January 1967 Jordan went to prison a second time. Under the new Race Relations Act of 1965, he was jailed for eighteen months for publishing an inflammatory pamphlet, *The Coloured Invasion*, which sought to promote racial strife. Upon his release Jordan revived the now defunct NSM as the British Movement in the summer of 1968. Compared to the parliamentary ambitions of the NF, the British Movement (BM) was to concentrate on mobilizing skinheads, football hooligans and young urban thugs against the left and colored immigrants in inner cities. This violent strategy harked back to the "tough squads" of Leese's Imperial Fascist League and, of course, the Nazi stormtroopers of the 1920s. The purpose of BM racial attacks was outright provocation of the West Indian and Asian minorities in the expectation that any counterattacks on whites would unleash a massive backlash, escalating into racial war.

Jordan was succeeded in 1974 as BM leader by Michael McLaughlin, a former merchant seaman from Liverpool. McLaughlin was ambitious and had evidently undermined Jordan's position while he held the office of chairman. In disgust, Jordan resigned from the BM altogether in 1975 to devote himself to writing on his farm at Greenhow Hill near Harrogate, Yorkshire. Throughout the 1970s the BM had close links with a political underground that fomented racial violence and sought contacts with European fascist terrorists. By 1980, it claimed to have twenty-five branches and a membership of four thousand, but these figures probably counted skinheads, football hooligans and other barely affiliated street fighters. But McLaughlin's fief was a difficult one to govern. The presence of a turncoat and *Searchlight* mole, Ray Hill, at its highest levels thwarted many BM attacks while leading to police investigations and much internal feuding. Once Ray Hill went public in 1982, the movement was severely demoralized. The very unruliness of the BM street forces frustrated any proper internal organization. Despairing of an undisciplined rabble, McLaughlin resigned the leadership and closed down the BM national office at Shotten in North Wales in late 1983.

This disbandment was rejected by the remaining organizers who began to salvage the movement, renaming it the British National Socialist Movement

(BNSM) at its 1985 annual general meeting. As the "godfather" of the Nazi underground, Jordan continued to intrigue for the revival of far-right terrorism. Inspired by *The Turner Diaries* and the militant example of The Order in the United States, Jordan penned a master plan for the future of British Nazism in the journal of the League of St. George in June 1986. Here Jordan claimed that the elite control of television ensured the survival of democracy through the ballot box and political parties. He rejected traditional party organization and called for its replacement by an "elite spearhead" or "task force" engaged in "war" and mentioned the example of the special units of Otto Skorzeny, the Third Reich's premier commando leader. This armed guerrilla activity should, Jordan argued, be matched by a racial populist party that slowly builds its respectability; meanwhile, others should infiltrate mainstream parties and public bodies. As illegal activity would often lead to capture and prison sentences, Jordan warned that "a strict separation of the personnel of the overt from those of the underground activities is absolutely essential."[19]

A handful of core BNSM activists evidently kept the flame alive in Jordan's sense. To begin with, there was a systematic re-recruitment of former members. Weapons training for BNSM members was fostered by placing them in gun clubs and Territorial Army units around the country. Several BNSM members with arms convictions became involved with Defence Begins At Home, a respectable right-wing pressure group, also known as the Hedgehogs, which lobbied between 1983 and 1986 for an increase in Britain's community defense capability. The Blood and Honour network of white power music fans numbering some eight hundred skinheads provided a further pool for the recruiting sergeants of the BSNM. However, after the Hungerford massacre in which the gun fanatic Michael Ryan ran amok, killing his neighbors and police officers, even some BNSM members began to worry. Following a tip-off, three leading BNSM gunmen—Jeff Carson, a scoutmaster from southwest London, David Philips from Essex and John Sullivan from London—were arrested while firing pump-action shotguns in the Hertfordshire woods.[20]

At this time, the increasing isolation of Northern Ireland in its nationalist struggle against both the Irish Republican Army (IRA) and a complaisant U.K. government had begun to attract the far right in Britain as a fertile ground for its own nationalist propaganda. The NF intensified its operations in the province and a massive, joint NF–Orange Order march was held in November 1986 at Bridgwater, Somerset, the constituency of Northern Ireland secretary Tom King, in protest of the Anglo-Irish Agreement.[21] The BNSM forged its own military links with Ulster Loyalist groups such as the Ulster Defence Association (UDA) and its terrorist units, the Ulster Freedom Fighters

(UFF) and the Ulster Volunteer Force (UVF). These groups operated both in Northern Ireland and in mainland Britain, where underground BNSM members were frequently involved in gun-running and in armed attacks against Republican targets. The Blood and Honour network also provided further BNSM recruits for the mainland cells of the Ulster units. John Nicholson, a lay preacher in the Protestant Church and a London UDA officer, arranged for the training of dozens of young men in southern England.

Finally, the BNSM cultivated close contacts with neo-Nazi groups on the continent. Et Wolsink (b. 1924), a former Dutch SS man, became the BNSM international liaison officer in addition to belonging to a string of neo-Nazi associations, including holding a senior office in the Dutch People's Union (DVU), the Dutch "Wiking Jugend," the Northern League and the Dutch section of the German neo-Nazi ANS-NA, headed by Michael Kühnen. Wolsink had a notorious Nazi past, having been sentenced in 1946 to eight years' imprisonment for his role in the SS Brandenburg division. A close friend of the widow of the Dutch Nazi leader Rost van Tonningen, Wolsink was able to bring more than one hundred members of the BNSM and its overseas supporters together at a secret location in Derbyshire in April 1989 for the hundredth anniversary of Hitler's birthday.[22] By 1990, the two to three hundred active BNSM members were concentrated in London, the Midlands and particularly in Yorkshire. Two leaders, Stephen Frost and Glyn Fordham, operated from P.O. boxes in Slaithwaite near Huddersfield and Heckmondwike. Living close by at his Yorkshire farm, Colin Jordan was always abreast of developments among the militant Nazis.

Jordan continued to supply articles to American Nazi publications on the contemporary relevance of National Socialism and the unique leadership of Adolf Hitler. In *National Socialism: World Creed for the 1980s* (1981), a booklet reprinted from an article first published in the WUNS periodical, Jordan dismissed nationalists, populists, Nazi fetishists ("Hollywood Nazis"), and skinheads (a sideswipe at those street fighters initially welcomed into the British Movement) as betrayers of National Socialism. Jordan exalted Nazism as a religion of life and nature, quite incompatible with Christianity. National Socialists, he concluded, were neither nationalists nor conservatives but racial revolutionaries summoning the white peoples of the world to unite for survival and supremacy. As a current tactic, he argued for disruptive sabotage of the system and the development of elite Nazi cadres through private Nazi schools, labor projects and small rural communities.[23]

This idea carried through to a back-to-the-land movement among the "Political Soldier" and "Third Way" activists who emerged from the breakup of the National Front in the mid-1980s. Nick Griffin, a former NF leader, trained cadres at his family farm in Suffolk. Seeking new alliances, the political soldiers made overtures to Qaddafi's Libya and to Iran and Iraq. The group also praised the Welsh nationalist bombers and arsonists, the Sons of Glyndwr. From his farm on the Welsh Marches, Griffin ran a "Smash the Cities" campaign implying a Nazi version of Pol Potism.[24] David Myatt, one of Jordan's devoted followers in the old BM, tried to set up a Nazi country commune in Shropshire. In the 1990s, the Order of Jarls Bælder, Myatt's Reichsfolk and the National Socialist Alliance mounted similar rural ventures to foster the elite Nazi spirit among the few who were expected to lead the masses when the established social and economic order ultimately collapses (see chapter 11).

In the early 1980s, Jordan revived Leese's periodical *Gothic Ripples* as his own occasional mouthpiece for articles on the Third Reich, Hess's "murder" in Spandau prison, and anti-Semitic and racist commentary on contemporary affairs. Eulogies of Hitler were also a staple item among these writings, reaching a climax in 1989, the centenary year of his birth. "Hitler was Right!," originally published in *Gothic Ripples* and then reprinted in George Dietz's special 20 April 1989 anniversary issue of *Liberty Bell*, upheld Hitler's accuracy on a whole range of issues, including the denunciation of democracy, the protection of the folk community, his allegedly preemptive attack on the Soviet Union, the lost opportunity of an Anglo-German alliance and his prophecy of the dark age that would follow his defeat.[25] In a commemorative article for Matt Koehl's New Order *NS Bulletin*, Jordan followed the exposition of Savitri Devi in presenting Hitler as a "Man against Time," a superhuman personality who, through the force of his own will, sought to oppose Aryan decline within the cycle of the ages. Another paean to Hitler was published in the magazine of the League of St. George, a leading far-right group in Britain.[26]

Embellished with the sombre muscular bronze statues of the Nazi sculptor Arno Breker, Jordan's booklets and articles on National Socialism are written for a literate readership. Beside the pious and enthusiastic offerings of the New Order, this native British testimony to Hitler and universal Nazism seems earnest and down to earth. In *A Train of Thought* (1989), Jordan returned to the theme of clandestine task forces to speed the breakdown of the social order, a hope that now reposed in the underground BNSM. In 1993 he lightened his touch with a satire, *Merrie England—2,000*, which paints a droll Orwellian view of a Britain at the end of the twentieth century dominated by the race-relations police, reeducation for the bigoted elderly, tax relief for mixed marriages, ritual obeisance for the guilty white population and in place of Nelson's Column a statue of Nelson Mandela in "Harmony Square." In recognition of his godfather status to the international Nazi movement over three decades, the European section of the WUNS in Denmark published a volume of Jordan's selected writings in 1993.

Combat 18, a guerrilla group active since the early 1990s, was another revival of Colin Jordan's plan for a militant Nazi underground. Directly descended from the BNSM, both in terms of personnel and methods, Combat 18 (C18) mobilizes thugs, boot boys and skinheads for physical attacks, bombings and arson against its perceived racial enemies. Its name is taken from the first and eighth letters of the alphabet, which signify Adolf Hitler. C18 specializes in intimidation, harassment and brutality. Attacks are usually accompanied by gloating phone calls and crude stickers carrying its black skull symbol and the caption "Combat 18 in the area." Illustrated fliers of a sinister trooper wearing a gas mask and toting powerful new weapons are captioned "C18 ready for ethnic cleansing" in cut-out letters. C18 is an armed criminal conspiracy that gathers intelligence and mobilizes its cells to carry out acts of violence against its chosen targets, which have included Labour politicians, MPs, green activists and members of Jewish organizations. By distributing hit lists of its enemies' private addresses and telephone numbers, it aims to strike fear into all opponents by showing that it is always ready to mount surprise attacks.

C18 began to form in late 1991 out of the BNSM, Blood and Honour skinhead groups and notorious racist football gangs including West Ham, Charlton, Leeds, Millwall and the Chelsea Headhunters. Harold A. Covington, the American Nazi, lived in London that winter and appears to have been instrumental in encouraging the emergence of a new militant Nazi alliance involving groups in Sweden, Germany and C18 in Britain, using computer communications and U.S.-style Nazi terrorism.[27] Another factor favoring the group was the need for tougher stewarding at BNP meetings and other events, such as lectures by the revisionist historian David Irving in November 1991. A brutal and bloody attack by C18 on Anti-Nazi League pamphleteers followed in February 1992 at Tower Hamlets. Old BNSM faces and known football hooligans began to guard the BNP as it canvased the London streets and ran election rallies in the run-up to the April 1992 general election. In view of its subversive and illegal activities, C18 gave an offshore mailing address in Raleigh, North Carolina, which was Covington's Dixie Press. Covington then passed the applications and inquiries back to Steve Sargent in Barnet, whose Resurgam Books also distributed the *Searchlight* article on Covington's earlier role in Britain.[28]

The unchallenged street leader of C18 was Paul David Sargent (b. 1960), better known as Charlie "Ginger Pig" Sargent on account of his hair color and plump figure. A typical working-class Nazi thug, Charlie Sargent was active in the BM during the 1970s and early 1980s, trailing a long record of violence. In 1978 he was convicted on offensive weapons and threatening-behaviour charges arising from public disorders. He proclaimed a "race war," inciting Muslims and blacks to retaliatory violence. If others did not follow him, he would know that "our race is too weak to survive and deserves to die."[29] His elder brother, William, was active in the National Front and organized illegal dogfights, while his younger brother, Stephen, ran Resurgam Books and published *Thor-Would*, a pagan C18 magazine, from his home in Barnet. Another top figure in C18 was Eddy Whicker, a South London garbage collector, one of the National Front's toughest street fighters in the 1970s. Later involved with the UDA, as was Charlie Sargent, Whicker has been a prominent steward in C18-minding activities alongside the BNP. John Merritt and Paul Ballard, both long-term members of the Croydon BNP branch, a former NF stronghold, were also senior C18 managers. Another C18 man, Steve Martin from Stamford Hill, also had BNP and strong Ulster loyalist links. Once charged with UVF gun running, he later became a full UDA member.[30]

The C18 *Redwatch* bulletins contained hit lists of enemies, a clear incitement to violence, injury and murder. The first issue (March 1992) was flagged as "a bimonthly report on the red front. Compiled by COMBAT 18" and carried the slogan "let them hate so long as they fear." Readers were encouraged to compile their own lists. The American Nazi model was evident in reference to the Aryan Militant group, unexpected attacks with knife and gun, and the injunction "to hide in the faceless hordes of ZOGs putrid, mud infested cities ... UNDERMINE-DEMORALIZE-DESTROY."[31] Many of the people listed in the second issue (May 1992) were not communists but Labour Party members, officers of refugee organizations and anti-apartheid activists. There was a press release of C18's arson attack on the *Morning Star* office, while the final page superimposed the words "race war" and "armed resistance" with the C18 skull logo over a portrait of Hitler and a sketch of a masked figure carrying an assault rifle. The fire at the communist newspaper served as a model for fresh attacks: two arsons in Birmingham, the Democratic Left office (August 1992) and the Sandwell Unemployment and Community Resource Centre (November 1992) were listed in subsequent *Redwatch* issues.[32]

In these scruffy and semi-literate bulletins, C18 flaunted its Nazi ideas. The third issue of *Redwatch* bore the symbol of the South African Afrikaner Weerstandsbeweging (AWB) movement and the caption "Zyklon-B: over six million satisfied customers. Manufactured by Combat 18" beside a picture of an Auschwitz poison gas canister. The hit list included several Communist Party organizers, ANC supporters and information on the left-wing group Militant.

The fourth issue included Ken Livingstone, the Labour council leader; Marc Wadsworth of the Anti-Racist Alliance; and Sir Ivan Lawrence QC, the Conservative MP and member of the Jewish Board of Deputies who had recently been appointed chairman of the Home Affairs select committee on race relations. The third issue of another C18 magazine entitled *Combat 18* contained detailed instructions on how to make powerful bombs, explosives and fuses. Beneath the slogan "Kill em all!," C18 target lists now included Paddy Ashdown, the Liberal Democratic Party leader; Glenda Jackson, the well-known actress and prominent Labour supporter; Alf Lomas, a member of the European Parliament; and Paul Condon, commissioner of the Metropolitan Police and a senior detective of the International and Organised Crime Branch, the unit specially assigned to deal with C18 crimes.[33]

C18 had two to three hundred members throughout Britain operating in military cells. They were responsible for hundreds of criminal incidents, including affray, arson and violent assault. Asian businesses were burned down in London, trades unionists' homes in Durham and Leeds were destroyed and a firebomb attack was made on a meeting in Milton Keynes being addressed by Leon Greenman, an eighty-year-old Holocaust survivor who was later harassed. A demonstration in Eltham (November 1992) was followed by affray in Nottingham (23 January 1993). Left-wing and anarchist bookshops in Kilburn, Whitechapel, Nottingham and Durham were attacked. On 15 January 1994, C18 organized a large international skinhead event involving neo-Nazi groups from Holland, Denmark and Germany that dissolved into running battles across London with left-wing protesters and the police. In August 1994 in Leeds, there were crossbow and firebomb attacks on ANL members, and Derek Fatchett, Labour MP for Leeds West, was twice granted police protection. Over a three-year period dozens of incidents occurred in London alone involving arson and vicious assaults against colored people. Many of these were reported with boasts of injury and damage in the successive issues of the new C18 magazines, *Putsch*, *Lebensraum* and *The Order*.[34]

Both *Putsch* and *Lebensraum* reflect the frustration and rage of white working-class youths displaced in their traditional neighborhoods by growing racial minorities. Thirty years and a whole generation after Jordan's first race riots, Britain now has large established Asian and black communities in London and the large cities of the North and Midlands. Mosques and Hindu temples replace old pubs and labor clubs, ethnic festivals overwhelm embattled white residents and Asian-language newspapers, cinemas and shops reflect the existence of large unassimilated groups. White youngsters form a tiny minority in many schools where rolls are almost exclusively made up of ethnic minority children. Housing allocations in such London boroughs as

Tower Hamlets overrepresent the ethnic population out of all proportion to their white residents, which has led to a "rights for whites" movement led by the British National Party. Labour-held councils now select Muslim candidates for office in areas of high Asian population, while many local authorities pander to blacks with respect to employment, special projects and facilities, and even for mayoral office. Working-class whites are directly confronted by the increasing cultural and political self-assertion of the minorities.[35]

John Cato's editorial line in *Putsch* plays on the fears of poor, white, working-class youth increasingly threatened with marginalization. He castigates liberal elites for conniving in their disinheritance through political correctness and public expenditure on multicultural festivals, black AIDS research, homosexual clubs, and police training in racial sensitivity and minority languages. He likens the lot of black slaves to the miseries of the Victorian proletariat and asks why the white working class should share the guilt of the liberal middle classes about racism. As white youth clubs close down and whole swathes of urban heartland are surrendered to the ethnic groups, the media and mass entertainment beam a constant barrage of positive multiracial images onto the British populace. Meanwhile, the national press constantly suppresses reports of black-on-white crime and racial strife in the inner cities. While rare white racist attacks on blacks receive copious coverage with guilt-laden moralizing, numerous white victims of black crime are simply attributed to poor "race relations." Cato demands wholesale repatriation of colored immigrants, arguing that the multiracial experiment is a complete catastrophe, propped up only by a managed media and pious liberal elites.[36]

The C18 hit lists, bomb-making instructions and escalating racial violence indicate the influence of American Nazi ideology and methods. In *The Order*, the magazine named after the U.S. terrorist group, editor John Cato paid fulsome tribute to its martyred leader, Robert Jay Mathews. It quoted Mathews's "declaration of war" against a "Jewish controlled mongrelized society, which is depriving White Aryans of their existence and homeland." The same issue featured a full exposition of Louis Beam's strategy of "leaderless resistance" for the war on ZOG.[37] In the pages of *Putsch*, Cato exults in Pierce's advocacy of individual acts of violence against blacks and Jews. After fleeing from Kent to Spalding in Lincolnshire, Cato started a new magazine, *The Oak*, which reprinted many of Pierce's articles. Paul Jeffries set up Life Rune Books in Leeds as the U.K. distributor for William Pierce's National Alliance. In June 1994 Cato and Jeffries formed the National Socialist Alliance (NSA) as a federation of C18, several rebel BNSM sections with their magazines *Sigrun* and *Europe Awake,* and the Blood and Honour groups in a British version of Pierce's American organization. By mid-1995, a number of smaller groups had joined the NSA, including David Myatt's National-Socialist Movement, Adrian Blundell's White Aryan Resistance and the Yorkshire-based Patriotic Women's League.[38]

The NSA adopted other American ideas besides terrorism, "leaderless resistance" and liaison with the National Alliance. The idea of an "Aryan white homeland," familiar from *The Turner Diaries* and Christian Identity doctrine, began to circulate among young British Nazis. An island off the coast of Scotland was rejected in favor of an area that was underpopulated, almost entirely white and yet within striking distance of the large cities where war could be waged against a multiracial society. It was decided to set up the racial homeland in Essex, between Chelmsford and the coast, near the Bradwell nuclear power station. The idea was further endorsed by Colin Jordan's former NSM aide, Wulstram Tedder, who was already running a small Nazi commune on the Welsh borders, and David Myatt, another violent former BM activist and Nazi satanist, who publicized the project as the "East Saxon Kindred." This was to be "an all-White neighbourhood and community, and thus an Aryan republic . . . where Aryans can live among their own kind . . . the territory will thus be ruled and controlled by Aryans who are National-Socialists."[39]

The NSA's formation coincided with increasing radicalism on the British far-right scene. The BNP gain (September 1993) and then loss (May 1994) of a council seat in Tower Hamlets led to frustration with electoral strategy, especially among younger members. Racist groups now felt embattled by the widespread acceptance of a multiracial society combined with stricter enforcement of race-relations legislation, involving the imprisonment of leaders and the censorship of its press. The flight into sectarian militancy and enclave doctrine paralleled the development of American Nazism in the late 1970s and early 1980s. Now British Nazis proclaimed an all-out battle for the very survival of the white race against the hated ZOG in tones of religious fervor and apocalyptic prophecy. The masthead of *Putsch* magazine carried the motto "we must secure the existence of our people and a future for white children," the "14 Words" of David Lane, a member of The Order now serving a life sentence for his part in the murder of a Jewish radio commentator in Denver. In early 1995 there were increasing regional defections from the BNP membership to the NSA, including the Halifax, Oldham, Scotland and Northern Ireland branches.[40]

Since its inception, C18 has been closely linked to neo-Nazi groups abroad. In 1992 contacts were forged by Harold Covington with the terrorist White Aryan Resistance (VAM) in Sweden. This underground group imitates The Order with bank robberies and the stockpiling of weapons as a preliminary step for "a racial holocaust" to "eliminate ZOG." Its declared enemies are the political parties, the police and the media, the Jewish community and anti-racists. In December 1993, neo-Nazi letter-bomb campaigns began in Austria against socialists and liberals soft on immigration. Cryptic communications from the Bavarian Liberation Army (Bajuvarische Befreiungsarmee, BBA) regularly cite heroes from Austria's military past in battles against the invading Avars, Slavs and Turks. Like VAM, the German anti-anti-fascist organization also publishes a hit-list bulletin, *Der Einblick*, across the border in Denmark. Both organizations foster contacts with C18 and the Danish National Socialist Movement (Dansk Nasjonal Sosjalistik Bewegung, DNSB) at the annual international Nazi festival in Diksmuide and the Rudolf Hess commemorations in Fulda. Leading members of the DNSB, VAM, NSA, and Norwegian and Austrian groups met in Copenhagen in March 1995 to coordinate their anti-anti-fascist activities.[41]

Striking evidence of these international links emerged when seven young Danish neo-Nazis were charged in January 1997 with planning an international letter-bombing campaign against targets in London supplied by C18. The packages were due to have been posted in Sweden. The letter-bomb technique was directly borrowed from the Austrian nationalists, but the British targets reflected the influence of American ideas of "race war." Among the intended recipients of the letter bombs were prominent British athletes in mixed-race marriages, including Kriss Akabusi and Derek Redmond.[42] The targeting of such "race-traitors" and their spouses was a pointed theme of William Pierce's novel *Hunter*, in which the Nazi hero stalked race-mixing couples with intent to kill, thereby spreading terror and demoralization throughout multiracial society. C18's mobilization of their Danish, Swedish and German allies for such a campaign of violence against politicians and public figures demonstrates the international scope of the hit-list strategy that intends to intimidate all supporters of multiracialism.

Only weeks after the bombing campaign was exposed, Charlie Sargent was charged with murdering a fellow activist and is now serving a lengthy prison sentence. C18 began to splinter. Meanwhile, Troy Southgate's National Revolutionary Faction was achieving prominence in the militant underground. Southgate had begun his political career in 1983 with the "Political Soldiers" faction of the National Front, then followed Griffin and others into the Italian-inspired International Third Position in 1989. This association lasted until September 1992, when Southgate formed the English Nationalist Movement (ENM). Between 1992 and 1998, the ENM returned to the revolutionary principles of the NF, with an emphasis on the writings of Otto Strasser and Walther Darré alongside the socialist ideas of William Morris, Robert Owen and William Cobbett. Renamed National Revolutionary Faction

(NRF) in 1998, the party is committed to "national revolution," advocates a strong Europe and has joined the European Liberation Front, a pan-European alliance of national revolutionaries based on the ideas of Otto Strasser, Francis Parker Yockey and Jean Thiriart. Like other groups in the Euro-American radical right, the NRF is committed to the fight against ZOG and the "New World Order," rejects the democratic process and aims to establish autonomous all-white zones. In August 2000 its strategy of infiltration led to joint actions alongside violent anti-hunt saboteurs of the Animal Liberation Front.[43]

David Myatt's National-Socialist Movement (NSM) absorbed many C18 activists when Charlie Sargent's younger brother, Steve, and a few dozen supporters joined the NSM in March 1997. A longtime devotee of right-wing extremism and satanism, David Myatt had begun elaborating a "religion of National-Socialism" in the early 1990s, advertising his writings in *The Oak*, edited by John Cato. Advocating direct action and sabotage of basic services including water, sewage and electricity, Myatt saw C18 as the street army from which an Aryan revolutionary movement could be built. Myatt's cultic view of Nazism embraced a Manichaean view of the racial struggle between Aryans and the growing numbers of colored groups in British cities: "Since these foreigners are an invasion force, since there is now a war, and since we do live under a tyrannical Zionist Occupation Government, we have no choice but to actively fight for our freedom, our race and our lands. We must fight the non-Aryan invaders who have settled in our lands."[44] As Myatt's strengths lay in political education and doctrine, the leadership of an expanded NSM passed in 1997 to Tony Williams (b. 1956), a wealthy young supporter of Nazi causes since the early 1980s.

Refounded in June 1997, the NSM remained true to Myatt's visionary Hitlerism and was committed to the establishment within Britain of an exclusive Aryan community. Rejecting the "conventionalities of electioneering," the NSM adopted the Nazi leadership principle to foster "national and racial solidarity, duty and honour." Tony Williams began publishing *Column 88*, a quarterly magazine in color, with his editorials, "Broadcasts from the Bunker," providing a flippant commentary on the state of liberal Britain as seen from the Third Reich. Historical articles on Nazi social welfare in prewar Germany and the life of William Joyce alternated with Myatt's views on the suppression of dissent in democracies and U.S. convict Steve Stein's eulogy of young German Panzer crews. Alongside features on NSM policy on racial identity and community values, the magazine ran an interview with Colin Jordan, excerpts from the writings of Savitri Devi, and heroic stories of German World War II military exploits.[45] While Williams concentrated on history and philosophy, Steve Sargent continued publishing *White Dragon*, a bimonthly magazine targeting skinheads and football fans with a white ethnic message.

The NSM attracted national publicity when it was discovered that the young man arrested for the three nail bombings in London in May 1999 had joined the group in late 1998. Living in the isolation of multiracial single room occupancy housing in East London, David Copeland (b. 1976) had embraced racist politics, joining the British National Party in spring 1997 and reading Christian Identity literature on the Internet. Already in 1996, Copeland had begun to think of a bombing campaign against ethnic groups in order to provoke a backlash and racial war in Britain. Seeking more radical contacts, he joined the NSM, being appointed an area leader in February 1999. His first nail-bomb attack on 19 April in Brixton, a largely black London borough, wounded thirty-nine people. On 24 April he struck in Brick Lane, an area of Asian population, leaving six wounded. On 30 April he bombed a public house patronized by homosexuals in Soho, which resulted in three deaths and horrific injuries to sixty-five people. Allegedly inspired by *The Turner Diaries*, Copeland acted as a lone wolf and had little involvement with the NSM.[46] Panicked by the discovery of the bomber's identity, Tony Williams disbanded the NSM in May 1999. However, Copeland's violent campaign was a textbook application of "leaderless resistance" and operation in "phantom cells."

The Nazi underground has remained active in Britain from the early 1960s right up to the present, persistently cultivating racist anti-Semitism and trying to provoke violent conflict between whites and people of color in Britain's cities. The noisy protests, inflammatory rhetoric and criminal acts of the original NSM, BM and C18 involving racial attacks, arson and sabotage have exercised an influence on the formation of anti-immigrant feeling and even on government policy that is out of all proportion to their actual memberships. Copeland saw his nail-bomb campaign as a provocation for racial war. This militant tradition owes much to Colin Jordan, the godfather of British neo-Nazism. Radicalized by his terms of imprisonment, Jordan has consistently advocated the growth of revolutionary Nazi activist cells and the eventual overthrow of liberal democracy in conditions of crisis. Like his American counterparts, Jordan blended an abiding love of Hitler and the Third Reich with a modern racist doctrine opposed to colored populations within white nations. In common with American neo-Nazism, this British Hitlerism aims at global white supremacy through a campaign of millenarian militancy against the perceived disorders of liberalism and multiracialism.

3

Julius Evola and the Kali Yuga

ON 2 AUGUST 1980, Italian neo-fascist terrorists took center stage as public enemies every bit as dangerous as extreme left-wing fanatics. At 10:25 A.M. a deafening bomb explosion rocked the main concourse of Bologna railway station. Eighty-five victims died either immediately or as a result of their injuries, and another two hundred were wounded, many horribly. The rationale behind the massacre was familiar yet incredible: the neo-fascist "strategy of tension" regarded such mayhem, horror and disorder as a trigger for a prerevolutionary situtation. Despite the difficulties of finding the actual perpetrators, the authorities found abundant confirmation that these bomb attacks against Italy's civilian order were indeed part of such a strategy of tension. As the police sought to question Paolo Signorelli, Franco Freda, Claudio Mutti and Stefano delle Chiaie, Italy's well-identified neo-fascist underground, a single name kept recurring in their investigations. This was a philosopher who had served the terrorists as an inspiration, mentor and guru figure. His name was Julius Evola.

The official effort to apprehend the terrorists after the Bologna bombing was thorough, and several members of the violent Nuclei Armati Rivoluzionari (NAR) fled to London and other foreign capitals to escape arrest. Wherever they made contact with far-right groups abroad, knowledge of Evola spread abroad. Julius Evola now became a cult figure, with his books and doctrines receiving increasing attention and discussion in the periodicals and conferences of the European New Right. An elegant, smooth-shaven face, a firm mouth and an imperious gaze with a flashing monocle: visual images of Evola began to appear in English, French and German far-right periodicals during the 1980s. His unqualified elitist posture and high-flown metaphysical critique of modernity attracted those who felt themselves profoundly alienated from the norms and values of liberal society. More importantly, his esoteric elitism and spiritual authoritarianism offered a sophisticated ideology to right-wing intellectuals who saw Anglo-American neo-Nazism as a crude creed with limited appeal.

Julius Evola (1898–1974) is today a prominent icon of fascist idealism. His ideal was the Indo-Aryan tradition, where hierarchy, caste, authority and state ruled supreme over the material aspects of life. Invoking the heroic and sacred values of this mythical tradition, Evola advanced a radical doctrine of anti-egalitarianism, anti-democracy, anti-liberalism and anti-Semitism. He scorned the modern world of popular rule and bourgeois values, democracy and socialism, seeing capitalism and communism as twin aspects of the benighted reign of materialism. During the 1930s, Evola had enjoyed the reputation of a bold and controversial theorist in Fascist Italy and had also been well known in Conservative Revolutionary circles in Germany during the Third Reich. Wounded at the close of the war, he had spent the postwar years in a wheelchair at his apartment on the Corso Vittoria Emanuelle in the center of Rome. Secluded from practical politics, Evola held the aura of a fascist sage untainted by the fall of Mussolini until his death in 1974. A young generation of neo-fascists was irresistibly drawn to this oracle of violence and revolution.[1]

Giulio Cesare Andrea Evola was born in Rome on 19 May 1898, the scion of a noble Sicilian family. He soon rebelled against his strict Catholic upbringing. Alongside his high school studies in industrial engineering, he cultivated a keen interest in the Italian literary avant garde, dominated at the time by Giovanni Papini and Giuseppe Prezzolini, and in Filippo Tommaso Marinetti's futurist movement in art. At the age of nineteen he joined the Italian army in the later stages of the First World War, serving as a mountain artillery officer at the Austrian front on the Asiago plateau in northern Italy. After the war, Evola found it hard to adjust to settled life. Beset by spiritual restlessness, he embarked on a quest for self-transcendence, which implied a break with the bourgeois values of the past. Dismissing futurism as loud and showy, he became the leading representative of the Dada movement in Italy. He gave readings of his avant-garde poetry in the Cabaret Grotte dell'Augusteo—Rome's answer to the Cabaret Voltaire in Zurich—and exhibited his paintings in Rome, Milan, Lausanne and Berlin.[2]

Repelled by the commercialization of avant-garde art and its hardening into convention, Evola gave up painting in 1922 and wrote three transrational philosophical books, which he published during the 1920s.[3] Evola's philosophical idealism of the absolute individual was but one expression of his quest for self-transcendence in a postwar age of shattered values and moral uncertainties. He also became interested in oriental studies and became a profound student of magic, the occult, alchemy and Eastern religions. He experimented with hallucinogenic drugs, discovered the ancient Theravadin Buddhist text, the *Majjhima-Nikaya*, and wrote the introduction to an Italian translation of the *Tao-Te-Ching* in 1923. He frequented the Italian Independent Theosophical League and was introduced by its president, Decio Calvari, to the study of Tantrism, which especially captured Evola's imagination. He began corresponding with Sir John Woodroffe, the learned British orientalist, who revealed the secrets of this esoteric Hindu school in *The Serpent of Power* and other books published under his pseudonym, Arthur Avalon. Evola presented his own study of Tantrism and kundalini yoga, based on Woodroffe's works and original texts, as *L'uomo come potenza* [The Yoga of Power] (1925).

Tantrism originated in India around A.D. 400 as a radical Hindu cult focused on women, goddesses and sexual energy. Rejecting customary Hindu abstinence, tantric rituals celebrated intoxicating beverages, meat, fish, mudras and ritual sexual intercourse. Tantrism revolves around the notion of breaking all ties or bonds (*pasha*). Individuals with an animal nature, enslaved by appetite, lust, custom and religious conformity are necessarily disqualified. By means of taboo and spiritually dangerous practices (orgies, intoxication), the superior adept (*vira*) can raise his consciousness to supreme levels of unity with the divine female power of Shakti, which animates and inspires the whole universe, thereby acquiring exceptional knowledge (*vidya*) and magical powers (*siddhis*). Tantric doctrine lays much emphasis on the the male god Shiva and his bride Shakti, whose sexual union is personified in ritual intercourse. While this act symbolizes the creative impulses of the cosmos, male ejaculation of semen is typically discouraged. In this way the energy of orgasm is supposedly channeled away from the propagation of organic life toward a powerful ascent experience.

Tantrism complemented Western idealism in Evola's quest for self-transcendence. Its secrecy and elitism essentially negated the modern world of rationalism and democracy. Evola wrote that the knowledge and powers pursued by the modern world are democratic, that is, available at educational institutions to anyone with enough intelligence. Likewise, technology is democratic: an instrument or weapon can be used by anyone with sufficient training. By contrast, the tantric magical powers (*siddhis*) are always personal and exceptional achievements accessible only to the few.[4] But Evola also thought Tantrism arose specifically in fifth-century India at a time of spiritual decadence when men could no longer achieve an otherworldly liberation from the world. Instead, they sought a full-blooded embrace of life's delights—liberty within the world. For this reason, Tantrism was more akin to Western modes of thought and also appropriate to the modern age characterized by density, coarseness and moral decline. Tantric rituals essentially transformed "poison into medicine" for the strong and liberated individual.[5]

During the 1920s Evola immersed himself in the study of the Western esoteric tradition. Through Theosophical and Masonic circles he met Arturo Reghini (1878–1946), a Roman occultist immersed in alchemy, magic and theurgy. Reghini edited two journals, *Atanòr* (1924) and *Ignis* (1925), whose contents embraced initiate studies from Pythagoreanism to yoga, from Hebrew Cabalism to Cagliostro's Egyptian Freemasonry. Evola contributed numerous reviews and articles on Tantrism, on the nature of woman, on Rudolf Steiner, and an essay on Dionysius. A circle soon gathered around Reghini and Evola. A strong anthroposophical influence came from Giovanni Colazza and Duke Giovanni Colonna di Cesarò. Close to the group, which adopted the name UR, were Guiliano Kremmerz (1861–1939), founder of the Fraternity of Myriam that had an interest in sex magic, and an Indian alchemist, C. S. Narayana Ariar Shiyali.[6] Between 1927 and 1929 the group published *Ur* (renamed *Krur* in 1929), a monthly journal of essays and rituals, which included many of Evola's magical studies.

Arturo Reghini sought the renewal of the classical tradition in a fiercely anti-Christian, pagan spirit. He was a powerful influence on Evola during the years 1924 to 1930, introducing him to the traditional texts of alchemy, whose symbolism they regarded as a universal key to the macrocosm of the universe and the microcosm of man. After presenting an initial study of alchemy in *Krur*, Evola published his book *La tradizione ermetica* [The Hermetic Tradition] (1931) on hermeticism as an ancient pagan tradition. Evola believed that the veiled symbolism of hermetico-alchemical cosmology described the outlines of a heroic, pre-Christian worldview when a warrior aristocracy reigned supreme. Evola instances the "tree" as a symbol of knowledge and immortality: in a heroic myth, one who succumbs in a bid to win the powers of the tree simply has more courage than luck; he may try again and regain his dignity. But in a postheroic religious era, he has sinned, and his action is a sacrilege and is damned.[7] Evola saw alchemy and hermeticism as an occult survival of the "Royal Art," a universal secret science of human and natural transformation according to heroic concepts, now buried beneath pusillanimous Christian priestcraft.

The anti-democratic and anti-modernist tenor of Evola's political thought may be traced to his readings of Plato, Nietzsche and Oswald Spengler, whose famous work *The Decline of the West* (1918–22) he later translated into Italian. But Reghini was a more immediate force. Both he and Evola regarded the Roman patrician world and the imperial constitution as a close approximation to their ideal state. This strict hierarchy was but a pattern of a higher, transcendental and absolute order. The leveling, egalitarian universalism of Christianity negated and ultimately dissolved this political order, heralding the disorder of the modern world. Writing in *Atanòr* in 1924, Reghini reflected that he had already fifteen years earlier predicted the rise of an Italian regime based on the ancient world and welcomed Fascism. The fasces—the bundle of rods containing an Etruscan bronze axe as the symbol of the magistrate's power in ancient Rome—was presented to Mussolini in 1923 by a member of an order dedicated to such a revival. The Group of UR also performed rituals intended to inspire the Fascist regime with the spirit of imperial Rome.

Evola began writing political journalism in 1925. His articles reproached Fascism for its proximity to the church, the careerism of its functionaries, and its dependence on the bourgeoisie and the masses: Evola sought to transform Fascism in accordance with his precepts of spiritual aristocracy and monarchy. These attacks reached a climax in the publication of his book *Imperialismo Pagano* [Pagan Imperialism] (1928), in which he celebrated the ideal of ancient Rome, denounced all the Christian churches, and scourged the secular universalism of both American democracy and Soviet communism. Mussolini, for his part, was sufficiently impressed and interested in these matters to write a journal article in reply to Reghini's exhortation for Fascism to initiate an era of "pagan imperialism." In the political realities of Italy, Mussolini could never have afforded to follow an anti-Christian line. The regime's goal of a concordat with the Catholic Church eventually led to the Lateran Treaty of 1929 with the Vatican, thus dashing the Group of UR's hopes of influencing the new order.

Evola underpinned his anti-modernist political doctrine through his oriental and esoteric studies. Through Reghini he discovered the work of the French orientalist René Guénon (1886–1951), who invoked the notion of a primordial Tradition, implicit in the metaphysical structure of the universe and reflected in the authentic religious traditions of East and West. Brought up in a Catholic family, Guénon studied philosophy at Paris before immersing himself in the French occult revival at the turn of the century. Besides a passing interest in Theosophy and Freemasonry, he was especially receptive to Advaita Vedanta, which was becoming better known in the West through Vivekananda, and studied Indian philosophy under Hindu teachers. In his books, *A General Introduction to the Study of Hindu Doctrines* (1921) and *Man and His Becoming According to the Vedanta* (1925), Guénon described the ultimate reality according to Vedanta. Beyond all reason or discursive thought, this metaphysical unity could only be grasped from the inward-directed point of view, the suprarational intellectual intuition by which the Self (*Atman*) communicates with the ego.[8]

Guénon considered that Hindu Vedanta represented a "primordial Tradition" whose transcendent truths were also preserved in the authentic religions of Islam and medieval Catholicism. The modern West, by contrast, had almost entirely lost any connection with the Tradition. In his seminal work of pessimism, *The Crisis of the Modern World* (1927), Guénon showed how the West had, since the end of the Middle Ages, succumbed to a spiritual decline. A process of materialization embraced all life; art and culture pursued mere externalities, while thought and science lost themselves in endless analysis, division and multiplicity. Western life was completely absorbed in "becoming," with its attendant focus on rational means, speed and technical efficiency. The "humanistic" concern with man's importance and consciousness, his social and political emancipation had displaced all transcendent references in an aberrant cult of individualism. Guénon regarded this decline as the fulfillment of the Hindu Puranic divisions of time. The four *yugas*, each of successively shorter duration, corresponded to the golden, silver, bronze and iron ages of classical antiquity. The West had now been passing through the fourth age, the Kali Yuga or "dark age," for more than six thousand years.[9]

Evola felt a deep affinity with Guénon's esoteric pessimism. Here, in sparse outline, he found all the reasons for the decay of a primordial heroic world based on sacred authority and metaphysical absolutes. He applauded Guénon's scathing attack on the vacuous relativism and chaotic liberalism of the modern world. Forthwith he began work on his own anti-modernist text, *Rivolta contro il mondo moderno* [Revolt against the Modern World] (1934), which remains his best-known and most important book. Here Evola described a metaphysical Aryo-Vedic tradition that allegedly governed the religious and political institutions of archaic Indo-European societies. He traced the accretion of golden age myths relating to polar symbolism and the Arctic origin of the white Aryan race through ancient Indian, Iranian, Greek and Amerindian texts, with acknowledgments to Bâl Gangadhar Tilak, a Brahman scholar, and Herman Wirth, the amateur prehistorian of an Atlantis culture and later director of Heinrich Himmler's Ahnenerbe.[10] The sacred nature of regal authority, the mystery of ritual, initiation and consecration, the divine origins of patrician rule, chivalry and a rigid caste hierarchy defined this traditional world in utter opposition to the secular, individualistic and liberal concerns of the modern world. Like Guénon, Evola subscribed to the Hindu cycle of the ages and equated the modern world with the dark age or Kali Kuga, in which all tradition is forgotten, disorder is rife and society is degenerate.

Evola's view of history and political theory were grounded in a fundamental "doctrine of two natures," the "primordial Tradition," which distinguishes the metaphysical order of things from the physical, the immortal from the mortal world, the superior realm of "being" from the inferior realm

of "becoming," the dominant, virile principle of spirit from the lower, feminine domain of matter.[11] For Evola, the predominance of spirit in Traditional
societies was evident in their strict hierarchy of functions, which still survived
in the caste system of Aryan-Hindu society. While the lower functions are
concerned with mere matter and organic vitality, the ascending functions are
progressively ruled by spirit. In the Hindu caste hierarchy, one finds the slaves
or workers (*sudras*), who are subordinated to the bourgeoisie or merchants
(*vaisyas*). Higher up one finds the warrior nobility (*kshatriyas*), and all are
subject to the spiritual authority of the priests (*brahmins*). This order, in
which powers of the spirit corresponded to caste, prevailed in all Traditional
societies; Evola cites its presence in Plato's *Republic*, in ancient Iranian society
and even in the social divisions of peasants, burghers, nobility and clergy in
the European Middle Ages.[12]

The priestly caste stood at the apex of the caste hierarchy. However, in the
world of primordial Tradition this was no professional priesthood but royalty
itself. In Evola's view, the roots of authority had a metaphysical character and
every temporal power proceeded from spiritual authority. Quoting the Aryo-
Vedic Laws of Manu, Evola claimed that the ruler was no "mere mortal" but "a
great deity standing in the form of a man" in societies still based on Tradition.
Thus, the Egyptian pharaoh was regarded as a manifestation of Ra or Horus,
while the kings of Rome were the incarnations of Zeus; the Assyrian kings, of
Baal; the Persian shahs, of the gods of light.[13] More especially, kings and the patriciate performed the sacred rites that linked the human domain with the
gods, thus forming a "bridge" to the supernatural realm. The possession and
practice of these sacred rites defined the priestly caste, who were simultane-
ously the leaders of the state, itself invested with the current of divine power.
"The supernatural element was the foundation of the idea of a traditional patriciate and of legitimate royalty: what constituted an ancient aristocrat was not
merely a biological legacy or a racial selection, but rather a sacred tradition."[14]

The doctrine of caste was closely linked in Evola's thought to the idea of
history as a process of regression or involution. Basing his cyclical view of history on the Puranic divisions of time, Evola asserted civilization inevitably declined from the Satya Yuga or golden age, where the primordial Tradition was
observed and upheld, through the successively shorter and more decadent
Treta and Dvapara Yugas, until the onset of the Kali Yuga or dark age, when
the Tradition is wholly forgotten. Social disorder, spiritual alienation and violence characterize this wretched epoch to a point of cataclysmic dissolution
when the next Satya Yuga once more begins its redemptive cycle. Evola recognized that this prehistoric account of a golden age and subsequent decline
hardly accorded with the evolutionist ideas of Darwin. He insisted that an-

cient testimonies and writings from all great world cultures make no mention of bestial cavemen but "more-than-human" beings in a better, brighter and superhuman ("divine") past. He speculates that the absence of fossil remains of a superior primordial mankind might indicate its existence prior to materialization. Evola ultimately dismisses evolutionism as a science typical of dark-age myth, which derives the higher from the lower and man from animal in total ignorance of Tradition.[15]

Evola offers a sweeping panorama of prehistoric cycles of civilization corresponding to the four traditional yugas. The epoch of remote prehistory corresponding to the golden age was a real location in the Arctic, accounting for the many polar myths of origin. Some spiritual disaster was matched by a catastrophic tilt in the earth's axis, causing a forced migration of a primal Hyperborean (extreme northern) race in a first wave toward North America and the northern regions of Eurasia, and then in a second wave toward a now lost continent in the mid-Atlantic. Using occult ideas from Helena Blavatsky's Theosophy, Evola speculated that a large Atlantean group became mixed with aboriginal Southern races of proto-Mongols and proto-Negroes who may have originated in the lost continent of Lemuria. In accordance with the doctrine of two natures, Evola tended to see "spirituality" as the prior determinant of a culture rather than its ethnic, racial population. However, since certain races were the carriers of Southern "spirituality," they were in turn identified as decadent factors. Thus, while the first wave of Hyperborean emigration remained wholly Nordic, the Western civilization of Atlantis absorbed many Southern-Lemurian traits, thus giving rise to the dichotomy of solar, male or Uranian spirituality (Northern-Atlantic races) and lunar, female or Demetrian spirituality (mixed Southern-Atlantean races).[16]

Evola adopted Bachofen's idea of matriarchy[17] not as a prior linear phase of evolution, but as an independent Southern world, inhabited by other races that eventually clashed with Northern-Atlantic traditions. This Southern "mother-culture" was later typifed by the Asiatic-Mediterranean goddesses of life, such as Isis, Ishtar, Cybele and Demeter, who subordinate the male, solar principle, and by images such as the child on the lap of the Great Mother. By contrast with the virile spirituality implicit in intelligible essences and dramatized in gods of war, sky and the sun, the "mothers" preside over a telluric and cthonic world of earth, darkness and moon. In accordance with the maternal principle, in which we are all children of the earth, this culture encouraged social structures of a collectivist nature with ideals of sharing, brotherhood and equality. Evola saw these "lunar" themes of peace and community as typical of Demetrism, representing the second silver age or Treta Yuga, in which a priestly caste ruled without virile, regal authority. He saw

further evidence of this feminized spirituality in ancient cults of emascula-
tion and even in priests wearing robes redolent of female attire.[18]

Evola's dualism of male-female spirituality owed an even greater debt to
the young Jewish philosopher Otto Weininger (1880–1903), whose famous
book *Geschlecht und Charakter* [Sex and Character] (1903) expounded a
metaphysical view of the principles of male and female sexuality.[19] Weininger
glorified higher reason, Platonic truth and Kantian imperatives while negat-
ing the fallen, mundane sphere of matter and nature. Only man aspires to the
eternal life of the spirit, while woman embraces the lower life of the earth and
the senses. Man may choose between that life which ends with physical death,
or that life for which death means a restoration of complete purity. Woman,
on the other hand, is part of the material world. Void of any higher spirit, she
knows nothing of logic and morality. She has no ego, no individuality but
leads a purely sexual, impersonal existence.[20] Man is a subject and woman is
an object whose only desire is to be formed and given meaning by male attention and sexual coitus. Ontologically, she is a nullity, and her existence
simply guarantees the continued reproduction of the material, sensate
world.[21] Evola's celebration of virile spirituality was rooted in Weininger's
work, which was widely translated by the end of the First World War.

Evola traced the progress of Northern-Atlantic heroic spirituality among
the ancient Aryans of India and Iran, commenting that in India the term *arya*
was a synonym for *dvija*, meaning "twice-born" or "regenerated." However, he
noted that India eventually followed a contemplative path and abandoned the
regal and solar path of a spiritual patriciate. Evola attributed the rise of a professional *brahmin* caste to the decay of the original dynasties responsible for
the Aryan conquest of India. The disintegration of the Aryan worldview in
India followed the identification of *Brahman* (God) with all nature in a pan-
theistic sense that reflected the spiritual influence of Southern races.[22] In Iran
the heroic spirituality led to the warrior cult of Ahura Mazda, the Aryan ethic
of truth and loyalty, and the view of the cosmos as an order maintained
through sacred rites. Some decline caused by lunar naturalism and decadent
priestcraft led to a solar reaction in the doctrine of Zarathustra, which Evola
compared to Buddha's reforming role in decadent Hindu India. Mithraism
again inaugurated a new heroic cycle of Aryan, solar spirituality opposed to
all telluric cults of earth and darkness.[23] Once Mithraism declined in Iran,
Evola saw its later revival in the Roman Empire as a spiritual path that the
West might have followed instead of Christianity, a speculation incidentally
shared with Carl Gustav Jung.[24]

Turning to Western history during the present Kali Yuga, Evola celebrated
the Roman Empire as a major attempt to reverse the forces of Mediterranean-

Southern decadence and forge a new unitary state based on heroic Aryan-Western spirituality. He speculated that Rome's new rigor and ascent were due to the influence of prehistoric immigrant "reindeer" and "battle-axe" peoples of Hyperborean origin, who formed regenerative nuclei among the aboriginal races of Etruscans, Sabines, Sabellians, Siculians and others in the pre-Roman Italian peninsula. Those aboriginal peoples who adhered to the worship of lunar, female deities typically formed the lower stratum of plebeians beneath a patriciate devoted to notions of authority and *imperium*. Roman spirituality was henceforth characterized by an absence of pathos and mysticism toward the divine. Its key virtues were duty, loyalty, heroism, order and dominion. The revolt of the Roman patriciate against the foreign Tarquin dynasty (509 B.C.), the fall of Capua, and the destruction of Carthage (146 B.C.) were representative events in Rome's methodical liquidation of the centers of earlier Southern influence.[25]

As Rome rose to imperial power, the virile idea of the divinely ordered state supplanted all earlier hieratic, Demetrian forms of society. The patriciate performed the sacred rites under a precise law, and all society was subject to strict paternal rights. Continuing his dualistic theme of Northern and Southern spirituality, Evola saw Rome maintain its heroic Aryan-Western culture of hierarchy and state through constant rejection of Dionysian and Aphrodistic influences, such as the banning of the Bacchanalia. Roman suspicion of mystery-religions of Asian origin and Pythagorean philosophers was likewise rooted in a spiritual antipathy toward Demetrian throwbacks, while its famous civil wars involving such figures as Pompeius, Cassius and Anthony were contests with Southern revisionism. Through its single-minded dedication to heroic civilization, "Rome shifted the centre of the historical West from the telluric to the Uranian mystery, from the lunar world of the Mothers to the solar world of the Fathers."[26] By the time of Augustus, the imperial cult had effectively restored the spiritual "genius" of the emperor as a bridge with the supernatural realm, while Roman universalism seemed to stretch to the limits of the known world.

Evola regarded the advent of Christianity as a process of unprecedented decline. The Christian ideal of a religion open to everyone irrespective of race, tradition and caste was a solvent of Roman order and hierarchy. By positing mere faith over heroic and initiatory spiritual growth, Christianity appealed to the plebeian mentality with promises of salvation from subjection, the world and even death. Christian egalitarianism, based on principles of brotherhood, love and collectivism, militated against all Roman ideas of duty, honor and command. The Christian God was not the god of the patricians, invoked while standing erect and carried in front of the legions, but a crucified god-man, to whom one prayed in the sense of sin and atonement. The spread of Christianity marked a shift from the masculine to the feminine, from the solar to the tellurian, from martial aristocratic values to mystical plebeian sentiment. Evola detected the revival of female, lunar spirituality in its myths of a sacrificed and regenerated (agricultural) god and the Virgin birth, and its iconography of Mother and Child. Nevertheless, Christianity was only a symptom of decline, as Evola believed the Roman heroic cycle was already exhausted in "ethnic chaos and cosmopolitan disintegration."[27]

Evola's "Northern" bias led him to regard the German peoples as a powerful countervailing force to Christianity's female culture. As descendants of Northern-Aryan racial stocks, the Germans had preserved their prehistoric purity outside the cosmopolitan late Roman Empire. Their Norse myths and tribal ethos preserved traces of the primordial Tradition. The god Wotan-Odin granted victory, possessed esoteric wisdom and had secrets not granted to any woman; he was the leader of the dead heroes. The oldest Nordic stocks regarded Asgard in the far north as the home of the gods, an ancestral memory that linked them with the Indo-Aryans in the East. Initially a barbarian force of destruction at the close of the Roman cycle, the German tribes brought warrior leadership, fealty and freedom into the medieval European political order. While laying the basis of feudal caste society, these values represented solar spirituality against the feminizing Church. Chivalry upheld the hero over the saint, the conqueror over the martyr. Loyalty and honor were the highest virtues, while cowardice was a greater evil than sin. Evola regarded the quest for the Grail and the Crusades as symbols of a solar tradition within Christian civilization. In the medieval struggle of popes and emperors for precedence, Evola identified the Ghibelline dynasty of Hohenstauffen emperors (1152–1272) as the Germanic champion of "sacred regality" in a revived Holy Roman Empire.[28]

Evola saw the Italian communes of the Renaissance as pioneers of the profane and anti-traditional idea of society based on economic and mercantile factors, leading to the Jewish trade in gold and the rise of banking and capitalism. Evola applauded Dante's condemnation of the revolt of the Lombard cities and the principle of self-government. The Hohenstauffen emperors fought over Italy, not for German aggrandizement, but "against the rebellious race of merchants and burghers in the name of honor and spirit." Evola thought it highly significant that the Renaissance should have started in Italy, not on account of its Roman heritage, but as the perennial crucible of the antagonism between North and South, between solar and lunar spirituality. In his view, the Renaissance did not represent a revival of classical civilization but only a borrowing of its decadent forms for a wholly new spirit of atomization and independence. Where emperors had once ruled by nobility and supernatural authority, the new political ideal was demonstrated by Machiavelli's *Prince*, where the individual can only rule in his own name by employing cunning, violence and diplomacy.[29]

Evola regarded Renaissance humanism as the harbinger of modern thought, limited to the exploration of the human dimension in the arts, philosophy and science. Humanism embraced individualism in this negation of the transcendent world by glorifying the "self" as an illusory center. The Reformation opposed Rome precisely because of its hierarchy and dogma, remnants of Tradition, and set up individual conscience as the sole authority in religion. The private interpretation of the Bible emphasized critical judgment and human reason, which would ultimately challenge all authority and metaphysical reality. Rationalism joined forces with empiricism and expermentalism to create modern science, whose sole object was the material world. Science is exclusively concerned with the physical dimension, the discovery of mathematical relations, laws of consistency and the calculation of outcomes. With its uniform criterion of truth based on "soulless numbers" and indifference to quality and symbol, science also paved the way for the rise of lower social orders by degrading and democratizing the idea of knowledge. Denying all transcendence, science vainly attempts to compensate the human spirit with power over material objects, titanic technology and huge industries.[30]

Evola traced the continued descent of the Kali Yuga in European politics. Emperors now foresook imperial consecration, and Frederick III was the last emperor to be crowned in Rome (1452). Kings and princes began to claim an absolute power, thus subverting the universal ecumene with the idea of the national state. Free cities and republics began to assert their independence, not only against imperial authority but also against the nobility. The principle of a common body of law declined, and chivalry decayed into a defense of temporal and territorial ambition. Raison d'état destroyed the foundation of Christendom and European unity with wars of kings against emperors, alliances with the sultan, and the rise of territorial princes in virtual independence from the empire. Royalty became increasingly secular, divorced from its former spiritual authority. With the Reformation, states themselves began to act as schisms from superordained authority. The assertion of the "divine right" of kings in Catholic states in the age of the Counter-Reformation after the Council of Trent was no more than an empty formula concealing the spiritual vacuity of kingship divorced from authentic universalism.[31]

Evola saw the rise of national monarchies as an intermediate stage in the cycle of decline. Just as national monarchies once asserted their own absolute power, they in turn would be confronted by individuals demanding emancipation in the name of their own free, sovereign autonomy. Spiritual secession from the sacred center ultimately weakened the very principle of hierarchy. The collapse of supernatural authority encouraged the emergence, revolt and liberation of lower strata in society. The atomization of the European imperial order presaged the rise of mercantile classes, ideas of popular sovereignty and the French Revolution, when all authority and law are only legitate as the will of the citizens. This principle of authority "from below" formed the basis of democracy and liberalism in modern bourgeois states.[32] A further stage in this process of egalitarianism led to the collectivism of mass consumer society or communism, typified by America and Soviet Russia. As this decadent downsweep in the Kali Yuga progresses, matter rules over form, leveling occurs on every plane, and anti-traditional values of secular humanism, hedonism and utilitarianism dominate.

Evola's involution or regression through the cycle of the ages was mirrored in the law of the regression of castes. Once the sacred regality of the mythical golden age is lost, power devolves upon the second warrior caste, represented in Europe by national monarchs and absolute sovereigns. Then in time, the aristocracy decays, and power shifts to the third caste (the mercantile class). The Italian communes, merchants and Jewish bankers of the Renaissance eventually led to the capitalist oligarchs and middle classes, who consolidated their power by exploiting liberal and democratic ideologies to drive bourgeois revolutions in the nineteenth century. By the beginning of the twentieth century, organized labor and communist revolution sought to transfer power to the fourth caste of slaves, reducing all values to matter, machines and the reign of quantity. This cycle of castes extended to the international arena. Evola regarded the First World War as a global struggle between the third caste (the Entente democracies) and the residual forces of the second caste (the feudal and aristocratic Central Powers). The Second World War began with the anti-democratic and authoritarian regimes of Germany and Italy challenging the plutocracies in the name of fascist collectivism, but eventually this war became a crusade of democracy, allied with the fourth caste of the Soviet Union, against "regression" to warrior castes. The outcome was the division of Europe, with America and Russia as the dominant mass societies, united in their crass materialist and utilitarian civilization.[33]

Evola's notion of race was spiritual, subject to spirit and tradition. He spoke of "a man of race," meaning "a man of breeding" with its aristocratic implications. Evola elaborated a tripartite racial thory of body, mind (religion and adherence to Tradition), and soul (character and emotions), in which the inner determined the outer forms.[34] Discussing Arthur de Gobineau's racial thought, Evola asserted that races only declined once their spirit failed.[35] Evola actually rejected Alfred Rosenberg and other biological racists of the Third Reich, implying that their physical anthropology was based on reductionist and materialist science.[36] Evola's interpretation of the word "Aryan" was similarly idealistic. In his book on Buddhism, he had translated *arya* to mean aristocratic or high caste and illuminated in a spiritual sense as well as related to the Nordic, light-skinned Aryan conquerors of India. It will be recalled that Evola's ideal of the "Aryan-Roman" race was essentially defined by its sacral and aristocratic quality. Mussolini actually adopted Evola's ideas as the official Fascist racial theory in 1938, when Italy enacted its own racial laws distinct from those of Nazi Germany.

Evola's anti-Semitism was also metaphysical, whereby he regarded Jewry as a symbol for the rule of money, individualism and economic materialism in the modern world. Here again one sees the influence of Otto Weininger, who defined Jewishness (*Judentum*) as an "intellectual tendency" or "psychic constitution" manifest in all individuals and races, but finding its fullest expression in historical Jewry. Weininger maintained that the Jews resembled women in their metaphysical essence. Like women, the Jews had neither a soul nor a need for immortality. Weininger highlighted the Jewish contribution to science as an urge to deny all transcendence through a mechanistic-materialist worldview. The Jewish devaluation of all higher meaning, he argued, was evident in their support of Darwinism and man's descent from the apes, Marxism and the economic interpretation of history.[37] The Jews lack all conviction, they are ambiguous and endlessly flexible.[38] Significantly, they have no desire for property but prefer coin and mobile capital so that they can quickly change direction for gain. Weininger regarded the modern age with its increasing emphasis on business and journalism as a social universe in the image of the Jews.[39]

Otto Weininger's critique of the "psychic constitution" of Jewishness was central to Evola's anti-modernist idealism. Evola detected the fatal Jewish influence in early modern Europe through rational calculation and banking. From its origin in the ghettos, the trade with gold and interest ultimately conquered and refashioned the world. But the Jews were not the sole pioneers, for Evola follows Karl Marx and Werner Sombart in seeing a revival of the "Hebraic spirit" in Protestant puritanism, rationalism and capitalism.[40] The Jews had only taken advantage of humanism and the Reformation to create the secularized scientistic and mechanistic world of modernity. However, it was the "Jewish spirit [which] destroys everything through rationalism and calculation, leading to a world consisting of machines, things and money instead of persons, traditions and fatherlands."[41] Much later, in 1970, Evola would describe Hitler's fanatical anti-Semitism as a paranoid idée fixe with tragic consequences and a stain upon the reputation of the Third Reich that would be hard to remove.

However, Evola's anti-Semitism also took the form of an attack on real Jews. Quoting the notorious text of Jewish conspiracy theory, *Protocols of the Learned Elders of Zion*, Evola sees the Jewish press and finance as systematic means of spreading the liberal virus, which would destroy the monarchical and aristocratic residues of Western culture. Evola published his own preface and an essay, "The Authenticity of Protocols as Proven by Jewish Tradition," in the Italian edition of the *Protocols*, which recycled contemporary anti-Semitic slurs and falsehoods. He found abundant evidence of the erosive influence of individual Jews in American banking and industry as well as in the Russian Revolution. Likewise, Jews were always at the forefront of modernistic ideas, such as Sigmund Freud and psychoanalysis, Albert Einstein and the theory of relativity, Emile Durkheim and the "sociology" of religion. Under stress, Evola could indulge in vicious anti-Semitism in his journalism. After the murder of his friend Corneliu Codreanu (1899–1938), the leader of the fascist Romanian Iron Guard, Evola railed against "the Judaic horde," describing a potential communist takeover in Romania as "the filthiest tyranny, the talmudic, Israelite tyranny."[42]

Finding Italian Fascism too compromising, Evola began to seek recognition in the Third Reich, where he frequently lectured from 1934 onward. Although National Socialism opposed liberalism and "Jewish culture," Evola was repelled by Nazi populism, plebeian culture and nationalism as manifestations of modernity. Nazi racism was rooted in biological materialism, and the Führer principle, whereby Hitler drew his legitimacy from the *Volk*, and likewise ignored all transcendent reality. Evola praised the SS as a vehicle of the state, of hierarchy, racial heritage and a new warrior elite, but the SS authorities rejected Evola's ideas as supranational, aristocratic and thus reactionary. Evola found his closest allies among the Conservative Revolutionaries in Germany and Austria such as Edgar Julius Jung, Wilhelm Stapel and Othmar Spann. Several of his books were translated into German, and many of his articles appeared in German conservative and right-wing periodicals between 1928 and 1943.[43] In August 1943 Evola conferred with the deposed Mussolini at Hitler's field headquarters in East Prussia and was involved in the short-lived Republic of Salò. Following his flight from Rome before the Allies in late 1943, Evola spent the remainder of the war in Vienna. Working with fascist leaders across Central Europe, he performed liaison services for the SS in recruiting a pan-European army for the defense of the Continent against the Soviet and American invaders. Severely injured in an air raid on 12 March

1945, he was permanently paralyzed in both legs. After his return to Italy he lived in Rome, the guru of the neo-fascist right, until his death in 1974.[44]

How did Evola's lofty mythological discourse and profound pessimism inspire neo-fascist activism and violence? In the early 1950s, Evola directed his writings more toward practical politics. His journalism and his pamphlet *Orientamenti* [Orientations] (1950) stressed the "legionary spirit" and "warrior ethic" while outlining how ideals, elites and order could be maintained with the Movimento Sociale Italiano (MSI) neo-fascist party, police and army taking over the state. In his book *Gli Uomini e le Rovine* [Men Among the Ruins] (1953), he restated his doctrine in terms of counter-revolution, the transcendent character of state against the economy, and the need for an anti-bourgeois, warrior's view of life. By the time Evola penned his work *Cavalcare la Tigre* [Riding the Tiger] (1961), he despaired of such remedies. The postwar economic miracle and consumerism were now sweeping away all that remained of tradition, hierarchy and order. Evola's critique was scathing: nothing in this final stage of the Kali Yuga was worthy of survival. Evola sets up the ideal of the "active nihilist" who is prepared to act with violence against modern decadence.

What did this mean in practice? While Evola held himself above all political parties, he exerted a strong influence on young right-wing Italians who despaired of Italy's return into the mainstream of liberal development. Many compared their fate to that of Dante, who had lamented the passing of the Ghibelline order.[45] Young postwar neo-fascists sat at Evola's feet to hear this oracle of aristocratic values and war with modernity. Guiliano Salierni, a young MSI activist in the early 1950s, recalled Evola's call for violence.[46] The neo-fascist Ordine Nuovo (ON) was founded in 1956 by Pino Rauti, one of Evola's closest disciples. ON ideology was replete with Evolan terminology, including aristocracy, hierarchy, elite rule, political soldiers and warrior asceticism. Its strategy corresponded to Evola's initial postwar ideas, namely the reinforcement of the state, including the seizure of power by police, armed forces, veteran groups and youth organizations.[47] Giorgio Almirante, the MSI leader, hailed Evola as "our Marcuse—only better," alluding to the Frankfurt School veteran Herbert Marcuse's status as the doyen of the 1968 student revolutions.[48]

The use of violence in Italian neo-fascism escalated with numerous bomb attacks and massacres, beginning with the Piazza Fontana explosion in Milan in April 1969. Adriano Romualdi, a leading young neo-fascist, identified Evola in 1971 as the intellectual hero of militant right-wing youth in Italy "because the teaching of Evola is also a philosophy of total war."[49] By 1975, the far-right underground adopted a leftist strategy in mounting attacks against the state itself (murders of officials, robberies in ministries). The trend toward violence continued, so that by the late 1970s a cult of action replaced ideology itself, elevating the idea of combat to an existential duty. Neo-fascist terrorists such as Franco Freda and Mario Tuti frequently reprinted and cited Evola's two most militant tracts, *Metafisica della guerra* (1935) and *Dottrina ariana* (1940), in praise of "heroic," "exemplary" action without an instrumental purpose. Inspired by these ideas of metaphysical stuggle, the underground bulletin *Quex* (1978–81) (from Hitlerjugend Quex, a Nazi youth hero) glorified Corneliu Codreanu's "legionaries" and "fulfillment in heroic death" in the same breath as Evola's "luminous forces against all tellurism and chaos."[50] Groups such as Movimento Revoluzionario Popolare, Terza Positione and Nuclei Armati Rivoluzionari subsequently unleashed a surge of black terrorism in Italy until the majority of militants had been captured or killed and a handful fled abroad.

In late 1980, a cell of Nuclei Armati Rivoluzionarice (NAR) fugitives arrived in London, where they made contact with Britain's far-right National Front (NF). Roberto Fiore, a close associate of the imprisoned Mario Tuti; Massimo Morsello and his wife Marinella Rita; and Amadeo de Francisci and Stefano Tiraboschi were all subsequently convicted in absentia by a Rome court for NAR terrorist offenses involving armed conspiracy. Inspired by Evola and Codreanu, Roberto Fiore would have a catalytic influence on the new ideological direction of the NF. After its dramatic increases in membership and success at the polls in the strife-torn 1970s, the NF had seen its support draining to the new Conservative government of Margaret Thatcher, which vigorously addressed industrial unrest, rising crime and weak immigration control. This weakening and isolation of the NF had a radicalizing effect on its leaders and their ideology. A younger generation of university-educated NF activists, represented by Nick Griffin, Derek Holland and Patrick Harrington, felt that the NF's soggy mixture of reaction, concern over law and order and the immigrant threat to jobs and homes lacked any theoretical sophistication. While the older NF leaders John Tyndall and Martin Webster were tainted by British neo-Nazism, the young men embraced the ideals of Italian neo-fascism.[51]

Roberto Fiore and his colleagues helped the NF forge a new militant elitist philosophy that foreswore electoral strategies in favor of educating and training a fanatical, quasi-religious "New Man" in select cadres for a national revolution. By 1983, this group—led by Griffin, Holland and Harrington—had broken away to form the NF "Political Soldier" faction. Cadres similar to Iron Guard legionary "nests" became the organizational unit, and training seminars were held at the Hampshire country house of Rosine de Bouneviale, the publisher of the Catholic anti-Semitic magazine *Candour,* originally founded by A. K. Chesterton. Backed by Fiore, the "Political Soldiers" published a new journal, *Rising* (1982–85), which emphasized the spiritual and cultural basis of a new social order. A revival of the countryside and a return to feudal values reflected Codreanu's prewar attack on the decadence and materialism of urban life; nationalist communes were planned in upland areas of Britain. Archaic woodcut art juxtaposed knights and rural idylls with consumerism and modernity. Evola's most militant tract was discussed, especially his call for a "Great Holy War" fought for personal spiritual renewal paralleling the physical "Little Holy War" on a material plane against national or ideological enemies. Like the hero of the *Bhagavad Gita,* Christian Crusaders, ancient Norse warriors and Roman legionaries were all united in the Aryan struggle for self-transformation and a nobler reality. Some indication of this struggle was given in a paean to Franco Freda, Italy's most notorious neo-fascist terrorist.[52]

Derek Holland published *The Political Soldier* (1984) as a manifesto of the new NF elite of racial nationalism to counter "the forces of Evil swamping the entire globe in an ocean of Filth, Corruption and Treason." Both the global dark age and the past failures of the NF could only be remedied by the Political Soldier, a "New Type of Man." Holland evoked Codreanu's Legionary Movement of the Romanian Iron Guard, with its cult of death, as the outstanding example of political soldiery in the twentieth century: "[Men] willing to sacrifice anything and everything for the victory of their Ideal."[53] The Islamic Revolutionary Guards of Iran were also cited as fanatical, spiritual warriors with a similar contempt for death. Evola's anti-modernity and warrior ethics of the "Holy War" led the NF "Political Soldiers," like their Italian models, to embrace pro-Islamic positions, with public support for the anti-Western, national revolutionary regimes of Muammar Qaddafi and Rûhollâh Khomeini in Libya and Iran. By the end of 1989, Nick Griffin, Derek Holland and the Italians had finally left the NF to establish the International Third Position (ITP).[54]

Evola's ideas had a much wider impact beyond this Anglo-Italian revolutionary nationalist sect. From the late 1970s, neo-fascist intellectuals sought to engage mainstream society in the discourse of the New Right. Following the founding of GRECE (Groupement de recherche et d'études sur la civilisation européenne) in Paris in 1969, new glossy magazines such as *Elements, Totalité, Vouloir, Diorama Letterario* and *Elementi* sprang up in France, Belgium and Italy to challenge liberal, egalitarian ideology. The market and utilitarianism were rejected in the name of a superior spiritual view of life. Organic community was compared favorably with capitalist society and its quantitative, abstract relationships. Racial origins, differences, and identity were mobilized to counter egalitarian and multiracial ideas. Again, Roberto Fiore and the Italians in London acted as catalysts in promoting this intellectual discourse in Britain. Fiore was a close friend of Michael Walker, a former NF organizer in central London who began publishing the journal *National Democrat* in late 1981 (renamed *The Scorpion* in spring 1983). As a linguist and translator, Walker was well placed to edit a New Right magazine in Britain, which offered readers articles on nationalism, anti-egalitarianism and the Conservative Revolution by Robert Steukers, the Belgian editor of *Vouloir*, and Alain de Benoist and Guillaume Faye of GRECE.

This new radical discourse had ample scope for Evola's ideas of tradition against progress, hierarchy against equality, rule from above against democracy and the primacy of aristocratic over plebeian values. Evola's contempt for America as the most advanced center of Western alienation from Tradition also interacted with a widespread mood of anti-Americanism during the 1980s. Both the left and right condemned the cultural colonization of Europe by U.S. multinationals, Hollywood film and American television soaps, and the rapid rise of American-style consumerism. McDonald's hamburgers and Coca-Cola became key symbols of a banal American mass culture and its massive penetration of the postwar vassal states of Europe. Widespread opposition to the United States' stationing of Pershing and Cruise missiles in Europe and attendant fears of the likely sacrifice of the Continent in any nuclear exchange between the superpowers also stoked these anti-American sentiments.

Michael Walker introduced Evola's life and work to a wider English readership in *The Scorpion* between 1984 and 1986. His spiritual theory of race, anti-modernity and views on Jewish influence were located within his "superior, heroic and aristocratic conception of existence."[55] The entire summer 1984 issue of the magazine was devoted to an attack on the secular, liberal notion of American statehood, divorced from any ethnic roots or culture. Among its articles was a translation of Evola's 1945 essay "American 'Civilization,'" which saw America as the final stage of European decline into the "interior formlessness" of vacuous individualism, conformity and vulgarity under the universal aegis of money-making. Its mechanistic and rational philosophy of progress combined with a mundane horizon of prosperity to transform the world into an enormous suburban shopping mall.[56] This anti-American theme was extended by Evola's ideas on a unified Europe's need for a spiritual and supranational basis. Only by opposing the current Westernization of the world could Europe challenge both superpowers for global hegemony.[57] Through these articles, Walker presented Evola as the champion of a European spiritual and national revival against the liberal, multiracial quagmire of the United States.

The international export of Julius Evola has added a vital strand to the contemporary radical right in the Anglo-American world and elsewhere. Once Evola had embraced the mythic ideology of cultural decadence and rebirth, he identified self-transcendence with the higher, timeless spirituality of a lost world, which could only be reborn through catastrophic change. Evola's studies in Tantrism, oriental religions and the Western esoteric tradition also offer new intellectual horizons and widening access to fascist idealism. His works on Zen and Taoism were matched by translations of Pascal Beverley Randolph's *Magia sexualis* and several of Gustav Meyrink's occult novels.[58] His dualist metaphysics of sex, derived from Otto Weininger, provided a key to world religions and occult doctrine highlighting the abyss of emancipatory, collectivist politics based on lunar spirituality. His notion of the "Jewish spirit," also from Weininger, has influenced Miguel Serrano's "Esoteric Hitlerism."

Evola's aristocratic world of Tradition, painted in the exotic colors of Hyperborean and Eastern mythology, juxtaposed with the "Jewish spirit," offers an esoteric mystique to reactionary discourse and is attracting new audiences. His rigorous New Age spirituality speaks directly to those who reject absolutely the leveling world of democracy, capitalism, multiracialism and technology at the outset of the twenty-first century. Their acute sense of cultural chaos can find powerful relief in his ideal of total renewal. The year 1998 witnessed a plethora of publications and conferences marking the anniversary of Evola's birth.[59] A major U.S. New Age publisher, Inner Traditions, has so far published English-language editions of eight of Evola's major monographs, while the right-wing Arun-Verlag has published several titles in German. *Kshatriya*, a Viennese intellectual right-wing journal devoted to Evola and Codreanu, provides a forum for Russian, German and Hungarian Evolans. Even Black Metal music has taken up Evola, and Michael Moynihan, a right-wing U.S. industrial musician, has translated *Men among the Ruins*.[60]

4

Imperium and the New Atlantis

FOR MORE THAN thirty years, James H. Madole (1927–1979) regularly harangued passers-by on the crowded streets of New York City with his urgent call for a fascist revolution in the United States. His appearances owed much to the customs of an open-air revival meeting and evangelical preaching. Flanked by his own stormtroopers clad in uniform black caps, gray shirts with lightning-bolt armbands and black trousers, Madole always wore a close-fitting suit jacket with all three buttons fastened and a ludicrous motorcycle crash helmet above his thick horn-rimmed glasses. The plump, middle-aged Madole stood upon a pulpitlike rostrum decorated with the lightning bolt symbol of his National Renaissance Party and emphasized his speeches with staring eyes, wild grimaces, and striking melodramatic poses. Throughout the 1960s and 1970s, the National Renaissance Party frequently hit the headlines by provoking violent protests and riots in districts of New York heavily populated by Jews and blacks, where Madole carried his missionary message of white supremacy and Aryan renaissance.

Madole was obviously a fanatic and could easily be dismissed as a wild eccentric pursuing a quixotic political campaign on the margins of postwar American society. However, his campaign strategies, his organization and, above all, his philosophy and doctrines of Aryan renewal identify him as an early and important figure in the development of esoteric fascism. His ideas were saturated with the fabulous mythology of science fiction and occult notions derived from Theosophy. He attacked Christianity and upheld the hierarchical caste society of Vedic India as the model for his "New Atlantis," the future fascist state of America. Ultimate authority would rest with philosopher-kings selected and schooled for rulership from childhood. His street-fighting stormtroopers, known as the Security Echelon, were supposed to be the living example of a new military caste of Aryan warriors. Madole also anticipated later fascist "Third Way" movements with his rejection of both capitalism and communism. In his opposition to the plutocracy and imperialism of the United States, Madole even sought alliances with Arab and black nationalists and encouraged them to hold joint meetings with the National Renaissance Party. By the mid-1990s, Madole was being celebrated by fascist and neo-Nazi groups as the "father of post-war occult-fascism."[1]

James Hartung Madole was born on 7 July 1927 in New York City. Two years after his birth, his parents separated and young James was brought up in Beacon, New York, by his mother, who held strongly anti-Semitic views. While in high school, the lonely youngster developed a passionate interest in science. He built his own laboratory at home and carried out experiments in chemistry and astronomy. As a youth, Madole envisioned the scientist in Faustian terms, a semi-divine sage seeking mastery of the earth and the whole universe. He considered that science was the only valid basis of culture and that society should be governed by scientist rulers. This naive belief in the omnipotence and certainty of science was heightened by Madole's enthusiasm for science fiction, a literary genre that had gained a remarkable hold over the popular American mind through mass-circulation magazines and pulp fiction in the 1930s and 1940s.[2] Science fiction frequently emphasized the elitist pretensions of the heaven-storming scientist, while its fantasy genre often described magical lands and authoritarian utopias on alien planets.

The elitism of science and science fiction (SF) drew Madole to fascism as a political philosophy. During his late teens, Madole sought out SF fans with fascist leanings and thus came to know Charles B. Hudson, an SF writer and veteran prewar American fascist, who was a leading defendant in the famous Sedition Act trials of 1941–43.[3] Hudson was a short, fanatic, plump man with a bald pate who had cultivated a Midwest fascist following during the 1930s with his bulletin, *America in Danger*. He worked in close collaboration with *Weltdienst*, the Nazi German press agency run by Lieutenant-Colonel Ulrich Fleischhauer in Erfurt under the auspices of Alfred Rosenberg. The agency sought to drum up overseas support for the Hitler regime by fostering an anti-Semitic international with a global ideology of resentment.

Hudson was an obsessive conspiracy theorist and peppered his bulletin with references to the "hidden hand" and ascribed to the Jews every calamity in American history from the assassination of Lincoln to the Johnstown flood. His pet phrase, "Judeo-Socialistic-Communistic Nu-Deal Organized-Jewry-Finance World-War I" encapsulated all the dangers he perceived in modern liberal society and was later abbreviated to the "synagogue of Satan." By 1940 Hudson's bulletin and Omaha base acted as major outposts in the Midwest for defeatist and appeasement propaganda in favor of the Third Reich. He promoted the pro-Nazi views of John B. Snow, James True, Colonel Eugene Sanctuary, Congressmen Jacob Thorkelson and Clare E. Hoffman; the charismatic radio priest, Father Charles E. Coughlin; Mrs. Leslie Fry, a Russian-born promoter of the anti-Semitic *Protocols of the Elders of Zion*; and Mrs. Elizabeth Dilling, the communist-obsessed agitator and lecturer.[4]

By the time Madole met Charles B. Hudson at the end of World War II, the latter had achieved notoriety for his indictment on sedition charges after Pearl Harbor and the outbreak of war against Japan and Germany. While many of his contacts were tried, convicted and imprisoned, Hudson had remained at liberty and continued to peddle anti-Semitic and anti-communist literature. In 1945 Madole formed the Animist Party as a right-wing political movement with its base among SF fans. Thanks to Hudson's influence, Madole enjoyed the support of several "America First" and patriotic groups surviving from the prewar period. He soon caught the attention of another patriot, Kurt Mertig, who had led the Citizens Protective League before the war. Mertig was a fat-jowled, heavily accented, German American shipping executive with the Hamburg-American Line. Together with Louis Zahne, a brusque Prussian and former member of the Friends of the New Germany (a precursor of the German-American Bund), Mertig held weekly mass meetings for Americans and Germans at the Turnhalle in Yorkville, New York, during the early 1940s. His anti-Semitic, anti-war and pro-German speeches left no doubt that the League was a Nazi front and in 1943 he was ordered removed 300 miles inland by the Army Exclusion Board as a security measure.[5]

In 1949 the elderly Kurt Mertig had founded the neo-Nazi National Renaissance Party with its headquarters in Yorkville. The party took its name from Hitler's *Political Testament*, where the Führer proclaimed that, from the sacrifice of his death, there would spring up "the seed of a radiant renaissance of the National Socialist Movement." Mertig was on the lookout for a successor and was impressed with Madole, who, though barely twenty-two years old, had already demonstrated dynamic powers of oratory in the Animist Party and the Nationalist Action League. Shortly after joining Mertig, Madole assumed leadership of the National Renaissance Party (NRP) and retained this position until his death thirty years later.[6] This party thus had its roots in the prewar German-American Nazi fronts of Yorkville, with its predominantly German population. Between 1937 and 1941, these streets had regularly witnessed the parades of Fritz Kuhn's "Bund Boys" under their ominous swastika standards. The NRP was to become Madole's lifelong career and the vehicle for his radical ideas of Aryan renaissance and occult fascism.

Madole began as a Nazi enthusiast, initially using the swastika as the party flag, although this was later superseded by the fascist symbol of a lightning bolt within a circle. He announced in his party bulletin that "what Hitler did in Europe, the National Renaissance Party intends to do in America." The NRP proposed to abolish Congress in favor of elite rule; it would protect the

Aryan race against racial contamination by deporting the colored races, and it would destroy communism by eliminating the Jews. However, during the 1950s Madole steered the NRP along novel lines of fascist development, involving a "Third Way" position rejecting both capitalism and communism. Instead of its former conventional radical right-wing position of anti-Semitism and anti-communism, the NRP later modified its view of the Soviet Union. Here, Madole was influenced by the American fascist intellectuals Francis Parker Yockey and Frederick Charles Weiss, both of whom favored a pro-Soviet position against the United States and world Jewry.[7]

Francis Parker Yockey (1917–1960) had acted as a legal assistant to the Allied prosecution at the Wiesbaden "second string" war crimes trials in 1946–47, only to resign in disgust at what he considered Allied hypocrisy. While in Ireland he wrote *Imperium* (1948), a voluminous account of Western heritage and destiny from a Spenglerian point of view. After making contact with the national bolshevist (pro-Soviet) neo-Nazi circle under Alfred Franke-Grieksch in Germany, Yockey went to London to influence the English Mosleyites of the Union Movement in this neutralist, anti-American direction. Here, Yockey founded the anti-Semitic European Liberation Front in 1949 and published *The Proclamation of London* as its manifesto. After falling out with Mosley, Yockey traveled in Europe. From the early 1950s until his suicide in FBI custody in 1960, Yockey was an active neo-fascist agent throughout Europe and the United States. He cultivated close links with a number of far-right groups and maintained the pro-Soviet bias in pursuit of his anti-American and anti-Zionist convictions. Yockey's analysis of Russia in *Imperium* was more favorable than that of America; he also wrote approvingly of Stalin's anti-Zionist campaign in Czechoslovakia for the NRP press in 1952 and was suspected of visiting East Germany, the Soviet Union and even Cuba.[8]

Born on 18 September 1917 in Chicago to a wealthy upper-middle-class family of Irish and German descent, Yockey was raised in Ludington, Michigan, and attended the Foreign Service School at Georgetown University and Northwestern University. He graduated with a law degree from Notre Dame University in 1941. Profoundly attracted by European traditions (his parents had lived in Paris before the First World War), Yockey felt repelled by the mediocrity of American culture and democracy. At an early stage he fell under the spell of Oswald Spengler, whose widely translated magnum opus, *The Decline of the West* (1918–22), explained the growth and decay of civilizations according to organic principles.[9] During the late 1930s, Yockey joined several domestic pro-German and fascist groups. He spoke at a gathering of William Dudley Pelley's Silvershirts in 1939 and was tipped by Mrs. De LaFayette Washburn to lead the National Liberty Party.[10] While serving in the U.S. Army in 1942–43, Yockey maintained his Silvershirt contacts and was suspected of Nazi sympathies. Going AWOL from a Georgia camp in November 1942, he undertook a Nazi intelligence mission in Texas and Mexico City. He subsequently obtained a medical discharge by feigning mental illness.[11] Following legal appointments in Detroit in 1944–45, he worked for eleven months on the War Crimes tribunal in Germany. After five months in the States, he settled at an inn in Brittas Bay, Ireland, to write his six hundred–page political opus.

Imperium scorns democracy, equality and the ideas of 1789. Its main theme is a metahistorical anti-Semitism, suggested by Spengler's The Decline of the West. In his monumental book on the periodicity of history, Spengler had contrasted the Western Faustian soul, whose prime symbol is dynamic energy in limitless space, with the Magian soul of Babylonian-Semitic culture, typified by algebra, mosaics and arabesques, the sacraments and scriptures of the Jewish and Christian religions.[12] Spengler described the Jews as a residual fossil of the earlier Magian civilization, stranded in urban ghettos among the settlements of medieval Europe. Landless, cynical and mercantile, the Jews represented the completed stage of an earlier civilization quite alien to the young Faustian culture of the West. It was not until Europe itself became intellectual and cosmopolitan in the eighteenth century that Jewry felt itself at home. Henceforth, the Jews contributed massively through commerce, art and philosophy to the acceleration of modernity but in a way that was critical and destructive of the native Western spirit.[13]

Yockey adopted these Spenglerian ideas for his analysis in Imperium. Just when the West should have been progressing toward the final stage of an empire, Jewry represented a fateful form of "cultural distortion." Mindful of their past oppression, the Jews vengefully exploited the new cultural forms of money thinking, rationalism, materialism, capitalism and democracy to destroy the traditions of the West and the authority of its old elites.[14] The Jews henceforth remade the modern world in their own image and interest. Yockey recounts the massive Jewish invasion of the United States from 1880 onward, bringing some 5 to 7 million immigrants from Eastern Europe. "The American Revolution of 1933"—the Democratic victory under Franklin D. Roosevelt—marked the Jewish seizure of political power in America. By contrast, German National Socialism represented "the European Revolution of 1933," which set the West back on course toward its proper fulfillment in a strong empire. However, the defeat of the Axis by extra-European forces—America and Russia—unleashed a new terror with war-crimes show trials. Yockey gives an early version of Holocaust denial by claiming that the gas chambers were faked to discredit the Nazis.[15] Imperium is dedicated to "the hero of the Second World War" (Adolf Hitler).

It is impossible to overestimate Yockey's importance in early postwar Nazi networks. In 1949 Yockey's Mosleyite circle included Guy Chesham, Peter Huxley-Blythe and Baroness von Pflugl, who financed the publication of *Imperium*. In 1949 Yockey published *The Proclamation of London* as the manifesto of his European Liberation Front, which opposed Washington and Tel Aviv with a pan-European fascist order. By fusing anti-Semitism with anti-Americanism, Yockey clearly identified the United States, rather than Russia, as Europe's main enemy. Thus, Yockey wanted to organize partisans against the Allied occupying powers in Germany and take direct action against American bases in England.[16] Already in the late 1940s, Yockey had organized the legal defense network of Rudolf Aschenauer, a leading figure in the German neo-Nazi Socialist Reich Party and legal counsel for the Malmedy war criminals. In October 1951 Yockey attended a fascist international conference in Naples; the following month he and the Italian neo-fascist Egido Boschi visited the Canadian fascist leader Adrien Arcand in Montreal. Yockey spent part of 1953 writing anti-Semitic propaganda in Cairo, having links to Otto Skorzeny, Hitler's top commando leader, now a military adviser to the Egyptian government. By the time of his death in June 1960 in San Francisco, Yockey's name was a byword in international Nazi intrigue.[17]

A close ally of Yockey in New York was Frederick Charles Weiss, who was also involved in the NRP. Born in Pforzheim, Germany, in 1886, Weiss had graduated from the University of Heidelberg and the Sorbonne. He first visited the United States in 1910 but returned to Germany, where he served as an artillery captain in the First World War. The son of a wealthy German industrialist whose fortune was lost by 1918, Weiss emigrated to America between the wars and settled in New York. After the Second World War he was deeply involved in Nazi and fascist intrigues on an international scale. According to the West German authorities, Weiss was another important contact man for renegade Nazis in Germany and overseas. He was said to correspond with prominent Nazi leaders, including Dr. Werner Naumann and Dr. Ernst Achenbach; General Heinz Guderian, Hitler's famous Panzer tactician; Dr. August Haussleiter, a prominent neo-Nazi politician in Bavaria; and Hans-Ulrich Rudel, the famous Stuka pilot hero who shuttled between Germany and Argentina, where he advised President Juan Perón. Weiss was closely linked to the postwar Socialist Reich Party (SRP) in Germany, while his aide H. Keith Thompson was instrumental in an American action committee to defend SS General Otto Remer of the SRP after the party had been officially banned. Thompson was also involved with several neo-Nazi presses in South America, which printed literature for clandestine circulation in occupied Germany.[18]

Just as Yockey had earlier attempted to solicit a pro-Soviet, anti-American line among the Mosleyites in London, Weiss also saw a Nazi future in an Eastern alliance. Through the National Renaissance Party press and his own publishing house, Le Blanc Publications, Weiss authored a stream of articles in praise of Russia from 1955 onward, which bore the unmistakable stamp of Yockey's influence. Here he argued that the "deep, instinctive religious antipathy of the Russian people toward Western economic forms" was a sign of their national health. The Russian aversion to the rule of money and the triumph of mercantile elites recalled the medieval European reaction to usury and Jewish banking practices. The Russian Revolution was viewed by Weiss as a violent reversal of Peter the Great's attempted Westernization of the country. Its only disadvantage was a Jewish leadership, which targeted the peasants, craftsmen and believers, in his view the true representatives of the Russian soul. However, the Revolution ultimately fanned the flames of Russian nationalism, and under Stalin's leadership nationalism fused with revolutionary communism.[19]

Madole accepted the views of Weiss and Yockey that the Soviet Union had by 1939 liquidated the original "Jewish Bolshevik" leadership of the Revolution in favor of Stalinism, which represented a strongly nationalist form of socialism. The NRP thus regarded Stalinism as a nationalist form of totalitarian rule and a valuable ally against the international Jewish menace and plutocracy, headquartered in the United States. The pro-Soviet stance of Yockey, Weiss and Madole was quite at variance with the traditional American far-right endorsement of the Cold War and the fight against world communism. In the same way, Madole admired various Third World dictators, typically vilified on the right as communists, for their staunch anti-imperialist hostility toward American capitalism and Zionism. He supported Nasser's "progressive nationalism" in Egypt and was contemptuous of the old Arab ruling families, whom he regarded as lackeys of U.S. imperialism. These sympathies gained the NRP support and financial backing from Arab nationalists, including diplomats in the United States. Abdul Mawgoud Hassan, press attaché of the Egyptian United Nations delegation, spoke at an NRP meeting.[20]

A further ideological alliance of the NRP indicative of its "Third Way" position involved the Greenshirts, a pro-Islamic nationalist movement. Founded in the early 1960s by John Hassan, a Euro-American convert to Islam, the Greenshirts were the action troops of the Ikhwan al-Kifah al-Islamiyya (IKI), the Fighting Muslim Brotherhood. The Greenshirts wore a uniform consisting of a forest green military shirt with dark red swallowtail collar insignia, a dark-red short fez with chin strap, black trousers, boots and belt. They met at Masjid Rabbil-Alamin, a Polish-Lithuanian mosque in Brooklyn, where a large portrait of their blond-haired, blue-eyed Imam was displayed. The inspiration of the Greenshirts was the Bosnian Muslim SS which was incorporated in the Waffen-SS during World War II and endorsed by the Grand Mufti of Jerusalem who resided in exile in Berlin. The Greenshirt insignia was the upraised scintian used by the 13th Waffen-SS Gebirgsdivision. John Hassan wrote a paper vindicating the Muslim SS formations for their part in Hitler's war machine. He believed that a new global Islamic movement was an essential weapon to expose and confront Zionism in the postwar world. Due to the overlap in their beliefs and international policy, the Greenshirts and the NRP collaborated in the 1960s.[21]

But it was in the field of doctrine that the NRP went beyond any ideology encountered on the postwar far-right scene. Madole's fascist philosophy was an extraordinary mixture of notions involving a considerable debt to the "Aryan" teachings of Hinduism and Theosophy. Madole probably first encountered the teachings of Helena Petrovna Blavatsky (1831–1891), the founder of modern Theosophy, through the world of science fiction and fantasy literature. Originally founded at New York in 1875, the Theosophical Society had survived charismatic Madame Blavatsky's death and established vigorous national societies in India, the United States, Britain and continental Europe during the late nineteenth century and the first decades of the twentieth. The success of the movement was largely due to the appeal of rediscovered ancient wisdom based on Egyptian and Hindu traditions, attractive to those individuals in the Anglo-American world who felt disturbed by the growth of agnosticism and the challenges of modern science.[22]

The key text of Blavatsky's mature formulation of Theosophical doctrine was written after the removal of the Theosophical Society to India in 1879 and her encounter with Hinduism and Buddhism. *The Secret Doctrine* (1888) was presented as a commentary on a secret text called the "Stanzas of Dzyan," which she claimed to have seen in a subterranean Himalayan monastery. Her weighty tome described the activities of God from the beginning of one period of universal creation until its end, a cyclical process that continues indefinitely over and over again. The first volume (*Cosmogenesis*) outlined the scheme according to which the primal unity of an unmanifest divine being differentiates itself into a multiformity of consciously evolving beings that gradually fill the universe. All subsequent creation passed through seven "rounds," or evolutionary cycles. In the first round, the universe was characterized by the predominance of fire, in the second by air, in the third by water, in the fourth by earth, and in the others by ether. This sequence reflected the cyclical fall of the universe from divine grace over the first four rounds and its following redemption over the next three, before everything contracted once again to the point of divine unity for the start of a major new cycle.

The second volume (*Anthropogenesis*) attempted to relate mankind to this grandiose vision of the cosmos. Not only was humanity assigned an age of far greater antiquity than that given by science, but it was also integrated into a scheme of cosmic, physical and spiritual evolution. These theories were partly derived from late-nineteenth-century scholarship concerning paleontology, inasmuch as Blavatsky adopted a racial theory of human evolution. She extended her cyclical doctrine of cosmic evolution with the assertion that each round witnessed the rise and fall of seven consecutive root-races, which descended on the scale of spiritual development from the first to the fourth race, becoming increasingly enmeshed in the material world. Here the Gnostic notion of a Fall from Light into Darkness was quite explicit. Evolution then ascended through progressively superior root-races from the fifth to the seventh.

According to Blavatsky, the modern white race constituted the fifth root-race upon a planet that was passing through the fourth cosmic round, so that an upward process of spiritual advance lay before mankind. She called this fifth root-race the Aryan race and claimed that it had been preceded by the fourth root-race of Atlanteans, which had largely perished in a flood that submerged their mid-Atlantic continent. The three earlier races of the present planetary round were proto-human, consisting of the first Astral root-race, which arose in an invisible, imperishable and sacred land, and the second Hyperborean root-race, which had dwelled on a vanished polar continent. The third Lemurian root-race had flourished on the continent of Lemuria that once lay in the Indian Ocean. It was probably due to this race's position at or near the nadir of the evolutionary racial cycle that Blavatsky charged the Lemurians with racial mixing entailing a kind of Fall and the breeding of monsters and inferior races.[23]

It was Blavatsky's mystical racism that appealed to Madole's taste for the fabulous landscapes of science fiction. Above all, Theosophical doctrine offered him a ready-made account of Aryan superiority against the debris of lower, unnatural half-breeds originating in racial defilement. Madole was also drawn to Blavatsky's account of her revelation. Throughout her account of prehistory she frequently invoked the sacred authority of elite priesthoods among the root-races of the past. She claimed she received her own initiation into the secret doctrine from two exalted *mahatmas*, or masters, in Tibet who had decided to impart their wisdom to Aryan mankind. After the Lemurians had fallen into racial sin and iniquity, only a hierarchy of the elect remained pure in spirit. This remnant became the Lemuro-Atlantean dynasty of priest-kings who dwelled on the fabulous island of Shamballah in the Gobi Desert.

These leaders were linked with Blavatsky's own masters, who were the instructors of the fifth Aryan root-race.[24] This elitism and sacred authority strongly attracted Madole, whose fascism was ultimately driven by religious fanaticism.

Madole elaborated an NRP program combining the metaphysics and philosophy of the Eastern Aryan tradition (Hinduism and Theosophy) with the science and technology of the Western Aryan tradition (the white European races) in order to create favorable circumstances for the emergence of the "God Man" (see below). From 1974 onward, Madole published his major occult-political treatise, "The New Atlantis: A blueprint for an Aryan Garden of Eden in North America," as a series of articles in the *National Renaissance Bulletin*. Drawing his inspiration from Theosophy, Madole claimed that the Aryan race was of great antiquity and had everywhere been worshipped by lower races as "White Gods." The proposed system of NRP government was based on the Hindu Laws of Manu, which sanctioned a caste system based on racial divisions and a pyramidal social structure ruled over by the priestly caste of *brahmins*. Below these stood the *kshatriyas*, a governing elite; then came the *vaisyas*, the merchant class; and finally the *sudras*, or workers. Madole regarded Vedic India as the archetypal model for Aryan statecraft. He believed that it had derived from Atlantis and continued in Brahmanic India, Pharaonic Egypt, Druidic Celtic Europe and Imperial Rome. He saw its revival in the "modern, streamlined, superbly efficient totalitarian states as manifested in National Socialist Germany, Fascist Italy and the Soviet Union." He regarded such hierarchy and racial segregation as a reflection of "Cosmic Law" and a guarantee of the harmony between the Macrocosm (the universe) and the microcosm (the body of man).[25]

Madole regarded all valuable esoteric teachings as Aryan in origin. Plato was credited with bringing the "Aryan Secret Doctrine" from Pharaonic Egypt back to Greece. His anti-democratic teachings underpinned the imperial achievements of Alexander the Great and ancient Rome. Madole quoted Blavatsky to the effect that the Jewish Cabala derived from Aryan sources in Central Asia. He further offered lengthy quotes from P. D. Ouspensky, Gurdjieff's successor in the teaching of the Fourth Way, and Eliphas Levi, the nineteenth-century French occultist, to support the aristocratic principle and the incompatibility of a society grounded in metaphysical wisdom with modern notions of equality and democracy in the age of the masses. He also quoted a diatribe of Aleister Crowley, the notorious English magician and occultist, along Social Darwinist lines: "We have nothing with the outcast and the unfit. . . . Nature's way is to weed out the weak. . . . At present all the strong are being damaged, and their progress hindered by the dead weight of the weak. . . . The

cant of democracy condemned. It is useless to pretend that men are equal."
Madole's slogan for the NRP state was even taken from the English Rosicrucian novelist, Sir Edward Bulwer-Lytton: "No happiness without order, no
order without authority, no authority without unity."[26]

Madole maintained that only a combination of fascist institutions and esoteric initiation could foster the development of the "God Man," an advanced
Aryan man representing "a forward step in the evolution of the incarnated
egos now embodied within the human race." This "New Adam" could come
only from the Aryan race, subject to a program of "selective breeding, cosmic
thinking, specialized training and Occult Initiation." The ancient Vedic system of philosopher-kings would govern the New Atlantis, and the inferior
racial elements of the masses would be eliminated by means of euthanasia
and eugenics. Madole stressed the anti-Semitic aspect of his beliefs by assert-
ing that "cosmic thinking" would replace "man-made Judaeo-Christian concepts of Reality." Cosmic Law, a combination of Hindu and Theosophical
tenets, was favorably contrasted with Semitic religious beliefs that "have
stressed the absurd argument that man's role is to overcome and enslave Nature." With a withering glance at the shortcomings of modern liberal society,
Madole claimed that "chaotic democracy and anarchy reflect the Judaeo-
Christian rebellion against Nature."[27]

Madole's hostility to the Judeo-Christian tradition involved a rejection of
Christianity itself. Whereas most right-wing American groups, from conservatives to Nazis, identified with Christianity, Madole saw Christianity as a
Jewish cultural product. He denounced "the national heritage of religious
twaddle handed down from the Pilgrims and the Puritans" and claimed that
"the Semitic heresies of Judaism and Christianity [existed] as alien and disruptive factors within the body of Aryan Europe." He condemned Christian
humanism together with liberal democracy, egalitarianism and "the nonsen-
sical belief in anthropomorphic deities" as products of the Jewish mind
"foisted upon Aryan humanity at the point of Roman swords under the ac-
cursed Christian Emperor Constantine." Madole fulminated against "the ignorant fanatics of the Christian clergy" who had destroyed the ancient Aryan
esoteric and scientific knowledge and thus ushered in the medieval Dark
Ages. The text was illustrated with Christians being thrown to the lions in the
Roman circus, over the caption: "The grim justice of Imperial Rome—death
to the Judaeo-Christian subverters of Aryan values, the foul criminals whose
later victory plunged Aryan Europe into the Dark Ages."[28]

Such open hostility toward Christianity led Madole and some of his NRP
followers to plumb the occult paths of paganism and satanism. Alongside
books on Theosophy, the NRP literature list included Gerald Gardner's *The*

Meaning of Witchcraft, Lewis Spence's *The History and Origins of Druidism*, Paul Carus's *History of the Devil and the Idea of Evil* and a number of books on runes. In his quest for the pre-Christian, pagan sources of Aryan religion, Madole made contact with satanist groups, and there was even some overlap in membership between these and the NRP. James Wagner, a former Security Echelon (SE) commander, recalls that relations between the NRP and the Church of Satan, founded in 1966 by Anton Szandor LaVey, were cordial. Madole and LaVey frequently met at the NRP office and in the Warlock Bookshop in New York. Madole is said to have erected a large satanic altar in his apartment, and Wagner has confirmed that an image of Baphomet, the sabbatic goat, hung there, and that Madole played LaVey's recording of the Satanic Mass at several NRP meetings. One NRP bulletin shows a picture of Madole and an SE trooper with the high priest of the Temple of Baal and some female acolytes at their temple. Seth Klippoth, the NRP Michigan State organizer, formed the satanic Order of the Black Ram with some other NRP members "to celebrate the ancient religious rites of the Aryan race."[29] These contacts between Madole's occult fascism and satanism anticipated the pagan alliances of neo-Nazis and satanists in the 1990s (see chapter 11).

Another leading member of the NRP, Eustace Clarence Mullins (b. 1923), provides a further indication of the occult ideas current within the party. Mullins had beome a devotee of Ezra Pound while the latter was interned in an American mental hospital for his pro-Axis stance during the war. Besides writing a book on Pound, Mullins authored an anti-Semitic history of the Jews and an exposé of the Federal Reserve system, a favored topic among right-wing conspiracy theorists. From his Chicago base, Mullins was associated with two organizations in the 1950s concerned with the mystique of Aryan eugenics: the Real Political Institute and the Institute for Bio-Politics.[30] It is possible that these research groups also reflected Yockey's eccentric biological political theories. Papers found at the time of his arrest included his own essays on the principle of polarity in the psyche, a book on palmistry and politics, and a bibliography of books on the "second body," on reincarnation and on cosmic rays.[31] Although these esoteric topics relate to Yockey's own interests, they also give a hint of the mystical fascist concerns within the NRP.

But Madole did not simply indulge sectarian religious ideas as a fantasy of a golden age in the distant past. Madole was an occult *fascist*. He wanted to translate mankind and the world into the authoritarian utopia of a revived Vedic hierarchy, employing violent and draconian means if necessary. The sectarian religion of Theosophy, borrowings from Hinduism, paganism and satanism, and mystical biological and eugenic ideas all served to explain and justify his militant attack on the democratic and liberal institutions of the modern world. Inspired by the Hindu stratification of society into castes, Madole modeled his stormtroopers on the *kshatriyas*, the warriors forming the second of the four main Hindu castes, subordinate only to the *brahmin* priests. He regarded his activists as "cosmic warriors" who were to uphold the order of the cosmos and ensure that the laws of race and eugenic selection became the basis of the New Atlantis. These men were imbued with a fighting spirit and were indoctrinated with classes, lectures and reading lists on fascism, Theosophy and Vedic India. Wagner relates that stormtrooper instruction included "unique mind training" and the discussion of Theosophical and Indo-Aryan metaphysics.[32]

These stormtroopers were initially known as the "Elite Guard," acting as street orderlies from 1954 onward to protect Madole's regular street meetings. In 1963 Madole renamed his warrior elite the Security Echelon and organized a number of battalions. Given the high Jewish proportion of the population in New York, Madole's NRP rallies represented a unique provocation with their strident Aryan zealotry and vicious anti-Semitism. As one of the first postwar fascist parties, the NRP was targeted for counterdemonstrations by communist and Jewish organizations in the city. There was a strange courage in Madole's tireless witness to his doctrines, with racial diatribes against the Jews and blacks in the heart of a multiracial and Jewish metropolis. Running street battles inevitably ensued between the SE units and the large masses of protesters. This emnity and tension served to heighten the self-regard of Madole's tough squad as an elite of cosmic warriors fighting the inferiors of a degraded world.[33]

One of the first and most notorious of the SE/NRP actions occurred on 25 May 1963, when the party held a rally in Yorkville, New York, a town that had seen vigorous prewar fascist activity on the part of the German-American Bund, the Christian Front and Kurt Mertig's Citizens Protective League. The rally drew a crowd of four thousand, including a counterdemonstration of a thousand Jews organized by the Jewish War Veterans. A massive riot began in the afternoon and continued into the evening after police lines failed to contain the Jewish protest and the SE men went into action. Madole used to counter-demonstrate with force whenever the Congress of Racial Equality (CORE) organized pickets at racially exclusive restaurants and other institutions during the civil rights campaign of the early 1960s. Another favored location for SE picket action was Astoria, New York, where the NRP formations frequently engaged the Maoists of the Progressive Labor Party in the years between 1973 and 1975. In 1974, the NRP ran a picket of the Israeli El Al Airlines office on Rockefeller Plaza in downtown Manhattan, which brought the expected news coverage. Madole won continuous publicity for the NRP as a

result of the many court cases brought against the party for affray, illegal so-
licitation of donations and the contested use of public halls.[34]

This strategy of militant confrontation was extended by Madole's adroit
manipulation of the media. Madole and his top officers successfully sought
radio and TV slots, such as the Pennsylvania cable broadcast "Interview with
a Fascist," where Madole appeared on the screen flanked by uniformed SE
troopers. In 1975 the NRP applied to hold a meeting at the Bicentennial Au-
ditorium in Virginia. The prospect of a fascist party dignifying its program
and views by association with a prestigious venue at a time of national celebrations swiftly mobilized a reaction among black, Jewish and liberal interest groups. The local Anti-Defamation League and the Black Urban League
threatened violence. Black members of the Bicentennial Commission and
Virginia State Senator Leroy solemnly promised to resign if permission were
granted to the NRP. The ensuing furor only served to create further publicity for the party which was, after all, allowed to hold its meeting in the au-
ditorium.[35]

Madole seldom appeared without a show of strength from the Security
Echelon. The stormtroopers wore black caps, gray shirts with lightning-bolt
armbands and black trousers; black jackets with epaulettes, collar insignia,
medals and badges of rank were worn by senior officers. These strong, well-
built uniformed men with short haircuts and of neat appearance created an
uncanny impression and a threatening martial presence. As Madole ran
through his racial invective against the Jews, blacks and other supposed inferiors, the Security Echelon exuded a sinister, brooding aura, a glimpse of the
fearful fascist regime that awaited onlookers if ever the New Atlantis, with its
neo-Vedic hierarchy of racial castes, were to be established on the ruins of a
multiracial America.[36]

Madole died of cancer at the age of fifty-one on 6 May 1979, and the NRP
barely survived its leader. His mother, Grace, attempted to keep the movement alive by encouraging other leaders. Andrej Lisanik, a tough SE commander who had earlier served as an officer in the wartime Czech Army, assumed the leadership, but he was killed by a mugger. As he was carrying the
bulk of the NRP records with him in his car at the time, these were scattered
and lost. By 1980 the NRP was defunct.[37]

The NRP provides an early postwar example of a fascist organization that
used sectarian religious ideas to elaborate a political theology of Aryan renaissance. Its adaptation of Theosophy for a fascist ideology was by no means
original or unique. Even before the First World War, occult-racist *völkisch*
sects in Austria and Germany had quarried the ideas of Theosophy for the
Aryo-Germanic cult of Ariosophy. Notions of elite priesthoods, secret gnosis,

a prehistoric golden age, the conspiracy of demonic racial inferiors and millennial prophecies of Aryan salvation all occur in the writings of Guido von List (1848–1919) and Jörg Lanz von Liebenfels (1874–1954) and their followers. Their ideas and symbols filtered through to several anti-Semitic and nationalist groups in late Wilhelmian Germany, from which the early Nazi Party emerged in Munich after the war. At least two Ariosophists were closely involved with Reichsführer Heinrich Himmler in the 1930s, contributing to his projects in Germanic prehistory, SS order ceremonial and his visionary plans for the Greater Germanic Reich in the third millennium.[38]

The attraction of Theosophy for Madole and the Ariosophists right up to the present lies in its eclecticism with respect to exotic religion, mythology and esoteric lore. The sources of Aryan and Germanic belief, customs and identity, so germane to nationalist thought, are thus placed within a universal and non-Christian perspective upon the cosmos, the origins of mankind and the races. Given the neopagan revivalism and frequent antipathy toward Christianity among fascists, Theosophy can offer such individuals a scheme of religious belief that ignores Christianity in favor of a mixture of mythical traditions and new scientific ideas from contemporary scholarship in anthropology, etymology, ancient history and comparative religion.

In the nineteenth and early twentieth centuries, Theosophy itself tended to be associated with liberal and emancipatory causes by its leaders in Britain and India. Here one recalls Helena Blavatsky's support of Garibaldi's struggle in Italy and Annie Besant's championship of the Indian National Congress. However, the very structure of Theosophical beliefs can lend themselves to illiberal adoption. The implicit authority of the hidden mahatmas from a Lemuro-Atlantean dynasty with superhuman wisdom is easily transmogrified by racist enthusiasts into a new hierarchical social order based on the mystique of the blood. And the notion of an occult gnosis in Blavatskyan Theosophy, together with the charge that alien (Christian) beliefs have obscured this spiritual heritage, also fits the need to ascribe a prehistoric pedigree to modern racial nationalism. A recent example of the neo-fascist potential in Theosophy is provided by the Nouvelle Acropole movement of Jorge Angel Livraga (b. 1930), the charismatic Argentinian Theosophist who by the 1980s had built up an ardent youth following in more than thirty countries. The structure, organization and symbolism of the Nouvelle Acropole is clearly indebted to fascist models.

The Theosophical inspiration of James Madole and the National Renaissance Party ably demonstrates the cultic and pseudoreligious underpinnings of a marginal postwar fascist movement. For a minute sect to uphold disgraced and abhorrent notions of anti-Semitism and Aryan supremacy in the wake of the recent defeat of the Axis powers was both extremist and radical; to persist in holding rallies and street protests at the heart of cosmopolitan New York in support of their discredited ideas required a racism that was religious in inspiration. The medley of Theosophy, popularized Vedic Hinduism, hostility toward Christianity and the neopagan posturing of satanism provided a composite doctrine of racial superiority. Thus armed, believers could vilify the Jews, blacks and other colored races while comforting themselves that they were in the militant vanguard of a powerful force for racial revolution and the coming victory of the Aryans in a fascist utopia.

5

Savitri Devi and the Hitler Avatar

THE UNDERGROUND WRITINGS of Savitri Devi (1905–1982), prophetess of Aryan rebirth and the Hitler avatar, have exercised a significant and
enduring influence on universal Nazism in the postwar Anglo-American
world and elsewhere. Her fervent devotion to Adolf Hitler, the high-flown
language of her books, the overt religiosity of her missionary zeal and her pilgrimages in Allied-occupied Germany made her an exemplar of the postwar
Nazi faith. Arrested in 1949 for disseminating illegal Nazi propaganda in the
ruined Reich, she was imprisoned in a British military prison. During the
1950s she entered the German nationalist underground, becoming close
friends with leaders of the short-lived neo-Nazi parties and visiting notorious
Nazi emigrés in Egypt and Spain. With her exotic Hindu background, she has
provided Nazi apologists with an unabashedly pagan, anti-Christian statement of the Hitler doctrine. Contemptuous of the man-centered beliefs of
liberty, equality and fraternity, she spurned Christianity, Judaism and Marxism and aspired to a pagan Aryan heritage drawn from the pantheons of classical Greece, ancient Germany, and Vedic India. Her books inspired Lincoln
Rockwell, William Pierce, Matt Koehl and Colin Jordan. She was among the
founding members of the World Union of National Socialists (WUNS) at the
Cotswold camp-conference of 1962 and remained a luminary on the international neo-Nazi scene until her death twenty years later.[1]

She was born Maximiani Portas on 30 September 1905 in Lyons and
brought up there in comfortable circumstances. Her mother, Julia Nash, came
from Cornwall and her father was of mixed Mediterranean heritage, having
an Italian mother from London and a Greek father who had acquired French
citizenship due to his residence in France.[2] As a young girl she felt a strong patriotic sympathy for classical Greece, and the hero of her youth was Alexander the Great. The scornful and pessimistic poetry of the French Parnassian
poet, Leconte de Lisle (1818–1894), especially his *Poèmes barbares* with their
eulogy of pagan peoples and their vanquished gods, made a deep and lasting
impression on her. Her growing alienation from Christianity was complemented by her rejection of the Jews and their religious legacy. By 1929, while

still a postgraduate student at Lyons and Athens, she already identified with the anti-Semitic and Aryan ideology of German National Socialism. In 1932 she traveled to India in search of its traditional Aryan-Vedic culture, whose Indo-European pagan gods and beliefs she considered undefiled by Judeo-Christian monotheism.[3]

Through her passage to India in search of the Aryan heritage, Maximiani Portas retraced the intellectual journey of many European philosophers and philologists who had begun to seek the origins of mankind in India from the mid-eighteenth century onward. During the Middle Ages and the Renaissance, European scholars had generally accepted the biblical account of creation in the Book of Genesis, which traced the descent of all the races initially from Adam and Eve in the Garden of Eden and then from Noah and his sons, Shem, Ham and Japhet. However, the discovery of the Americas and many previously unknown aboriginal peoples placed an increasing strain upon this biblical explanation. During the Enlightenment, the *philosophes* expressed the anti-clerical and anti-biblical mood of a rational age by dissenting from the old Hebraic account of human origins in favor of a more exotic yet universal source. The location of this source in India provided a background to this quest for a new Adam. The subsequent development of this postbiblical anthropogeny gave rise to the Aryan myth in the nineteenth and twentieth centuries. It exercised a powerful and fatal influence on Nazi racial doctrine.

In his highly influential essay *Über die Sprache und Weisheit der Inder* (1808), the German Romantic thinker Friedrich Schlegel (1772–1829) paid fulsome tribute as a philologist to the beauty, antiquity and philosophical clarity of Sanskrit. But in the final part of the book he aired his anthropological ideas about a new masterful race that had formed in northern India before marching down from the roof of the world to found empires and civilize the West. In his view, all the famous nations of high cultural achievement sprang from one stock, and their colonies were all one people ultimately deriving from an Indian origin. Although he wondered why the inhabitants of fertile areas in Asia should have migrated to the harsh northern climes of Scandinavia, he found an answer in Indian legends relating to the tradition of the miraculous and holy mountain of Meru in the Far North. Thus, the Indian tribes had been driven northward not out of necessity but by "some supernatural idea of the high dignity and splendor of the North." The language and traditions of the Indians and the Nordics proved that they formed a single race.[4]

The new anthropogeny of the gifted white European races was complete by 1819, when Friedrich Schlegel applied the term "Aryan" to this as yet anonymous Indic-Nordic master race. The word had been derived from

Herodotus's *Arioi* (an early name for the Medes and Persians) and was recently used by French and German authors to designate these ancient peoples. However, Schlegel's new usage caught on as he linked the root *Ari* with *Ehre*, the German word for honor. Philologically he was quite correct, since one also finds the same root with a similar meaning in the Slavic and Celtic languages. However, the anthropological implications of the new word for the ancestral European race were much more exciting and flattering: as Aryans, the Germans and their ancient Indian ancestors were the people of honor, the aristocracy of the various races of mankind. It should be noted that Friedrich Schlegel was neither an extreme German nationalist nor an anti-Semite. Nevertheless, his ideas in due course stimulated the boldest ideas about Aryan supremacy among German, French and English scholars.

Throughout the first half of the nineteenth century, famous and obscure German philosophers and philologists alike worked tirelessly to develop and refine the Aryan myth. Many more speculations were supplied by Julius von Klaproth (who coined the term "Indo-Germanic"), Georg Wilhelm Friedrich Hegel, Jacob Grimm and Franz Bopp. In 1820 the geographer Karl Ritter described the Indian armies breaking through to the West across the Caucasus. As the originator of the famous dictionary, Grimm exercised a lasting influence on literary and historical textbooks. He described the arrival of the Greeks, Romans, Celts and Germans in Europe in successive waves of immigration from Asia. However, the Aryans were not yet set against the Jews in these accounts. The outlines of the Aryan-Semitic dualism first became apparent in 1845, when Christian Lassen (1800–1876), the pupil and protégé of the Schlegel brothers, contrasted the Semites unfavorably with the Indo-Germans, depicting them as unharmonious, egotistical and exclusive. His emphasis on biology, the triumph of the strongest, the youthful and creative nature of the most recent species, and the superiority of the whites provided the basic ingredients of all subsequent thinking about the master race. Such notions were soon combined with a virulent anti-Semitism by the famous composer and author Richard Wagner (1813–1883), who enjoyed an enthusiastic mass following in Germany and Austria.[5]

Given the existence of entries for "Aryans" and "Indo-Europeans" in standard encyclopedias and textbooks in France, England and Germany from the late 1860s onward, there is nothing remarkable about Maximiani Portas's adoption of the racial Manichaeanism based on an Aryan-Semitic dualism. However, her ideas about the original Aryan homeland owed more to European romanticism and native Indian scholarship than to the modern theories of German racist and nationalist authors. Instead of seeking out the heirs of the pristine race in northern Europe, she traveled to India, "that easternmost and southernmost home of the Aryan race." In this respect, her thinking was quite traditional. For example, Max Müller had believed that the purity with which the Hindus had preserved the Aryan language and religion showed that those Aryans who had migrated to India had been the last to leave their highlands in Central Asia. Maximiani Portas's enthusiasm for the Aryan Indians was thus firmly grounded in the Aryan myth as it had developed in Europe since the time of the German Romantics.

Her ideas concerning the origins of the Aryans were drawn directly from the books of Bâl Gangadhar (Lokmanya) Tilak (1856–1920), who was widely acclaimed as "the father of Indian unrest."[6] After completing his education at Poona University, Tilak had spurned a career in government service and devoted himself to the cause of national awakening. Besides his radical political activities, Tilak was an accomplished scholar of ancient Hindu sacred literature. As an Indian nationalist, he was particularly interested in the Vedas as the earliest document of the Aryan Indians and the oldest writings in the history of mankind. During a brief term of imprisonment for sedition in 1897–98, Tilak immersed himself in Vedic study and duly published his major statement concerning the age and original location of Vedic civilization, *The Arctic Home in the Vedas* (1903).

On the basis of astronomical statements in the Vedas, Tilak concluded that the Aryan ancestors of the Vedic writers had lived in an Arctic home in interglacial times between 10,000 and 8000 B.C., enjoying a degree of civilization superior to that of both the Stone and the Bronze Ages. Owing to the destruction of their homeland by the onset of the last Ice Age, the Aryans had migrated southward and roamed over northern Europe and Asia in search of lands suitable for new settlement in the period 8000–5000 B.C. Tilak believed that many Vedic hymns could be traced to the early part of the period between 5000 and 3000 B.C., when the Aryan bards had not yet forgotten the traditions of their former Arctic home. During the period 3000–1400 B.C., when later Vedic texts including the *Brahmanas* were composed, the Arctic traditions were gradually misunderstood and lost. Regarding Aryan prowess, Tilak concluded that "the vitality and superiority of the Aryan races, as disclosed by their conquest, by extermination or assimilation, of the non-Aryan races with whom they came in contact . . . is intelligible only on the assumption of a high degree of civilisation in their original Arctic home."[7]

Tilak's ideas of Aryan Arctic origins, together with the conventional Aryan myth, strongly influenced Maximiani Portas's view of India, its culture and its peoples. She imagined the Aryan invasions of India as having occurred over a longer period during the fourth and third millennia B.C. However, in common with European scholars, she preferred to view the Aryans as gifted barbarians whose military skills in horsemanship and use of wheeled chariots enabled them to dominate the Dravidians and other dark-skinned races they encountered in the more advanced Indus civilization in northwest India. From the Vedas it was possible to reconstruct a great deal about these light-skinned proto-Nordic invaders. After entering northern India through the passes in the Hindu Kush mountains, the Aryans had settled the Punjab and then gradually penetrated along the river courses throughout the Gangetic plain of northern India. They lived initially as seminomadic pastoralists on the produce of cattle. The cow was thus a very precious commodity and often an object of veneration. The Vedic hymns describe the Aryans as a vigorous warrior aristocracy more interested in fighting than in agriculture. Great prestige and pleasure was attached to battle, chariot racing, drinking the intoxicating *soma*, music making and gambling with dice.[8]

Maximiani Portas was, above all, interested in the caste system of Hinduism, which she regarded as the archetype of racial laws intended to govern the segregation of different races and to maintain the pure blood of the fair-complexioned Aryans. When the Aryans first invaded India, they were already divided into three social classes: the warriors or aristocracy, the priests, and the common people. The Aryans spoke contemptuously of the dark-skinned, flat-nosed folk of Dravidian and aboriginal stock whom they conquered, calling them Daysus (meaning "squat creatures," "slaves" and even "apes"). A more exclusive development of the caste system followed this encounter, which involved both fear of the Daysus and anxiety that assimilation with them would lead to a loss of Aryan identity. The Sanskrit word for caste is *varna*, which actually means color, and this provided the basis of the original four-caste system comprising the *kshatriyas* (warriors and aristocracy), the *brahmins* (priests), and the *vaishyas* (cultivators); the fourth caste, the *sudras*, were the Daysus and those of mixed Aryo-Daysu origin. Maximiani Portas venerated the Aryan race for its racial purity as the zenith of physical perfection and for its outstanding qualities of beauty, intelligence, willpower and thoroughness. She regarded the survival of the light-skinned minority of Brahmans among an enormous population of many different Indian races after sixty centuries as a living tribute to the value of the Aryan caste system.

For Maximiani Portas, Hinduism was the custodian of the Aryan and Vedic heritage down through the centuries, the very essence of India. In her opinion, Hinduism was the sole surviving example of an Indo-European paganism once common to all the Aryan nations: "If those of Indo-European race regard the conquest of pagan Europe by Christianity as a decadence, then the whole of Hindu India can be likened to a last fortress of very ancient ideals, of very old and beautiful religious and metaphysical conceptions, which have already passed away in Europe. Hinduism is thus the last flour-ishing and fecund branch on an immense tree which has been cut down and mutilated for two thousand years."[9] She imagined that Indian society could also show how the world would appear around A.D. 8000 once the New Order of Nazism had prevailed for six thousand years.[10]

Years before, on a visit to Palestine, she had resolved to honor the pagan gods and fight the Judeo-Christian legacy of the West. Imagining herself as a pioneer of Nazi ideals in the East, she now resolved to do all in her power to maintain the Hindu traditions against Christianity and all other philosophies of equality. Maximiani henceforth regarded India as her home. After exten-sive travels throughout India in the period from 1932 until the middle of 1935, she lived from July to December 1935 at Rabindranath Tagore's ashram in Shantiniketan at Bolpur in Bengal, renowned for its cosmopolitan mem-bership. The negligible cost of living at the ashram outweighed her aversion to its liberal spirit and the presence of émigré German Jews. Here she learned Hindi and perfected her command of Bengali. She then taught English and Indian history at Jerandan College, not far from Delhi, and worked in a sim-ilar capacity at Mathura, the holy city of Krishna during 1936. Ever more in-volved in the life and customs of Hinduism, she adopted a Hindu name, Sav-itri Devi, in honor of the female solar deity, by which we will henceforth refer to her in this account. She richly evokes the colorful diversity of India in *L'Étang aux lotus* [The Lotus Pond] (1940), a book recording her early im-pressions of the country in the years 1934 to 1936.[11]

At this time, the future of Hinduism in India was directly affected by the political institutions of late British rule as these made provision for represen-tation in state legislatures by quotas based on the numbers of each religious group in the population. Several Hindu political organizations, notably the Hindu Mahasabha and the Rashtriya Swayamsevak Sangh (RSS), achieved major prominence in the interwar period by addressing the problem of de-clining Hindu influence and seeking conversions among non-Hindus and the return to the fold of former apostates.[12] Savitri Devi's Aryan-Hindu enthusi-asm now interacted with this militant expression of Hindu nationalism. After settling at Calcutta in late 1936, she discovered the Hindu Mission there, to which she immediately offered her services.

When quizzed by its president, Srimat Swami Satyananda, about her own religious beliefs, Savitri Devi explained that she was an Aryan pagan and re-gretted the conversion of Europe to Christianity. She wanted to prevent the sole remaining country honoring the Aryan gods from falling under the spir-itual influence of the Jews. She also added that she was a devotee of Adolf Hitler, who was leading the only movement in this Aryan pagan spirit against the Judeo-Christian civilization of the West. Satyananda was interested and impressed by the young Greek woman and her intense eyes, outspoken manner, and fluent command of Hindi and Bengali. He also shared many educated Hindus' interest in Hitler because of his Aryan mythology and use of the swastika, the traditional sign of fortune and health. He told her that he considered Hitler an incarnation of Vishnu, an expression of the force preserving cosmic order. In his eyes, the disciples of Hitler were the Hindus' spiritual brothers. With this evident meeting of minds, Satyananda engaged Savitri Devi as a lecturer. Her duties involved speaking at the Mission headquarters in Calcutta and traveling to give lectures throughout Bengal and the neighboring states of Bihar and Assam.[13]

These pro-Nazi views of the Hindu Mission brought Savitri Devi into contact with the nationalist Hindu Mahasabha Party. After the German invasion of Czechoslovakia in March 1939, the Hindu Mahasabha adopted a particularly strong pro-German position, assuming a close congruence between the Aryan cult of Nazism and Hindu nationalism. As one Mahasabha spokesman declared:

> Germany's solemn idea of the revival of Aryan culture, the glorification of the Swastika, her patronage of Vedic learning and the ardent championship of the tradition of Indo-Germanic civilization are welcomed by the religious and sensible Hindus of India with a jubilant hope. . . . Germany's crusade against the enemies of Aryan culture will bring all the Aryan nations of the world to their senses and awaken the Indian Hindus for the restoration of their lost glory.[14]

While moving in these circles, Savitri met Asit Krishna Mukherji, a Hindu publisher with strong pro-German sympathies. He was the editor and proprietor of *The New Mercury*, a fortnightly National Socialist magazine published with the support of the German consulate in Calcutta from 1935 until 1937, when it was suppressed by the British government. She had already noticed this publication, which was the only Nazi paper in India, during her earlier travels around Bengal and read its contents with great interest. Mukherji's editorial line was unabashedly pro-German and pro-Nazi, yet he also stood for a pan-Aryan racism with a strong Indian element. The articles ranged from Hitler's views on the nation and architecture and translated excerpts of *Mein Kampf* to studies on the original Aryans, the origin of the swastika, and the Arctic homeland of the Aryans. On the eve of his departure for a new assignment in 1938, the German ambassador, Baron Eduard von Selzam, wrote in a secret communiqué to all German legations in the Far East that no one had rendered services to the Third Reich in Asia comparable to those of Sri Asit Krishna Mukherji.[15]

Mukherji admired the growing might and influence of the Third Reich. He was deeply impressed by the Aryan ideology of Nazi Germany, with its cult of Nordic racial superiority, anti-Semitism and race laws. He approved of the German emphasis on the Hellenic ideal of physical strength and beauty, so well displayed in the Olympic Games held at Berlin in the summer of 1936. He recognized the Nazi flag—a black swastika upon a white circle on a red background—as a close relative of the Pan-Hindu flag with its immemorial Aryan symbols of swastika, lotus and sword. Likewise, he saw the parallels between the martial spirit of the Third Reich and the old Hindu warrior tradition of the Marathas and other Indian races, between M. S. Golwalkar's RSS Hindu youth formations and the Hitler Youth that had been his inspiration. Just as the Hindu nationalists were protesting against colonial rule, Germany was also on the march in defense of Aryandom and had already challenged Britain and France, her sworn enemies, for an end to the ignominious Versailles settlement and, more, for the leading position in Europe.[16]

Savitri Devi's encounter with Mukherji was a pivotal event in her life. She had at long last found a pan-Aryan activist who shared her belief in the Aryan revival of India. He was to become her husband. With the outbreak of war in September 1939, her position as a Greek passport holder in Calcutta became problematic. As a Hindu Mission lecturer, she was known to the British authorities as an alien with Nazi sympathies and ran a clear risk of deportation or detention. In early 1940 Mukherji had therefore proposed that they marry in order that she become the wife of a British subject and so remain at liberty. It was, she claims, not a romantic match but one based on their cordial friendship and shared ideals. The date that was set for the wedding coincided with news of the British evacuation from Dunkirk and the imminent fall of France. Resplendent in her best gold and scarlet sari, Savitri Devi was married to Asit Krishna Mukherji in a Hindu ceremony on 9 June 1940 in Calcutta. She spent the rest of the war in joyful anticipation of an Axis victory and the division of India between Germany and Japan. Her husband was involved in espionage activities on behalf of the Japanese in India and Burma.[17]

By the end of the war, Savitri Devi had assimilated many notions from Hinduism into a heterodox form of National Socialism that glorified the Aryan race and Adolf Hitler. In the first place, she adopted the Hindu cycle of the ages described in the *Vishnu Purana*, one of the ancient legends forming part of popular Hindu scripture. According to this cyclical doctrine, four ages, or yugas, of decreasing length characterize the world's decline from a golden era to the utter decadence of dark age, or Kali Yuga. This pessimistic cosmology of entropy and exhaustion perfectly matched her acute feelings of hostility toward liberalism, democracy and modernity. She was profoundly convinced that the world had entered that dark age by about 3000 B.C. The religious prominence of Jewry, its universalistic successor in Christianity, and above all the modern world and the rational ideas of 1789—freedom, equality and brotherhood—were but signs of its accelerating degeneration.[18]

Against the dismal cosmology of the Kali Yuga, she developed her own doctrine of Men in Time, above Time and against Time. These three kinds of historical personalities represented three quite distinct responses to the bondage of Time as understood in the cycle of the ages. Of the three types, Men in Time were the essential and most active agents of the Kali Yuga. Their egoism, violence and power-seeking ambitions typify the Dark Age and all its vicissitudes; she identified Genghis Khan (1157–1227), the medieval Mongol chieftain whose lightning victories brought him brief dominion across Eurasia in the thirteenth century, as a leading example of the Man in Time. Men above Time were properly at home in the undisturbed perfection of the Satya Yuga or golden age. As unworldy mystics and sages, their divine revelation ideally shone upon an ordered realm that knew no strife. The solar mystic and Egyptian pharaoh Akhenaton (c. 1370–1340 B.C.), she believed, was an eminent Man above Time. But Men against Time combined the qualities of the other types, lightning and sun, by acting with ruthless violence in an attempt to restore the conditions of the coming golden age at the end of the dark age. These martial heroes were the saviors of the cycle of the ages; by means of war, revolution and annihilation, they worked to redeem the world from the thrall of the Kali Yuga and so initiate a new time cycle.[19]

She linked these ideas to the theistic Hindu notion of the *avatara* (avatar), who incarnates the periodic descent to earth of the deity, typically Vishnu, in a human, superhuman or animal form. This mediator between God and men was a development from the extra-human gods of the Vedic period. The origin of the concept of avatar is obscure, and precursors have been traced to Aryan Iran in the *Bahram Yasht*, a Zoroastrian text, which may even show traces of Chinese influence and mythology. However, in none of these beliefs does the concept play such an important part as it does in the post–Vedic Hindu thought of the epics and the *Bhagavad Gita*. Both the *Ramayana* and the *Mahabharata* describe the descent of avatar in the form of Rama and Krishna, both of whom reappear as the favorite incarnations of Vishnu. In the *Puranas*, these avatars also appear between the ages as yuga avatars.[20] The Kalki avatar appears as the tenth and final incarnation of Vishnu. In a manner redolent of Judeo-Christian apocalypse, he arrives in the form of a sword-bearing rider on a white horse to vanquish the dark age and start a new golden age.

Savitri Devi believed the greatest Man against Time in all recorded history was Adolf Hitler, the divinely appointed leader of the Aryan world in the West. His demand for German national unity in a strong new Reich in defiance of the humiliating Versailles Treaty clearly identified him to her as a champion of the old tribal principle against the degenerate capitalist and cosmopolitan order of the Allies. His adoption of racist ideas, his anti-Semitism and his implementation of the Nuremberg laws forbidding inter-marriage and sexual relations between Aryans and Jews convinced her that he intended to seek the revival of the Aryan caste system on a worldwide scale. Adolf Hitler's ruthless use of military violence against his enemies in a resistant fallen world, and his uncompromising plan to exterminate the Jews, the age-old adversary and counter-image of the heroic Aryans, characterized him as the essential Man against Time. Like a fiery comet from the heavens, he burst through the gloomy pall surrounding the earth in the Kali Yuga to herald the spreading sunshine of a new order of perfection, divine justice and righteousness.[21]

Savitri Devi is unquestionably the first Western writer to identify Adolf Hitler as an avatar. She frequently quotes from the *Bhagavad Gita* with reference to the German leader: "When justice is crushed, when evil is triumphant, then I come back. For the protection of the good, for the destruction of evil-doers, for the establishment of the Reign of Righteousness, I am born again and again, age after age."[22] Her eulogy of Adolf Hitler's life and political career in *The Lightning and the Sun* (1958) begins with the incarnation of the divine collective Self of Aryan mankind as "the late-born child of light" at Braunau am Inn in 1889. Her description of his youth and dawning sense of mission is based on August Kubizek's account of their adolescent friendship in Linz and Vienna during the years 1904 to 1908. Whether enthusing over the ancient Germanic sagas and the magical power of Wagner's music or busily outlining plans for new cities, buildings and monuments, Hitler is always for her the true friend of his people, ever inspired by the inner vision of a healthy, beautiful and peaceful world, an earthly paradise reflecting cosmic perfection.[23]

Savitri Devi was sure that Hitler had realized he was an avatar while still a youth. She found compelling proof of this in August Kubizek's description of young Adolf's dramatic reaction to a performance of Wagner's *Rienzi* that they had seen together during November 1906 in Linz. Both boys were caught up in the great epic of Rienzi's rise to become the tribune of the people of Rome and his subsequent downfall. When the performance ended, it was past midnight. Hitler, usually very talkative after an exciting opera, was silent and withdrawn. He led his friend through the cold, foggy streets up the Freinberg hill on the western side of the town. Kubizek recalled how Hitler strode on, looking pale and sinister, until they reached the summit. They were no longer engulfed by the fog, and the stars shone brilliantly overhead. Then Hitler began to speak, his words bursting forth with hoarse passion. Kubizek was utterly amazed. Hitherto he had always understood that Hitler wanted to become an artist, a painter or an architect. None of that mattered now. It was as if another Self spoke through him in a state of ecstasy or complete trance. "In sublime, irresistible images, he unfolded before me his own future and that of our people. . . . He now spoke of a mandate that he was one day to receive from our people, in order to lead them out of slavery, to the heights of freedom."[24] Postwar American neo-Nazis William Pierce and Matt Koehl would later pay tribute to Savitri Devi's revelation of Hitler's avataric illumination on the Freinberg.[25]

Armed with this curious mixture of Hindu-Aryan myth and Nazi conviction, Savitri Devi returned to Europe in October 1945. Consumed with bitter regret and self-reproach that she had not experienced the "great days" of the Third Reich, she was determined to make her belated contribution to German National Socialism. In London she took casual employment as a wardrobe manager with a traveling Indian dance company and hit upon the idea of distributing pro-Nazi leaflets while passing through Germany by train in June 1948. Returning through France and entering Germany at Saarhölzbach, she spent some three months between 7 September and 6 December 1948 distributing a further six thousand leaflets in the three Western occupation zones and the Saarland.[26] In preparation for her third propaganda sortie to enemy-occupied Germany, she had printed in London a small German-language handbill headed with a swastika. Here she exhorted the Germans to remain true to their Führer, who was alleged still to be alive, and to rise up against the Allied forces that now were stationed throughout the country. Her sense of mission, her Nazi piety and her self-proclaimed membership of a tiny gathered remnant of Hitler loyalists is evident from the text:

> German People
> What have the democracies brought you?
> In war time, phosphorous and fire.
> After the war, hunger, humiliation and oppression;
> the dismantling of the factories;
> the destruction of the forests;
> and now, — the Ruhr Statute!
> However, "Slavery is to last but a short time more."
> *Our Führer is alive*

And will soon come back, with power unheard of.
Resist our persecutors!
Hope and wait.

Heil Hitler!

S.D.

This eccentric appeal coupled with apocalyptic hopes surrounding the reappearance of Hitler was followed by a stanza of a well-known Nazi marching song.[27]

Given the utter defeat and demoralization of postwar Germany, its shattered industries, depleted workforce, the hungry cities and the growing dependence on the occupying forces, such an appeal was at best symbolic. It chiefly served Savitri Devi's burning need to demonstrate her solidarity with Nazism, her loyalty to Adolf Hitler, and her loathing of the West and its supposed superiority. She began distributing the handbill on the night of 13–14 February 1949 in Cologne and soon found a young ex-SS man to help her. By the time she was finally caught a week later, she had successfully distributed 11,500 leaflets and handbills in West German cities in five months of clandestine activity. At a hearing it was decided that Savitri Devi had a case to answer under Article 7 of Law No. 8 of the Occupation Status, which forbade the promotion of militarist and National Socialist ideas on German territory subject to the Allied Control Commission. The maximum penalty for the breach of this law was the death sentence. She was detained at the British military prison for women at Werl until her formal trial, which was fixed for 5 April 1949.[28]

Besides offering a non-Christian religious mythology for Nazism, Hinduism also supplied Savitri Devi with a style of worship for her Hitler cult. During her time in India she had always been impressed by that eclecticism which allowed orthodox Hindus to decorate their domestic shrines with photographs of Hitler and Stalin, figures admired in defiance of the British Raj, beside the familiar images of Vishnu and Shiva. This *bhakti* form of devotionalism became the hallmark of her own Hitler cult, complete with prayers, contemplation and rituals. Examples of this devotionalism abound in the memoirs of her Aryan-Nazi mission to occupied Germany from 1948 onward. At pious gatherings of die-hard Nazis in bare garrets amid the ruined cities, she gave fervent expression to her undying loyalty to Hitler, the savior of a chosen race. There were emotional readings from *Mein Kampf*, the giving and receiving of precious Nazi souvenirs, clandestine Hitler salutes and secret signs of recognition, and an exalted sense of community with fellow believers awaiting the vanished Führer's triumphant return.[29] She thereby expressed an intense spirituality focused on Hitler as a redeemer-figure and her over-whelming desire to form a part of his congregation.

After her arrest, this sense of community with the Nazi faithful only in-creased. She repeatedly professed her Hitlerism in terms of religious inspira-tion and conviction to her amazed interrogators and patient lawyer. Her hopes of martyrdom soared as her trial approached. "I would walk to the place of execution singing the Horst Wessel Song. . . . Stretching out my right arm, firm and white in the sunshine, I would die happy in a cry of love and joy, shouting . . . the holy words that sum up my life-long faith: 'Heil Hitler!' I could not imagine for myself a more beautiful end."[30] Back in her cell, she whispered fervent prayers to Shiva while clasping his Hitler's likeness in a locket to her breast. She derived further solace from reading the Nazi Party program and the *Bhagavad Gita*.[31] Once she had been sentenced to three years' imprisonment, she felt she had truly joined the persecuted faithful. Her chief pleasures in prison were close friendships with convicted Belsen camp wardresses and overseers and the surreptitious writing of her propaganda mission memoir.[32]

Bonds of great affection and respect linked Savitri Devi to the female war criminals in Werl. Condemned by the world at large following the defeat of Nazism, these Belsen convicts and other prisoners represented to Savitri Devi the fearless, unflinching loyalty of committed Nazi womanhood dedicated to the creation of a wonderful, beautiful Aryan world of the future in accordance with the vision of Adolf Hitler. Their disgrace, ill-treatment and imprison-ment only confirmed their status as martyrs to the Nazi cause in Savitri Devi's eyes. She was proud to be associated with them and to share their hardships at Werl. For her part, the fanatical Savitri Devi enjoyed a high regard among her fellow Nazi and SS prisoners for her high-flown rhetoric, her insistence on the idealistic philosophy of Aryan rebirth, and her pious Nazi spirituality. She gave a more profound meaning to their cause, often lightly embraced during the opportunist days of Nazi power, and sustained them in their present hard-ships. Regarded as a firebrand by the prison authorities, she was later re-stricted in her contacts with the other political prisoners.[33]

Upon her early release in August 1949, she was expelled from Germany and went to stay at her old hometown, Lyons. In April 1953 she returned to Germany, this time as a pilgrim on a personal tour of places in the "Aryan Holy Land" most hallowed by association with Hitler and the National So-cialist movement. Her pilgrimage began in Leonding and Linz, where Hitler had spent his childhood and youth, followed by a visit to his birthplace on 20 April 1953, the sixty-fourth anniversary of his birth. From here she traveled on to Berchtesgaden in Bavaria, where she wandered on the site of the

Berghof, Hitler's Alpine retreat on the Obersalzberg. In Munich she paid her respects at such shrines as the taverns where Hitler first held party meetings, the Feldherrnhalle for its memories of the 1923 putsch, and the site of the Brown House on Königsplatz. She sought the physical proximity of war criminals at Landsberg, the principal penitentiary for convicted Nazis in the former American zone. Her next station of remembrance was Nuremberg. At the Luitpoldarena and Zeppelinwiese she imagined the exultant party rallies of the 1930s; in a sombre mood she visited the Palace of Justice where the surviving members of the top Nazi leadership were tried before the International Military Tribunal in 1945–46.[34]

Her pilgrimage ended on a wider mythical and pagan note with a visit to the prehistoric sun temple and the rock cliffs of the Externsteine, traditionally identified as an ancient Germanic sacred site. Here she performed cultic rituals to speed the coming of the next Reich. In darkness, she experienced a spiritual death and rebirth in a stone tomb; at sunrise she shouted the names of Vedic gods and Hitler from the top of the rocks.[35] Her record of this pilgrimage was dramatic and emotionally charged. Through her visits to the shrines of Nazism and ancient Germany, Savitri Devi dwelled upon the meaning of these places and their significance for her own lifelong allegiance to the pagan Aryan ideal. Together with the earlier memoirs of her propaganda mission and imprisonment, *Defiance* (1950) and *Gold in the Furnace* (1951), *Pilgrimage* (1958) has become a renowned example of Nazi devotional literature and a favorite in the neo-Nazi underground.

The relative isolation of Savitri Devi in India during the Third Reich, coupled with the intensity of her underground zealotry, suggest that she and friends celebrated their secret Nazi gnosis in postwar Germany like members of a persecuted sect. But Savitri Devi, ever outspoken, was also burning for active witness and action. This urgency ultimately led to her achievement of notoriety and influence in the neo-Nazi movement. In the first place, she quickly established herself as a confidante and fellow-traveler among the leaders of the reviving nationalist scene in Germany. Once de-Nazification had been sacrificed to the Allies' fresh interest in wooing the Germans for the Cold War against the Soviet Union, new political parties began to spring up in Germany that owed much of their inspiration to National Socialism. After the Sozialistische Reichspartei (SRP) was banned in 1952, the Deutsche Reichspartei (DRP) became the most influential electoral force on the extreme right, with some 16,000 paid-up members, a few seats in the Land diets, and about half a million votes across the country in federal elections. Led by Adolf von Thadden, the DRP boasted such former celebrities of the Third Reich as Werner Naumann, a former Nazi secretary of state and Hitler's choice to succeed

Goebbels; the SS general, Wilhelm Meinberg; a number of Wehrmacht generals; and the Luftwaffe ace, Colonel Hans-Ulrich Rudel.[36]

From the early 1950s onward, Savitri Devi frequently visited Rudel at Hanover and came to know him well, completing her manuscript of *The Lightning and the Sun* there in March 1956. In 1945 Rudel had fled to Argentina, where he became a popular and prominent member of the country's large Nazi community, which enjoyed the protection of the Peron government. The wartime hero here turned his mind to devising plans for assisting Nazi fugitives and war criminals to escape from Europe, and he became the head of such a rescue organization called the Kameradenwerk. On his return to Germany in 1951, Rudel publicly declared his undying admiration for Adolf Hitler and his vision of a resurrected, strong Germany. This outspoken loyalty to the Third Reich, backed by the wartime legend of his Luftwaffe exploits, firmly established him as the idol of the reviving neo-Nazi movement. He became a committee member of the DRP while his nationalist views found a regular outlet in the *Deutsche Soldaten-Zeitung* (est. 1951), which was edited by former officials in Goebbels's propaganda ministry and by SS officers.[37]

When Savitri Devi first met Rudel, he was already perhaps the most popular and visible figure of the neo-Nazi scene in the young German republic. With his extensive émigré contacts, he remained a key player in the Nazi clandestine groups abroad; with his fellow-conspirators Otto Skorzeny and Eugen Dollmann, Rudel played an important role in recruiting large numbers of former Nazi fugitives from Argentina for key posts in the new republican regime of Egypt. Rudel was impressed by Savitri Devi's praise of Nazism as an international racist movement, a notion well suited to the clandestine and dispersed nature of postwar Nazi conspiracy. Thanks to Rudel's introductions, Savitri Devi was launched into the international die-hard network and subsequently able to meet leading Nazi émigrés in the Middle East and Spain. In the spring of 1957 she stayed for some time near Cairo with Johannes von Leers, Goebbels's former anti-Semitic propaganda expert, now ensconced as the head of Nasser's anti-Jewish broadcasting service. He in turn was able to introduce her to many old Nazis and SS officers who had found a sympathetic refuge in Egypt. Later, in 1961, she was the guest of Otto Skorzeny in Madrid. This famous commando leader masterminded Mussolini's escape in 1943 and since the end of the war had built up an extensive commercial and intelligence operation in Spain, South America and Egypt involving American and German interests.[38]

While teaching at Montbrison in France in the 1960s, Savitri Devi spent her summer holidays at Berchtesgaden and continued to cultivate her old

Nazi friends in Bavaria. However, she was soon to make a greater impact on the international neo-Nazi movement, which began to grow from the 1960s onward. Early in the spring of 1961 she made her first contact with the British neo-Nazis. While spending her Easter holidays with an old friend in London, she quickly learned of the widespread publicity that the British National Party was attracting as a result of its confrontational stunts and demonstrations over the increasing levels of colored immigration into Britain. The growth of these fringe movements committed to racism, virulent anti-Semitism and folkish nationalism fired her enthusiasm, and she lost no time in meeting Andrew Fountaine, the president of the British National Party (BNP). She soon became familiar with John Tyndall and Colin Jordan and corresponded with the latter following her return to France. It was through this early contact that she was able to follow the subsequent wranglings in the BNP between Fountaine and Bean, on the one hand, and the brazen neo-Nazi tendency of Jordan and Tyndall. The latter commanded her instinctive allegiance, and in due course she became their devoted supporter in the National Socialist Movement (NSM).[39]

In August 1962 Savitri Devi attended Jordan's much-publicized camp-conference in Gloucestershire and was a founder-signatory of the Cotswold Agreement that set up the World Union of National Socialists (WUNS). Her involvement with the WUNS was the starting point of her subsequent prestige in international neo-Nazi circles. She became close friends with Françoise Dior, who was married to Jordan in 1963 and became involved in NSM undercover activities in Britain. Back in France where Savitri Devi lived, Dior headed up the national section of the WUNS. Through the camp, Savitri Devi also met Lincoln Rockwell, who was evidently impressed by her Hindu-Aryan mythology as a basis for universal Nazism.[40] Once Rockwell succeeded Jordan as leader of the WUNS, he launched *National Socialist World* as the smart party magazine; here his editor, William Pierce, gave pride of place to a condensed edition of Savitri Devi's *The Lightning and the Sun*. Not only had Pierce decided to publish her alongside Rockwell and Jordan, the leaders of the WUNS, but devoted nearly eighty pages of the inaugural issue to her.[41]

For Savitri Devi, this publication represented her first major debut in international neo-Nazi circles. Hitherto, her books extolling National Socialism had been published privately in Calcutta and in limited editions. These had been given or distributed by means of personal contacts in England, France and Germany, especially through her old Nazi contacts like Hans-Ulrich Rudel and Otto Skorzeny, as well as the numerous sympathizers and Nazi widows she regularly visited in the 1950s. But through Rockwell and Pierce, her ideas about National Socialism as a religion of nature, the Hindu cycle of the ages and Hitler's world significance as an avatar were brought before a much wider readership in Western Europe, the United States, South America and Australia. In the third issue, Pierce announced that the magazine had received such an enthusiastic response to the publication of *The Lightning and the Sun* that he had decided to offer their readers some more of her writings: there followed excerpts from two chapters of *Gold in the Furnace* in 1967 and from *Defiance* in 1968.[42] Her reputation was henceforth assured among the American Nazis. Her devoted admirer Matt Koehl approvingly quoted her "religion of nature" and dilated on Hitler's revelation on the Freinberg.[43]

Following her retirement from teaching in France, Savitri Devi decided to eke out her small state pension back in India, where she still had the friendship of her husband and his family, even if they had long lived separate lives. After working on her new memoirs at Dior's home in Normandy for nine months, she returned to live with Mukherji in New Delhi in August 1971. Although far away from the activities of European and American neo-Nazism, she still busily corresponded with Colin Jordan, Matt Koehl and other Nazi enthusiasts in Europe and America.

In the late 1970s, Ernst Zündel, the German-Canadian publisher of Holocaust denial texts, promoted a series of taped interviews with her and set about producing new editions of her books, commencing with *The Lightning and the Sun*. The Italian neo-fascists were also fascinated by her violent Aryan mysticism. Franco Freda, the notorious Italian neo-fascist who was finally tried in 1978 for his part in the terrorist bombings of 1969, published a German translation of her postwar memoir, *Gold in the Furnace*, under his imprint Edizioni di Ar in 1982. Founded in 1964 to cultivate the idea of a prehistoric Indo-European heritage, Edizioni di Ar also publishes an annual review, *Risguardo* (1980–), which contains articles on the ancient Aryans, the New Europe and Third Position. Its fourth volume carried an article by Lotte Asmus and Vittorio De Cecco that was devoted to Savitri Devi as the "missionary of Aryan paganism," with a review of her life, works and influence.[44] A co-edition of her memoir was distributed in Germany by Thies Christophersen's Kritik-Verlag at Mohrkirch in Schleswig-Holstein. As a German eyewitness working in the vicinity of Auschwitz, Christophersen became notorious for his publication of *Die Auschwitz-Lüge* (1973), which denied its status as an extermination camp. This book became a much-quoted source among other Holocaust denial writers, including Arthur R. Butz and Robert Faurisson.[45]

Savitri Devi's work had first appeared in Italian translation with the publication of *L'India e il Nazismo* by Edizioni all'insegna del Veltro of Parma in 1979. The publisher, Claudio Mutti, is a prominent member of the Italian far right. An admirer of Islamic fundamentalism and Franco Freda's brand of armed right-wing terrorism to provoke revolution, Mutti styles himself a "Nazi Maoist." His own imprint, Veltro, offers a wide range of books on symbolism, tradition, golden age myths, paganism and Islam, together with works by Nazis and fascists, including Horia Sima, Corneliu Codreanu, Robert Brasillach, and Holocaust denial texts. Steeped in the anti-modernist sentiment of Julius Evola, Mutti is drawn to the works of Traditionalists René Guénon and Frithof Schuon as a negation of the secular world. As a Muslim convert and Third Positionist, Mutti combines anti-Semitism with virulent anti-Westernism, mirrored in his editions of Rûhollâh Khomeini, the Iranian *mujâhidîn* and its declaration of a Holy War against the infidels.

In his introduction to Savitri Devi's *L'India e il Nazismo*, a translation of the tenth chapter of her *Souvenirs et réflexions d'une aryenne* (1976), Mutti claims that while "the spiritual dimension of Nazism has been ignored in the West," it is intuitively understood by those traditional peoples of India, North Africa, Japan and Afghanistan who have a concept of Holy War. He suggests that Savitri Devi's "Hitlerian esotericism" throws new light on the Hindu regard for Hitler as an avatar of Vishnu, and sees a similar motive in his honorific title *hâjj* (pilgrim) among Muslims. Mutti mentions Hitler's own recognition of his providential status among non-European peoples ("Already Arabs and Moroccans are mingling my name with their prayers"; *Hitler's Table Talk*, 12–13 January 1942). Mutti wholeheartedly agrees with Savitri Devi's conception of Hitler as a Universal Restorer of a pristine order akin to the Kalki avatar or the *mâhdi*.[46] By this means, Claudio Mutti assimilates Savitri Devi into his own neo-fascist war against the profane West. It is perhaps noteworthy that Mutti first encountered Savitri Devi through reading the fervent prose of *Pilgrimage* as an idealistic teenager. Further Italian translations of her work have been published in *Arya*, an émigré neo-fascist journal published by Vittorio de Cecco in Montreal.[47]

Invited by Matt Koehl to lecture before New Order audiences in the United States, Savitri Devi died on 22 October 1982 while visiting an old friend en route in England. Colin Jordan sent Tony Williams and two other young British Nazis, all dramatically dressed in black, to the simple cremation ceremony at Colchester, Essex. By a prior arrangement, an inscribed urn containing Savitri Devi's ashes was sent to Matt Koehl, who placed them in the New Order hall of honor in Milwaukee, Wisconsin, allegedly next to those of Lincoln Rockwell. Thus did Savitri Devi, the nomadic pan-Aryan Nazi and Hitler worshipper, enter the neo-Nazi Valhalla of the former American Nazi Party.[48]

Savitri Devi's chief importance lies in her supplying the postwar neo-Nazi movement with a mystical pan-Aryan myth that embraces white people across the world. It is obviously ironic that Savitri Devi enfranchised the Indians in her vision of a pan-Aryan world under Nazi rule, when chief Nazi theorist Alfred Rosenberg thought the Indo-Aryans had long dissipated their Nordic blood among the indigenous dark-skinned peoples of the subcontinent.[49] It is equally evident that racist groups in Britain and America hardly distinguish between Asian and black ethnic minority groups as unwanted aliens. Nevertheless, Savitri Devi's fervent Hitler cult offers a global Aryan mystique for defenders of an embattled white world. As noted earlier, this was precisely George Lincoln Rockwell's ambition in founding the World Union of National Socialists, and it is notable that her writings first came to prominence among the American neo-Nazis. Such universal Nazism offers a powerful mythic rationale for resistance to colored immigration in the predominantly white nations of Europe, North America, Australia and New Zealand.

Through underground channels, her ideas continued to reach a new generation of cultic neo-Nazis in the 1980s and 1990s. An important publicist of her work has been the Chilean author-diplomat Miguel Serrano (b. 1917), whose "Esoteric Hitlerism" assimilated the Hitler avatar to a composite Manichaean cosmology of anti-Semitism (see chapter 9). Serrano has praised Savitri Devi extravagantly as a pioneer of Esoteric Hitlerism and as "the priestess of Odin."[50] He in turn has served as an inspiration to a loose network of Nazi pagans and satanists in Britain, France and New Zealand under such names as the Black Order and the Infernal Alliance (see chapter 11). One of the Combat 18 magazines catering to racist skinheads in Britain has featured a eulogy to Savitri Devi.[51] *The Lightning and the Sun* was republished in 1994 by a Nazi satanist press in New Zealand, which also devoted a special number of its magazine to her as the "Priestess of Hitlerism."[52] Lionized by mystical fascists and racist pagans as the "foremother" of international neo-Nazism, Savitri Devi has now attained the status of an Evita figure for opponents of multiracial society. Her books are increasingly hot tips among racist pagans, skinheads and Nazi metal music fans in the United States, Scandinavia and Western Europe.

6

The Nazi Mysteries

THE IMMEDIATE POSTWAR years were all too heavily burdened with the tragic consequences of the Third Reich for its image to be anything but negative among the Western Allied nations. The wholesale destruction of Europe through German militarism and the gruesome extermination of the Jews combined to make Hitler and National Socialism the objects of universal condemnation and horror. The German population's swift repudiation of its former ideology of power and conquest, coupled with the abject behavior of the major war criminals at the Nuremberg trials, completed the shame of Nazi Germany. However, the former idolization of Hitler by the Germans, the regime's dramatic but short-lived continental dominion, and the irrationality and macabre nature of its anti-Semitic racist policies also set National Socialism quite apart from other periods of modern history. Outside a purely secular frame of reference, Nazism was felt to be the embodiment of evil in a modern twentieth-century regime, a monstrous pagan relapse in the Christian community of Europe. The total defeat of the Third Reich and the disappearance, suicides and executions of its major figures lent a further uncanny aura to the image of Nazism.

By the early 1960s, this quasi-religious evaluation of Nazism had begun to exercise a horrid fascination upon the Western mind. Whereas straightforward revulsion and horror had formerly attached to the Third Reich, one could now clearly detect a mystique of Nazism, a sensational and fanciful presentation of its figures and symbols. The trappings of Nazism, shorn of all political and historical context, began to penetrate the milieu of popular culture through thrillers, nonfiction books and films. Stories of Nazi fugitives, including Martin Bormann, Josef Mengele, even a resurrected Heinrich Himmler or Adolf Hitler (survivors, after all) amid the Amazon jungles, in the desert capitals of the Middle East or down obscure back streets of London and New York, became the stock-in-trade of paperback fiction and speculative nonfiction works.[1] Like some monstrous and obscene survival of an earlier dreaded era, these paper Nazis lived a shadowy existence on the margins of the modern postwar world bristling with its own problems, conflicts and political forces. Often the fugitives turned plotters, seeking by means of a conspiratorial revival to subvert our apparently safe liberal world and to restore their sway in a Fourth Reich.

The notion of unholy relics is closely related to the phenomenon of fugitives real and fictional. Soon after the war, Nazi regalia, uniforms, decorations and documents became collectible and soon after commanded high prices. But the biggest prices of all were reserved for the artifacts of the Nazi leadership. For these collectors, an uncanny aura hangs over the Brown House dinner service, laid for many a high-level junket at party headquarters in Munich, but a talismanic quality inheres in the paintings or supposed personal diary of Hitler himself. Such journalistic scoops and fiascos concerning Hitler memorabilia ably demonstrate the fascination of these relics, culminating in the scurrilous *Stern* magazine Hitler Diaries affair of 1983.[2] These magical tokens of a vanished dispensation are joined by secret Nazi treasure. The leaders of the Third Reich were notorious lovers of art, and booty was seized on a vast scale from all the occupied states of Europe. Much of it has been successfully located and restored to its rightful owners, but stories of Nazi loot sunken in lakes or buried in mines or glaciers still abound.[3] The fugitives, the unholy relics and the hidden hoards of treasure posited notions of Nazism's secret survival and, by implication, excited a frisson in the liberal but romantically tempted spirit about its dreaded revival.

The mystique of secret survival and potential revival was made fully explicit in the modern mythology of "Nazi Mysteries." In this case, Nazism was mystified and romanticized into a neo-Gnostic religion with links to Theosophy, secret centers in Tibet, cultic rituals and all the paraphernalia of black magic. Taking their cue from the seminal French bestseller by Louis Pauwels and Jacques Bergier, *Le matin des magiciens* (1960), later widely translated into many foreign languages, numerous popular books published in Britain, France and the United States linked Hitler and the Nazis with secret societies, the occult and magic from the early 1960s onward, with a peak around the mid-1970s.[4] Again, the effect was to dehistoricize the facts of dictatorship, terror, war and oppression into a mythological tableau of demonic mission and planetary change. The occult mythology also charged Nazi artifacts and relics with magical powers of revival and restoration. Fictional themes such as the recovery of Hitler's ashes or the location of a secret Nazi colony in the Himalayas henceforth jostled with the older stories of Nazi survival. Although originally a literary phenomenon, the perverse theology of the "Nazi Mysteries" became a potent element in mystical neo-Nazism during the 1980s and 1990s.

These popular books have persistently represented the Nazi phenomenon as the product of arcane and demonic influences. The remarkable story of

Hitler's rise to power is directly linked to supernatural powers. According to this mythology, the appeal of Nazism cannot be explained adequately by secular or material considerations. No empirical analysis of social and economic factors could ever account for its nefarious irrationalism and early lightning successes. The modern mysteriosophy of Nazism chooses rather to explain the rise of the Third Reich in terms of an absolute but secret power that supported and controlled Hitler and his entourage. This hidden power is characterized either as a discarnate entity (e.g., "black forces," "invisible hierarchies," "unknown superiors") or as an occult elite in a distant age or remote location, with which the Nazis were in contact. Recurring themes in this popular tradition have been Hitler's mediumistic possession, a Nazi link with hidden masters in the East, and the Thule Society and other occult orders as channels of black initiation. All writers in this genre thus document a secret history of the Third Reich, unknown to conventional historians, as the instrument of dark powers for the achievement of satanic ends.

Hans Thomas Hakl has done pioneering work in identifying the early French sources for a Hitler guided by occult forces. Writing in 1934, René Kopp, a Christian mystical author, sought the secret of the success of Napoleon, Mussolini and Hitler in "destiny" as "the totality of invisible spiritual forces which influence mankind.... The masters of the world (especially Hitler) have been placed on earth by these powers with intent." Analyzing photographs of Hitler over time, Kopp decided that his face had changed and that he showed signs of somnambulism, indicating the possibility of "possession by a spirit of unknown origin." Another French writer, Edouard Saby, writing in the spring of 1939, also alluded to Hitler as a medium, a magician and initiate, finding proof of Hitler's magical activity in his vegetarianism, his self-discipline, his artistic development and his magical gaze and gestures. Saby adduced the history of the Vehm (a secret medieval court), and an alleged member of the "order" was quoted as saying: "We trained, encircled and led Hitler, we Brothers of the Holy Vehm; we, the Seven Commanders of the Rosy Cross of Bavaria; we, the High Initiates. . . ."[5] Here one finds the prewar seeds of the myth of Nazi occult forces.

As the largest Roman Catholic nation in western Europe and the cradle of the Enlightenment, France has always tended to view militant and nationalist developments in Germany both in terms of Christian teachings and the new religion of reason. Hostile movements in her neighbor across the Rhine are often disqualified as irrational, but if categories of religious thought predominate, German motives can be seen as evil and ungodly. The attribution of potentially demonic inspiration to Hitler indicates the latter viewpoint among French Christian and esoteric writers. Here it should be remembered that

Hermann Rauschning's book, *Hitler m'a dit* (1940), appeared in French just as the German Army was invading the country. As the air-raid sirens whined and the population of Paris was gripped by panic at the prospect of renewed occupation by the dreaded "Boche," these alleged conversations with Hitler were intended to show dramatically that the German enemy was more than a common foe but infernally inspired. Rauschning's book offered strong moral propaganda: France would prevail, it could be thought, because God was on her side against the devil.

In this mythology, Hitler's demonic possession is directly linked to his Nietzschean vision of a new species of mankind, the Aryan superman who will become a god among mere mortals. The breeding of this divine mutation is the task of National Socialism, which is thus no mere political movement but is concerned with transforming the very nature of life on earth. The original source for these ideas was Hermann Rauschning (1887–1982), a member of the conservative Prussian ruling class and the former president of the Danzig Senate who broke early with the Nazis. After emigrating from Germany in 1936, he wrote several books exposing the vulgar leadership and base methods of the Nazis for English, French and American publication. Allegedly based on a long series of personal conversations with the German dictator, *Hitler Speaks* (1939) was intended to reveal his nihilism, fanaticism and warmongering ambitions as well as an unstable and prurient personality. Although recent scholarship has almost certainly proved that Rauschning's conversations were mostly invented, his record has an uncanny note of veracity, recording the authentic voice of Hitler by inspired guesswork and imagination.[6]

Rauschning's importance to the later mythology of Hitler's demonic possession is evident from a few sample quotations: "Hitler was abandoning himself to forces which were carrying him away—forces of dark and destructive violence. He imagined that he still had freedom of choice, but he had long been in bondage to a magic which might well have been described, not only in metaphor but in literal fact, as that of evil spirits." This satanic compact is linked to the blasphemous Nazi ambition of breeding an Aryan superman. In a chapter entitled "The Human Solstice," Rauschning reports Hitler's musings on the magical evolution of a higher human species, the opening of the Cyclopean eye as an organ of supernatural perception and other occult powers: "Man is God in the making. . . . Those who see in National Socialism nothing more than a political movement know scarcely anything of it. It is more even than a religion: it is the will to create mankind anew." Hitler adds triumphantly: "The new man is among us! He is here! . . . I will tell you a secret. I have seen the vision of the new man—fearless and formidable. I shrank from him!" Another episode records Hitler waking in the night, screaming and shaking with terror at the apparition of an unnamed presence, presumably a demonic vision of the superman.[7]

Rauschning's conversations were to have the most potent influence in inspiring the 1960s mythology of a demonic Hitler, first in France. With a lost war, collaboration and Allied liberation in recent memory, the demonic interpretation of Hiler and Nazism could also serve as an excuse for defeat at an unconscious level and a bandage for wounded French pride. How could mere mortals have armed themselves against these monstrous powers of darkness? In support of their thesis of Hitler's awesome plans for a mutation of the human race, Pauwels and Bergier quoted extensively from Hermann Rauschning: Hitler's pronouncements about magical consciousness, the fearsome new man, the cyclical development of humanity, the end of its "solar period" and the dawn of a new race in nothing less than a planetary crisis.[8] These and similar passages from Rauschning frequently appear in the books of Trevor Ravenscroft, James Herbert Brennan and subsequent exponents of the new "Nazi Mysteries."[9] The purpose of such Rauschning quotations is typically twofold: on the one hand, to demonstrate Hitler's surrender to evil powers; on the other, to suggest a Nazi satanic compact to achieve a magical transformation of consciousness and even the physical nature of life on earth, the inauguration of a new aeon.

The literature of the "Nazi Mysteries" quickly mixed up such demonism with the myth of a Nazi link with the Orient which had a complex pedigree of Theosophical and French provenance. Originally rooted in Tibetan and Mongolian mythology, the notion of hidden sacred centers in the East was first popularized to Western audiences by Helena Petrovna Blavatsky, the founder of modern Theosophy. In *The Secret Doctrine* (1888), based on the "Stanzas of Dzyan," which she claimed to have read in a secret Himalayan lamasery, Blavatsky maintained that there existed many similar centers of esoteric learning and initiation; magnificent libraries and fabulous monasteries were supposed to lie in mountain caves and underground labyrinths in the unexplored regions of Central Asia. Notable examples of these centers were the subterranean city of Agadi, thought to lie in Babylonia, and the fair oasis of Shamballah in the Gobi Desert, where the divine instructors of the Aryan race were said to have preserved their sacred lore.[10] Other Theosophical writers later extended these speculations. Annie Besant and Charles Leadbeater described "Shambhalla" as a city founded c. 70,000 B.C. by the leader of the Aryan race on the shores of a now-vanished Gobi Sea, while Alice Bailey identified "Shamballa" as the seat of the "Lord of the World," again in the Gobi Desert, who watches over the evolution of men until all have been saved.[11]

The legend of Agartha, the other hidden sacred center in the East, was developed by French occultists writing from the late nineteenth century onward. Louis Jacolliot (1837–1890), a French official at Chandernagore in India under the Second Empire, wrote a trilogy on Indian mythology and its relationship to Christianity. In *Le fils de Dieu* (1873) he relates local Brahmans' stories of "Asgartha," a prehistoric solar capital, which was the seat of the chief priest of all Brahmans and the manifestation of God on earth. Later taken by the invading Aryans, the city was finally destroyed by the Norsemen around 5000 B.C.[12] This mythology was greatly elaborated by the French occultist, Joseph Saint-Yves d'Alveydre (1842–1909), who described the secret city of Agartha as an underground theocracy in the Himalayas that guided the course of world history. Originally on the surface of the earth, Agartha was transferred underground and concealed from the rest of humanity at the beginning of the Kali Yuga, dated to around 3200 B.C. Here a technologically and spiritually superior society of millions is ruled by a supreme pontiff. Once the surface world has reached a sufficiently advanced level of enlightenment, Agartha will reveal itself in all its glory and complete the epiphany of mankind in a global transformation.[13]

After the First World War, the Polish adventure and travel writer Ferdynand Ossendowski presented a further version of the myth of Agartha. In an account of his journey through Siberia and Mongolia after the Russian Revolution, Ossendowski related local Buddhist beliefs, which referred to the subterranean kingdom of "Agharti," where the King of the World reigned. This utopian realm was credited with supernatural powers that could be unleashed to destroy an evil mankind and transform the surface of the entire planet. Apocalyptic prophecies suggested that the King of the World would manifest when the time had come for him to lead all the good people of the world against the bad. However, in 1890 the King of the World was said to have appeared at Narabanchi monastery and foretold a forthcoming period of war, hunger, disease and dreadful crimes, at the end of which he would send a people, now unknown, to lead men in the fight against evil, who would found "a new life on the earth purified by the death of nations." Finally, in the year 2029 the peoples of Agharti would swarm forth from their subterranean caverns onto the surface of the earth.[14] The French esotericist René Guénon (1886–1951) was intrigued by Ossendowski's account and later published his own book on the spiritual center of the world as *Le roi du monde* (1927).

These ideas of a secret theocracy in the East were supplemented by the spiritual power of *vril* in the "Nazi Mysteries." In his novel *The Coming Race* (1871), Sir Edward Bulwer-Lytton had attributed this power to a subterranean race of men, the Vril-ya, psychically far in advance of the human species. The powers of *vril* (most likely derived from the Latin *virile*) included telepathy and telekinesis. This purely fictional notion was quoted by Madame Blavatsky in *Isis Unveiled* (1877) as but one name of the mysterious, all-pervading force known to man since the ancient theurgists.[15] The *vril* was understood to be an enormous reservoir of psychic energy not only in the world at large but also in the human organism, only accessible to initiates. It was believed by some occultists that whoever became master of the *vril* force could, like Bulwer-Lytton's underground race of Vril-ya, enjoy total mastery over all nature. Willy Ley, who emigrated to the United States in 1935 after a short career as a rocket engineer in Germany, wrote a short account of the pseudo-scientific ideas that had found some official acceptance during the Third Reich. Besides Hörbiger's World Ice Theory and a Hollow Earth Doctrine, both of which found leading Nazi patrons, Ley recalled a Berlin sect that had engaged in meditation exercises focusing on a bisected apple, in order to penetrate the secret of *vril*.[16]

Pauwels and Bergier cited this article in their *Le matin de magiciens* and exaggerated the significance of this obscure Berlin sect in order to claim that the Nazi leadership was determined to establish contact with an onmipotent subterranean theocracy and gain knowledge of its power. It was supposed that this power would enable Germany to conquer the whole world and transform human life in accordance with an apocalyptic vision:

> Alliances could be formed with the Master of the World or the king of Fear who reigns over a city hidden somewhere in the East. Those who conclude a pact will change the surface of the Earth and endow the human adventure with a new meaning for many thousands of years. . . . The world will change: the Lords will emerge from the center of the Earth. Unless we have made an alliance with them and become Lords ourselves, we shall find ourselves among the slaves, on the dungheap that will nourish the roots of the New Cities that will arise.[17]

Pauwels and Bergier claimed that Hitler and his entourage believed in such ideas. In their account, the Berlin sect was known as the Vril Society or the Luminous Lodge, and it was credited with the status of an important Nazi organization. A French psychiatrist was quoted to the effect that "Hitler's real aim was to perform an act of creation, a divine operation . . . a biological mutation which would result in an unprecedented exaltation of the human race and the 'apparition of a new race of heroes and demi-gods and god-men.'"[18] In this way, racism was linked with the *vril* force and the occult mythology of an Eastern theocracy to evoke a millenarian image of the Nazi future.

Commenting on the Nazis' religio-mythological thinking backed by science and technology, Pauwels and Bergier described Hitlerism as "Guénonism plus tanks."[19]

The "Nazi Mysteries" reserve a special place for the Thule Society and certain of its members as the occult center of the Nazi movement and a channel of black magical initiation for the mediumistic Hitler. Founded in Munich in July 1918 by Rudolf von Sebottendorff (1875–1945), the Thule Society was a *völkisch*-racist group named after Ultima Thule. This northern land was recorded by the Greek navigator Pytheas of Marseilles circa 400 B.C. and tentatively identified as Iceland. As the homeland of the Eddas, Iceland was regarded by Guido von List and other German nationalists at the turn of the century as the last refuge of ancient Teutons who rejected Christianity. The Thule Society certainly acted as an important focus for nationalist and racist circles at the end of the First World War and provided military support against the left-wing revolution in Bavaria during the spring of 1919. It may justifiably be regarded as a ginger-group and predecessor of the National Socialist German Workers' Party. Organizational and personal links passed directly from the Thule Society via a Political Workers' Circle to the German Workers' Party, the precursor of the Nazi Party. Such later leading Nazi personalities as Rudolf Hess and Hans Frank were members of the Thule, while Dietrich Eckart and Alfred Rosenberg were guests.[20]

Pauwels and Bergier singled out two particular individuals as Hitler's occult mentors in Munich during the early 1920s. Dietrich Eckart (1868–1923) was a bohemian playwright who achieved some renown for his translation of Ibsen's *Peer Gynt*. He was also a rabidly anti-Semitic journalist and prominent in the nationalist circles of Munich as the editor of his newspaper, *Auf gut deutsch*. He is also known to have frequented the Thule Society in 1919. Eckart and Hitler probably first met in November 1919 while working on the German Workers' Party program and became close companions throughout 1920 and 1921. The experienced and well-connected Eckart not only gave force and focus to Hitler's burgeoning anti-Semitism, but also introduced the young party leader to people in moneyed and influential social circles. Eckart's influence waned with Hitler's growing renown and self-confidence after 1922; he was not even involved in the plans for the Munich putsch and died shortly afterwards on 26 December 1923. However, Hitler remained devoted to his old friend, honoring him with various memorials within the party and a dedication in the second volume of *Mein Kampf*.[21]

According to Pauwels and Bergier, Hitler's other alleged occult mentor and a powerful Thule initiate was Karl Haushofer (1869–1946), the central figure in German geopolitics. After a military career leading to the rank of major-general in the Reichswehr in the First World War, Haushofer had devoted himself to the study of political geography, subsequently gaining the Chair of Geopolitics at Munich University, where Rudolf Hess was his student assistant. When Hitler and Hess were imprisoned at Landsberg after the putsch, Haushofer is known to have visited his former pupil and also met Hitler. Hitler is supposed to have been impressed by Haushofer's geopolitical theories claiming that the "heartland" of Eastern Europe and Russia ensured its rulers a wider dominance in the world.[22]

Haushofer had also spent the years 1908–10 in Asia and cultivated a life-long interest in the Far East, especially Japan. Assigned as military attaché to the German Embassy in Tokyo, he had also traveled in India, Burma, Korea and China. But these links with the East were sufficient grist for the "Nazi Mysteries" mill. Already in 1954, Pauwels had written a book on the Caucasian thaumaturge George Ivanovitch Gurdjieff (1866–1949), in which he claimed that Haushofer met Gurdjieff in Tibet in 1903, 1905, 1906 and 1908. Back in Germany in 1923, Haushofer had supposedly founded the Thule Society, modeled on similar groups in Tibet, with a philosophy based on the two cities of Agarthi [sic] and "Shampullah" [sic]. Pauwels described the latter as a city of violence, ruled by the King of Fear, with whom an alliance could be made to rule the world. He alleged that the Thule group formed such an alliance with "Shampullah" in 1928 through a colony of Tibetan monks in Berlin.[23] In rebuttal of this legend, it should simply be pointed out that Haushofer had never traveled outside Europe prior to 1908, and that his well-documented movements in the Far East precluded any visit to Tibet.[24] Pauwels's only source for this alleged contact between Haushofer and Gurdjieff is Jacques Bergier, who claimed to have received his information from German officers with whom he was imprisoned at Mauthausen camp.

According to Pauwels and Bergier, the influence of Eckart and Haushofer upon Hitler chiefly related to the communication of arcane knowledge derived from unknown powers. Shortly before his death, Eckart is reported to have said: "Follow Hitler. He will dance, but it is I who called the tune. We have given him the means of communicating with Them. Do not mourn for me: I shall have influenced history more than any other German." Eckart's role as an occult mediator was thus explicitly linked to invisible hierarchies.

Thule was thought to have been the magic centre of a vanished civilization. Eckardt [sic] and his friends believed that not all the secrets of Thule had perished. Beings intermediate between Man and other intelligent beings from Beyond, would place at the disposal of the Initiates [i.e., the members of the

Thule Society] a reservoir of forces which could be drawn on to enable Germany to dominate the world . . . [its] leaders would be men who knew everything, deriving their strength from the very fountain-head of energy and guided by the Great Ones of the Ancient World. Such were the myths on which the Aryan doctrine of Eckardt and Rosenberg was founded and which these prophets . . . had instilled into the mediumistic mind of Hitler. [The Thule Society] was soon to become . . . an instrument changing the very nature of reality . . . under the influence of Karl Haushofer the group took on its true character as a society of Initiates in communion with the Invisible, and became the magic centre of the Nazi movement.[25]

This wholly spurious account also claimed that Haushofer was a member of the Luminous Lodge, a secret Buddhist society in Japan, and the Thule Society.

According to the legend with which Haushofer no doubt became acquainted in 1905, and the version which René Guénon gave of it in his *Le Roi du Monde*, after the cataclysm of Gobi the lords and masters of this great centre of civilization, the All-Knowing, the sons of Intelligences from Beyond, took up their abode in a vast underground encampment under the Himalayas. There, in the heart of these caves, they divided into two groups, one following the "Right Hand Way," and the other the "Left Hand Way." The first of these had its centre at Agarthi, a place of meditation, a hidden city of Goodness, a temple of non-participation in the things of this world. The second went to Schamballah, a city of violence and power whose forces command the elements and the masses of humanity, and hasten the arrival of the human race at the "turning-point of time."

It was thus as an initiate of the Eastern theocracy, rather than as a geopolitician, that Haushofer is supposed to have proclaimed to Hitler the necessity of "a return to the sources" of the human race in Central Asia. He was therefore advocating the Nazi conquest of Turkestan, Pamir, Gobi and Tibet in order to secure Germany's access to the hidden centers of power in the East.[26] This sensational image of the Thule Society and its members is almost entirely a fictional invention. Hitler never attended a single meeting of the Thule Society. While the founder of the Thule Society, Rudolf von Sebottendorff, was certainly interested in the occult, a detailed diary of its regular meetings from 1918 to 1925 maintained by its secretary, Johannes Hering, mentions only two lectures on such topics. On 31 August 1918, Sebottendorff gave a talk on dowsing, of which Hering disapproved, commenting that occultism brought dubious members into the Thule from time to time; and on 23 February 1919 a certain Wilde lectured on occultism. All other lectures and excursions were devoted to such themes as megalithic culture, the original homeland of the Teutons, Germanic myths and poetry, the Thule legend, the Jews and Zionism, and current political issues. Eckart was only a guest, once giving a reading from his plays *Lorenzaccio* and *Ahasver* on 30 May 1919, and there is no evidence whatsoever to link Haushofer with the group. Far from growing in importance as an occult group behind the Nazi Party, the Thule Society was politically insignificant by 1920 and lapsed into complete inactivity after 1925.[27] Throughout its heyday of 1918–19 and afterwards, the Thule Society was defined by its nationalist and anti-Semitic ideology and a solid Munich middle-class membership.

Once Pauwels and Bergier had provided this basic stock of myths relating to the occult inspiration of Nazism, further authors were tempted into a sensational field that promised evident commercial success. In Germany, Dietrich Bronder repeated the story of the Haushofer-Gurdjieff link, including the former's initiation into Tibetan mysteries and the Berlin colony of monks; in fact, the 1939 SS expedition of Ernst Schäfer was said to have gone to Tibet with the express purpose of establishing a vital radio link between the Third Reich and the lamas. Bronder was the first to write in this vein about Sebottendorff, who, despite his occult interests, had not been mentioned by Pauwels and Bergier. He capped his account of the Nazi occult background with a spurious membership roll of the Thule Society that wrongly included Hitler, Mussolini, Goering and Himmler.[28] In France, many books devoted to the mysteriosophy of Nazism rolled off the presses. Accounts of Hitler's mediumship, Dietrich Eckart and a sinister link between Nazi Germany and a theosophically imagined Tibet, indicating the Vril Society, the ill-used Haushofer, Sebottendorff and the Thule Society, were busily repeated in Pierre Mariel's *L'Europe païenne du XXe siècle* (1964), René Alleau's *Hitler et les sociétés secrètes* (1969), Werner Gerson's *Le Nazisme, société secrète* (1969) and Jean-Claude Frère's *Nazisme et sociétés secrètes* (1974).

Only one part of Pauwels and Bergier's book addressed Nazi occultism in a work that was otherwise concerned with fabulous vistas of prehistory, ancient science and lost civilizations. This mixture has proved to be a successful market formula. The popular books of Robert Charroux also explore the mysteries of the ancient civilizations of Egypt, Hyperborea, Atlantis, Mu and the American Indians. Born in 1909, Robert Charroux served as Minister for Cultural Affairs in the French Vichy government; from 1960 onward he devoted himself to archaeology, prehistory and a reintepretation of ancient civilizations, suggesting a familiarity with Julius Evola's ideas. In *Le livre des* secrets trahis (1964) he speculates on whether the Hyperboreans were extra-terrestrials from Venus who became the tutors of early mankind. The emnity of the Hyperboreans and the Hebrews, the myth of the Black Sun, the Thule Society and Agartha all appear in his work.[29] Originally published in France and translated into many languages, Charroux could boast of more than two million readers by the 1970s. Sharing with Erich von Däniken an interna-tional reputation for the literature of gods and ancient astronauts, Charroux extended the "Nazi Mysteries" into a wider mythology of Aryans and their semi-divine ancestors.

Probably the single most influential "Nazi Mysteries" book in the English-speaking world was The Spear of Destiny (1972), written by Trevor Raven-scroft (1921–1989). A British commando in the North African campaign dur-ing World War II, Ravenscroft was captured and imprisoned at a POW camp in Germany from 1941 to 1945. He subsequently became a journalist on the Beaverbrook Press and worked for the International Publishing Corporation. Sometime after the war, Ravenscroft claimed he met Walter Johannes Stein (1891–1957), a Viennese Jew who had emigrated from from Germany to Britain in 1933, to whom he falsely attributed a most amazing story of Hitler's demonic inspiration.[30]

Before the establishment of the Third Reich, Stein had taught at the Wal-dorf School in Stuttgart, which was run according to the anthroposophical principles of Rudolf Steiner. During his time there, Stein wrote a curious and learned book, Weltgeschichte im Lichte des Heiligen Gral (1928), which gave a spiritual interpretation of history and its Christian fulfillment based on the legend of the Holy Grail. In particular, Stein argued that the Grail romance of Wolfram von Eschenbach's Parzival (c. 1200) had been based on the histori-cal background of the ninth century, and that the fabulous characters of the epic corresponded to real persons who had lived during the Carolingian Em-pire. For example, the Grail king Anfortas was named as King Charles the Bald, the grandson of Charlemagne; Cundrie, the sorceress and messenger of the Grail, was considered to have been Ricilda the Bad; Parzival himself was named as Luitward of Vercelli, the chancellor of the Frankish court; and Klingsor, the evil magician and owner of the Castle of Wonders, was identi-fied as Landulf II of Capua, a man of sinister reputation due to his pact with the heathen powers of Islam in Arab-occupied Sicily. The battle between the Christian knights and their evil adversaries was understood as an allegory of their enduring struggle for possession of the Holy Lance, the Spear of Longi-nus that pierced the side of Christ at his Crucifixion.[31]

On the basis of his possible contact with Stein and knowledge of his work, Ravenscroft developed his own occult account of Nazism, which revolved around Hitler's supposed obsession with Grail mysteries and the Spear of Longinus. In *The Spear of Destiny*, Ravenscroft described how the young student Stein had discovered a worn, secondhand copy of Eschenbach's *Parzival* in an occult bookshop in the old quarter of Vienna in August 1912. This volume contained numerous handwritten jottings in the form of a commentary on the text, which interpreted the Grail epic as trials of initiation upon a path to the attainment of transcendent consciousness. This interpretation was supported by many quotations in the same hand drawn from oriental religions, alchemy, astrology and mysticism. Stein also noted that a strong theme of anti-Semitic hatred and pan-German racial fanaticism ran through the entire commentary. The name written on the inside cover of the book indicated that its previous owner was one Adolf Hitler.[32]

His curiosity aroused concerning the jottings, Stein allegedly returned to the bookshop to ask the proprietor if he could tell him anything about this Hitler. Ernst Pretzsche informed Stein that the young Hitler was was an assiduous student of the occult and gave him his address. Stein sought Hitler out. In the course of their frequent meetings, in late 1912 and early 1913, Stein learned that Hitler believed that the Spear of Longinus could grant its owner unlimited power to perform either good or evil. The succession of previous owners allegedly included Constantine the Great, Charles Martel, Henry the Fowler, Otto the Great and the Hohenstauffen emperors. As the property of the Habsburg dynasty since the dissolution of the Holy Roman Empire in 1806, the Holy Lance now lay on view in the Treasure House of the Hofburg in Vienna. Hitler was determined to gain possession of the lance in order to guarantee the success of his own bid for world domination. Ravenscroft also included the sensational story that Hitler had accelerated his occult development through the use of hallucinogenic peyote, which he had been given by Pretzsche, who had worked until 1892 as an apothecary's assistant in the German colony in Mexico City.[33]

Much of this might seem plausible. Hitler's knowledge of the Grail romances and the Spear of Longinus could easily be attributed to his ardent enthusiasm for the operas of Richard Wagner (1813–83), whom he idolized as the greatest interpreter of the Germanic folk-spirit. The Grail and its knights play a central part in *Lohengrin* (1850), which Hitler first saw at age twelve in Linz and again more than ten times during his time in Vienna between 1907 and 1913. *Parsifal* (1882), Wagner's last work and the only one to involve the Spear, was based on Eschenbach's Grail story but fused the original Christian symbolism with the blood mystique of the Aryan racial myth. Here Parsifal was the chaste champion of Aryan manhood who alone could retrieve the sacred spear that had penetrated Christ's side and thus preserve the Grail, the talisman of the German race. Since Hitler studied all the Wagner librettos, he would have been well aware of the racial overtones of *Parsifal*. During the 1930s he declared that this opera was the basis of his racial religion and a Rauschning conversation refers to "the holy grail of pure blood."[34] Ravenscroft's allusions to Hitler's occult reading matter in Vienna was already endorsed by Alan Bullock's masterly biography, which referred to his appetite for books on "the Eastern religions, yoga, occultism, hypnotism, astrology."[35] The only trouble with all this is that Ravenscroft was lying about his source. Stein never knew Hitler personally in Vienna or anywhere else, while the figure of Ernst Pretzsche was plainly invented.[36]

Ravenscroft described an equally fanciful social network of people supposedly involved with occult lore in Munich, Hitler's next station in life. Dietrich Eckart was described as an occult initiate who had traveled in Sicily to find the castle of Landulf II at Caltabelotta, where this putative model for Klingsor had performed satanic rituals of Arabian astrological magic that were said to have appalled the Christians of southern Europe. Landulf was supposed to have invoked the spirits of darkness through the torture and sacrifice of human victims; Ravenscroft suggested that the Thule Society, under the direction of Eckart, performed similar rituals on Jews and communists who had unaccountably disappeared in Munich during the early postwar years. Ravenscroft even recruited for his "Nazi Mysteries" the person of Aleister Crowley (1875–1947), the notorious English magician, who established his antinomian Abbey of Thelema at Celafù in 1921. Crowley was alleged to have hunted for clues at Caltabellotta, while Eckart made a study of Crowley's Gnostic sex-magic and its symbolical connections with Landulf's satanic practices. This jumble of links between twentieth-century occult Nazism and ninth-century Sicily was crowned by the claim that Hitler believed himself to be the reincarnation of Klingsor-Landulf, a modern vessel for the spirit of the Anti-Christ.[37]

Ravenscroft concluded that Eckart and Haushofer initiated Hitler into black rituals designed to establish contact with evil powers:

> Dietrich Eckart contrived to develop and open the centres in the astral body of Adolf Hitler, giving him the possibility of vision into the macrocosm and means of communication with the powers of darkness . . . utilising his memories of a past incarnation as the Landulf of Capua in the ninth century. . . . By divulging *The Secret Doctrine*, Haushofer expanded Hitler's time-consciousness . . . [and] awakened [him] to the real motives of the Luciferic Principality which possessed him so that he could become the conscious vehicle of its evil intent in the twentieth century.[38]

The centers of the astral body, vision into the macrocosm, the Luciferic Principality and its imminent manifestation as the Anti-Christ are all concepts derived from Anthroposophy. Here it can be seen how Ravenscroft bowdlerized the materials of Rudolf Steiner and Walter Johannes Stein for a quasi-anthroposophical account of a demonic Hitler and the occult powers of Nazism. With the appearance of Eckart and Haushofer, one may detect the influence of Pauwels and Bergier, whose twin Eastern theocracies of Agarthi and Schamballah also appear in Ravenscroft's book, this time as demonic mystery centers representing the powers of Lucifer and Ahriman in anthroposophical doctrine.[39] Spiritualism also features in Ravenscroft's fantastic account of the Thule Society. Obscene seances with a naked female medium were said to have been held by Eckart, Rosenberg and Sebottendorff as a means of contacting the shades of the Thule hostages murdered by communist revolutionaries in April 1919. Both Prince von Thurn und Taxis and Countess Heila von Westarp proclaimed from beyond the grave that Hitler would be the next claimant of the Spear of Longinus and lead Germany into a disastrous bid for global conquest.[40]

The Spear of Destiny was translated into several languages and has now been in print for a quarter of a century, a recurrent stimulus for new authors and readers alike. The Spear of Longinus, the Grail romance of Parzival and their central importance to Hitler's conception of demonic world-rule have reappeared in a number of other books. Francis King's popular study of the influence of the occult on the rise and fall of Nazi Germany, *Satan and Swastika* (1976), mentions the story, while Dusty Sklar quotes Ravenscroft's account of Thule seances, Hitler's racist interpretation of Grail symbols, and Haushofer as an authority on *The Secret Doctrine*.[41] James Herbert, the bestselling British horror writer, was tempted into the lucrative "Nazi Mysteries" market. His gruesome thriller *The Spear* (1978) was based on the plot of a present-day Thule Society for a right-wing military coup in the strike-torn, troubled Britain of the late 1970s, when the National Front was making electoral gains. The spear was the talismanic centrepiece of satanic rites to resurrect the corpse of Heinrich Himmler at a replica Wewelsburg in North Devon. A ritual involving the lance at the real Wewelsburg in Westphalia also marked the climax of Russell McCloud's *Die schwarze Sonne von Tashi Lhunpo* (1991). Howard A. Buechner, a distinguished American physician, has written two books describing the transfer of the Holy Lance and Hitler's ashes to a secret Nazi shrine in Antarctica at the end of the war and their recovery in 1979.[42]

In this quest for sensational mystification, Heinrich Himmler and the SS eventually surpassed the Thule Society as a black order of satanic initiation. Pauwels and Bergier had already alluded to Hitler's plans, according to

Rauschning, for *Ordensburgen*, elite schools for the new leadership of the party, which they confused with Himmler's SS. At these medieval castle-schools, the pride of young Aryan manhood would be drilled in fanatical belief, loyalty and self-sacrifice, pronouncing vows and embarking on an "irreversible, superhuman destiny." The SS itself would form an international order at the apex of a hierarchical society consisting of overlords, party members, the anonymous masses and, below them, the modern slaves of the conquered foreign races. In their account, the concentration camps were a form of imitative magic, a model for the social order of the future. The crematorium ovens of Auschwitz were accorded mere ritual for a magical act of demonic creation.[43]

While Hitler was linked to the Holy Lance, the Holy Grail entered the "Nazi Mysteries" via the SS. As early as 1960, Pauwels and Bergier credited the German commando ace Otto Skorzeny with a plan to steal the Grail. However, it was the French adventurer and writer A. de Saint-Loup who elaborated this legend fully. In a book about the Cathars and their mountain fortress Montségur, Saint-Loup related the story of the young German scholar Otto Rahn (1904–1939), who had made a study of Grail traditions in Provence in the early 1930s. When Rahn joined the SS, Himmler encouraged his research, impressed by the idea that Catharism represented a Germanic dualist heresy of ancient Aryan origin. Saint-Loup spun the tale that Himmler believed the Grail still lay undiscovered in the Montségur area after Rahn's death in 1939. Accordingly, the SS had returned to find the Grail. Their mission successful, they had flown the priceless relic to the "Grail Castle," Hitler's Kehlsteinhaus, or Eagle's Nest, at Berchtesgaden. At the end of the war, the Grail was taken by German commandos and hidden in a glacier below the 3,000-meter Hochfeiler peak in the Zillertal, Austria.[44] This story combined all the essential ingredients of Nazi mystery, including religious heresy, the subversion of sacred symbols and hidden postwar treasure.

Saint-Loup was himself an SS man in the French Charlemagne Waffen-SS division, which had fought in the final stages of the Battle of Berlin. Born in 1908 as Marc Jean Pierre Augier, he spent the 1930s in a series of overseas adventures. He had crossed the Sahara on a motorcycle, explored in the Arctic, and visited the Soviet Union and Franco's Spain. After his military service in the SS, he emigrated to Argentina for several years, advising the government on mountain warfare and writing a book on life in Tierra del Fuego. His subsequent books on Montségur and the legend of an SS mission to find the Grail stimulated new French publications on the Nazi-Cathar connection. Under the joint pseudonym Jean-Michel Angebert, Michel Bertrand and Jean Angelini wrote a bestselling book on this aspect of Nazi mythology, *Hitler et la tradition cathare* (1971), which was quickly translated into English under the title *The Occult and the Third Reich* (1971), reprinted in 1974. The story of Otto Rahn, the SS quest for the Holy Grail and Skorzeny's successful mission to secure it was recyclyed with new variations in Howard Buechner's fanciful book *Emerald Cup—Ark of Gold* (1991).[45]

By focusing on Himmler, the mythologists were on firmer ground, for it is true that, unlike Hitler, Himmler was absorbed in esoteric traditions and by Atlantis and Aryan origins. Pauwels and Bergier were early to discover Heinrich Himmler's SS Ahnenerbe (Ancestral Heritage) organization. The Ahnenerbe was in fact an important and representative institution within the SS. In 1933 Himmler encouraged the foundation of a new research group of scholars in the humanities (prehistory, archaeology, linguistics, ethnography and symbology), natural science and medicine, all directed toward the vindication of the Aryan racial worldview of Nazi and SS ideology. After 1935 the Ahnenerbe grew rapidly, embracing more than 50 departments. It published two scientific periodicals and maintained several publishing houses in Germany, the occupied Low Countries and Norway. Foreign expeditions were planned to exotic locations in Asia, Africa and South America. Scholars from German universities edited studies on Indology, Sanskrit texts, the Cathars and the Holy Grail, the Rosicrucians and the mysteries of Tibet. Scientific research embraced biology, heredity and genetics on rare breeds of animal life in Central Asia and the Caucasus.[46]

The SS expedition to Tibet in 1938–39 was originally planned as a private project, but Himmler offered limited funding in order to place it under Ahnenerbe auspices. His occult ideas on the semi-divine origins of the Aryan race were a strong motive for his interest in Tibet. The expedition leader, Dr. Ernst Schäfer, was the son of a wealthy Hamburg industrialist. As a student in 1931–32, Schäfer had already joined an expedition to Tibet led by the young American Brooke Dolan for the Academy of Natural Sciences, Philadelphia.[47] After joining the SS in 1933, Schäfer went on the second Dolan expedition to eastern and central Tibet in 1934–36, when he was in charge of the scientific work. The success of this expedition brought Schäfer to Himmler's attention. At their first meeting in June 1936, Himmler explained his interest in the World Ice Theory, according to which primeval floods had submerged the ancient continent of Atlantis. He also mentioned his belief that the Nordic race did not evolve, but had descended from the heavens to settle on Atlantis. Himmler believed that Aryan emigrants from Atlantis had founded a great civilization in Central Asia. He was therefore most interested in Schäfer's studies and wished to facilitate his next expedition to Tibet.[48]

Ernst Schäfer's third Tibet expedition took place between April 1938 and August 1939 under SS auspices. Given Schäfer's academic expertise in zoology and botany, with some background in geography and ethnology, his report offers a panoramic survey of the fauna and flora of the remote country on the roof of the world. There is no mention of Himmler's esoteric interests in Aryan origins, although careful anthropological measurements of Tibetan nomads were taken. Color photographs document the magnificent Himalayan landscapes and solitary desert plateaus of the Tibetan interior, including pictures of fortresses, monasteries, temples and the splendid Potala in Lhasa. There is also rich documentation of the cultural and religious festivals of the Tibetan people. These include portraits of the aged abbot of the Taschilunpo monastery, the seat of the Panchen Lama, processions of Buddhist monks, masked impersonations of Tibetan deities and demons and lamas summoning the gods with the strange sounds of their long horns and drums.[49] Schäfer returned to Germany with many species of animals and 108 volumes of Tibetan sacred scripture, the *Kangschur*, a gift from the Dalai Lama.

However, the presence of a Nazi scientific expedition in the fabled land of Tibet could only lend credence to the imaginary occult links between Hitler, Nazism and the eastern theocracy of Agartha. Pauwels and Bergier noted Schäfer had made contact with a number of lamas in various monasteries, as well as bringing back "Aryan" species of horses and bees to Germany.[50] Bronder alluded to the German links with Tibetan Buddhism already made by Haushofer and Hess. A certain Karo Nichi, the ambassador of Tibetan Agartha in Berlin, was said to have led the Schäfer expedition in order to deliver radio equipment for communications between Berlin and Lhasa.[51] The perennial fascination of these tales of strange Nazi missions to remote destinations has remained a constant in popular culture. Himmler's esoteric projects even feature in the highly successful Indiana Jones films of Stephen Spielberg. In *Raiders of the Lost Ark* (1981), the American archaeologist is assigned to find the Ark before the Nazis can obtain it for their own evil use, while in *Indiana Jones and the Last Crusade* (1988), the race is on to secure the Holy Grail. Images of uniformed Nazis pursuing such objects of power as the lost Ark of the Covenant and the Grail have created a worldwide awareness of the SS's interest in ancient and exotic traditions.

Heinrich Himmler's conception of the SS as an elite military religious order spearheading an Aryan crusade to reconquer the East found many echoes in his romantic view of medieval German history. On 2 July 1936, Himmler convened a special religious service over the tomb of Henry the

Fowler at Quedlinburg cathedral. The date was the thousandth anniversary of the death of Henry the Fowler (875–936), the German king who founded the royal Saxon dynasty and pushed the Slavs eastward across the River Elbe. In a mood of mystical pilgrimage, Himmler spoke of Henry as a paragon of Germanic valor and piety, and swore to continue his mission in the East.[52] Occultist writers would later dwell at length on Himmler's interest in spiritualism and his belief that he was the reincarnation of King Henry.[53]

But it was Himmler's castle, the Wewelsburg, which established the reputation of the SS as an esoteric chivalrous order. During the electoral campaign of early 1933, Himmler had traveled through Westphalia, "the land of Hermann and Widukind," and was deeply impressed by the mythical atmosphere of the Teutoburger Forest. Ever inspired by romantic medieval models, he began to think of acquiring a castle in this region for SS purposes. The Wewelsburg near Paderborn was duly taken over by the SS in August 1934. It began its career as a museum and SS officers' college for ideological education within the Race and Settlement Main Office, but was then placed under the direct control of the Reichsführer-SS Personal Staff in February 1935. This transfer reflected Himmler's new idea for making the Wewelsburg into an SS-order castle, comparable to the Marienburg Castle of the medieval Teutonic Knights in Prussia. During the late 1930s Himmler and the castle commandant, Manfred von Knobbelsdorff, held pagan wedding ceremonies at the Wewelsburg for SS officers and their brides and organized spring, harvest and solstice festivals for the garrison and the village.[54]

Himmler's plans became increasingly ambitious. The massive north tower of the castle was enlarged with labor from a nearby purpose-built concentration camp. Here, in the large circular upper hall surmounted by a domed cupola, were to hang the coats-of-arms of dead SS-*Gruppenführer*, while its marble floor was decorated with a large sun wheel composed of twelve zigzag sig-runes. In the vault below twelve pedestals flanked the interior wall at regular intervals around a paved circular recess on the stone floor. In the wings of the castle, study rooms were named and furnished after figures representing Nordic mythology such as Widukind, Henry the Fowler, Henry the Lion, King Arthur and the Holy Grail. Plans dating between 1940 and 1942 provided for the relocation of the village some distance away and the building of an enormous architectural complex consisting of halls, galleries, towers, turrets and curtain walls on a radial layout around the hillside, with the great northern tower of the medieval castle as its focus. At this early stage of the war, Himmler evidently conceived of the Wewelsburg as a future SS vatican built on a gigantic scale to represent the center point of a new Aryan world order.[55]

The mythological and cultic aspects of the castle, not so much its construction by slave labor, were the highlight of its occult interpretation. Ravenscroft lingered over the interior design and symbolic decoration of the castle with its rooms named after Germanic heroes, including Otto the Great, Henry the Lion, Friedrich Hohenstauffen and Philip of Swabia. Others imagined the meditations of the twelve top *Gruppenführer* as latter-day Jesuit superiors in high-backed pig-skin chairs that bore the occupant's name on silver plates, placed around the huge oak table, reminiscent of King Arthur's Round Table, in the great hall. Down in the large stone crypt, the "realm of the dead," symbolic ceremonies were easily imagined. Whenever a top SS leader died, his heraldic device would be ritually cremated in the central recess and the ashes placed in an urn on one of the twelve pedestals surrounding the circular walls.[56] By the late 1970s, the Wewelsburg also featured in thriller literature as Himmler's Camelot, the mysterious ceremonial center of the SS.[57]

Himmler's organization spread terror throughout Nazi-occupied Europe, but in *Occult Reich* J. H. Brennan gave it another meaning: "With its runic doctrines, its inner circles, its ritual festivals and its Black Jesuit Grand Master, the SS was a magical order in every sense of the word."[58] By emphasizing Himmler's occult whimsies and these mystifications, the authors of the "Nazi Mysteries" give weight to the pseudoreligious image of the SS. By contrast, the police and security services, the cruelty of their slave labor programs, and the terrible extermination camps are diminished. Romantic details such as the alleged search for the Holy Grail, the meditations of the inner leadership, comparisons of the Black Order to the Jesuits of St. Ignatius Loyola, Arthurian and Germanic symbolism and the strange ceremonies for the dead at the Wewelsburg all tend to obscure the brutal, violent nature of the SS behind an aura of magic and mystery.

Alan Baker has recently sought to document and analyze this genre of Nazi occultism. The subject is complicated by the fact that early (pre-Nazi) *völkisch* and Pan-German racist groups before and after the First World War were definitely influenced by esoteric ideas. The construction of the Aryan myth indicating the polar origins of the Nordic race certainly had deep roots in European Romanticism and late nineteenth-century Theosophy, and flourished in such movements as Ariosophy. Despite this ideological affinity, Baker accepts that evidence that Hitler and other leading Nazis practiced black magic is very weak. Once again, one travels through the tangled mythology of the post-1960 genre attributing occult powers to the Nazis, including Trevor Ravenscroft's *The Spear of Destiny*, the fringe cosmologies of Hanns Hörbiger's World Ice Theory and the Hollow Earth Theory and ongoing sagas of secret Nazi activities involving Antarctica and UFOs. It is, as Baker argues, a valid field of inquiry, irrespective of the dubious nature of this latter-day literature. Just as the Nazis mythologized the history of their putative Aryan ancestors in order to legitimize their claims to racial superiority, so the Nazis themselves have been mythologized as a uniquely evil force by modern writers in the fields of occultism and conspiracy theory.[59]

The lightning successes of the Nazis, both electorally and later militarily, together with their manifest evil, stimulated notions of their demonic inspiration as early as the mid-1930s among esoteric writers in France. The destructiveness of Nazism and the macabre irrationality of the Holocaust begged a religious interpretation involving a dualistic war in heaven, satanic inspiration and the use of dark forces. Initially canvassed from the 1960s onward in popular literature, this fanciful demonization of Nazism has created and perpetuated an occult image of Hitler, National Socialism and the Third Reich. But while the authors of the "Nazi Mysteries" write in a speculative spirit, their readers are often less skeptical. Once thriller writers borrowed its materials, the "Occult Reich" became even more commonplace in popular discourse. In this process, Nazism was credited with the status of a perverse theology, complete with doctrine, prophecies, rituals and ceremonies. In the course of the 1970s and 1980s, mystical neo-Nazis commandeered this sensational mysteriosophy of the Thule Society and Wewelsburg to create new Nazi cults involving Gnosticism and satanism. The original stigmatization of Nazism as pure evil was thus inverted to celebrate the very taboos of the liberal democratic world as the forbidden gods of a dark realm.

7

Wilhelm Landig and the Esoteric SS

VIENNA WAS A gray city in the aftermath of the Second World War. Its Habsburg glories, the charm and gaiety of its music and theaters were a thing of the past. For some eight years since the *Anschluß*, Austria had formed a mere province of the Third Reich. In the closing months of the war, Vienna was badly bombed and the Red Army had fought its way into the city. From 1945 to 1955 the capital was divided up into sectors among the Allies. Russian, British, American and French military personnel were responsible within their respective sectors for administration, police work and security. The Four Powers each presided in turn for a month at a time over the Inner City within the Ringstrasse and its battered statuary and public buildings. Food, fuel and medicine were in short supply. Black market trading, prostitution and espionage were a means of survival for the local population. The gloomy, wintry atmosphere of Graham Greene's famous novel, *The Third Man* (1950), hung like a heavy pall over the defeated and occupied city.

Most Austrians now viewed Hitler and German rule as a nemesis and the bringers of catastrophe. However, a significant minority of Nazi loyalists found defeat intolerable after the power and exuberance of Germany's continental dominion. In the early 1950s, an Aryan-Nordic mythology took root in Vienna that was in marked contrast to the flagrant Hitler worship of postwar Anglo-American Nazi cults. Since Hitler and politics were now such painful memories, this mythology was characterized by speculations about ancient Nordic races, Thule and Atlantis, and Germanic religion. Also important was the rediscovery of ideas and individuals in the Ahnenerbe, Heinrich Himmler's SS office that researched Aryan archaeology and anthropology from 1935 to 1945. Apocalyptic hopes for national resurrection and salvation focused on wild speculations about the supposed existence of German miracle weapons, including flying saucers and secret polar bases at the end of the war. These ideas were very much a product of the grim desolation prevailing in postwar Vienna. They provided the seeds of the neo-Nazi mythology of the Black Sun which has been circulating in the far-right German underground since the 1990s.

The origins of this mystique lie in a small occult-racist circle that first gathered for discussions at the studio of the designer Wilhelm Landig (1909–1997) in the Vienna IV district in 1950. Born in Vienna in December 1909, Wilhelm Landig was a staunch pan-German nationalist. As a schoolboy he had joined the youth section of the Freikorps Roßbach and later fought in the Freikorps "Deutsche Wehr" in Vienna, two of the many private armies formed after the First World War to defend Germany's borders and suppress left-wing revolts. He served in the Third Reich first in 1937–38 at the Labour Science Institute in Berlin, then until 1941 in a government department in Vienna. From 1942 to 1944 he fought with the Waffen-SS in the Balkans, receiving German and Croatian decorations in fierce anti-guerrilla campaigns against partisans. In 1944 he was directed from Belgrade back to Vienna for "special tasks" involving new military technology. In autumn 1945 he was subject to automatic arrest as a former SS man and interned in a British POW camp until 1947. Upon his release he entered the world of inter-Allied espionage, hawking low- and medium-grade Soviet intelligence to Western security services. Another member of the circle, Rudolf J. Mund (1920–1985), had been an illegal Nazi stormtrooper in Vienna while in his teens and later served on the Russian front and in the Ardennes as a lieutenant in the Waffen-SS. He too had been imprisoned and subject to postwar disqualifications.

These fighting men were drawn to occultism and racist myths as a way of transcending their defeat and the humiliation of the German Reich. The focus of their discussions was a secret center in the Arctic known as the Blue Island, which could serve as a source point for a renaissance of traditional life. This idea was taken from Julius Evola, whose *Erhebung wider die moderne Welt* [Revolt against the Modern World] (1935) became the Bible of the Landig group. Landig's *völkisch* ideology of Ario-Germanic superiority was embedded within the high-flown metaphysics of Evola's primordial Tradition. Only the Northern Atlantic races, especially the Aryan Germans, understood the sacred nature of regal authority, the mystery of ritual, initiation and consecration, the divine origins of patrician rule, chivalry and a rigid caste hierarchy. Evola's polar mythology of Thule and trenchant anti-modernity had already been current among German conservative and right-wing periodicals during the Third Reich. As a Waffen-SS officer, Landig may also have met Evola during the last year of the war. After June 1944, Evola had worked in Vienna, helping to recruit a pan-European army of Waffen-SS volunteers from all over Europe to defend the continent against the invasion of the United States and the Soviet Union.

The Vienna group also hungrily devoured the ideas and books of Herman Wirth (1885–1981), the Dutch-German lay scholar of ancient religions and symbols. Born on 6 May 1885, the son of a schoolmaster in Utrecht, Wirth embraced pan-German ideas early and served as a German volunteer in the First World War. After moving to Germany in 1923, Wirth began to write and published his major works on Germanic prehistory, *Der Aufgang der Menschheit* (1928) and *Die Heilige Urschrift der Menschheit* (1931–36). By comparing the scripts of the Mediterranean countries and the Orient, the symbols of North and West Africa, the languages of the North American Indians and the Eskimos, Wirth posited the existence of a former great civilization of the proto-Germanic Thuatas in the North Atlantic basin. He discovered the oldest remains of this Nordic-Atlantean culture in the carved symbols of the Old Stone Age in southwestern Europe. Wirth's methods and conclusions were rejected by most university academics, and he attracted further controversy by editing *Die Ura Linda Chronik* (1932), a Friesian manuscript generally regarded as a nineteenth-century forgery, as a chronicle of Germanic life in the sixth to first centuries B.C. But these Nordic speculations brought Wirth the favor of Heinrich Himmler, and in 1935 he was invited to found and direct the SS Ahnenerbe institute for anthropological and archaeolgical research.[1]

Owing to Wirth's predilection for ancient matriarchy—evidence of his intellectual debt to the Swiss scholar Johann Jakob Bachofen—and archaic collectivism, which seemed sympathetic to socialist ideals, he subsequently fell from Nazi grace and left the institute in 1937. However, Wirth's following and influence among German *völkisch* groups was considerable from the outset. His vision of an ancient high Thuata civilization from which the Nordic sea peoples had set forth in their swan and dragon ships to colonize the Atlantic world reflected a utopian imperialism for those who bewailed the impotence and demoralization of the Weimar Republic. Pessimists and opponents of the present were drawn to his idea that a revival of this Thuata-Atlantean culture would signal the rebirth of the Germanic race and the liberation of mankind from the curse of modernity. Besides his major works and a host of controversial brochures, Wirth lectured widely in Germany, wrote numerous articles for the learned and popular press and presided over his own "Herman Wirth Society" in Berlin.[2] He survived the Second World War and cautiously resumed work on Germanic prehistory. Wilhelm Landig was an early admirer of his books and, once he had founded his own Volkstum-Verlag in Vienna in 1958, began to publish new works by the antediluvian prophet, who lived at Marburg on the Lahn until his death at age ninety-five on 16 February 1981.

But the interests of the Landig circle were not simply confined to cultural pessimism and nostalgia for a lost golden age. These men believed that spiritual contact could be made with the Blue Island, the hidden polar center. Another member of the circle, the Swiss engineer Erich Halik, supervised the pouring of large plaster casts for mediumistic purposes, and meditation exercises were undertaken in an effort to tune in. Halik claimed that esoteric circles of the SS had sought the favor of this spiritual world center. These SS "heretics" were particularly interested in the Cathar tradition and directed their quest toward the Arctic and Tibet. Halik cited the work of Otto Rahn, the Grail scholar commissioned by Himmler to study the polar traditions of the Cathars in southern France. Halik saw world history in profoundly esoteric terms. German bases on Greenland represented the attempt of SS "heretics" to reach the "Midnight Mountain" of polar tradition, while the UN flag with its blue polar symbol indicated the inspiration of rival Rosicrucian groups in California (on the Allied side). Halik speculated that the "militant esotericism" of the SS was also inspired by Ossendowski's tales of Agharti and the mystical fascism of Julius Evola. Halik was also the first to link the esoteric SS with the "Black Sun" roundel insignia carried by German aircraft in the polar region at the close of the war.[3]

Halik was especially excited about the contemporary postwar UFO sightings. In a series of articles published in the Austrian esoteric magazine *Mensch und Schicksal* between 1951 and 1955, Halik related the flying saucers to the Black Sun myth. He identified the saucers as manifestations of the Grail, "a cultic vessel used by the supreme hierarchy of Christian Gnostics." He analyzed the etheric constitution of flying saucers on the basis of their glowing concentric rings.[4] At the same time, Halik seemed to believe that the Germans had indeed established "polar empires" in both the Arctic and Antarctic, under the signs of the "Golden Sun" and the "Black Sun." While the former represented a Luciferic, solar quest (linked with Otto Rahn and the SS Cathars), the latter was driven by Saturnine, satanic lodges of the SS.[5] Halik understood the UFOs not so much as a technical invention as the application of a metaphysical and alchemical principle. The alchemical metaphor of *sol niger* (Black Sun) was said to represent occultation, blackening, a sinking into the mystery of self-discovery. This was the supposedly idealistic message of SS "heretics" operating from the Blue Island, harbingers of a millenarian world transformation.[6]

The literary and intellectual interests of Rudolf Mund cast further light on the occult-nationalist heritage of the Landig group. While held in an American POW camp at St. Avold in 1945, Mund was thrilled to discover a fellow inmate in Edmund Kiß, an author whose books he had avidly read before the war. A surveyor in the town of Kassel, Kiß had penned a series of novels that combined epic tales of life in prehistoric Atlantis, the Thuata culture of Herman Wirth and the World Ice Theory of the maverick Austrian cosmologist Hanns Hörbiger (1860–1931). First published in 1913, the World Ice Theory held that all stellar and planetary phenomena were the result of violent encounters between fire and ice. Besides the origin and movements of the heavenly bodies, the theory also offered an account of earth history and prehistoric mankind. Hörbiger maintained that the earth had captured several planets as moons before our present Moon and that these had successively crashed onto the earth, accompanied by geological upheaval and flood. He posited the existence of men in the Tertiary era, the rise of the oceans due to the approach of the former moon, and the subsequent establishment of asylum cultures in Mexico and the South American Andes.[7] While the World Ice Theory attracted mythologists of lost continents, its elemental cosmology seemed to mirror the Nazi ideology of struggle and was officially sponsored by the Brownshirts (Sturmabeteilung, or SA).[8]

An early supporter of the World Ice Theory, Kiß had already traveled in 1928 to Peru and Bolivia, where he sought evidence of such a late-Tertiary asylum culture in the Andes. With the émigré German professor Arthur Poznansky, long employed by the Bolivian government, Kiß studied the ancient ruins of Tiahuanaco on Lake Titicaca. He was convinced that the carved relief on the sun gate of the city was an astronomical calendar confirming prehistoric human experience of the most recent lunar catastrophe and subsequent flood. In the cordillera he found a gigantic sculpture of a Nordic head hewn out of the rock, for him striking evidence of earlier Atlantean migration and colonization when the oceans had encircled this high Andean plateau. Once he had returned to Germany, Kiß wrote a number of scientific works devoted to his speculations on Hörbiger's theories.[9] Even more influential, however, was Kiß's tetralogy of best-selling novels that popularized the Nordic Atlantis hypothesis and the heroic-catastrophic events of upheaval, inundation and Nordic migrations to a wide public. In these works, Atlantis and its submergence became a political symbol for the social chaos of the Weimar Republic or even Oswald Spengler's doom-filled prediction of Western decline. Only the Germans—the last people of the heroic Nordic race—could restore order in this disjointed world by means of their powerful will to survive and prevail.

His first novel, Das gläserne Meer (1930), described the catastrophic earthquakes and floods following the downfall of the first Tertiary moon. Driven out by glacial conditions and hunger, the Nordics migrate over an ice bridge to the hospitable climes of the southerly continent. This blue-eyed, blond master caste of Atlantis keeps its dark-skinned slaves in strict subjection and secures the survival of the white race by plundering women from adjacent lands. The novel Frühling in Atlantis (1933) is set against the golden age of Atlantean civilization. The pure-blooded, Nordic "Asen" number only two million out of the sixty million inhabitants of the state, the rest being "darks" and partial citizens. The rulers' chief task lies in breeding the Nordic type to guarantee their authority, but the inferiors are restive and eventually murder the young leader, Baldur Wieborg of Thule, a hero of climatic disasters and eugenic policy. This ominous political note was clearly intended to reflect Kiß's own anxieties about the threat of the Slavs or other racial inferiors to German superiority.[10]

Kiß's next novel, *Die letzte Königin von Atlantis* (1931), is set against the background of the sinking of Atlantis due to the climatic disasters resulting from the capture of our present Moon some 14,000 years ago. Remnants of the Nordic master race, former creators of an empire and high civilization, migrate to conquer the highlands of South America, including the Peruvian plateau of Atzlan. Here in this asylum they practice strict eugenics to maintain the purity of their blood, while condemning the inferior races to menial labor. In this book, Kiß brings the Nordic head he discovered to life as Godda Apacheta, the astronomer of Atzlan, who is the narrator. In the final novel of the series, *Die Singschwäne aus Thule* (1939), all the surviving Asen, under their blue banner with a silver swastika, attempt to return to the ancestral Arctic home. But instead of a perpetual spring as in former moonless times, a terrible cold prevails and hardens them anew. After many years they swarm forth again southward to Hellas, where they found the famous high Greek culture of the first millennium B.C. And so the cycle begins again. Throughout all history, the Nordic Germans will always send forth their supernumerary populations to colonize, found new states and breed up the declining inferior races.[11]

Renowned as the "poet of Atlantis," Edmund Kiß was also drawn by Heinrich Himmler into the SS Ahnenerbe. Already in July 1936, Kiß and others signed the Pyrmont Protocol agreeing to the official SS patronage of the World Ice Theory. The project was established as a meteorological section of the Ahnenerbe, in which Philipp Fauth, Hörbiger's prewar co-author, played an important part. When, in August 1936, Kiß began to plan a new expedition to the highland of Abyssinia to find traces of the human civilization of the Tertiary period and remains of the earlier moon, Himmler was swift to promise Ahnenerbe support. The Ahnenerbe was also involved in Kiß's plans for a further research trip to Peru, scheduled for 1940 but ultimately abandoned due to the war.[12] One might add that the World Ice Theory achieved near official endorsement in the Third Reich: Hitler's own enthusiasm for it is mentioned several times in his *Table Talk* and illustrated by his promise to build an observatory at Linz, representing "the three great cosmological conceptions of history—those of Ptolemy, Copernicus and Hörbiger."[13] Kiß then joined the Waffen-SS, achieving the rank of SS *Obersturmbannführer*, and later served as commandant of the guard at Hitler's headquarters. At the end of the war he hoped to lead a group of commandos to Tibet, where it was intended to gather the support of Mongolian tribes for a struggle that would commit Soviet forces to a Central Asian theater and thus relieve the embattled Reich.

During the cold, dark nights of late 1945, Rudolf Mund listened with rapt attention to the old explorer's tales. The ruined cities on the Marajo island in the Amazon delta, Tiahuanaco and Lake Titicaca, the mausoleum of Puma Punku and the astronomical observatory of Kalaseseya rose before his mind's eye. Kiß's epic storytelling gifts briefly banished the misery of defeat in the wretched camp. Nordic heads in the Andean cordillera, wide-ranging SS expeditions to confirm prehistoric high-Nordic civilizations in Africa and South America, and the huge timescale of Hörbiger's World Ice Theory conjured a world of immemorial Aryan superiority against which the defeat of the Third Reich seemed a minor setback. The catastrophic nature of these distant events suggested a world of violent struggle and renewal deeply attuned to the Nazi view of nature. That an ancient Nordic people had survived such upheavals, floods and ice ages only served to confirm the perennial heroism of the Germans in the face of enormous challenges.[14]

In April 1946 Mund met Kiß again in another camp at Augsburg. Learning of the young Waffen-SS lieutenant's plan to escape, the elderly Kiß gave him a hundred marks. Once more, fate brought them together at Dachau. Although weak and ill, Kiß expressed his intention to travel to Tibet upon his release. Mund was deeply impressed by these encounters, which somehow held the promise of far horizons beyond the present calamity of German defeat. Mund remained ever attracted to the esoteric Aryan mystique which he believed had lain behind the SS. As a young Waffen-SS soldier he had no direct contact with mystical SS circles during the Third Reich. However, the comradeship, heroism and sacrifice of his frontline experience in the Waffen-SS were the formative experiences of his life. He had believed the myths of this "first volunteer European army" in which the bravest young men of Germany and other Western nations had fought a crusade against Soviet communism. Defeat, capture, the shocking discovery of Nazi atrocities and the disgrace of his SS uniform drove him in search of a noble SS that had championed the utopian Aryan world against all that was dark, chaotic and inferior. Throughout the postwar years, Mund pursued his occult-*völkisch* investigations in an attempt to make sense of his former ideals.

These romantic researches led Mund to the works of the young SS-*Unterscharführer* Otto Rahn, who was deeply interested in the medieval Cathars and Grail legends. Originally intending to write a dissertation on Kyot, the

Provençal troubadour whose lost Grail poem served Wolfram von Eschenbach as a source for *Parzival,* Rahn had gone to the Languedoc in 1931. He soon identified the Grail knights with the Cathars and Montségur castle as Montsalvat. He settled at Ussat-les-Bains, where he was encouraged by the local neo-Cathar expert, Antonin Gadal, to explore the caves of Sabarthès, where the Cathar treasure was supposedly hidden. In his book *Kreuzzug gegen den Gral* (1933), Rahn ultimately fused the troubadour and Minnesang traditions, the Cathar heresy and the legends of the Grail to posit an underground Gnostic religion of Aryan-Visigothic origin, which had been brutally suppressed by the Catholic authorities in 1244. His quest for a Germanic religious tradition based on heresies and legends interested Himmler, who sought his collaboration in SS-sponsored research. In March 1936, Rahn joined the SS and undertook a research tour of Iceland under SS auspices. He subsequently published the travel journal of his quest for the ancient Cathar-Visigothic tradition across Europe as *Luzifers Hofgesinde* (1937).[15] Here in the whimsical ideas of Himmler and the passionate quest of Otto Rahn, Rudolf Mund found evidence of the mystical mission of the SS.

In 1958 Mund joined the Order of the New Templars (ONT), a racist chivalrous sect that cultivated a heretical dualist Ario-Christian theology of blond heroes in eternal struggle with the inferior beast-men. Originally founded on Christmas 1900 by Jörg Lanz von Liebenfels, the ONT achieved some influence in Vienna before and during the First World War, when Lanz was publicizing his Ariosophy, a conflation of Aryan racism, Gnostic Christianity and Theosophy in his *Ostara* magazine. These mystical racist brochures are reputed to have strongly influenced the young Hitler. The sect expanded from Austria into Germany and Hungary during the 1920s but went underground in Vienna after 1945.[16] Mund immersed himself in the archives of this Aryan cult, studied the writings of the early Church fathers and the history of the Knights Templar, and later wrote a hagiographical book about Lanz von Liebenfels.[17] In 1979 Mund succeeded Walter Krenn as prior of the ONT.

Through his research into the ONT, Mund also became interested in the mystical rune theories of Karl Maria Wiligut (1866–1946), the so-called Rasputin of Himmler. By virtue of his alleged possession of ancestral memory and an inspired representation of archaic Germanic traditions, Wiligut became the favorite mentor of Heinrich Himmler on mythological subjects and was given an official assignment for prehistorical research in the SS between 1933 and 1939. Consulted by his patron on a wide range of issues, Wiligut's influence extended to the design of the death's-head ring worn by members of the SS, the conception of the Wewelsburg as the order castle of the SS, and the adoption of other ceremonial designed to bestow a traditional aura upon the SS ideology of elitism, racial purity, and territorial conquest. Wiligut's ideas were similar to those of Guido von List, the runic occultist and Ariosophist close to Lanz von Liebenfels, and Wiligut had links with members of the ONT from as early as 1908. His introduction to Himmler was effected by Richard Anders, an SS officer who was also an ONT brother. Mund was delighted to find a further source of SS esotericism and produced a biography of Wiligut, which was published by Landig's Volkstum-Verlag.[18]

Wiligut also provided a further source for the myth of the Black Sun. In one of his Halgarita mottos, a series of cryptic religious revelations written for Himmler in the 1930s, Wiligut described an ancient sun called Santur. Wiligut's contemporary adepts, Emil Rüdiger and Werner von Bülow, interpreted this heavenly body as a second sun that shone 230,000 years ago upon the Hyperboreans in the North Pole and promoted their spiritual development. Santur still orbits in the vicinity of our planet today as an extinct star, thus invisible, but as a Black Sun it still emits a powerful intelligence.[19] Wiligut's reconstruction of a prehistoric Germanic "Irminist" religion was at least partially inspired by Guido von List's Armanism, the ancient faith of the Ario-Germans, which reflected a kind of Germanized Theosophy in the *völkisch*-occult underground of the era prior to the First World War.[20] By tracing Wiligut's own inspiration back to this period, one discovers an even earlier source for the Black Sun in Theosophy, which had been highly influential in German esoteric circles since the turn of the century.

In her major opus *The Secret Doctrine* (1888), Helena Blavatsky occasionally mentioned a "central sun" in the Milky Way, "a point unseen and mysterious, the ever-hidden center of attraction of our Sun and system." As the energetic center of the galaxy or even the universe, this dark central sun represents the mass of potential energy prior to the Big Bang of modern cosmology. While the Jewish Cabala described its "black light," Eastern initiates of Aryan tradition regarded it as the source of "creative light" and the "center of Universal life—Electricity."[21] Blavatsky thus emphasized a distinction between the Semitic and Aryan cosmogony: the former materializes and humanizes the mysteries of nature; the latter spiritualizes matter. Blavatsky's ideas were taken up by *völkisch*-theosophical authors in Germany before the First World War and after. Guido von List wrote of an invisible "primal fire" as the ancient Ario-Germans' notion of the highest divinity.[22] Peryt Shou (1873–1953), a German occult writer, had described humanity's heightened receptivity to the ultraviolet spiritual light of the "central sun" in the Age of Aquarius and related this to Germany's future in the troubled postwar era.[23]

If Mund was primarily an esotericist, Landig was a political activist. In the mid-1950s he was the Austrian representative of the European Social Movement (ESB), the fascist international organization founded at Rome and Malmö, which sought German alliance with a worldwide league of non-aligned nations, especially the Arab states, between the two superpowers. In 1955 Landig was in regular contact with Per Engdahl, the Swedish neo-Nazi leader, and Karl-Heinz Priester, a former Hitler Youth leader who had extensive contacts in the German nationalist underground. In 1958 Landig founded his own nationalist press, Volkstum-Verlag, whose logo featured an Ostrogothic eagle brooch dating from the reign of Theoderich the Great in the fifth century. In the same year he also began publishing his monthly international news service *Europa-Korrespondenz*, which adopted a nationalist and anti-communist line. It was speculated that Johannes von Leers, the former Reich propaganda ministry official who had sought refuge in Nasser's Egypt, was involved in the latter's funding.[24] In 1970 Wilhelm Landig became the Austrian representative of the World Anti-Communist League (WACL), founded in Taiwan in 1967 after a merger of the Asian People's Anti-Communist League and the Anti-Bolshevik Bloc of Nations. This was arguably the most important far-right network in the world and accounts for Landig's highly informed international news service.

However, it was Wilhelm Landig's own novels that ensured the revival of occult-nationalist themes among a younger generation of neo-Nazis in the 1990s. The ideas and interests discussed by the Landig group in the 1950s found permanent expression in Landig's trilogy of Thule novels. The first of these, *Götzen gegen Thule* (1971), was begun in the late 1950s and incorporated the thought of Julius Evola and Herman Wirth. Theories of Aryan polar origins and Atlantis are mixed with powerful new nationalist myths of "the last battalion," secret German UFO bases in the Arctic, alchemy, Grail myths and Cathar heresies, and a Nazi-Tibetan connection involving Himalayan masters and an underground kingdom in Mongolia. In this novel and especially in its successor, *Wolfszeit um Thule* (1980), a global Jewish conspiracy always lurks in the shadows, seeking to foil the revival of Nordic German rule, but its Judeo-Christian idols are powerless against the resurgence of the Black Sun. The last novel of the series, *Rebellen für Thule* (1991), is a wishful fantasy of right-wing radicalism among German youth. A former SS officer, the hero of the second novel, is invited to lecture on the Atlantean heritage of the Aryans at a German secondary school. The pupils reject the liberal views of their despised left-wing history teacher and hungrily embrace the new nationalist myths of Thule.

Götzen gegen Thule is an allegory of the Landig circle's attempts to make contact with an esoteric center of Nordic traditions, the legendary realm of Thule, the final bastion of the Germanic world in defeat. The story describes the world odyssey of a small group of SS soldiers and Luftwaffe airmen across four continents in the immediate aftermath of the Second World War. In the first part of the novel the two airmen, Recke ("beserker") and Reimer ("bard"), are sent from Norway to Point 103, a secret base that has been established by the esoteric SS elite in Arctic Canada, unknown to the Allies and also to most German authorities. Point 103 is a large underground complex equipped with highly advanced technology, including flying saucers whose apparent mission is to maintain the spirit of German defense after the final surrender of the Reich. But Point 103 is also a combatant in a metaphysical war between hidden forces on a spiritual plane. In this great power struggle, the secret base seeks the proximity and support of the esoteric world center of ethically positive forces located somewhere nearby at the Midnight Mountain of polar myth. Its symbol is the alchemical Black Sun, a round disk that is not exactly black but the deepest violet.[25]

Like Landig's bloc of unaligned nations against the superpowers, Point 103 seeks to promote an international alliance for the ideals of the Black Sun. Many foreign delegates attend a great conference held in the assembly hall of the base decorated with astrological symbols and an enormous icon of Mithras slaying the Bull. The delegates have all been flown to the conference by means of the V-7, a German flying saucer with a speed of 4,000 kilometers per hour and a range of 2,000 kilometers. These include a Tibetan lama, Japanese, Chinese, and American officers, Indians, Arabs, Persians, an Ethiopian, a Brazilian officer, a Venezuelan, a Siamese and a full-blooded Mexican Indian. The Arabs speak darkly of secret Islamic brotherhoods, the Indians and Persians invoke old Aryan traditions, the Orientals allude to their occult orders and a mysterious world center. Attired in their uniforms or national dress, many of the delegates make speeches identifying their national myths and ideals with those of the Thule and pledge their full support when the time comes for action.[26]

Recke and Reimer are accompanied by an enigmatic Waffen-SS officer, Gutmann ("Good Man," a descendant of German Cathars or "perfect ones"), who acts as their guide and mentor, initiating them into the Thulean philosophy. He quotes the Iranian *Avesta* and the theories of the Munich paleontologist Edgar Dacqué as evidence of a golden age when the Arctic region was green and fertile, the primaeval homeland of the Aryans. He mentions the sinking of Atlantis as a result of a lunar collision according to Hörbiger's World Ice Theory, and the subsequent forced exodus of the Aryans due to sin-

ful egoism and climatic disaster. Kiß's researches in the Andes and his discovery of the stone head with Nordic features in Bolivia offer proof of these
Aryan migrations. The Dogger bank area around Heligoland was known as
"Holy Land" in old annals, sure evidence of a sunken Aryan-Atlantean culture, for wherever they settled in Europe, Iran and India, the Aryans sought
to re-create their lost paradise and recalled its memory in their myths, legends and place-names. Gutmann considers that the flood myth of the Bible
is simply derived from ancient Hindu texts and the Gilgamesh epic, implying
that the Old Testament is a merely local Jewish adaptation of worldwide
Aryan traditions. Following Herman Wirth, he claims that the ancient
Tuathas and Germans are blood heirs of the old Atlantean race on the European continent.[27]

Following the formal German surrender in May 1945, the chief of staff at
Point 103 orders that all German insignia be removed from uniforms: the
Black Sun disk is now the symbol of their secret independent Reich and is
substituted for German markings on their aircraft and flying saucers. He fol-
lows this announcement with a pep talk offering a panoramic review of
Thulean prehistory and destiny, based on Herman Wirth and Julius Evola.
The Arctic and Atlantean Nordic races created the oldest German state, the
Tuatha empire of Doggerland with its neolithic long barrows. The solar deity
and a belief in cycles of cosmic regeneration are manifest in the bull-slaying
Iranian warrior cult of Mithras, the heroic religion of the Age of Taurus,
which the new Thuleans of Point 103 practice. But the virile horned son of
God, the ancient revelation, gave way to the pale "fish head" of Jesus Christ:

> [The Age of Pisces initiated] the demolition of the aristocratic principle with
> the revolt of the slaves, the disinherited, those lacking heritage and tradition
> and with a grudge against everything which signified energy and leadership.
> As Evola recognized, the poison of proselytizing fanaticism sweeping over an-
> cient Rome in a barbarian Semitic wave, was simultaneously a reinforcement
> of all Asian-southern factors of decline, which had already penetrated the ed-
> ifice of pagan imperialism, and the germ of western affliction. The collapse of
> Rome opened the gates for all subsequent aberrations and degeneration lead-
> ing to the present state of Europe.

Faced with the current German military defeat, the chief of staff takes solace in these long-term cosmic cycles of decline and renewal. The Age of
Aquarius is approaching, and Europe, the land of the white man, awaits a
spiritual revival. The modern German heirs of the Tuathas must once again
rise to the historic challenge of a cosmic crisis. The black uniforms of the SS

and the Black Sun symbolize the winter solstice of the Aryan race, harbingers of a glorious new era. The supernatural glowing, flying disks ("manisolas") are portents from the hidden esoteric world center near the pole that proclaim the advent of global changes on a vast scale. The Thuleans will meanwhile develop their technical and military potential in seclusion at Point 103 for a further five years before intervening on a metaphysical plane in alliance with other friendly organizations for a global Aryan revival. When this apocalyptic transformation is complete, their symbol of the Black Sun will turn a shining silver-white.[28]

Sustained by this vision of Nazi revival, the German servicemen initially fly to the French Pyrenees to bring a French collaborator named Bélisse (from Bélisane, sun god of the Gauls), back to assist the alchemical experiments in the laboratories at Point 103. Living near Montségur, Bélisse is a neo-Cathar deeply versed in Grail lore, who supposedly helped Otto Rahn in his prewar researches. Due to his family allegiance to the old heresy of Visigothic origin, he recognizes the Germans as spiritual and racial kinsmen. He is also an authority on the manisolas, allegedly attributed by the Cathars to the Grail as the signatures of the highest love (*Minne*).[29] By means of these allusions, Landig recruits the Cathars and the cult of love among the medieval troubadours, symbolized by the shining disks of light, for the invisible forces of the Thule in their global struggle against evil and decay. However, after Bélisse is killed in a mountain fall, the mission is abandoned. Unable to regain contact with their aircraft, the Germans travel on to Spain for further instructions. As the novel proceeds, they embark on an odyssey halfway around the world through France, Spain, Morocco, Egypt, Lebanon, Syria, Iraq, Kuwait, Iran, Pakistan, India and Tibet, always trying to find a means to return to Point 103. Throughout their journey they meet many foreign allies, with whom they discuss Indo-European mythology and their common Aryan roots.

Behind the defeat of the Third Reich and the emergent new world order of the superpowers stands Israel, the deadly enemy with which the Thuleans are locked in a Manichaean conflict. According to Gutmann, this rivalry extends far back into prehistoric times, when black magicians of Semitic origin ruled over the Aryan Atlanteans in an interregnum. At this time the Jews set up their own Baal gods beside the Atlantean god Poseidon and later celebrated Mount Sinai as a bowdlerized version of Mount Meru or the Midnight Mountain in the Arctic. The restless Jewish tendency to migrate northward and westward from Israel is explained as a kind of nostalgia or folk-memory of their brief dominion over the Aryans and a desire to rule once again from the North. Gutmann alleges that this contest for the pole between the Jews and the Indo-Aryan groups that aspire to an Atlantean renaissance will ultimately result in victory for one or the other side.[30] The flag of the United Nations, founded in October 1945, reveals the Jewish determination to encircle the pole and usurp the esoteric world center from the Aryans. Its design, featuring a map of the world centered on the North Pole, contains cabalistic symbolism and is displayed in the telltale Israeli colors of blue and white.[31]

At a meeting with an old Jewish rabbi in Toledo, Gutmann expands on this immemorial rivalry between Semites and Aryans in the context of the new superpowers. The black magical power of the Jews is opposed to the white magic of the Aryans, and their battlefield is the rest of the world which, with the defeat of the Third Reich, is now a gray magical circle with a black center at Mount Sinai. According to Gutmann, the Ark of the Covenant is an accumulator for astral energies used in magical operations.[32] This paranoid myth is compounded with references to cults and Freemasons. A similar Ark is said to be guarded by the American Shriners in New York. Their headquarters in Chicago control all Masonic lodges dedicated to the goal of One World government. Both Roosevelt and Churchill belonged to this brotherhood and were always working for its aims. This world brotherhood gathers all powers within its network and works with them all to conquer the Midnight Mountain. On the one hand, this magic works to buttress the Jewish racial substance, on the other it dissolves other peoples into a multiracial chaos.[33]

In the final part of the novel, Landig introduces a Nazi-Tibetan connection as a further dimension of world conspiracy and mystery. Passing references are made to the cordial German-Tibetan relations established by the SS Ahnenerbe-sponsored expedition of Ernst Schäfer to Tibet in 1938–39.[34] But if Tibetan secrets were withheld from the Nazis, the presence of a Tibetan lama at the Point 103 conference suggests a continuing interest. When the German servicemen are abducted from India by Mongols and flown to a Tibetan monastery high in the snowbound Himalayan ranges, they recall the Mongolian legend that these people await the coming of the Lord of the World from the hidden underground city of Agartha. This revelation will usher in a yellow world empire that will stretch as far as Mount Meru at the pole, thus creating another rival for the Aryan Thule and Point 103. The Tibetans, it seems, were allies of the Germans against common enemies in the war, but in the end they too must pursue their imperial vision according to their own racial myth.[35]

The Tibetan abbot, Ngön-kyi Padma Dab-yang, gives another account of Mongolian mythology, which Landig has evidently borrowed from Louis Pauwels and Jacques Bergier's sensational account of Nazi occultism, *Le matin des magiciens* (1960). He describes two cities as the respective realms of material and spiritual energies. Revered by the secret brotherhoods and lodges of the West, Shambala is the terrestrial city of power and might, the source of material energies on the left-hand path, ruled over by a King of Fear. Agartha is the inner, underground realm of contemplation and spirit, the right-hand path, presided over by the Lord and King of the World, who will at the appointed time lead good men against the evil ones and establish the Mongol Empire. The abbot reproves the German soldiers, saying that certain figures in the Third Reich broke the Nazi-Tibetan treaty by allying themselves exclusively with the energies of Shambala and its naked violence, and thus played into the hands of its agent, Stalin. Both sources must be balanced, otherwise evil will result. Tibet has lost years of work through the fall of the Third Reich, and now the dark clouds of communism are gathering in the East. However, he urges the Germans to join them as there is an old prophecy that a Great Khan will once again come to the West and establish a great empire, and the time for its fulfillment is close at hand.[36]

With these revisionist legends, Landig wishes to imply that a few traitors in the Reich leadership betrayed the Nazi cause and brought about Germany's downfall. Eventually, the German servicemen succeed in escaping from their courteous Tibetan captors but are finally picked up by the British in India and interned in a prisoner-of-war camp. Repatriated to Germany and Austria, they find a sullen, gray world of defeat, evasion and distrust. The former Aryan-Nazi vision is forgotten, atrocity propaganda has invented the extermination camps, the Nuremberg executions are a pretext for a Jewish ritual of vengeance, and German girls sleep with black American soldiers. The storm of the idols against the Thule has begun. At a reunion in Salzburg, the soldiers ruefully accept the withdrawal of Point 103 from world affairs. They concede that the Aryans, scattered and dispossessed, have now become the new Ahasverus (the traditional name for the Wandering Jew). They can only be patient and wait until the blue and gold banner of the Aryans flies again, when "Greater Thule will become the new spiritual concept for all white men in the northern world, an ideal empire above all states, in Europe and America . . . the Fourth Reich of the Germans!"[37]

Landig's second novel, Wolfszeit um Thule (1980), describes a similar odyssey in the wake of German defeat. Here the narrative follows the adventures of two naval officers, Krall and Hellfeldt, and SS-Major Eyken, formerly stationed at Point 103. Assigned to a flotilla of German U-boats which leaves Norway in early May 1945, they achieve a devastating victory over an Allied naval convoy in the North Atlantic. The flotilla collects all equipment and personnel from Point 103, which is then evacuated and totally destroyed. During the voyage their conversations touch on the Midnight Mountain and its connection with the legendary Blue Island in the Arctic Ocean. Rumors from earlier expeditions regarding landmass below the polar ice cap and chance sightings by Canadian pilots of "monastic structures" recall Evola's ideas of a lost Hyperborean civilization in the Far North.[38] With the official surrender of the Third Reich, the northern world is forfeited and the flotilla sets sail for the South Atlantic to make contact with the new bases of the Black Sun, the epithet of the shadow Reich government in exile. The geographical focus of this novel thus indicates the shift of Nazi survival toward Latin America and Antarctica, the new Thule of the Southern Hemisphere.

Landig uses the dialogue of his characters to convey his own brand of esoteric Nazi political theory. Major Eyken explains that the North Pole is the *theonium* of the world, associated with Lucifer, the light-bearer of the north, and Prometheus and represents the spiritual source of all Aryan strength. As its counterpart, the South Pole is the place of greatest materialization and all demonic energies. Using the ying-yang symbol as a model, he indicates that this "white" northern spiritual zone has spawned a "black" point: materialist forces of high finance and Masonic lodges prevail in the United States superpower; the Americans are usurping the Aryans with their own "Thule" base in Greenland; and the Soviets are seeking to develop their own military presence in the Arctic. The Aryans must therefore shift their spiritual potential southward and form a "white" point in the "black" spiritual zone in order to tap its powers for their own purposes in the reclamation of the North. Their goal is the repurified, white sun, the sol invictus of Mithraism, which will ultimately succeed the Black Sun, their present symbol of revanchist military power.[39]

Although Argentina had declared war on Germany in March 1945, the fugitives find support in Buenos Aires and travel on to La Paz, Bolivia. Here they receive confirmation of Edmund Kiß's high standing in Bolivia on account of his prewar investigations of the Nordic-Aryan heritage of Tiahuanaco, the mausoleum of Puma Punku and the observatory of Kalasasaya. Eyken enlightens the others regarding the full breadth of Kiß's work on the prehistoric calendar with the aid of Hörbiger's World Ice Theory to prove that the Nordic Atlanteans founded the first Egyptian civilization. When their local contact confirms the presence of Aryan bloodlines among the Quecha Indians of Bolivia, who have blond hair and blue eyes, the conversation turns to other ancient and medieval European colonizations of Latin America, long before the much-vaunted discovery of the "half-Jew," Christopher Columbus.[40]

Kiß's research in Bolivia links up with new developments. Along the western side of the Andes mountains he discovered an extensive tunnel system stretching from the Atacama Desert as far as Ecuador, attributing it to a mysterious people with unimaginable technology many thousands of years ago. Here among the dense forests, deep inside the Andean labyrinth, several hundred German military and technical personnel have established a secret base called Mime's Smithy as a companion to Point 211 in Antarctica. (Mime, a figure in Norse mythology, is the smith who forges Siegfried's sword in Wagner's *Rheingold*.) Eyken and his comrades spend many months at this site, marveling at the advanced technology brought by German scientists who have escaped the American and Soviet dragnets for Third Reich miracle weapons researchers. Another, smaller secret base in the Andes has been established in the Brazilian forest near the Beni Valley. While the dark powers of the postwar world condemn the old Nazi leadership to death at Nuremberg in October 1946, a new Thulean Reich, a provisional "Aggartha of the North," is growing deep inside the Andes.[41]

Meanwhile, Landig also describes a sinister new episode in the hoary myth of the Elders of Zion. Following the founding of the state of Israel in May 1948, members of the American Jewish elite gather one hot July day at a secluded villa off Riverside Drive in Manhattan to discuss the progress of their world dominion. Since the Elders' historic nocturnal meeting in the Prague Jewish Cemetery in 1787—the tale in Goedsche's novel *Biarritz*, which inspired the notorious *Protocols*—the Jews have realized their ambition of controlling both gold and the press. Through communism and liberalism, they are now breaking the influence of white elites worldwide. With the slogan "Nazism" they have brought everything Germanic into disrepute and can disarm any resistance to their plans. A banker reviews the growth of Jewish power through the Federal Reserve system. The Bretton Woods agreement of 1944 only served to internationalize public debts owed to Jewry, while the Marshall Plan shall create a complaisant and materialist postwar Germany, forgetful of its higher ideals. A scientist then outlines the future of humanity with a shocking description of genetic engineering, mind control through electronics and drugs, robot policemen and the creation of a docile population subject to Jewish world government.[42]

Landig's intrepid resistance fighters now turn their attention to a postwar alliance with anti-communist forces in the Far East. Earlier links with Tibet are now weakening due to the ascendancy of Red China, and their hopes are now focused on Mongolian exiles in Japan, Korea and Taiwan. Traveling across the Pacific by V-7 flying disk, the trio arrives in Hong Kong to make contact with the Green Dragon, a Chinese nationalist league with former links to the Thule in Germany. When Eyken is kidnapped by the Maoist Red Dragon order, which tries to recruit him as a German communist agent, Taiwanese members of the Green Dragon come to his rescue. Along the way they meet a sympathetic Briton, and conversations range over such themes as the cabalistic design of the U.S. Pentagon, British-Israelism, and the hostile secret elites such as the Council on Foreign Relations. Eyken explains their esoteric mission to their new friends:

> A circle of initiates within the SS bear the Black Sun as a secret insignia for Thule. It is the sol nigra of alchemy. . . . The Greek mysteries already recognized a secret sun besides the golden disk of Atlantis. This was the star Antares in the sign of Scorpio. . . . The deep purple color of the Black Sun is not without illumination, but the pervasive splendor which illuminates the initiate. According to ancient Germanic tradition, God is omnipotent and invisible. Light perceptible to the human eye is material, a shadow of the invisible, spiritual light and fire, a tiny spark of which still glows in the Age of the Wolf around Thule and awaits rekindling. . . . The Black Sun is the sign of invisible divinity which stands above the material golden glow of daylight, once the golden sun of the Atlanteans was usurped by the servants of Mammon and Freemasonry. The deep purple disk represents the accomplishment of divine will and law against the presumptive power of gold, together with its masters and slaves. . . . Charged with secret knowledge, this symbol was seen on the military aircraft of the SS shortly before the end of the Second World War. The Black Sun illuminates a Reich and will never set.[43]

Their companion regrets that Britain remains ignorant of this Aryan heritage and still serves the stars of David and Moses. He sees the spiritual confidence of the Germans and fears that noninitiates (i.e., the former Allies) will be overwhelmed by an apocalypse.

In South Korea, Eyken meets the Gusdä Menen Tudun, an anti-communist and former senior officer of the Mongolian Army who fled when the Russians established a puppet regime in his homeland. Eyken explains their interest in the secrets of the Gobi Desert and Shambala and outlines the racial anthropogeny of Blavatskyan Theosophy, already known to Tibetan initiates 10,000 years ago. Tibetan traditions also indicate an Atlantean myth of seven subraces, including the Aryans, Akkadians, Toltecs, Turanians, Rmoahalians, Tlavatlians and Mongolians. The swastika symbol emerged at the time of the Aryans' dominance on Atlantis, prior to their prehistoric migration to the Himalayas. Ever since, the Aryans have retained a secret longing for Mount Meru and Hyperborea, their original homeland in the Far North. The Güsda recognizes Eyken as an initiate of the secret doctrine that unites these esoteric Nazis with the mysteries of the Orient. The free Mongolians believe that the Eagleland (Germany) is their

ally in the West, for Hitler was believed to be a descendant of a great warrior in the entourage of Genghis Khan, while Stalin is a changeling from
the tribe of the "yellow eyes" and a family of Japhetic priests and backed by
black magicians. He also relates how the Bogdo Hutuchtu, the living Buddha of the red cap lamas in Mongolia, has been deposed by the communists, and how no one now dares speak about the realm of Agartha or the
King of the World. But he is biding his time and will appear at the appointed time to lead the good of this world against the bad.[44]

Shortly afterward, the Germans are captured by Korean communist insur-
gents from the North and interned together with an American, a Czech and a
Japanese. The captives find a common cause in anti-communism in the new
Cold War world order. Following the outbreak of the Korean War on 25 June
1950, the Germans manage to escape and make their way to Hadong. Their
mission in the Far East is now accomplished. Besides discovering a shared esoteric heritage, the warriors of the Black Sun have established the presence of
potential allies among the victims of Soviet and Chinese communist expansion, thus mirroring Landig's own interest in the World Anti-Communist
League (WACL) with its strong base in the Far East. WACL originated in the
Asian People's Anti-Communist League, founded in Taiwan by the Chinese
nationalist Kuomintang in 1954, which joined with East European émigré organizations in 1966 to form WACL, with world headquarters in South Korea.
By seeking friends in Taiwan and Korea, the Thule is seeking to become a third
force between the West and the communist world.

Meanwhile the German servicemen are unable to renew contact with the
bases in the Andes and decide to return to Europe. In late 1950 they arrive in
Allied-occupied Vienna to find Hellfeldt's property confiscated and family
apartment occupied by strangers, reflecting Landig's own bitter experience of
the postwar regime and its harsh treatment of former Nazis. Under the pall of
defeat, occupation and restrictions, the old soldiers form a circle of undying
loyalty to their ideals. Once again, they recall the secret lore of Thule and the
Far North and its evangel for the German Reich. The mob rule of democracy,
they comfort themselves, will be but short lived. Hitler was not a Thulean initiate but left the secret gnosis of the North to special circles within the SS, to
whom he offered his protection. Eyken equates the esoteric symbolism of the
Grail according to Evola with the Hyperborean doctrine of a sacred center in
the North, with its powerful legends of root-races, Atlantis and all-conquer-
ing Aryans. The quest for the Grail is identical to the Aryan longing for contact with the Midnight Mountain. At the twilight of the gods in Norse
mythology, everything falls into the jaws of the wolf Fenrir, bringing chaos
and darkness. The Thuleans must now endure the Age of the Wolf, for when

the Third Reich sank in flames, all forces that ranged against the North triumphed, and evil overcame good.[45]

In *Rebellen für Thule* (1991), Landig traces the origins of the Black Sun to Babylonian religion. An ancient cuneiform inscription makes explicit reference to the Black Sun "shining within us, you give us the power of understanding." Landig recalls the vision of Marduk grieving over the collapse of the empire until the goddess Ishtar commands the stars to shine a new invisible light. Landig sees this prophecy as referring to the temporary defeat of the German Reich and its restoration through the esoteric illumination of the Black Sun. "The Black Sun shines above the Midnight Mountain. The human eye cannot see it—and yet it is there: Its light shines within. The bold and the righteous are solitary but they have divinity."[46] The knowledge of the Black Sun was lost through Christianity, until the Templars rediscovered its lore in the Levant. Their knowledge was lost by the Freemasons, and finally only a small circle of SS esotericists cultivated the Black Sun as the "inner light." Like the Templars and Cathars, the SS were persecuted after the war primarily as heretics in Landig's mythology.[47]

This German *völkisch* interest in Babylon can be traced back to the turn of the century when Friedrich Delitzsch (1850–1922), the famous Assyriologist, argued that the Old Testament and Jewish monotheism were derived from Babylonian religion. His initial lecture, "Babel und Bibel" (1902), aroused widespread controversy, as it clearly weakened Jewish claims of divine revelation and election.[48] Taking the debate a stage further, Houston Stewart Chamberlain and Herman Wirth regarded Babylonian culture as a heritage of the Sumerians, whom they identified as early Aryan colonizers of Mesopotamia. Landig's interpretation of the Gilgamesh epic and inscriptions from Babylon follow this Nordic-Sumerian line by highlighting their correspondences to the Edda and old Norse sources. Landig also referred to Peter Jensen's scholarly interpretation of Gilgamesh as a Babylonian cosmology focusing on the constellation of Taurus and its major star Aldebaran.[49] The supposed common Aryan ancestry of the Sumero-Babylonians and the Germans would lead to a lively esoteric discourse in the 1990s involving ancient Babylon, German flying saucer technology, and extraterrestrial ancestors from Aldebaran.

Landig's ariosophically colored novels have greatly popularized Aryan mythology and occult anti-Semitism. The names and doctrines of Julius Evola, Herman Wirth, Edmund Kiß and Hans Hörbiger, hitherto scattered shards of Third Reich memory, are here skilfully woven into adventurous narratives and presented anew to a modern readership. Throughout the books of Landig's Thule trilogy, the Black Sun is a mystical symbol for an esoteric order within the SS, the refined distillate of the Nazi spirit, temporarily eclipsed but still potent during the postwar ascendancy of the Jews and their superpower puppets. According to this neo-Nazi mythology, the lost war of 1939–45 is but a prelude to an even greater metaphysical conflict.[50] However, like all powerful symbols, the Black Sun is many-sided. Besides the myth of alchemical occlusion, signifying the latency of Thulean-Nazi power, Landig also identifies the Black Sun as the source of spiritual light and inspiration, a symbol of divine illumination and coming salvation.[51] Gathered from such diverse sources as the Gilgamesh epic, secret Templar legends, and esoteric SS lore involving Otto Rahn, Cathars and a Luciferic polar world center, Landig's Black Sun is a powerful myth invoking the Nazi gnosis in the darkness of defeat.

The myth of the Black Sun was elaborated further with the publication of another occult-Nazi thriller, *Die schwarze Sonne von Tashi Lhunpo* [The Black Sun of Tashi Lhunpo] (1991) by Russell McCloud. It is the first decade of the twenty-first century and the European Union and the United Nations together administer a New World Order devoted to democracy and economic prosperity. The assassinations of the president of the European Bank and a leading member of the UN Security Council are linked by a brand mark of the Black Sun on the foreheads of the victims. In this case, the symbol is a sun wheel, a black disk surrounded by twelve radial sig-runes.[52] This unique SS sun wheel design actually exists at the Wewelsburg castle near Paderborn, originally acquired by Heinrich Himmler in 1934 as an SS staff college whose special emphasis was on the Germanic heritage and Nordic religion. Between 1936 and 1942, Himmler rebuilt and expanded the Wewelsburg as a ceremonial place, where his top SS leaders would celebrate pseudoreligious rituals. Himmler regarded the castle as the magical omphalos, marking the center of the Germanic world, and planned ultimately to develop the whole site as an SS vatican of Aryan spirituality. The large circular sun wheel with twelve sig-rune spokes decorates the white marble floor of the *Gruppenführer* hall in the northern tower.[53]

McCloud is the first writer to identify the Wewelsburg sun wheel with the Black Sun myth, thereby indicating the esoteric influence of Wiligut and the SS heritage of Aryan-theosophical lore at the heart of Himmler's imaginative world. However, it has been suggested that this twelve-spoke sun wheel derives from decorative disks of the Merovingians of the early medieval period and are supposed to represent the visible sun or its passage through the months of the year. These disks were discussed in scholarly publications during the Third Reich and may well have served the Wewelsburg designers as a model.[54] Moreover, the fact that Peryt Shou and Wilhelm Landig described the Black Sun as deep purple seems to contradict its representation at the Wewelsburg as a mottled dark-green pattern on white. But if the Black Sun is the cosmogonic source of all creative energy in the universe, the Wewelsburg symbol surely evokes both the rotational and explosive power of the Big Bang at the creation of the universe.

In the novel, the journalist hero follows a lead from the Wewelsburg to Tibet, where he finds Karl Steiner, a former SS man living in a Himalayan hermitage a day's march from the Tashi Lhunpo monastery, the seat of the Panchen Lama and the yellow-hat monks. Although youthful in appearance, Steiner is over ninety years old and came to Tibet on the final (fictional) SS Ahnenerbe expedition of 1942. His explanation of world history places the Nazi-Tibetan link in the familiar context of the Thule and Mongolian myth. The prehistoric Thuleans were originally the offspring of the gods: one party wanted to remain aloof and use mortal men as cattle, the other decided to educate and improve mankind. These parties divided into the camps of Schamballah and Agarthi. McCloud reveals a certain Nazi sympathy by identifying Schamballah with the secret governors of the "New World Order," the UN secret service, the European Union and the Freemasons. But the Nazis, we are told, made their alliance with Agarthi, for it was their plan to transform men into supermen. The Third Reich, the Second World War and the recent wave of assassinations are thus mere episodes in the perennial battle of Agarthi and Schamballah regarding the destiny of man. The climax of the novel is reached with a winter solstice ritual at the Wewelsburg attended by Steiner and highly placed agents of Agarthi intended to restore Nazi world dominion.[55]

Between 1971 and 1991, the Black Sun thus developed from Landig's signature of eclipsed Nazi power at Thule to the Wewelsburg SS sun wheel, identified as the symbol of Agartha, a secret Himalayan realm embedded in Nazi, Tibetan and Theosophical myth. Charged by these exotic references to remote or hidden centers of power and initiation, the Wewelsburg Black Sun has become an esoteric symbol among younger neo-Nazis from Austria to the international scene since the 1990s. Arun-Verlag in Engerda (in the former German Democratic Republic) has published further editions and a film script of McCloud's book, while the *Nation Europa* book mail-order catalog offers Black Sun stickpins and a wristwatch with a Wewelsburg sun wheel face. Kadmon (a pseudonym for Gerhard Petak), an industrial musician in Vienna, publishes *Aorta* (1991–95), a periodical devoted to pagan traditions and the neo-fascist avant garde. His music label, Allerseelen, has released a CD, *Gotos=Kalanda* (1995), adapted from Wiligut's pagan calendar cycle of poems presented to Himmler in 1937. The Wewelsburg Black Sun is prominent on Petak's letterhead and the Allerseelen label.[56]

In his study of far-right esotericism in Germany, Rüdiger Sünner suggests the Wewelsburg Black Sun has become a key symbol in the neo-Nazi cults. An image in *Elemente*, the journal of the Kassel-based Thule-Seminar, a research association for Indo-European culture, shows a martial warrior holding a shield decorated with the Wewelsburg sun wheel. His upheld sword proclaims the struggle for a "rebirth of Europe" against the "holocaust of peoples on the altar of multiracialism." The German *völkisch* magazine *Sol invictus* uses the symbol as its masthead. The issue devoted to "Midnight" (Black Sun) shows two somber knights standing guard beneath the sun wheel symbol, whose invisible power prevails against the gloom, cold and pain of the interregnum. An accompanying verse reads: "As knights of the sun we are returning home/we will be the new nobility/rare scions of our own rank/we were orphaned and the journey was long/the darkness did not swallow us/we rose up/the children of the sun, when they see us/will understand the words of fire!"[57] The Wewelsburg sun wheel is also the logo of German Thule-Netz on the Internet, which has offered widespread access to far right and racist websites in Europe and America since 1992. The SS sun wheel is widely discussed in neo-Nazi underground magazines in Germany and on their international links. Black Sun badges are now even sold by a group in New Zealand.[58]

Rüdiger Sünner has also made a documentary film entitled *Schwarze Sonne* about the occult background of National Socialism. His treatment extends from the Ariosophists and Thule Society as mystical Nazi precursors through Himmler's SS ceremonial to the current neo-Nazi cults.[59] While filming at the Wewelsburg, he was threatened by a skinhead, brandishing his fist with a Black Sun tattoo. He regarded Sünner's film a desecration. Just as the Black Sun symbolized Landig's "last battalion" of the Thuleans at Point 103 in the frozen North in the early postwar months, this emblem has come to signify the magical evocation of a lost homeland among young neo-Nazis. The enigmatic symbol of the Black Sun indicates the faraway ideals of Thule, an alternative world in total opposition to a multiracial Europe.

8

Nazi UFOs, Antarctica and Aldebaran

FOLLOWING THEIR APPEARANCE in the early postwar years, flying saucers swiftly established themselves as a major cultural icon in popular mythology. These futuristic discoid aircraft, capable of amazing speeds and maneuvers, initially impinged on public awareness following an incident on 24 June 1947. Kenneth Arnold, flying his private plane through the Cascade Mountains in Washington State, saw a formation of nine objects in flight at about 9,000 feet. He estimated their speed at 1,700 miles per hour—an incredible figure before ultrasonic flight—and described the strange craft flipping up and down "like a saucer would if you skipped it across the water." Arnold's sighting was not the first, as nearly forty had been recorded earlier that year. However, this was the incident that sparked a major wave of journalism on flying saucers, and further reports from forty-eight states were received that summer alone. American fears of communism and Russian aggression—the Cold War was just gearing up with the establishment of communist regimes in Eastern Europe—fueled interest and anxiety. As the number of saucer sightings mounted all over the Western world, it was realized that the saucers' performance far surpassed all known technology and human endurance. Belief in the extraterrestrial origin of the flying saucers soon became widespread.[1]

Public fear of Soviet superweapons or extraterrestrial visits clearly necessitated an official response. The US government notably took an ambivalent view of the saucers, seeking to debunk them if at all possible while strenuously denying any possibility of their origin on earth. Founded in December 1947, a monitoring investigation called Project Sign examined 237 sightings under the direction of Allen Hynek, then professor of astronomy at Northwestern University. In February 1949, Project Grudge was commenced by the United States Air Force. Renamed Project Blue Book in March 1952, and advised by Hynek, this project represented the official U.S. investigation of the UFO phenomenon ("Unidentified Flying Object" was by then the preferred technical and more neutral term) until its closure in 1969. Meanwhile, civilian investigation groups were founded in America, Britain and Europe. Waves of sightings continued unabated. Science fiction magazines and films, a fast-growing genre in America and Europe during the 1950s, reinforced the imagery of flying saucers and the likelihood of alien visitation.[2] A new dimension was added once direct meetings with extraterrestrial aliens were claimed. A new contactee literature developed after George Adamski's story of his encounter with an alien in the Californian desert in November 1952.[3]

Fifty years of the UFO phenomenon have turned into a global mythology transcending national frontiers. Stephen Spielberg's enormously successful film, *Close Encounters of the Third Kind* (1977), initiated a widespread belief in government coverup and conspiracy regarding its knowledge of UFOs and aliens. A veritable UFO industry flourishes today. Hundreds of books are published each year covering sightings, abductions, crash retrievals and even alien autopsies. Scores of specialist magazines minutely analyze data and evaluate rumors, claims, photographs and eyewitness accounts. The film *Independence Day* (1996), featuring an alien invasion on earth with the Roswell, New Mexico, crash story of July 1947 in the background, and the television series *The X-Files*, highlighting the investigation of the paranormal, have generated vast profits and a huge interest in UFOs within a complex mythology involving extraterrestrial life, apocalyptic expectations, religious hopes and government conspiracy against the people. Posters, T-shirts, and other merchandise, together with advertising and visual references in popular media, have created a discourse on UFOs and aliens accessible to everybody.

Esoteric Nazism has found its own niche within this powerful and universal mythology. As early as the 1950s, rumors began to circulate among certain German nationalist circles that the postwar flying saucers were in fact German superweapons that had already been under development and tested during the Third Reich. At the time of Germany's surrender in May 1945, this technology was supposedly shipped to safety in the Arctic, South America and Antarctica. The abundance of UFO sightings was thus attributed to a hidden Nazi presence in remote and inaccessible regions of the world. By the late 1970s, neo-Nazi writers were claiming that the "Last Battalion," a massive Nazi military force of highly advanced UFOs, was in possession of a vast tract of Antarctica. At any moment, this fleet of Nazi UFOs could sally forth to deliver the benighted world from the yoke of the two superpowers as well as the postwar ills of democracy and liberalism. From the early 1990s these myths of advanced Nazi technology were conflated with alternative energy sources and alliances with an extraterrestrial civilization in the remote solar system of Aldebaran. Jan van Helsing, the notorious German conspiracy theorist and anti-Semite, now uses these myths, together with the Black Sun, in his best-selling books on secret societies and their power in the twentieth century.

The roots of Nazi UFO mythology lie in the closely related Hitler survival myth. Early myths of German revanche were linked with the idea that Adolf Hitler had escaped from the Berlin bunker during the closing days of the war and made his way to safety abroad. Conflicting accounts of events in the Bunker, circumstantial evidence, and early Soviet suggestions that Hitler was alive created widespread speculation regarding his fate.[4] Stories of Hitler's last-minute marriage to Eva Braun and their flight to a new life began to circulate in the international press during the summer of 1945. On 16 July a sensational article in the *Chicago Times* had Hitler and Eva Braun landing in Argentina and living on a German-owned estate in Patagonia. The story was reprinted by every major American and European paper, including the *New York Times*, the *Baltimore Sun*, *The Times* of London, and *Le Monde*. The story was most likely prompted by the late surrender in early July of the German U-530 submarine at the Argentine port of Mar del Plata. Several Buenos Aires papers reported earlier clandestine landings by rubber boats along the coast. However, on 17 July the newspaper *Critica* stated that the Führer and Eva Braun had landed from the U-530 in Antarctica, noting that the possible place of disembarkation was Queen Maud Land, the destination of a German Antarctic expedition in 1938–39.[5]

The late surrender of German submarines in Argentina during the summer of 1945 played a key role in focusing press interest on Hitler's escape to the Southern Hemisphere. The U-530 had given itself up at Mar del Plata on 10 July with an excessively large crew of fifty-four men, considerable stocks of food and an odd cargo—more than five hundred large drums containing cigarettes. On 17 August 1945, three months after the capitulation of the Third Reich, another German submarine, U-977, surrendered at Mar del Plata. Captain Heinz Schäffer had only thirty-two men under his command on board. The logs of both submarines showed that both had left Kristiansund, Norway, on 2 May 1945. As in the case of the U-530, the crew were all exceptionally young and unmarried men. A third submarine had meanwhile surrendered at Leixoes on the coast of Portugal on 5 June. The mystery of the submarines' long voyages, young crews, exceptional supplies and unknown whereabouts during the intervening months before their surrender fed speculation that the submarines had been involved in a "phantom convoy" bringing Hitler and other top Nazis with auxiliary forces to a secret hideout in Antarctica.[6]

Admiral Richard E. Byrd's massive international mission to Antarctica in 1946–47 offered another suggestive piece of evidence for the Allies' apparent concern with a postwar Nazi military presence in Antarctica. On 2 December 1946 a United States fleet of thirteen ships, equipped with four thousand navy troops, amphibious tanks, helicopters and two hundred airplanes, sailed from Norfolk, Virginia, to join up with Anglo-Norwegian and Soviet task forces to monitor Antarctica, ostensibly for the purposes of scientific research and to establish territorial claims. On arriving in Antarctica, the expedition quickly ran into difficulties. Byrd lost four airplanes and hastily withdrew, abandoning the whole operation. A Chilean journalist, Lee Van Atta, quoted Byrd to the effect that he was concerned about the threat to US security from unidentified enemies in the polar region who could fly from one pole to the other.[7] A Hungarian exile living in Argentina, Ladislao Szabó, authored a book, *Hitler esta vivo* [Hitler Is Alive] (1947), which described the abortive U.S. Antarctic mission and the captured U-boats in the context of Hitler's escape to a secret Antarctic Nazi base. The book was immediately translated into French and sponsored a spate of sensational magazine stories from 1947 into the early 1950s.[8]

The next stage in Nazi UFO mythology was the link between postwar saucer sightings and the revelation that German engineers had worked on flying disks during the Third Reich. In March 1950, *Flugkapitän* Rudolf Schriever (b. 1910) gave an interview to the German news magazine *Der Spiegel*. He described how he had begun pondering solutions for vertical take-off while working as a chief pilot at Eger (now Cheb) in 1942. He designed a central domed cabin for the crew and controls that was surrounded by a circular plane of rotating turbine blades driven by three jets mounted below. The whole disk had a diameter of 49 feet (14.4 meters). The turbines could develop 1,650–1,800 rpm with a thrust of 100 meters/second. Schriever calculated that his 3-tonne disk could achieve a flying speed of 4,200 kilometers/second with a range of 6,000 kilometers. Once the Messerschmitt jet became available in 1942, the project began to be developed by him and his team at the BMW works at Prague. Schriever stated here that he worked on his designs until 15 April 1945 but fled before the Russian advance into Czechoslovakia. Living with his parents-in-law at Bremerhaven-Lehe, he related how his workshop was burgled in August 1948, and his designs for the flying disk and a model were stolen. He was convinced that Czech engineers had since reconstructed his flying disk for a foreign power.[9]

More details soon emerged. According to a later report, the Schriever flying disk was actually built and rolled out of the hangar for a test flight in April 1945: "A fantastic creation of nearly 15 meters in diameter, in its center the plexiglass cupola of the control room glistening in the sunlight." A slight technical fault and an air-raid warning postponed the flight indefinitely. The works shut down on 9 May in the midst of a Czech revolt. Schriever and his colleagues blew up his flying disk and he escaped, driving his BMW into the

Bavarian Forest in the American zone. Here he repaired agricultural machinery for a while, until his belongings, including the designs, were plundered.[10]

In early 1953, the A. V. Roe Company in Canada announced its development of a circular jet aircraft with a speed of 1,500 mph. Another German engineer, Georg Klein, former special commissioner in Albert Speer's Ministry of Armaments and Munitions, claimed that such designs were already current in the Third Reich. He identified at least two classes of German flying disks. The first was developed at Breslau by Richard Miethe, a V-2 rocket engineer, and consisted of a non-rotating disk 42 meters in diameter. This disk fell into Russian hands, while Miethe fled via France to the United States, where he joined the A. V. Roe Company. The other model was the disk of Rudolf Schriever and Klaus Habermohl built in Prague, consisting of a broad, flat ring of moving turbine blades around a fixed, globe-shaped pilot's cabin. Astonishingly, Klein recalled that he had been present at this disk's first manned test flight on 14 February 1945, when the craft reached an altitude of 12,400 meters within three minutes and developed a maximum speed of 2,200 kilometers/hour in horizontal flight.[11]

It was in the period 1951 to 1955 that Erich Halik, a member of Wilhelm Landig's circle, published his articles in *Mensch und Schicksal*. He was certain that postwar sightings of flying saucers related to German craft. He devoted careful analysis to George Adamski's account of a cigar-shaped mother ship, from which a saucer flew forth in November 1952. Halik argued that the naive American, Adamski, could neither interpret the "Black Sun" insignia nor recognize the swastikas in an "alien" inscription. In the science fiction idiom of his day, Adamski had attributed both craft and crew to Venus, an identification which obviously suited the authorities. As we have seen in chapter 7, Halik concluded that German flying saucers were now operating from secret polar bases in the Arctic. Halik's publication in an Austrian esoteric magazine attracted little notice at the time, but here in outline was the kernel of the Nazi UFO mythos: the flying disks were an important part of a German plan to create an extraterritorial state prior to a renewed attack on the Allied enemies after 1945. As we shall see, Nazi ufologists in the late 1980s would recycle Halik's articles and match Adamski's photographs with new "discoveries" of wartime SS designs.[12]

In 1955 a book published in South Africa gave more details of the Miethe disk. Known as the V-7, it had no rotating parts and was driven by twelve adjustable jets, five rearward for forward flight and the other seven for directional steering. With a range of 13,000 miles, the V-7 was able to reach 1,500–2,000 miles per hour. One of these craft was flown from the V-rocket base Peenemünde and crashed on Spitsbergen. Another fell into Russian hands at Breslau and was shipped, togther with two technicians, to a site in Siberia. A flying disk with Russian inscriptions was reported to have landed in Pomerania in July 1953, while the motive power of the A.V. Roe design was based on the V-7. Besides emphasizing the advanced German contribution to aeronautical engineering during the Second World War, these stories implied that foreign powers had seized this German technology and were now secretly developing flying disks—hence the wave of saucer sightings.[13]

As the war receded into the past, more technical experts from Germany and Italy published substantial accounts of German secret weapons research and development during the Second World War. In 1959 Major Rudolf Lusar, who had worked at the German Patent Office, wrote a lengthy account of the extraordinary variety of missiles, flying bombs and long-range rockets in operational use before the end of the war. He also discussed the flying disks of Schriever, Habermohl and Miethe, who were supported by an Italian physicist called Bellonzo.[14]

The Italian connection was strengthened by Renato Vesco, an Italian aircraft engineer, who had worked with the Germans at Fiat's immense underground installations at Lake Garda, producing advanced aeronautical devices that were tested at the Hermann Goering Institute in Riva del Garda. Vesco described an astonishing variety of advanced secret weapons in wartime Germany, including explosive gases, blower cannons, television-guided bombs, and pilotless fighter planes. Foremost among these for subsequent UFO speculation was the *Kugelblitz*, an unmanned circular aircraft with gyroscopic stabilization, and the *Feuerball* ("foo fighter") antiradar device, a spherical armored shell that could follow enemy bombers. Its fiery halo overionized the atmosphere in the vicinity of the plane, disabling its radar and sometimes interfering with engine ignition. Allied air crews had first become afraid of these huge fireballs pursuing them across the German night skies in the autumn of 1944. Invisible to radar themselves, the fireballs could fly in formation at high speeds, approach, disappear and regroup. In Vesco's view, the *Feuerball* was an early antecedent of the flying saucers.[15]

Vesco also documented the titanic industrial effort that the Third Reich made in 1944–45 in order not to succumb. In August 1944 Hitler turned planning and construction of new weapons over to the SS, whereupon Himmler appointed SS-*Gruppenführer* Hans Kammler as director of secret war production. Besides its own private research and testing centers, the SS now had full access to other governmental sites. As Allied strategic bombing intensified, huge underground installations were rapidly built, many with slave labor. These included the enormous underground complexes of Nordhausen and Kahla in the Harz-Thuringian Forest area. With two major tunnels a mile long connected by sixty-two transverse tunnels, the Mittelwerke factories at Dora near Nordhausen provided a total of twelve miles of underground installations. In February 1945 the famous V-weapons center at Peenemünde on the Baltic coast was partially evacuated to the neighboring village of Bleicherode Ost. Shortly before the German surrender, the Dora complex had begun the large-scale manufacture of V-2 rockets and V-1 flying bombs, while the Bleicherode site developed the giant rocket-torpedo A-9/A-10 to bomb the United States.[16]

The first connection between postwar flying saucers and Nazi fugitives in the Southern Hemisphere was made by Michael X. Barton in a couple of sensational books published in Los Angeles. His first book, *We Want You: Is Hitler Alive?* (1960), was based on the U-530 and U-977 stories in the *Police Gazette* articles of the early 1950s. Barton claimed that Hitler was in Argentina, where UFOs were being developed in secret underground installations by German scientists, and he also alluded to the existence of neo-Nazis in West Germany and Lincoln Rockwell's American Nazi Party in the United States. However, these UFOs were allegedly modeled on the silent "electro-magnetic" bell-shaped flying saucers built of copper at Vienna by Viktor Schauberger, an Austrian inventor, in 1940.[17] Barton's second book, *The German Saucer Story* (1968), described the Schriever-Habermohl and Bellonzo-Schriever-Miethe disks, concluding that German scientists were now busy assembling large-size flying disks in underground factories, comparable to the wartime facilities in Nordhausen and Bleicherode, in remote areas of South America, South Africa and possibly Antarctica.[18]

During the 1970s, Wilhelm Landig and Ernst Zündel, both neo-Nazi publishers and authors, blended these stories, hints and suggestions into a powerful and elaborate myth of Nazi resurgence. In novels and nonfiction works they described how, during the war, the Third Reich had succeeded in establishing secret bases in the Arctic and Antarctica. Naval convoys had brought labor, expertise and material to the icy wastes of the polar regions, where huge underground factories were built to produce the flying saucers for continued hostilities in the event of a Nazi defeat in Europe. The remoteness and inhospitality of the polar regions, surrounded by pack ice and stormy seas, is juxtaposed with a technocratic utopia. Here, throughout the postwar era, SS and Luftwaffe officers and soldiers live and work under strict discipline, while their ever more advanced saucers fly covert sorties across the world. The fearful nature of the Third Reich and the burden of its defeat are thus deflected in a science fiction vision of German technical and racial superiority as the huge saucers rise above the brilliant white snows of an icebound Shangri-La.

In 1971 Wilhelm Landig published *Götzen gegen Thule*, the first novel in his Thule trilogy. As we have already seen, this epic adventure of three German servicemen across the world at the end of the war combines Aryan myths from the works of Julius Evola, Herman Wirth and Edmund Kiß with Nazi revanchism. Subtitling his book "A Romance Full of Realities," Landig weaves Nazi UFOs into his narrative in an almost routine manner. The men are flown in a V-7 disk to Point 103, the secret base in Arctic Canada established by the Black Sun division of the SS. There are references to similar disk construction projects in Prague and Breslau. The men also witness a "manisola," another kind of disk powered by metaphysical, anti-gravitational energy. Equipped with extensive floodlighting, workshops and living quarters, the secret base is a large site with rocket-launching pads and caves excavated from the surrounding mountain range to serve as hangars for advanced aircraft.[19] The men then fly to Prague to evacuate Schriever, his colleagues and the disk from the BMW plant in the midst of a Czech uprising and Soviet tank advance.[20] Landig's first novel only mentioned these late wartime disks and a major Arctic base, but it clearly served to inspire a much-expanded Nazi UFO mythology from Ernst Zündel.

Zündel was well known as a German Canadian publisher in Toronto specializing in neo-Nazi literature for worldwide distribution, especially in West Germany. By the late 1970s, he was swamping the German Nazi underground with books, fliers, audiotapes and videos that glorified Hitler and the Third Reich, promoted Holocaust denial and drew attention to Allied war crimes. Born in the Black Forest in 1939, Ernst Christof Friedrich Zündel had trained as a graphic artist in Germany and emigrated to Canada in 1958. In 1961 he befriended the veteran French Canadian fascist Adrien Arcand, under whose influence he became an ardent German nationalist concerned with rehabilitating the Third Reich. He founded his own publishing house, Samisdat Publications in Toronto, to publish *The Auschwitz Lie* (1974), a translation of Thies Christophersen's notorious essay on Holocaust denial published in Germany the preceding year. An immediate best-seller among far right and anti-Zionist groups, the book established Samisdat as a flourishing underground Nazi publishing concern. By the summer of 1979, more than 100,000 copies of the book had been sold in five languages.[21]

Zündel now wanted to reach new audiences with a revamped and exciting image of Hitler and National Socialism. In the economic recession following the rise in oil prices in 1973–74, hopes for left-wing revolution were giving way to "New Age" ideas of spiritual renewal, fantasy and the occult. This period notably witnessed the publishing peak in the modern mysteriosophy of Nazi occultism. At this time, the books of Erich von Däniken, Robert Charroux, Raymond Drake and others about gods, ancient astronauts and flying saucers were achieving huge worldwide sales in several languages.[22] The widespread UFO phenomenon was increasingly being co-opted by religious sects in the English-speaking world such as the Aetherius Society as evidence of divine instructors.[23] Zündel exploited this new mood for the purposes of neo-Nazi revisionism. The Hitler survival myth, UFOs and secret postwar Nazi bases in Antarctica provided fantastic and sensational topics for his next Samisdat books. Eventually, in a powerful myth of national salvation and Hitler's messianic world role, he would claim that the Nazis had extraterrestrial origins or guidance.

His first offering was *UFOs: Unbekanntes Flugobjekt? Letzte Geheimwaffe des Dritten Reiches* (1974), written by Willibald Mattern, a German émigré living in Santiago de Chile. The book was an unashamed paean to the Third Reich with extensive quotes from Hitler's *Mein Kampf* and denunciations of a Jewish world conspiracy. But the Reich was apparently not dead. On 24 February 1945 Hitler had declared: "In this war there will be neither victors nor vanquished, only the dead and the survivors, but the Last Battalion will be German!" This postwar German battle force, active and ready to resume world combat, was directly linked to the postwar wave of flying saucers.[24] Recycling stories from the South American press, Ladislao Szabó's *Hitler esta vivo* (1947), and Michael X's *We Want You: Is Hitler Alive?* (1960), Mattern dwelled at length on the two U-boats that had surrendered at Mar del Plata months after the German surrender in the summer of 1945. Providing full crew lists, Mattern commented on the youth of the crew and on their lack of living relatives. U-530 and U-977 were supposedly just the stragglers of a ghost convoy of U-boats that had carried Hitler and other top Nazi leaders from Norway to permanent UFO bases in Antarctica.[25]

In 1975 Ernst Zündel next published an expanded English-language version of the Mattern text, followed by his own books on the German Antarctic theme, *Secret Nazi Polar Expeditions* (1978) and *Hitler am Südpol?* [Hitler at the South Pole?] (1979). The official German Antarctic Expedition of 1938–39 assumed a long-term strategic importance. Led by Captain Alfred Ritscher, a veteran Arctic explorer, this scientific expedition carried out extensive geographical, meteorological and zoological research in Queen Maud Land, which had formed part of the Norwegian territorial claim on Antarctica since 1930. Two large flying boats of the Dornier-Wal type flew daily from the expedition ship *Schwabenland*, taking over 11,000 photographs, occasionally landing, covering in all some 600,000 square kilometers and photomapping 350,000 square kilometers. The discovery of high alpine peaks (Mühlig-Hofmann Mountains) and a group of warm-water oases (Schirrmacher

Lakes) amid the frozen wastes was of particular interest as it suggested that there were hospitable microclimates within the icebound continent. At regular intervals of 20 kilometers, the airplanes dropped thousands of metal marker flags bearing swastikas to claim the newly surveyed territory for Germany, which was henceforth called Neuschwabenland. Congratulatory messages from Hitler and Hermann Goering greeted the expedition on its return to Hamburg in April 1939.[26]

Zündel and Mattern regarded this expedition as the first step in a far-reaching German policy to develop the polar continent into both a future refuge and a power base from which the Nazis could wage war even after defeat in Europe. More than this: the global phenomenon of flying saucer sightings, first noted in 1947, confirmed the presence of a Nazi colony with highly advanced technology in Antarctica. As the saucer projects in Bohemia and Silesia progressed and the military situation in Europe deteriorated, evacuation plans were put in hand. The saucer factories and test sites were dismantled and shipped to Antarctica by regular U-boat convoys. In this powerful myth of national resurrection, both authors hinted that the Germans had built up a gigantic yet secret complex of underground factories, saucer silos and armed garrisons in the warm oases of Neuschwabenland toward the end of the war.[27]

After the fall of the Third Reich, the secret Nazi colony in Antarctica continued to develop the flying saucers in complete security deep below the three-mile-thick icecap. With the advent of the worldwide UFO phenomenon, consternation grew in the victorious Allied camp. Both Mattern and Zündel cite "Operation Highjump," Admiral Richard E. Byrd's Antarctic mission with combined American, British and Soviet forces in 1946–47, as compelling evidence of the threat posed by the Nazi "Last Battalion." Byrd himself was quoted that the intention was "to break the last desperate resistance of Adolf Hitler . . . in the Queen Maud Land region, or to destroy him."[28] Bases were established, mapping missions flown and thousands of photographs taken. The German response was swift and deadly. In the vicinity of the secret Nazi base, American airplanes suffered instrumental failure. Within forty-eight hours, four aircraft had been lost. Byrd hastily aborted the operation, and the entire fleet returned to the United States.[29] Since 1947, Antarctic Nazi power has remained inviolate. Against a scenario of increasing racial chaos and economic catastrophe, thousands of Nazi UFOs will one day fly forth to restore German world power in an apocalyptic act of deliverance.[30]

Like Landig's first novel, the Samisdat titles quickly became hot tips among neo-Nazis in West Germany. Zündel also spiced his abridged English language version of the Mattern book with esoteric ideas, linking German millenarian myths with extraterrestrial visitations. Did the Nazis in Antarctica discover access to the "Inner Earth," long ago described in Nordic legends and sagas and assiduously cultivated by the Thule Society? Had the Nazis discovered long-hidden secrets on their expeditions to the Himalayas and Tibet? Perhaps extraterrestrials from other galaxies had assisted the Germans with the saucer projects, having recognized their receptiveness to the new technology. Perhaps this collaboration was based on some shared ancestral kinship. He recalled Reinhold Schmidt's UFO contactee account of a "Saturnian" spacecraft whose crew spoke German and behaved like German soldiers, and speculated whether the German nation was indeed a colony of Saturn, long since settled on Earth. Why were the Germans so "different"? Could this explain why the Germans always excel as soldiers, engineers and technologists? Was Hitler planted on this planet to pull back Western civilization from the brink of degenerate self-extinction?[31]

Back in Vienna, Landig swiftly elaborated these ideas in *Wolfszeit um Thule* (1980), the second action-packed novel in his Thule trilogy. As indicated in chapter 7, the book describes the voyage of a huge "phantom convoy" of German U-boats from Norway to Antarctica in May 1945. The earlier Arctic base, Point 103, is destroyed, and all the men and materiel are evacuated. V-7 flying saucers accompany the convoy as it travels down into the South Atlantic.[32] From Bouvet Island, midway between the Cape of Good Hope and the Antarctic mainland, most of the German U-boats proceed to Neuschwabenland, the 600,000 square kilometer German Antarctic territory formerly claimed by the Ritscher expedition of 1938–39.[33] A returning eyewitness describes how, in this enormous land mass the size of Germany, the forces of the Black Sun are building an impregnable military fortress, backed by the miracle weapons and flying saucers of the Third Reich. The secret bases are concentrated in the area bounded by the Wohlthat Massif, the Conrad Mountains and the Ritscher Peak near the warm-water Schirrmacher Lakes. This southern successor of Point 103, far larger and impregnable, will serve as the "last German Battalion" in a continuing standoff with the (temporarily) victorious Allies.[34]

The new Antarctic bases remain veiled in mystery as Landig's tale then follows the remaining German submarine to Argentina, where a small commando group is put ashore at night by rubber boat on the Rio de la Plata. The historical record is matched by the surrender of U-530 a few days later in July 1945, followed by U-977, another straggler of the "phantom convoy."[35] The three men then travel from Buenos Aires in friendly Argentina to La Paz in Bolivia. Contacts bring them southward to a large underground factory on the west side of the Andes in Chile, known as Mime's Smithy, located within the huge, prehistoric tunnel systems earlier discovered by Edmund Kiß. Here, several hundred engineers and scientists under German command are developing the V-7 flying saucers, with which regular contact is maintained with Point 211, the Antarctic base.[36] Landig alludes to further secret German bases in Brazil, including one colony at the headwaters of the Rio Purus. This was the remnant of a wartime Waffen-SS expeditionary force of two thousand men, who landed by U-boats in 1942 with plans to seize the Panama Canal.[37] In early 1947 the colony at Mime's Smithy exults in the rapid repulsion of Admiral Byrd's military invasion by their comrades in Neuschwabenland.[38]

The mythical power of these stories of German saucer bases in the Andes and Antarctica was wholly dependent on worldwide curiosity about UFOs throughout from the early 1950s through the 1970s. During this period, thousands of UFO sightings over North and South America, Europe and Asia were reported. Photographs of clearly recognizable saucer craft were published in magazines and books.[39] The Cold War, the superpower space race, and a plentiful supply of science fiction created a demand for such stories in the press. Recurrent scares of government cover-ups regarding the UFOs—did the authorities know much more than they were telling?—created a psychic space within which the UFO phenomenon could be linked with conspiracy theory. In this view, both the Americans and Russians were anxious to deny that the UFOs were man-made craft operated by renegade German Nazi forces. Nazi UFOs linked with Antarctica supplied a powerful myth of German revanchism against the hegemony of the superpowers.

The idea of Nazi UFOs caught on fast. The Belfast-born British author W. A. Harbinson wrote a best-selling novel, *Genesis* (1980), on the theme, which reprinted five times in three years.[40] An American aviation genius emigrates in 1935 to the Third Reich to profit from the resources of a totalitarian state. Nazi slave labor working day and night hews out the huge underground factories of the Harz and Thuringia, where his amoral thirst for technical achievement knows no limits. Backed by the SS, he constructs a huge saucer in the enormous rock tunnels at Kahla. As the war closes in, trains daily transport slaves and materiel to Kiel, where they disappear to the "wilderness." When the Third Reich finally collapses, the ruthless genius finally escapes with top SS fugitives Hans Kammler and Artur Nebe to their long-prepared fortress in Antarctica. As the postwar years pass, a New Order state arises, manned by "implanted" human robots, a secret scientific utopia rid of all humanity. The concentration camps, SS guards, whips and barking dogs lie far in the past; futuristic flying saucers flashing across the snowy peaks are a potent symbol of victorious fascist inhumanity.[41]

During the 1980s the mythos was elaborated by further neo-Nazi publications on miracle weapons, Nazi UFOs and secret German bases in Antarctica by the Hugin-Gesellschaft and Teut-Verlag in the small town of Wetter in the Ruhr. D. H. Haarmann's three-volume *Geheime Wunderwaffen* [Secret Miracle Weapons] (1983–85) dilated on the by now familiar topics of the Ritscher expedition, the "phantom convoy" and Operation Highjump. Further Allied Antarctic invasions had been mounted in 1955–56 and again under cover of the International Geophysical Year in 1958, when atomic weapons were used in vain against the hidden German enemy. Haarmann saw the Antarctic Treaty of December 1959 as a ploy of the United Nations Organisation, conceived in 1942 to achieve Allied war aims against the Axis Powers as well as a nefarious world conspiracy.[42] His subsequent volumes took up the themes of worldwide saucer sightings in the 1950s, especially the (historical) incident when seven disks flew over the White House in Washington on 20 July 1952, interpreted by Haarmann as a show of German capabilities, and Reinhold Schmidt's encounter with a German-speaking saucer crew in November 1957. Haarmann also linked UFO cover-ups and the extraterrestrial hypothesis with a "secret government" conspiracy of invisible elites such as the Council on Foreign Relations.[43]

This conspiracy not only concerned a blackout on Nazi resurgence but on alternative energy technology. How else could the modern saucers execute such astonishing feats of speed, acceleration, rapid changes of direction with soundless flight and the complete absence of exhaust? Here, the wartime work of Viktor Schauberger, the Viennese inventor, on electromagnetic flying saucers is cited as the prototype of antigravitational power. Evidently, the secret German saucer industry is using free "implosive" energy from the earth's gravitational and magnetic fields rather than the "explosive" technology of fossil fuels with all their harmful ecological consequences. Knowledge of the Nazi saucers and their free energy power is thus being suppressed by a (Jewish) conspiracy of banks, oil and automobile industries in the postwar world economy. Haarmann even considers the mystical sources of such "implosive" technology, citing Miguel Serrano's speculation that the SS found the Cathar Grail treasure in southern France, an idea that connects with Erich Halik's thoughts on "manisolas" and Julius Evola's idea of the Grail as an Aryan-Nordic mystery tradition.[44] Such a world conspiracy against alternative energy would become a major theme of New Age literature in the 1990s.

Richard Schepmann, the publisher of Teut-Verlag, is the son of the former SA staff officer Wilhelm Schepmann. In 1983 he was sentenced to a six-month suspended sentence and heavy fine for inciting racial hatred. The Hugin-Gesellschaft and Teut-Verlag continued to present revanchist German nationalism in an esoteric context, introducing the first volume of Miguel Serrano's "Esoteric Hitlerism" trilogy to a German readership in 1987. Serrano had ready access to Spanish-language literature in South America bearing on the Hitler survival myth and Nazi *OVNIs* (UFOs) cultivated by neo-Nazi groups in Chile. Through Serrano, the Nazi UFO subculture was also able to extend its esoteric references to the history of secret societies, the Grail, Templars and Rosicrucians. Hugin's program also included other Nazi UFO publications, such as the two-volume work *Deutsche Flugscheiben und U-Boote überwachen die Weltmeere* (1988–89) by O. Bergmann and a complete dossier of press cuttings on UFO sightings from the 1950s to the present. The millennial nationalist ideology behind all publications was evident from an announcement in large print: "German Volk awake! You are at the threshold of an incomparable golden age, not at the end of your long history."[45]

Nazi UFO mythology has a serial character, whereby earlier details are constantly elaborated into new concepts and ideas. In the early 1990s, the Austrians Norbert Jürgen-Ratthofer and Ralf Ettl developed new Nazi UFO myths involving ancient Babylon, Vril energy and extraterrestrial civilization in the solar system of Aldebaran. These colorful ideas are integral elements of a dualist Marcionite religion propagated by Ralf Ettl through his Tempelhofgesellschaft (Temple Society) in Vienna, identified as a secret successor to the historic Templars, who had absorbed Gnostic and heretical ideas in the Levant. Marcion established his own religious community in Rome in the second century A.D., whereupon sister churches spread through the east and west of the empire. Marcion's theology was dualistic. In the gospel he found a God who is goodness and love, and who desires faith and love from men. In the Old Testament, he saw a just, stern, jealous and wrathful God who requires obedience, fear and righteous conduct from his servants. Marcion taught that man was created out of matter by the just and wrathful god and fell under the curse of the Demiurge, until a higher God took pity on the wretched race of mankind and sent his Son down to earth to redeem men.

This strict distinction between the Christian God of the gospel and the Jewish God of the Old Testament was the basis of Marcion's doctrine. Marcion championed Paul, who alone was supposed to understand the gospel. Paul opposed the original apostles with their Judaistic doctrines. Marcion followed in Paul's footsteps, setting aside the spurious gospels, purging the Gospel of Luke from judaizing interpolations, and restoring the Pauline epistles. Marcion taught that all should put their trust in the good God and renounce their allegiance to the Demiurge. The true Christian should shun all things sensual and perishable, which are the works of the evil Demiurge. God redeems only the spirit of man, as all matter perishes (an influence from contemporary Gnosticism). The Marcionite churches enjoyed a golden age between A.D. 150 and 250, when they represented a vital challenge to the Church.

Thereafter, they declined, with many Marcionites going over to the Manichaeans in the east and providing impulses for the Gnostic Paulicians, Bogomils and ultimately the Cathars in the west. By identifying the Jews as evil antagonists in a dualist cosmology, modern Marcionites are typically anti-Semitic.

Jürgen-Ratthofer and Ralf Ettl claim that Rudolf von Sebottendorff discovered old texts or oral traditions on his travels in the Middle East relating to this dualist rejection of El Shaddai (Jahve), the god of the Old Testament, whom Jesus identified as the devil (John 8:44). Sebottendorff also allegedly found Persian and Babylonian references to a millennial battle between good and evil, which inspired his (spurious) book *Der interkosmische Weltenkampf* (1919). Sebottendorff was supposed to be acquainted with the prophecy of the "Third Sargon" by the Babylonian seeress Sajaha (c. 650 B.C.), which told of terrible woes and the inversion of all values until the avenging emperor would arrive from the north (Midnight) and destroy all evil by fire. Recalling that Christ told the Jews that the Kingdom of God would be taken from them and given to a people who would produce its fruit (Matthew 21:43), Sebottendorff learned that Jesus later told Germans serving in a Roman legion that they were the chosen people.[46] In Jürgen-Ratthofer's fictional account, Sebottendorff was the first individual to understand that this cosmic battle between the forces of darkness and light would reach its climax in the twentieth century with the advent of the Age of Aquarius.

In August 1917, according to Jürgen-Ratthofer and Ettl, Rudolf von Sebottendorff, Karl Haushofer, the medium Maria Orsic from Zagreb and the pilot Lothar Waiz held a meeting with the old prelate Gernot of the Societas Templi Marcioni at a café in Vienna. Their discussions turned on astrology and apocalyptic predictions in Indian, German and Babylonian traditions. Gernot was highly impressed and invited Sebottendorff to visit the secret estate of his Templar order known as the "Die Herren vom Schwarzen Stein" (DHvSS) [Lords of the Black Stone] at Marktschellenberg in Bavaria. The DHvSS was supposedly founded by the Knight Commander Hubertus Koch in 1221 as a Marcionite Templar order. Its dualist and Gnostic "Babylonian" doctrine told of the dominion of evil on earth and the battle between light and El Shaddai based on the revelations of the goddess Ishtar. The Black Sun is the divine source of energy accessible to initiates through a hierarchy of spiritual intermediaries. Through the DHvSS, Sebottendorff understood that Marcionite anti-Judaist teachings ultimately came from the much older Babylonian doctrine common to all Aryan peoples. The cosmic challenge of the age demanded the defeat of El Shaddai and the Jews.[47]

Jürgen-Ratthofer and Ettl next latched onto the Vril references in the occult Nazi mythology of Louis Pauwels and Jacques Bergier. These, it will be recalled, go back to Willy Ley's report of a Vril Society in Berlin. German researchers have recently established that such a group did exist in association with the astrological publisher Wilhelm Becker. This wholly obscure "Reichsarbeitsgemeinschaft 'Das Kommende Deutschland'" published a short brochure *Vril: Die kosmische Urkraft* (1930), which described the Atlanteans as possessors of a spiritual "dynamo-technology," superior to the mechanistic notions of modern science. Based on Vril energy, this technology also enabled the Egyptians and Aztecs to build their pyramids. The brochure claims that this knowledge of the ancients should now be applied for the benefit of modern mankind. The group's second brochure, *Weltdynamismus* (1930), rejected explosive technology and spoke of the release of free energy. A chapter headed "The World Apple" described a bisected apple as a map of the universal free energy field. It is quite probable that Willy Ley's record of the Vril group recalled this very detail as a meditational object.[48]

In Jürgen-Ratthofer and Ettl's account, this group of esotericists concerned with Atlantis and free energy becomes a powerful UFO research agency. Between 1917 and 1919, Sebottendorff built up the Germanenorden and the Thule Society as true to secret Aryan-Babylonian doctrine. When the Thule was involved in the Bavarian revolution of May 1919, a separate section for spiritual and esoteric studies was founded as the Vril Society. In December 1919 an inner group of the Thule and Vril held a joint meeting at Ramsau near Berchtesgaden, where the medium Maria Orsic presented transcripts in an old Templar script of communications she had received telepathically. These proved to be written in Sumerian, the language of the founders of the oldest Babylonian culture. These channeled communications allegedly came from the planet Sumi-Er in the solar system of Aldebaran, the brightest star in the constellation of Taurus, sixty-eight light years away from earth. Jürgen-Ratthofer and Ettl claim that the DHvSS and its modern successor, the Vril Society, received mediumistic confirmation that the Sumerians were a colony of superior beings sent from Aldebaran to earth 500 million years ago. The Aldebaran language not only resembled Sumerian but also German, since both peoples shared the same Aldebaran ancestry.[49]

With mounting excitement, the Vril Society was supposed to have examined the old archives of the DHvSS and concluded that Hubertus Koch and his followers had established esoteric contact with the Aldebaran people back in the Middle Ages. The apparition of the Babylonian goddess Isais was possibly even a visit by an Aldebaran woman. The grand seal of the DHvSS showing a winged bull clearly reflected Aldebaran's location in Taurus, while Isais was the Aldebaran empress. All the Aldebaran traditions indicated "a kind of National Socialism on a theocratic basis." The Vril Society concluded that this exclusive contact between the German Marcionite order, themselves and Aldebaran signified that the Aldebaran people were "the Germans in the sign of Taurus" and thus allies in the great cosmic battle against the Jewish forces of darkness.[50] In fulfillment of this esoteric alliance across the galaxy, Maria Orsic next received channeled instructions for the construction of a time-travel machine. A leading member of the Vril, Dr. W. O. Schumann, pioneered the development of electromagnetic fields through rotating disks, and a prototype was constructed near Munich in 1922. Over the following decade, this research and development led to an entire range of German flying saucers based on the principle of anti-gravitational levitation.[51]

In June 1934 Lothar Waiz flew the first RFZ 1 (Rundflugzeug) at Brandenburg. The stimulus of military innovation quickly led to highly advanced craft. Thereafter, the Thule Society took a hand by establishing the SS Development Department E-IV for advanced saucer technology. These larger and much more powerful craft took the series name "Haunebu." Driven by a "Thule-Tachyonator," the Haunebu I had a 25-meter diameter, a speed of 4,800 kilometers/hour, a range of eighteen hours and carried a crew of nine men. Developed in November 1943, the Haunebu II was slightly larger and could travel at 6,000 kilometers/hour for fifty-five hours. The massive Haunebu III had a diameter of 71 meters and could reach a speed of 40,000 kilometers/hour with a range of eight weeks, carrying a crew of thirty-two men. The Schumann group produced two smaller saucers, Vril-1 and 2, as fighters. Jürgen-Ratthofer and Ettl reproduce detailed technical drawings, ostensibly from the SS department E-IV and Schumann's Vril group. Apparently seven craft of the Haunebu II type were built, one each of the other Haunebu types, and seventeen Vril-1 craft.[52] In late 1944, the SS E-IV also designed the Andromeda vessel, 139 meters in length and 30 meters high. Powered by four "Thule-Tachyonators" and four "Schumann-Levitators," this long-distance spaceship could transport a Haunebu II and two Vril 1 saucers in its internal hangars. This huge cigar-shaped mother ship and its accompanying saucers were supposed to be responsible for George Adamski's famous sighting in California in 1952.[53]

Through their elaborate mythology of Sumero-Aldebaran links, Jürgen-Ratthofer and Ettl attribute German flying saucer technology to semi-divine guidance from extraterrestrial civilization. They also claim that National Socialism and anti-Semitism are closely bound up with channeled communications from a highly advanced society ethnically related to the Germans and following a political model similar to the Third Reich. According to these communications, the population of the Aldebaran solar system has long been organized on racial lines. The master race of "light godmen" (Alpha-Aldebarans) lives on the planet Sumi-Er, while the lesser races are confined to the planet Sumi-An. These racial differences arose through the colonization of former planets with different climates. Atomic wars also created mutations among the colonists into "apemen." (A commentary adds that the ancient Assyrians thought Negroes were the result of a prehistoric conflagration and bemoans the intellectual decline of America due to racial mixing.) Aldebaran is also supposed to be at war with the empires of Capella and Regulus, culturally inferior but with larger populations. (Again the commentary speculates whether earth has also received colonies from these solar systems, thus accounting for the white, yellow and black races on earth).[54] The idea that the Germans are the direct descendants of Alpha-Aldebarans simply translates the "ario-heroic" godmen of Lanz von Liebenfels's Ariosophy into the modern science-fiction idiom of planetary colonization from a distant star.

Jürgen-Ratthofer and Ettl also articulate a sci-fi millenarianism, whereby the Nazis are supposed to have sent flying saucer missions to seek extraterrestrial support for the Axis against the Allies, even years after the latter's victory. On Christmas 1943, the Vril and Thule held a major conference at the Baltic resort of Kolberg (now Kołobrzeg), where desperate military measures were discussed. Vril staffs were now working on a spaceship that could switch into another dimension and thus reach Aldebaran, sixty-eight light-years away. After discussions with Hitler and Himmler, the Vril group launched an advanced Vril-Odin (Vril-7 or Vril-8) saucer in early 1945 into the "transdimensional canal," which enables travel at 900,000 kilometers/second (three times the speed of light). After a voyage lasting only several weeks (on board), Vril-Odin is supposed to have reached the Aldebaran solar system in 1967. The Aldebaran regime then dispatched an enormous interstellar armada consisting of 280 battle cruisers of various classes, ranging from 1.5 to 6 kilometers in length and capable of carrying between 4 and 810 flying saucers apiece. Depending on its speed after emerging from the "transdimensional canal" in the asteroid belt, this armada is to arrive on earth sometime between 1992 and 2005 to resume the Second World War.[55]

Two Nazi-UFO videos are widely circulated in the neo-Nazi and New Age milieus today. *UFO—Das Dritte Reich schlägt zurück?* [UFO—The Third Reich Strikes Back?] tells the story of the Black Sun, illustrated with reliefs and statues from ancient Babylon. The film also shows impressive images of recent sightings of UFOs with German markings, compared with technical drawings of Haunebu and Habermohl-Schriever saucer designs. It ends with a pathetic account of the joint German-Japanese last-ditch mission in April

1945 to seek military aid from Mars. After an eight and a half month voyage, the Haunebu III lands on Mars in January 1946, only to find the deserted pyramid city and "Face," signs of a bygone higher civilization. "What disappointment must these men have felt, when they realized that all was in vain!"[56] The other video, also written by Jürgen-Ratthofer, *UFO—Geheimnisse des Dritten Reichs* [UFO—Secrets of the Third Reich], covers the Thule-Vril story with its background in Sebottendorff's meeting with the Marcionite Templars. The Thule created the secret society of the Black Sun within the SS. Actors stage the mediumistic séances, the young Hitler is shown studying in a library and American UFO experts are interviewed. The line between archival sources and fiction is constantly blurred, giving the impression of a documentary. Where did the German saucers go at the end of the war? One solution, we learn, is that they traveled back in time through the "transdimensional canal" to safety in ancient Babylon, where the German crews were feted as "white gods" from another world.[57]

Jürgen-Ratthofer and Ettl's books were first published by Michael Dämbock, who edits the magazine *Pen Tuisko*, "letters for German pagans," as a mixture of Germanic mythology, runelore and astrology. Jürgen-Ratthofer has published further books on time machines and the Aldebaran galactic empire. His most important recent book is *Lichtreiche auf Erden* [The Reichs of Light on Earth], in which he speculates on an alliance between Iraq and the Greater German Reich during the 1991 Gulf War. As Iraq lies in Mesopotamia, its elite are also descended from the Sumerians and thus related to the Germans. As German territory was a nuclear hostage to the Allies after 1945, the Nazi UFOs could only pursue a limited clandestine war against selected targets. Meanwhile, the Cold War and the Strategic Defense Initiative (SDI) can only be understood as the postwar Allied response to this threat. Nevertheless, only the Nazi UFOs, the "Reichs of Light," have prevented an atomic war being fought in Europe as well as in Korea, Vietnam, the Falklands and the Persian Gulf.[58] The Nazi UFO books of Jürgen-Ratthofer and Ettl are widely distributed by the Andromeda mail-order bookshop in Nuremberg, which issues monthly catalogs in which similar material is listed alongside the literature of conspiracy theory, channeling, New Age spirituality and redemption.

In the mid-1990s this quasi-ariosophical lore of Aldebaran-German linkage penetrated the international UFO scene. The best-selling books of the leading German conspiracy theorist, Jan van Helsing, recapitulated the imaginary history of Vril flying saucers, the settlement of Aldebaran colonists in Sumeria, and the German mission to Aldebaran.[59] Through UFO conferences, Helsing's revelations have encouraged a new wave of Aldebaran channels. In his new book *Unternehmen Aldebaran* [Operation Aldebaran] (1997), Helsing describes how a Bavarian family recalled their contacts with extraterrestrials, involving abductions and implants, while under hypnotic regression. Karin and Rainer Feistle describe a UFO commander showing them enormous "embryo farms" for the breeding of a "new race" that will secure mankind's future.[60] Helsing uses these hints to elaborate on human history. Arriving on earth 735,000 years ago, Aldebaran colonists bred "slaves" for menial tasks (Helsing uses Lanz von Liebenfels's term *Tschandale*), but these inferiors revolted and mixed with other races. When the Aldebarans revisited earth much later, they saw that the race-mixing slaves had caused wars, revolution and political upheaval. The Aldebarans decided to breed up the race on earth by means of the Germans as their closest relatives. They therefore helped the Germans develop advanced technology during the 1930s, while the Feistles' testimony indicates the ongoing Aldebaran project for a German master race.[61] This tableau involving the revolt of inferiors, harmful race mixing and the creation of an Aldebaran-German elite reflect the updating of Ariosophy through a modern mythology of semi-divine extraterrestrial guidance.

Anglo-American contributions to Nazi UFO mythology also exist: witness the success of W. A. Harbinson's thrillers in the "Projekt Saucer" series. In June 1977, the U.K. independent television company Anglia broadcast a spoof television program *Alternative 3* about colonies on Mars erected to avoid ecological catastrophe on earth. Nearly twenty years on, Jim Keith, the veteran U.S. conspiracy theorist, elaborated a complex account of how German scientists and industrialists, brought to America under Operation Paperclip after World War II, may have already established secret bases on Mars pending the evacuation of elites from a polluted and congested earth. (The secret nature of this scenario recalls the clandestine Nazi buildup in Antarctica.) Although carried out under U.S. auspices, this project represents the perpetuation and eventual realization of Third Reich policy for the acquisition of German *Lebensraum* (living space). Recalling postwar German involvement in varied forms of totalitarian control such as intelligence, security, psychiatry and genetic engineering, Keith wonders whether the Nazis are still implementing schemes for their final triumph "by constructing bases on Mars or the moon to carry the ancient Grail of Aryan racial purity away from what they conceive as a cataclysm-doomed Earth."[62]

Actual Anglo-American identification with the manifest German mission of the Nazi UFOs is rarer. The German Research Project at Gorman, California, directed by Henry Stevens has published excellent documentation on Nazi UFOs, but eulogies of the SS, references to the Dark Power (Jews), the New World Order and the sham of democracy indicate a sympathy for the

Third Reich.[63] The Nazi UFO myth has also found support in the British far right. For example, Tim Hepple (b. 1967) joined the "Political Soldier" faction of the National Front in 1984, before moving on to the British National Party in 1986. Although a university music student with a middle-class background, Hepple was a hardened street fighter and organized the Dewsbury race riot in June 1989.[64] In 1992 he changed his name to Matthews and began to infiltrate the British ufology scene.[65] After initially taking the prevailing line that UFOs were extraterrestrial in origin, he supported the thesis of man-made UFOs with a paean to the pioneering achievements of the Third Reich. Here Matthews cited the delta wing designs of Alexander Lippisch (1893–1976), the "black triangles" (prototypes of "stealth" aircraft) of Reimar and Walter Horten, "foo fighters," and the flying disks of Schriever, Habermohl and Miethe.[66] Matthews's enthusiasm for the Nazi origins of flying saucers suggests an ideological allegiance beyond technical admiration.

Flying saucers are ambiguous. C. G. Jung interpreted their mandala form as a symbol of the self and absolute wholeness.[67] But radiant steel surfaces and lightning speeds also suggest an aesthetic of armored, invincible identity. This image of the flying saucers may reflect deep-seated fascist notions of technology, gender and sexuality. Fascination with technology was a key element in Italian futurism, whose founder, F. T. Marinetti, looked forward to the melding of man and machine in a world of speed, violence and contempt for woman. "The Futurist hero was the man of iron, the aviator and the engineer."[68] After the First World War, Ernst Jünger celebrated a sleek aesthetic of the machine, military technology and efficiency through his literary works and photo essays. Shells, tanks and aircraft—metallic, armored and high velocity—are threatening projections of symmetrical order upon a sensual, vegetative natural world.[69] Nazi flying saucer mythology certainly shares in this symbolism, reflected by the glittering, lifeless, icy wastes of Antarctica, where all-male military communities labor in saucer silos to reconquer the world.

Armed with this symbolism, Nazi UFO mythology always identifies the Germans as the master race. In its first period, 1950 to 1970, chief emphasis was laid on the myth of Nazi survival, German technical prowess and the construction of miracle craft and secret bases in Antarctica and South America. These tales served a consoling function for the defeat of the Third Reich and division of postwar Germany while promising a revanchist Nazi millennium. But the UFOs are also vehicles for a futuristic Aryan cult. In the period 1970–85, Wilhelm Landig and Ernst Zündel embroider the technical scenario with Gnostic Thulean-Jewish struggles and the Black Sun mythos. By the 1990s, Miguel Serrano, Norbert Jürgen-Ratthofer, Ralf Ettl and Jan van Helsing present Nazi UFOs within a new Ariosophy of semi-divine Aryan origins, along with channeling, conspiracy theories and New Age beliefs. Sumerian and Templar secrets, wise extraterrestrial guides, spiritual purity and the dazzling perfection of spinning luminous saucers offer positive archetypal symbols. These not only erase the cruel memory of the Third Reich, but suggest that the Nazis were interesting, spiritual people. Such is the power of UFO mythology to reconfigure Nazism for the twenty-first century.

9

Miguel Serrano and Esoteric Hitlerism

A NEW HITLER CULT with extraordinary mythological force was articulated by the Chilean diplomat, explorer and poet Miguel Serrano from the late 1970s onwards. Stimulated by the "Nazi Mysteries," Serrano's neo-Nazi mythology traces its roots to his wartime enthusiasm for Hitler, anti-Semitism, and initiation into a Chilean esoteric order practicing meditation, yoga and Tantrism. His Gnostic doctrine describes the celestial origin of the Aryans, the bearers of divine light, and a global conspiracy against them by an evil demiurge, the regent of our planet and all base matter. The Hindu-Nordic inspiration of Serrano is evident in his assimilation of the Aryans' polar home, Sanskrit terminology and yoga, together with runes and Germanic myths. Serrano's cult is especially indebted to the Jungian theory of archetypes, and like Savitri Devi he identifies Hitler as an avatar.

Far from being an eccentric phenomenon, Miguel Serrano's mystical Nazism is a major example of the Thulean mythology's successful migration to South America in the postwar period. When Mussolini and Franco were in power, parties and movements in Latin America combined native populism with fascist models, as in the regimes of Juan Perón in Argentina and Getúlio Vargas in Brazil. But even though Chile and Argentina had sizable minorities of German descent, prewar Nazi organizations in these countries were relatively small. Arriving in large numbers after 1945, Nazi fugitives sought a new myth of *völkisch* identity relating to German settlement in Latin America. According to Serrano's myth, the Nazis' flight recapitulated prehistoric voyages of discovery made by Aryan ancestors. The homeless Nazis could thus cast themselves as heirs of an original Aryan population in Chile and Argentina. The Nazi fugitive organizations found support among native elites, businessmen and admirers of Hitler and Mussolini. Given traditional racist attitudes toward the Indian and mixed-race populations, Chileans and Argentinians of European descent were also drawn to myths of Nordic origin. The mulitiracial composition of Latin America thus interacted with anti-Semitic Nazi racism to elaborate a new Thulean myth of Aryan settlement in the Southern Hemisphere.[1]

Miguel Juaquin Diego del Carmen Serrano Fernández was born in Santiago on 10 September 1917. On the maternal side he is a descendant of the countesses of Sierra Bella, whose extensive estates lay in the south around Las Condes. The Serrano family itself was noted for gifted poets, political idealists and diplomats. His mother, Berta Fernández Fernández, died when he was five; three years later he lost his father, Diego Serrano Manterola. Miguel was brought up, together with two younger brothers and a sister, by his paternal grandmother, Fresia Manterola de Serrano, in a townhouse in Santiago and at a romantic seventeenth-century country mansion on the foot slopes of the Andes in the Claro Valley. From 1929 to 1934, Miguel Serrano was educated at the Internado Nacional Barros Arana. This school was noted for its German affiliation since the influx of Prussian army instructors and educators to Chile following Bismarck's support of Chile in the Great Pacific War (1879–82) against Peru and Bolivia. Serrano attributes his admiration of all things German to this education. He also traces his blue eyes and fair hair through an Aryan bloodline to the Basque and Cro-Magnon races of northern Spain.[2]

At school, Serrano and his friends formed literary circles initially innocent of politics. However, in the late 1930s, a time of political polarization in Chile, his close friend, the budding poet Hector Barreto, joined the socialists out of sympathy with the poor but was killed at the age of eighteen in a brawl with uniformed right-wing Chilean Nazis (Nacistas). Serrano reacted to this tragedy by embracing Marxist sympathies and began writing for the left-wing journals *Sobre la marcha*, *La Hora* and *Frente Popular*. His diplomat-poet uncle, Vicente Huidobro, strongly encouraged Serrano to join the Republicans in the Spanish Civil War. However, Serrano soon rejected Marx and became disillusioned with the communists in Chile, owing to their shadowy connections to Moscow and even to the American CIA.[3]

He was then drawn to the Nacistas (Movimento Nacional Socialista de Chile) following their abortive coup on 5 September 1938, when sixty-two young supporters were shot dead while they occupied the social security building near the presidential palace La Moneda in Santiago. Originally founded in 1932, this Chilean Nazi Party was modeled on European fascist parties, particularly the National Socialist German Workers' Party. Led by the mercurial German-Chilean firebrand, Jorge González von Mareés (1900–1962), the party held a special appeal for the German-descended people of the southern part of central Chile but also recruited members from other sectors of the population.[4]

Like other fascist parties, the Nacistas organized mass marches of its uniformed stormtroopers, giving Nazi salutes, singing battle songs and bearing flags and insignia. The charismatic personality of *El Jefe* (leader) was a potent factor in the movement. Serrano was deeply impressed by the male comradeship, the staunch patriotism and the fascist mythos of the Chilean Nazis. Their heroic martyrdom in the massacre of September 1938 overcame his revulsion at the murder of his best friend. In July 1939 Serrano publicly associated himself with the Nacistas (now renamed Vanguarda Popular Socialista), began writing for the party journal *Trabajo*, and accompanied the leader on speaking tours across the country.[5]

As Chile remained neutral at the outbreak of the Second World War, the Nacistas were at liberty to express their solidarity with the Axis powers. However, the reformed party was losing its fire, while González von Mareés, chastened by his term of imprisonment after the failed coup, was now conciliatory toward liberal-bourgeois politicians. Following the German invasion of the Soviet Union, Serrano threw himself directly into pro-Nazi propaganda with the publication of his own fortnightly political and literary review, *La Nueva Edad*, from July 1941 onward.

Among the regular contributors were René Arriagada of the national daily *El Mercurio*, who was interested in Oswald Spengler, General Francisco Javier Díaz, a devoted supporter of Hitler, and Hugo Gallo, the cultural attaché at the Italian Embassy. Articles ranged from discussions of German philosophy and ideology to epic accounts of German military campaigns and the destruction of Soviet communism. The Third Reich was consistently glorified. Serrano cultivated close links with the Nazi personnel at the German Embassy in Santiago which supported his periodical. From an SS man, formerly adjutant to the director of the Reich Chancellery in Berlin, Serrano learned about extensive Nazi documentation on the power of secret societies, discovered by Alfred Rosenberg in old Masonic lodges in Paris after the Occupation. This material was also published and discussed in *La Nueva Edad*.[6]

These early hints of conspiracy were powerfully reinforced when Serrano was introduced to the myth of Jewish world conspiracy in the autumn of 1941. Two Chilean artists, readers of his magazine, brought him a Spanish-language edition of the *Protocols of the Elders of Zion*. This discovery marked a crucial point in the development of Serrano's Nazism. Prior to 1941, neither the Chilean Nazis nor Serrano had embraced anti-Semitism as part of their radical nationalist and fascist ideology, which saw its enemy primarily in Marxist communism. Now, at a single reading, Serrano became utterly convinced that the Jews were behind a worldwide plot to subvert all order, tradition and national independence. On the basis of these beliefs, Serrano became a fervent anti-Semite and began publishing material from the *Protocols* in his magazine beginning in early November 1941.[7] In the later, Gnostic elaboration of his

Hitler cult, Serrano transmutes the Jewish world conspiracy into an evil demiurge, the lord of darkness who rules over our fallen planet.

Besides this apocalyptic anti-Semitism, Serrano mixed his Nazi politics with ideas from esotericism, Hinduism and kundalini yoga. In late 1941, Hugo Gallo suggested to Serrano that the war could also be fought on other, inner planes and introduced him to a Chilean esoteric order. Owing allegiance to a mysterious Brahmanical elite supposedly based in the Himalayas, this order had been founded by a German immigrant, "F. K.," to Chile around the turn of the century. The order practiced techniques of ritual magic, tantric and kundalini yoga for the achievement of mystical unions and visions. The master of the order emphasized the importance of the subtle or astral body, which could be awakened and activated through rituals and spiritual exercises. By means of yoga meditation, the serpent power (*kundalini*) was drawn up from the base of the spine through the several energy centers (*chakras*) of the subtle body to the crown of the head, in order to awaken the superconscious ego. This ascent experience was linked with Nietzschean notions of the will to power and fascist activism. Deeply impressed by the master's esoteric wisdom, Serrano was initiated into this mystico-martial order in February 1942.[8]

The order related its esoteric spirituality directly to Hitler and Nazism. While the remote Brahmanical leadership of the order indicated its Vedic-Aryan origins and doctrine, cult members were united in an admiration for Hitler as a savior of the Aryan (Indo-European) race. Astral travel and higher states of consciousness were regarded as the ancestral heritage of the pure-blooded ("twice-born") Aryans. The master often made oracular statements concerning Hitler and the global conflict he had unleashed in the Second World War: Hitler was described as an initiate, a being of boundless and unprecedented willpower (*shudibudishvabhaba*). He had voluntarily incarnated on earth as a highly developed being (*boddhisatva*) in order to overcome the dark age, or Kali Yuga. On several occasions, the master established astral contact with Hitler: once they conversed about German colonial claims, another time the master saw him at his Eagle's Nest high upon the Kehlstein at Berchtesgaden. After the war had ended, the master encountered Hitler deep inside the earth, sure evidence that he was alive and had survived the Berlin bunker.[9] In the light of these revelations, Serrano regarded Adolf Hitler and the mass cult of the Third Reich as archetypal forces whose active intervention in history promised a qualitative leap into a new era.

After the defeat of the Third Reich, Serrano continued to believe that Hitler had escaped from the ruins of Berlin and found a refuge either in the warm oases of Antarctica or deep below the ice cap. Already suggested by his master, this idea was widely rumored in the Latin American press during the summer of 1945.[10] Serrano devoured the speculations of Ladislao Szabó's book, *Hitler esta vivo* (1947), that Hitler had been brought to safety by a U-boat convoy to the warm oases in Queen Maud Land originally discovered by the Ritscher expedition of 1938. An obscure urge led him to accompany the expedition of the Chilean Army and Navy to Antarctica in 1947–48 as a journalist. The bleak and uninhabited wastes of the polar region made a lasting impression on him. He read books by Carl Gustav Jung on the collective unconscious and mused on the proximity of his idol. On his return he published a short book, *La Antártica y otros Mitos* (1948), which repeated Szabó's claims.[11] Hitler continued to obsess him. During his first visit to Europe in 1951, he visited the ruins of the Berlin bunker, where Hitler had vanished from the stage of world history; he gazed long at the walls of Spandau Prison, where Rudolf Hess and other top Nazis were immured; he lingered over the ruins of Hitler's Berghof in Bavaria, anticipating Savitri Devi's pilgrimage after its final demolition.[12]

But the visit to Europe also opened up new prospects. In Switzerland, Serrano met and befriended Hermann Hesse, the well-known German romantic writer who had received the Nobel Prize in 1946. A later encounter and ensuing friendship with C. G. Jung led to an ardent exchange of ideas concerning myths and archetypes. In 1953 Serrano, following a family tradition, had entered the Chilean diplomatic corps in order to obtain a posting to India, which he regarded as an important source of esoteric truth. Eventually promoted to ambassador, he remained in India until 1962, all the while immersing himself in India's rich spiritual heritage. A recurrent leitmotif of this Indian period was his search for the secret Brahmanical order of his Chilean master. He traveled to remote Himalayan shrines and met numerous gurus. However, as the order was supposed to be have its seat at Mount Kailas in Tibet, it remained inaccessible to him in Chinese-administered territory.[13] Through his diplomatic role he met many leading personalities and became a personal friend of Nehru, Indira Gandhi and the Dalai Lama of Tibet. He now published literature devoted to mythological and spiritual themes, including *The Visits of the Queen of Sheba* (1960), with a preface by C. G. Jung, and *The Serpent of Paradise* (1963) about his quest in India.

Miguel Serrano subsequently held prestigious postings as Chilean ambassador to Yugoslavia (1962–64), with simultaneous accreditation in Bulgaria and Romania, and ambassador to Austria (1964–70) as well as representative to the International Atomic Energy Commission and the United Nations Organisation for Industrial Development (UNUDI), both based in Vienna. However, in late 1970 Serrano was dismissed from the Chilean diplomatic service by Salvador Allende, the newly elected Marxist president of Chile. He resolved to live as an exile, renting an apartment at Casa Camuzzi, the house in which Hermann Hesse had lived from 1919 to 1931 at Montagnola in the Swiss Ticino. Serrano spent the next years in Europe, enjoying the life of a writer wandering in the forests and on the mountains. In this new carefree phase of life Serrano initially devoted himself to a poetic treatment of religious myths. His first book from this period, *El/Ella: Book of Magic Love* (1973), was an allegory of man's search for unity. Themes of Tantrism, Catharism and the reunion of the male animus and female anima guaranteed the work translation into many foreign languages. A second book, *Nos: Book of the Resurrection* (1980), was a Jungian autobiography based on similar themes and Nietzsche's idea of eternal return.[14]

However, the abrupt and unexpected end to his public career, coupled with the communist takeover in his country, also attracted Serrano to Nazism again. In the early 1940s he had absorbed the myth of a secret world conspiracy involving Jews, secret societies and communists. The new revolutionary regime in Chile now appeared to confirm these fantasies. During his time in Switzerland, he increasingly pondered on the dualist implications of Catharism, anti-Semitism and the Jungian idea of the projection of the "shadow." While his poetic work sung of unity and spiritual integration, Serrano became a hostage to the idea of opposing archetypes of light and darkness. He began work on his remarkable Hitler Trilogy, which eventually comprised *El Cordón Dorado: Hitlerismo Esotérico* (1978), *Adolf Hitler, el Último Avatāra* (1984) and *Manú: "Por el hombre que vendra"* (1991). Drawing his inspiration from his earlier involvement in Chilean Nazism, the *Protocols* and the esoteric Brahmanical order, Serrano now assimilated a medley of revelational, occult and "Nazi Mysteries" literature from the 1960s and 1970s to elaborate his own political mythography of "Esoteric Hitlerism."

The ascent experiences and visions Serrano underwent through yoga and other rituals under the guidance of his master form the esoteric core of Serrano's Gnostic religion. Through a magical heightening of consciousness, Serrano believes that it is possible to achieve a union with divine forces extraneous to man and nature. He claims this is not a matter of the unconscious mind, but some form of superconsciousness, whereby the ego is "taken over" by one or other of the gods, as imagined by the ancient Greeks. These ideas were focused by his readings of C. G. Jung and were further developed by his extensive conversations and correspondence with the eminent Swiss psychoanalyst between 1957 and 1961. These are of considerable interest and have been published as *C. G. Jung and Hermann Hesse: A Record of Two Friendships* (1965) in a number of languages.

Jung had begun to develop his theory of the archetypes and the collective unconscious during the First World War. In his later work, Jung would present the archetypes in scientific terms, describing them as "primordial images," "an instinctive trend," or "archaic remnants" arising from the collective unconscious of mankind and rooted in its long phylogenetic evolution. However, Jung first identified the archetypes in more religious language as "the Ruling Powers, the Gods."[15] Confronted by the rise of Nazism and the mass enthusiasm of the German people for Hitler, Jung published in 1936 an essay entitled "Wotan" in which he suggested that the Germans were once again possessed by the archetype of the Germanic god of storm and frenzy. He saw precursors of this pagan exuberance in the Dionysian, irrational philosophies of Friedrich Nietzsche, Alfred Schuler and Ludwig Klages, and in the poetry of Stefan George. The Wandervögel youth movement, völkisch nationalism, and various attempts to "Germanize" Christianity traced a decline in the talismanic power of the Cross and the return of the *furor teutonicus*, a formerly dominant archetype.[16]

But if the German masses had indeed been seized by the Wotan archetype, then Hitler was the ultimate personification of Wotan. In other articles and interviews of the interwar period, Jung focused on the phenomenon of Hitler himself. He described how Hitler was possessed by this archetype of the collective Aryan unconscious and could not help obeying the commands of an inner voice. In a series of interviews between 1936 and 1939, Jung characterized Hitler as an archetype, often manifesting itself to the complete exclusion of his own personality. "Hitler is a spiritual vessel, a demi-divinity; even better, a myth. Mussolini is a man." At a military review witnessed by the two leaders, Hitler reminded Jung of a sort of wooden scaffolding in clothes, an automaton with a mask, a robot or someone with the mask of a robot. "Hitler seemed like the 'double' (*Doppelgänger*) of a real person, as if Hitler the man might be hiding inside like an appendix, and deliberately so concealed in order not to disturb the mechanism. . . . You know you could never talk to this man; because there is nobody there. . . . It is not an individual; it is an entire nation." Jung likened Hitler to Mohammed, the messiah of Germany who teaches the virtue of the sword. "His voice is that of at least 78 million Germans. He must shout, even in private conversation. . . . The voice he hears is that of the collective unconscious of his race."[17]

Jung's suggestion that each race had its own collective unconscious and archetypes interested Serrano especially, for this meant that Hitler could inspire all members of the Aryan race. However, Serrano believed that Jung was merely "psychologizing" an ancient, sacred mystery with such concepts as archetypes and the collective unconscious.[18] For Serrano, the archetypes *are* the gods, independent metaphysical powers that rule over their respective races and occasionally possess their members. In his opinion, the Aryan collective unconscious was literally the "memory of Aryan blood," an esoteric construction of biological racism. As his master had claimed, the individual person may travel in the astral, thereby evacuating his body for archetypal possession. Serrano claimed that this frequently occurred in Hitler's case. The Aryan archetype had sought out its most effective agent in order to intercede in the world. Impressed by Hindu mythology and Savitri Devi's *The Lightning and the Sun*, Serrano identified Hitler as an avatar of the gods Vishnu, Shiva or Wotan, come to lead the heroic Aryans back to their long-lost divinity.[19]

But who exactly are the gods, and what do they want with men? In order to explain the purpose of the Hitler avatar, Serrano elaborates a sci-fi cosmology involving a fabulous pageant of divine extraterrestrials and their galactic contest with a universal adversary. The gods dwell at a remote place in the galaxy, perhaps even beyond, illuminated by the Black Sun, which is beyond our golden sun and invisible from earth. Sometimes Serrano suggests that this place is beyond time and space, in another, non-existent universe, in the Green Ray. The gods are eternal, omnipotent, omniscient, through their possession of *vril* power and the Third Eye; they reproduce asexually by means of plasmic emanations from their ethereal bodies; the divine light of the Black Sun courses through their veins.[20] It is Serrano's claim that these beings are the divine ancestors of the Hyperborean, Nordic or Aryan races on earth.

Hundreds of thousands of years ago, the gods' cosmic dominion was challenged by the demiurge, an inferior godlet, who had imitated and faked a lower form of creation in matter and begun to establish his rebellious realm on the planet earth. Some of the gods (Serrano often uses the tantric term *divyas* for god-men) thus embarked upon a heroic spiritual adventure by descending to earth to combat this cosmic revolt. The *divyas* arrived from this other universe in their divine form through the cosmic aperture of Venus, clothed themselves in matter and settled on a ring-shaped polar continent around the North Pole, which they called Hyperborea in memory of their original homeland near the Black Sun and in the Green Ray. In this exile of matter, the *divyas* found a strange and terrible world. The fake creation of the demiurge was subject to entropy and involution. Lacking divine inspiration, the demiurge's bestial creatures, variously described as "robots," "golems" and "slaves of Atlantis," only degenerated while endlessly multiplying themselves on the physical plane. Trapped in the world of the demiurge, these beast-men were condemned to futile self-reproduction in matter, an endless repetition in the Circle of Circles.[21]

Serrano states that the intervention of the gods, coincident with the beginning of the cycle of the ages, was intended to reverse the process of involution and decay. Now known as the Hyperboreans, the gods began to train the colored races of the demiurge in a caste system and attempted to spiritualize the earth and all nature.[22] However, these efforts were frustrated and betrayed by treason among some Hyperboreans, who consorted with "the daughters of men" (i.e., the beast-men of the demiurge). This sinful miscegenation recapitulated the cosmic emnity of the demiurge. Now bastard races arose on earth, the divine blood was diluted, the awareness of divine origins diminished, involution and entropy accelerated.[23] Further catastrophes struck with the fall of a moon or comet upon the earth, which caused a deluge and the inversion of the poles, and many pure-blooded Hyperboreans sought refuge at the South Pole. The continent of Hyperborea became invisible and vanished as it receded into the interior of the hollow earth, where other Hyperboreans reestablished their divine order in the secret underground cities of Agartha and Shamballah.[24]

Serrano finds mythological evidence for the extraterrestrial origins of man in the *Nephelin* of the Book of Genesis, while the story of an original racial sin comes from the Book of Enoch. A Greek myth records that Apollo returned to Hyperborea in the Far North to rejuvenate his body and wisdom every nineteen years. Aztec cosmology describes the descent of Quetzalcoatl from Venus, while Irish legends identify divine ancestors in the Tuathas of Dannan.[25] Serrano suggests that the sudden appearance of Cro-Magnon Man with his high artistic and cultural achievements in prehistoric Europe records the passage of one such *divya*-descended race alongside the abysmal inferiority of Neanderthal Man, an abomination and manifest creation of the demiurge.[26] In particular, he cites Lokamanya Bâl Gangadhar Tilak on the Arctic home of the Indo-Aryans, their migrations and subsequent preservation of blood purity through the caste system.[27] Of all the races on earth, the Aryans alone preserve the memory of their divine ancestors in their noble blood, which is still mingled with the light of the Black Sun. All other races are the progeny of the demiurge's beast-men, native to the planet.[28]

Serrano's story of how mankind came about is a variety of Gnosticism. The *divyas* represent the incorruptible world-soul, a fragment of which descends and is entrapped in matter. His cosmology is but a tale of the spirit's separation from the Supreme Deity and exile in the bondage of matter, while the original divine inspiration becomes ever weaker in a progressively more corrupt world as it passes through the yugas of the Hindu cycle of the ages. But since the *divyas* came to do battle with the evil demiurge, this fall and entrapment in matter are not final but part of a redemptive scheme. Salvation will be achieved once the Hyperborean Aryans or *vîras* (the tantric term for a semi-divine hero) repurify their blood, thus restoring their memory of divine ancestry. When the Aryan *vîras* reclaim their divine inheritance and become *divyas* again, they will defeat the demiurge and transform the whole earth into a paradise.[29]

The origin of evil poses a fundamental problem in most religions. Serrano prefers the idea that the demiurge originates in a fall, war or rebellion following Creation to a strictly Manichaean dualism whereby Good and Evil are co-eval and equal opposites. Here Serrano follows the Gnostic tradition of the Cathars (fl. 1025–1244) by identifying the evil demiurge as Jehovah, the God of the Old Testament. As medieval dualists, these eleventh-century heretics had repudiated Jehovah as a false god and mere artificer opposed to the real God far beyond our earthly realm.[30] This Gnostic doctrine clearly carried dangerous implications for the Jews. As Jehovah was the tribal deity of the Jews, it followed that they were devil worshipers. By casting the Jews in the role of the children of Satan, the Cathar heresy can elevate anti-Semitism to the status of a theological doctrine backed by a vast cosmology.[31] If the Hyperborean Aryans are the archetype and blood descendants of Serrano's *divyas* from the Black Sun, then the archetype of the Lord of Darkness needed a counter-race. The demiurge sought and found the most fitting agent for its archetype in the Jews.[32]

According to Serrano, the Jews have stolen the divine birthright of the Hyperboreans. Everywhere in their history he finds evidence of their imposture, imitation and bowdlerization of an authentic racial tradition. As a primitive, illiterate tribal group, the Jews first received spiritual instruction from the lowly Chaldean artisans of Ur, whose myths they plagiarized as the Book of Genesis. Neither Abraham nor Moses were Jews, and the Hebrews were a Hyperborean people whose traditions were also appropriated by the Jews. According to Serrano, the Jews are not even a biological race, but a bastard people formed by centuries of interbreeding between Canaanites, Edomites, Aramaeans, Moabites, Hittites, Amorites, Samaritans, Galileans, Phoenecians and Philistines. Only with the return from Babylon and the construction of the second temple did the Jews attempt to consolidate their racial identity and exclusivity in the thousands of strict laws and regulations found in Deuteronomy. At the same time, they claimed a divine vocation over all other peoples through Ezra's new covenant with Jehovah.[33]

The Jews' attempt to place themselves in the center of God's plan and world history could only succeed through their falsehood and conscious obliteration of the truth. This is allegedly the reason for emnity between the Aryans and the Jews: Serrano accuses the Jews of foisting their national history and synthetic pseudo-religion upon the rest of mankind while denying and obscuring all knowledge of its Hyperborean and extraterrestrial origins, in order to assuage their own terrible guilt of racial sin, which is even further ritualized in bestiality.[34] This whole project is assimilated to the demiurge's dark cosmic purpose:

> This is the meaning of the Jewish method: not to keep the blood pure with the intention of reviving the original *Minne*-memory . . . and thus to transcend materialization in the highest realms, but only to attract to himself materials and images appropriate to the beast-man, his hate-filled resentments and lust for revenge. [The Jew] attributes these to a "god" who is nothing but a golem . . . which has seized possession of a group of terrestrial beings to perpetuate his own existence as an incubus. . . . That is the counter-initiation which has changed the course of things in the history of mankind.[35]

For Serrano, the Jew is but the concrete manifestation of the antagonist in a cosmology structured by the battle of opposing archetypes. Serrano traces this conspiracy of the Jews against the Hyperborean Aryans throughout all history, with a particular focus on Spain and the Americas. The Goths who migrated from southern Sweden into eastern Europe around 800 B.C. represent "the holiest community of the Germanic Aryans." Between the second and sixth centuries A.D., the Ostrogoths colonized Russia and Central Europe, while the Visigoths (according to Serrano, a corruption of "white gods") ruled Spain from A.D. 418 to 713, but their racial stock and political influence persisted in the North long after the Arab conquest.[36] Many Jews from the Levant soon followed in their wake. Serrano traces the history of the Jews in Spain, indicating their rapid attainment of wealth and high office in Church and state against a background of insincere conversions and recurrent expulsions. The Visigothic elite eventually instituted the Inquisition against the Jews of Spain, and the Jews were finally expelled in 1492. Many avoided this fate by conversion while remaining "secret Jews" (Marranos). Meanwhile, the refugees and the Marranos spread throughout the Mediterranean and northern Europe as the new merchant elite in the early capitalist era. Serrano regards the story of the Jews in Spain as an instructive rehearsal for the twentieth-century German conflict with Jewry in the Third Reich.[37]

As a Chilean of European descent, Serrano was especially eager to claim a Hyperborean heritage in the Americas. Just as the original Hyperboreans fled to the South Pole, other Aryan initiates were supposed to have traveled to America long before Columbus. Serrano suggests that Cro-Magnon Man and the Trojans came to America in prehistoric times. He also describes medieval Friesian and Viking settlements in Central and South America and their involvement with the Incas and other Indian peoples. The Knights Templar also supposedly started colonies in America between 1272 and 1294. After the suppression of the order in Europe in 1307, the Templar fleet disappeared from La Rochelle, France, and sailed to Mexico.[38] The later Spanish colonization of South America and Chile in particular was led by warriors of Visigothic and Basque–Cro-Magnon blood, to whom Serrano proudly traces his own ancestry, blue-blond Aryan features and "blood memory."[39] His is the America of the White Gods.

Here Serrano's mythology directly interacts with the new Thulean ideology of German Nazis in South America. His idea of ancient Aryan settlement in South America extends Jacques de Mahieu's earlier idea of a Viking empire in pre-Columbian South America. Born in 1915 in Paris, De Mahieu emigrated after the war to Argentina, becoming director of the Institute of Anthropology in Buenos Aires. By the spurious application of ethnology, archaeology and linguistics, De Mahieu identified many sites of Viking settlement throughout Latin America. His story begins with the landing of a Viking named Jarl Ullman from Schleswig in the Gulf of Mexico in 967. Regarded by the Indians as the white god Quetzalcóatl, he then conquered the Toltec empire. When his army began to mix with the local population, Ullman pressed on to Venuzuela and Columbia. A later Viking leader, Naymlap, colonized Peru, which later served as the center of the Inca empire ruled by Nordic elites.[40] Although the original Viking invaders numbered only some five hundred persons, De Mahieu calculated a population of some 80,000 by the year 1290. De Mahieu finds the heritage of these lost Vikings in the pale skin, blue eyes and fair hair of many Indians, as well as in putative runic inscriptions and even swastikas.[41] Published originally in French, his books were translated into German by Wilfred van Oven, Goebbels's former deputy, who fled to Buenos Aires after the war.

Serrano claims that the Jews always followed hard on the heels of the Aryans either to steal their wisdom or to subvert the Nordic heritage. The lost tribes of Levi and Reuben came to America in ancient times, and pernicious Jewish influences could be observed among some primitive Indian tribes.[42] The later "discovery" of America by Columbus was a planned Jewish operation to tail the Templars and their Grail treasure: the Jews were frightened that a Hyperborean restoration was under way in the unknown Western Hemisphere and at the South Pole. In the sixteenth and seventeenth centuries, both Marranos and orthodox Jews from the Netherlands entered America, establishing secret societies under cover of their trading companies and *Kahal Ka-*

dosh (Holy Associations) from Brazil to New York.[43] Serrano sees this Jewish diaspora in America as a demonic crusade against the White Gods of America. Aided by the "white treason" of Christianity and Freemasonry, both Americas have become "the seething, monstrous melting-pot of mestizos and mulattos" of modern times. The White Gods have remained secure only in the secret cities of the Andes, in the hollow earth and the oases of Antarctica which the enemy can never penetrate.[44] As "the black shadow of the white gods," the Jews act as the Gnostic adversary throughout Serrano's improbable account of American history. Here Serrano demonstrates the ideological symbiosis between native Latin American racism and Nazi ideas.

Serrano's occult history of the New World finds a natural ally in the myth of Masonic or Jewish world conspiracy embraced from the French Revolution onward by anxious monarchists, aristocrats, clerics and many other social groups beset by the rapid changes and dislocations of modernity. *The Protocols of the Elders of Zion* detailed horrific Jewish plots to overthrow all existing thrones and religions, to manipulate and enslave the entire gentile world through international banking, wars, artificial slumps, anarchy and revolution. If democracy, liberalism and socialism was supposed to serve the Jews as a means to erode traditional authority, their ultimate plan was to destroy all states and create a world empire ruled by a monarch from the house of David, who would be the anti-Christ.[45] Describing the power of the Jews in the modern period, Serrano quotes whole protocols verbatim: the Jews expect to rule the earth; they will reduce the gentile nations to subservience by means of speculation, ruinous borrowing, and the artificial stimulation of economic crises; the international network of Masonic lodges advances their aims; if any nation ever tries to escape their clutches, the Jews will destroy such opposition by inciting war with its neighbors.[46]

Like most anti-Semitic readers of the *Protocols*, Serrano believes that these plans for Jewish world domination were first leaked at the Zionist Congress held in August 1897 at Basel and subsequently passed via Paris to Russia, where they were edited by Sergei Nilus in 1905. He has published a commemorative group portrait of the congress delegates and menacing photographs of their venue at the Dreyfus Brodsky mansion.[47] Serrano identifies Achad Ha'am, alias Asher Ginzberg (1856–1927), as the editor of the *Protocols* at Odessa in the 1880s, a speculation that may be traced to Lesley Fry (Mrs. Shishmarev), a Russian American woman writing in the 1920s.[48] Ginzberg was a mystical Zionist, who saw Jerusalem as the future cultural focus of Jewry and opposed Theodore Herzl's more secular brand of nationalism. This makes him even more sinister to Serrano: such secret and symbolic Zionism strove to create a "terrestrial *chakra*" for the unification of Israel and the conquest of the universe through the counter-avatar of the Lord of Darkness.[49] Needless to say, Serrano discounts Ginzberg as an elder; members of this secret group always remain wholly secret and anonymous; nowadays they wait concealed beneath the earth, safe from the atomic holocaust they may at any time unleash upon mankind.

Serrano is also deeply impressed by the novel *Biarritz* (1868) by Sir John Retcliffe, a pen name for Hermann Goedsche, who served on the editorial staff of the conservative *Kreuzzeitung* in Berlin. One of its chapters, entitled "At the Jewish Cemetery in Prague," describes a secret nocturnal meeting of the twelve representatives of the Jewish tribes who gather every hundred years at this "Cabbalistic Sanhedrin" to report on their progress toward world domination. The eerie background, midnight gloom and satanic allusions of this fictional narrative lend an uncanny aura to these conspiratorial revelations. The delegates each speak in turn about the massive concentrations of Jewish capital in each of the European capitals. Plans for the future include the acquisition of land and urban property, the degradation of craftsmen and promotion of mass manufactures, the achievement of full civic equality and intermarriage with the Goyim (non-Jews) to infiltrate the aristocracy and influential families, and the control of the law, medicine and the press. "We will prescribe to the world, what it is to think and to believe, to praise or to condemn. . . . We will destroy our enemies' belief in everything they hold dear."[50]

The date and content of this book almost certainly reflect conservative apprehension about the growing freedom and acceptance of Jews in German society after the revolution of 1848, culminating in their full emancipation in the years from 1867 to 1871. Desirous of these benefits, the Jews had associated themselves with the forces of political liberalism and soon played a highly prominent role in business, banking, the professions, academe and journalism in proportions excessive to their numbers in German and Austrian society. This rapid advance owed much to the long exclusion of Jewish talent from civil society, which suddenly found free rein in public careers and the expanding commercial opportunities of both empires.[51] The fantasy of a Jewish plot was thus able to make a career in the ensuing reaction to liberalism. Goedsche's thriller soon turned into a forged document known as *The Rabbi's Speech*, which was frequently published in Russia, Austria-Hungary and Germany between 1872 and the early 1900s. It may well have served the czarist secret police in their forgery of the *Protocols* in the late 1890s; in any case, it was often printed together with them and cited as proof of their authenticity.[52] The telling chapter of *Biarritz* lent further support to Nazi anti-Semitism: Johannes von Leers published a booklet edition in 1933 and three

American Nazi Party leader George Lincoln Rockwell addresses a rally in Chicago in 1966. (Courtesy of AP/Wide World Photos)

Matt Koehl as leader of the National Socialist White People's Party (NSWPP) in 1970. (Courtesy of New Order, Milwaukee)

Colin Jordan's White Defense League and John Bean's National Labour Party hold a joint demonstration in Trafalgar Square, London, on 24 May 1959. Inset: WDL propaganda. (Courtesy of Searchlight Magazine Ltd.)

Colin Jordan, his wife Françoise Dior, and a friend demonstrate against the pro-immigration Labour Party candidate at the Leyton by-election, January 1965.

Baron Julius Evola in the 1930s.

Cover of *Rising*, No. 3
(1983), the magazine
of the Evola-inspired
"Political Soldier"
faction of the
National Front.

Francis Parker Yockey in court in San Francisco, June 1960.

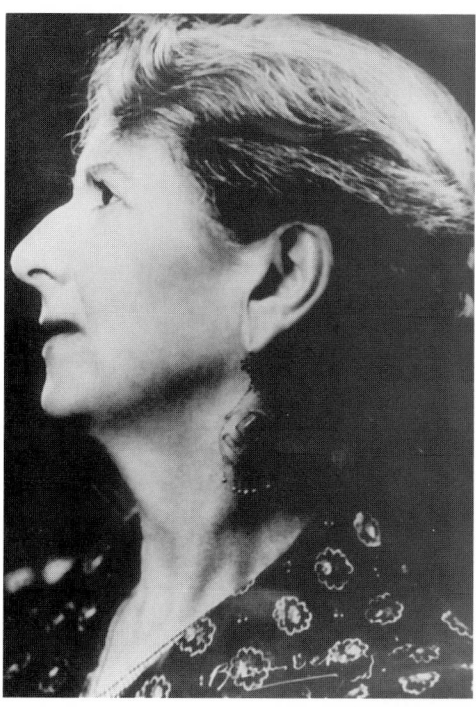

Savitri Devi.
(Courtesy of New Order,
Milwaukee)

Miguel Serrano.
(Courtesy of Miguel Serrano)

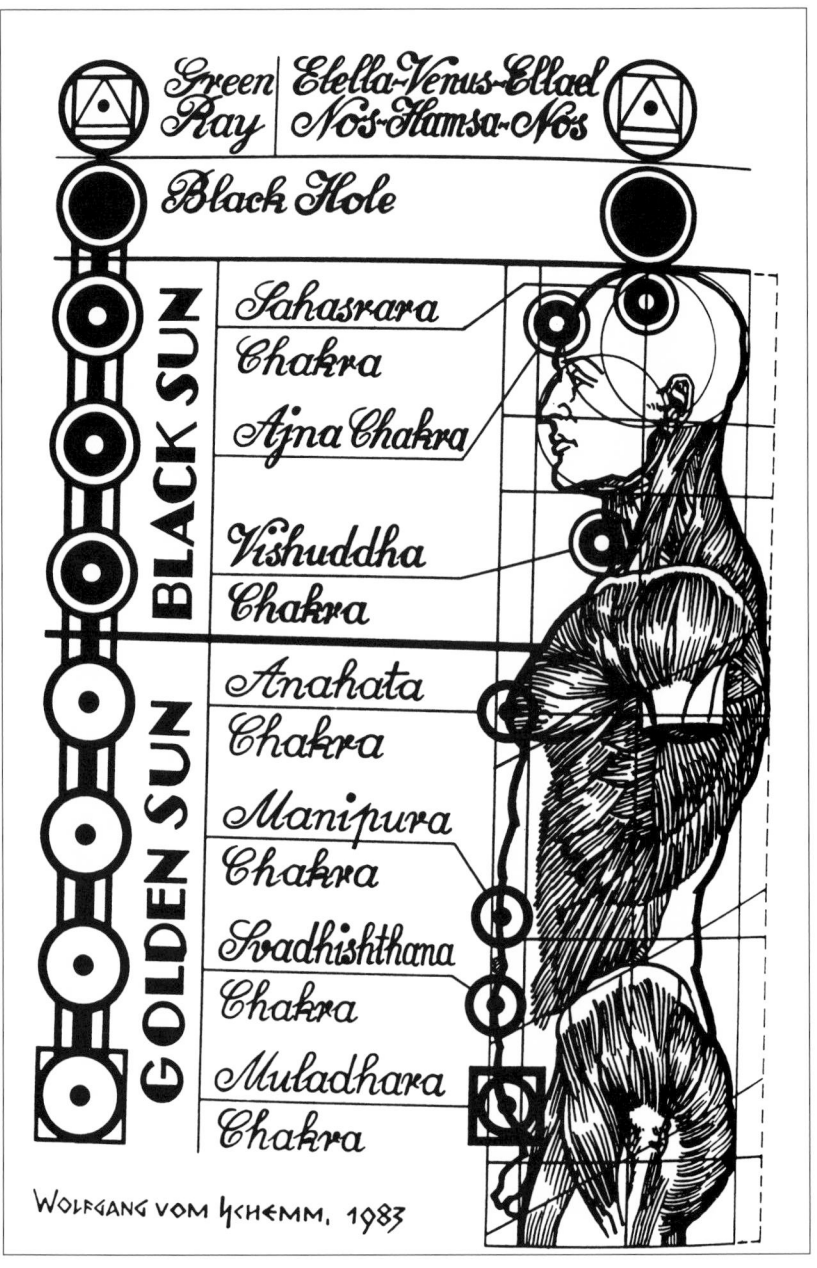

Hindu-Nordic esoteric anatomy in Miguel Serrano, *Adolf Hitler, el Último Avatāra* (1984). (Courtesy of Wolfgang von Schemm)

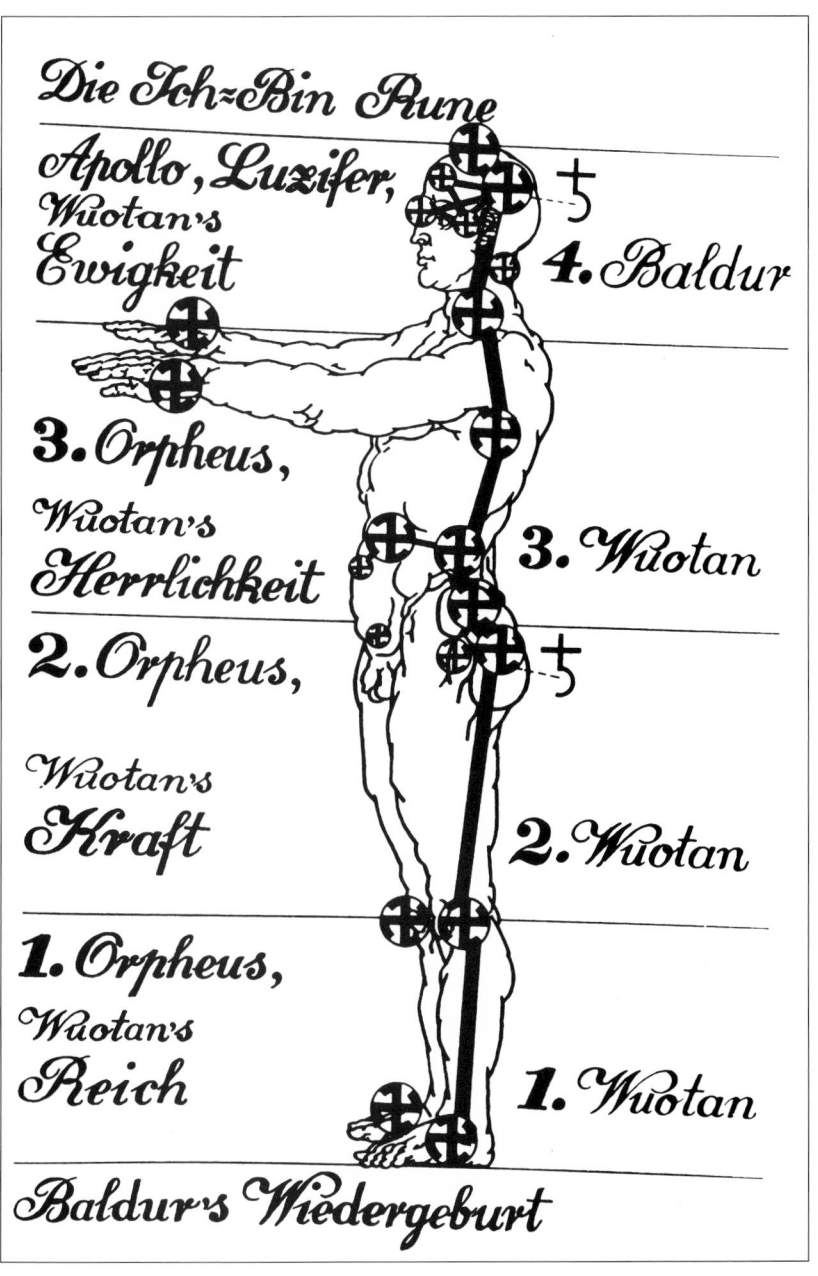

Die Ich=Bin Rune

Apollo, Luzifer,
Wuotan's
Ewigkeit

♄

4. Baldur

3. Orpheus,
Wuotan's
Herrlichkeit

3. Wuotan

2. Orpheus,

♄

Wuotan's
Kraft

2. Wuotan

1. Orpheus,
Wuotan's
Reich

1. Wuotan

Baldur's Wiedergeburt

NAZI UFO PUBLICISTS

Wilhelm Landig

Willibald Mattern

Ernst Zündel

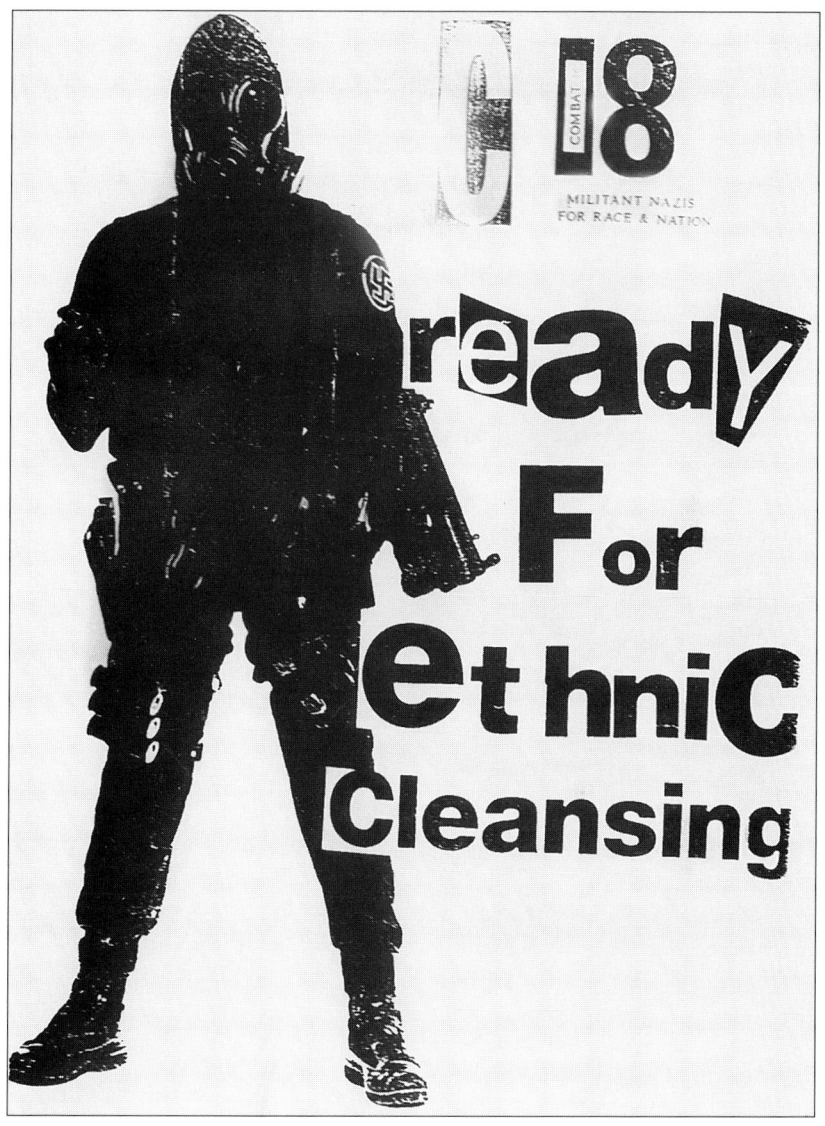

Combat 18 Leaflet, c. 1993.

Advertisement for Aryan Nations (1997).

The Reverend William Butler presides over a wedding in the Aryan Nations compound at Hayden Lake, Idaho, 1998.

Ben Klassen, later Pontifex Maximus and Founder of the Church of the Creator, as a Florida state legislator, 1966.

the
FLAMING **SWORD**

Membership Bulletin of The Black Order

February 1995

No. 5

Cover of *The Flaming Sword*, No. 5 (February 1995), showing the Ku Klux Klan as an ancient Germanic secret tribunal, *Vehmgericht*, passing judgment on a racial enemy.

Cover of *The Order*, No. 14 (early 1996). Combat 18 magazine using "ZOG" (Zionist Occupation Government) terminology from the U.S. extreme right.

Resistance, No. 7 (1996).

The White Dragon, No. 18 (October 1999), spoof on the wave of asylum seekers at British ports.

David and Katja Lane with Ron McVan, the founders of Wotansvolk and the 14 Word Press. (Courtesy of Katja Lane)

Masthead of *Focus Fourteen*, No. 704 (April 1997) (courtesy of Ron McVan).

Art for the 14 Word Press; cover design for *Creed of Iron* (1997) (courtesy of Ron McVan).

other editions appeared during the Third Reich, one of which served Serrano as a source.

Serrano is aware of the charges of forgery against the *Protocols*, based on their plagiarism from the political pamphlet by Maurice Joly, *Dialogue aux Enfers entre Montesquieu et Machiavel* (1864), which presented the case for liberalism against the despotism of Napoleon III. Nevertheless, Serrano's utter conviction in the existence of a universal Jewish plot of demiurgic inspiration precludes any doubts. He wonders where Goedsche could have obtained his information and finds it suggestive that neither Joly nor the *Protocols* use key material in Goedsche or *The Rabbi's Speech*. He decides that the latter is the common source for all the accounts with a date prior to 1864. As the documents exist, it follows for him that their obscure but authentic prototype must also have existed. This, he claims, had long circulated among Russian rabbis at Simferopol and was kept in their court archives at Odessa. Serrano regards the *Protocols* as the only known legacy of an obscure tradition whose traces have almost been obliterated.[53] The Jewish world conspiracy is the cornerstone of his Gnostic cosmology and thus resistant to all proofs of forgery, plagiarism, historical motive and purpose.

Besides these crude, paranoiac fantasies of conspiracy, Serrano has also assimilated the metaphysical anti-Semitism of Otto Weininger and Julius Evola. Quoting Claudio Mutti's introduction to the *Protocols*, Serrano sees Weininger's "Platonic idea" of Jewry as the "intellectual tendency" or "psychic constitution" of modernity as an archetype in fundamental opposition to the Hyperborean hero. Serrano agrees with Evola's characterization of the Jewish spirit as abstraction, calculation and mechanistic thinking. Taking his cue from Evola's *Tre aspetti del problema Ebraico* (1936), Serrano sees Albert Einstein's theory of relativity as an atomistic Jewish cosmology, "dissolving and exploding the integrated Aryan universe into a thousand reflecting mirrors." Serrano also quotes Evola's list of Jewish mathematicians and physicists— Tullio Livi-Civita, Hermann Weyl and Max Born—who developed the quantum theory. Their reduction of all existence to subatomic particles in mathematical and algebraic formulas empties the world of all sense and spirit.[54] Here Serrano co-opts "Jewish" modernity as a demonic principle that disinherits the Aryan heroes from their spiritual birthright in a higher cosmos.

With regard to the present, Serrano is a profound cultural pessimist. Enthralled by the demiurge and its Jewish agents, the modern world is in an advanced state of degeneration corresponding to the Kali Yuga. Serrano rejects Christianity, the Enlightenment and rationalism. Art and tradition are dead; the human population proliferates in living silos and cement ant heaps. The zoological promiscuity of the lower races, the racial chaos of South America, the rule of the masses and markets, materialism and industry, the overriding concern with quantity, the atomistic futility of contemporary civilization are objects of his savage scorn. Money, electronics and numbers substitute for value and hierarchy on all sides. "The Fourth Estate will be the rule of the collective, machine-slaves, automatons, a planetary bureaucracy, robots and ant-men."[55] Serrano links redemption with a tangled mythology involving the Gnostics, the Druids, the Cathars and the Knights Templars and the Grail, all of which he regards as the secret agents of the Hyperborean gnosis through a benighted age.

Conspiracy and war are the two recurring motifs of Esoteric Hitlerism. Only a Great Cosmic War of the Worlds can account for the original fall of Hyperborea and the end of the golden age.[56] But wars also possess redemptive force. The great wars of the Koravas and the Pandavas in the *Mahabharata*, the wars of the Vanir and Aesir in Norse mythology, above all the Great War of 1939–45 are but punitive campaigns against those who have interbred and defiled their divine blood.[57] Following Savitri Devi, Serrano regards Adolf Hitler as an avatar, a divine intermediary between the Hyperborean gods and men (the Aryan race alone). He also describes Hitler as a *bodhisattva* or *tulku*, namely, a divine being in Mahayana Buddhism worthy of nirvana who has chosen to return to the human plane to help men to salvation. The Aryan-Hyperborean archetype incarnated in Hitler, in order to defeat the demiurge, breaks the Circle of Circles and redeems the white race. Following his victories in the West and Scandinavia and the dashing of his hopes for a settlement with Britain after the failure of Rudolf Hess's flight, Hitler attacked the communist Soviet Union and declared war on the United States, both supposed bastions of Jewish power in the modern world. His aim was an all-out avataric battle against the demonic hosts of the Kali Yuga in order to turn the cycle from the dark age into a new golden age.[58]

As a Latin American with no direct memory of Nazi atrocity, Serrano sees the Third Reich in millennial terms. With Hitler's seizure of power in 1933, Germany suddenly entered "the Esoteric Reich of the *Víras*" through a "click" into another dimension. Serrano sees Hitler as the center of an archetypal field of energy, not as a despot atop a hierarchical pyramid, and dismisses Evola's critique of the plebeian nature of National Socialism. He especially reveres the SS as an esoteric order of initiates seeking the the Holy Grail of Hyperborean blood. He dwells at length on the symbolic architecture of the Wewelsburg, where Himmler evoked the memory of Parsifal and the knights of the Grail. Here the SS supposedly practiced yoga and secret rites to restore their memory of the magical Aryan blood and thus achieve their alchemical "Great Transmutation" into god-men. For Serrano, the murderous activities of the SS take place on the symbolic level of a cosmic war in heaven. For him, the figure of six million Jewish victims of the Holocaust is only significant because the figure 6 is an archetype of the Jewish collective unconscious. He denies the Holocaust, stating that the six million figure is no human invention but rooted in the "cabalistic" planetary conspiracy of Jehovah.[59]

In Serrano's view, the defeat of the Third Reich in 1945 is only a temporary loss in the outer world. The Nazis had already prepared a secret refuge beneath the ice cap of Antarctica, possibly in alliance with the Hyperboreans who had long ago colonized the interior of the hollow earth. Their advanced technology, based on implosion and antigravity, accounts for the countless postwar UFO sightings and also anticipates a new civilization that will ennoble rather than despoil the earth. Hitler remained for some time in the warm Antarctic oases, but he has probably long since traveled by UFO through the "window" of Venus back to the archetypal home of the Black Sun and the Green Ray beyond the galaxy.[60] Elsewhere, Serrano mentions "parallel universes" and "astral wormholes" to justify his belief in the survival of Hitler in another dimension and the imminent transfiguration of our world.

Pending the intervention of the Hitler avatar in renewed cosmic conflict, Serrano believes that Gnostic redemption can be achieved on the inner planes of consciousness. This inner battle against the demiurge involves methods of magical ritual and tantric yoga for the transmutation of the individual Aryan *vîra*. Serrano assimilates the *chakras*, mudras and mantras of yoga and the Nordic runes into a physiology of the astral body. Personal salvation can be achieved by yoga and meditation. The resultant repurification of the blood to its former quality of divine light activates and "tunes" the *chakras*, transforming the Aryan hero into a god-man. In a series of complex illustrations, Serrano interprets the Hitler salute with an outstretched right hand as a yogic mudra for drawing cosmic energy into the *chakras*, depicted as mystical centers of swastika-spinning energy.[61] This bodily redemption is complemented by a transformation of nature into a paradise. Serrano implies that this process takes place in a parallel world or another dimension, which is opened up as the spell of the demiurge is broken. Long entrapped in the illusion of matter, the Aryans will once again be able to see the Hyperborean *divyas*, the Black Sun and the Green Ray "on the other side of their senses," through a "click" in the time-space continuum, which may be experienced at any time.[62]

Serrano has long practiced yoga and meditation as a means of raising his consciousness beyond the grasp of the demiurge and for making contact with the higher Aryan intelligences. On at least one occasion Serrano and his friends have visited the Wewelsburg castle in Westphalia to perform Nazi religious rituals. Here in the crypt of the great northern tower of the castle,

Serrano and his companions assumed the positions of runes and intoned "Nordic" mantras. Serrano's account of these rituals describes how their deep vibrations filled the acoustic space, designed on the principles of "Aryan mathematics," to suspend mundane reality and enable them to reach another universe. Serrano himself spoke the mantras of greeting, summoning the brahmans of his old order to unite once again as in the war with the SS leaders and support Hitler in his struggle against the forces of darkness, against the Lord of the Shadows and his supporters on the planet. Serrano even related this campaign to the esoteric symbolism of the architectural plans for the completed north tower, the center of this SS vatican and the omphalos of the Germanic world. In a bizarre parody of St. Peter's in Rome, a small throne room with the seat number 13 was to have occupied the lantern upon the tall cupola. Here, the "Führer-Parsifal" would give the order for the final assault on the demiurge and his planetary legions.[63]

Given the highly personal and eclectic nature of Serrano's Nazi mythology, one must ask how he is regarded within the movement and how influential are his ideas. Already during his years as Chilean ambassador to Austria (1964–70) and subsequently in Switzerland, Serrano cultivated strong ties of friendship with renowned surviving Nazis, including Léon Degrelle, Otto Skorzeny, Hans-Ulrich Rudel and Hanna Reitsch, the famous aviatrix. He visited Julius Evola in Rome and Herman Wirth, the aged ex-director of Himmler's SS Ahnenerbe, in West Germany and Wilhelm Landig in Vienna. He paid court to the American poet and fascist sympathizer Ezra Pound in Venice. He was friendly with the French former Waffen-SS man, Saint-Loup, whose stories of Otto Rahn, Montségur and Skorzeny's mission to find the Grail gave him inspiration. He quarried books on extraterrestrial gods by Robert Charroux, a leading French fantasy writer who had served as a minister in the Vichy government of wartime France. Serrano appears to have been especially close to Léon Degrelle, whom he eulogized in a fascist magazine interview that printed a photo of the two men together in Spain.[64]

Returning to Chile after the military coup of September 1973, Serrano found little sympathy for his ideas among the Pinochet regime. Henceforth, Serrano cast himself in the role of intellectual gadfly to the Nazi die-hard faithful in Chile and abroad. In May 1984 he conspicuously gave the Hitler salute at the Santiago funeral of SS Colonel Walter Rauff, who had long eluded West German justice in Chile.[65] During the war, Rauff had served in the SS Reich Main Security Office, where he masterminded the mobile killing operations using gas vans in the early stages of the Holocaust. Held responsible for the deaths of 97,000 Jews, he successfully contested extradition with the financial and legal aid of Das Reich network. Serrano also regularly organizes anniversary celebrations of Hitler's birthday at a country retreat in Chile on 20 April each year. In 1986 he published his political manifesto for National Socialism in the Southern Cone of Latin America.[66] A familiar figure in his black leather coat, he convened a major Nazi rally in Santiago with swastika flags and marches on 5 September 1993. This event was staged in honor of Rudolf Hess and in memory of the Chilean Nazi martyrs of 1938. He maintains a lively correspondence with neo-Nazi leaders overseas and is on calling terms with Matt Koehl of the New Order, the successor organization to Lincoln Rockwell's American Nazi Party. It is likely that old Nazis welcome Serrano's Nazi enthusiasm and unswerving loyalty to their hero, Adolf Hitler, even if many find his mythology fantastic.

The picture is somewhat different when one considers Serrano's image among a younger generation of neo-Nazis. Here Nazism is already detached from the historic context of the Third Reich and re-presented as a global, racist ideology of white supremacism. A coloring of pop mythology, Hinduism, and extraterrestrial Aryan gods adds sensational appeal to the powerful myths of elitism, planetary destiny and the cosmic conspiracy of the Jews. A German translation of El Cordón Dorado was published in 1987 by Richard Schepmann's Teut-Verlag in Wetter, Western Germany, which specializes in reprints from the Nordland-Verlag of the Ahnenerbe and dossiers on Nazi UFOs. An English translation has now been published by the 14 Word Press of Wotansvolk in the United States (see chapter 13). Serrano was the subject of a long, in-depth illustrated interview in the Greek far-right magazine TO ANTIΔOTO and has more recently been featured in the underground literature of the Black Order, a small international neo-Nazi organization with lodges in Britain, the United States, Italy, Sweden, Australia and New Zealand. The Black Order combines Hitlerite mythology with a variety of Nazi satanism in a Nordic pagan denial of the Christian roots of Western civilization.[67]

In these interviews, Serrano seeks to engage a younger audience by juxtaposing his magical and millennial vision of National Socialism with a corrupt, saturated image of modern liberalism. Using heroic and epic metaphors, describing himself as a "warrior-troubadour" (a reference to Catharism), and his work as "extra-stellar poetry," Serrano opposes an Aryan mystique of ancient Germanic gods, lost lands, polar mysticism and extraterrestrial deities to the Jewish "black magic" of money, economic exploitation, nuclear power and ecological degradation. His anti-Semitism assumes a cosmic function, identifying the Jews as the root cause of all alienation and inhumanity in the world. Abstraction, the reign of quantity, computerization of all aspects of life, the assault on nature—trends that disturb many in an increasingly automated, regulated society—are attributed to the demonic

Jewish spirit.[68] For him, all sin, suffering and disorder are the work of the Jews, intent on enslaving and ultimately destroying the earth and its creatures. In this way, Serrano offers a mystical Nazism that glosses over the facts of tyranny, torture and repression in the Third Reich with a medley of myths about SS heroes, fabulous cities and a magical Aryan millennium. In their New Age costume, these myths of Gnostic world rejection and the projection of all fault and sin onto a hated adversary act on young minds as a powerful distillate of Nazism.

10

White Noise and Black Metal

WESTERN ECONOMIES ARE again attracting increased numbers of im- migrants and asylum seekers from developing countries. Meanwhile, existing ethnic minorities claim a greater political and economic stake in their host states. The resulting pressure on native lower-income groups is giving rise to a new politics of white identity, which finds violent expression in white power music. Bound for Glory, Skullhead, Svastika, Battle Zone, Violent Storm, Celtic Warrior are just a few of the white power bands that regularly tour Eu- rope and perform at venues packed with hundreds of skinheads in Valencia, Stockholm, Rome and Bremen. A CD release of the British band No Remorse is entitled *Barbecue in Rostock*, a gloating reference to the notorious arson at- tack on a German refugee hostel in August 1992. The lead singer, a skinhead called Jacko, his whole torso covered with tattoos of snakes, spiders and swastikas, belts out hateful lyrics laced with threats to murder the "wogs," "pakis" and "Yids." There are presently at least several hundred bands in West- ern and Eastern Europe that act as recruiting sergeants for the racist far right among the alienated young, and possibly there are as many again in the United States, Australia and New Zealand.

A violent mood of racist extremism, intolerance and misanthropy is widely current among certain sections of urban white working-class youth. Much of this aggression is a compensation for feelings of personal inadequacy and failure. A high proportion of skinheads come from broken families, have low educational achievement and seek both identity and peer recognition within a skinhead group. Youngsters with a sense of inferiority in an increas- ingly skilled and automated society can find relief in the abuse and assault of other races, immigrants, even the elderly and disabled. They feel frustration and resentment at the apparent indulgence of liberal elites toward ethnic mi- norities. Community politicians are seen as demanding and receiving ransom payments from a guilt-ridden liberal society, which appear to perpetuate the dependence of an unassimilated underclass. The new misanthropes regard blacks in the United States, colored immigrants in Europe and even disabled people as a growing burden upon the resources of a teeming and polluted world. Hitler cults and ideas of Aryan identity are finding new audiences among white working-class youth beset by an increasing sense of disenfranchisement in multiracial Western societies.

Both the skinhead movement and white power music have their origins in Britain, where urban youth gangs have continuously been in fashion from the 1950s onwards. Teddy Boys, Mods and Rockers, Hell's Angels each in turn created a cult of distinctive clothing, gang feuds and rebellion against their parental generation. The skinhead movement first emerged in 1968–69 when young males adopted the uniform of shaven head, turned-up jeans worn with braces and heavy toe-capped boots. Tattoos were also favored, with a preference for shocking or gruesome motifs. Intolerance and aggression, menacing behavior and physical attacks were their trademark. While not originally linked with any neo-Nazi groups, both the National Front (NF) and the British Movement (BM) began to recruit the skinheads as street-fighting troops in the 1970s.

The Nazi music scene in Britain was the offspring of this alliance. From the mid-1970s onward, left-wing and anti-fascist groups had used popular music to mobilize the young against the advance of the NF. Impressed by the success of this "Rock against Racism" movement, the NF mounted a counter-offensive called "Rock against Communism" (RAC), which sought to propagandize skinheads through gigs and large events, fan magazines and star performers. Ian Stuart Donaldson and his band, Skrewdriver, swiftly emerged as one of the NF's chief assets in promoting this racist, anti-Semitic music. Born in 1958, Stuart came from a middle-class background in Blackpool. His first band, The Tumbling Dice, formed in 1975 and was renamed Skrewdriver in 1977. Reacting against the left-wing milieu of the punk groups, with whom he often shared venues, Stuart joined the NF in 1979 but initially found that he was losing his following. However, with the effective retreat of the NF from electoral politics after its defeat in the 1979 election, the stage was set for the NF to attract more marginal, violent support.[1]

Once Skrewdriver was reformed in 1981, it began to attract large attendances and helped transform RAC into a buoyant youth organization. In the following year, the "Political Soldier" faction of the NF, under the leadership of Nick Griffin, Derek Holland and Patrick Harrington, set up White Noise Records to produce and market Skrewdriver's music. This new elite NF leadership, steeped in the tactics of the fugitive Italian terrorists and the doctrines of Julius Evola, saw the skinheads as a pool of paramilitary irregulars who would appear legally independent of the NF but in reality serve as their ground troops for street battles, football hooliganism and racial attacks in inner cities. To cultivate this alliance, the NF regularly held spring and summer gigs for Skrewdriver and other bands on the Griffin family farm at Hunt-ingfield in Suffolk, which were attended by hundreds of skinheads. The an-nual Yuletide gig of the White Noise Club held at a large pub in Morden in southwest London acted as a high point in the Nazi music calendar and at-tracted a large following from across Europe during the mid-1980s.[2]

Music and song have always possessed an extraordinary power to articu-late myth and sentiment. This militant youth culture, exulting in gut feelings of anger, aggression and xenophobia, has been particularly susceptible to fas-cist myths of patriotic revolution, anti-communism and racial identity. Stu-art himself once observed that a pamphlet is read only once, but a song is learned by heart and repeated a thousand times. Skrewdriver's lyrics fulfilled this role and became the common refrain of thousands of skinheads and young neo-Nazis across the world: "We are Mother Europe's sons . . . I want my freedom in this world today" (Mother Europe's Sons); on German reunifi-cation, "Once the land so proud and free until the war: the shame came down on Germany—Deutschland, and now you're one land: free once again" (One Land); "So many lives have been wasted . . . with half of Europe ruled by the red beast, while the other half were fooled to thinking they were free, as kosher power ruled at every feast" (Europe on My Mind); "New order, our time will come" (Our Time Will Come).[3]

However, in late 1987 Stuart and the former BM skinheads under the leadership of Nicky Crane broke with the NF following disagreements over money and politics. Stuart and the skinheads increasingly resented the NF's condescending attitude toward them, and it was claimed that thousands of pounds were owed to the bands and the record company. Stuart and Crane then founded the Blood and Honour network as a rallying point for racist skinheads and followers of the white power bands. Within Britain this net-work acted as Stuart's own music company for the production and distri-bution of new recordings, songbooks and a fan magazine, Blood and Hon-our. However, over the next half-decade, Blood and Honour, backed by the growing international reputation of Stuart and Skrewdriver, acted as a pow-erful inspiration to fascist skinheads in both the United States and conti-nental Europe. After Stuart was killed in a car crash in September 1993, his organization was swiftly taken over by the Sargent brothers and their neo-Nazi paramilitary group, Combat 18, which subsequently established Blood and Honour "franchises" in Norway, Sweden, France and the new states of Eastern Europe, including the Czech Republic, Slovakia, Slovenia and Serbia.[4]

More than fifteen years since the relaunch of Skrewdriver, there were by 1995 at least twelve white power bands with a hardcore following of about five hundred Nazi skinheads in Britain. Combat 18 played a major role in the organization of gigs and derived substantial income from the performances and recordings of the bands No Remorse (London), Sudden Impact (London), Chingford Attack (London), The Order (London), Warlord (London), Razor's Edge (West Bromwich), Avalon (Coventry), Celtic Warrior (Cardiff) and Storm Section (West Country). Founded in 1991 as a pan-Nazi initiative of Harold Covington, the leader of the NSWPP in the United States, Combat 18 combined the tactics of a protection racket with organized crime in its drive to control this lucrative business in Britain, Sweden, France and the United States. Combat 18 also established I.S.D. Records besides the Blood and Honour network as a recording company and promoted the publication of several skinhead magazines including *Blood and Honour, Blood and Honour Scotland, British Oi!* and *Rampage.* Some bands remained outside the C18 fief, including English Rose (Leicester), Squadron (South London) and Paul Burnley's breakaway No Remorse, which has made joint recordings with Svastika of Sweden.[5]

The skinhead scene is a major feature of militant neo-Nazism in Germany and expanded dramatically after reunification. With about two thousand committed Nazi skinheads and as many as double that number of supporters, Germany may be the largest and best-organized Nazi music market in Europe. There are at least fifty bands with a public profile, including a number that have already existed for more than a decade. Endstufe, founded in 1984, claims to have sold more than 100,000 CDs of its recordings, while Asgard, Holsteiner Jungs, Kraftschlag, Noie Werte, Radikahl and Störkraft have also found an international following. The Nazi skinzine *Rock Nord* has a circulation of about 10,000 copies, and there at least thirty further fanzines with circulations between one hundred and ten thousand copies. Throughout the 1980s, distribution was dominated by Rock-A-Rama Records of Cologne, but following its official suppression in 1993, this market position was taken by Funny Sounds of Düsseldorf, though there are at least six other record companies. All together, the German Nazi music companies produce more than one hundred new CDs each year with a turnover of more than one million DM.[6]

The growth of the German skinhead movement was related to several acute domestic problems. In the dilapidated eastern regions of the former German Democratic Republic (DDR) there was growing mass unemployment, economic misery and the difficulties of adjusting to capitalism and competition. But these problems were compounded by a further strain, namely, the arrival of hundreds of thousands of asylum seekers from strife-torn and underdeveloped countries taking advantage of Germany's liberal

constitution at a time when Britain and France were tightening their immigration policies. Throughout the early 1980s, the number of applicants for
asylum in West Germany had remained around 30,000 to 50,000 per annum,
but this figure began to skyrocket by the end of the decade with 121,318
(1989), 194,063 (1990), then 256,112 (1991) and over 400,000 in 1992.[7]
Politicians appeared helpless, and reception centers and asylum hostels
mushroomed across the country, in some cases nearly doubling the size of the
local community. While the economic uncertainty and large-scale factory
closures in the east had fueled xenophobia, this reaction was exacerbated by
the new regions having to take their "fair share" of the country's arriving asylum seekers.[8]

Germany wore an ugly face in the period between 1991 and 1994, with
skinhead groups roaming the towns in search of immigrant and asylum-
seeker victims. Violence toward the refugees (Gypsies, Kurds, Romanians,
Africans, Tamils) soon spilled over against the country's long-standing Turkish and Yugoslav guest-worker population (and the much smaller North Vietnamese, Mongolian and Mozambique groups in the former DDR). The riots,
arson attacks and murder at Hoyerswerda (September 1991), Rostock (August 1992), Mölln (November 1992) and Solingen (May 1993) were only the
most conspicuous flashpoints of mayhem. Overall, the number of reported
violent attacks attributable to the far right increased by 400 percent, from 270
in 1990 to 1,483 in 1991. In 1992 the number had risen to 2,639, a 77 percent
increase over the previous year.[9] Although the number of neo-Nazi and right-
wing extremist organizations remained steady at around sixty-five groups,
their membership rose from 4,300 to 5,600 between 1990 and 1993. However,
the additional number of militant extremists outside formal organizations,
especially skinheads, reached 6,400 in 1992, and it was also evident that these
extremists were very young. Until 1985, the median age of those involved in
extreme-right violence was about twenty-seven, but it was barely over nineteen in 1991–93, with many juveniles in the early and mid-teens in the skinhead movement.[10]

German police, social workers and teachers were universally overwhelmed
by the growth and ferocity of juvenile violence. The skinheads armed themselves with baseball bats with which they mercilessly beat their helpless victims, often to death. Arson attacks on hostels, explosions, and shootings became commonplace with a fatality on average every three weeks.[11] The sheer
outnumbering of police coupled with tacit approval among German citizens
for the attacks against foreigners created a situation in which the state was
hard-pressed to control an epidemic of neo-Nazi juvenile delinquency. The
crucial role of the skinhead and Nazi music scene in first attracting youngsters

into the far-right milieu was quickly recognized by the German government. Fanzines with titles such as *White Power, Glorreiche Taten, Möh—der Glatzenreport, Proißens Gloria* and *Skinhead-Zeitung* incited racial hatred and violence while offering tips on organization and law evasion. Meanwhile, the Nazi music bands propagated the racial war on foreigners: "Battledog, the beast of German blood, bad times coming for the scum," sang Störkraft.[12]

The Nazi skinhead scene is also very active in Sweden, tracing its origins to British inspiration. In 1985 Tommy Edwards, a Liverpool NF skinhead, helped establish a local branch of RAC in Södertälje, an industrial town south of Stockholm. His Swedish contacts, Peter Rindell and Göran Gustavsson, began publishing *Streetfight*, a "patriotic" skinzine which gave a heavy profile to English skins and their bands, especially Ian Stuart's Skrewdriver, for which Swedish tours were arranged in 1987 and April 1989. Blood and Honour together with the Swedes then launched a new extremist political skinzine *Vit Rebell*, proclaiming a "white revolution without mercy" and calling for a Swedish stormtroop to make an armed onslaught against Zionists, capitalists and communists. In its second and third issues the magazine threatened that this race war was about to be unleashed in Sweden. American neo-Nazi and Christian Identity apocalyptic were manifest in discussions of Ben Klassen's Church of the Creator and Ian Stuart's enthusiastic recommendation of William Pierce's *The Turner Diaries* and *A Candidate for the Order* by Michael Hoffman II, Ernst Zündel's biographer, as both books "really give inspiration to white revolutionary nationalists."[13]

Although the Swedish authorities suppressed *Vit Rebell* at the end of 1989, the Swedish Nazi skinhead movement grew from five hundred in 1991 to more than three thousand in 1995. In that year there were eight Nazi murders and a high level of public disorder. The white power bands, including Storm, Odium, Totenkopf, Division S, Spandau and Vit Aggression, are chiefly based in Stockholm and Gothenburg. Large concerts were held during 1994 and 1995 in Stockholm and Alingsås, the latter in conjunction with the largest Nazi demonstration organized in Sweden since 1945, when about six hundred supporters from Scandinavia, Germany and Britain gathered to hear Svastika, No Remorse and Celtic Warrior on 30 April 1994. Some five hundred participants from the same countries and the United States watched Asar, Swastika and Squadron perform at one of the largest rock cafés in central Stockholm in August of that year, and another concert featuring four bands was held in the capital in February 1995. Videocassette recordings of these and many other performances are marketed by Freedom Videos in Britain; such availability greatly enhances their propagandistic effect over time.[14]

At least five record companies in Sweden produce racist music for the skinhead market, ranging from Last Resort in Stockholm, Ultima Thule (the band of this name had gained a large following by 1994) in Neköping, Svea Music in Askersund, Ragnarock in Helsingborg and Nordland, which publishes its own skinzine *Nordland* as well as records and videocassettes under the label 88. Other scene periodicals include *Valhall* (Gothenburg), *Viking Order* and *Skinzine Norr*. Both *Nordland* and *Valhall* work closely with Resistance Records, the largest Nazi music supplier in the United States. As in Germany, there are now some signs that the authorities are combatting the growth of this Nazi youth movement. During 1996 many arrests took place, followed by internal dissension among the Swedish skinheads, whose numbers have meanwhile dropped to around two thousand.[15]

Both France and Italy also generated highly active Nazi skinhead movements. French bands included Bifrost, Stormcore and All Spyz, while the leading skinhead organization was the Charlemagne Hammerskins (CHS), run by Hervé Guttuso, who was aligned with Combat 18 and lived in Britain. The CHS published a series of national and regional skinzines, including *W.O.T.A.N.* (Will of the Aryan Nation), *Terreur d'Élite*, *88/14* (Gironde), *Death before Dishonour* (Calais) and *Une Balle dans la tête* (Montpelier). Other figures in the French Nazi music scene included Greg Reemers, who ran the skinzine *Viking*. After breaking with Combat 18, he produced *Sang et Honneur* as the flagship of an independent Blood and Honour section in France. Other French skinzines include *Un Jour Viendra, Militants Blancs, Blitzkrieg, Rêve de Gloire* and *Eostre.*[16] In the late 1980s there were several thousand Nazi skinheads in France, but now there are far fewer and many signs that the Black Metal music scene has become a more favoured target for Nazi politicization.

After the founding of the Veneto Front Skinheads in the mid-1980s, Italy witnessed the rise of numerous Nazi skinhead bands, including ADL 122, Peggior Amico, Corona Ferrea, Nomina Dresda, Legione dell'Odio, Soluzione Violenta and Supremazia Bianca. Although discouraged by the passing of the Mancino Act against the incitement of racial hatred in 1993, the skinhead groups have returned to prominence with an umbrella organization in the north called Azione Lombarda Skinhead 88. There are also a number of commercial operations with shops in Rome, Milan and Bologna selling badges, T-shirts, records and videos. Italy has also hosted some of the largest international white power rock concerts in Europe. Over the August bank holiday of 1991, hundreds of revolutionary nationalists from all over the continent gathered near Bassano del Grappa, significant as communist partisan territory in the closing months of the 1939–45 war, to hear Peggior Amico and

Skrewdriver give a concert called "Return to Camelot." Peggior Amico and Skullhead from Consett on Tyseside put on a show for a massive skinhead audience at Grottaferrata near Rome in May 1992.[17]

Nazi skinheads first appeared in the United States in 1984, clearly patterned on the dress and behavior of the British model. By the late 1980s there were some one thousand across the States, but by the mid-1990s their numbers had grown to about four thousand, with a larger group of over ten thousand sympathizers. The Anti-Defamation League, a watchdog group monitoring Nazi and anti-Semitic activity, published its first report in November 1987 and has since produced six more on this growing racist menace. The 1993 report recorded a dramatic increase in the number of murders committed by Nazi skinheads, with twenty-two killings in the preceding three years, the victims chiefly being Hispanics, blacks and Asians. Skinheads also committed thousands of lesser crimes including stabbings, shootings, thefts, synagogue desecrations, street disorders and mayhem. There is no single national skinhead organization, but rather loosely linked networks of gangs that affiliate under such names as American Front, Northern Hammerskins, Confederate Hammerskins, Aryan Resistance League and SS of America. These in turn have occasionally formed local alliances with the Ku Klux Klan, White Aryan Resistance, the Church of the Creator, and such Christian Identity groups as Aryan Nations.[18]

White power music has been a vital driving force in forging American skinhead identity through records, CDs, songbooks and zines that provide band interviews, eulogies of Nazi heroes and the dissemination of symbols and ideology. Founded in 1994, the Detroit-based record company Resistance Records dramatically upgraded the Nazi skinhead scene with a high-quality music production and a glossy magazine *Resistance* (1994–), which runs to more than sixty pages. Bands that have recorded with Resistance Records include Aggravated Assault (Atlantic City), The Voice (Pennsylvania), Centurion (Milwaukee), Bound for Glory (St. Paul), Max Resist and the Hooligans (Detroit), Nordic Thunder (Delaware) and Beserkr (Oklahoma). Their violent hate-rock albums carry such titles as *Crush the Weak, Born to Hate, Behold the Iron Cross* and *The Voice of Our Ancestors*, while their cover artwork features Viking warriors, German soldiers in World War II battle scenes and Nazi rallies. Resistance Records maintains a slick marketing operation with credit card sales and a website that features visuals and sound clips of selected albums.

The founder of Resistance Records was George Eric Hawthorne, a young Canadian of Italian descent now in his early thirties, whose real name is George Burdi. Brought up a Catholic, Hawthorne early rejected the universalism of Christianity, immersed himself in Nietzsche and was attracted to an ideology of white supremacy. In Toronto he assisted the Holocaust revisionist Ernst Zündel at the Samisdat offices and became a local chapter leader of the Church of the Creator, a radical religious organization founded by the Ukrainian-born Ben Klassen in 1973 that deifies the white Aryan race. A chance encounter with a tape of *Hail the New Dawn* by Skrewdriver revolutionized Hawthorne's conception of the white revolutionary movement. Popular music, the sound of his own generation, would bring youth, vitality and aggression to a movement previously supported by middle-aged and elderly reactionaries. In 1990 he founded his own band, RAHOWA, its name derived from the Church of the Creator motto "RAcial HOly WAr," which released its first major album under the title *Cult of the Holy War* in 1996.[19]

Resistance publicized the ideology of white power to a growing readership of music fans. Launched in spring 1994 with a five thousand circulation, the magazine first featured interviews with American and European bands, including Aryan, Svastika, Centurion, Nordic Thunder, Bound for Glory and Das Reich. By the second issue, circulation was up to ten thousand and Hawthorne's editorials dilated on the coming white revolution and racial will to power. Articles embraced varied topics, including anti-racism, political correctness, the "genocide against the white race," David Duke's impressions of India, the Swedish white power scene, and a paean to Robert Jay Mathews, the founder of the terrorist Brüders Schweigen group, or The Order, killed by the FBI in 1984.[20] National and cultural traditions are emphasized with a Celtic festival favorably compared with the "artificial, prepackaged, soda-pop culture" of the pastless present. Against what it sees as the multiracial eclipse of Aryan ancestry, RAHOWA "resurrects the spirit of ancient Europe," while Hawthorne and its other members are proud of their Scottish, Germanic, Balt and Slav origins.[21] History is also prominent, with features on the racist and populist ideas of Jack London, Charles Lindbergh and a youth memoir of the Russian front by a Dutch Waffen-SS man in his seventies.[22] Nordic and Third Reich imagery jostles with anti-black and anti-Jewish cartoons.

Hawthorne's white revolutionary racism and the American Nazi skinhead movement represent a desperate negation of the rapidly changing racial demography of the United States. Since the early 1980s, affirmative action and positive racial discrimination coupled with fast increasing levels of non-European immigration and the rise of a black underclass have dramatically revised the image of a predominantly white, Anglo-Saxon America. Hawthorne and other white power groups regard desegregation and multiracial policies in Western countries as the secular outcome of Christian sympathy for the weak, disadvantaged and inferior. Their pro-white racism is thus overlaid by a trenchant critique of Christianity, which is also a legacy from the biological monism and "laws of nature" preached by the Church of the Creator. Hawthorne and his skinhead supporters believe that they are now fighting for the very racial survival of the European races against a flood of colored peoples both across the world and in the formerly white countries that now have growing colored populations.[23]

In Hawthorne's view, the white race must now abandon the "false morality" of Christianity, which causes it to act against its own interest in tolerating the growing numbers and power of other races. Any liberal or humanitarian hostility to white power is interpreted as weakness, cowardice or guilt, fostered by a treacherous (Jewish) media campaign preaching tolerance, integration and racial harmony. This ideology is underpinned by the superman mythos of Friedrich Nietzsche and the "law of the jungle" taken from Social Darwinism. *The Anti-Christ*, Nietzsche's trenchant rejection of Christianity written in 1888, is now current as an anti-Christian manifesto among white power activists in America and Europe. Here Nietzsche juxtaposes the will to power against Christian moralizing: "What is good?—All that heightens the feeling of power. . . . What is bad?—All that proceeds from weakness. What is more harmful than any vice?—Active sympathy for the ill-constituted and weak—Christianity." Page after page, Christianity is relentlessly stigmatized as a pitiable antithesis to the tonic emotions enhancing the feeling of life; a myth offering spiritual consolations in place of tangible gains; a contradiction of all natural urges toward assertion and victory.[24]

Ragnar Redbeard is another major inspiration to the white power movement in the United States, Australia and New Zealand. His classic work, *Might Is Right; or The Survival of the Fittest*, first published in Chicago in 1896, outlines the case for Social Darwinism, with scathing attacks on Christianity, democracy and socialism.[25] For Redbeard, the natural world is a world of unremitting struggle, the natural man is a warrior and the natural law is tooth and claw. In this war of all against all, there are only a small number of victors strong enough to conquer and make the rules. The great mass of people have no initiative and are born to be subjects and slaves. Redbeard heaps scorn upon Christianity: "A god begging his bread from door to door!—A god without a place to lay his head!—A god executed by order of a stipendiary magistrate!" All collectivist politics, with their sentimental appeal to the masses, are but the humbug of the agitator who desires to rule and enrich himself through the State, just as the priest once did through the agency of the Church.[26]

The white power bands mobilize these trenchant Social Darwinist ideas against the tolerance of left-wing and liberal values. They believe that white

America is now a hostage to its colored populations where an affluent society seeks to appease its growing underclass. They oppose the welfare support of single black mothers with large families, which is seen as only encouraging their proliferation. Life, they argue, is a ruthless competition for scarce resources. Every individual, clan and tribe must secure its territory and propagate itself in order to survive; liberal societies are fated for extinction with their positive racial discrimination and never-ending subsidy of racial enemies, the weak and infirm. In an interview, Hawthorne extravagantly praised Redbeard's poem about war, arms and power.[27]

> Might was Right when Caesar bled upon the stones of Rome
> Might was Right when Joshua led his hordes o'er Jordan's foam
> And Might was Right when German troops poured down through Paris gay;
> It's the Gospel of the Ancient World and the Logic of To-Day.
> The Strong must ever rule the Weak, is grim Primordial Law -
> On earth's broad racial threshing floor, the Meek are beaten straw -
> Then ride to Power o'er foeman's necks let nothing bar your way:
> If you are fit you'll rule and reign, is the Logic of To-Day.[28]

While racism, right-wing extremism and violence were originally confined to white power music, the misanthropic *zeitgeist* later caught on against the brutal percussion and deafening crescendos of black metal music. In their recordings, performances and fan magazines, some of these groups brazenly display motifs of racial hatred, misanthropy, apocalyptic destruction, fascism and Nazism. Black metal music derives from the heavy metal genre which included such well-known commercial bands as Black Sabbath, Iron Maiden, AC/DC, Kiss and Motörhead, beginning as early as the 1970s. These groups also flaunted "Gothic" motifs of death and darkness, but in the case of black metal this "nightside" symbolism has often developed into a complete philosophy of negation. Formed in 1981, the Danish band Mercyful Fate was an early representative of black metal, led by the practicing satanist, King Diamond, who performed with a demonic mask of black and white face paint. The British band Venom was formed in Newcastle, England, in 1980 to offer fans a coarse fare of anti-Christian blasphemy and satanic posturings. The Swedish band Bathory (named after the homicidal sadistic Hungarian countess of the seventeenth century) started up in 1983. By the end of the 1980s, the genre was beginning to mix its transgressive satanism with Norse mythology as a "dark" pre-Christian native tradition.[29]

In the mid-1980s a new wave of satanic black metal began in Norway. Inspired by Venom and Bathory, Øystein Aarseth founded his band, Mayhem, in Oslo in 1984. Soon after changing his name to Euronymous, Aarseth re-launched his own record label and opened a music shop called "Helvete" (the Norse word for hell). In his songs and in his life-style, Euronymous cultivated a philosophy of nihilistic hatred, colored by the brooding, depressive morbidity often associated with the negative side of the Scandinavian psyche. A circle of black metal fans and performers gravitated to this dismal cellar with its satanic decor, and new Norwegian bands called Emperor, Immortal, Enslaved and Arcturus were formed. The groups Satanel and Darkthrone followed in 1990. Scandinavian folklore, grotesque monsters and a malignant atmosphere provided an uncanny background to their cacophonous music with obscene satanic and nihilist lyrics. Wearing black clothes and white face paint, Euronymous's demented and anti-social rants were matched by the other groups' profane acts involving blasphemy and aggression before shock-hungry audiences. Very shortly, these fantasies of slaughter and apocalypse were followed by genuine mayhem, with suicides, feuds and murders.[30]

In 1991 Satanel split into two bands, Burzum and Immortal. Burzum was the musical vehicle of a young Norwegian ex-skinhead, Kristian Víkernes (b. 1973), who called himself Count Grishnackh after one of the evil "orc" characters in J. R. Tolkien's fantasy trilogy *The Lord of the Rings*, while Burzum meant "darkness" in the orc language. Víkernes also legally changed his given Christian name to Varg, Norwegian for wolf. He wrote morbid lyrics about night, Jesus' death, and the coming of Christianity as an enervating plague among the heroic northern peoples in his CD release *Filosofem*. Having introduced a devil-worshiping cult into Norwegian black metal, Euronymous and Víkernes began to proclaim their readiness to commit outrages. On 6 June 1992 the beautiful old wooden stave church of Fantoft, one of Norway's architectural treasures dating from the twelfth century, was burned to the ground by arson. By January 1993, fire attacks had occurred on at least seven other major Norwegian stave churches. Víkernes was subsequently convicted of the murder of Euronymous in August 1993 and of three of the church arsons; he was sentenced to twenty-one years in jail. Sensational publicity during the trial period guaranteed Víkernes the media role of an arch-satanist.[31]

While in jail, Víkernes began to formulate his nationalist heathen ideology using materials from Norse mythology combined with racism and occult National Socialism. These essays were published in various underground publications and in *Filosofem*, a neo-Nazi magazine published by Vidar von Herske, another member of Burzum, who had migrated to France. Víkernes's articles typically revolved around esoteric interpretations of myths in the *Edda*, with discussions of Odin, his magical ring, ravens and wolves. Víkernes identified himself with Wotan or Odin: "I am his flesh and blood, his soul and spirit; for

I am his posterity and the archetypes in our race are his." Other articles focused on Norse cosmology and magical practices.[32] With his increasing racial
nationalism, Víkernes sees himself as a successor to Vidkun Quisling, the Norwegian political leader who headed the collaborationist government during
the Nazi occupation of the Second World War. In particular, Víkernes is interested in Quisling's mystical doctrine of "Universism," which combines pan-
theism with a Nietzschean will to power. He has also written a book *Vargsmål*,
underlining his role as chieftain of his Norwegian Heathen Front.[33]

The black metal scene has since exploded into an international phenomenon, with hundreds of bands in Norway, Sweden, Finland, France, Germany,
Austria and the United States. With names such as Bathory, Possessed, Slayer,
Sodom, Enslaved, Moonfog, Soulgrind, Ragnarok and Helheim, the groups
cultivate a dread image with black clothes, long hair and white facial "corpse-
paint." Performances are wild and frenzied and the magazines are filled with
skulls, ravens, werewolves, runes and magical sigils. America's leading black
metal magazine, *Descent*, published in Seattle, focuses on dark and occult topics alongside interviews with Storm, Blood Axis, Allerseelen and Sol Invictus.
In Norway itself, Andrea Meyer-Haugen publishes *Horde of Hagalaz* as "the
voice of northern witches, warlocks and warriors," to express "myths and
magic of the cold, northern heathen ground and the understanding of the
dark side of human nature." An explicit link to Nazi ideas is often present.
One Australian group, Spear of Longinus (inspired by Trevor Ravenscroft's
Spear of Destiny), describes its music as "Nazi occult metal" and features pictures of Himmler's Wewelsburg castle on its fliers. The New Zealand zine *Key
of Alocer* includes articles on Nazism and satanism, while *Trumpeter of Evil* in
Holland has glorified the Dutch SS.[34]

George Eric Hawthorne was eager to foster the links between black metal
and white power music, with special praise for the groups Burzum, Storm,
Moonspell and Graveland. *Resistance* has run features on the Norwegian
black metal scene and on the Polish group Graveland. Stephen O'Malley, editor of *Descent*, reviews the Scandinavian bands, their personalities and oc-
cult-Nordic outlook with an opening quote from Varg Víkernes: "I am natu-
rally affiliated with 'Nazism,' for it is based on our archetypal values. . . . Too
bad the holocaust is a lie. . . . Burn what you spurn, strife is life. Lay waste to
the Jew's world."[35] Darken, the leader of Graveland, dresses as a medieval Polish warrior, praises Hitler, and foretells the rebirth of an "Aryan Pagan Empire." His views are unabashedly fascist: the pagan spirit underlies all reaction
to Christianity, democracy and technical civilization, where money takes the
place of gods. The Holocaust was the culmination of this reaction. Yet modern politicians, he claims, try to deprive Europe of its true traditions and

identity. Graveland awaits the resurrection of buried archetypes and their terrible vengeance: "The Pagan Spirit sleeps in every one of of us, it is very strong but dormant. Once awakened, it shall resent and destroy that which denied it life all these centuries."[36]

The black metal scene in Germany also acquired a Nazi wing. The band Absurd was formed by sixteen-year-old Hendrik Möbus (aka Jarl Flagg Nidhoegg) and two others in Sondershausen in the former East Germany. Styling themselves as leaders of a local satanic cult, the three murdered a classmate, Sandro Beyer, in April 1993. While Möbus served an eight-year sentence for murder, Graveland released the Absurd tape *Thuringian Pagan Madness* with a cover photograph of Beyer's gravestone, thus garnering the group further notoriety in the Nazi black metal scene. Released on parole in August 1998, Möbus stated that Beyer was killed as a "race defiler," thereby emphasizing the band's Nazi politics.[37] Möbus aligned himself further with the Norwegian black metal Nazi movement by becoming head of the German branch of Varg Víkernes's Heathen Front, which now has chapters in Norway, Sweden, Finland, Germany, Russia, the Netherlands and the United States. Möbus also founded Darker than Black (DTB) Records and cultivated links with the Saxonian Hammerskins, resulting in DTB reaching a distribution deal with Germany's Hate Records, one of the largest white power music promoters in Europe. In October 1999, the German authorities raided DTB Records. Möbus was already serving a short prison sentence for displaying Nazi symbols; as a result of his part in DTB, he was sentenced to a further eighteen months. At this point Möbus went on the run, only to resurface in the American Nazi underground the following summer.[38]

The widening influence of this nihilist, satanic subculture is evidenced by the Black Circle, a loose network of national socialist black metal bands. For the anniversary of Hitler's birthday in 1999, Absurd produced a CD in collaboration with an American Nazi band called Birkenau, named after the Nazi extermination camp. Möbus also contributed to a CD medley of Nazi black metal music entitled *Night and Fog* in association with the bands SS1488 (Austria), Kristallnacht (France), Fullmoon, Wineta and Thunderbolt (all from Poland). While Wineta proclaims its opposition to "niggers, Jews and all other sub-human mongrels," Kristallnacht's leader "has spent time in ZOG controlled prisons for his beliefs and cadaver desecration." In 1998 Jon Nodtveidt, the Swedish singer of the band Dissection, was jailed for the murder of an Algerian man in Gothenburg. The Russian Black Metal Brotherhood has meanwhile emerged in the East and claimed responsibility for a variety of criminal acts.[39] Founded in 1993, Misanthropy Records in Suffolk, England, produces a dozen black metal bands through its own label and distributes a further fifty. As the principal promoter of Varg Víkernes's Burzum material, Misanthropy has a website linked to the Heathen Front and the German neo-Nazi Thule Netz. Misanthropy has close links with Stephen O'Malley, editor of *Descent*, and also distributes industrial music by the American band Blood Axis and the Austrian project Allerseelen.[40]

The Oregon-based industrial musician Michael Jenkins Moynihan (b. 1970) and his group Blood Axis have released a CD entitled *The Gospel of Inhumanity* (1995). The cover picture is taken from the apocalyptic painting *Der Krieg* by the nineteenth-century German Decadent artist Franz von Stuck. It shows a naked warrior with a banner over his shoulder riding a black horse across a field littered with human corpses. The music and lyrics celebrate the realization of a violent will-to-power. Highlights include readings from Friedrich Nietzsche's *Thus Spake Zarathustra* and spoken excerpts from writings of Charles Manson and the fascist poet Ezra Pound. Reviews hail the piece as full of brute force, esoteric wisdom and a call to arms: "the infernal shadowside of pagan Europe." Some idea of Moynihan's political affiliations may be gleaned from an interview in *Aorta*, an esoteric fascist booklet series edited by the writer-musician Kadmon of Vienna. Here he speaks of his interest in Mithraism, the martial religion popular among the Roman Legions combining "the harsh reality of struggle and spiritual light." He is fascinated by the mythos of the Archangel Michael as a violent solar deity rather than as a Christian saint and interprets Charles Manson as a Gnostic and a kindred spirit of the Nazi philosopher Alfred Rosenberg. Both are claimed as champions for recognizing the "polar symbiosis of creation and destruction."[41]

Moynihan's first musical project Coup de Grace lasted from 1984 to 1989, combining violent electronic recordings with illustrated booklets. In 1988 he brought out a special edition of Nietzsche's *The Anti-Christ* and became interested in Charles Manson and the Californian Church of Satan. These stations mapped his exploration of a pagan philosophy based on nature, race and a blood mystique. In 1989 he founded Blood Axis, taking as its symbol the *Kruckenkreuz*, which had been used by Jörg Lanz von Liebenfels as the symbol of the Order of the New Templars; the cross was also used by the Austrian Vaterländische Front and later became the national emblem of Austria under the regime of Chancellor Dollfuß. He has also collaborated with Boyd Rice, an industrial musician, who is both a priest in the Church of Satan and a member of Bob Heick's American Front of Nazi skinheads. In 1992, under his imprint Storm, Moynihan published a complete anthology of James N. Mason's militant articles from *Siege*, the periodical of the National Socialist Liberation Front, which called for terrorist attacks on the "Jewish power-structure" of the United States.[42]

In his Universal Order, a bizarre cult that has even alienated many American Nazis, Mason idolizes Manson as the outlaw hero who long ago declared
war on the "system" by murdering Hollywood celebrities. Given Manson's infamous reputation as a convicted mass killer serving a life sentence, he also at-
tracts black metal satanists as an "establishment" demon or taboo figure.
Moynihan has since conducted a major interview with Charles Manson in jail
that appeared in a popular metal magazine.[43] Moynihan also has extensive
European links. While running Coup de Grace, he lived for part of the time
in Antwerp and toured Germany and Holland. He is also co-editor of
Filosofem, published by Vidar von Herske in France. His own articles in the
journal have included essays relating Hermann Hesse's novel *Demian* to
Gnosticism and fascism, as well as a study of the runes and the cosmic significance of the "Wolfsangle" or Eiwhaz-rune, which serves as the emblem of the
Black Order, an international neo-Nazi sect, since renamed the White Order
of Thule.[44] Moynihan has since highlighted the far right and racist affiliations
of black metal in his book, *Lords of Chaos* (1998), co-authored with Didrik
Søderlind, which features extensive interviews with members of the Norwegian and German bands concerning their church burnings, murders, neo-pa-
ganism and Nazi ideas.[45]

The Austrian industrial musician Kadmon (Gerhard Petak) has attracted
an English and German-speaking following through his tracts on themes of
paganism, mysteries and fascism in the *Aorta* series. Topics have included
Kenneth Anger's film *Lucifer Rising*, inspired by the English magician Aleister
Crowley; the Romanian fascist leader Corneliu Codreanu; the blood lamp
cult of Alfred Schuler in Munich around 1900; the mystical side of the SS as
represented by Otto Rahn's quest for the Holy Grail at Montségur; the ancient
cult of Mithras; and Karl-Maria Wiligut, Heinrich Himmler's private magus
on matters of ancient Germanic spirituality. Individual tracts have also been
devoted to Moynihan and Blood Axis and to Norwegian black metal, which
Kadmon relates to Scandinavian *Oskorei* mischief folklore. *Aorta* has been followed by a new series *Ahnstern*, with tracts on the Austrian UFO engineer
Viktor Schauberger (1885–1958), Ernst Jünger and his Great War novels.[46]
Kadmon is inspired throughout by a dark romanticism, the occult and mythical and chthonic elements of European culture.

Through his music label Allerseelen, Kadmon has released the *Gotos=
Kalenda* verses that Wiligut had originally dedicated to Himmler in 1937.
Kadmon's logo is the "Black Sun," the circular sun wheel of twelve sig-runes
at the Wewelsburg. This symbol has become widespread among neo-Nazi
youth in Germany and abroad as a more esoteric sign than the common
swastika. Moynihan and Kadmon have issued a joint recording, *Walked in*

Line/Ernting, which features the stomp of soldiers' marching boots and Wiligut lyrics. Kadmon has given Moynihan many ideas and images from German fascism and militarism, including Wehrmacht battle scenes, Ernst Jünger's verse, Waffen-SS graves with rune stocks and Lanz's New Templar *Kruckenkreuz*. Kadmon's European influence is also evident in Moynihan's plans to publish a translation of Julius Evola's *Men among Ruins* and a selection of Wiligut's runic writings.[47]

Other American bands are less esoteric in their references. Of the several hundred black metal bands across the States, a significant minority flirt with Nazi and fascist ideas. A group called Ethnic Cleansing has released two EPs under the titles *Piles of Dead Jews* and *Hitler Was Right*, with shouted hate ditties about non-whites and the state of the nation. The satanic band Acheron, led by Vincent Crowley, has released a CD entitled *Hail Victory*; Crowley also edits a zine, *Order of the Evil Eye*, and is a member of the Church of Satan. Bob Heick, the American Front leader, has also recorded cassettes under the name Robert X. Patriot with the White Devil Conspiracy. Boyd Rice and his band NON have a CD, *Might!*, an interpretation of Ragnar Redbeard's misanthropic classic with electronic cacophony and grating frequencies. The American black metal scene is publicized by a number of magazines, including Aaron Garland's *Ohm Clock* (Las Vegas) and Beau Lippincott's *Warcom Gazette* (San Jose), which contain long interviews with bands on their satanist and Nazi philosophy as well as many pages devoted to reviews of music recordings and other zines in the underground scene. Crude Social Darwinism jostles with obscenity, nihilism and fantasies of mass destruction.

The potent attraction of the black metal underground to alienated youth was demonstrated dramatically by the school massacre at Littleton near Denver, Colorado, on 20 April 1999. On Hitler's birthday, Eric Harris and Dylan Klebold, both aged eighteen, unleashed a blood bath at Columbine High School with automatic weapons and pipe bombs. After their four-hour rampage of indiscriminate shootings and explosions, twelve fellow students and a teacher lay dead, many more were wounded, and the two assailants had shot themselves. It subsequently emerged that the two young killers were members of a school clique known as the Trenchcoat Mafia, which affected long leather coats, listened to black metal music, and indulged a fascination with the occult, evil, Nazism and Hitler. This behavior was apparently motivated by their hatred of the school's mainstream culture of money, popularity and success, epitomized by its star football team members ("jocks") and academic highflyers. The killers' favorite metal musician was Marilyn Manson, a transvestite shock-rocker who took his name from Charles Manson with all its associations of rebellion, murder and mayhem. Marilyn's records included such songs as "Antichrist Superstar," while other lyrics celebrated grenade explosions, suicide and evil.

Although members of the clique were generally among the brighter students at the school, their disaffection from the mainstream led them to embrace transgressive modes of conduct as a token of their alienation. In their yearbook entry, members inscribed the message, "Who says insanity is crazy? Insanity is healthy." The Trenchcoat Mafia's marginal identity found powerful expression in black metal and "Gothic" (darkside) music. Besides the leather coats, some members wore T-shirts with far-right and pagan insignia. The preoccupation with guns, death and Hitler were all so many statements of a profound rejection of the comfortable, liberal American mores of the Denver suburbs. Students at the school recalled how Harris during the past year wore black clothes in a Gothic style, affected to speak German, and was obsessed with anything about the Nazis and the Second World War. Harris had also set up his own website with descriptions of how to make pipe bombs, referring to a "chilling day to come"; he also published a song by the German band Kein Mitleid mit der Mehrheit (No Sympathy with the Majority), which said, "What I don't do I don't like. What I don't like I waste." The school massacre evidently represented Harris and Klebold's real-life enactment of anti-social, destructive fantasies fueled by a sense of failure and backed by Marilyn Manson's lyrics of doom, satanism and suicide.[48]

Another episode of Nazi fantasy and gun obsession concerned three young Britons who traveled to America and committed suicide in February 1996. Jane Greenhow and Ruth Fleming were both students at Leicester University, where they met Stephen Bateman, a young man working at a local company. A love triangle formed and they later shared a house in Andover, Hampshire. In January, the trio flew to Detroit. Fleming and Bateman traveled right across the States before shooting themselves in a suicide pact on 21 February at a shooting range in Mesa, Arizona. Greenhow shot herself several hours later in a separate incident on the shore of Lake Shasta in northern California. Subsequent investigations revealed a mysterious trail of clues linking the victims to neo-Nazi groups. There had been local talk in Andover of their traveling to a neo-Nazi training camp in the United States. Neighbors recalled their wearing Nazi-style uniforms and boots and listening to far-right music; an SS cap, Gestapo trousers and two toy German tanks were later found on the premises, while gun catalogs and photos of people in black military-style uniforms were left behind at their London hotel. Greenhow left behind eighty to one hundred pages of writing revealing her dedication to neo-Nazi and citizens' militia causes and bemoaning German defeat in the Second World War. The presence of Resistance Records in Detroit added further circumstantial evidence, while a Combat 18 magazine published an obituary. While no crime was committed, one can only speculate at the morbid fantasy and alienation that led these young people to their death.[49]

The authorities are increasingly conscious of the power of Nazi music bands to incite racial hatred and violence. In April 1995 George Eric Hawthorne was convicted for the assault of an anti-racist protestor after the disruption of his concert in Ottawa, and he was sentenced to one year in jail. Resistance Records continued trading, but in April 1997 the Anti-Defamation League successfully brought pressure to bear and Michigan State and Canadian police closed down the operation in Detroit and in Ontario, confiscating all stocks of CDs and tapes. Bunkruptcy loomed, but William Pierce of the National Alliance intervened by buying the company, refinancing the operation and reestablishing it under Erich Gliebe's management at his own base in Hillsboro, West Virginia. Pierce sees white power music as a powerful element in his campaign to influence a younger generation against multiracialism. "There is a growing revolutionary spirit among our young, creative musicians," says Pierce, "and they need a medium to express themselves."[50] Given Pierce's own creative expression in the violence-filled pages of *The Turner Diaries*, with their graphic accounts of race war in the United States, his distribution of albums such as *Crush the Weak, Born to Hate, Behold the Iron Cross* and *The Voice of Our Ancestors* leaves no doubt as to the message he is broadcasting.

William Pierce also demonstrates the close interaction between the white power and the black metal underground music scenes. Describing his plans for Resistance Records, Pierce announced his intention of broadening the spectrum of "White resistance music" to include such genres as Gothic and black metal, while the spring 2000 issue of *Resistance* ran an article "Is Black Metal a White Noise?" This article featured Hendrick Möbus, leader of the German black metal band Absurd, who had already served a five-year prison term for murder and was again on the run from German justice. It transpired that Möbus had flown to the United States in December 1999 before shuttling between Nathan Pett, the publisher of *Fenris Wolf*, a fanzine combining esoteric Nazism and paganism, in Spokane, Washington, and the White Order of Thule, a similar outfit in Richmond, Virginia. In early 2000 Pett affiliated his fanzine to the Pagan Front, a coalition of organizations, record labels, bands and individuals promoting the Nazi black metal underground. In June 2000 Möbus arrived at Pierce's National Alliance headqaurters in Hillsboro, West Virginia, and stayed for two months. During his stay, Möbus helped Pierce secure entry into the black metal scene in the United States and Europe, involving a deal with Cymophane Records, an American-Swedish black metal label with access to mainstream distribution channels. Möbus was arrested by the U.S. Marshals' Service at Lewisburg, West Virginia, on 29 August 2000, and Pierce promptly helped him apply for political asylum and fight extradition to Germany.[51]

Skinhead gangs, white power and black metal bands are a youth phenomenon dominated by young males between the ages of fifteen and the late twenties. As such, these social groups are notoriously volatile, constantly forming, breaking up and re-forming. Strong leadership, personality clashes and opportunistic alliances largely dictate their growth and development. Organizational links with neo-Nazi parties and groups are likewise tenuous and fluid. Ian Stuart's break with the National Front and the formation of the independent Blood and Honour network prefigured the recurrent fission and assertion of autonomy in the skinhead and Nazi music scenes. However, the neo-Nazi co-option and infiltration of this youth subculture was never intended as an organizational strategy to boost their own card-carrying membership. Their aim is to broadcast racism and contempt for liberalism and democracy among a new constituency of alienated white youth. From this point of view, the skinhead movement, carried by its concerts, recordings and zines, has proved a hugely effective ideological asset for the international Nazi underground. Nietzschean anti-Christianity, Social Darwinism, racial intolerance and white supremacy are now the common passwords in a right-wing youth culture that extends through North America, Europe and Australasia. By entering a youth culture that has subsequently generated its own distinctive media of music and magazines, neo-Nazism has achieved a popular outreach among the young generation on an international scale.

11

Nazi Satanism and the New Aeon

BLACK METAL MUSIC with its transgressive attacks on Christianity, tolerance and democracy is proving an attractive front for fascist and Nazi propaganda among the young. Cacophonous crescendos and pagan lyrics serve to make white power and blood mythos seem chic. But the bands and concerts are only the public face of this nihilistic assault on civilized values. Still more secret initiations are on offer to an alienated youth. Behind the violent bands and their frenzied fans lurks an international network of small extremist groups devoted to Nazi satanism, Nordic cosmology, magic and occultism. In this shadowy underground, Nazi ideas come packaged in the strident tones of Nietzsche and Ragnar Redbeard, freely mixed with the Black Mass and Aleister Crowley's magick. A core belief of this Nazi satanism concerns the advent of a new elite of supermen who will sweep away the inferior masses with their "slave religions and moralities" and so usher in a new aeon of planetary evolution.

The writings of the English magician Aleister Crowley offered many hints of authoritarian and illiberal doctrine. In 1904 in Cairo, a spirit called Aiwass had dictated to Crowley his holy writ, *The Book of the Law*. This revelation proclaimed the new Aeon of Horus, an era of force, global wars and universal bloodshed, which had superseded the old age with its moribund Christian religion. One phrase from the book became Crowley's lifelong maxim and the basis of his own religion of Thelema (will): "Do what thou wilt shall be the whole of the law." He later combined this Nietzschean imperative with notions of empowerment derived from yoga and tantric sex-magic, which he first discovered in 1912 on joining the Ordo Templi Orientis (OTO), a fringe Masonic organization in Germany. In 1920 Crowley founded an Abbey of Thelema with a handful of disciples at Celafù in Sicily and later found supporters in Germany and the United States.[1] Martha Künzel, one of Crowley's German devotees, believed that Hitler was following Crowley's precepts and became an enthusiastic Nazi. Crowley later flattered himself by noting parallels between the prophecies of *The Book of the Law* and Hitler's alleged utterances in Rauschning's *Hitler Speaks*.[2] The English thriller-author Gerald

Suster introduced these speculations to a younger generation of occultists. Writing in the "Nazi Mysteries" genre, he interprets the two World Wars and the authoritarian states of the twentieth century as the grim fulfillment of Aiwass's new aeon.[3]

Contemporary satanism began when Anton Szandor LaVey (1930–1997) officially founded the Church of Satan in San Francisco in April 1966. LaVey first worked in the circus, carnival and burlesque houses as a lion tamer and musician. Drawn to the macabre and dark side of life, he immersed himself in the occult, including such topics as vampires, hauntings and the magic of Aleister Crowley. In the late 1940s LaVey was already corresponding with Jack Parsons, a Crowleyan lodge leader in Pasadena, and he frequented a branch of the Church of Thelema (est. 1934) in Berkeley, California, in 1951. However, he was chiefly influenced by Kenneth Anger (b. 1930), Parsons's close associate, who enjoyed cult status in Hollywood for underground films such as *Inauguration of the Pleasure Dome* (1954), based on Crowley and his own visit to the Abbey of Thelema at Celafù. In 1961 LaVey and Anger began hosting regular parties in San Francisco for friends interested in magic and the supernatural. This "Magic Circle" was the precursor of the Church of Satan, a rationalist cult of self-gratification, personal power and success. LaVey cultivated a Mephisto image with his shaven head and hooded black cape, while his temple was decorated with the sign of the inverted pentagram and goat's head, skulls and black candles. The sensational nocturnal ceremonies attracted widespread interest in the novelty-seeking atmosphere of California in the late 1960s.[4]

The sources of LaVey's satanism were both traditional and modern. "The Nine Satanic Statements" identify Satan as the principle of egoism, carnality, and self-gratification, while "The Book of Satan" indicates the influence of Social Darwinism, with quotes from Ragnar Redbeard's *Might Is Right*.[5] LaVey's main ritual imitated the Black Mass of seventeenth-century France with its parody of Church liturgy and ceremonial involving a nude female altar, black candles and polluted sacraments as a form of psychodrama intended to destroy any residual Christian piety or guilt. The alleged blasphemies of the Templars are glorified in "The Ceremony of Stifling Air." Another ritual, "*Das Tierdrama*," allegedly borrowed from the eighteenth-century anti-clerical Illuminati, celebrates the animal nature of man. An overall debt to Crowleyan magic is attributable to Anger's involvement. But LaVey was also drawn to the evil aura of the Third Reich. The Church of Satan's "Law of the Trapezoid" was prefaced by the Nazi anthem "Germany Awake" written by Dietrich Eckart. Alongside garbled references to the Vril, Thule and Ahnenerbe, LaVey claims that "*Die elektrischen Vorspiele*" rituals were based on the distorted angles of German expressionist film and performed in Nazi Germany by the elite of the SS.[6]

Membership of the Church of Satan grew rapidly between 1967 and 1970 to about two thousand persons in groups or "grottos" around the United States. In the early 1970s it was still one of the larger occult organizations in the United States with a stable membership of around five hundred, which could support a regular newsletter, *The Cloven Hoof*. But the cult was soon rent by a number of defections by grotto leaders, who started small rival cults, including the short-lived Ordo Templi Satanis and the Church of Satanic Brotherhood. Another splinter was the Order of the Black Ram, founded in Detroit by Douglas Robbins, another ex-leader from the Church of Satan. This group cultivated close links with the fascist National Renaissance Party of James Madole. Then in 1975 Michael A. Aquino (b. 1946), a major in the U.S. Army Reserve and a Magister Templi of the main cult, led a major rebellion against Anton LaVey's authority. Together with Lilith Sinclair, the New York grotto leader, he carried a majority of the Church's membership into his new religious organization called the Temple of Set. Dedicated to Set, the ancient Egyptian deity believed to have provided the model for the Satan of Christian belief, Aquino's cult offered a more occult and intellectual form of satanism than the theatrical posturing of the Church of Satan.

While LaVey simply saw Satan as a symbol of man's egoism, Aquino believed in the objective reality of the devil. The theurgic rituals of the Temple of Set invoked the Prince of Darkness as a sinister supernatural power. On 21 June 1975 Michael Aquino received a direct revelation from Satan, later published as *The Book of Coming Forth by Night* (1985). This revelation presented the twentieth century as the beginning of a new satanic dispensation. Tribute was paid to Aleister Crowley's earlier prophecy of a new Age of Horus characterized by power politics and mass destruction. Aquino's ritual practices included Crowleyan magic and the conjuring of intelligent evil entities. Impressed by the power and conquests of the Third Reich, Aquino also flirted with the myth of Nazi occultism. While careful to reject anti-Semitism (many Temple of Set members were Jewish), Aquino regarded Heinrich Himmler as a satanic initiate. Inspired by the popular myth of the SS as a secret occult order, Aquino imagined the Wewelsburg as a major terrestrial focus of evil powers and conducted a satanic working there in 1981. Here at the black heart of Himmler's SS empire, Aquino claimed a higher initiation, later published as *The Wewelsburg Working* (1982).[7]

These American experiments in exploiting the shock value of Nazism have been superseded in the 1990s by Nazi satanic cults that combine paganism with praise for Hitler and the Third Reich. In Britain, the Order of

Nine Angles (ONA) was founded by David Myatt, onetime bodyguard of the veteran British Nazi Colin Jordan and street activist in his British Movement during the early 1970s. The ONA celebrated the dark, destructive side of life through anti-Christian, elitist and Social Darwinist doctrines. The link with neo-Nazism was implicit in Myatt's extensive writings on the "religion and spirituality of National-Socialism." In France, Christian Bouchet combines an interest in Aleister Crowley's magic with the anti-Semitic and fascist ideas of Francis Parker Yockey. In New Zealand, there are the Ordo Sinistra Vivendi and the Black Order, which claims a worldwide membership and publishes magazines such as *The Heretic, The Flaming Sword* and *The Nexus* (now *Western Destiny*).

Common to all Nazi satanist groups is an utter contempt for the values of Christianity and liberal society. The highest praise is reserved for the warrior spirit, heroic courage and pride of pagan barbarian peoples, especially the Teutonic and Celtic natives of Northern and Western Europe, prior to their conversion to Christianity. Nietzsche is regarded as a prophet for his celebration of the Anti-Christ and denunciation of Christianity as a "religion of slaves." The supposedly weak, humble and guilt-ridden nature of Christian morality is constantly held up to ridicule. Its secular heritage is held responsible for the prodigious growth of an inferior humanity composed of racial inferiors and fearful weaklings who claim the protection of democracy and liberalism against the fierce and powerful. Most of mankind is regarded as a wasteful burden upon the planet. The Jews and Christians are regularly pilloried for promoting a pacifist, materialist, cosmopolitan society (the so-called New World Order) in which a homogeneous and blinkered one-world citizenry obediently consume standardized products for the profit of the plutocracy. The erosion of all gender, racial, national and cultural differences is seen as a grave threat to human evolution, which, it is claimed, can only progress through struggle and war.

The chief representative of Nazi satanism in Britain is David William Myatt, whose thought has been a major influence on this international cult. Born in 1952, Myatt was brought up in East Africa and Singapore, where he was fascinated by spirit-dancing and martial arts. In 1967 Myatt came to England to complete his secondary education, while his father returned to Africa. The young Myatt made contact with a coven in Fenland the following summer and later joined secret groups in London practicing the magic of the Golden Dawn and Aleister Crowley. Around this time the activities of Anton LaVey and the Church of Satan became widely known. Yet Myatt remained unimpressed by what he saw of ritual magic and occultism. He sought something altogether more exciting, dangerous and truly evil. At the same time, he began to think of satanism as a means to create a new fearless individual, a higher human type in a Nietzschean sense.[8]

In 1969 Myatt first encountered the British Movement (BM) started by Colin Jordan the previous year. While on his way to a magical temple, Myatt chanced upon a street fracas following a skinhead rally. Ever in search of adventure and tests of nerve, Myatt felt instinctively drawn by the comradeship of these young fighters engaged in a struggle against superior numbers of left-wing protesters. He joined the movement and regularly attended BM rallies and meetings, acting on occasion as Colin Jordan's bodyguard. Myatt was impressed by Jordan's writings on National Socialism and was also introduced by Jordan to the writings of Savitri Devi, whose book, *The Lightning and the Sun*, enthralled him with its eulogy of Nazi values.[9] In his own mind, Nazism and satanism were both representative of Nietzschean self-overcoming and the creation of bold, fearsome warrior type: "To me, at that time, Adolf Hitler and his movement seemed to embody some of the ideals I believed magick should achieve—they seemed to represent a Satanic spirit, an urge to conquer, discover and extend . . . a zestful, life-enhancing character, a dynamism and charisma."[10]

After completing his school education in 1970, Myatt studied for a physics degree at Hull University and later moved to Leeds, where he continued to support the BM. In January 1974 he came to prominence on the far-right scene here when he formed his own radical group, the National Democratic Freedom Movement (NDFM), with his followers Joe Short and Eddie Morrison. Starting in October that year, the NDFM briefly published a monthly bulletin, *British News*, under the subtitles "For Race and Nation" and "The Newspaper of White Power." Its propaganda was crudely racist and anti-Semitic, and NDFM members were involved in a series of violent attacks on colored people and left-wingers.[11] During this time, Myatt wrote propaganda, organized meetings and rallies, and regularly spoke in public, once even taking his message to Hyde Park Corner. Myatt was twice arrested in political street fights and convicted for public-order offenses, receiving six-month prison sentences on both occasions.[12]

Myatt's activity on the far-right political fringe proceeded in tandem with his deepening involvement with the black arts. In 1973 he met a woman who led the ONA, a small satanist-wicca group whose tradition and practices greatly excited his interest. The ONA claimed descent from a cult surrounding a dark, violent goddess who prevailed in Albion (England) as early as 4000 B.C. As a pagan nature-religion, its rites were related to the flow and ebb of cosmic energies, the rising of certain stars in the spring and autumn, and ceremonies were performed at henges and stone circles. From these supposed neolithic origins, the cult had declined with the advent of Christianity into a clandestine folk way practiced and handed down by a handful of individuals since medieval times, especially on the Welsh Marches, the place of its supposed prehistoric origin. The modern history of the ONA began in the 1960s when this woman united three obscure neopagan temples called Camlad, The Noctulians and Temple of the Sun as a new order.[13]

Following the cult leader's emigration to Australia, Myatt took over the order and threw himself into the task of codifying and extending its teachings into a fully developed system of initiation and training for adeptship. His early ONA rituals employed a satanic mass that invoked Adolf Hitler as a noble savior as a form of "positive blasphemy."[14] Other ONA practices used crystals and sound vibrations, known as Esoteric Chant, physical ordeals, the undertaking of dangerous tasks or difficult occupations (Insight Roles) designed to develop personality and leadership. Ceremonies involved magical acts based on the Tree of Wyrd, a septenary symbol of astrological and alchemical correspondences between the individual psyche and the natural order. Between 1976 and the early 1990s, Myatt wrote more than ten ONA ritual books, including *The Black Books of Satan, The Deofel Quartet, Naos, Hostia* and *Hysteron Proteron*. Beginning in 1988, the ONA also published a periodical, *Fenrir*, named after the wolf in Norse mythology.

Myatt rejects the quasi-religious organization and ceremonial antics of the Church of Satan, the Temple of Set and other satanic groups. He believes that traditional satanism goes far beyond the gratification of the pleasure-principle and involves the arduous achievement of self-mastery, self-overcoming in a Nietzschean sense, and ultimately cosmic wisdom. His conception of satanism is practical, with an emphasis on individual growth into realms of darkness and danger through practical acts of prowess, endurance and the risk of life. Nature is regarded as a theater of chaotic amoral forces—both light and dark—which drive evolutionary progress through conflict, struggle, death and survival. The true satanist must therefore transcend his own limitations in the causal, physical world to make direct contact and identify with this suprapersonal sphere of acausal, sinister forces in the cosmos. Access to the acausal realm is provided through "nexions," gates or angles on the Tree of Wyrd, which provide the name of the order. These nexions are created by evil acts and blasphemous rituals.

Myatt derives the word "evil" from the Gothic term "ubils," meaning "going beyond the due measure" for his teaching of self-overcoming.[15] He asserts that satanism requires the performance of acts that are generally regarded as forbidden, illegal and evil if the initiate is to experience the amoral and acausal realms of sinister forces. A prime example of this ONA teaching is the practice of human sacrifice as a form of initiation and rejection of human morality. Myatt has written guidelines on the selection and testing of "opfers" (victims) prior to their ritual execution. Such "human culling" is supposed to heighten the satanist's own contact with the dark acausal forces, because war, killing and bloodshed are held to possess a powerful, sinister and evolutionary value. Although he claims that the chosen victims are already reviled by society, his mention of Christians and journalists as potential candidates suggests otherwise. Human sacrifice is related to a prehistoric ONA tradition that victims were offered to propitiate the goddess Baphomet at the time of the spring equinox and the rising of the star Arcturus in the autumn.[16] Myatt's defense of human sacrifice has led to acrimonious exchanges and condemnation by Aquino and others, who seek to make satanism socially acceptable.[17]

The ONA possesses a graded hierarchy designed by Myatt—the Seven-Fold Way—for the training of satanists. The Neophyte concentrates on private study of order literature and self-development. The Initiate takes a magical companion of the opposite sex and practices with the ONA system of spheres and pathways on the Tree of Wyrd described in the ritual book *Naos*. This system derives from the cabalistic Tree of Life, familiar to Myatt from Golden Dawn ceremonial magic. The Star Game, a three-dimensional system of occult correspondences, is used for the magical achievement of specific desires and aims. Challenging tests of physical stamina and endurance develop determination and vitality. In the next grade of initiation, the External Adept is expected to found his or her own magical group or temple and assume the leadership role in order to develop authority over followers. Manipulation of others, the charisma of power, sexual and material pleasure are experienced through active practice. As an Internal Adept, the satanist studies and trains in Esoteric Chant and practices an advanced form of the Star Game involving its esoteric influence on history and politics over long periods (known as Aeonics). The grade ritual of the Abyss involves a ritual retreat, living totally alone in an isolated natural setting for three months with only basic food and shelter. The three higher grades are Master of Temple/Mistress of Earth, Magus/Magistra and Immortal.[18]

Compared to the eclectic nature of American satanism, many ideas and rituals of the ONA recall a native tradition of wicca and paganism. The frequent reference to "wyrd," the Anglo-Saxon term for destiny, indicates a native pre-Christian tradition, while the rhythm of the seasons is upheld by holding ceremonies at the equinoxes, the rising of stars and other astronomical events. The burning of incense made from the twigs and leaves of hazel, beech and other indigenous trees similarly suggests a rootedness in English nature. An oral transmission is attributed to a few older individuals in the rural community; the physical sites of prehistoric ceremonial activity, especially in Shropshire and Herefordshire, are specially sought out for "black pilgrimages." In his narrative accounts of "traditional satanism" among rural populations in the nineteenth century and earlier, Myatt evokes a world of witches, outlaw peasant sorcerers, orgies and blood sacrifices at lonely cottages in the woods and valleys of this area where he has lived since the early 1980s.[19]

"Aeonics" is a form of ONA magic directly concerned with history and politics. Myatt's ideas on this subject were inspired by his reading of Arnold Toynbee, A Study of History (1933–61), which maintains that every higher civilization passes through an organic life cycle of growth, challenge, maturity and decay. Adapting the scheme to his magical worldview, Myatt introduces an "aeon" as the temporal manifestation of acausal energy expressed in the particular archetypes, ethos and religious cult of each civilization. Following Toynbee's analysis, Myatt identifies a common periodicity in the major civilizations of Egypt, Sumeria, the Hellenic world, India, Japan, China and the West. Each civilization lasts between 1,500 and 1,700 years. After about 800 years of growth, a civilization is subject to some form of challenge which initiates a Time of Troubles lasting on average 398 to 400 years. The final stage, typified by a strong military and imperial regime, lasts for a further 390 years, after which the civilization finally falls. The Universal State or Imperium of the West, which Myatt associates with a Nazi revival, should commence in the period 1990-2011 and last until 2390 A.D.[20]

This imperial future is jeopardized by the intrusion of a magical energy, both foreign and hostile to the native archetypes of the Western aeon. Here Myatt borrows the ideas of the "Magian soul" from Oswald Spengler and Jewish "cultural distortion" from Francis Parker Yockey. Magian interference in a Faustian culture has led to an inversion of heroic, confident and vigorous attitudes into feelings and ideas based on anxiety, guilt and deference to inferiors and competitors. Myatt claims that the "Nazarene/Magian" ethos produces Christian faith and dogma, moral and political abstractions rather than embracing action and real experience of the world. This allegedly negative spirit has morbidly influenced Western civilization: "From being a pioneering entity, imbued with elitist values and exalting the way of the warrior (and thus enshrining a 'master-morality'), it has become essentially neurotic, inward-looking and obsessed." "The dogma of racial equality," "the sham of democracy," and "the myth of the holocaust," together with humanism, communism and capitalism, he defines as Nazarene (i.e., Christian) archetypes opposed to the fulfillment of Western destiny in an Imperium.[21]

In his prophecy of the Imperium, *Vindex: The Destiny of the West* (1984), published by George Dietz's Liberty Bell, Myatt follows Yockey in denouncing the role of modern Jewry in Europe and America. Marxist communism and Freudian psychoanalysis, the rise of the social sciences, the abstraction and ugliness of modern art, atonal music and the counterculture of the 1960s have two common factors: they all, directly or indirectly, contradict the Faustian, assertive ethos of the West, and all are creations of Jews, "the last representatives of the decayed Magian soul."[22] Myatt asserts that "Aeonics" can oppose this current. By using satanic ritual to channel acausal, sinister energy into the political present, Myatt seeks to destroy Nazarene archetypes and values. Christianity and Magian decadence will recede. The return to older and truly Western values will witness the coming of Vindex, a Caesar-avenger figure (also redolent of Savitri Devi's Kalki), who will establish the Imperium. Beyond this age lies a new Galactic Aeon—a time of Promethean adventure involving space travel and interstellar colonization.[23]

According to Myatt, interwar fascist movements represented a bid by Left Hand Path Adepts (i.e., black magicians) to disrupt Nazarene/Magian forms, found a satanic empire and fulfill the wyrd of the West. "Seen in esoteric terms, National-Socialist Germany was a practical expression of Satanic spirit: led by [Hitler] who was able to utilize acausal energy and 'earth' it to achieve political goals . . . NS Germany was a burst of Luciferian light—of zest and power—in an otherwise Nazarene, pacified and boring world."[24] The Third Reich was such an affront to Nazarene domination that it had to be "uprooted from the psyche of the West" by inventing the guilt-laden myth of the Holocaust. But Myatt argues that the period of Nazi rule has opened a nexion for acausal, sinister influence; its archetypal energy has been stored and awaits further use. Hence, the satanic rationale of Myatt's fascination with Hitler and early involvement with Jordan's British Movement.

A neo-Nazi revolution is the catalyst for the Imperium and a new aeon. Using Toynbee's terms, Myatt identifies colored immigrants as a massive "barbarian horde" within the territories of Western civilization. However, he regards the skinheads as "internal barbarians" who resent the immigrant presence and form warrior bands and clans to fight for territory. These "young Aryans" reject bourgeois-liberal morality and ways of living; the skinhead clans have the potential to destroy what is decaying and diseased, and so usher in a new beginning. For Myatt, the skinheads and Nazi metal bands are "among the best of our race . . . real warriors who 'think with their blood.'"[25] They are the heralds of Vindex and the approach of the western Imperium.

From the late 1970s onward, Myatt encouraged the growth of several ONA temples around Britain from his caravan base in Norfolk. His own life sketch describes a period as a tramp and violent interludes as a mercenary in a minor African war, some involvement in Ulster and assignments as a contract killer. Meanwhile, his spiritual search has embraced such diverse experiences as a novice at a Benedictine monastery in Britain, studying the Koran in Egypt, exploring Taoism and martial arts and joining the Buddhist Society.[26] He has published slim booklets of poetry about life on the roads and his experiences of love and war. The pagan, warrior ethos of ancient Greece also features in his thinking, and he has made original translations of Homer, Sophocles and Aeschylus. After marrying and settling in Church Stretton in Shropshire, he attempted in 1983 to set up a rural commune within the framework of Colin Jordan's "Vanguard Project" for neo-Nazi utopias publicized in *Gothic Ripples*.[27] Given the highly secretive nature of the ONA, it is difficult to estimate its numbers and influence. However, its cellular structure has encouraged growth and attracted young leaders. In 1990 Myatt nominated one Christos Beest as his successor, in order to devote himself more to active neo-Nazism. It is possible that the ONA has provided a pool of recruits, especially among the young and violent, for Myatt's new political groupings.

David Myatt became active again on the neo-Nazi scene in the 1990s, associating himself with Combat 18 and the National Socialist Alliance on the extremist wing of the British far right. In 1993 he commenced publishing the Thormynd Press National-Socialist Series, which so far numbers fifteen tracts devoted to such topics as the "nobility," "wisdom," "numinosity," "enlightenment," "religion" and "revolutionary holy war" of National Socialism. Hitler's "divine revelation," "folk and fatherland," a traditional life rooted in the soil and nature all reflect the "honour, loyalty and duty" of National Socialism, which he opposes to the life of isolated consumers in liberal, capitalist society.[28] Besides this appeal to roots and an organic community, Myatt still dreams of an authoritarian-military Imperium led by Vindex, to be followed by the conquest and colonization of distant planets in other galaxies.[29]

In early 1995 Myatt began publishing *The National-Socialist*, a bimonthly desktop periodical, proclaiming the struggle of all Aryan individuals against their extinction beneath the tide of inferior races abetted by liberal race traitors. Here, Hitler worship, elitism and racial nationalism combine with an apocalyptic call for armed revolution against what Myatt sees as a tyrannical, anti-Aryan society based on consumerism, race mixing and multiculturalism. The paper supported the National Socialist Alliance and its policy of creating an "Aryan homeland" as a white racial enclave.[30] Addressing himself to skinheads and Blood and Honour bands, Myatt called for a racial holy war against the Negro and Asian invaders of "our Aryan fatherlands." All colored people are regarded as an invasion force sanctioned by the Zionist Occupation Government (ZOG), the term among the American racist right for the hated "system": "We must fight the non-Aryan invaders who have settled in our lands. We must fight the Aryan traitors in our midst who have betrayed our race. We must fight those who fraternize with the invaders. We must fight anyone who sides with the enemy, who enforces the tyrannical anti-Aryan laws of the enemy."[31]

In 1996 Myatt started a militant Nazi sect called the Reichsfolk. Based at York in England, this national organization aimed to create a new Aryan elite, "The Legion of Adolf Hitler," and so prepare the way for a golden age in place of "the disgusting, decadent present with its dishonourable values and dishonourable weak individuals."[32] Its warriors must be prepared to face imprisonment and death; they must make their home among their comrades in barracks and on the battlefields. Another series of pamphlets is devoted to "Aryan revolution," covert tactics, weapons and vigilante action. Reichsfolk publishes a desktop journal, *Das Reich*, named after the 2nd SS Division in Nazi Germany and seeks to emulate the SS ethos: "the proud, healthy, racially aware Aryan warrior." Myatt inveighs against the global environmental crisis: the majority of humanity is deemed "worthless" and a "parasitical infestation," which is plundering and despoiling the planet; even nature itself and evolution are in jeopardy. The superior Aryans must throw off the "diseases" of Christianity, pacifism, liberalism and race-mixing socialism—all anti-evolutionary dogmas and contrary to the laws of nature—and become hard and natural, thriving, prospering and expanding at the expense of inferiors. The population of Britain must be reduced from 55 to 10 million while its white surplus begins a new wave of Aryan world conquest.[33]

This sudden reemergence of David Myatt in the mid-1990s as the spiritual rector of the far-right fringe in Britain was linked to its transformation into a highly radicalized, militant underground. Frustrated by the electoral failure of nationalist parties, censorship and arrest due to the ever-tightening application of race laws, many younger neo-Nazis deserted from the BNP. In June 1994 they formed the National Socialist Alliance (NSA), which included the skinhead formation Combat 18 and its magazines *Putsch*, *The Order* and *Thor-Would*; the Blood and Honour Nazi metal bands; the British National Socialist Movement (BNSM) and its journals *Sigrun* and *Europe Awake*; Myatt's former National-Socialist Movement and Adrian Blundell's White Aryan Resistance. Taking its cue from *The Turner Diaries* and American far-right terrorism, the NSA eschewed mass electoral strategies in favor of a violent revolutionary struggle against the ZOG "system." The American idea of a white racial enclave was also adopted with plans for an Aryan homeland (East Saxon Kindred) around Chelmsford and Maldon in Essex, a scheme

also endorsed by Myatt.[34] The sense of increasing marginality and the imprisonment of leaders have created an atmosphere of idealism, self-sacrifice
and apocalypse, which is sustained by Myatt's "Aryan religion" and the
Manichaean battle against desperate odds.

The Order of the Jarls of Bælder (OJB) is another pagan-satanic movement on the British far right having an international membership. Founded
in September 1990 at Reading, Berkshire, by Stephen Bernard Cox, the OJB
combines magic and folkish nationalism in a pan-European fraternity of
knowledge, martial arts and physical adventure for young males. Inspired by
the growing assertion of regional identities in the European Union, the collapse of the Soviet Union and the reemergence of former nations in Eastern
Europe, the OJB encourages the varied traditions and "resurgence of the European tribes." The membership declaration refers to the presencing of the
"Old Gods," ancient lore and native ethos, Nietzschean self-overcoming and
the development of a warrior elite. Using terms already familiar in this subculture, the OJB claims it is training new leaders to achieve the "aeonic" destiny of Europe and the Imperium of the West, ultimately the emergence of
Homo Galactica. All "alien and messianic forms" (i.e., the Judeo-Christian
tradition) are dismissed in favor of acausal, sinister energies and the evolution
of the elitist Superman. The OJB symbol comprises a pattern of three inter-
lacing triangles and the zodiacal sign for Gemini within a broken curved-
armed swastika.

Stephen Cox has developed courses in Teutonic, Celtic and Viking history
and culture, magic, runic paths, "Aryan Living" and grade rituals for the
order, but the principal attraction of Bælder for youth lies in its adventure initiatives. Cox intends these activities to foster a new male ethos to counter the
lack of competition and military ethos among the young in liberal society.
These include the European Youth Pioneers, a new pan-European scout
movement which revives the memory of Sir Robert Baden-Powell, the German Wandervögel and Bündische Jugend, with sports, woodcraft, tree lore,
folk dance and music, archery and stave fighting, signaling, orienteering,
camping and survivalism. A Spartan Sports League offers a range of sports
and body training techniques (Gymnos, Kouros, Runic Body Work) based on
Greek, Spartan and German bündisch models, with a strong emphasis on
male bonding and homoeroticism. The magical interest is evident in expeditions to remote sites, satanic rituals and shamanic "shape-shifting." Embedded within Bælder is Fraternitas Loki (FL), a secret inner order concerned
with sinister forces and the Aeonic mission. As in the ONA, FL missions involve personal risk and danger and may even overlap with the violent activities of Combat 18.[35]

Cox rails against the contemporary Western culture of blandness, conformity and political correctness; liberalism has created an aimless, rootless, undisciplined youth. The absence of any positive direction for the innate dynamic energies of young males has led to football hooliganism, gang warfare, street violence, drug rackets and crime waves.[36] With its pagan magic and emphasis on Aryan identity, coupled with Dartmoor camps and trials of skill and strength, Bælder aims to give such youngsters a new collective purpose. The new elite will thus develop a strong cadre loyalty, racial pride, physical hardiness and athletic prowess. The OJB also provides its members with correspondence courses and a reference library comprising over four thousand sources in magic and occultism, paganism, mythology, and Nordic and Greco-Roman culture. The library also acts as a deposit library for the rituals of other Nazi-satanic orders, including the ONA, the Ordo Sinistra Vivendi and the Black Order, and the homosexual Ordo Templi Baphemetis led by James M. Martin. There is also a bimonthly double-issue magazine *Bælder*, which contains order news such as solstice rituals at stone circles in Ireland, articles on mythology and ancient sites, book reviews, library accessions and details of courses, activities and scholarships.

Although much of Bælder's cultural activity is concerned with pagan magic and prehistory, Cox's political interests are evident from his own publications. *Freyr's Oceanic Western Kingdom* (1995) and *The Aryan Arctic Atlantis* (1995) offer a mystical reappraisal of the Nordic origins of the European peoples reminiscent of the Aryan-Atlantean novels of Edmund Kiss and the speculations of Alfred Rosenberg. Another Cox title, *Sleepwalkers versus the Übermenschen* (1996), outlines the aeonic cycles from heroic Atlantis down to the present crisis of monotheism, materialism and liberalism. Regionalism, Green ideas and the New Age are related to racial folk memory and the emergence of a new pagan elite for the healing of the planet and the future of Europe. *The Occult Cycle of the Third Reich* (1997) dismisses the "old aeon" stereotypes that condemn fascism and instead presents the "Nazi Mysteries" as a "creative surge of folk archetype of immense innovation and vision": the familiar topics include Vril power, Black Sun, UFOs, the "aeonic insights" of Hitler and Himmler, and Darré's blood and soil ecology. The OJB library contains many works on the Third Reich, Holocaust denial, most Reichsfolk publications and David Myatt's outpourings on "the religion of National-Socialism."[37]

Since 1990 the OJB has allegedly grown swiftly, with many hundreds of members in Britain and Ireland, France, Holland, Belgium, Germany, Austria, Norway, Sweden, Denmark, Finland and Italy. Members are also resident in Canada, the United States, Australia, South Africa and New Zealand. It is noteworthy that there are also active lodges in Poland, Lithuania and elsewhere in Central and Eastern Europe (camps also offer teaching in English as a foreign language). OJB members are drawn from among right-wing youth groups and skinhead bands that have been successfully politicized. They include many metal musicians and editors of zines in their respective countries. Mixing the colorful baits of magic and satanism with the attractions of physical sports and outdoor adventure, Cox has successfully promoted national pride, folk tradition and Aryan racial awareness as an international project for alienated youth.

France has also boasted an active Nazi-satanist-pagan scene. Vidar von Herske, close associate of convicted arsonist and murderer Varg Víkernes, left Norway for Metz, where he records for his band, Burzum, and publishes the pagan Nazi journal *Filosofem* (1994–) with support from the Nordland Forlag of the Danish Nazi Party. The contributors include himself and Víkernes, Hawk Helsson, Michael Moynihan, Kerry Bolton, Stephen Cox and David Myatt on Aryan origins and Norse religion, the Viking ethos and the glories of the Third Reich. In 1991 Christian Bouchet (b. 1955) founded Nouvelle Resistance, a revolutionary nationalist movement, and the European Liberation Front, which revives the ideas of Francis Parker Yockey for a fascist continental bloc. He visited Savitri Devi earlier in India and now busily liaises with Libyan nationalists and Mexican national revolutionaries while his magazine, *Lutte du Peuple*, promotes the idea of an alliance between Third Way movements in Britain, Spain, Italy, Germany and Russia. He has issued editions of the writings of Yockey, D'Annunzio, Thiriart, Blanqui, de Rivera, Drieu La Rochelle and Brasillach. But Bouchet is also deeply involved in magic, fringe Masonry and Gnosticism. Through reading Julius Evola he discovered Aleister Crowley and the Western Tantrism of the Ordo Templi Orientis. He publishes an esoteric journal *Thelema*, while his imprint carries titles by Aleister Crowley, Jack Parsons, Frater Achad and Austin Osman Spare.[38]

A worldwide Nazi satanist network revolves around the activities of Kerry Raymond Bolton, who operates from Wellington in New Zealand. A former leader of the far-right Nationalist Workers' Party committed to white supremacy and authoritarian rule, Bolton became frustrated by the electoral futility of fringe politics in the late 1980s. Attracted by the satanic-Nietzschean synthesis of the ONA, he embraced the new Social Darwinism and started to publish his occult-political zines, *The Realist*, *The Watcher* and *The Heretic*, which has featured a Charles Manson interview, a eulogy of Yukio Mishima and a review of satanic arson in Norway by Varg Víkernes. In 1992 Bolton founded the Order of the Left Hand Path, which was renamed the Ordo Sinistra Vivendi (OSV) in 1994. Totally rejecting the "moral dualism" of the

Western collective unconscious originating in "Zoroastrian-Judaeo-Christian belief," the OSV practices satanic rituals while advocating heresy and the sinister way to restore a balance between creation and destruction. Man is a carnal animal and the satanist must free himself from all dogma and assert the instincts of his animal nature. LaVey, Crowley and Nietzsche are each praised for their attack on Christianity and "all slave moralities, religions and ideologies which would level mankind down into an egalitarian, undifferentiated herd." National Socialism is celebrated as the collective realization of this ethos.[39]

In January 1994 Bolton set up the Black Order, which claimed a global network of national "lodges" in Britain, France, Italy, Finland, Sweden, Germany, the United States and Australia, dedicated to fostering National Socialism, fascism, satanism, paganism and "other aspects of the European Darkside." Bolton has proclaimed an international "occult-fascist axis" and identifies a new cultural revolution among youth, coalescing around satanism, the New Right and "industrial" music, with the latter providing the impetus and a worldwide audience. He compares this new synthesis to the role of futurism eighty years ago in preparing the ground for the emergence of Fascism, and he pays tribute to Boyd Rice of NON, Michael Moynihan of Blood Axis (both Church of Satan priests) and the Austrian musician-writer Kadmon as leaders of this avant garde. The Black Order is intended not merely as a study group or publishing enterprise, but as an activist front to mobilize bands and political groups to fulfill the "Wyrd of our Civilization and the post-Western Aeon." Its symbol is an Iwaz rune, the Yew Tree of Life and Death, surrounded by the self-devouring world serpent. From Kadmon, Bolton has also adopted the Wewelsburg Black Sun symbol for his Black Order, a telling example of the rapid internationalization of this German neo-Nazi symbol.[40]

Through the pages of the Black Order quarterly membership bulletin *The Flaming Sword* (1994–95) and its successor zine *The Nexus* (1995–), subtitled the "Journal of the Kulturkampf, Realpolitik, Esoterrorism," Bolton caters for a full range of interests across the satanic-Nazi-metal movement. There are in-depth interviews on the American scene with Charles Manson, James Mason, Robert N. Taylor, George Eric Hawthorne and Michael Moynihan, and also with David Myatt, Christos Beest, Kadmon, Christian Bouchet and Miguel Serrano. Articles range from explorations of pagan Norse mythology, the runes and the mysteries of Hela, Loki and Fenriswolf to studies of Thulianism, Himmler's Wewelsburg and tributes to old SS leaders, William Dudley Pelley, James Madole, Céline, Marinetti and D'Annunzio. There is a complete reprint of the ONA Mass of Heresy, which includes a Nazi creed, and a ritual invocation for the 1994 anniversary of the Munich putsch, complete with Himmler portrait, skull, black candles, Iwaz rune banner and the Wewelsburg Black Sun symbol. There are contributions from David Myatt on the galactic empire, aeonic strategy and the cosmological magic of National Socialism. Holocaust denial and Social Darwinism jostle with Indo-Aryan mythology relating to Shiva, the "satanic" god of destruction and the reign of casteless *chandala* (untouchables) at the end of the *Manvantara*.

Kerry Bolton denounces Christianity as a "slave religion" in contrast to Nietzschean elitism. He revels in the strength and solitude of the Superman while pouring scorn on democracy and the "herd." Some samples from his text, "The Foundations of the Twenty-First Century," are indicative of his thought. In praise of the elite: "Humankind is as much a part of the food-chain as any other organism: better be the predator than the prey"; "the Superman's instinct creates his morality"; "What is 'good' is whatever strengthens; what is 'bad' is whatever weakens"; "the Superman is not constrained by the moralities and superstitions of the herd." On democracy: "The common religion of the inferiors is equality and the Welfare State: these give [them] an unjustified sense of worth and an unearned sense of security"; "the ignorant vote of the herd disenfranchises the informed vote of the few"; "the dominant morality and religion of the west has a common basis: universal equality; from this spring the dogmas of democracy and Socialism"; "the crusaders for 'human rights' . . . toil to keep alive what would, and should, perish." He calls for a new age of epic heroism, new prophets and gods to match man's Faustian destiny toward higher forms of evolution.[41]

More recently, Bolton has rediscovered the Nietzschean credentials of Aleister Crowley. Bolton is impressed by the "aeonic model" of *The Book of the Law*, together with its strident condemnations of Christianity, democracy and humanitarianism. Crowley's Aeon of Horus is an age of "force and fire" where the strong (who have realized their true will) shall rule over the slaves (whose weakness causes self-enslavement). In 1996 Bolton founded the Thelemic Society, not as another rival Crowleyan magical order, but as a fascist vanguard group to assert Thelema as a "fighting creed." Couched in the familiar tones of apocalypse, the manifesto refers to global changes and epochal upheavals: "It is now vital for Thelemites to declare our holy war upon the vestiges of the Old Aeon; to clear the way for the New, the Aeon of Force and Fire, of the Crowned and Conquering Child." New publications in support of this Crowleyan fascism include *Aleister Crowley and the Conservative Revolution* (1996) and *The Warrior Mage* (1996), a biographical sketch of General J. F. C. Fuller, member of the British Union of Fascists and Crowley's onetime follower, both penned by Frater Scorpio, and *Thelema Invictus* (1996) by Siatris. By invoking Crowley, Bolton emulates

LaVey, Anger and Aquino, each of whom regarded the English magician as an important inspiration for Nietzschean satanism.

But Bolton also vigorously attacks the rampant individualism of selfish satanism as nothing more than an extension of Whig liberalism and unbridled laissez-faire economics. The "Puritan-Jewish plutocracy" hankers after the messianic vision of a "New World Order" in which their elites will preside over the docile, obedient mass of humanity. These elites seek to undermine all national, cultural and ethnic differences in order "to reduce humanity to a mass of interchangeable economic units, produce-and-consume automatons, in a World State." Bolton regards capitalism as the negation of evolution, as it levels mankind into one huge global consumer market undifferentiated by gender, culture or race. He sees fascism and Nazism as the only genuine rebellion against these leveling forces of democracy, Marxism and plutocracy, hamburgers and Coca-Cola. Their racial collectivism fulfills the biological and cultural ascent of mankind in accordance with the Nietzschean and Faustian imperative. Bolton applauds the Russian nationalist Vladimir Zhirinovsky's goal of a New European Order free from "Zionization" and "Americanization." The Nazi satanist must deploy a sinister dialectic of crisis creation to disrupt all messianic trends toward one-worldism.[42]

Through his imprints Realist Publications and Renaissance Press, Bolton has published a variety of texts in furtherance of his "sinister dialectic." The list includes *Dietrich Eckart: Hitler's Occult Mentor* (1995), *Lovecraft's Fascism* (1995) and *Blood and Soil: A Heathen Manifesto* (1996), all by Wulf Grimwald, a former Grand Master of the Black Order, and calculated to appeal to a youth readership interested in dark and sci-fi subjects. Bolton himself has written books on James Madole, Marinetti and futurism, as well as his own anti-Christian commentary on Nazism, *Hitler, Christianity and the Third Reich* (1993). Bolton has also issued a new edition of Savitri Devi's *The Lightning and the Sun*, a study of Miguel Serrano and Esoteric Hitlerism, and acts as the international distributor for David Myatt's ONA and Thormynd Press's National-Socialist series. Besides reprints from Oswald Mosley, Arnold Leese, William Joyce and Francis Parker Yockey, there are Nazi and Black Order pendants, patches, banners, fascist music, and rune and Celtic ogham sets for sale. The writings of Nietzsche and Ragnar Redbeard promote the new Social Darwinism and contempt for Christianity.

Bolton's publishing enterprise is also important as a notice board and contact directory for the worldwide satanic-Nazi-metal scene. In each of *The Nexus* issues he offers nutshell reviews of the skinhead, industrial metal and Nazi fanzines. There are regular analyses of *Resistance, Greystorm, Revolutionary Nationalist, The New Order, Power* (Ernst Zündel), *Gambanreidi Statement*

(Odinist/NS), *Rise, Ohm Clock,* and *Warcom Gazette* (Gothic-industrial/Niet-zschean/Darwinist/fascist) from North America. Satanic interests in the United States are covered by *The Order of the Evil Eye* (Acheron), *Devilcosm, The Devil's Advocate, The Scapegoat, The Black Flame* and *The Cloven Hoof* (these last two from the Church of Satan). The Nazi-satanist and industrial music scene in France is represented by *Filosofem* and *The Burning Ground* (NS/pagan/satanic), *Napalm Rock* (music/pagan/Third Way), *Lutte du Peuple* (Bouchet's Nouvelle Resistance) and *Ravens Chats* (pagan/satanist/indus-trial). Other European offerings include *The Scorpion* (Michael Walker), *Aorta* and *Ahnstern* (Austrian industrial/blood mysticism), *Trumpeter of Evil* (Dutch metal/satanist/NS), *Sabbath Stone* (Belgian occult/satanist), *Mimer* (Sweden), *Horde of Hagalaz* and *Sepulchral Noise* (both Norwegian satanist metal fanzines) and *Revenge of Metal* and *Golden Dawn* (NS/pagan both from Greece). In Britain there are *Compulsion* (industrial music), *Fenrir* (ONA), *Bælder* (OJB) and David Myatt's *N.S. Review, The National-Socialist* and *Das Reich.* From the Antipodes come *Renewal* (Odinist), *Key of Alocer* (satanic/Nazi) and *Suspire* (Ordo Sinistra Vivendi). Both the OSV and the Black Order had joined the Internet by November 1996.

Bolton has continued to publish *The Nexus*. Several numbers have been devoted to such figures as Savitri Devi, Julius Evola and Ezra Pound. Follow-ing Bolton's increased interest in Francis Parker Yockey as a "Third Way" the-orist, the magazine has recognized the communist revolutionaries Mao-Tse-Tung and Che Guevara as allies against the globalist capitalism of "American plutocratic world hegemony."[43] Seeking left-wing and right-wing allies in his battle against the "New World Order," Bolton thereby underlines his affinity with new "national socialist" or brown-red alliances in post-communist Rus-sia and in such groups as Bouchet's Nouvelle Resistance and Troy Southgate's National Revolutionary Faction in England.[44] Bolton also celebrates Stalin as a strong nationalist leader. Seeking to recruit Stalin for his roll of great au-thoritarian figures in the West, Bolton claims that Stalin destroyed the old Bolshevik revolutionary elites as "Zionists" and "agents of international cap-italism."[45] In his quest for rebels against the "New World Order," Bolton praises developing nations such as India and Malaysia for rejecting free-trade policies in return for loans from the International Monetary Fund. Western intervention in Kossovo is condemned as the attempt of the "New World Order" to subdue a sovereign nation seeking to maintain its ethnic homo-geneity against globalization and multiracialism.[46]

Bolton continues to publish *The Nexus* along the lines of this "Third Way" alliance between collectivist and nationalist reaction to globalism, changing the title to *Western Destiny* in 2000 to reflect his Yockeyan ideology. Meanwhile, his Nazi satanic projects have passed to others. Harri Baynes, a young follower in New Zealand, has taken over the OSV, while in 1997 the international Black Order was renamed the White Order of Thule, based in Richmond, Virginia. Originally led by Peter Georgacarakos and Michael L. Lujan, the White Order of Thule (WOT) promotes Nietzschean notions of the Superman against Judeo-Christian religion, alongside the "sinister" or "darkside" aspects of the pagan northern soul. The magazine *Crossing the Abyss* emphasizes the Nietzschean project in its reference to man's self-transcendence in daring, risk and advanced forms of evolution: one cover illustration shows a striking image of a hammer-wielding Nordic hero chiseling himself into being from a rough block of undressed stone. There are articles on Savitri Devi, Odin as a god of death and paganism as "an Aryan science."[47] There are numerous reviews and advertisements of Black Metal music. The art work is typically Gothic and gloomy, with a preponderance of swords, skulls, ravens, runes and Norse warriors. The WOT has since moved its operations to Deer Park, Washington.

Nazi satanism is surely the most extreme example of the cultic revival of fascism. Taking their cue from LaVey and Aquino, these neo-Nazi groups combine satanic rituals and magical invocations with Hitler worship and Nazi ideology. The Nazi satanist attack on Christianity, even more vehement than its anti-Semitism, reiterates Nietzschean notions of the Superman and the Social Darwinist concern with power, conquest and the survival of the fittest found in old National Socialist doctrine. Socially, however, these practices represent the transgressive behavior of extremist sects that actively embrace their own marginalization. Indeed, this self-conscious association of Nazism with sacrilege is specifically intended by its devotees to highlight the very blasphemy of Nazism. When Nazi satanists perform their sinister rituals with Hitlerite references, they embrace a dark will to power and rehearse a murderous intent toward their enemies. In this cultic milieu, the trappings of Hitler and Satan both represent charged symbols for elitism combined with anger and aggression toward the "New World Order," capitalism, Christianity, democracy, other races and humanity in general ("the herd"). The swastika and Third Reich imagery join black candles, skulls and magical pentagrams in a tableau of ritualized transgression and exclusion from the rest of society.

12

Christian Identity and Creativity

HIGH UP IN the Idaho panhandle in the Pacific Northwest, majestic mountains rise above large forest-rimmed lakes. From the remote settlement of Hayden Lake, a dirt road leads to a heavily armed compound where signs warn "Whites Only" and German shepherd dogs patrol. Filled with Third Reich memorabilia, the 20-acre compound resembles a military camp surrounded by high fences and razor wire. The dominant feature is a 29-foot-high wooden watchtower draped with a huge Nazi swastika flag. But this eerie throwback to a concentration camp in Hitler Germany is actually home to numerous families and couples who have pledged themselves to living in a white world. Sympathizers live in nearby villages and meet each Sunday for a religious service held at the church within the compound. The service is held by the Reverend Richard Butler, who established this white racial utopia known as Aryan Nations in 1974. He begins the service with an outstretched right arm salute before launching into a sermon about the rising tide of color and the "niggers" who are getting preferential treatment as whites become an endangered minority in their traditional ethnic homelands.

Butler inveighs against the political class that is destroying the white race. Americans have not been conquered by the Jews, blacks, Mexicans or Asians, but they have been deceived by their own weakness and allowed nineteen million white babies to be butchered by abortion. Affirmative action, he claims, effectively bars any white man from full citizenship in the United States. All over the world, in Germany, England and Canada, the white race is declining in numbers due to falling birth rates, and colored immigration is encouraged to replace the population. Only whites have ever heeded calls to curb population growth, and white women have been neglecting child-bearing in favor of careers and making money. Advertising, media images and television encourage white women to take black husbands, while education, books and memorials promote ethnic minorities to the detriment of white majority heritage and culture. Butler ends his sermon with his rallying call: "As long as this alien tyranny evil occupies our land, hate is our law and revenge is our duty."[1]

After the service, the families speak of their desire to escape the ethnic swamping of their former home towns, where Latin American immigrants began arriving in the 1980s to work for low wages in the local factories. "Mexicans and blacks overran the whites," one young woman says. "You're not supposed to mix races. The Bible says that. But people listen to nigger music, they dance like niggers. Nobody cares anymore." Her new husband adds: "Every time you turn around you see white girls with niggers, slowly destroying our pure race." In the compound, children grow up in a secure, communal world quite apart from multiracial metropolitan life. They hardly ever see a colored face and are quite innocent of the political correctness and affirmative action that dominates contemporary American society. Sexual roles at Aryan Nations are strongly traditional. Women cook and do the housekeeping, while the men protect, respect and provide for the women and children. Due to past attacks on the compound by opponents, men carry shotguns or assault rifles and wear a paramilitary blue uniform.[2]

Aryan Nations rose to prominence on the white supremacist scene in the mid-1970s, when the influence of the Ku Klux Klan was on the wane. Its advocacy of a white power revolution and call for a white racial homeland in the Pacific Northwest set a new agenda for the racist far right that was increasingly concerned with viable responses to the rapid growth of multiracialism in the United States. Richard Butler, an enthusiastic pastor of the racist, anti-Semitic Christian Identity movement, preached a radical doctrine at his Church of Jesus Christ Christian on the Aryan Nations compound. He told his followers that Christian Identity gave whites "divine permission to hate." Adopting the symbols of Nazi Germany, Butler held an annual Aryan World Congress at Hayden Lake that attracted a wide range of extremists, including Klansmen, militant tax protesters, neo-Nazis and Identity believers from all over the United States and even overseas. By the early 1980s, Aryan Nations' sphere of influence included such notorious far-right leaders as ex-Texas Grand Dragon Louis Beam, National Alliance leader William Pierce and White Aryan Resistance founder Tom Metzger.

Aryan Nations became the theological college from which the most violent racist radicals would graduate. In 1983 a group called the Brüders Schweigen embarked on a campaign of robberies and assassination over an eighteen-month period. Many members of the group had been Aryan Nations members and drew their inspiration from Butler's preaching. The leader, Robert Jay Mathews, was killed at a shoot-out with federal agents in December 1984, while twenty-four members of the group were convicted of racketeering and other offenses. Members of the Aryan Republican Army, another terrorist group with ties to Aryan Nations, carried out some twenty-two bank robberies in the mid-1990s to fund a white supremacist revolution. Another terrorist group, the New Order, was also associated with Aryan Nations. In 1998 four members pleaded guilty to charges in connection with an alleged plot to blow up the Southern Poverty Law Center, a watchdog monitoring U.S. hate groups; kill its director Morris Dees; poison cities' water supplies and bomb state capitol buildings.

What was the content of Butler's gospel that could motivate young men to commit reckless acts of insurrection against the multiracial Leviathan? Why could the racist right, so often characterized by pessimism and despair, embrace a vision of active millenarian combat against the hated political and social order of the United States? The answer to these questions lies in the unique doctrine of Christian Identity that represents one of the most powerful doctrinal statements of the Nazi cult in contemporary society. Briefly stated, Christian Identity regards the white Aryans as the descendants of the biblical tribes of Israel who are on earth to do God's work. By contrast, the Jews are quite unconnected to the Israelites but rather the very children of the Devil, the spawn of an illicit sexual relation between Satan and Eve in the Garden of Eden. Alongside these dualist notions, Identity doctrine is also vigorously millenarian by believing that the world is on the verge of a final apocalyptic battle between good and evil.

Christian Identity clearly reflects the global dominance of the Anglo-Saxon peoples in the nineteenth and early twentieth centuries. The colonial achievement of the British Empire and the rapid white settlement of the United States posited the idea that the white European races were the "chosen people" of biblical narrative. The corresponding elaboration of the Israelite identity of the Aryans, matched by the relegation of the Jews, created an Aryan mystique grounded in biblical Christianity. The universalism of the New Testament is thus subordinated to the tribal covenant and racial exclusivity of the Old Testament, in which the Aryans claim God's favor in lieu of the Jews as God's chosen people. This gospel is logically mirrored by virulent anti-Semitism. The Jews are regarded as the cosmic arch enemy for they have stolen this birthright and are bent on vanquishing the Aryans through economic enslavement, colored immigration and race mixing. The growth of Christian Identity in the United States after the Second World War indicates the Americans' strong attachment to Christianity to guarantee their status as pilgrims, pioneers and settlers of the promised land.

Christian Identity combines a contemporary appeal to white supremacism with the two-thousand-year-old tradition of Christian anti-Semitism. The notion that the Jews, together with the colored pre-Adamic races or "mud people," have conspired against the white Adamic peoples throughout all time is strengthened by the belief that the world is now almost entirely in the grip of these anti-Aryan forces. The United States government is seen as the manifestation of this evil tyranny, generally known by Identity followers as ZOG (Zionist Occupation Government). Christian Identity has no central organization but consists of numerous small churches, Bible study societies and associated political groups. Estimates of the number of people involved with Identity are thus uncertain, though they range from two thousand to over fifty thousand.[3] Still, the marginal political status of Identity in American society belies its capacity to offer a theological rationale for militant opposition to multiracial society that can erupt in acts of millennial violence.

Christian Identity traces its origins to British-Israelism, a sectarian religious movement originating in nineteenth-century England under such leaders as John Wilson (?–1871) and Edward Hine (1825–1891). In his *Lectures on Our Israelitish Origin* (1840), Wilson claimed that the British were the lineal descendants of the "ten lost tribes" of the northern kingdom of Israel, whose religious election was illustrated by the increasing world dominion of the Anglo-Saxon and Celtic peoples. The British were deemed to be the descendants of Ephraim, while the settlers of North America sprang from Manasseh. However, the movement was itself originally philosemitic. The Jews themselves were deemed heirs of the two tribes in the southern kingdom of Judah, whose destiny was linked to the British Israelites in a millennial vision of the future. The reuniting of All-Israel, a prerequisite of the Last Days, required that the ten tribes of Israel, namely the British, should once again join the descendants of the remaining tribes—that is, the Jews—in the Holy Land. Throughout the early twentieth century, the joint enterprise of the Anglo-Jewish resettlement of Palestine remained an important part of British-Israelite millennialism.[4]

British-Israelism spread to America through the activities of Lieutenant Charles Totten of New Haven, supported by the missionary travels of Edward Hine in the United States between 1884 and 1888. By the end of the 1920s, British-Israelism acquired a national organization as the Anglo-Saxon Federation of America under the leadership of Howard B. Rand (1889–1991). Rand was a vital link between British-Israelism and its later American variant, Christian Identity, for he not only consolidated the movement in the United States but also opened it to the right-wing and anti-Semitic influences that became dominant in the postwar period.

A key figure in this development was William J. Cameron (1878–1955), whom Rand involved in federation meetings in Detroit in 1930. Cameron was a notorious anti-Semite who had begun his career as a writer for Henry Ford's weekly newspaper, the *Dearborn Independent*. He became its editor in 1921 and ran a weekly series of anti-Semitic articles, later collected in a four-volume work under the title *The International Jew*. These articles introduced the American public to *The Protocols of the Elders of Zion*, the czarist invention that has become the most famous anti-Semitic book of the twentieth century.[5] By the mid-1920s he was Henry Ford's press relations manager, a position he held until the early 1940s. In 1933 Cameron was a member of the national executive committee and became president of the Anglo-Saxon Federation of America in 1937. He brought substantial resources to the movement, including the prestige of his close relation with Henry Ford, media skills and a high-powered network of business contacts. His combination of the myth of Jewish world conspiracy with British-Israelism was a signal episode in the rightward, anti-Semitic shift of its membership and discourse.

But early British-Israelism's fraternal attitude toward the Jews often betrayed a patronizing tone. John Wilson had claimed that the Jewish tribes of Judah had intermarried with spiritually inferior peoples known as the Edomites.[6] In 1934 Cameron took this disenfranchisement of the Jews a stage further by elaborating on the "Esau race," "an anti-Israel power that endures to this day." According to Cameron, this formerly separate Esau race had "amalgamated with the Jews, and began their terrible work of corrupting the Jewish religion from within." The Esau people became the Edomites and later the Idumeans, the ancestors of Herod. All this suggested that whatever remained of the tribes of Judah in the Jews had been corrupted by the blood of the Esau race, until the Jews were biologically linked with Jesus' persecutor. Another British-Israelite writer, Frederick Haberman, described the Jews' intermarriage with the Edomites, Idumeans and Syrians, causing them to acquire the dark complexion of these peoples, in marked contrast to the tall and fair Israelites, "the cream of the Aryan race."[7]

The geographical shift of British-Israelism toward the West was another critical factor in its radicalization. In 1937 a Canadian group at Vancouver broke its ties with Toronto and London and began cultivating contacts on the West Coast, cemented by a series of annual conferences in Vancouver, Portland (Oregon) and Los Angeles between 1939 and 1947. Vancouver-based writers embraced markedly conspiratorial and anti-Semitic ideas, which became a dominant influence in California. A pseudonymously authored novel, *When? A Prophetical Novel of the Very Near Future* (1944), contained one of the earliest statements maintaining that the Jews are the offspring of Satan. Another apocalyptic tract, *When Gog Attacks* (1944), presented a number of key Christian Identity ideas: Cain as the founder of the "synagogue of Satan"; the "Turko-Mongol" origins of the Ashkenazic Jews; and the historical truth of the *Protocols of the Elders of Zion*. By 1947, Los Angeles had become the new center of the British-Israel movement, where its increasing radicalism inter-sected with the career of America's best-known anti-Semitic agitator, Gerald L. K. Smith, who had been Huey Long's henchman in the 1930s. Smith culti-vated close links with the California leaders of the movement, including Bernard Comparet, William Potter Gale and Wesley Swift. Under his influ-ence and their leadership, British-Israelism was finally transformed into Christian Identity.[8]

The tendency of British-Israelism in America to diminish the ties between the Jews and All-Israel was largely attributable to the factors of American Jew-ish immigration and political Zionism. British-Israelism absorbed the wide-spread nativist reaction to the high immigration levels of East European Jewry from the late nineteenth century onward. Resented and perceived as unassimilable, these Ashkenazic Jews provoked hostile theories concerning their racial origins. Lothrop Stoddard, the leading racial theorist of the inter-war period, had described two races of Jews. The "aristocratic" Sephardic Jews, who had entered the Mediterranean world, were the genuine Semites. However, the Ashkenazic Jews were a mixture of diverse bloods, whose fea-tures reflected intermarriage with the Hittites. These eastern Jews had mi-grated into southern Russia, where they then blended with the Khazars, whom Stoddard regarded as a combination of Turkish and Mongoloid peo-ples.[9] Although Stoddard had no connection with British-Israelism, the movement readily adopted the Khazar identity of the Jews as a further means of invalidating their claim to be the descendants of the biblical Hebrews.

By the 1960s, when Christian Identity was established as a force on the ex-treme right, the Khazar ancestry of the Jews was a firm article of faith. Two books, widely read in this milieu, came to excercise a strong influence in this regard. John Beaty's *Iron Curtain over America* (1951) focused especially on the roots of Russian Jewry. He claimed that the reforms of Czar Alexander II gave the "Judaized Khazars," who had converted in the seventh century, the opportunity to infiltrate and corrupt Russia. Wilmot Robertson's *Dispos-sessed Majority* (1972) repeated the Khazar thesis of Stoddard. Christian Identity teachings readily seized on this negative reference to Russian Jewry, but backdated Jewish intermarriage with the Khazars into biblical times. In *A Short History of Esau-Edom in Jewry* (1948), the Vancouver writer C. F. Parker had claimed that a tiny remnant of "true Judah" was pitted against a larger group of Idumean-Hittites who masqueraded as the true seed of Abraham and sought to expel the descendants of Jacob. These Esau-Hittites are the Ashkenazim, concentrated in Eastern and Central Europe and America. The old religious language also lent itself to new political contexts. Edom meant "red," and Parker hinted that most Russian communist revolutionaries were descendants of Esau-Edom, an association also repeated by others, including Howard Rand and Wesley Swift.[10]

The hostility of British-Israelism toward Zionism also worked to associate Jews with racial impurity. When the British Army invaded Palestine in 1917, the famous Balfour Declaration was issued, promising that the British would facilitate the establishment in Palestine of a national home for the Jews. In 1922 British-Israelite prophecy seemed again confirmed when the League of Nations gave Britain a mandate to rule Palestine and secure that objective. However, while Jewish settlement was necessary for divine fulfillment, the concept of a sovereign Jewish state was anathema. Once Zionism articulated its demand for an exclusively Jewish state, the withdrawal or expulsion of the British would imply that Palestine would be left with Judah but Israel would be absent. The novel *When?* describes an apocalyptic military climax to the Second World War set in Palestine. After the British retreat from Jerusalem, the city is captured by the evil forces of Gog, aided by Zionists—none other than inauthentic Jews who are the descendants of ancient intermarriages with impure races. One of the hero's informants claims that the Sephardim are the true Jews, while the Ashkenazim are not. "There was great animosity between the real Semitic Jews and the greater part of the Zionists [who] were usurpers of Gentile blood."[11]

In 1948, the year of the creation of the state of Israel, C. F. Parker repeated the view that there were two races of Jews. He considered the Zionists to be almost exclusively Ashkenazim and therefore "Esau-Edomites." If the Sephardim were pious and apolitical, the Ashkenazic Zionists shamelessly mobilized the financial and political influence of European and American Jewry to support their campaign for a sovereign state. "The newly declared Jewish State of 'Israel' is as ersatz and barren as its predecessor, the Herodian-Jewish nation, for it still rejects Jesus Christ. . . . The Jews have seized the Holy Land from the rightful owners [Israel-Britain]."[12] Howard Rand also fulminated against the new state, branding it the work of "renegade Jews," not "true Israelitish Jews." He described these "renegades" as the same impostors who had led the Russian Revolution thirty years earlier. In a later article, he identified the Zionists with "a Great Conspiracy" and "programme of evil," whereby the Jews had deceived Christians, so that Jews appeared to be the rightful heirs to the state of Israel. This grand deception, he argued, had extensive ramifications among the Nihilists, the Illuminati, the Fabians and the House of Rothschild.[13]

Christian Identity doctrine progressively removed the Jews totally from the domain of humanity. As we have seen, from the 1930s onward, movement writings increasingly called into question the religious authenticity and racial homogeneity of the Jews. Even the originally philosemitic English movement limited the Jews to the tribes of Judah, while the Anglo-Saxon-Celtic tribes of Israel assumed the senior partnership in the quest for Jewish conversion and the millennial resettlement of All-Israel. Then it was suggested that Jews had intermarried with the offspring of Esau to become the Edomites. Canaanite and Hittite blood was supposed to have further compromised their racial identity, until their Semitic inheritance was drowned in the Asiatic gene pool of the Khazars. As Michael Barkun has observed, while the Anglo-Saxons claimed for themselves the biblical role of Israel, the Jews' claims were progressively delegitimated. First, they needed the protection of the European Christian tribes of Israel; then they lusted after strange peoples to become carriers of tainted and alien blood; finally, they were mere impostors masquerading as the heirs of a biblical people and credited with plots and revolutions compatible with the *Protocols of the Elders of Zion*.[14]

However, British-Israelism went a stage further in the demonization of the Jews. This worldview was based on nineteenth-century theories of a pre-Adamic race of inferior, bestial creatures quite separate from Adam, who was regarded as the son of God and the first white man. But the Adamic race was threatened by evil. In this narrative, the Devil assumed humanoid form as the "serpent" and sexually seduced Eve. This primal sin not only resulted in the first couple's expulsion from Eden, but in the creation of a hybrid creature called Cain. While Cain's birth began a human "seedline" linking his descendants with satanic paternity, Cain himself was supposed to have fled eastward to establish a colony together with colored pre-Adamite peoples. Here—a preferred location was East Turkestan—Cain initiated his followers into the Devil's plan for earthly dominion. As the myth crystallized, the Jews were increasingly linked with Canaanites, the putative descendants of Cain, rather than the Edomites. If the tribes of Judah were supposed to have intermarried with Cain's descendants, it followed that the Jews were the literal offspring of the Devil through the original satanic seedline of the "serpent" as well as the descendants of sundry black and brown pre-Adamic races.[15]

These ideas began to coalesce into a logical theology by the mid-1940s, but the first full versions were not published until around 1960 by Conrad Gaard, Betrand Comparet, William Potter Gale and Wesley Smith, who represented the first generation of Christian Identity preachers associated with Gerald L. K. Smith. Already in the novel *When?*, Cain was said to have founded a secret society to do the Devil's work on earth, which was continued by the Askhkenazim Jews.[16] Conrad Gaard described the "serpent" as a pre-Adamite acting on Satan's orders to father Cain.[17] William Potter Gale was less ambiguous in his booklet, *The Faith of Our Fathers* (1963): "Satan seduced Eve and she had a son by him who was named Cain." As Cain was unacceptable to the Creator, he joined Satan's hosts and became a member of a pre-Adamite non-white society deriving from Lucifer and his fallen angels who dwelled upon earth. Gale considered the Jews to be Cain's descendants who had intermarried with Judah. Judah's son by a Canaanite woman produced Shelah, who "was of the mongrelized seed, some white from Judah and the balance of Negro and Asiatic mixture." He posited a millennium in which the war between God and the Devil was enacted by final conflict between the children of Adam and the Jews.[18]

Wesley Swift, the seminal influence upon Richard Butler, elaborated a similar quasi-Gnostic anthropogeny involving the Adamic race as the direct spiritual offspring of God, created before the creation of the solar system. The non-white pre-Adamites also had an extraterrestrial origin in the rebellion of Lucifer, who had come to earth with his fallen hosts from elsewhere in the galaxy. Swift asserted that Lucifer seduced Eve, who gave birth to Cain, whose progeny, "the sons and daughters of Lucifer," "are the people you know today as Jews." The Adamites were identified as the Aryans of central Asia, whose divine vocation was to combat the Luciferians, whose ranks included both the original pre-Adamite nonwhites and the demonic seedline of Cain. Beset by fearful images of white submergence in a colored flood, masterminded by satanic Jews, Swift's identification of evil ultimately embraced the entire non-white world. The Jews themselves were shape-shifters, a plastic form of evil in the most varied racial forms: "The jews are Hittites and Amalekites and Canaanites. They are red, black, yellow, and brown, as well as off-coloured white."[19]

Swift's millennialism invoked a panorama of evil dominion based on the whore of Babylon riding on a beast with seven heads and ten horns, as described in the seventeenth chapter of the Book of Revelation: "And the woman was arrayed in purple and scarlet color, and decked with gold and precious stones and pearls, having a golden cup in her hand full of abominations and filthiness of her fornication: And upon her forehead was a name written, MYSTERY, BABYLON THE GREAT, THE MOTHER OF HARLOTS AND ABOMINATIONS OF THE EARTH."[20] Swift saw this apocalyptic image as a metaphor for the Jewish world conspiracy. This system of "Mystery Babylon" was headed by Jewry, the direct descendants of Lucifer, who had enslaved the white Aryan world by economic means. However, Swift already envisaged the coming millennium, when an uprising would finally destroy this conspiracy and the terrible power of world Jewry. "When Mighty Babylon falls, it will be the falling of the symbolic mystery system that controls all pagan religions and false theology, and philosophies, and economic manipulation—all parts of the Luciferian kingdom, Great will be the fall of that kingdom."[21]

Wesley Swift (1913–1970) was the most important figure in the early postwar history of Christian Identity, and it was he who introduced Richard Butler to the movement. Born in New Jersey, the son of a Methodist minister, Swift had come to California in the early 1930s and probably encountered British-Israelism at the Kingdom Bible College in Los Angeles. He founded his own church as the Anglo-Saxon Christian Congregation in Lancaster, California, in 1946, where he established himself as a gifted preacher. Alongside his religious witness, he was also politically active through the Christian Nationalist Crusade of Gerald L. K. Smith, with whom he closely collaborated. In 1956 he met William Potter Gale (1917–1988), with whom he founded the Christian Defense League (CDL) in the early 1960s as a Christian Identity vehicle. The first president and national director of the CDL was Richard Butler, whom Gale had brought to Wesley Swift's church. As Butler wrote, his meeting with Swift was nothing short of a revelation: "He [Swift] was the total turning point in my life. The light turned on. He had the answers I was trying to find."[22]

Richard Girnt Butler was born on 23 February 1918 in Bennett, Colorado, the son of a machinist of German-English ancestry. As a youngster he was fascinated by the novel *The Red Napoleon*, serialized in *Liberty Magazine*, which described the invasion and conquest of the United States by race-mixing Bolsheviks. In the Depression years, the family moved to Los Angeles, where Butler studied aeronautical engineering at the City College and took a part-time job with the Consolidated Vultee Aircraft Company. Posted by the company in 1941 to Bangalore to overhaul airplanes for the Royal Indian Air Force, Butler was given the honorary rank of captain and a Hindu valet. In India, Butler was deeply impressed by the caste system and its notion of racial purity. After the Japanese attack on Pearl Harbor, Butler returned to Los Angeles and enlisted in the Army Air Corps, where he instructed mechanics but saw no active combat.[23] Given his anti-communist and racist sympathies, Butler found it hard to accept Nazi Germany as America's enemy. Later he would recall how thrilled he was to see newsreels of marching Germans, avidly sharing Hitler's hatred of communists.

After the war, Butler's politics matured into extremism. He was enthralled by Senator Joseph McCarthy's anti-communist hearings, supported his campaign, and became convinced that America was beset by "Jewish communism." Forsaking his earlier American heroes, he now regarded Hitler as the second greatest man to live after Jesus Christ. While organizing a signature campaign of the California Committee to Combat Communism, Butler met

William Potter Gale, a former senior officer on General Douglas MacArthur's staff, who had been ordained an Identity minister by Swift in 1956. Gale brought Butler to Swift's Anglo-Saxon Christian Congregation at Lancaster in 1961, whereupon Butler immersed himself in Identity teachings, studying intensively with Swift and absorbing the racist-millennial theology into his own Nazi outlook. These religious and political milieus had already overlapped when senior Identity figures collaborated with Lincoln Rockwell to launch the National States Rights Party in 1958. Butler himself introduced Rockwell to Christian Identity in the early 1960s. In June 1964, Rockwell met with Wesley Swift to discuss a close working relationship, motivated by Rockwell's view that the American Nazi Party needed a pseudo-Christian theology to attract more members.[24]

From 1946 to 1964 Butler organized and ran a plant for the manufacture and machining of automotive engines and aircraft parts, alongside his presidency of the CDL and Identity preaching. In 1968 he became a senior marketing engineer with Lockheed Aircraft Company at Palmdale, California, where he was involved in the production of the L-1011 jumbo jet aircraft. During this time he became the co-inventor of a rapid repair system for airplane tubeless tires, royalties from which considerably boosted his financial position. Following Swift's death in 1970, Butler took over as pastor at the Lancaster church, but the congregation began to dwindle. Butler felt that a new start had to be made away from multiracial California. Holding a private pilot's license, he began making flights up to the Pacific Northwest and thought of creating a white homeland in that part of the country. He retired from Lockheed at age fifty-five and in 1974 moved to Hayden Lake near Coeur d'Alene, Idaho, and purchased an old farmhouse. In 1977 he formed the Church of Jesus Christ Christian with a political arm known as Aryan Nations.

Much Aryan Nations literature echoes the biblical concerns of British-Israelism since its transformation into modern Christian Identity. Butler's credo states that "the Bible is the true Word of God . . . the family history of the White Race, the children of Yahveh placed on earth through the seedline of Adam." Adam is described as the father of the white race only. The credo asserts that the true, literal children of the Bible are the Twelve Tribes of Israel, now scattered throughout the world and known as the Anglo-Saxon, Teutonic, Scandinavian, Celtic, Basque, Lombard, Slavic and kindred peoples. A chart shows how yesterday's tribes of Israel correspond to today's Aryan nations based on the traditional association of Great Britain with Ephraim, Canada and the United States with Manasseh, Sweden with Asher, Dan with Denmark, France with Zebulun, Italy with Gad and so on. In view of Jewry's complete relegation, all *twelve* tribes are included, as the two Jewish tribes of the southern kingdom, Judah and Benjamin, are now identified as the ancestors of Germany and Iceland. The credo repeats the charge that the Jews are Satan's spawn: "There are literal children of Satan in the world today . . . the descendants of Cain, who was a result of Eve's original sin, her physical seduction by Satan."[25]

God's intended purpose, according to the credo, was that "His racial kinsmen were to be in charge of this earth." Christ's redemptive work ended on the cross, and the Aryan race was henceforth commissioned to fulfill his divine purpose and plans, which are presented in terms of a final millennium to be established on earth. In his political manifesto, Butler outlines twelve points for the establishment of a state for the Aryan racial nation. This begins by stating that no such state of the "Adamic Aryan race" presently exists. Given the duty of the Aryans to preserve their race, culture and people, it follows that redemption consists in a return to the eugenic law, which alone guarantees the creative "life spirit" of the Adamic Aryan through the purity of the blood of the race in the current generations. Only "the single united will of the people of the racial nation" can produce the racial state, while there can be no separation between "spiritual" worship and the political state. Aryan Nations is described as a "White Racial 'Theopolitical' movement . . . a 'geopolitical' movement for the re-establishment of White Aryan sovereignty over the lands of Aryan settlement and occupation."[26]

The Aryan Nations catalog includes a wide range of Christian Identity literature, with numerous booklets and tracts by E. Raymond Capt, Wesley Swift, Bertrand Comparet, and Howard Rand. The theme of Anti-Christ is prominent in books on communism, the Illuminati, the Federal Reserve System, and the *Protocols of the Learned Elders of Zion*, all illustrating the varied assaults of the Jews in their cosmic war against the Adamite Aryans. A whole section is devoted to the Third Reich and National Socialism, with eulogies of Adolf Hitler and Reinhard Heydrich, glowing accounts of Nazi policy, art and culture and Leon Degrelle's *Story of the Waffen SS*. Holocaust denial also features with Richard Harwood's *Did Six Million Really Die?* and the Auschwitz titles of Wilhelm Staeglich and Thies Christophersen. *The Aryan Warrior* by Richard Butler is required reading for all Aryan Nations members. Here, Butler describes Christianity and race as the twin foundation of "the will to power and world leadership inherent in the soul of the seed of Adam." The pages devoted to the spiritual, mental and physical education of Aryan youth are profusely illustrated with Third Reich posters from the 1930s promoting the Hitler Youth and League of German Maidens. All land and industrial capital shall be subject to public control in the national and racial interest. The financial system of international Jewish capitalism will be ended and there will be no interest-bearing debt.

In 1981 Butler hosted his first annual Aryan Nations World Congress at Hayden Lake, which drew numerous Identity and non-Identity white racialist groups from all over America. Christian Identity millennialism was now in the ascendant against a background of increased immigration, high non-white birthrates, forced school busing and white urban flight. Groups such as Dan Gayman's Church of Israel (COI) and James Ellison's Covenant, Sword and Arm of the Lord (CSA) had adopted a survivalist stance by retreating to remote, rural compounds to await the impending cataclysm (a time of Tribulation preceding redemption of God's chosen) away from the criminality and racial chaos of large cities. At Schell City in Missouri, Gayman gathered a COI congregation of some hundred in his plan to organize self-sufficient groups upon the land. In 1974 Ellison had established the most fortified of all Identity settlements at the 224-acre CSA compound called Zarephath-Horeb beside Bull Shoals Lake on the northern border of Arkansas. By 1984 its increasingly militant stance against outside society led to confrontation with the authorities, which climaxed in an FBI raid in 1985. A huge stockpile of weaponry was seized, and Ellison was sentenced to twenty years' imprisonment.[27]

Increased tension in relations with the Soviet Union under the Reagan presidency also played a part in the renewed millennialism of Identity in the early 1980s. In a manner similiar to the religiomilitary scenario of *When?*, Bernard Comparet outlined a new Cold War version of the Last Days in 1982. The Russian Gog would form a grand coalition with the Islamic world, aided by "the mixed breeds of Asia and Africa and India, who . . . will ally themselves with anything which promises them that they can rape and pillage in the lands of the White Man." The multiracial forces of Gog will then attack on two fronts, occupying the eastern Mediterranean and the Suez Canal to stop the supply of oil before invading the United States across the Bering Strait, supported by missile, submarine and aircraft. After the "Asiatic hordes roll in like a flood in our northwestern States," God will intervene with all manner of natural catastrophes to defeat the invaders. Here, the former British-Israelite focus on Palestine gives way to an enormous conflict centered on the United States, whose invasion by Asian forces is described as a multiracial inundation.[28]

Apocalyptic survivalism soon metamorphosed into outright millennial insurrection. In September 1983 a militant racist sect called The Order was founded at Metaline Falls, Washington. Also known as the Brüders Schweigen or Silent Brotherhood, this terrorist group was led by Robert Jay Mathews (b. 1953), who had a long history of far-right links, including the John Birch Society and tax resistance. His plan was the creation of a small cell that had the will and resources to attack and overthrow the "Zionist Occupation Government" (ZOG) of the United States. For this purpose he required funds to buy arms for a guerrilla campaign against the state, which, it was expected, would lead to a mass revolt of the white population. The Order began its operations with large-scale counterfeiting and armed robbery, stealing $3.8 million from a Brinks armored car in Ukiah, California, in July 1984. Other acts of violence included the assassination of Alan Berg, a Jewish radio presenter in Denver known for his outspoken opposition to right-wing groups. Mathews was killed by the FBI in a siege on Whidbey Island, Washington, in December 1984, while the remaining Order members were apprehended in 1985 and 1986.[29]

Mathews had discovered Butler's church in early 1982. He had his adopted son baptized there and encouraged friends to attend. During that year he conceived the "White American Bastion" and advertised in the right-wing press, believing that if he could attract enough like-minded settlers, whites would become the dominant political and economic force in the Pacific Northwest. In June 1983 Butler held an Aryan Nations rally at Spokane, Washington, where Mathews played a leadership role in deterring hostile protests. The following month he attended the annual Aryan World Congress at Hayden Lake, where Louis Beam gave a moving address about white men securing the future for their children. During the various sessions, there was much talk of "time for action" in establishing an Aryan homeland, but no one seemed ready to act. In September 1983, at William Pierce's National Alliance convention in Arlington, Virginia, Mathews delivered a rousing oration on Aryan resurgence in the Pacific Northwest. He then returned home to Metaline Falls and founded his own secret circle to secure that objective.

Mathews initiated his first nine members into The Order as they clasped hands by candlelight in a circle around a participant's baby daughter, symbolic of the white future, and pronounced the following oath: "I, as a free Aryan man, hereby swear an unrelenting oath upon the green graves of our sires, upon the children in the wombs of our wives, upon the throne of God Almighty, sacred be His name . . . to join together in holy union with these brothers in this circle and to declare forthright that from this moment on I have no fear of death, no fear of foe; that I have a sacred duty to do whatever is necessary to deliver our people from the Jew and bring total victory to the Aryan race." While Mathews's own religious inclination was latterly more Odinist than Christian Identity, a quarter of the Order's recruits had Identity associations with Aryan Nations and Church of Jesus Christ Christian. David Lane, who drove the getaway car after the Berg murder, was an Identity church member and also founded the 14 Word Press, whose motto has become a mantra for white supremacist groups across the world ("We must secure the existence of our people and a future for white children").[30]

Mathews was a charismatic and visionary leader, capable of inspiring strong bonds of loyalty among his band, which grew from the original nine to two dozen men, all subsequently indicted for their part in the criminal operations of The Order. Mathews's apocalyptic despair and millennial fervor are evident in his "declaration of war," sent to leading newspapers throughout the United States a few days before the siege in which he lost his life:

> It is now a dark and dismal time in the history of our race. All around us lie the green graves of our sires, yet, in a land once ours, we have become a people dispossessed. . . .
>
> While we allow Mexicans by the legions to invade our soil, we murder babies in equal numbers. Were the men of the Alamo only a myth? Whether by force of arms or force of the groin, the result of this invasion is the same. Yet our people do not resist.
>
> Our heroes and our culture have been insulted and degraded. The mongrel hordes clamor to sever us from our inheritance. Yet our people do not care.
>
> Throughout this land our children are being coerced into accepting nonwhites for their idols, their companions, and worst of all their mates. A course which is taking us straight to oblivion. Yet our people do not see. . . .
>
> All about us the land is dying. Our cities swarm with dusky hordes. . . .
>
> The water is rancid and the air is rank. Our farms are being seized by usurious leeches and our people are being forced off the land.
>
> . . . We say: "Rise and join us! . . . The Aryan yeomanry is awakening. A long forgotten wind is starting to blow. Do you hear the approaching thunder? It is that of the awakened Saxon. War is upon the land. The tyrant's blood will flow.[31]

In a final open letter addressed to his local newspaper, Mathews described the process of his own politicization. He recalled the profound impression Oswald Spengler's *Decline of the West* and William Gayley Simpson's *Which Way Western Man?* had made on him, while he subscribed to numerous periodicals concerned with the decline of white America:

> The stronger my love for my people grew, the deeper became my hatred for those who would destroy my race, my heritage, and darken the future of my children. By the time my son had arrived, I realized that White America, indeed my entire race, was headed for oblivion unless White men rose and

turned the tide. The more I came to love my son the more I realized that unless things changed radically, by the time he was my age, he would be a stranger in his own land, a blonde-haired, blue-eyed Aryan in a country populated mainly by Mexicans, Mulattos, Blacks and Asians. His future was growing darker by the day.

I came to learn that this was not by accident, that there is a small, cohesive alien group within this nation working day and night to make this happen. I learned that these culture distorters have an iron grip on both political parties, on Congress, on the media, on the publishing houses, and on most of the major Christian denominations in this nation, even though these aliens subscribe to a religion which is diametrically opposed to Christianity. . . .

Thus I have no choice. I must stand up like a White man and do battle.

A secret war has been developing for the last year between the regime in Washington and an ever growing number of White people who are determined to regain what our forefathers discovered, explored, conquered, settled, built and died for. . . .

. . . I will leave knowing that I have made the ultimate sacrifice to ensure the future of my children.

As always, for blood, soil, honor, for faith and for race.[32]

The cultural pessimism of Spengler, Simpson and Yockey are here directly linked to the decline of the white Aryan race. Only the clarion call for an insurrection against ZOG can now restore a white world.

Mathews fell far short of his goal of inciting a white revolution and thus unifying the radical right in a race war. His millennial challenge to ZOG was answered by a hail of FBI bullets and his incineration in the house on Whidbey Island. Such failure is underlined by the arrest and conviction of his closest followers, who were indicted on major charges, and their imprisonment, many for terms in excess of one hundred years. However, the war of the Brüders Schweigen against ZOG had several important consequences. First, it showed Identity Christians and other racial radicals that terrorist offensives could be taken against a tyrannical establishment. Then, in consequence, Mathews is now the principal hero and martyr of far-right folklore, while other members of the Brüders Schweigen enjoy an emblematic status in underground magazines. At the same time, its example also divided the far right with some groups endorsing such violence and terrorism, and others distancing themselves. Richard Butler stated that the men of the Silent Brotherhood "will become heroes to our grandchildren," but defections and overwhelming state surveillance reduced the Aryan Nations to a shadow of its former strength by the late 1980s.

Butler soon forged new alliances to restore Aryan Nations to its former front-line role on the far right. Seeking to capitalize on the growing neo-Nazi skinhead movement, Aryan Nations staged annual Aryan Youth Festivals at the Hayden Lake compound between 1989 and 1996. Held on the weekend closest to Hitler's birthday, the prime attraction was bands playing white power music. Butler has described the "skinhead phenomenon as a 'natural biological reaction' of white teenagers banding together after being taught that 'non-white kids are great and white kids are scum.'"[33] At the same time, Butler resumed his former diplomacy among far right groups to bring other white supremacist groups within the Aryan Nations fold. In 1994 Aryan Nations formed an alliance with Gary Lauck's National Socialist German Workers Party—Overseas Organization (NSDAP-AO) based in Lincoln, Nebraska. As the most prolific worldwide distributor of neo-Nazi literature, NSDAP-AO offered Aryan Nations access to international support that had previously remained beyond its reach. By 1995 Aryan Nations was operating in twenty-six states and had established European chapters in Italy, Finland and Denmark. Aryan Nations evidently presented Christian Identity racial theology within a context that was acceptable to a broad spectrum of Nazi and other extremist right-wing groups.

A further reversal in the fortunes of Aryan Nations occurred in October 2000, when Butler was compelled to surrender his Hayden Lake property to satisfy part of a $6.3 million judgment against him as a result of a civil suit for negligence brought by Victoria and Jason Keenan, who were shot at and assaulted by Aryan Nations security guards in 1998. Butler and his supporters allege that damages were set at such an exorbitant level expressly in order to bankrupt him and Aryan Nations. However, he still intends to remain politically active. He has since moved to a house provided by Vincent Bertollini, a wealthy supporter, in nearby Hayden. Bertollini and his associate, Carl Story, run an organization called the Eleventh Hour Remnant Messenger, which is also committed to the anti-Semitic, Aryan supremacist theology of Christian Identity. They have used wealth amassed from their Silicon Valley computer ventures to finance mass mailings and other church activities. As the lawsuit also stripped Butler of the right to use the name Aryan Nations, the organization is now known as Aryan National Alliance.[34]

Like Lanz von Liebenfels's Ariosophy in prewar Austria and Germany, Christian Identity embeds white Aryan nationalism and its reactionary fervor within a fundamentalist Christian doctrine. From the perspective of the racist right, the policies of the U.S. federal government are all working for the extinction of the Aryan race. Welfare programs and privileges for special interest (i.e., ethnic) groups are funding the promotion of a non-white America through the hard-earned taxes of the white majority. Identity Christians see the unholy alliance of the Jews and the pre-Adamite "mud peoples" behind the ceaseless advocacy of racial integration, race mixing, abortion and homosexuality in politics and the media. Government programs to subsidize drug abusers, to offer welfare to immigrants and asylum seekers, and to provide sexual education due to fear of AIDS are seen as conspiracies to debilitate and debauch the American population to the point of total dependence on a Jewish sovereign elite presiding over a New World Order.

Identity Christians believe that liberal, multiracial society virtually outlaws the discussion of racial inequalities such as black educational achievement, criminal demography, and the relative ethnic percentages of the prison population. Any such inequalities are deemed evidence of white racism. Meanwhile, they condemn any reverse discrimination which grants black and other ethnic groups special racial privileges. They see the authorities as indulging the expression of ethnic racial identity and even antipathy toward whites while imposing severe penalties on protagonists of white power and white separatism. Identity Christians are inured to being held up as objects of scorn and branded as bigots through the mainstream media, which constantly preach a message of integration and race mixing, together with the acceptability of abortion and homosexuality. They see the permissiveness of democratic society as clear evidence of the Jewish conspiracy to lead the Adamic Aryan people astray from God's laws in order to enslave them. Identity Christians ultimately see the politics of liberalism and racial equality in terms of demonic deception, for the underlying issue at stake is not so much white supremacism, but the threatened submergence of God's chosen people, White Israel, in the dark gene pool of the pre-Adamic "mud races." Their Manichaean belief in a satanic antagonist is absolute and the defining feature of their political outlook.

Although theologically quite distinct from Christian Identity, the Church of the Creator (COTC) is motivated by similar fears for the survival of the white race in an America subject to mass Third World immigration. To secure the future of whites against racial submergence, the Church of the Creator calls for a "Racial Holy War" against the colored races in the United States, together with the Jews who are supposedly using the blacks, Hispanics and other "mud" races to degrade the white race. The COTC rejects Christianity as a "suicidal religion," which the Jews originally introduced to demoralize and ultimately destroy the Roman Empire through race mixing and universalism. The militant, anti-Christian, racist ideology of the COTC has proved a magnet to violent skinhead groups across the United States, with a result that the

COTC has become a largely urban-based movement claiming some three thousand members with overseas groups in Canada, South Africa, Australia and Europe. A number of terrorist conspiracies to assassinate ethnic leaders and violent racial killings have been linked to COTC members, inspired by its crusade for a "whiter and brighter world."[35]

The COTC was founded in 1973 by Ben Klassen (1918–1993), a wealthy real estate developer, in order to promote "Creativity," a new religion dedicated to the resurrection and redemption of the white race. The idea of a racial religion was the culmination of Klassen's odyssey through the American far right in search of solutions to the nation's ills. Born into a large German-speaking Mennonite farming community in the Ukraine on 7 February 1918, Klassen spent his early years in a country ravaged by revolution, civil war and a famine instigated by the Bolsheviks. In June 1924 the family decided to emigrate, first settling in Mexico before moving to Saskatchewan, Canada, in December 1925, choices dictated by then prevailing restrictions on immigration to the United States. During his youth, Klassen's sympathies were already with Germany. He read Hitler's *Mein Kampf* in 1938 with approval, and intended to study engineering at Heidelberg. However, once war intervened he enrolled at the University of Sakatchewan in Saskatoon from 1939 to 1943. After emigrating to the United States in 1945, he made a fortune through the invention of an electric can opener and built up real estate companies in California, Nevada and Florida.[36]

The first stirrings of Klassen's postwar political consciousness concerned liberal attacks on Joseph McCarthy's campaign in 1953–54 to expose communists in government. The forced racial integration by government troops of schools in Little Rock, Arkansas, in 1957, a similar incident at the University of Mississippi in 1961, and Governor George Wallace's defense of schoolhouse segregation in Alabama in 1962 awakened Klassen to the dangers of the civil rights movement and revived his memories of Hitler's racial creed.[37] In 1963 Klassen joined a local Florida chapter of the John Birch Society. Initially impressed by its diagnosis that communism was infiltrating the West, Klassen soon noted that the Jews and the race question were taboo subjects in the John Birch Society. In November 1966 he ran successfully for election as a Republican Florida state representative but found that his concern with the "Jewish problem" and opposition to civil rights drew the fire of the press and even criticism from fellow Birchers. After losing his seat the next year through redistricting, Klassen next took a leading role in a third party seeking the election of George Wallace to the U.S. presidency as a segregationist in 1968.[38]

Klassen was repeatedly disappointed that none of his political affiliations would recognize that it was the Jews rather than communists or liberals who were at the root of the conspiracy to destroy America. Even though top Birchers admitted as much in private, they took the view that charges of anti-Semitism would finish the Society.[39] After exploring the Ku Klux Klan, Matt Koehl's National Socialist White People's Party, Gerald L. K. Smith's movement, and the National States Rights Party, Klassen founded his own Nationalist White Party (NWP) in November 1970. He initially defined his patriotic third party as a movement of "White Christian people who conquered America [and] don't intend to be relegated to second-class citizenship."[40] The fourteen-point program of the NWP, tellingly described as a "creed," claims that the white race was created in the image of the Lord as his noblest and highest creation. However, the white race is now in mortal danger of being "mongrelized and enslaved by a diabolical worldwide conspiracy," as set forth in the Jewish Talmud, the *Protocols of the Elders of Zion* and Karl Marx's *Communist Manifesto*.

The program evidently owed much to Klassen's reading of *The International Jew* by Henry Ford:

> The Jew has been a blood-sucking parasite on the backs of the White people since the dawn of history, promoting the collapse and destruction of every civilization the White man has ever built. The White Race has now become the most persecuted, abused, plundered and mistreated people on the face of the earth . . . the White people of America alone, who have never known military defeat, have been forced by their treacherous Jewish controlled government under the pretext of foreign aid, welfare, and other hoaxes to pay more tribute to hostile colored races at home and abroad than all the vanquished peoples of the earth have paid to their conquerors. The White man has lost control of his land, his government, his schools and his money.

Such traditional discourse of Jewish world conspiracy was updated through the claim that the Jews were exploiting the colored races to undermine white, Gentile Americans through the civil rights movement and rising levels of immigration:

> Since the African Negroes were brought to America as slaves, largely by Jewish slave traders, they have been a serious problem to White America, and a spreading cancer in our midst, greatly aggravated by the Jewish drive to mongrelize the White Race. Their presence here in America is a dire threat to the very survival of the White Race itself. Under the present course of events, America will be a polluted brown mongrelized mass of riff raff and scum by the end of the century, reduced to a level of degradation where our White

civilization will collapse. We are determined that this must not happen to God's finest and noblest creation—the White Race.[41]

Despite Klassen's initial focus on "white Christian" opposition to the Jews and civil rights for blacks, he soon began to identify Christianity as a major part of the problem. In his correspondence with potential NWP supporters he noted that Christians were inhibited from criticizing the Jews in view of their shared religious heritage. Klassen soon went further in a complete rejection of Christianity. He regarded Christ's Sermon on the Mount with its teachings "judge not," "love your enemies," "turn the other cheek," "sell all thou hast and give it to the poor," and "resist not evil" (Matthew 5–7) as "suicidal" advice concocted by the Jews for Gentile consumption. By charging the Jews with using Christianity to destroy Roman morale and civilization, Klassen presents a simplistic, anti-Semitic version of Evola's critique of Christianity's effect on the Roman Empire. By ignoring its transcendent dimension, Klassen impugns Christianity as an anti-natural ideology that has ever since weakened white European peoples by preventing them from acting effectively in a competitive natural world. Klassen decided that the white race needed "a new religion based on the concepts of preserving the White race, not a rehash of old Jewish shibboleths."[42] This kind of "Aryan Judaism" for the exclusive benefit of the white race would act as a counterpart to the tribal identity and powerful influence of the Jews in their host societies.[43]

Accordingly, Klassen founded the Church of the Creator on 16 August 1973 in Lighthouse Point, Florida. By this time he had already published *Nature's Eternal Religion* (1973), the first text of his new religion of Creativity based on Darwinist ideas of natural selection and evolution. Here Klassen sees all nature obeying the laws of the survival of the fittest. By constantly subdividing species into subspecies and encouraging their competition, nature seeks to refine and upgrade superior species while allowing inferior ones to decline and become extinct. As the white race is held to be the crowning creation of nature, Creativity posits an ethical scheme in which whatever is good for the white race is the highest virtue, and whatever is bad is the ultimate sin. Like earlier Aryan myths, Creativity holds that the white race is the sole originator of all worthwhile culture and civilizations in world history, while the Jews have always acted as their deadly enemy by preying as parasites on their white host societies. Klassen regards both the Egyptian and Aryan Indian civilizations as proud creations of the white race. Their eventual decline into multiracial chaos and squalor is a fate that shortly awaits the United States unless it can resist race mixing by adopting his new racial religion.[44]

Klassen effectively deifies the white race (always capitalized in his writings) as the crown of creation. The logo of the COTC shows a letter "W," signifying the white race, surmounted by a crown to symbolize its place in nature, above this a halo to represent its holy status. Its destiny is to expand and repopulate the whole world while shrinking the numbers and territory of its enemies—the inferior, uncreative, colored races. Klassen has nothing but contempt for blacks, whom he regards as shiftless, lazy and stupid. The black African, he claims, invented nothing, domesticated no animals, and never produced a written language. The Jewish-directed media foment black racial awareness while constantly preaching "brotherhood" to whites. Black underachievement in modern American society is constantly countered by Jewish media calls for more equality, enforced by the integration of housing and busing to mixed schools. Klassen notes that schools have since become hotbeds of crime, knifings, beatings, lawlessness and anarchy. The Jews are driving the civil rights movement with the aim of promoting interracial marriage, as they see the mongrelization of the white race as a crucial step toward achieving Jewish dominance over a debased Gentile humanity.[45]

Klassen repeatedly pays tribute to Adolf Hitler as "the greatest leader the White Race has ever produced." Hitler, Klassen believes, struck a major blow for the white race in his near-destruction of the Jewish conspiracy.[46] But Klassen also distinguishes Creativity from National Socialism. He sees nationalism and Pan-Germanism as divisive of the white race, while Creativity should embrace all whites. Klassen also believes that the situation in contemporary America is quite different from Weimar Germany. Burgeoning colored minorities, crime, welfare, and racial integration require a new religion based on the white *Volk*, rather than a mere political ideology. Klassen sees the race problem in a global context. He recalls that in 1920 the white race was outnumbered two to one in the world. It was outnumbered seven to one by 1973, when the United Nations predicted that whites would be outnumbered forty-nine to one in a further twenty years. Klassen conjures a terrible vision of the future, when the colored races, "agitated and controlled by the Jews," have enough physical power to slaughter the white race in their own lands.[47]

By the early 1980s Klassen had published his second Creativity text, *The White Man's Bible* (1981), and a health book, *Salubrious Living* (1982), co-authored with Arnold DeVries. As early as 1974, Klassen had considering building a "world center" for the COTC. Disgusted by the increasing immigration of Cubans, Haitians and Latin American refugees to South Florida, together with its growing black and Jewish population, Klassen decided to purchase land in North Carolina. On 10 March 1982 the new COTC center was founded in a valley of the Blue Ridge Mountains near Otto, a few miles north of the Georgia state line. Klassen celebrated the American "winning of the West" with its pioneering values of white colonization and the subjugation of the native American Indians with a wooden building reflecting the architectural style of old Western towns in Colorado, Arizona and California. Together with a succession of editors, he published a periodical *Racial Loyalty*, a populist inflammatory tabloid that attracted urban skinhead groups to the COTC with its rhetoric of racial violence against the "mud" races now rapidly colonizing American cities. Styling himself the Pontifex Maximus of his church, Klassen established his mail-order ministry by recruiting ministers for the COTC on a nationwide basis. Branches of the COTC were chiefly encouraged to spread the racial gospel through street actions involving leafleting, marches, banners and displays. An "Operation Skinhead" was specifically mounted to attract white youth to its open challenge of ethnic groups in American cities. A COTC initiative was also started in South Africa in an attempt to stave off black-majority rule.[48]

Using the term "Rahowa" (RAcial Holy WAr) as the COTC battle cry for white world domination, Klassen's apocalyptic vision is evident in his book *Rahowa! This Planet Is All Ours*:

> RAHOWA! In this one word we sum up the total goal and program of not only the Church of the Creator, but of the total White Race, and it is this: We take up the challenge. We gird for total war against the Jews and the rest of the godamned mud races of the world—politically, militantly, financially, morally and religiously. . . . We regard it as a holy war to the finish—a holy racial war. Rahowa! is INEVITABLE. It is the Ultimate and Only solution.

Faced with the threat of racial inundation by blacks and other colored races, the "racial holy war" against the "mud" races is the only road to the resurrection and redemption of the white race:

> No longer can the mud races and the White Race live on the same planet and survive. It is now either them or us. We want to make damn sure it is we who survive. This planet is from now on all ours, and will be the one and only habitat for our future progeny for all time to come.[49]

Here Klassen's militant prophecy uncannily recalls Lanz von Liebenfels's call in his pre-1914 *völkisch* Ariosophy for Aryans to wage a global race war against the "apish" lower races.[50]

During the 1980s, Klassen sent out feelers to many leaders within the white race movement including Tom Metzger, the founder of White Aryan Resistance in Fallbrook, California; Matt Koehl and his New Order; William Pierce of the National Alliance; and DeWest Hooker, a close associate of George Lincoln Rockwell in the early years of the American Nazi Party. Klassen's overriding concern was, however, to find a successor and financial patron to carry on the leadership of the COTC. Between 1990 and 1992, Klassen appointed three short-lived successors, Rudy Stanko, Charles Altvater and Mark Wilson, before choosing Rick McCarty in January 1993. After Ben Klassen's death in August 1993, the movement floundered as a loose association of skinhead groups until Matt Hale took over its remnants in 1996, renaming it the World Church of the Creator (WCOTC).

Born on 27 July 1971, Matt Hale had already attracted notoriety by founding an American White Supremacist Party while a student in 1990. In 1992 he started the National Socialist White Americans Party, achieving 14 percent of the vote in city council elections in East Peoria, Illinois. After gaining a degree in political science from Bradley University in 1993, Hale completed law school and passed his bar examination in 1998. Besides publishing a periodical, *The Struggle*, Hale hosts a substantial website, appears regularly on talk radio shows and markets an extensive range of WCOTC audiotapes, videos and literature, including all of Klassen's "holy books of Creativity." His lead editorials in *The Struggle* address flashpoint issues of immigration, rampant black crime, and the discriminatory effects on whites of affirmative action.[51] Website testimonials from converts similarly reflect their relief and newfound sense of purpose in discovering a movement that challenges the media's ceaseless insistence on white guilt and multiculturalism. With his organizing ability and intellectual leadership, Hale has successfully expanded the number of active WCOTC state chapters from eight to over thirty, with overseas organizations in Belgium, France, Sweden, Canada and Australia.

Despite their doctrinal divergence over Christianity, Christian Identity churches and the Church of the Creator indicate an important trend in the development of the postwar white racial movement. As Jeffrey Kaplan has shown in his several masterly discussions of these groups, they are distinct in presenting themselves as religions, typically organized as sects and embracing millenarian hopes of a white racial utopia.[52] Despite the massive delegitimation of racial discrimination after the atrocities of the Third Reich, postwar Nazi parties in America and Britain still sought a political platform on the far right to denounce civil rights and colored immigration in the 1950s and 1960s. However, the advancing ascendancy of liberal elites in these societies since then has systematically narrowed their political space through an ideological program of anti-racism, egalitarianism, and now multiculturalism in education, media and government. Nationalist parties in Europe already risk a legal ban in those countries with specific laws against discrimination on racial grounds, inciting racial hatred, anti-Semitism and Holocaust denial.

Confronted by the entrenchment of multiculturalism and affirmative action in liberal society, certain white nationalists feel so embattled and disinherited that they can express their ideology only in terms of sacred, absolute affirmations: hence their flight into sectarian "churches" underpinned with racial theologies of white identity and supremacy. Their abandonment of political parties with the National Socialist label, indeed their avoidance of political activity as such in a liberal society profoundly hostile to their views, suggests a certain historical parallel. The intellectual origins of National Socialism can be traced to the German *völkisch* groups and sects espousing nationalist and anti-Semitic doctrines in Austria and Germany at the turn of the last century. Discouraged by liberal political establishments, these groups incubated reactionary ideologies of German racial identity, which then found overt political expression after the privations and loss of the First World War. It seems likely that these new religions of white identity in the United States and other white nations facing growing ethnic minorities are performing a similar incubatory function, all the more virulent for their political marginalization and repression.

13

Nordic Racial Paganism

IF CHRISTIAN IDENTITY remains the major religious expression of white Aryan racial identity in the United States, several new racial religions on the American far right simply reject the Christian heritage of the West altogether. Regarding Christianity itself as a Jewish cultural product with its origins in the Middle East, the Odinist movement articulates an unabashed racial paganism, invoking the gods of the Norse and Teutonic pantheons. By reviving the festivals, rituals and customs of the ancient Indo-European peoples, they wish to break what they regard as the alien, imposed dominion of Christianity after two thousand years. This spiritual rediscovery of the Aryan ancestral gods is intended to embed the white races in a sacred worldview that supports their tribal feeling and partial view of humanity.

Odinism today represents the battlefront of racist paganism in support of a white Aryan revolutionary path in the United States with associated branches and chapters in Europe, South Africa and Australia. Its devotees practice imaginative forms of ritual magic and ceremonial forms of fraternal fellowship based on Norse and Germanic models while embracing the ideals of white supremacism and National Socialism. In this chapter we will trace the German origins and history of Odinism in the English-speaking world before focusing on several examples of the movement: Wyatt Kaldenberg and his Pagan Revival network, which focuses on Odin's warrior aspect and advocates a cult of violence; Jost Turner and his NS Kindred, which celebrates Odin as a master of mysteries in a devotional cult of Aryan mysticism with meditation and yoga; and the Wotansfolk movement of David and Katja Lane with Ron McVan, which elaborates a full-blown Wotanist cult for the millenarian salvation of the endangered Aryan race.

The origins of Odinism as a self-conscious reconstruction of pre-Christian Teutonic beliefs lie in nineteenth-century Germany. Against a background of burgeoning nationalism, *völkisch* writers speculated on the Germans' spiritual resources in resisting Roman conquest and their recalcitrant conversion to Christianity under Charlemagne. In his widely read novel, *Ein Kampf um Rom* (1867), the historian Felix Dahn lauded the ancient Germans for their manly heroism, valor and defiance, in contrast to Christian humility, repentance and sense of sin. From the 1880s onward, the Germanic gods Odin, Donar, and Thor became popular subjects of lithographic art by G. E. Doepler and F. W. Heine. In 1893 the Viennese folklorist Guido von List began writing about the Wotanist priesthood and attempted to salvage its ancient religion from the Norse sagas, with special emphasis given to Odin (Wotan) and his runic wisdom. List's early attempt to revive Wotanism through his books and his High Armanist Order (HAO) was emulated in 1912 by a secret nationalist group, the Germanenorden, which performed quasi-Masonic rituals based on the figures of ancient Germanic mythology.[1]

In 1911 Otto Sigfrid Reuter founded the Deutsche Orden and the Deutschreligiöse Gemeinschaft (renamed the Deutschgläubige Gemeinschaft after 1918) as Germanic religious groups dedicated to a god closer to national identity. In 1924, members of these groups and the Jungborn, a league within the German Youth Movement, combined to form "Die Nordungen" as the leading neo-Germanic religious circle of the Weimar era. Otger Gräff, a leader of the Youth Movement, explained the role of ancient Germanic mythology in this new religiosity: "Donar and Baldur, Loh and Froh are but names by which the Teuton signified the divine mystery he felt within himself." The ancient Germanic gods were no antiquarian constructs but rather archetypes accessible to contemporary Germans who realized their true spiritual identity. The first issue of *Nordungen* declared: "Balder-Sigfrid still lives today in the best of our people, his essence of sunlit liberation is alive in all our longings and ambition, and who would deny that Wotan, the eternal wanderer and Faustian seeker of experience, is still alive as once in Nordic man?"[2]

During the 1920s many *völkisch* and Youth Movement groups followed a neopagan cult with solstice festivals and pious invocations to the Germanic deities as archetypes and forces of nature. The new *deutschgläubige* faith was elaborated by numerous writers, including Jakob Wilhelm Hauer, Bernhard Kummer, Alfred Conn and Adolf Kroll, who sought to define Germanic religion as an innate spirituality, inherited from one's racial forbears, a living counterpart of the homeland, one's blood, feeling and thinking.[3] It was thus irreconcilable with the universalist claims of Christianity to absolute truth. However, German neopaganism in the Weimar era usually recognized that a naive revival of the ancient Wotan cult was impossible for modern man. It rather sought a synthesis of German spirituality from the Norse sagas and the Icelandic Edda, together with the German mystical tradition and the idealist philosophy of Kant, Schelling and Fichte.[4] In his famous essay on neo-Germanic spirituality, Carl Gustav Jung characterized this restless quest for a new Germanic spirituality as the eruption of the archetype "Wotan", as a "living and unfathomable tribal god" among the Germans after the First World War.[5]

In the following account of racial paganism in modern America, I am heavily indebted to Mattias Gardell, who has allowed me to make use of a chapter in his forthcoming work, *Gods of the Blood: Race, Ethnicity and the Pagan Revival*, to be published by Duke University Press. According to Gardell's research, Odinism began its modern career with the establishment of the Odinist Fellowship in 1969 by Else Christensen. Born at Esbjerg on the Danish west coast in 1913, Else Oscher was involved in revolutionary union-ism and politics in Copenhagen during the 1930s. She was eventually at-tracted to the left-wing Strasserite wing of the emerging Danish National So-cialist Workers' Party, and in 1937 married Alex Christensen, who had served as a senior aide to the party leader later ousted in 1933. Following the Nazi oc-cupation of Denmark in 1940, Alex was briefly imprisoned as a dissident. In 1951 the Christensens emigrated to Canada, where they settled in Toronto. Else Christensen's interest in racial radicalism brought her into contact with Willis Carto, a leading figure of the American far right, and James K. Warner, New York organizer of Rockwell's American Nazi Party. Carto introduced her to the writings of Francis Parker Yockey, Oswald Spengler's American eulogist and author of *Imperium*. Abandoning the idea of using Odinism as the reli-gious counterpart of National Socialism in America, Warner gave Christensen his Norse material, which included the writings of Alexander Rud Mills.[6]

Mills was an Australian lawyer and Nazi sympathizer who promoted a racial pagan religion within the context of the British Empire of the 1920s. In his most influential book, *The Odinist Religion: Overcoming Jewish Christian-ity* (1930), he described how the Nordic races had built the civilizations of Sumeria, Egypt, Persia, Greece and Rome. Weakened by "foreign immigration and miscegenation," these racial paragons then absorbed the false Jewish-Pla-tonic idea of a transcendent God and eventually progressed to the Christian belief that all men were created equal.[7] Mills sought to restore the racial vigor of the pre-Christian English people through his Anglecyn Church of Odin, which was intended to replace all British-Anglican-Christian insitutions with an Anglo-Saxon racial religion. During the 1920s and 1930s, Mills helped cre-ate small Odinic polygamist colonies in Australia, Great Britain, South Africa and North America, but these pagan communes probably soon lapsed. In the 1950s, Mills launched the First Church of Odin, again with little lasting suc-cess.[8] Mixing Odinism with occult and Masonic notions, Mill's writings re-mained his only tangible legacy, which Else and Alex Christensen discovered in the early 1960s while immersing themselves in the writings of Yockey and Spengler.

Following Spengler, Yockey had argued that all cultures follow an organic pattern by passing through the successive phases of birth, growth, maturity, fulfillment and death. Each culture has a soul that determines its religion, science, art, politics and morality throughout its life span. Races are the raw material for cultural expression, differing in their degree of will to power. Anticipating the future fulfillment of Western culture in a powerful Eurasian imperium, Yockey expected to see the emergence of a robust, white Western race.[9] However, this outcome was presently frustrated by the spiritual malaise of the West, which Yockey elaborated as the pathologies of culture-parasitism, culture-distortion, and culture-retardation. Culture-parasitism denotes the presence of alien groups that cannot participate in the historical destiny of a culture. Yockey believed that black and Asian peoples in the West replaced an unborn indigenous white population, thus depriving the Western culture of proper raw material for the fulfillment of its destiny.[10]

Yockey saw the Jews as the most dangerous form of parasitism in the West, namely culture-distortion, when "outer life-forms are warping the Culture from its true Life-path."[11] During the Middle Ages, the Jews had remained secluded in their ghettos, an inert organism outside the mainstream of Western development. But once Western culture reached its maturity in the age of rationalism around 1750, the Jews sensed their opportunity. With their distorting ideas of materialism, economics and usury, and opposition to absolutism, they undermined the spirit and traditional elites of the West. Seeking their own advantage and emancipation, they furthered democracy, equality, feminism, capitalism and socialism during the nineteenth century.[12] As a colony of Western culture, America had been especially vulnerable to this influence, which was exacerbated by high levels of Jewish immigration from the 1880s onward. Succumbing to this culture-distortion, America was subverted from its historical destiny and was induced to intervene in Europe when Hitler initiated the first phase of the new authoritarian Imperium.[13]

Yockey saw the defeat of the Axis as a terrible lost opportunity for Western revival. Writing in 1948, he noted that "a deep yearning is going through the western world to be free from the dirt and uncleanness of party-politics, class-war, financial usury, and the complete absence of the heroic spirit." The future state form, he was certain, was the resurgence of authority. Honor, religion and a stern socialism will sweep away the distortions of democracy, money power and finance capitalism. This new racial state will undertake a massive war for the survival of Western civilization, while its "new, total, political, organizatory, authoritarian Imperialism [. . .] will plant the Western banner on the highest peaks and the most remote peninsulas."[14]

Else Christensen's ideas for an Odinist revival of Aryan culture were directly inspired by her reading of Yockey, Mills and Jungian psychology.[15] She agreed with Yockey that Western civilization was in a late degenerate phase, undermined by Christianity, capitalism and communism. Noting Yockey's emphasis that "disease to a culture can only be a *spiritual* phenomenon," she believed that only a religious antidote could arrest and reverse the current decline of the Aryan West.[16] This remedy lay in Mills's revival of Norse paganism as the primordial expression of the Aryan Folk Soul: "The role of Odinism is clear—the pathogens must be destroyed, and healthy organisms raised to serve the purposes of Aryan spiritual liberation and all-round advancement."[17] Christensen identified the seeds of an Aryan cultural revival in "the subconscious elements of Urd," interpreted in Jungian terms as the genetic transmission of the collective unconscious. By plumbing the archetypes of the racial unconscious, white people could discover their ancestral wisdom. Race and religion are thus organically related. The source of Odinism is thus biological, and "its principles are encoded in our genes. . . . Odinism embodies [. . .] the reality of multifaceted struggle [to defeat our enemies] and fulfill our destiny."[18]

According to Gardell, Else Christensen became the most public voice of Odinism in the United States from the early 1970s onward, regularly publishing *The Odinist* newsletter and traveling widely from her base at Crystal River, Florida. During the 1980s she established a prison outreach ministry in the state, but the Odinist Fellowship tended to focus on literature and ideas rather than ceremonies. Besides the celebration of Hitler's birthday, only four seasonal meetings were held with a ritual Norse sumbel (drinking ceremony). Her politics remained left of center. Her call for Aryan religion, freedom, consciousness and self-determination was embedded in a program for "retribalization," with the decentralization of authority to small, local self-governing units of free Aryan individuals.[19] She praised the early left-wing nationalist ideology of Mussolini and the Strasserite element in National Socialism, and saw totalitarian government as a betrayal of both movements' original revolutionary promise. Her anarchist tendencies are always colored by racial collectivism, whereby the individual's needs must be subordinate to tribal welfare. "Man is a social animal, capable of self-realization only within a community of racial and ethnic kin."[20] As racial purity was a paramount requirement, all race mixing was strictly forbidden in these free Odinist communes.[21]

While Christensen was advancing her racial Odinism in the 1970s, the alternative movement of Ásatrú, more concerned with the practice of rituals and Norse magic, was started by Steve McNallen in Texas. Ásatrú is an

Icelandic word meaning "belief in the Æsir (gods)." Their memberships often overlapped, but by the end of the 1970s, the political divide between Odinism and McNallen's Ásatrú Free Assembly (AFA) had become acute. The presence of racists and Nazis was an embarrassment to McNallen and other AFA members, whose racial pride was secondary to an exploration of spirituality. In 1978 he demanded that all AFA members forgo Nazi uniforms and insignia, but the underlying political tension in the organization eventually led to its demise in 1987. Successor organizations were Mike Murray's Ásatrú Alliance and Edred Thorsson's Ring of Troth. Mike Murray had been a young member of Rockwell's American Nazi Party, then joined Christensen's Odinist Fellowship, eventually serving as vice-president, before coming to the ritual spirituality of the AFA. His Ásatrú Alliance has disowned racial affiliations, although individual Odinists continue to interact with the Alliance in its magazine *Vor Trú* and at Althings (annual gatherings). By contrast, the Ring of Troth is aligned with the wiccan and neopagan communities, where multiracialism is not at issue.[22]

McNallen's attempt to weed out Nazis from the AFA led to more radical initiatives in the Odinist movement. Among those who left were Jost Turner, whose NS Kindred is the subject of later discussion. Other former AFA Aryanists Sigi Hubard, Tom Paget, Wyatt Kaldenberg and others built the Greater Los Angeles area chapter of the Odinist Fellowship. Tom Paget invited Tom Metzger, a notorious white racist then leading the White American Political Association, to speak at the chapter's Folk Moot, after which Metzger was a frequent guest at Odinist meetings. However, Else Christensen thought Metzger too racist, and members of the Arizona Kindred also wanted the Fellowship to be pro-white but not hostile to colored races and Jews. With Christensen urging restraint and a low profile, racist Odinists within the Los Angeles chapter wanted less ambiguous allies: Redbeard formed the racialist Thor's Hammer Kindred; Elton Hall broke with the Arizona Kindred and formed the Jomsviking Kindred; Tom Paget and Wyatt Kaldenberg joined Metzger's newly formed White Aryan Resistance (WAR). Wyatt Kaldenberg became editor of Metzger's periodical *WAR* and promoted Odinism through his articles.[23]

Gardell informs us that Wyatt Kaldenberg was born in 1957, the son of a Mormon family in a small California town. His early left-wing political involvement with the Young Socialist Alliance was soon overlaid with racial awareness through fights with black fellow students, including Black Muslims. Impressed by the black separatist creed of the Nation of Islam, Kaldenberg sought a white racial religion for himself. He joined the AFA in the late 1970s but was disgusted by McNallen's stand against Nazi sympathizers and quickly gravitated toward Tom Metzger's combative racism. Kaldenberg's

WAR articles spewed a stream of abusive misanthropy and violent rhetoric to promote a white revolution. His pagan worldview is essentially Manichaean, seeing history and politics as a cosmic battle between the divine Aryans and demonic, unnatural forces of Judeo-Christianity. The Aryans once lived in harmony with nature and a golden age prevailed, but Judeo-Christianity plunged the world into a dark age. The Aryan race is identified with the Earth, life and nature, while the mud races are "death," "the decay of winter" and "the maggots which feed on life." The Aryans must defeat this darkness, otherwise winter will reign for an eternity.[24]

Pagan Revival started in the early 1990s as an irregular, untitled, open typewritten letter distributed to friends and fellow pagans. After a short phase as an e-zine on the Internet, Kaldenberg began publishing the magazine as a pulp paper tabloid in 1998. The periodical is described a "a voice of the Eurocentric polytheistic communities," whose main goal is to promote the religion of Ásatrú, which worships the living gods and goddesses of the Norse pantheon, including Odin, Thor and Frigga. Articles range from scholarly comparisons of the ancient Germanic, Zoroastrian and Vedic pagan religions to an economic analysis of the growing Hispanic population of the southern United States. Interspersed with these varied reprints and outside contributions are popular reviews of white power, industrial and metal music and zines, and a busy section containing Kaldenberg's extensive e-mail and postal correpondence on religion, politics and sex.

Kaldenberg's own vicious tirades and macho language in articles and published letters are clearly targeted at alienated youth seeking a straightforward justification for violent acts against Jews and colored people. "We must kill all who threaten our survival. We must crush dissent," Kaldenberg asserts. "Mass murder is a sad thing, but Nature dealt the White Race a raw hand. If we do not remove the dark ones from our land, then sooner or later, all White nations will end up as dark as India."[25] He castigates Christianity for renouncing aggression, violence and conquest. As an alien Jewish import, Christianity has emasculated the pagan Aryan peoples by alienating them from the vital forces of their own gods and goddesses. "White people are so fucked up that we have demonized our native belief system and glorified the fables and mythology of foreigners . . . the deranged rants of the termite Jesus devour the structures of our inner self. Christianity is the theology of self-hating. . . . Praise Jesus and his cult of universal brotherhood. Thanks to Jesus, soon we won't even have a White race."[26] He blames the Jews for Christianity, which has killed off 300 million European pagans over two thousand years. Faced with such an enemy, he has little use for Holocaust denial, and asks, "Why we didn't grease the

Jews sooner?" The Holocaust should rather be celebrated: "Auschwitz and Dachau [should be] religious shrines because evil died there."[27]

Despite the left-wing inspiration of his youth, Kaldenberg despairs of the majority, even of whites. His ideal society is structured on an ancient Viking meritocracy with a ruling caste of Jarls, or warriors, with "the courage to fight and die to defend the Volk." From their ranks, all royalty and aristocracy were selected, so that "the greatest Aryan men and women had the freedom to excel to the top of society." The middle caste was the Karls, or workers, who did not fight but were the silent white majority of their day, "the mindless White sheep herd." Beneath them were the Thralls, a criminal slave caste.[28] Kaldenberg's Aryan revolution has no time for folksy, egalitarian moots. Power must be concentrated in the hands of the aristocratic warrior elite: "Our principal adversary in the battle for White survival is the White majority. . . . Only the rule by a tribal council made up of the best, most active, and most devoted will free the sheep from the tyranny of themselves. . . . The masses will always be sheep, waiting to be exploited by someone. . . . The White sheep herd were born to serve The Illuminated Ones."[29]

Kaldenberg's Odinism, unlike the Ásatrú movement from which he defected, has little spirituality and few ceremonies. His vehement rejection of Judeo-Christianity on political and sexual grounds leads to the celebration of Odinism chiefly as a cult of aristocracy, power and the propagation of the white race. As "the Pagan law of tooth and claw made our race great," Kaldenberg directs most of his polemic against the liberal, cowardly and pusillanimous whites who are not prepared to work, to fight for space and to win suitable Aryan mates for the multiplication of their race. His rails against Christian Identity for fatally misdirecting the energies of Aryan revival toward a false Jewish cult. However, given the armed superiority of the established authorities, he discourages the millennial insurrection of *The Turner Diaries* as a suicide mission. More recently, he has endorsed the idea that Aryan revolutionaries should form a new corporatist elite, suggesting that Odinists take up capitalism, invest in the stock market, and thus control the means that control the masses. "Whoever controls the Blue Chip companies controls America. Who controls America, controls Europe, NATO, and the United Nations. Who controls the United Nations controls the Earth."[30] Ultimately, only power and numbers count for Kaldenberg.

Jost Turner was a communal Odinist pioneer and also articulated a racialist Odinism that places great emphasis on spirituality and consciousness-raising. According to Mattias Gardell, he established his National Socialist Kindred during the 1980s on a folkish "back-to-the-land" Odinist commune called Volksberg in the mountains of northern California. In his teaching known as Aryan Kriya, Jost combines Aryo-Vedic beliefs, Norse mythology and Hindu Tantrism to direct the spiritual evolution of the Aryan individual in accordance with racial archetypes. Born in 1946, Jost served for two years in a combat role with a reconnaissance platoon of the 101st Airborne in the Vietnam War. Embittered and traumatized, he returned to his native California in 1967 and began exploring occultism and oriental religions at the height of the "flower power" era. At this time, he encountered the *Autobiography of a Yogi* by Swami Parmahansa Yogananda, an Indian who had led a Hindu mission to the United States during the 1920s. Jost trained in Kriya yoga with Yogananda's Self-Realization Fellowship and lived for two years at an ashram in Northern California.[31] By the mid-1970s Jost became interested in Norse paganism and occult National Socialism and was involved with the Ásatrú Free Fellowship. He married Stephen McNallen's sister-in-law and the families remained close even after Jost left the AFA.

Jost sympathized with the hippies' idea of "dropping out" and destroying the system by non-participation. When hippies began to form self-sufficient communes in the country, Jost was impressed by their mastery of homesteading, animal husbandry, and craft skills. Deciding to break with urban society, Jost and his family joined the commune movement and learned these same skills. The hippie communes embraced an idealism based on left-wing solidarity, oriental religion and a tolerance for drugs. Jost regarded their lack of discipline and the rise of marijuana cultivation with its easy profits as the chief factors that eventually destroyed both the ideals and the community spirit. Once the former utopianism embraced a readiness for armed resistance to outside interference, a defensive attitude led to an alliance between armed hippie cultivators and right-wing revolutionaries. In this world of outlaw rural enclaves, Jost saw the seeds of a back-to-the land movement for racially conscious whites:

> Today, the mountains are waiting for a new back-to-the-land movement, one imbued with a true idealism, and a sound spiritual philosophy. This time it will not be the pressures of White middle class materialism that will spur a back-to-the-land movement. This time it will be the awesome pressure of mass non-white immigration, and White second-class citizenship.
>
> All of the elements for building an Aryan Folk community are here. The time is now ripe. There is little future for White youth in any city. The cities are becoming more and more non-white. Economically, it is getting more and more difficult to survive in the city. The social welfare system is becoming more and more anti-white. The schools are sorely anti-white. Today, the disenfranchised Aryan youth are beginning to stir. The Skinhead movement is a

reaction to the growing non-white terrorism, and White indifference. It pains me to see our youth in government prisons for smashing a few degenerate heads in a futile attempt to fight back against overwhelming oppression. How much more useful it would be to put their energy into hewing themselves a homestead, and ultimately an Aryan community, out of the unsettled mountains. . . . Why not take up the old hippy slogan to "drop out," and begin by destroying this anti-white system by non-participation?[32]

Jost lived for two years among the scattered barns and teepees of the hippies, but in the mid-1980s he began to lay the basis of the Volksberg commune, a folkish utopia for his National Socialist Kindred (NS Kindred) based on Odinist principles. Located on a symbolic 88-acre plot in the hilly forests of northern California, Volksberg achieved economic self-sufficiency through farming and handicrafts, providing a small Wotan School for the commune children. In Jost's view, National Socialism was a modern revival of Aryan tribalism structured along the lines of decentralized communalism. But this collective vision was no mere peasant idyll, since Jost believed that such new Folk-communities were the bridges to a more highly evolved species of Aryan mankind. Only these *Übermenschen* (supermen) could lead the world back into harmony with Nature and toward the golden age envisioned by Adolf Hitler.[33] In this way, Jost's thought elaborated Else Christensen's idea of the awakening archetypes to include New Age notions taken from yoga and Hinduism. During the Volksberg years, the NS Kindred published numerous tracts on National Socialism and racialist Odinism, with a growing emphasis on self-development.

Inspired by Savitri Devi's devotional work, *The Lightning and the Sun*, Jost regarded Hitler as a semi-divine religious leader who had indicated the Aryan spiritual future in the higher collective of the Folk. Like Savitri Devi, Jost also embraced Hitler as an evangelist of love. "His words, his actions, his entire existence is testimony to his selfless love of his Folk. . . . Everything that he did was done for the benefit of the Folk. The welfare and higher evolution of the Folk is the only reason for the existence of National Socialism."[34] Jost's eulogies of National Socialism as a selfless religion could easily be describing an idealized form of Christianity or Hindu Vedanta. He attributed the failure of National Socialism to the selfishness and materialism of the unregenerate Aryans rather than the Jews and regarded Hitler as a martyr whose sacrifice to these negative forces should awaken the Aryans to their real destiny. Once the Aryan discovers true love, he clearly sees that the enemy images of colored races, international finance and the Jews are "all just symptoms of a deadly disease of selfishness."[35] This equation of National Socialism with a religion of selflessness shows how far Jost had managed to combine his Odinism with the teachings of Yogananda.

Disappointed with the poor quality of recruits to the Volksberg commune, Jost abandoned the name "NS Kindred" in 1995 and concentrated his efforts on publishing books on Aryan Kriya. His system of Aryan spiritual self-development was based on the tantric Hinduism of Yogananda, Norse mythology, and the Hindu-Nordic ideas of Savitri Devi and Miguel Serrano, whose ideas had begun to spread in the pagan subculture by the early 1990s. Jost claimed that Yogananda's autobiography and ideas had been edited by disciples to gain acceptance in liberal America. Jost declared that Yogananda was not anti-Hitler and supported the non-interventionist America First Movement during the Second World War. He upheld the Korean War against communism and "foresaw the massive problems" of multiculturalism.[36] After reading Savitri Devi's account of Aryan Hinduism, Jost was convinced that Kriya sprang from kindred blood. Its teaching reflected Odinism, while its "path of accelerated evolution was what was symbolized by the allegories of Wotan, Thor, Yggdrasil."[37]

Gardell writes that Jost pursued the story of Yogananda's own guru, Babaji Nagaraj, a supposedly immortal Aryan *siddha* (self-realized divine being). Legend records that Nagaraj ("king of the serpents" signifying mastery of Kundalini) was born in A.D. 230. Practicing kundalini yoga, he achieved the highest state of human evolution, physical immortality and divine enlightenment at the age of sixteen. Supposedly still alive today, Nagaraj leads an ashram of fellow immortals in the Himalayas. According to Jost, this ashram was the secret center sought by Miguel Serrano during his years in India.[38] Many gurus, besides Yogananda, claim to have been sent by Nagaraj to teach mankind the consciousness-raising techniques of Kriya yoga. Through his own practice of Kriya, Jost came to feel that Nagaraj was now directing him to take up the struggle against the forces of the dark age, or Kali Yuga. After receiving instruction in the original 144 Kriyas (practices) by another American disciple of Nagaraj, Jost was told to open an Aryan Kriya path "especially for Aryanists, Odinists, National Socialists, and other true heirs to the ancient Aryan science of accelerated evolution."[39]

Like Savitri Devi, Jost understood history in terms of the Hindu Puranic divisions of time, but his system was more complex, involving two interacting cycles. The equinoctial cycle comprised two sets of four yugas, first declining then ascending over a period of 24,000 years, while the galactic cycle takes an awesome four million years to complete. The Satya Yuga, or golden age, corresponds to the Norse Axe Age, the Treta Yuga to the Sword Age, the Dvapara Yuga to the Wind Age, and the Kali Yuga to the dark or Wolf Age.

According to Jost, the last equinoctial Satya Yuga reached its climax around 11,500 B.C., when Aryan supermen created the ancient civilizations of Egypt, Europe and South America, characterized by pyramids and megalithic monuments. The last equinoctial Kali Yuga lasted from A.D. 500 to 1600, with the Renaissance marking the renewed ascent of the Dvapara Yuga. However, this ascent is frustrated by the superimposition of the galactic time cycle, whereby we are now entering a coincident galactic Kali Yuga lasting 400,000 years. This has the effect of retarding planetary evolution by four hundred years, so that selfishness and materialism are still more dominant than they would normally be in the ascending Dvapara Yuga.

This imminent upswing of the equinoctial cycle recalls Savitri Devi's apocalyptic expectation of the end of the Kali Yuga. But Jost also argues that Aryan man can even surmount the vicissitudes of the galactic Kali Yuga stretching far into the future, thanks to the ancient science of accelerated human evolution developed by Babaji Nagaraj in a former golden age. "Even during the dark ages of this earth men and women of sufficient physical development could, by self-effort, attain super-consciousness in their life time." Anticipating the galactic Wolf Age, Nagaraj and his brotherhood of immortal *siddhas* also remained on earth "to preserve the ancient Aryan science" for a future revival of the race, which Jost is now undertaking.[40]

Aryan Kriya is based on the precepts of classical yoga involving a set of moral requirements to purify body and mind through correct body posture (*asana*) and meditation (*dhyana*). In the *Yoga Sūtras* of Patanjali, these prescriptions are summarized as a list of eight "limbs": (1) abstention, comprising non-violence (*ahimsa*), truthfulness, non-theft, celibacy and non-greed; (2) observance, comprising cleanliness, contentment, austerity, self-study and attentiveness to God; (3) posture; (4) breath control; (5) sense withdrawal; (6) concentration; (7) meditation; (8) contemplation. However, Jost differs from Patanjali and most yoga teachers by claiming that celibacy is a Christianized distortion of true Aryan Kriya during the dark age. *Ahimsa* has also been wrongly interpreted to mean one should harm no living creature. Jost claims that one must be prepared to take up arms in a revolutionary war against the oppressors. In the spirit of the *Bhagavad Gita*, "we may be compelled by duty to harm or kill [but] it is important that our mind be kept clear of hatred, animosity and any desire for revenge."[41]

The regime of Aryan Kriya involves daily baths, a macrobiotic diet, and a rural life-style in harmony with nature. The Aryan should practice various yoga techniques that recall Miguel Serrano's Hindu-Aryan yoga of swastika-spinning *chakras*. Seated in the "swastika posture" (*swastikasana*), the adept can rouse the kundalini energy at the base of the spine and circulate it through the *chakras* by concentrating on images of the runes or the swastika, and by chanting mantras like *aum* for the sixth *chakra*, called the Eye of Wotan. Daily practice of these techniques together with a natural diet will eliminate all disease, prevent aging and raise one's level of consciousness.[42] Its goal is the self-realized Aryan man-god who is "One with Wotan." This self-development toward the highest state of human evolution also has a cosmological significance. Aryan man is a microcosm corresponding to the macrocosm of the sun and the twelve houses of the zodiac. The spiritual advance of the microcosm has a beneficial effect on the racial group and the outer world during the galactic Wolf Age. Jost recalls that the ancient Aryan *siddhas* "recognised that humans of high evolution were absolutely indispensable to keep the planet from degenerating into chaos and complete destruction during the dark ages."[43]

By translating notions of white supremacy into a discourse of spiritual evolution, yoga and the teachings of ancient Hindu-Aryan masters, Jost offers a form of racial Odinism closely related to the millennial piety of New Age religion. Only the Wolf Age could obscure the cosmic truth that individuals and races are unequal, with the immortal Aryan masters representing the peak of evolution. Through Aryan Kriya, Jost offers a means for Aryan individuals to realize their higher spiritual evolution and thus transcend the present dark age. "The siddhas are counting on all of us to use this technique to advance our own evolution so that we can advance the evolution of the world and pull it up from its tailspin into degeneracy."[44] Aryan Kriya was hardly launched before Jost died of cancer in 1996. However, this mystical form of Odinism survives in the practice of small groups in the United States, Canada, Western Europe and Scandinavia. The ardent young Swedish National Socialist and former COTC supporter, Tommy Rydén, has also translated Jost's works into Swedish for distribution through his DeVries Institute (named for Arnold DeVries, the co-author of Ben Klassen's *Salubrious Living*).[45]

Founded by David and Katja Lane and their friend Ron McVan in 1995, Wotansfolk is a highly prominent racial Odinist group in the United States today. Following his conviction for the homicide of Alan Berg while a member of the Brüders Schweigen, David Lane was sentenced to 190 years' imprisonment. The notoriety of the group and his enormous sentence have combined with his prolific output of revolutionary writings in prison to make him perhaps "the best known White political prisoner in the world today." David Lane also coined the 14 Words motto, "We must secure the existence of our people and a future for White children," based on the rising tide of color in global population. Repeated in all Wotansfolk literature, this credo has now spread throughout the magazines and music of the racist underground across the world. With a background in music and the creative arts, Ron McVan joined the couple's 14 Word Press at St. Maries, Idaho, in 1994 and has since been a seminal influence in the development of the Wotansfolk religious philosophy. Through tireless correspondence and the publications of the 14 Word Press, Katja Lane has created a successful prison outreach program with hundreds of prison kindreds in the United States. A website set up in 1995, and subsequently expanded, has enabled Wotansfolk to establish kindreds in many foreign countries.

David Eden Lane was one of four children born to an itinerant farmworker in 1938 at Woden, Iowa (hence his pagan nom de plume, Wodensson). By 1943 the father's desertion and family poverty had put the children in an orphanage, where young David was adopted by a traveling Lutheran minister and his wife. Subjected to endless hours of services, prayers and Bible studies, Lane early rejected Christianity and regarded his adoptive father as an "obnoxious buffoon." During the 1960s he became increasingly disenchanted with mainstream political parties and the betrayal of American commitment to the Vietnam War. A brief association with the John Birch Society introduced him to a conspiratorial view of politics and media power. By 1978 he was convinced that the Western nations were ruled by a Zionist conspiracy, which seeks the extermination of the white Aryan race in order to dominate the inferior races. Lane's thought was thus primarily racialist, as a response to the Jews' alleged goal of their racial dominion and Aryan extinction. He lost his Colorado real estate broker's license by refusing to sell homes to colored people in white areas, a penalty he attributed to Jewish power, and in 1981 he attracted the attention the Anti-Defamation League by distributing thousands of copies his leaflet "The Death of the White Race" in Denver and surrounding towns.[46]

David Lane's political education was strongly colored by Christian Identity. His natural sister, Jane Eden, was engaged to the Pennsylvania state leader of Aryan Nations, and she also worked for Richard Butler's church in Idaho. Lane subsequently became involved in Aryan Nations as Butler's "information minister." Lane's "The Death of the White Race" leaflet and his booklet, *Under This Sign You Shall Conquer*, a study of "true Christianity and racism," were distributed by Aryan Nations. He also attended Pete Peters's Laporte Church of Christ, an important Identity congregation near Fort Collins, Colorado. Lane first met Robert Jay Mathews at the Aryan Nations world congress in July 1983 and was sworn into the Brüders Schweigen at its inauguration on 22 September 1983. Lane also introduced Mathews to his mistress, Zillah Craig, and brought Mathews to Peters's church.[47] In June 1984 Alan Berg, a Jewish radio talk-show host notorious for his baiting of far-right groups, was shot at his home in Denver by members of the Brüders Schweigen. Lane was an early suspect and was captured on 31 March 1985. He was tried in Seattle with other Brüders Schweigen members accused of counterfeiting and of Berg's murder and given forty years for racketeering and conspiracy. In November 1987 he was convicted in a federal court in Denver of violating Alan Berg's civil rights by killing him and given another 150 years.[48]

Constantly radicalized by his struggle against racial integration and the federal authorities, Lane sees the world in apocalyptic and Manichaean terms. After the Seattle trial, Lane defined The Order's mission in Identity terms as the battle between the divine seedline and the Devil's progeny.[49] Protesting that he was innocent of involvement in the Berg killing, Lane is convinced that he was the victim of the government's perjured hearsay testimony and that he was given a double jeopardy arraignment for the same offense. During his years in high-security prisons at Marion, Ohio; Leavenworth, Kansas; and Florence, Colorado, Lane penned his Aryan revolutionary works to show how the Zionist American establishment was using racial integration, backed by the media, education and a punitive justice system, to demoralize and destroy the white race. During these years, his writings increasingly moved away from Identity toward a racialist pagan viewpoint, which sees the natural laws of the universe as divine. These laws are essentially defined as the preservation of one's own race, and a race is judged superior or inferior by its will and ability to survive. A people that allows racial aliens to dwell in its midst will perish through racial interbreeding as "no race of People can indefinitely continue their existence without territorial imperatives in which to propagate, protect, and promote their own kind."[50]

Besides this deistic naturalism, Lane also wrote on the Western esoteric tradition, utilizing numerology and such occult devices as initiate schools and secret knowledge to trace a hidden heritage in the history of religion. Druids, Egyptian priesthoods, Pythagoras and Plato, the Christian Gnostics, Cathars, Knights Templar, Rosicrucians and other Hermetic philosophers are all deemed initiates or heirs of the mystery religions that had flourished in the first millennium B.C. as Odinism, Mithraism, Zoroastrianism and Gnosticism. These mystery or pagan religions pursued a deeper knowledge involving the abstract principles of natural law, while the vital forces of the universe were personified in the gods and goddesses of their various pantheons. Disaster struck in 325 when the Romans, under Emperor Constantine, colluded with the Jews to adopt the universal religion of Christianity throughout the empire. The Jews usurped and distorted the wisdom of the ancient mystery schools in order to erect a spiritual tyranny for all time and places in which they would be recognized as "God's chosen people."[51] Lane uses numerology, the "coding system" of the King James Bible (allegedly written by Sir Francis Bacon) and magic squares to decipher the true universal scheme hidden in the Bible and in pagan mythologies.

Lane's overriding concern remains the defensive assertion of white racial survival. He rails against the liberal multiracial and race-mixing policies of the white nation-states in North America, Europe and Australasia, while colored races already account for over 90 percent of the world population. Lane states that only 8 percent of the world's population is white, and only 2 percent is white female of child-bearing age or younger, a crucial statistic for the reproduction of the race. Seen in the context of global demography, the inevitable result of affirmative action for so-called ethnic minorities and racial integration in the remaining white homelands is genocide for the white race. In Lane's view, the white race is being denied white ethnic states by the denial of white schools, white neighborhoods, and any other white organizations for maintaining their biological and cultural identity. Racial integration inevitably leads to an increase of interracial matings each year, which will lead to white racial extinction if unchecked.[52] The 14 Word credo is his incessant response to this planned assault on the white race. His militant racialism has earned him the unqualified praise of Colin Jordan as an "[exemplary] warrior for the survival and revival of the White peoples of this world."[53]

Always resisting invasions of racial aliens, the Aryan race has created a civilization comparable to their earlier Roman empire. "The White race has suffered invasions and brutality from Africa and Asia for thousands of years," declares Lane, "so the attempted guilt-trip placed on the White race by civilization's executioners is invalid under both historical circumstance and the natural Law which denies inter-species compassion. . . . All races have benefitted immeasurably from the creative genius of the Aryan people."[54] Lane vilifies America under its Zionist Occupation Government (ZOG) for a deliberate policy of white genocide over many years. He interprets the Second World War as a Jewish plot to use "the white men of America and England . . . [to destroy] the racial basis of our ancient European homeland." Nazi Germany was actually attempting to perform its historic function as defender of the Aryan race, just as it had repelled invading Moors and Mongols during the Middle Ages.[55] The ensuing Cold War with the Soviet Union was a mere hoax to "use America's racially integrated military to mix races near bases all over Europe and America."[56]

Lane frequently cites the harrowing examples of enforced racial integration in the United States, such as the 101st Airborne's use of bayonets to integrate Southern schools, and the police's use of clubs to beat the white moth-

ers of South Boston when they protested the integration of their neighborhood schools. The government is said to sanction homosexuality and abortion to depress white births. Young white females are constantly bombarded
by race-mixing propaganda, affirmative action displaces whites from employment and taxes impoverish the whites while financing the breeding of
colored races. Summoning images of innocent white children bused into lawless black ghettos, the decay and criminality of urban America and white
flight to the suburbs and country towns, Lane concludes that America is no
longer a white country. While the government admits a figure of 70 percent
white, Lane thinks that with Hispanics, Jews and illegal aliens, America may
just still be 50 percent white. However, in another generation, America will resemble Africa and other colored areas of the world. "The day is coming, if
there is not a revolution soon that American police and military powers
under the command of the Jews and comprised of Negroes, Mexicans, Orientals and vicious race traitors will attempt to murder the last true White
men." In an apocalyptic vision recalling medieval Mongol hordes with herds
of captive women, Lane predicts "the last true White women and children will
be carried off for recreation and sport."[57]

Backed by its global economic and military power, the United States has
become a catalyst to re-create the world in its own multiracial image. Indicating the telltale Zionist mottos on the Great Seal of the United States, "E
pluribus unum" (one out of many), and "novus ordo seclorum" (new order of
the ages, or New World Order), Lane relates how America has intervened militarily to enforce this order in the Southern states, in Latin American countries, in Italy, twice in Germany, and in Korea, Vietnam, Libya, and Iraq. Eastern Europe under communism was long isolated from the liberal multiracial
experiment of the West, but now intervention has begun in Yugoslavia. Lane
condemns the "anti-White slaughter of innocents in Serbia" and quotes General Wesley Clark, NATO's supreme commander during the war in Kossovo,
as saying: "Let's not forget what the origin of the problem is. There is no place
in modern Europe for ethnically pure states. That's a nineteenth-century idea
and we are trying to transition into the twenty-first century, and we are going
to do it with multi-ethnic states."[58] Lane considers it no coincidence that a Jew
should express this American determination to mix and destroy the integrity
of every race and nation on the globe to create the New World Order.

Turning to religion, Lane believes that the white race cannot share gods
or religions with other races. Alien gods destroy a race's sense of uniqueness
and also its capacity for survival. Abandoning Christian Identity, he believes
Wotanism is the best religion for the white race today. Using terms from
mythology and Jungian psychology, Lane declares that Wotan is the best

representation of the creative force and folkish needs. "Wotan awakens our racial soul and genetic memory. He stirs our blood." Religion should serve the paramount goal of racial survival. Lane contrasts the New Testament's "Ten Commandments for Racial Suicide" with Wotansvolk wisdom for Aryan man. To "Blessed are the meek: for they shall inherit the Earth" (Matthew 5:5), he answers, "Fortune smiles on a people whose visions are brave, bold and determined." Concerning sex, "Whosoever looketh on a woman to lust after her hath committed adultery in his heart" (Matthew 5:28), Wotansvolk rejoins, "If our males do not lust after our women strongly enough to fight to the death for women and territory, then we as a race will perish." "Love your enemies, do good to them which hate you" (Luke 6:27) is countered with, "Smite your enemies and the enemies of your people with the hammer of Thor. Feed their bodies to vultures in the market place, that your next enemy depart in fear." For Lane, religion is ultimately a political weapon: "Render unto Caesar the things that are Caesar's" (Mark 12:10), to which Wotansvolk replies, "Cut off ZOG's head and feed it to the dogs. Government beyond the consent of the governed is tyranny and theft."[59]

While David Lane supplies the driving political ideology of white survival behind Wotansvolk, Gardell's research shows that Ron McVan has developed its artistic, devotional and philosophical content. Born in Philadelphia in 1950, McVan moved in the world of rock music and worked as an artist. Religiously motivated, he was drawn to Buddhism until he read Ben Klassen's books *Nature's Eternal Religion* and *The White Man's Bible*. This encounter led to his involvement in white racialism. He contributed articles and artwork to the Church of the Creator (COTC), later editing its periodical, *Racial Loyalty*, and becoming martial arts instructor of its paramilitary White Berets at the COTC headquarters at Otto, North Carolina. While McVan shared Klassen's anti-Christian mission, he found Creativity shallow and started a Wotan's Kindred in the Pacific Northwest in 1992. In 1994 McVan moved to St. Maries, Idaho, to work with the Lanes' newly established 14 Word Press, and in 1995 the three founded Wotansfolk as an Odinist movement to foster the spiritual awareness of Aryan identity and destiny.

According to McVan, Wotanism is rooted in the white race's genetic character and collective identity. "Our ancient, White ancestors understood that to ensure our heritage and racial survival, expansion and advancement we must initiate means to galvanize our Folk Consciousness. Allegories and myths were developed along with a variety of archetypical gods which best represented Nature's Law and the collective unconscious of the Folk. Foremost and most consistent among all these archetypes was the Teutonic God, Wotan."[60] Describing Wotanism as "the inner voice of the Aryan soul," McVan relates how the irruption of the Wotan spirit united and transformed the German people with an "amazing and almost instant iron will and productivity" in the 1930s. The Wotan spirit has been notably quiescent in the decades following 1945, when a deliberate genocide of the white race, its culture and traditions, was launched in multiracial states. However, McVan sees a "metamorphosis of the gods" taking place in our time, "a calling of the blood." Because all Aryans, to a greater or lesser degree, still retain an element of Wotan consciousness, this spirit is their protectorate and strength and "the surest means to unify our common purpose and destiny."[61]

Wotansvolk sees its mission as a continuation of the earlier efforts of such individuals as Richard Wagner, Friedrich Nietzsche, Guido von List and Carl Gustav Jung to restore the Aryans to their potent collective unconscious. McVan cites Lanz von Liebenfels's claim that the Knights Templar were an armed guard of Ariosophy until their suppression by the Church in the fourteenth century. However, by the end of the nineteenth century, many *völkisch* groups had sprung up to foster the "ancient Teutonic, Gnostic wisdom and ritual practice." This revival of Teutonic mythology was enhanced further by Wagner's inspirational music and Nietzsche's heroic philosophy, which cast new light on "the long-suppressed Aryan consciousness." McVan recounts how Wotanism and Ariosophy were rediscovered by Guido von List and Jörg Lanz von Liebenfels, and their example was followed by Karl Maria Wiligut, Rudolf von Sebottendorff, Theodor Fritsch and Dietrich Eckart, who forged a new Aryan self-consciousness among the Germans in anticipation of National Socialism.[62]

Wotansvolk's inspiration in the work of Carl Gustav Jung is primarily attributable to his famous essay of 1936, in which he described the Wotan archetype as an autonomous psychic factor producing violent and restless effects in the collective life of the Germans. Jung recalled the earliest signs of its outbreak before 1914 in the German Youth Movement with its sun worship, solstice rituals and pagan symbolism. After 1933, Jung saw the enthusiastic masses of the Third Reich as being seized by the full flood of the Wotan archetype after centuries of its repression.[63] In a letter written to Miguel Serrano in 1960, Jung expanded on the perennial potency of the Wotan archetype:

> When, for instance, the belief in the god Wotan vanished and nobody thought of him anymore, the phenomenon originally called Wotan remained; nothing changed but its name, as National Socialism has demonstrated on a grand scale. A collective movement consists of millions of individuals, each of whom shows the symptoms of Wotanism and proves thereby that Wotan in reality never died, but has retained his original vitality and autonomy. Our

consciousness only imagines that it has lost its Gods; in reality they are there still and it only needs a certain general condition in order to bring them back in full force.

Turning to the postwar present, Jung then commented that the weakness of orthodox Christianity and the challenge of communism placed the world in a similar spiritual predicament to pre-Nazi Germany in the 1920s, "i.e. we are apt to undergo the risk of a further Wotanistic experiment. This means mental epidemy and war."[64]

Wotansvolk literature approvingly quotes Jung on Wotan but omits any mention of his dire warnings after the Nazi era. In this respect, Wotansvolk identifies with an early Jung who supposedly drew inspiration from contemporary irrationalism and *völkisch* nationalism. In his controversial books, Richard Noll has related Jung's early intellectual development to the neoromantic intellectual climate of German fin-de-siècle culture, when pessimistic notions of decline and decadence were matched by Nietzschean calls for rebirth and renewal. Following explorations of spiritualism and Theosophy, Jung became interested in the Aryan-Mithraic religion and the solar mysticism of German *völkisch* nationalists.[65] Jung borrowed evolutionary biologist Ernst Haeckel's theory that the stages of individual development recapitulated the evolution of the human race in order to articulate his own evolutionary theory of the unconscious. To Jung, fantasies and dreams recorded the prehistoric and ancient religious experience of mankind. In 1909 Jung set about excavating the unconscious of his Swiss and German patients in the light of ancient Aryan mystery religions and their solar symbols. If Jung initially had regarded the eruption of the unconscious strata of the mind as a pathology, by 1916 he believed that the conscious mind could only be revitalized by cutting through the repressive Christian overlay of European civilization to the archaic pre-Christian levels below.[66]

Wotansvolk celebrates Jung as seen by Noll: the rediscoverer of the Aryan mysteries of the European peoples, especially the Germans, before the imposition of an alien, Semitic Christianity that severed them from their primordial sources of life, their gods, myths and archetypes. Using Jung's imagery of archetypal eruption, McVan claims that "Jung predicted that the Aryan race would soon enter a resurgent age of Wotan, who would rise within the folk conscious mind of his people, like a dormant volcano to new activity." Only through a spiritual act, "in which the White race rediscovers its myth and legend," can Aryan man survive as a species.[67] Gardell shows how most of McVan's work is directed toward this rediscovery. He has re-created full Wotanist rites of blot (ceremony) and sumbel (toasting). His artistic talent has fashioned mead horns, Thor's hammers in brass and silver, oak and antler rune staffs, spiral armbands and other runic jewelry, all retailed through the 14 Word Press to Wotansvolk kindreds worldwide. His distinctive artwork featuring Viking warriors, Wotan and ancient megalithic ceremonial sites adorns the pages of 14 Word Press publications, including the monthly newsletter *Focus Fourteen*. His impressive wooden sculptures of Norse gods and goddesses, wolves, dragons and ravens are scattered over the headquarters site at St. Maries, together with a wooden temple (*Hof*) dedicated to the memory of Guido von List.

Besides his digest of Wotansvolk wisdom, *Creed of Iron* (1997), McVan has also authored and illustrated numerous pamphlets on the mystery of the blood, Old Norse poems, Wagner and Jung. Wotansvolk religion offers a spiritual and ceremonial dimension in support of Lane's strident insistence on Aryan power, propagation and survival, and it is notable in this context that the 14 Word Press has issued its own edition of Ragnar Redbeard's *Might Is Right*. But Wotansvolk also recommends song, dance and meditation to bring Aryan man and woman into harmony with cosmic energies. McVan also revives the esoteric notion of the Odic force, first discovered by Karl von Reichenbach (1788–1869), to show how Aryans can fully realize their creative potential.[68] McVan's most recent publication, *Temple of Wotan: Holy Book of the Aryan Tribes* (2000), is a lavishly illustrated large-format repertoire of Wotanist sacred rites, art, poetry and runes, and it includes the full text of C. G. Jung's "Wotan" essay. This Wotanist "bible" is dedicated to Miguel Serrano, who also supplies the foreword. Here Serrano dilates on Wotanism as the original religion of the divine Aryans. He recalls the Externsteine in Germany as a major shrine and the importance of the Germann SS in reviving the cult at the nearby Wewelsburg. The volume also contains reprints of the Jung-Serrano correspondence, including the prophetic letter already quoted.[69] In Wotansvolk, Serrano appears to have found a major promoter in the English-speaking world. The 14 Word Press has recently published the first English-language edition of Serrano's *The Golden Chain: Esoteric Hitlerism*.

In its racial focus on immigration and white submergence, latter-day Wotanism sees the loss of white ethnic identity as the main consequence of globalization. Wotansvolk rejects metropolitanism and large-scale industry as the causes of congestion, immigration and race mixing, pollution, and rampant crime. Led astray by rationalism and materialism, modern man feels that he must ceaselessly consume manufactured products so that the machines that enslave him may grow. Wotansvolk demonstrates its tribalist antipathy toward economic liberalism by arguing that folk community living is the sole antidote to disorders of life in overpopulated and polyglot cities. Cooperation, kinship and constructive emotions, along with a simplified unstressful life-style, are essential factors for the development of a healthy race. "The world struggle for the future is only now just beginning. As the sickness of this lost society becomes too much to bear, the need for neo-tribalism and a return to our folk gods will become ever more apparent. To this, the Aryan path of Wotanism [. . .] provides a dynamic storehouse of ancestral knowledge and ethnic identity."[70] In its opposition to cities, liberalism, and international cap-italism, Wotansvolk revives the idyll of rural *völkisch* utopias sought by early twentieth-century German pagans.

14

Conspiracy Beliefs and the New World Order

THE 1990s WITNESSED political developments in both America and Europe that lent credence to a fear of big government and corporatism. The fall of the Soviet Union and the end of communism in 1990 signalled the beginning of a new phase of U.S. world hegemony, backed by frequent calls for a "New World Order" by both President Bush and also Russian leaders. The Gulf crisis and the dispatch of a U.S. led-United Nations taskforce for the war against Iraq (February 1991) unleashed further rhetoric about supranational government. Government regulation, already growing under the Republican administration of George Bush, received a further boost from the Democratic victory of Bill Clinton in 1992. After the external threat of Soviet communism had vanished, the increasing democratic deficit of government became a focus for nationalist fears of creeping socialism and bureaucratic authoritarianism. American patriots were especially concerned when President Clinton began campaigning for tighter gun control in the summer of 1993, and firearms purchases were restricted by the Brady Law of February 1994. Fears of incipient government tyranny fomented conspiracy myths among independent social groups wary of bureaucracy and increased regulation. The increasing pace of federal integration in the European Union, signposted by the Maastricht Treaty of 1993, fanned similar fears about administrative rule and a loss of national sovereignty in European states.

On 19 April 1995, the blast of a massive 7,000-pound bomb ripped through the Alfred P. Murrah Building, a nine-story federal government office block which housed more than 500 employees in Oklahoma City. Timothy James McVeigh, a twenty-seven-year-old Gulf War veteran, was arrested two days later and charged with the then worst terrorist atrocity in United States history, which claimed the lives of 168 people and injured more than 500. McVeigh had earlier ties to the citizens' militia movement, which began forming around 1992 to practice weapons training and "survivalism" in remote forests. The militias saw themselves as the defenders of American values and were opposed to rising taxes, growing government regulation and plans

279

for ID cards. Above all, they resisted President Bill Clinton's attempts to tighten up America's gun laws. The right to bear arms (enshrined in the Second Amendment of the Constitution) was regarded as a safeguard for liberty and an essential deterrent to the abuse of government authority.

Citizens' militias existed in more than forty states from California to Pennsylvania, with a particular concentration in the North and Midwest. However, the militias were only the armed wing of a much broader patriot movement, which included anti-tax protesters, advocates of "sovereign" citizenship (denial of U.S. federal authority), Christian fundamentalists and anti-abortionists, involving perhaps 5 to 12 million people. United by a profound suspicion of big government and its intentions, their ideology drew on a bizarre range of conspiracy theories involving hidden elites, banks, secret societies and international organizations. These ideas were fueled by hostility toward the increased levels of federal government interference and regulation under the Clinton administration. As McVeigh journeyed through the netherworld of gun clubs, militias and far-right groups, he had absorbed these paranoid fantasies of government's war against the people. The Oklahoma bombing not only demonstrated the terrible power of such ideas to motivate murder and mayhem, but also revealed how widespread such cultic beliefs had become in 1990s America.[1]

These conspiracy theories revealed secret plots behind everything from UFOs to gun control, from Freemasonry to AIDS, from CIA mind-control experiments to the establishment of "one-world government" by the United Nations. By the early 1990s, conspiracy culture could support a small but fast-growing sector of the publishing trade. With sales of over half a million copies, *The New World Order* (1991) by Pat Robertson, founder of the Christian Broadcasting Network, reveals that the New World Order (NWO) will eliminate America's sovereignty with the aid of UN troops. An elite of godless conspirators is intent on ruling the world, and computer technology and microchips are part of the NWO enslavement plan. Jack McLamb's *Operation Vampire Killer 2000* (1992) describes how America is to be overrun by foreign UN troops and turned into a socialist police state. His "vampires" are the bloodsucking secret elites that are undermining the Constitution, in order to rule over a racially mixed and docile society. Other favorites were Gary Kah's *En Route to Global Occupation* (1991), detailing the clandestine moves to suspend the Constitition and establish one-world government, and Jeffrey Baker's *Cheque Mate: The Game of Princes* (1993), giving extensive details of the plans of bankers, corporate leaders and leading families to rule over a helot world. John Coleman's *Conspirators' Hierarchy* (1992) documents the Committee of 300, a powerful group of international bankers, industrialists and oil magnates intent on world control. Jim Keith's *Secret and Suppressed* (1993) includes chapters on the Jonestown, Guyana, massacre as a CIA mind-control effort, on brain implants, AIDS and on secrets from the Pentagon and the Vatican library. In *Psychic Dictatorship U.S.A.* (1995), Alex Constantine gave horrific details of involuntary mind-control experiments by government agencies in America.

Besides a battery of magazines, including *The Free American, USA Patriot Magazine, Patriot Report* and Don McAlvany's *Intelligence Advisor*, the conspiracy subculture communicated busily through the Internet and on the airwaves of small independent shortwave and FM radio stations. Anthony J. Hilder, a broadcaster with Radio Free World in Los Angeles, invoked the terrifying specter of complete governmental control over U.S. citizenry: "You are the victim! You are the spoils! They want your home, your family, your mother, your children; they want to inject your children with a number!" Hilder speaks about UFOs as a ploy of the U.S. Department of Defense, "a crisis creation project," and the preamble to "a mock invasion designed to panic the population of the planet into accepting global government upon the ashes of American sovereignty." Hilder mentions Adolf Hitler's call for "One Reich, One People, One Leader" as a precursor of the New World Order. Just as the Wall Street bankers earlier financed both Nazism and Soviet communism, the elite's goal today is a totalitarian slave state of controlled citizens.[2]

As the leading legal spokesperson of the U.S. militia movement, U.S. attorney Linda D. Thompson had long charted the progress of the encroaching New World Order.[3] An early conspiracy convert, she was intensely radicalized after witnessing the siege of the Waco Branch Davidian sect by members of the Bureau of Alcohol, Tobacco and Firearms (BATF). She produced a video, *Waco: The Big Lie* (1993–94), which documents the background of the sect, the legal preparations of the government to justify its assault on the Waco compound, and the ensuing hostilities from February to April 1993. Throughout the film, the sect is portrayed as the hapless victim of an unprovoked attack, while the BATF recalls the jack-booted stormtroopers of Nazi times. Summary shootings, gas attacks, and the final destruction of the compound by fire and the death of virtually all inside demonstrated that "not since the Nazi occupation of Europe were innocent people subjected to such stark, lawless atrocities at the hands of government as those at Waco."

Since beginning her investigation of the Waco debacle, Linda Thompson claimed that she was subject to pursuit and harassment by unmarked "black helicopters" that hovered over her home and attacked her office with an ultrasonic weapon, debilitating her and her staff. These mysterious "black helicopters" have since become a staple ingredient of New World Order conspiracy fears, variously linked to UFOs, UN troop movements across America, and the Federal Emergency Management Agency (FEMA) as the cover organization for a police-state.[4] Linda Thompson was also concerned about the construction of concentration camps across America linked by the railroad system. She identified one such camp at El Reno near Oklahoma City, which turned out to be the prison where McVeigh was charged with the bombing of the federal government building.

Timothy McVeigh read widely in patriot literature and was strongly influenced by its paranoid fantasies concerning federal government totalitarianism and a United Nations takeover. He was deeply preoccupied by the Waco siege and visited the site twice, during and after the confrontation. According to witnesses, McVeigh repeatedly viewed the Thompson video and often talked about a revenge attack on a government building. It is highly significant that the Oklahoma City bombing was carried out on the exact anniversary of the Waco siege. McVeigh was also impressed by the nightmare vision of total citizen control in a satanic social system, with the injection of numbers and the issue of bar codes to individuals. McVeigh even believed he was himself the victim of a mind-control project, claiming that the federal government had earlier implanted a microchip in his buttocks to monitor and control him during army service. According to the conspiracy theorists, the bombing itself was an FBI crisis creation project to panic the population into further surrender to the government.[5]

Conspiracy theories have long prevailed on the radical right in America. Following their rediscovery of the notorious English conspiracy theorist Nesta Webster (1876–1960), the John Birch Society and other right-wing groups identified European secret societies and Freemasonry in the eighteenth century as the ferment behind the French Revolution and subsequent challenges to traditional authority in modern times.[6] At the center of these speculations were the Bavarian Illuminati, a secret society founded at Ingolstadt on 1 May 1776 by a young Jesuit professor, Adam Weishaupt (1748–1830). The social vision of the founder was rational, egalitarian and anti-clerical. By targeting existing Masonic lodges for penetration, the order successfully spread its revolutionary ideas through Germany, Austria, Italy and into France. The Illuminati were dramatically exposed when the Bavarian authorities banned the order, and hundreds of papers and Weishaupt's letters were seized in 1786. A flood of confessions, self-justifications and official protocols ensued. Once the French Revolution broke out, a mass of circumstantial evidence already existed to link this watershed event of European history with the activities of secret societies.[7]

Without the influence of Nesta Webster, it is likely that few Americans today would have heard of the Illuminati. Due to the re-publication of her books and the popularization of her ideas among the radical right, the Illuminati became a major theme of American conspiracy literature from the late 1960s onward. Here, it is widely believed that the Illuminati had a malign influence on the founders of the United States through Benjamin Franklin, Thomas Jefferson and John Adams, who are alleged to have been members. Their influence is alleged to be visible in the occult symbols of pyramid and eye on the reverse side of America's Great Seal and on the dollar bill, originally designed by the Founding Fathers.[8] The Illuminati even entered popular culture through such underground classics as *The Illuminatus Trilogy* (1975) and *The Illuminati Papers* (1980) by Robert Anton Wilson. By the 1980s, the pre-revolutionary Illuminati of Bavaria had metamorphosed into supranational insiders bent on controling all national money systems and governments.[9]

From the 1970s onward, revelations about Jewish banking families, the American ruling class, and the secret goals of private and state agencies created a flood of books on conspiracy-theory for right-wing fundamentalist readerships. Gary Allen's book, *None Dare Call It Conspiracy* (1971), discussed the Rothschilds, the Warburgs and the Federal Reserve banking system before pinpointing the Council on Foreign Relations, a private foreign policy think-tank founded in 1921, as the prime mover for an unelected world government. Des Griffin, another leading American conspiracy theorist, traced the Illuminati up to Cecil Rhodes, the Round Table and the Rockefeller family in his highly influential book, *Fourth Reich of the Rich* (1976). These ideas were extended through new combinations in the books, bulletins and periodicals of conspiracy buffs. The National Security Agency, Central Intelligence Agency, Federal Bureau of Investigation and Inland Revenue Service were obvious targets. More attention was paid to the idea of elites behind the scenes, with exposés of the Council on Foreign Relations and the Trilateral Commission and their interlocking memberships with the boards of the Federal Reserve, leading energy companies, industrial multinationals, banks, media groups and top personnel in government departments and academe. The prestigious Bilderberg Group under the chairmanship of Prince Bernhard of the Netherlands, which has been convening discreet international conferences for policymakers and industrialists from America and Europe since 1954, is another object of deep suspicion. According to conspiracy theorists, the covert aim of all these secret elites is a "New World Order" that will manipulate and control the whole of mankind.[10]

In the early 1990s, the doyen of U.S. conspiracy cults was Milton William Cooper of St. Johns, Arizona, who wrote a compendium for the conspiracy-millenarian movement with the apocalyptic title *Behold a Pale Horse* (1991). Bill Cooper was born in 1943, the son of an airforce officer, and grew up at various overseas postings. After leaving secondary school in Japan in 1961, he joined the United States Air Force, later transferring to the navy in 1965. While serving on a submarine in the Pacific, Cooper had his first sighting of an enormous flying saucer, which emerged from the ocean and flew into the clouds. Although the saucer was repeatedly seen by other crew members and officers, Cooper alone was allegedly threatened with imprisonment for any future disclosure of what he had seen. From 1968 onward, he was assigned to Naval Intelligence with a high security clearance. Here he discovered the existence of a high-level conspiracy against the citizens of the United States. He was convinced that Naval Intelligence had participated in the assassination of John F. Kennedy, and by 1972 he had amassed disturbing classified information on UFOs, the navy, the secret government, the coming ice age, Project Galileo, and the plan for the New World Order.[11]

Following his honorable discharge in 1975, Cooper attempted to leak this kind of information to the press. He claims that the hidden powers were quick to suppress him. His car was forced off a cliff in California by a black limousine, after which two men climbed down to the wreckage. As one bent to feel his carotid pulse, the other asked if he was dead. When the first replied that he soon would be, the other expressed satisfaction that the job was done. A month later, Cooper was forced into another accident by the same mysterious car. This time he lost a leg. He was visited in hospital by two men who threatened him with a final accident if he persisted in trying to publicize secret information. Combined with his shocking discoveries of covert actions on the part of the military and the government, these near-fatal encounters utterly convinced Cooper of the realities of global conspiracy and cover-up. While continuing to collect material, he determined to expose the truth of this plan to enslave mankind in a New World Order. This intention was realized by the publication of his book, described by Cooper as "closer to that truth than anything previously written."[12]

Behold a Pale Horse is a chaotic farrago of conspiracy myths interspersed with reprints of executive laws, official papers, reports and other extraneous materials designed to show the looming prospect of a world government imposed on the American people against their wishes and in flagrant contempt of the Constitution. The first chapter comprises an allegedly secret government memorandum entitled "Silent Weapons for Quiet Wars." First discovered in an IBM copier at a surplus sale in July 1986, this document has become a hot favorite among the conspiracy cults. Here we learn that the elite decided in 1954 to exploit operations research, computer technology and finance to model a wholly predictable and manipulable society in order to transfer wealth from the undisciplined and irresponsible many to the worthy and intelligent few. Inferior mass education would keep the people undisciplined and ignorant, while the trivial concerns of media and banal entertainments would render them confused, disorganized and distracted. The piece is written in a technical jargon that likens social and economic engineering to electronics to suggest that all individuals in a society can ultimately be programmed, for "people who will not use their intelligence are no better than animals [without] intelligence. Such people are beasts of burden and steaks on the table by choice and consent."[13]

Bill Cooper identifies the document as a formal declaration of war by the Illuminati against the citizens of the United States. He asserts that peaceful citizens are justified in taking any measures, including violence, to identify, counterattack and destroy the enemy.[14] The second chapter, "Secret Societies and the New World Order," represents Cooper's own investigations and reflections on the global plot against independence and liberty. The roots of the Illuminati conspiracy are traced to an ancient Brotherhood of the Snake and thence through the Templars and the Freemasons. Cooper believes that most modern secret societies are really one society with a single purpose. A monolithic conspiracy to enslave mankind is masked by their apparent variety and plurality:

> The Order of the Quest, the JASON Society, the Roshaniya, the Qabbalah, the Knights Templar, the Knights of Malta, the Knights of Columbus, the Jesuits, the Masons, the Ancient and Mystical Order of the Rosae Crucis, the Illuminati, the Nazi Party, the Communist Party, the Executive Members of the Council on Foreign Relations, The Group, the Brotherhood of the Dragon, the Rosicrucians, the Royal Institute of International Affairs, the Trilateral Commission, the Bilderberg Group, the Vatican, the Russell Trust, the Skull & Bones, the Scroll & Key [secret societies of Harvard and Yale Universities], the Order are all the same and work towards the same ultimate goal of a New World Order.[15]

Cooper's obsessive analysis of these groups, both imaginary and real, piles detail upon detail to suggest the awesome power of interlocking elites across the world. Following Gary Allen's lead, pride of place is accorded to the Council on Foreign Relations and the Bilderberg Group. According to Cooper, the Council on Foreign Relations (CFR) controls the U.S. government. Its members have infiltrated the entire executive branch, State Department, Justice Department, the CIA and the top ranks of the military. Every director of the CIA and also most presidents since Roosevelt have been members of the CFR. Most top American journalists and press barons are members of the CFR. With traditional nativist American distrust of Britain, Cooper traces the CFR to the Royal Institute of International Affairs; he is also deeply suspicious of Oxford University and All Souls College. However, in his opinion, the most powerful secret organization in the world is the Bilderberg Group, whose three committees comprise members drawn from the Illuminati, the Freemasons, the Vatican and the old aristocratic families of Europe: "These are the men who REALLY rule the world."[16]

Cooper attaches Illuminati significance to the numbers 3, 7, 9, 11, 13 and 39. He finds these repeated in the number of articles of the U.S. Constitution, the original number of states, the number of members of the Constitutional Convention and the date of the Declaration of Independence. He detects further cabalistic evidence of Illuminati influence on the foundation of the United States in the Great Seal. The all-seeing eye in the pyramid represents Lucifer and is also the ancient symbol of the Brotherhood of the Snake. The motto "Novus Ordo Seclorum" betrays the project of the Illuminati for a New World Order, while the incidence of 13 in the number of leaves in the olive branches, the bars and stripes, the arrows, the letters in "E pluribus unum," the stars in the green crest, the stones in the pyramid and the letters in "Annuit Coeptis" indicate the signature of this most powerful of all secret societies. Worst of all, he also discovers that these numbers are repeated in the three groups of thirteen members in the committee structure of the Bilderberg Group, thus proving beyond all doubt its Illuminati inspiration.[17]

Cooper finds extensive evidence of the U.S. government's plans to impose totalitarian socialism in the abuse of presidential powers. He alleges that much legislation is introduced by the executive power through secret National Security Decision Directives that are neither reported nor made available to the public. By means of these "secret laws," the president (then George Bush) assumes the power to initiate covert actions, declare war, combat terrorism and suspend the Constitution in a state of emergency without reference to Congress.[18] Cooper passes on to the Federal Emergency Management Agency (FEMA), which in any national emergency is authorized to assume control of the media, food, energy and transportation, while mobilizing all citizens into work brigades under government supervision. William R. Pabst of Houston supplies a paranoid report on the Department of Defense's plans for a total takeover, on the police state, and details the location of a dozen concentration camps already established for the detention of political prisoners. "When your family is split up and spread across the United States to do slave labor and you never see your loved ones again, it will be your fault because you did nothing to prevent it."[19]

The ruling elite believes that only covert and totalitarian government can solve the problems of the age. Apparently, their paramount concern is overpopulation. In order to control population growth, the U.S. government continues to wage war on its own citizens through the introduction of diseases, harmful chemicals and radioactive substances among the population. The ruling elite specifically decided to target undesirable elements of society, including Negroes, Hispanics and homosexuals. The smallpox vaccine was introduced to Africa in order to decimate the black population. The hepatitis B vaccine was used to infect the U.S. population. The AIDS virus is a government weapon; tobacco fields are dusted with nuclear wastes to induce lung cancer; dioxin and other pollutants proliferate in the face of official denials.[20] A secret federal installation known as Mount Weather near Bluemont, Virginia, is described as an underground city for the shadow government-in-waiting, ready at any moment to take over the United States in a self-proclaimed emergency. Patriots, nationalists and right-wing groups are the primary targets of these repressive measures. Cooper warns patriots of their impending roundup and advises all right-thinking men to stay away from their homes over holiday periods (when arrests are presumably made).[21]

UFOs and extraterrestrials play an apocalyptic part in William Cooper's conspiracy cult. Alien spacecraft are alleged to have visited the United States with increasing frequency between early 1947 and the end of 1952. Crashed UFOs, dead and live aliens were recovered at Roswell in New Mexico and elsewhere and studied by top scientists under USAF and CIA auspices, while a massive security blanket, confused rumors and disinformation still keep the public in ignorance. Cooper appears to believe that the extraterrestrial humanoids came to Earth in search of genetic material to bolster their own declining species. President Eisenhower is supposed to have met the aliens officially in February 1954, and a formal treaty was signed between them and the U.S. government: in exchange for their advanced technology, the aliens were granted permission to abduct and examine limited numbers of humans for their genetic project. All covert state relations with the aliens are subject to a committee known as MAJESTIC-12, whose secret briefings Cooper allegedly read as an intelligence officer with the U.S. Pacific Fleet in the early 1970s. Huge joint alien-government airbases for flying saucers were secretly licensed at Dreamland or Area 51 near Rachel in the Nevada desert.[22] Area 51 has since become a prime destination for both ufologists and conspiracy cultists. Anthony Hilder has recorded an audiotape, *The Panic Project*, about UFOs stationed at the Dreamland base.[23] The ruling elite has secretly allied itself with extraterrestrials against the rest of the human population.

Bill Cooper's millenarianism is quite literal. By the year 2000, secret government measures against the people will escalate into overt hostilities. At the same time, the UFOs and extraterrestrial presence will be officially revealed as a kind of Second Coming. A spacecraft called Galileo, presently on its way to Jupiter, will deliver a plutonium payload into the heart of the giant planet, generating an atomic reaction and the birth of a new star, which is to be called Lucifer. A massive program of media manipulation will interpret this phenomenon as a sign of immense religious significance. The whole world will expect the fulfillment of ancient prophecy. At this point, a vault containing the ancient records of Earth will be opened at the Great Pyramid of Cheops in Egypt, where George Bush will be present for an occult celebration of the millennium and proclamation of the New World Order.[24]

Bill Cooper is motivated by an anarcho-libertarian spirit of rebellion against a government he identifies as unconstitutional, criminal and despotic. The same applies to Anthony J. Hilder, Linda Thompson and many other spokespersons of the U.S. conspiracy-millenarian cults. Given that the cults frequently identify German National Socialism inter alia as a precursor of the New World Order, one may wonder what any of this has to do with esoteric Nazism. The answer lies in the cults' obsession with secrecy and conspiracy. By declaring war on a secret ruling elite that enslaves innocent people, the conspiracy theorists invoke a lethal projection. The elite is identified as totalitarian, anti-democratic, contemptuous of the people; the people are portrayed as helpless, unsuspecting victims of vicious plots, alien abductions, implantations and all manner of personal violations. The accusation of such an awful occult tyranny vindicates a corresponding explosion of violence to demolish the massive edifice of lies, deception and oppression. The formerly docile victims are justified in fighting and destroying the elite by any means necessary. Covert actions, violence, terrorism—all the means the elite stand accused of employing themselves—are permitted to the victims as well so they may exterminate the conspirators and recover their lost autonomy.

The close psychological parallels between the U.S. conspiracy cults and Nazi patterns of thought become obvious when one finds that a complete reprint of the *Protocols of the Wise Men of Zion* forms the fifteenth chapter of *Behold a Pale Horse*. The text is taken from the first English-language edition, translated by Victor E. Marsden, which was originally published by the

Britons Publishing Society, a notorious anti-Semitic group, in 1921. Although Cooper quotes Mayer Amschel Rothschild (1743–1812) as saying, "Give me control over a nation's currency, and I care not who makes its laws," he does not attribute the *Protocols* exclusively to a Jewish world conspiracy. He suggests that any reference to the "Jews" as the conspirators should be replaced with the word "Illuminati," while the word "Goyim" denoting the Gentile dupes and victims should be read as "cattle"—the preferred term of contempt for honest but naive people.

Despite their late-nineteenth-century prose, many of the *Protocols* offer disturbing evidence of the conspiracy cultists' fears and anxieties about secret government and the New World Order. The Jews (Illuminati) create ferments, discords and hostility between states to increase their indebtedness and provoke wars against their opponents (Protocol 7): hence constant minor wars since 1945. The Jews (Illuminati) aim to bewilder public opinion through contradiction (Protocol 5); the Jews (Illuminati) will distract the masses from their real objects with amusements, games, pastimes, passions, people's palaces (Protocol 13). These strategies reflect the artificial party-politics and futile consumerism of the present. The Jews (Illuminati) will appoint a puppet ruler from among their slaves. He will have the right to propose emergency laws, to vary the constitution and declare a state of war (Protocol 10): hence the National Security Decision directives and the mobilization of FEMA to establish a police state. The Jews [Illuminati] shall create an intensified centralization of government in order to control all mankind (Protocol 15): hence the New World Order.

Conspiracy theories always flourish when people feel excluded from the political process. The worldwide growth of big government, the rise of a political class, and the widening gap between elites and electorates all work to stimulate conspiracy beliefs. The new American vogue in conspiracy beliefs rapidly found audiences in Europe, due to the advancing integration of the European Union and its federal institutions in the 1990s. In particular, the "alternative" movement, with its suspicion of powerful government, big business, and orthodox medicine has proved susceptible to conspiracy theories. The magazine *Nexus* (not to be confused with *The Nexus* of Kerry Bolton), a major success on the New Age scene, offers striking proof of this trend. Founded in Australia in 1990 and now commercially distributed in both the United States and Britain, it already claims a worldwide readership of more than 130,000. *Nexus* offers a fascinating mixture of "prophecies, UFOs, Big Brother, the unexplained, suppressed technology, hidden history and more." Articles on macrobiotic cooking, aromatherapy and the ozone hole jostle with exposés on fluoride treatment of water, CIA mind-control experiments and pharmaceutical drug rackets. Here it is already noticeable how alternative concerns with health, environment and right livelihood are tinged with fears and anxieties about secret abuses and government plots.

Nexus is also a propaganda journal for the concerns and conspiracy theories of the U.S. militias. Earlier issues have included a call by Linda Thompson for a march on Washington to arraign congressmen for treason. She demanded that militia members wear insignia and be armed, in order to be treated as prisoners of war. Her video on the Waco siege, which allegedly influenced McVeigh, was distributed by *Nexus* in Europe. In June 1994 the magazine published an in-depth analysis of the film and a prophetic review: "There is a very big underground movement building up in the United States at the moment. Every night somewhere in the USA, someone is showing this video to a bunch of friends. Nobody remains unaffected after seeing it. It is contagious, so beware!"[25] *Nexus* also published an article on FEMA by Linda Thompson. Here she dilated on the black helicopter traffic and the wide-ranging responsibilities of FEMA in the case of an emergency. However, she states that only 6 percent of the FEMA budget is spent on emergency management; the bulk of its funding is used to construct secret underground government facilities and new detention centers. She lists fourteen executive orders authorizing FEMA to take over all aspects of civilian life once the Constitution is suspended.[26]

Mark Koernke, a senior member of the Michigan Militia, has also written for *Nexus* on America's secret police forces. Claiming a background in military intelligence and command experience in special warfare units,[27] Koernke brings apparent authority to his account of FEMA, MJTF (Multi Jurisdictional Task Force) and FINCEN (Financial Crime Enforcement Network) and their widespread deployment around the United States for search and seizure; separation and categorization of men, women and children; and transfer to detention camps. Koernke asserts that these special forces use street gangs and thugs as law enforcement agents; UN and foreign military personnel are deployed across the country pending the declaration of an emergency; the government anti-gun and drugs campaigns and actions are a foretaste of the general mobilization against the populace.[28] The BBC television program *Panorama* showed a film of Koernke gloating at the prospect of lynching politicians. After the Oklahoma bombing, he was sought by the FBI and went on the run before being questioned and released.

In Britain, David Icke, the former professional soccer player and TV sports presenter, achieved star status in the New Age movement with the publication of his book *The Robots' Rebellion* (1994). Here he praised *Nexus* as incomparable and excellent for its provision of "hard-to-get information on the transformative changes in society." His book combines an anti-elitist, ecological and spiritual gospel with the complete battery of far-right conspiracy theories and militia concerns: secret societies and Freemasons, banking and hidden elites, the New World Order, microchip mind control, extraterrestrials and gun control. He has also resurrected the *Protocols of the Elders of Zion* with an extensive quotation of each protocol and a commentary on how its terrible plans have been realized in current political developments. Icke recognizes that Hitler used the *Protocols* to incite anti-Semitism in Nazi Germany, but his belief in their authenticity is unassailable: "Just because Hitler used knowledge for negative reasons doesn't reflect on the knowledge itself." Moreover, Icke notes the irony that "Hitler and the nazis were brought to power by the very Brotherhood plan which the *Protocols* so powerfully predicted."[29] Icke's speaking tours take him to all major U.K. cities. *The Robots' Rebellion* went through its third reprint before it had been out a full year, and he appeared at the October 1994 *Nexus* conference in Amsterdam, which also featured militia leader Linda Thompson.

While preaching a spiritual message of global love and enlightenment, *The Robots' Rebellion* repeats the familiar beliefs and paranoid clichés of the U.S. conspiracy cults. The American Federal Reserve was a creation of the Illuminati. The Brotherhood elite (Icke's alternative term for the Illuminati) includes the Rothschild and Rockefeller empires. It has six front organizations, namely the Council on Foreign Relations, the Trilateral Commission, the Club of Rome, the Bilderberg Group, the Royal Institute of International Affairs and the United Nations. The aim of the Illuminati is the introduction of a world government to which every continent would be subject. John F. Kennedy was assassinated because he opposed the Brotherhood's critical interests: the CIA, the Federal Reserve and the Vietnam war. The American Gun Control Act of 1968 is word for word the Nazi gun control law of 1938. Humans are to be bar-coded, in order to be "read" at supermarkets and banks. There are passages on FEMA, MJTF, FINCEN and the role of extraterrestrials. Icke quarries much of his material on the New World Order from Bill Cooper and expressly acknowledges *Behold a Pale Horse* as his source.[30]

It is clear from Icke's book that he is a transmitter of this information rather than its originator. Throughout the process of his spiritual awakening, Icke feels "[he is] being guided to an area of knowledge that needs to be made public." This is particularly true in the case of the New World Order. With disarming honesty he admits that he had only vaguely heard of this term until, over a period of three weeks, all the information about it in his book was put into his hands by a variety of different people. "Those on the higher levels who are guiding me wanted this information put in the book, and made

available to the public."[31] Who is then guiding Icke and his New Age following toward the beliefs of the millenarian-conspiracy cults? How does Icke
come to be quoting extensive excerpts from Bill Cooper and U.S. militia
sources? Who are the people who put this information into his hands? Recent
investigations by Matthew Kalman and John Murray of *Open Eye* magazine
suggest that far-right and neo-Nazi groups are pursuing a strategy of entry-
ism by targeting the credulous Icke for the dissemination of their own ideas
within the Green and New Age milieus.

The London-based New Age magazine *Rainbow Ark* maintains a close and
influential relationship with Icke. It has printed conspiracy excerpts from Icke
and also helped to organize his lectures and meetings. The magazine also betrays a surprising range of far-right supporters and links. These include its
former landlord, Mary Stanton, a British-Israelite; Anthony Chevasse, a promoter of C. H. Douglas's Social Credit movement; and Donald Martin, the
anti-Semitic publisher of Bloomfield Books and leader of the British League
of Rights. Martin has a long record of running ultra-right groups, including
the British Federation for European Freedom and the U.K. arm of the World
Anti-Communist League. British National Party leader John Tyndall regards
Martin and his organizations as allies in opposing the immigration of alien
peoples, and Martin has published in Tyndall's magazine, *Spearhead*. The editor of *Rainbow Ark* has steered Icke toward meetings with militant U.S. patriots, organized public meetings on conspiracy theories and rebellion and
recommended Bloomfield Books for information. The same editor has also
boasted of their manipulation of Icke's interests. "Icke's not ready for this yet,"
he commented on a spoof document entitled *Further Protocols* with out-
landish plans of "secret Zionism" for the "Goyim."[32]

The far-right links of *Nexus* have been exposed in Australia in the wake of
its articles on the U.S. militias. Formerly a Green alternative magazine with an
interest in New Age, health and Third World issues, *Nexus* took up the present line under its new editor, Duncan M. Roads. Roads visited Qadaffi in
Libya in 1989 and is a close friend of the right-wing Libyaphile Robert Pash.
A convert to Islam, Pash has tried to forge a link between the extreme right
and left in Australia. In the late 1970s he was the Australian contact for the
U.S.-based Aryan Nations and distributed Ku Klux Klan material. In the late
1980s he was the Australian distributor for Qadaffi's *Green Book* and helped
the "Political Soldier" faction of the National Front in Britain make top-level
contact with the Libyan regime.[33] As chairman of the Australian Peoples Congress, Pash is also closely involved with the Australian League of Rights, the
ultra-right anti-Semitic organization, which Donald Martin represents in
Britain. Among Pash's other introductions to Libya is John Bennett, historical

revisionist and president of the Australian Civil Liberties Union. Bennett is an associate of David Irving and Willis Carto; he serves on the editorial committee of *Journal of Historical Review*, which is concerned with Holocaust denial. *Nexus*'s British agent is also a devotee of the *Protocols*, an admirer of David Irving and he denies the existence of gas chambers in Auschwitz.

The impact of American conspiracy beliefs has been even more dramatic in Germany, where the *Protocols* enter a discourse of Nazi occult societies, extraterrestrial aliens and time travel. In 1993 Jan van Helsing published *Geheimgesellschaften und ihre Macht im 20. Jahrhundert* [Secret Societies and Their Power in the Twentieth Century], backed by a massive publicity campaign in esoteric magazines. The book quickly proved to be a best-seller, selling over 100,000 copies in Germany, Austria and Switzerland, with translations into English and French. Jan Udo Holey, the author, was born at Dinkelsbühl, Bavaria, in 1967. He had been a punk rocker, an anti-fascist activist and traveled on all five continents. Most recently, he had qualified in complementary medicine. For his debut as a conspiracy theorist, he had chosen a pseudonym with symbolic meaning. Professor van Helsing is the vampire hunter in Bram Stoker's famous novel, *Dracula*. Like Jack McLamb, the U.S. patriot author of *Operation Vampire Killer 2000*, Jan van Helsing sets out to expose the bloodsuckers behind the scenes. He identifies these archenemies of mankind as the Illuminati, a secret worldwide lodge, which oppresses states and ordinary people through wars and economic enslavement. However, Helsing's apparent concern for humanity and New Age ethos mask anti-Semitic motives.[34]

Helsing traces the origin of the conspiracy against mankind back to 300,000 B.C., when a Brotherhood of the Snake arose in Mesopotamia. High initiates first appeared in Germany during the fourteenth century, when they were known as Illuminati. Helsing finds the modern roots of the conspiracy in 1773, when Mayer Amschel Rothschild met twelve wealthy Jews (the Elders of Zion) at a secret meeting in Frankfurt. Here they devised a plan to control the entire wealth of the world. Helsing then reprints the *Protocols of the Elders of Zion* with extensive reference to Bill Cooper's comments on their current plausibility.[35] The Rothschild bank commissioned "the Bavarian Jew" Adam Weishaupt to found the secret order of the Bavarian Illuminati, which taught the "New Testament of Satan" and swiftly recruited leading figures in finance and industry. As the sworn enemies of monarchy and the Church, the Illuminati made a pact with the Freemasons to work for a "New World Order" through the American and French Revolutions. The First World War was engineered to bring Russia under Illuminati control; the Second World War exploited "differences of opinion between

German nationalists and political Zionists" to expand the Russian sphere of influence and legitimize the state of Israel; the Third World War will lead mankind to embrace the "Luciferic doctrine."[36]

Helsing's breathless survey of Illuminati progress through the ages is extensively sourced from Gary Allen, Des Griffin and Anthony C. Sutton. Short chapters on Freemasonry in America, the City of London, the Russian Revolution, and the Federal Reserve pile up alarming details of Jewish ownership and control behind the scenes. Zionism calls the tune to which the powers dance. The Rothschilds were behind the British declaration in support of a national Jewish home and the United States' entry into the First World War. In 1919 Rothschild agents Colonel House and Bernard Baruch attended the Versailles peace conference, which gave birth to the Rockefeller-controlled Council on Foreign Relations, "the most influential background organization in the USA today." During the 1920s the Dawes and Young Plans were instigated by Jewish and American interests to facilitate German reparations but their monopoly capital served only to build up the German arms industry. Despite his confused account, Helsing reassures the reader that "everything was planned down to the last detail . . . but only the Insiders knew."[37]

Turning to National Socialism and the Third Reich, Helsing borrows heavily from Jürgen-Ratthofer's *Das Vril-Projekt* with its fantastic account of links between the Thule Society, the Vril Society and extraterrestrial intelligences. Sebottendorff learned from the Gnostic Marcionite Templars that a world transformation was imminent according to the movement of the zodiac around the Black Sun. The Kingdom of God would be taken from the Jews and given to the Germans. According to the Thule Society, the Old Testament god, El Shaddai, commanded the Jews "to make hell on earth," which is why the world is always consumed by war and conflict. The Thule Society, Helsing claims, knew all about the Jewish world conspiracy and the *Protocols*. As the forerunner of the Nazi Party and the SS, the Thule pledged itself to fighting the Jewish banks and lodges and creating a "realm of light" on earth. According to the Babylonian revelation of Isais, Thule initiates believed in the coming of a messiah, the "Third Sargon," who would restore Germany to greatness with a new Aryan culture. Helsing adds further colorful passages on Hitler's search for the subterranean realm of Agarthi in order to make contact with the heirs of the Aryan aliens from Aldebaran-Hyperborea.[38]

Helsing expands on Karl Haushofer's links with Tibet before claiming that the SS and its inner Black Sun circle was a religious order, dedicated to the practical realization of the Thule Society's esoteric ideas. "Countless young men were trained by the Black Sun at the Wewelsburg and sent to Tibet, where they are preparing for Armageddon at the end of this century." At this point, Helsing dilates on the Vril Society's telepathic contacts with the aliens in the solar system of Aldebaran, sixty-eight light-years distant from earth in the constellation of Taurus. The extraterrestrials reveal that their master race of fair god-men began colonizing other planetary systems over 500 million years ago. Within our own system, they settled on Mallona (now forming the asteroid belt), Mars (as evidenced by the great pyramids and the Face at Cydonia), and on earth in Mesopotamia, where they formed the ruling caste of the Sumerians. Similiarities between the Aldebaran-Sumerian and German languages attest to the extraterrestrial origins of the Aryan Germans. Aided by the Aldebarans, the Vril Society built a time machine on anti-gravitational principles. This technology led to the amazing German flying saucers of the Haunebu and Vril classes built under SS auspices.[39]

Helsing's postwar account closely follows Des Griffin's bestselling *Descent into Slavery* (1980), which documents how the power-crazed Internationalists are steering all nations toward social and financial ruin in preparation for their ultimate absorption into a worldwide dictatorship. Unsurprisingly, we learn that only Illuminati elites benefited from World War II, but Helsing introduces a revisionist theme. He reproduces familiar neo-Nazi material about the 1933 Jewish declaration of war on Germany, Polish provocations, and the Morgenthau plan to pastoralize a defeated Germany.[40] He alleges that German and Japanese offers of peace were systematically ignored so that both countries could be reduced to rubble. The resulting destruction created enormous investment opportunities, and global reorganization signposted the New World Order.[41] Helsing's account of Germany's postwar experience in this process of internationalization is strongly nationalist. Under the guise of democracy and liberalism, the Illuminati planned the denationalization and moral degradation of Germany. Postwar "reeducation" (democratic and liberal instruction) to de-Nazify German attitudes and institutions defamed a parental generation, encouraged youth revolt and fostered moral relativism. Egoism, consumerism, and the neglect of history in the school curriculum has created a German youth ignorant of their past.[42]

Page after page addresses controlled media, newspapers and parapsychological methods of indoctrinating civilian populations. Helsing supplies membership lists of his key Illuminati organizations, including the Committee of 300, Council on Foreign Relations, Skull & Bones, the Round Table, the Bilderbergs, the Trilateral Commission, the Club of Rome, and the United Nations Organisation (UNO). At their apex stands the Rothschild family. Seals and symbols of organizations and companies are analyzed numerologically to find evidence of Illuminati direction. The links of the United Nations with the Rockefeller family and the CFR evidently indicate its strategic importance in the constantly overlapping elites behind the plan for world domination. The Knights of Jerusalem are close to the English royal family—here Helsing uses John Coleman's *Conspirators' Hierarchy*—and supply the leadership of the Committee of 300, whose innermost circle is the Order of the Garter. Circles within circles and names are named: for instance, Lord Carrington, former British foreign secretary, is a Garter Knight, head of NATO, and chairman of the Bilderbergers.[43]

In 1995 Helsing published *Geheimgesellschaften 2* in the form of extended responses to interview questions. Here he denies the charge of anti-Semitism, claiming Jewish friends and colleagues, before making the disingenuous distinction between Semitic Hebrews and Ashkenazi Jews or Khazars, who are his real antagonists in the persons of Rothschilds, Warburgs, the English royal family (!), Marx, Lenin, Stalin, etc. This ploy recapitulates the progressive disqualification of Jews from their Israelite heritage in Christian Identity doctrine. He then reprints several pages of Dr. Johannes Pohl's vicious translation of the Talmud that was published by the Nazi Party in 1943 as anti-Semitic propaganda.[44] On the *Protocols*, Helsing simply denies that their authenticity is an important issue: they exist and they are being applied. To complete his anti-Jewish rotomontade, he reveals that former Chancellor Helmut Kohl was born Henoch Kohn and shows how George Soros is ruining East European economies through his liberal economic writ.[45] Helsing's dubious sources, his constant repetition of Jewish names as members of private and public organizations, and above all his emphasis on the assets and powerbroking influence of the Rothschilds as the top Illuminati family leave no doubt that his conspiracy theories are aimed at Jewish targets.

Helsing's breathless search for conspirators continues among the "Black Nobility"—the aristocratic and royal families of Europe. Given their landowning interests, they are supposed to be working to create a new feudalism through deindustrialization and the reduction of the human population.[46] This leads to the Club of Rome, described by Helsing as a secret Rockefeller circle founded at the private Rockefeller foundation in Bellagio, Italy. Its membership comprises the oldest European families of the Black Nobility and top Illuminati families in America, all dedicated to a world government run by the elite.[47] In order to reduce the population, Club of Rome founder Dr. Aurellio Peccei, former chairman of Fiat, proposed the secret introduction of an epidemic. Helsing copies Bill Cooper's account of how the AIDS virus was artificially produced for this purpose at Fort Detrick, Maryland. The virus was introduced to the African population under cover of a WHO pox vaccination program in 1977 before being used to target "undesirable" groups in the United States such as blacks, Hispanics and homosexuals from 1978 onwards.[48] Helsing knows Bill Cooper personally and also reprints his entire account of the MAJESTIC-12 material and secret U.S. government treaties with evil aliens. The CFR and Trilateral Commission have complete control over alien technology as well as the economy. This joint human/alien power structure aims at the enslavement of the human race.[49]

Helsing's Illuminati-Jewish world conspiracy is extensively borrowed from the American patriot movement, but is applied to German nationalist concerns. He argues that this cosmic plot can be foiled only by a restoration of the German Reich. Helsing quotes Mattern and Landig's accounts of the Antarctic "phantom convoy" and the fruitless American attempts to subdue the Germans on Antarctica in 1947 and 1958. Helsing repeats the neo-Nazi adage that the German Reich did not capitulate, but only the German armed forces under Grand Admiral Dönitz. The German Reich is still legally in existence and the present regimes of Poland, Austria and the German Federal Republic are merely provisional governments. The German Reich presently controls huge areas of sovereign territory in Antarctica and the San Carlos de Bariloche province of Argentina. Helsing also claims contacts with members of the Black Sun. One such interviewee was allegedly born in Neuschwabenland and lives today with three million other Reich Germans in a subterranean city. Further bases exist on the Canaries, in the Bermuda Triangle and in the Himalayas. In all, the Reich Germans today have a standing army of 6 million soldiers, including immigrant Aldebarans, and an armada of 22,000 flying saucers. This "Third Power" may prove mankind's only defense against Illuminati enslavement.[50]

Helsing regards the United Nations intervention in Iraq and the ensuing Gulf War as another major instance of the Illuminati offensive against any remaining opposition to its New World Order. As "the Germans of the Orient," the Iraqis are long-standing allies of the German Reich, which built the country's defenses and maintains flying saucer bases there. Sustained UN air attacks against Basra and Nedschef had the main purpose of destroying German saucer bases. It is no accident that Helsing should admire fundamentalist and pariah states that pursue the politics of identity with ethnic cleansing against national minorities (e.g., Iraq, Serbia), as these states have no stake in a global economic order of liberal capitalist states under American hegemony. In fact, Helsing praises Iraq for its educational, welfare provision and other achievements under a "fascist" social system. Iraq is a major regional power posing a major threat to Illuminati goals in the Middle East. Helsing extols Saddam Hussein as the "new Hitler" who is far more beloved by his people than any career politician in the democracies.[51]

Helsing presents anti-Semitism and German nationalism within a wholly novel discourse of aliens, free energy, time travel, and New Age religion. He quotes the free-energy books of Nikola Tesla and David Hatcher Childress. Helsing is also especially interested in the Montauk Project, a literary invention of Preston B. Nichols, Peter Moon and Alfred Bielek. These American authors have developed a series of time-travel books on the basis of the "Philadelphia Experiment." The latter concerns a destroyer, USS *Eldridge*, said to have disappeared in August 1943 from its dock in the Philadelphia Naval Yard for several minutes, materialized at Norfolk 250 miles away, and then reappeared in Philadelphia through the practical application of Einstein's unified field theory.[52] In 1989, Alfred Bielek introduced himself at Timothy Beckley Green's UFO–New Age conference in Phoenix, Arizona, as a surviving crewman of the experimental ship. His account involved two parallel biographies in time. His story was quickly taken up by Beckley Green's Inner Light Publications, which publishes books by himself, Brad Steiger and Commander X on UFOs, alien earth bases and secret government cover-ups.[53]

From 1992 onward, Nichols and Moon authored a series of books about an imaginary research program at Montauk Point, Long Island, between 1969 and 1983 for investigating mind control techniques. Subsequent discoveries in telepathy and interdimensional transfer led to the manipulation of time and matter. Eventually, a time travel vortex was opened back to 1943 and to the original Philadelphia Experiment.[54] This sensational interface between secret research, official suppression and alternative realities fit perfectly with Helsing's wonderland of cosmic conspiracy. Following his first meeting with Bill Cooper in Hawaii, Helsing attended Timothy Beckley Green's 1991 conference in Phoenix, where he met Alfred Bielek and was deeply moved by his account of time travel. Following the publication of *The Montauk Project* (1992), Helsing acquired the German publication rights and met Peter Moon and Duncan Cameron, another alleged survivor of the Philadelphia Experiment. Helsing became close friends with this circle, who claim United Nations Organization (UNO) and Rockefeller agents have threatened them with death unless they keep silent. Undeterred, Peter Moon has now extended the Montauk mythology with Nazi and Tibetan connections based on Helsing's information about the Thule Society and the Black Sun.[55]

By presenting secret societies and Jewish world conspiracy as an extraterrestrial struggle over the destiny of our planet, Helsing succeeds in reaching a

New Age readership with his Manichaean anti-Semitism. For example, more than sixty new esoteric-conspiracy titles appeared in Austrian bookshops during the first quarter of 1995 alone. The success of his conspiracy books also coincides with a widespread reaction among many Austrians against the European Union since the country joined the EU in 1992. As in the case of the U.S. patriot movement, bigger government and foreign interference greatly increase the demand for conspiracy theory. This reaction has been exacerbated by the EU boycott of Austria in 2000 over the electoral success of Jörg Haider's populist Austrian Freedom Party. As already noted, Helsing's books remain best-sellers in Germany through the Andromeda mail-order bookshop and similar New Age outlets. The Swiss authorities have since banned Helsing's books for infringing the new anti-racism law of 1995. Following complaints from German Jews, the Mannheim public prosecutor arraigned author and publisher for spreading anti-Semitic propaganda in September 1996 but dropped the action in January 1997 as neither reside within its jurisdiction. Meanwhile, the Ewertverlag set up shop on Grand Canary Island as a precaution and published a new book dismissing the charges. Helsing has since published further best-selling books on the Third World War and German contacts with Aldebaran.[56]

The endemic spread of conspiracy theories in the New Age milieu is a disturbing phenomenon. An anarcho-libertarian interest in tracing CIA mind-control experiments, federal government covert operations and links with UFOs and aliens can suddenly switch into a pessimistic discourse of hidden elites, the Council on Foreign Relations, Trilateral Commission, the Bilderbergs and Rothschilds, leading to reprints of the *Protocols of the Elders of Zion*. How can one explain the drift from an open, anti-authoritarian, egalitarian outlook to an anxious myth of hostile elites and hidden threats? Some New Agers may well feel contempt for a society that has failed to transform itself spiritually in line with their aspirations in the 1970s. At that time, the secular social critique was Marxist, with rational explantions of capital concentration and corporate power. New Agers eschewed this in favor of inner transformation, but now, after Thatcher, Reagan and Bush, many may wonder what is holding up the arrival of the New Age. The pressures of globalization and automation, the escalating export of jobs, the backlash against affirmative action and political correctness all evidence a growing strain on the middle classes. Spiritual fixes via candle burning, tarot, runes and Druid workshops to calm the inner world can easily mix with "anti" fantasies about what (or more often "you know who") is spoiling things out there.

The compatibility of conspiracy theories with New Age ideas is not new. The *völkisch*-racist movement and Wandervögel groups of interwar Germany mixed nature worship and ecological and health issues with anti-Semitism, racism and national revival. Today many New Age groups rehearse the nativist aspects of *völkisch* thought in a eulogy of the primitive: Native Americans, African bushmen and Australian aborigines are credited with a natural wisdom long lost among the rational, technologically advanced peoples of the West. As long as the idealized groups were perceived as marginal, foreign or oppressed, such New Age sentiment was generally left-wing or liberal. However, once the models were sought closer to home in the prerational, mythical past of Western culture, *völkisch* ideas could make a fashionable return. In the New Age movement numerous groups and workshops are now devoted to reviving the lore of the ancient Celts and Teutons. Books on ogham, runes, prophecy and pagan gods proliferate. Shamanism, magic and superstition are in. Nostalgia for a lost golden age and apocalyptic hopes of its revival recall the ideological foreground of earlier demands for fascist renewal.

The U.S. militias, conspiracy cults, and New Age cultural pessimism represent varied strands of popular radicalism that are deeply hostile toward liberalism in modern politics and society. Some New Age ideas eulogize nature and primitive peoples in a gilded vision of the ancient past, while environmental extremists question the value of human civilization. These ideas originally had their roots in left-wing dissent, but their increasing tendency toward conspiracy beliefs and despair indicate their susceptibility to millenarian and mystical ideas on the far right. Discouraged by the impervious advance of modern technological society and the global economy, many have retreated to mental subcultures in which all manner of fantastic and threatening plots seem plausible to the extent that enables the *Protocols* to find new readers and believers. As yet, the New Age has little room for Hitler worship or Nazi UFOs, but it is noteworthy that *Rainbow Ark* has already speculated that many old Nazis have reincarnated in the bodies of modern Israelis as a way of karmically balancing former hatreds. Among such marginal beliefs, all kinds of revaluation are possible.

As we have seen, conspiracy theory may be traced to ancient religious ideas involving humanity's thrall to an evil, lower god who created matter and the inferior realm. Only the intervention of a higher, merciful god can enable man to attain spiritual redemption. These dualist ideas were integral to Gnosticism, Marcionism, Manichaeanism and other heretical movements in the early history of Christianity. Within a religious worldview, all suffering, disorder and strife posit the existence of evil. Personified as the Devil or Anti-Christ, with the Jews often cast as his representatives on earth, such dualist dynamics offered a powerful demonology in medieval Christianity. The patriot movement discourse of the Illuminati spreading AIDS, negotiating with evil extraterrestrials and enslaving mankind through microchip mind control in a demonic New World Order openly proclaims its inspiration in the *Protocols of the Elders of Zion*, the modern nineteenth-century rendition of medieval anti-Semitic fantasies. Just as the *Protocols* found a massive readership among the displaced and the disinherited in a changing world before and after the First World War, this new conspiracy discourse finds new converts among those bewildered and frustrated by the results of globalization at the beginning of the new millennium.

This chapter began with the Oklahoma City bombing in April 1995 in the context of conspiracy beliefs amongst patriot, militia, and far right groups in the United States. These beliefs are often rooted in anti-Semitic stereotypes but also involve a wider rejection of bureaucracy and a mistrust of elites, be they political, corporate or financial. A more recent and far worse terrorist atrocity in the United States demonstrates the far right's growing hatred of government and society.

On 11 September 2001, Islamic militant suicide-pilots highjacked three civil airliners and flew them into the World Trade Center in New York and the Pentagon in Washington D.C. In unforgettable scenes of catastrophe, the two 110-storey towers collapsed, bringing the combined death toll of the attacks to over 5,700 civilian lives. The U.S. government set about building a strategic coalition with European and many Muslim states to destroy the leading terrorist groups behind these crimes and their protecting states (notably the Taliban regime of Afghanistan). Attention was chiefly focused on Osama bin Laden and his al-Qa'eda group as the chief suspects, but other terrorist groups were also targeted, including the Egyptian Islamic Jihad, the Algerian Armed Islamic Group (GIA), the Islamic Resistance Movement (Hamas), Palestinian Islamic Jihad and Hizbollah in the Levant. Members of these groups had been responsible for attacks on the U.S. Marine barracks in Beirut in 1983, the Luxor tourist massacre of 1997, and the bombing of the U.S. embassies in Kenya and Tanzania in 1998. These groups go beyond their motive of creating a Palestinian state and the destruction of Israel by turning on its American protector. In their call for a *Jihad* (holy war) against the "Great Satan" of America, the supposedly demonic representative of secularization and materialism, these militant Islamicists enact a counter-crusade against the Jews and Christians. Their struggle reflects Samuel P. Huntington's "clash of civilisations" as the key flashpoint of this new century.

The far right exempted itself from the outrage that swept the United States and Britain. Instead, many sympathized with the Islamic militants against the "East Coast," code for American Jewry's influence in world finance and foreign policy relating to support for Israel. Some American neo-Nazis went so far as to praise the terrorist attacks. Tom Metzger of White Aryan Resistance (WAR) called the WTC attacks an example of "Victory or Valhalla" for Aryans to take note of, while a member of the National Alliance said "the enemy of our enemy [i.e., the Jews] is, for now at least, our friend" and wished that his comrades had half as much fortitude as the Islamic suicide-pilots. As indicated in previous chapters, the American, British and German far right has often courted rogue states such as Libya, Iran and Iraq against the Jews and the West in their search for allies against the "New World Order." Lincoln Rockwell and American neo-Nazi groups of the 1960s were actually ultra-conservative and loyalist patriots. By contrast, the far right today sees itself not only at war with the U.S. government but with the American people themselves. The neo-Nazis even seek alliances with enemies whose totalitarian, theocratic and millennial instincts are a mirror of their own.

Conclusion

The Politics of Identity

RACE IS THE lodestone of the Aryan cults and esoteric Nazism, the guiding principle of their historical and political worldview. American neo-Nazism, represented by George Lincoln Rockwell and his successors, adopted the Nazi view of the Jews as the ferment of liberal society, variously promoting communism, civil rights and race mixing. However, by the late 1950s such neo-Nazism was primarily driven by white opposition to civil rights for blacks, integration, busing, and affirmative action. Similarly, British neo-Nazi groups arose as a response to the fast-rising levels of colored immigration from the late 1950s onward. The American neo-Nazi slogan "white power" was paralleled by the call to "keep Britain white." As American blacks began to benefit from civil rights legislation and colored immigrants began to establish themselves politically in Britain in the 1980s, neo-Nazi groups began to suggest that white racial dominance was threatened in the ancestral homelands of white ethnic stock.

However, the racist far right has not grown in a vacuum. Although liberal opinion in the United States and Britain is determinedly opposed to racism, a number of factors in Western politics have worked to reintroduce race as a legitimate category of group identification. During the 1960s black power groups and radical critics called for the official recognition of "minority" group status and restitutive action by the state. The instititionalization of these demands led to extensive programs of equal opportunities and affirmative action in the provision of public services, employment and education to favor American blacks. A gradual transmutation of civil-rights law has led to the reorientation of these programs from equal opportunities toward the equal outcomes of racial quotas. This attribution of special benefits and privileges on the basis of ascriptive group membership is an unprecedented and remarkable deviation from the Anglo-American tradition of individual rights.[1] The discriminatory effects of these policies on whites, both potential and actual, has understandably caused some resentment among whites.

Government-mandated privileges on the basis of race have in turn fostered the growth of the racist far right.

But liberal support for affirmative action has gone further in producing a climate of white guilt. The causes of black crime, drug involvement and welfare dependence are often sought in white racism. Black on white crime in terms of murder, rape and robbery with violence is many times greater than white on black crime. However, the national media typically highlight instances of white racial attacks, while many reports of black crime are "colorblind" and mostly confined to the local press. The massive overrepresentation of blacks in the penal system, evident testimony of black crime, violence and underperformance are largely ignored by the liberal media, or otherwise invoked as further evidence of black disadvantage and white racism.[2] The comparative high performance of Asian minorities in education and employment, and their corresponding underrepresentation in prison statistics, demonstrate the untenability of attributing black failure to white racism. The precoccupation with white responsibility for the failure of race relations also ignores the high incidence of interethnic crime and violence. This disabling of white criticism through accusations of individual and "institutional" racism, coupled with a compensatory attitude toward black identity, has been a further factor in the stimulation of the racist far right.

Aryan cults and esoteric Nazism posit powerful mythologies to negate the decline of white power in the world. The cultural pessimism of Julius Evola, Savitri Devi and Miguel Serrano all express the fear of (Aryan) white submergence in a degenerate age dominated by social and racial inferiors. Their adoption of Hindu chronology is intended to plot the curve of that decline into the Kali Yuga with the millennial promise of regeneration through a new golden age in the cycle of the ages. Francis Parker Yockey likewise articulates a mythic philosophy of history, whereby the European races are (temporarily) disabled by alien Jewish influences and prevented from fulfilling their destiny in a powerful new Imperium or world empire. Addressing a more narrow German-speaking audience, Wilhelm Landig elaborates a neo-*völkisch* mythology of Aryan origins in northern Thule, in order to prophesy the recovery and resurrection of Nazi Germany. The Black Sun and Nazi UFO myths perform a similar if provincial function for German neo-Nazis who lament the loss of World War II and the triumph of liberalism in the international order.

However, while George Lincoln Rockwell, Colin Jordan, Wilhelm Landig and Ernst Zündel hark back to Nazi models and an epic narrative of World War II to counter postwar liberalism and its supposed Jewish architects, their recent successors, especially in the United States, tend to invoke quasi-*völkisch* mythologies of white identity and destiny. Our review of Christian Identity groups, the Church of the Creator, and Nordic racial pagans indicates a more diffuse defensive ideology than that of straightforward German National Socialism. Commentators have noted the rise of a new nationalism as a culture of resistance to the recent forces of globalization and immigration. It is thus highly significant that the Aryan cult of white identity is now most marked in the United States, where the challenges of multiculturalism and Third World immigration have been the greatest.

Race relations based on the civil rights of American blacks and the assimilation of New Commonwealth immigrants in Britain have long since been overtaken by the rise of Third World immigration, refugees and asylum seekers. The Immigration Reform Act of 1965 in the United States abolished the national-origins system of 1924 and has arguably changed America more than any other legislation in the twentieth century. This law was initially intended to redress the imbalance of immigrant stock between northern and southern Europe, when racial quotas had perpetuated immigration to match the dominant north European immigrant stock of 1920. However, by the mid-1970s the south European backlogs were depleted and the economic reconstruction of Europe reduced further immigration from that source. By 1980, only 5 percent of legal immigration came from Europe, while Asians (chiefly Filipinos, Koreans, Vietnamese and Indians) accounted for nearly half. Immigration from Latin America (chiefly Mexico) constituted about 40 percent. Fueled by a family preference system, the new immigration pattern reached record levels in the 1980s, while a surge of illegal Hispanic immigration was perceived as a loss of control over the nation's borders.[3]

Writing after the First World War, the American racial theorist Lothrop Stoddard perceived the threat of immigration in both economic terms—forcing down the level of wages—and its cultural consequences, affecting religion, rules of conduct, laws and customs. By 1940—in the middle of the Great Restriction of immigration—*Time* found it fashionable to mock Stoddard's fear of the "yellow peril" as a delusion. Nowadays, the same magazine predicts the inevitable eclipse of the white, Western world.[4] The 1965 legislation in favor of source-country universalism has led to a sustained wave of Third World immigration. Today, annual legal immigration in the United States of about 1 million, including 100,000 refugees and 100,000 applying for political asylum, is overwhelmed by an estimated 2 to 3 million illegal entries into the United States in every recent year. Conservative opponents of mass Third World immigration have highlighted how such recent non-European immigration is already transforming the U.S. demography quite dramatically. One might only consider that the proportion of southern and eastern European immigrants, which derived from post-1870 immigration and provoked the

Great Restriction of 1924–1965, only amounted to about 13 percent of the total U.S. population in 1930. By comparison, the proportion of post-1970 immigrants was already over 8 percent by 1990, and rising.[5]

The question of whether the United States can actually assimilate such immigrants is begged by policies of bilingualism and multiculturalism in the education system. Assimilation is further undermined by the expansion of affirmative action, originally intended to benefit blacks as a result of civil rights legislation, into a government-mandated discrimination against white Americans (but also blacks in practice) in favor of Third World immigrants. The ascendancy of international human rights over notions of national sovereignty has also led to a progressive erosion of citizenship, whereby illegal aliens are granted welfare, education, government subsidies and even voting rights.[6] These issues are a matter of deep concern to conservative groups in the United States, who see no particular reason to transform the demography of the United States, given its wholly unforeseeable consequences. The conversion of the United States into a "colony of the world" or a "universal nation" is without precedent in the modern world. Similar forces are at work in Europe, especially Britain, where multiculturalism is promoted by left-wing and liberal political agendas in the quest for the electoral support of the growing ethnic minorities. A recent report on the future of multi-ethnic Britain has even questioned whether the national epithet "British" carries a racist taint.[7]

As we have seen in the preceding chapters, the far right in the United States and Britain has gathered renewed vigor from the 1980s onwards. This trend was initially surprising as the first generation of postwar neo-Nazi leaders was aging and the memory of the Axis challenge to Western liberalism was fast slipping into history. However, the rise of skinhead racist gangs, white power music, and the transformation of neo-Nazi racism into new folkish religions of white identity clearly mirror the rising levels of immigration into Western countries and the ensuing pressures toward multiculturalism. It is these latter trends that prompt my comparison with *völkisch* German nationalist groups in multinational Austria before the First World War. But for the rise of fascism in the 1920s and 1930s, there would be scant interest in tracing these precursors of National Socialism. We cannot know what the future holds for Western multicultural societies, but the experiment did not fare well in Austria-Hungary, the Soviet Union and Yugoslavia. The multiracial challenges in liberal Western states are much greater, and it is evident that affirmative action and multiculturalism are even leading to a more diffuse hostility toward liberalism. From the retrospective viewpoint of a potential authoritarian future in 2020 or 2030, these Aryan cults and esoteric Nazism may be documented as early symptoms of major divisive changes in our present-day Western democracies.

Notes

NOTES TO CHAPTER I

1. The following biographical details are drawn from William L. Pierce, "George Lincoln Rockwell: A National Socialist life," *National Socialist World*, No. 5 (Winter 1967), 13–36, and his own autobiography, *This Time the World* (Arlington, Va.: American Nazi Party, 1962). Two recent studies of Rockwell and the American Nazi Party offer extensive background: Frederick J. Simonelli, *American Fuehrer: George Lincoln Rockwell and the American Nazi Party* (Urbana and Chicago: University of Illinois Press, 1999), pp. 5–12; William H. Schmaltz, *Hate: George Lincoln Rockwell and the American Nazi Party* (Washington, D.C.: Brassey's, 1999), pp. 5–11.

2. Simonelli, *American Fuehrer*, pp. 16–17; Schmaltz, *Hate*, pp. 12–14.

3. Simonelli, *American Fuehrer*, pp. 18–19; Schmaltz, *Hate*, p. 15.

4. Simonelli, *American Fuehrer*, pp. 19–21; Schmaltz, *Hate*, pp. 15–18.

5. George Lincoln Rockwell, *White Power*, 2d ed. (Reedy, W.Va.: Liberty Bell Publications, 1977), pp. 130–33; Schmaltz, *Hate*, p. 19–21.

6. Rockwell, *This Time the World*, pp. 154–55.

7. Quoted in George P. Thayer, *The Further Shores of Politics: The American Political Fringe Today*, 2d ed. (New York: Simon and Schuster, 1968), p. 27.

8. Rockwell, *This Time the World*, p. 173; Simonelli, *American Fuehrer*, pp. 23–24; Schmaltz, *Hate*, pp. 23–24.

9. Simonelli, *American Fuehrer*, pp. 24–26; Schmaltz, *Hate*, pp. 25–29.

10. Simonelli, *American Fuehrer*, pp. 27–28; Schmaltz, *Hate*, pp. 29–34.

11. Rockwell, *This Time the World*, pp. 296–302. Rockwell's communications with the Atlanta suspects are discussed in Melissa Fay Greene, *The Temple Bombing* (London: Jonathan Cape, 1996), pp. 219–23.

12. Rockwell, *This Time the World*, pp. 309–10; Simonelli, *American Fuehrer*, pp. 30–31; Schmaltz, *Hate*, p. 41.

13. Simonelli, *American Fuehrer*, pp. 36–37.

14. Simonelli, *American Fuehrer*, pp. 44–47; Schmaltz, *Hate*, pp. 71–78.

15. Simonelli, *American Fuehrer*, pp. 72–75; Schmaltz, *Hate*, pp. 133–35.

16. Rockwell, *White Power*, pp. 259–69.

17. Extensive details from the life of Rockwell and the numerous incidents involving the American Nazi Party are also recorded in Mark Sherwin, *The Extremists* (New York, 1963), pp. 139–55; Thayer, *The Further Shores of Politics*, pp. 13–33;

Charles Higham, *American Swastika* (New York: Doubleday and Co., 1985), pp. 274–80.

18. Simonelli, *American Fuehrer*, p. 86; Schmaltz, *Hate*, pp. 146–50.

19. Schmaltz, *Hate*, pp. 232–33.

20. Simonelli, *American Fuehrer*, pp. 87–95.

21. Gottfried Feder, "The Twenty-Five Points," *National Socialist World*, No. 3 (Spring 1967), 13–24; Matt Koehl, "Adolf Hitler: German Nationalist or Aryan Racist?" *National Socialist World*, No. 4 (Summer 1967), 13–22; Robert F. Williams, "The Black Plague: Race War in America," *National Socialist World*, No. 5 (Winter 1967), 67–84.

22. "Editorial," *National Socialist World*, No. 4 (Summer 1967), 8–11.

23. Schmaltz, *Hate*, pp. 304–5, 319.

24. Simonelli, *American Fuehrer*, pp. 131–37.

25. Biographical details of Matt Koehl are in Simonelli, *American Fuehrer*, pp. 77–79. In May 1958 Matt Koehl established an NSRP Atlanta group, some of whose members were arraigned for the attack on the synagogue in October. Greene, *The Temple Bombing*, pp. 209–10.

26. Koehl, "Adolf Hitler," pp. 15, 17.

27. Matt Koehl, "Some Guidelines for the Development of the National Socialist Movement," *National Socialist World*, No. 6 (Winter 1968), pp. 8–17 (pp. 12, 14f).

28. Matt Koehl, "Resurrection," New Order brochure, reprint of an editorial in *NS Bulletin*, April 1987.

29. Matt Koehl, "Hitler: Man and Symbol," New Order brochure giving abridged transcript of speech held on 14 August 1991.

30. Matt Koehl, *Faith of the Future*, 2d ed. (Milwaukee, Wis.: New Order, 1995), p. 31. The first edition was originally published as "Hitlerism: Faith of the Future," *The National Socialist*, Spring 1982.

31. "We fought on the wrong side," New Order brochure, reprint of editorial in *NS Bulletin*, Second Quarter, 1995.

32. Original NSLF propaganda and flyers are reprinted in *Siege: The Collected Writings of James Mason*, edited and introduced by Michael M. Jenkins [i.e. Moynihan] (Denver: Storm Books, 1992), pp. xix, 7, 19, 24.

33. *Siege*, pp. xi–xxvii.

34. *Siege*, pp. 281–322.

35. Elizabeth Wheaton, *Codename GREENKIL: The 1979 Greensboro Killings* (Athens, Ga.: University of Georgia Press, 1979).

36. Frank P. Mintz, *The Liberty Lobby and the American Right: Race, Conspiracy and Culture* (Westport, Conn.: Greenwood Press, 1985), pp. 129–31. Robert S. Griffin, *The Fame of a Dead Man's Deeds: An Up-Close Portrait of White Nationalist William Pierce* (New York: Barnes and Noble e-book, 2000), offers a comprehensive account of Pierce's ideology and career.

37. *Action: Internal Bulletin of the National Alliance*, No. 49 (March 1976), pp. 2–3. The Savitri Devi quotation is from "The Lightning and the Sun," *National Socialist World*, No. 1 (Spring 1966), pp. 13–90 (p. 61).

38. The standard account of this racist sectarian movement is Michael Barkun, *Religion and the Racist Right: The Origins of the Christian Identity Movement*, rev. ed. (Chapel Hill, N.C.: University of North Carolina Press, 1997).

39. Andrew Macdonald (i.e., William L. Pierce), *The Turner Diaries*, 2d ed. (Arlington, Va.: National Vanguard Books, 1980), pp. 152, 160–67, 195, 112, 196, 210.

40. Macdonald, *The Turner Diaries*, p. 209.

41. Macdonald, *The Turner Diaries*, p. iii.

42. Macdonald, *The Turner Diaries*, p. 111.

43. Kevin Flynn and Gary Gerhardt, *The Silent Brotherhood: Inside America's Racist Underground* (New York: Free Press, 1989), offers an extensive narrative account of The Order, its members and operations.

44. Barkun, *Religion and the Racist Right*, pp. 228–33.

45. Barkun, *Religion and the Racist Right*, pp. 233–39.

46. Richard Abanes, *American Militias: Rebellion, Racism & Religion* (Downers Grove, Ill.: InterVarsity Press, 1996), pp. 147–53. Cf. the FBI office bombing in Macdonald, *The Turner Diaries*, pp. 38–41.

47. "Lone Wolves and Live Wires," in *Siege*, 189–225.

48. Macdonald (i.e., William L. Pierce), *Hunter* (Hillsboro, W.Va.: National Vanguard Books, 1989).

49. Richard Kelly Hoskins, *Vigilantes of Christendom: The Story of the Phineas Priesthood* (Lynchburg, Va.: Virginia Publishing, 1990), p. 32.

50. Louis Beam, "Leaderless Resistance," in "Special Report on the Meeting of Christian Men Held in Estes Park, Colorado, October 23, 24, 25, 1992, Concerning the Killing of Vickie and Samuel Weaver by the United States Government," pp. 20–23.

51. Details of the formation and development of Combat 18 are in Gerry Gable, "Britain's Nazi underground," in *The Far Right in Western and Eastern Europe*, edited by Luciano Cheles, Ronnie Ferguson and Michalina Vaughan, 2d ed. (London and New York: Longman, 1995), pp. 258–71.

52. Winston Smith, "Should We Hold Our Noses and Vote for Bill Clinton?" *Resistance*, No. 90 (30 September 1996), p. 1; Winston Smith, "The Coming of the American Liberal Dictatorship," *Resistance*, No. 92 (14 October 1996), p. 1.

53. Winston Smith, "The Struggle That Dare Not Speak Its Name," NSWPP leaflet [n.d.].

54. Michael Cox, "Beyond the Fringe: The Extreme Right in the United States of America," in *The Extreme Right in Europe and the USA*, edited by Paul Hainsworth (London: Pinter, 1992), pp. 286–309 (pp. 300–302).

55. Jim Saleam, "American Nazism in the Context of the American Extreme Right, 1960–1978" (unpublished M.A. thesis, University of Sydney, 1985), pp. 115–16.

NOTES TO CHAPTER 2

1. Angelo del Boca and Mario Giovana, *Fascism Today: A World Survey* (London: Heinemann, 1970), pp. 89–90.

2. Jordan's early biographical data are taken from Colin Jordan, *Merrie England—2,000* (Harrogate, U.K.: Gothic Ripples, 1993), back cover.

3. Colin Jordan, *Fraudulent Conversion: The Myth of Moscow's Change* (London: Britons Publishing Society, 1955). It is most likely that Jordan wrote the book to refute Francis Parker Yockey's claims that the Soviet Union was not under Jewish control. Kevin Coogan, *Dreamer of the Day: Francis Parker Yockey and the Postwar Nazi International* (New York: Autonomedia, 1999), pp. 510–11.

4. Arnold Leese, *Out of Step: Events in the Two Lives of an Anti-Jewish Camel Doctor* (Guildford, U.K.: Author, [1951]), p. 52. Leese was a veterinary surgeon by profession. While working in the colonies, he had specialized in the treatment of camels. The autobiography describes his earlier membership in the British Union of Fascists, his election to the council in Stamford as a fascist and his foundation of the Imperial Fascist League.

5. David Baker, *Ideology of Obsession: A. K. Chesterton and British Fascism* (London: I. B. Tauris, 1996), p. 197.

6. The ensuing account of far-right political groups associated with Colin Jordan in the period 1958–62 is based on Martin Walker, *The National Front* (London: Fontana, 1977), pp. 25–50. An insider's view of the League of Empire Loyalists, National Labour Party, the White Defence League, and (first) British National Party is offered by John Bean, *Many Shades of Black* (London: New Millennium, 1999), pp. 119f, 126–30, 139–53 and passim.

7. For John Bean's account of the split, see Bean, *Many Shades of Black*, pp. 147–56.

8. John Tyndall, *The Eleventh Hour: A Call for British Rebirth*, 2d ed. (London: Albion Press, 1988), pp. 7–8, 26–40, 49–56.

9. Colin Jordan, *Britain Reborn: The Policy of the National Socialist Movement* (London: National Socialist Movement, [1962]).

10. Details of how Tyndall and Jordan smuggled Rockwell into Britain via Ireland are given in William H. Schmaltz, *Hate: George Lincoln Rockwell and the American Nazi Party* (Washington, D.C.: Brassey's, 1999), pp. 146–48.

11. Newspaper coverage of the camp included "Home Office Ban Entry of Nazi Delegates," *The Times*, 2 August 1962, p. 10; "Foreign Nazis Banned," *The Daily Telegraph*, 2 August 1962, p. 1; "Secret 'Nazi' Camp," *The Daily Telegraph*, 6 August 1962, p. 9; "Inquiry on Visit by U.S. Nazi," *The Times*, 7 August 1962, p. 8; "Yard Search for U.S. Nazi Leader," *The Daily Telegraph*, 7 August 1962, p. 1; "Jackboots in an English Glade," *The Daily Telegraph*, 7 August 1962, pp. 1, 16.

12. "U.S. Nazi Caught in London," *The Daily Telegraph*, 9 August 1962, p. 1; "American Nazi Detained in London," *The Times*, 9 August 1962, p. 8.

13. "2-hour Yard Raid on Nazi HQ," *The Daily Telegraph*, 11 August 1962, p. 1.

14. Richard C. Thurlow, *Fascism in Britain: A History, 1918–1985* (Oxford: Basil Blackwell, 1987), pp. 268–69.

15. Colin Jordan, "National Socialism: A Philosophical Appraisal," *National Socialist World*, No. 1 (Spring 1966), 5–7.

16. Richard Thurlow, *Fascism in Britain*, pp. 269f; Gerry Gable, "Britain's Nazi Un-

derground," in *The Far Right in Western and Eastern Europe*, edited by Luciano Cheles, Ronnie Ferguson and Michalina Vaughan, 2d ed. (London and New York: Longman, 1995), pp. 258–71 (p. 259).

17. Stan Taylor, *The National Front in English Politics* (London: Macmillan, 1982), pp. 18–49.

18. Thurlow, *Fascism in Britain*, p. 270.

19. Colin Jordan, "Party Time Has Ended," *National Review*, No. 45 (June 1986). For commentary, see "Nazi Blueprint for 'Total War,'" *Searchlight*, No. 133 (July 1986), pp. 8–10.

20. "British Movement Reborn—Armed and Dangerous," *Searchlight*, No. 173 (November 1989), pp. 10–11; No. 174 (December 1989), pp. 10–11.

21. "Front's 'Fixer' with Paramilitaries Moves Full Time to Northern Ireland," *Searchlight*, No. 137 (November 1986), pp. 3–4; "1986—the Final Tie-up with Loyalist Terror," *Searchlight*, No. 139 (January 1987), pp. 11–12.

22. "SS Man Is BM's Top Dog," *Searchlight*, No. 177 (March 1990), p. 11.

23. Colin Jordan, *National Socialism: World Creed for the 1980s* (Harrogate, U.K.: Gothic Ripples, 1981), pp. 6–8, 9f, 14. (First published in *The National Socialist*, No. 3 [Winter 1981].)

24. "1986—The Year of the Political Soldier," *Searchlight*, No. 139 (January 1987), pp. 9–10; "The New Axis," *Searchlight*, No. 147 (September 1987), pp. 3–4; "The Political Soldiers," *Searchlight*, No. 151 (January 1988), p. 10; "1988—The Year of the Mad Dogs," *Searchlight*, No. 163 (January 1989), pp. 9–11; "Wales and Northern Ireland: NF Heads 'Where the Terror Is,'" *Searchlight*, No. 166 (April 1989), p. 9; "Smash the Cities" sticker, *Searchlight*, No. 215 (May 1993), p. 8.

25. Colin Jordan, "Hitler was Right!" *Gothic Ripples*, No. 20 (1989), reprinted in Colin Jordan, *National Socialism: Vanguard of the Future* (Aalborg, Denmark: Nordland Forlag, 1993), pp. 13–23.

26. Colin Jordan, "Adolf Hitler: The Man against Time," *NS Bulletin* (1989), and "Adolf Hitler: Man of the Century," *League Sentinel*, No. 3 (1989), both reprinted in Jordan, *National Socialism*, pp. 25–29, 31–34.

27. "Top Nazi Poses an Early Problem for New M15 Boss," *Searchlight*, No. 204 (June 1992), pp. 3–5; "Covington: Mastermind of Terror," *Searchlight*, No. 214 (April 1993), pp. 12–13.

28. Gerry Gable, "Britain's Nazi Underground," in *The Far Right in Western and Eastern Europe*, pp. 258–71 (p. 262).

29. Charlie Sargent interview with the French Nazi magazine *Terreur d'Elite*, No. 4 (Winter 105 [1994]), quoted in *Searchlight*, No. 235 (January 1995), p. 4.

30. "Nazi Terror Comes to Britain: The Inside Story of Combat 18," *Searchlight*, No. 214 (April 1993), pp. 3–11.

31. *Redwatch*, No. 1 (March 1992), excerpts in *Searchlight*, No. 215 (May 1993), p. 4.

32. *Redwatch*, No. 2 (May 1992), reproduced in *Searchlight*, No. 214 (April 1993), pp. 3–4.

33. *Redwatch*, Nos. 3–6 (1992–93), excerpts in *Searchlight*, No. 213 (April 1993), pp. 4–7, 14. *Combat 18*, No. 3 (late 1994), excerpts and commentary in *Searchlight*, No. 236 (February 1995), p. 3.

34. "Invitation to Kill: C18 Urges Its Followers to Murder," *Searchlight*, No. 235 (January 1995), pp. 6–7.

35. *Putsch*, No. 11 (April 1994), pp. 12–13; No. 12 (May 1994), p. 16; No. 13 (June 1994), p. 22; No. 14 (July 1994), p. 27; No. 15 (August 1994), p. 33.

36. *Putsch*, No. 10 (March 1994), pp. 6–7; No. 11 (April 1994), p. 11; No. 12 (May 1994), p. 16; No. 15 (August 1994), pp. 32, 34, 38–39; No. 16 (September 1994), p. 41.

37. *The Order*, No. 4, excerpts and commentary in *Searchlight*, No. 223 (January 1994), pp. 3–5.

38. *Searchlight*, No. 226 (April 1994), p. 5; "C18's Violence in Theory and Practice," *Searchlight*, No. 231 (September 1994), pp. 3–4; *Searchlight*, No. 232 (October 1994), p. 5; *Putsch*, No. 18 (November 1994), pp. 55f; *Searchlight*, No. 234 (December 1994), p. 3; "Britain in 1995: Watershed on the Far Right," *Searchlight*, No. 241 (July 1995), pp. 2–4.

39. *The National-Socialist*, special edition (April 106yf [i.e. 1995]), quoted in *Searchlight*, No. 239 (May 1995), pp. 1–2.

40. "Britain in 1995," pp. 2–4.

41. *Searchlight*, No. 214 (April 1993), pp. 16–17; *Searchlight*, No. 223 (January 1994), pp. 6–10. The Copenhagen summit was reported in *The Order*, No. 11, p. 8, reproduced in *Searchlight*, No. 240 (June 1995), p. 10.

42. *The Times*, 20 January 1997, p. 4.

43. "The Shape of Things to Come: An Interview with Troy Southgate," *The English Alternative*, No. 10 (1999), pp. 4–8.

44. *The National-Socialist*, No. 17 (9 November 1996), p. 2.

45. "The Secret of Greatness: Part 2 of Extracts from Savitri Devi's Gold in the Furnace," *Column 88*, No. 3 (May 1998), pp. 17–18; "The Irish-American They Hanged for Being British," *Column 88*, No. 3 (May 1998), pp. 23–26; "A Tiger Never Tamed: Michael Wittmann—Claws of Steel," *Column 88*, No. 4 (August 1998), pp. 12–16; "Tony Williams Interviews Colin Jordan," *Column 88*, No. 4 (August 1998), pp. 23–26.

46. Graeme McLagan and Nick Lowles, *Mr Evil: The Secret Life of Racist Bomber and Killer David Copeland* (London: John Blake, 2000), pp. 20–38, 51–56, 66f, 78–87.

NOTES TO CHAPTER 3

1. Further detailed information in English about Julius Evola's life, thought and influence may be found in Richard Drake, "Julius Evola and the Ideological Origins of the Radical Right in Contemporary Italy," in *Political Violence and Terror: Motifs and Motivations*, edited by Peter Merkl (Berkeley: University of California Press, 1986), pp. 61–89; Richard Drake, in "The Children of the Sun," *The Revolutionary Mystique and Terrorism in Contemporary Italy* (Bloomington: Indiana University Press, 1989), pp. 114–34. An analysis of his philosophy and its reception by the Italian far right is also offered by Roger Griffin, "Revolts against the Modern World: The Blend of Literary and Historical Fan-

tasy in the Italian New Right," *Literature and History* 11 (Spring 1985), 101–23, and Franco Ferraresi, "Julius Evola: Tradition, Reaction, and the Radical Right," *European Journal of Sociology* 28 (1987), 107–51.

2. Raimund Meyer, Judith Hossli, Guido Magnaguangno, Juri Steiner and Hans Bolliger, *Dada global* (Zurich: Limmat Verlag, 1994), pp. 65–69.

3. These works are *Saggi sull'idealismo magico* (Rome: Atanòr, 1925); *L'individuo e il divenire del mondo* (Rome: Libreria di Scienze e Lettere, 1926); *Teoria dell'individuo assoluto* (Turin: Bocca, 1927); and *Fenomenologia dell'individuo assoluto* (Turin: Bocca, 1930). Influences from Schopenhauer, Hegel and Nietzsche combined in his philosophical idealism to assert "the ability to be unconditionally whatever one wants" and "the world is my representation."

4. Julius Evola, *The Yoga of Power: Tantra, Shakti and the Secret Way*, translated by Guido Stucco (Rochester, Vt.: Inner Traditions International, 1992), p. 16.

5. Evola, *The Yoga of Power*, pp. 186–88.

6. On the Group of UR, see the historical foreword by Renato del Ponte in Julius Evola/Gruppe von UR, *Magie als Wissenschaft vom Ich: Praktische Grundlegung der Initiation* (Interlaken, Switz.: Ansata, 1985), pp. 10–22; H. T. Hansen, "Die 'magische' Gruppe von UR in ihrem historischen und esoterischen Umfeld," in Julius Evola/Gruppe von UR, *Schritte zur Initiation: Magie als Wissenschaft vom Ich*, Band II: *Theorie und Praxis des höheren Bewußtseins* (Interlaken, Switz.: Ansata, 1997), pp. 7–27, also contains extensive biographical details of Guiliano Kremmerz, Arturo Reghini and the members of their groups.

7. Julius Evola, *The Hermetic Tradition: Symbols and Teachings of the Royal Art*, translated by E. E. Rehmus (Rochester, Vt.: Inner Traditions, 1995), pp. 2–12.

8. The best introduction to Guénon and his thought in English is Robin Waterfield, *René Guénon and the Future of the West: The Life and Writings of a 20th-Century Metaphysician* (Wellingborough, U.K.: Aquarian Press, 1987).

9. René Guénon, *The Crisis of the Modern World*, trans. Marco Pallis and Richard Nicholson, 2d ed. (London: Luzac, 1962), pp. 1–14.

10. For these references, see Julius Evola, *Erhebung wider die moderne Welt* (Stuttgart: Deutsche Verlags-Anstalt, 1935), pp. 167–89, and notes, pp. 438–45.

11. Julius Evola, *Revolt against the Modern World*, translated by Guido Stucco (Rochester, Vt.: Inner Traditions, 1995), p. 3.

12. Evola, *Revolt against the Modern World*, pp. 89–90.

13. Evola, *Revolt against the Modern World*, pp. 7f.

14. Evola, *Revolt against the Modern World*, pp. 35–37.

15. Evola, *Revolt against the Modern World*, pp. 177–83.

16. Evola, *Revolt against the Modern World*, pp. 188–89, 195–210.

17. In his work, *Das Mutterrecht* [Matriarchy] (1861), Johann Jakob Bachofen (1815–1887), a private scholar in Basle, postulated that the human race passed through three stages. In the first stage humans lived in primitive, nomadic groups with neither agriculture, marriage nor social institutions. The second stage was known as matriarchy, when agriculture developed and society was based on egalitarian values and a worship

of Mother Earth. Bachofen regarded the Greek goddess Demeter and the Eleusinian mysteries as derivatives of this cultural era. The third and present stage of evolution was patriarchy, in which the rule of law and the intellect prevail. The sun becomes the dominant symbol, represented by the Greek god Apollo. Bachofen's ideas influenced Nietzsche, Freud and Jung, as well as the bohemian counterculture, which wanted to redeem industrial society through a return to nature. Richard Noll, *The Jung Cult: Origins of a Charismatic Movement* (Princeton, N.J.: Princeton University Press, 1994), pp. 160–69.

18. Evola, *Revolt against the Modern World*, pp. 211–17.

19. A short biography of Otto Weininger by Dr. Moriz Rappaport appears in Otto Weininger, *Über die letzten Dinge*, 6th ed. (Vienna: Wilhelm Braumüller, 1920), pp. v–xxiv.

20. Otto Weininger, *Geschlecht und Charakter*, 19th ed. (Vienna: Wilhelm Braumüller, 1920), pp. 106–11, 185–88, 232, 372–75, 381.

21. Weininger, *Geschlecht und Charakter*, pp. 337–45, 378, 386, 391–93.

22. Evola, *Revolt against the Modern World*, pp. 230f, 246–47.

23. Evola, *Revolt against the Modern World*, pp. 249–52.

24. Richard Noll, *The Aryan Christ: The Secret Life of Carl Gustav Jung* (London: Macmillan, 1997), pp. 134, 309.

25. Evola, *Revolt against the Modern World*, pp. 263–75.

26. Evola, *Revolt against the Modern World*, p. 275.

27. Evola, *Revolt against the Modern World*, p. 286.

28. Evola, *Revolt against the Modern World*, pp. 290–301. In 1937 Evola published his full-length work on chivalry and the Grail as an initiatory, Hyperborean mystery. In particular, he regarded the Grail as a symbol for the Ghibelline project of reorganizing the West as an empire based on sacred regality. Julius Evola, *The Mystery of the Grail: Initiation and Magic in the Quest for the Spirit*, translated by Guido Stucco (Rochester, Vt.: Inner Traditions, 1997). Evola's admiration of the Hohenstauffen dynasty was strongly influenced by Ernst Kantorowicz, *Kaiser Friedrich der Zweite* (Berlin: Bondi, 1927). As a member of the poet Stefan George's circle of spiritual elitists, Kantorowicz's definitive biography celebrated Frederick II as the hero of a "secret Germany."

29. Evola, *Revolt against the Modern World*, pp. 307–11.

30. Evola, *Revolt against the Modern World*, pp. 312–20.

31. Evola, *Revolt against the Modern World*, pp. 302–4.

32. Evola, *Revolt against the Modern World*, pp. 306–9.

33. Evola, *Revolt against the Modern World*, pp. 327–44.

34. For a full discussion of Evola's racial ideas, see H. T. Hansen, "Julius Evolas politisches Wirken," in Julius Evola, *Menschen inmitten von Ruinen* (Tübingen: Hohenrain, 1991), pp. 7–131 (pp. 88–100).

35. Julius Evola, *Heidnischer Imperialismus* (Leipzig: Armanen-Verlag, 1933), p. 55; Julius Evola, *Grundriß der faschistischen Rassenlehre* (Berlin: Runge, 1943), pp. 43–47.

36. Julius Evola, "Paradossi dei tempi: Paganesimo razzista =Illuminismo liberale," *Lo Stato* 6, No. 7 (July 1935), pp. 530–32, and "Osservazioni critiche sul 'razzismo' nazional-socialista," *Vita Italiana* 21, No. 248 (1933), pp. 544–49, cited in H. T. Hansen,

"Julius Evolas politisches Wirken," in Julius Evola, *Menschen inmitten von Ruinen*, pp. 7–131 (pp. 92–94).

37. Weininger, *Geschlecht und Charakter*, pp. 416–18.

38. Weininger, *Geschlecht und Charakter*, pp. 425–32.

39. Weininger, *Geschlecht und Charakter*, p. 441.

40. Evola, *Erhebung wider die moderne Welt*, pp. 323–24, 480, 482.

41. Julius Evola, *Tre aspetti del problema ebraico* (Padua: Edizioni di Ar, 1994), pp. 35–36 (first edition published in 1936).

42. Julius Evola, "La tragedia della 'Guardia di Ferro,'" in *La vita italiana* 309 (December 1938), quoted in Franco Ferraresi, "Julius Evola: Tradition, Reaction, and the Radical Right," in *European Journal of Sociology* 28 (1987), 107–51 (pp. 129–30).

43. Hans Thomas Hakl, "Julius Evola und die deutsche Konservative Revolution," *Criticón*, No. 158 (April–June 1998), pp. 16–32. A bibliography of Evola's publications in German has been compiled by Karlheinz Weißmann in Evola, *Menschen inmitten von Ruinen*, pp. 403–6.

44. On Evola's wartime career, see Richard Drake, in "The Children of the Sun," *The Revolutionary Mystique and Terrorism in Contemporary Italy*, pp. 119–20; T. H. Hansen, "Julius Evolas politisches Wirken," in Evola, *Menschen inmitten von Ruinen*, pp. 7–132 (pp. 61–65).

45. Drake, *The Revolutionary Mystique and Terrorism in Contemporary Italy*, p. 125.

46. Drake, "Julius Evola and the Ideological Origins of the Radical Right in Contemporary Italy," pp. 77–78.

47. Franco Ferraresi, "Julius Evola: Tradition, Reaction, and the Radical Right," *European Journal of Sociology* 28 (1987), 107–51 (p. 135).

48. Giorgio Galli, *La Crisi italiana e la destra internazionale* (Milan: Mondadori, 1974), p. 20.

49. Adriano Romauldi, *Julius Evola: L'uomo e l'opera* (Rome: Volpe, 1971), pp. 7, 92.

50. Ferraresi, "Julius Evola," 138–40.

51. Roger Eatwell, "The Esoteric Ideology of the National Front in the 1980s," in *The Failure of British Fascism: The Far Right and the Fight for Political Recognition*, edited by Mike Cronin (Basingstoke, U.K.: Macmillan, 1996), pp. 99–117.

52. "Evola: The Aryan Doctrine of Fight and Victory," *Rising*, No. 3 (1983), p. 4; "Freda: A Martyr for Our Cause," *Rising*, No. 4 (1983), p. 3.

53. Derek Holland, *The Political Soldier: A Statement*, 2d ed. (London: International Third Position, 1994), pp. 10–11.

54. *Searchlight*, No. 163 (January 1989), p. 10; *Searchlight*, No. 168 (June 1989), p. 3; *Searchlight*, No. 247 (January 1996), pp. 11–14. See also *From Ballots to Bombs: The Inside Story of the National Front's Political Soldiers* (London: Searchlight, [1989]), pp. 7–12.

55. Mario Aprile, "Julius Evola: An Introduction to His Life and Work," *The Scorpion*, No. 6 (Winter/Spring 1984), pp. 20–21.

56. Julius Evola, "American 'Civilization,'" *The Scorpion*, No. 7 (Summer 1984), pp. 17–19.

57. Julius Evola, "United Europe: The Spiritual Pre-Requisite," *The Scorpion*, No. 9 (Spring 1986), pp. 18–20. Other articles on Evola included Luis Chester, "Riding the Tiger," *The Scorpion*, No. 8 (Spring 1985), pp. 30–32, and Marotta Salvatore, "*Suum Cuique*: Evola's Notion of the True State," *The Scorpion*, No. 10 (Autumn 1986), p. 37.

58. Julius Evola, *Taoism: The Magic, the Mysticism*, translated by Guido Stucco (Edmonds, Wash.: Holmes, 1994); Julius Evola, *Zen: The Religion of the Samurai* (Edmonds, Wash.: Holmes, 1994).

59. H. T. Hansen, "Nachlese zum Evola-Jahr," *Criticón*, No. 161 (March 1999).

60. Guillermo Coletti, "Against the Modern World: An Introduction to the Work of Julius Evola," *Ohm Clock*, No. 4 (Spring 1996), pp. 29–31.

NOTES TO CHAPTER 4

1. "A salute to James Hartung Madole (Father of Post-war Occult-Fascism)," *The Nexus*, No. 2 (November 1995), pp. 22–27.

2. Biographical details of James Madole and an overview of the National Renaissance Party are documented in William Goring, "The National Renaissance Party: History and Analysis of an American Neo-Nazi Political Party," *National Information Center Newsletter* (December 1969–January 1970). This periodical was published at Springfield, Massachusetts.

3. Goring, "The National Renaissance Party," p. 5.

4. For Charles B. Hudson and his extensive contacts in the patriotic and pro-Nazi groups of prewar America, see John Roy Carlson, *Under Cover: My Four Years in the Nazi Underworld of America* (New York: Dutton, 1943), pp. 132–53 and passim.

5. Details of Kurt Mertig and his prewar political activities may be found in Carlson, *Under Cover*, pp. 43–44, 266–68, 270, 389, 502.

6. Goring, "The National Renaissance Party," p. 6.

7. Kerry R. Bolton, *Phoenix Rising: The Epic Saga of James H. Madole* (Paraparaumu Beach, New Zealand: Renaissance Press, 1996), p. 2.

8. Ulick Varange (i.e., Francis Parker Yockey), *Imperium: The Philosophy of History and Politics*, 3d ed. (Torrance, Calif.: Noontide Press, 1983), pp. 578–86. The definitive study of Yockey's life and underground political activities is Kevin Coogan, *Dreamer of the Day: Francis Parker Yockey and the Postwar Fascist International* (New York: Autonomedia, 1999).

9. Coogan, *Dreamer of the Day*, pp. 48–73.

10. Coogan, *Dreamer of the Day*, pp. 92–100, 103. On Mrs. Washburn and the National Liberty Party, see Carlson, *Under Cover*, pp. 361–67.

11. Coogan, *Dreamer of the Day*, pp. 105–26.

12. Oswald Spengler, *The Decline of the West*, 2 vols. (London: George Allen and Unwin, 1926–28), vol. 1, pp. 183–216.

13. Spengler, *Decline of the West*, vol. 2, pp. 315–23.

14. Varange, *Imperium*, pp. 381–90.

15. Varange, *Imperium*, pp. 395–97, 493ff, 570ff, 533.

16. Francis Parker Yockey, *The Proclamation of London of the European Liberation Front*, 2d ed. (Reedy, W.Va.: Liberty Bell Publications, 1981), pp. 28–29; Coogan, *Dreamer of the Day*, pp. 167–81.

17. Coogan, *Dreamer of the Day*, pp. 227, 230–36, 240, 378–90.

18. Biographical information on Frederick Charles Weiss and H. Keith Thompson is in Coogan, *Dreamer of the Day*, pp. 252–60. Weiss is also discussed in Arnold Forster and Benjamin R. Epstein, *Cross Currents* (New York: Doubleday, 1956), Part 2, pp. 201ff and passim. His contacts are also mentioned in Kurt P. Tauber, *Beyond Eagle and Swastika*, 2 vols. (Middletown, Conn.: Wesleyan University Press, 1967), vol. 2, p. 1091 (VII/40).

19. Frederick Charles Weiss's articles "Russia" and "Kto Kovo—Who-Kills-Whom," quoted in Coogan, *Dreamer of the Day*, pp. 440–41.

20. Bolton, *Phoenix Rising*, p. 2.

21. John Hassan, "White Muslims: The Greenshirts," *The Nexus*, No. 4 (May 1996), pp. 10–11.

22. For the origins and history of Theosophy, see Bruce F. Campbell, *Ancient Wisdom Revived: A History of the Theosophical Movement* (Berkeley: University of California Press, 1980); Sylvia Cranston, *HPB: The Extraordinary Life and Influence of Helena Blavatsky, Founder of the Modern Theosophical Movement* (New York: G. P. Putnam's Sons, 1993).

23. Helena Petrovna Blavatsky, *The Secret Doctrine*, 2d ed., 2 vols. (London: Theosophical Publishing Company, 1888), vol. 2, pp. 6–12, 300f, 433–36. The myth of Lemurian miscegenation is discussed in vol. 2, pp. 184, 266f.

24. Blavatsky, *The Secret Doctrine*, vol. 2, p. 318f.

25. Bolton, *Phoenix Rising*, p. 4.

26. These references are drawn from "The New Atlantis: A Blueprint for an Aryan Garden of Eden in North America," published in serial form in *National Renaissance Bulletin* in 1974. Parts 2, 3, 4, 7, 9, 10 were reprinted in Bolton, *Phoenix Rising*, pp. 15–46 (pp. 33–35, 37–39, 45–46). The Bulwer-Lytton quote is taken from his novel *Vril: The Power of the Coming Race* (1871), an important source in the modern mythology of Nazi occultism (see chapter 6).

27. James H. Madole, "The New Atlantis" (Parts 9 and 10), in Bolton, *Phoenix Rising*, pp. 32–39, 39–46 (pp. 36–37, 45–46).

28. Madole, "The New Atlantis" (Part 10), in Bolton, *Phoenix Rising*, pp. 39–46 (pp. 40–41).

29. "A salute to James Hartung Madole (Father of Post-war Occult-Fascism)," *The Nexus*, No. 2 (November 1995), pp. 22–27 (pp. 25–26), reprinted in Bolton, *Phoenix Rising*, pp. 1–6 (pp. 4–5).

30. Goring, "The National Renaissance Party," pp. 7–8.

31. Coogan, *Dreamer of the Day*, p. 27.

32. Bolton, *Phoenix Rising*, p. 8.

33. This account of the Security Echelon and its street fighting campaigns and pickets is drawn from "America's Ksyatrias," *The Nexus*, No. 4 (May 1996), pp. 6–10, reprinted in Bolton, *Phoenix Rising*, pp. 7–14 (with additional photographs).

34. Bolton, *Phoenix Rising*, pp. 9–11.

35. Bolton, *Phoenix Rising*, pp. 10–11.

36. Bolton, *Phoenix Rising*, pp. 7, 12–14.

37. Bolton, *Phoenix Rising*, p. 5.

38. The contribution of Theosophy to the German *völkisch* movement is fully documented in Nicholas Goodrick-Clarke, *The Occult Roots of Nazism: Secret Aryan Cults and Their Influence on Nazi Ideology: The Ariosophists of Austria and Germany 1890–1935*, 2d ed. (New York: New York University Press, 1992).

NOTES TO CHAPTER 5

1. A full biography of Savitri Devi is provided by Nicholas Goodrick-Clarke, *Hitler's Priestess: Savitri Devi, the Hindu-Aryan Myth, and Neo-Nazism* (New York: New York University Press, 1998).

2. Savitri Devi, *Defiance* (Calcutta: A. K. Mukerji, [1950]), pp. 12, 58.

3. Goodrick-Clarke, *Hitler's Priestess*, pp. 19–25.

4. Léon Poliakov, *The Aryan Myth: A History of Racist and Nationalist Ideas in Europe* (London: Sussex University Press and Heinemann, 1974), pp. 190–92.

5. Poliakov, *The Aryan Myth*, pp. 192–99.

6. Savitri Devi, *Gold im Schmelztiegel: Erlebnisse in Nachkriegsdeutschland*, translated by Lotte Asmus (Padua: Edizioni di Ar, 1982), p. 21.

7. Bâl Gangadhar Tilak, *The Arctic Home in the Vedas* (Poona: Kesari, 1903), pp. 453–55, 464.

8. A concise account of the Aryan settlement of India appears in Romila Thapar, "The Impact of Aryan Culture," in *A History of India*, vol. 1 (Harmondsworth, U.K.: Penguin, 1966), pp. 28–49.

9. Savitri Devi, *L'Étang aux lotus* (Calcutta: Author, 1940), pp. 19–25 (p. 25).

10. Savitri Devi, *Defiance*, p. 69.

11. Goodrick-Clarke, *Hitler's Priestess*, pp. 39–40.

12. The origin and development of these movements are discussed in Christophe Jaffrelot, *The Hindu Nationalist Movement and Indian Politics: 1925 to the 1990s* (London: Hurst, 1996), pp. 11–35.

13. Savitri Devi, *Souvenirs et réflexions d'une aryenne* (New Delhi: Author, 1976), pp. 35–40.

14. Quoted in Milan Hauner, *India in Axis Strategy: Germany, Japan, and Indian Nationalists in the Second World War* (Stuttgart: Klett-Cotta, 1981) (Publications of the German Historical Institute, London, vol. 7), p. 66.

15. Savitri Devi, *Souvenirs et réflexions d'une aryenne*, pp. 41, 274f; Jean Parvulesco, *La spirale prophétique* (Paris: Guy Trédaniel, 1986), p. 99.

16. Goodrick-Clarke, *Hitler's Priestess*, p. 69.

17. Savitri Devi, *Defiance*, pp. 149–51, 226.

18. Savitri Devi, *The Lightning and the Sun* (Calcutta: Author, 1958), pp. 18–19.

19. Savitri Devi, *The Lightning and the Sun*, pp. 36–55.

20. The complex mythology and theology of the avatar receive their definitive study in Geoffrey Parrinder, *Avatar and Incarnation*, 2d ed. (New York: Oxford University Press, 1982).

21. Savitri Devi, *The Lightning and the Sun*, pp. 229–49.

22. Bhagavad Gita, VI, verses 7–8. This couplet is quoted by Savitri Devi repeatedly in *Pilgrimage* (Calcutta: Author, 1958), pp. [v], 7, 28, 31, 52, 173, 188–89, 261, and in *The Lightning and the Sun*, p. 416 and passim.

23. Savitri Devi, *The Lightning and the Sun*, pp. 215–16, 222–24.

24. Savitri Devi, *The Lightning and the Sun*, pp. 349–51. August Kubizek, *Young Hitler*, 2d ed. (Maidstone, U.K.: George Mann, 1973), pp. 64–66.

25. William L. Pierce, "George Lincoln Rockwell: A National Socialist Life," *National Socialist World*, No. 5 (Winter 1967), 13–36 (p. 26); Matt Koehl, *Faith of the Future*, 2d ed. (Milwaukee, Wis.: New Order, 1995), p. 28. A condensed version of Savitri Devi's *The Lightning and the Sun* appeared in Pierce's *National Socialist World*, No. 1 (Spring 1966), pp. 13–90 (Kubizek account, p. 84).

26. Goodrick-Clarke, *Hitler's Priestess*, pp. 131–32.

27. Text of handbill quoted in English in Savitri Devi, *Defiance*, pp. 1ff. The German original appears in Savitri Devi, *Gold im Schmelztiegel*, p. 261.

28. Goodrick-Clarke, *Hitler's Priestess*, pp. 137–38.

29. Savitri Devi, *Gold im Schmelztiegel*, pp. 239–46, 315–40, and *Pilgrimage*, pp. 244f.

30. Savitri Devi, *Defiance*, pp. 188f.

31. Savitri Devi, *Defiance*, pp. 169, 104, 190.

32. Details of the female wardresses appear in Savitri Devi, *Gold im Schmelztiegel*, pp. 128–30. The Auschwitz service of Hertha Ehlert, her best friend at Werl, is mentioned in *Defiance*, p. 273.

33. Goodrick-Clarke, *Hitler's Priestess*, pp. 140–46.

34. Goodrick-Clarke, *Hitler's Priestess*, pp. 140–46.

35. Savitri Devi, *Pilgrimage*, pp. 318–54.

36. The political context of these far-right parties in the early postwar years receives attention in Martin Lee, *The Beast Reawakens* (London: Little, Brown and Company, 1997), pp. 49–52, 115–17.

37. Hans-Ulrich Rudel describes his experiences in the postwar period 1945 to 1951 in *Trotzdem: Kriegs- und Nachkriegszeit* (Preußisch Oldendorf: Karl-Schütz-Verlag, 1987) and *Mein Leben im Krieg und Frieden* (Rosenheim: Deutsche Verlagsgesellschaft, 1994).

38. Goodrick-Clarke, *Hitler's Priestess*, pp. 176–79, 181–86.

39. Goodrick-Clarke, *Hitler's Priestess*, p. 190.

40. Goodrick-Clarke, *Hitler's Priestess*, pp. 195–203.

41. Savitri Devi, "The Lightning and the Sun (condensed edition)," *National Socialist World*, No. 1 (Spring 1966), pp. 13–90.

42. Savitri Devi, "Gold in the Furnace," *National Socialist World*, No. 3 (Spring 1967), pp. 59–71; Savitri Devi, "Defiance" (excerpts), *National Socialist World*, No. 6 (Winter 1968), pp. 64–87.

43. Matt Koehl, "Adolf Hitler: German Nationalist or Aryan Racist," *National Socialist World*, No. 4 (Summer 1967), pp. 13–22 (p. 22), and "Hitler and We," New Order brochure reprint of speech before Midwest comrades on 20 April 1992.

44. Lotte Asmus and Vittorio De Cecco, "La 'missionaria' del paganesimo ariano," *Risguardo* 4 (1984), pp. 64–70.

45. Pierre Vidal-Naquet, *Assassins of Memory: Essays on the Denial of the Holocaust* (New York: Columbia University Press, 1992), pp. 21, 43.

46. Savitri Devi, *L'India e il Nazismo* (Parma: Edizioni all'insegna del Veltro, 1979) (Quaderni del Veltro 11), pp. 5–7.

47. Arya of Montreal has published *Omaggio a Savitri Devi* as *Arya* 2 (1978). An Italian translation of her book on Paul of Tarsus, introduced by "Wittekind," was published under the title *Cristianesimo e Giudaismo (Paolo di Tarso), Arya* 5 (January 1981).

48. *Searchlight*, No. 91 (January 1983), p. 3; *Searchlight*, No. 97 (July 1983), p. 10.

49. Alfred Rosenberg, *Der Mythus des 20. Jahrhunderts* (Munich: Hoheneichen-Verlag [Franz-Eher-Verlag], 1934), pp. 660–64.

50. Goodrick-Clarke, *Hitler's Priestess*, pp. 219–22 (p. 220).

51. "Heart of Gold, Spirit of Light, Will of Steel," *The Order* [No. 14, early 1996?], cover headline: "No Surrender to ZOG!" [pp. 5–7].

52. Savitri Devi, *The Lightning and the Sun*, 3d ed. (Paraparaumu Beach, New Zealand: Renaissance Press, 1994); cover title and article "Priestess of Hitlerism: Savitri Devi," *The Nexus*, No. 9 (August 1997), pp. 1–4.

NOTES TO CHAPTER 6

1. The following novels illustrate the increasing popularity of Nazi fugitive and thriller fiction from the early 1960s onward: Jack Higgins, *The Testament of Caspar Schultz* (1962); Philip K. Dick, *The Man in the High Castle* (1962); Helen MacInnes, *The Salzburg Connection* (1968); Frederick Forsyth, *The Odessa File* (1972); Norman Spinrad, *The Iron Dream* (1972); Michael Sinclair, *A Long Time Sleeping* (1975); Ira Levin, *The Boys from Brazil* (1976); John Gardner, *The Werewolf Trace* (1977); Trevor Hoyle, *Through the Eye of Time* (1977); George Markstein, *The Goering Testament* (1978); Duncan Kyle, *Black Camelot* (1978); James Herbert, *The Spear* (1978); Robert Ludlum, *The Holcroft Covenant* (1978); Harold King, *Closing Ceremonies* (1980); Richard Hugo, *The Hitler Diaries* (1982); Gordon Stevens, *Spider* (1984); Pierre Salinger and Leonard Gross, *The Dossier* (1984); Maurice Sellar, *The Front Man* (1985); Joseph Heywood, *The Berkut* (1987); Greg Iles, *Spandau Phoenix* (1993). More serious literature concerning the imaginative legacy of Nazism would include: George Steiner, *The Portage to San Cristobal of A.H.* (1979); William Styron, *Sophie's Choice* (1979); D. M. Thomas, *The White Hotel* (1981). A critical evaluation of the Nazi thriller genre and its inspiration has been undertaken by Saul Friedlander, *Reflections of Nazism: An Essay on Kitsch and Death*, trans-

lated by Thomas Weyr (New York: Harper and Row, 1982), and Alvin H. Rosenfeld, *Imagining Hitler* (Bloomington: Indiana University Press, 1985).

During the 1970s, non-fiction books about Nazi-hunting in Latin America (with special reference to Martin Bormann) included William Stevenson, *The Bormann Brotherhood* (New York: Harcourt Brace Jovanovich, 1973), and Ladislas Farago, *Aftermath: Martin Bormann and the Fourth Reich* (London: Hodder and Stoughton, 1975), while the search for Josef Mengele, the infamous Auschwitz doctor, was covered by Erich Erdstein, *Inside the Fourth Reich* (London: Robert Hale, 1977).

2. The best account of the *Stern* affair is provided by Robert Harris, *Selling Hitler: The Story of the Hitler Diaries* (London: Faber and Faber, 1986).

3. Ian Sayer and Douglas Botting, *Nazi Gold: The Story of the World's Greatest Robbery and Its Aftermath* (London: Granada, 1984), and Arthur L. Smith, Jr., *Hitler's Gold: The Story of the Nazi War Loot* (Oxford: Berg Publishers, 1989), document the mystery of the missing Reichsbank reserves. The looting and fate of European art collections is treated in Charles De Jaeger, *The Linz File: Hitler's Plunder of European Art* (Exeter: Webb and Bower, 1981); Lynn H. Nicholas, *The Rape of Europa: The Fate of Europe's Treasures in the Third Reich* (New York: Alfred A. Knopf, 1994); *The Spoils of War: World War II and Its Aftermath: The Loss, Reappearance, and Recovery of Cultural Property*, edited by Elizabeth Simpson (New York: Harry N. Abrams, 1997).

4. These speculative non-fiction works typically focus on Hitler's charismatic powers as a kind of demonic possession, and the supposedly all-powerful occult Thule Society in Munich (est. 1918) and other secret lodges as channels of black initiation. Leading examples of the genre include: Dietrich Bronder, *Bevor Hitler kam* (Hanover: Hans Pfeiffer, 1964); René Alleau, *Hitler et les sociétés secrètes* (Paris: Grasset, 1969); Werner Gerson, *Le Nazisme société secrète* (Paris: N.O.E,, 1969); Jean-Michel Angebert [i.e., Michel Bertrand and Jean Angelini], *Les mystiques du soleil* (Paris: Laffont, 1971); Jean-Michel Angebert, *Hitler et la tradition cathare* (Paris: Laffont, 1971); Jean-Michel Angebert, *The Occult and the Third Reich* (New York: McGraw-Hill, 1971); Trevor Ravenscroft, *The Spear of Destiny* (London: Neville Spearman, 1972); Jean-Claude Frère, *Nazisme et sociétés secrètes* (Paris: Grasset, 1974); J. H. Brennan, *Occult Reich* (London: Futura, 1974); Francis King, *Satan and Swastika* (St. Albans, U.K.: Mayflower, 1976); Dusty Sklar, *Gods and Beasts: The Nazis and the Occult* (New York: Thomas Y. Crowell, 1977).

5. Hans Thomas Hakl, *Unknown Sources: National Socialism and the Occult*, translated by Nicholas Goodrick-Clarke (Edmonds, Wash.: Holmes, 2000), pp. 22–26. The references quoted are René Kopp, "Le secret psychique des maîtres du Monde: Bonaparte, Mussolini, Hitler," *Le Chariot: Revue Mensuelle de Psychologie Expérimentale et d'Occultisme*, No. 54 (June 1934), pp. 86, 111; Edouard Saby, *Le Tyran Nazi et les Forces Occultes*, 2d ed. (Paris: Editions de l'Ecole Addéiste, 1944), pp. 98, 104. The work was first published as *Hitler et les Forces Occultes* in 1939.

6. Theodor Schieder, *Hermann Rauschnings "Gespräche mit Hitler" als Geschichtsquelle* (Opladen, Germany: Westdeutscher Verlag, 1972); Wolfgang Hänel, *Hermann Rauschnings "Gespräche mit Hitler": Eine Geschichtsfälschung* (Ingolstadt, Germany: Zeitgeschichtliche Forschungsstelle, 1984).

7. Hermann Rauschning, *Hitler Speaks* (London: Thornton Butterworth, 1939), pp. 213, 240–43, 251.

8. Louis Pauwels and Jacques Bergier, *The Morning of the Magicians*, translated by Rollo Myers (St. Albans, U.K.: Mayflower, 1971), pp. 149f, 176–78, 195, 203. The French authors link Hitler's ideas of magical consciousness and a future mutation of the species to his enthusiasm for Hanns Hörbiger's World Ice Theory, which they discuss at length on pp. 153–70, 176–79. Rauschning attributed Hitler's interest in the myths and visions of early man, lapsed forms of perception and supernatural powers (Cyclopean eye) and their revival in a higher stage of human development to the writings of Edgar Dacqué, a Munich professor of geology and paleontology, who based his speculations on Hörbiger's theory, Hermann Rauschning, *Hitler Speaks*, pp. 240–41.

9. Trevor Ravenscroft, *The Spear of Destiny: The Occult Power behind the Spear Which Pierced the Side of Christ* (London: Neville Spearman, 1972), pp. 38n, 159f, 170–71, 175–76, 189–90, 244, 250; J. H. Brennan, *Occult Reich* (London: Futura, 1974), pp. 58–59, 101–2.

10. Helena Petrovna Blavatsky, *The Secret Doctrine*, 2d ed., 2 vols. (London: Theosophical Publishing Company, 1888), vol. 1, pp. xxiii–xxv; vol. 2, p. 319.

11. The myths of Agartha and Shamballah, and their many versions, are extensively analyzed in Joscelyn Godwin, *Arktos: The Polar Myth in Science, Symbolism and Nazi Survival* (Grand Rapids, Mich.: Phanes, 1993), chapters 7 and 8. The sources for a Theosophical Shamballah in the Gobi region are Annie Besant and Charles Leadbeater, *Man: Whence, How and Whither: A Record of Clairvoyant Investigation* (Adyar, India: Theosophical Publishing House, 1913), pp. 249–51, and Alice A. Bailey, *Initiation, Human and Solar* (New York: Lucis Publishing, 1974), p. 33. (First edition, 1922.)

12. Joscelyn Godwin, *Arktos*, p. 81. The reference is to Louis Jacolliot, *Le Fils de Dieu* (Paris: Lacroix, 1873), pp. 237, 264, 309–11, 326–27.

13. Joseph Saint-Yves d'Alveydre, *La Mission de l'Inde en Europe* (Paris: Dorbon, 1910), p. 27. For further details of Saint-Yves's life and thought, see Joscelyn Godwin, "Saint-Yves d'Alveydre and the Agarthian Connection," *The Hermetic Journal*, No. 32 (Summer 1986), pp. 24–34; No. 33 (Autumn 1986), pp. 31–38; also *Arktos*, pp. 83–86.

14. Ferdinand Ossendowski, *Beasts, Men and Gods* (London: Edward Arnold, 1926), pp. 299–316 (pp. 313–14).

15. Helena Petrovna Blavatsky, *Isis Unveiled*, 2 vols. (New York: Bouton, 1877), vol. 1, pp. 64, 125.

16. Willy Ley, "Pseudoscience in Naziland," *Astounding Science Fiction* 39 (1947), pp. 90–98.

17. Pauwels and Bergier, *The Morning of the Magicians*, p. 146f.

18. Pauwels and Bergier, *The Morning of the Magicians*, p. 148n.

19. Pauwels and Bergier, *The Morning of the Magicians*, p. 180.

20. The original source for the Thule Society is Rudolf von Sebottendorff, *Bevor Hitler kam: Urkundliches aus der Frühzeit der national-sozialistischen Bewegung* (Munich: Deukula-Verlag, Grassinger & Co., 1933), which includes a complete membership list. The origin, history and activities of the Thule are documented in Reginald H.

Phelps, "'Before Hitler Came': Thule Society and Germanen Orden," *Journal of Modern History* 25 (1963), pp. 245–61; Nicholas Goodrick-Clarke, *The Occult Roots of Nazism: Secret Aryan Cults and Their Influence on Nazi Ideology: The Ariosophists of Austria and Germany 1890–1935*, 2d ed. (New York: New York University Press, 1992), chapter 11; Hermann Gilbhard, *Die Thule-Gesellschaft: Vom okkulten Mummenschanz zum Hakenkreuz* (Munich: Kiessling, 1994), and Detlev Rose, *Die Thule-Gesellschaft: Legende— Mythos—Wirklichkeit* (Tübingen: Grabert, 1994).

21. Dietrich Eckart's life and thought, with special reference to his links with Hitler and the Nazi Party, are the subject of Ralph Max Engelman, "Dietrich Eckart and the Genesis of Nazism" (Ph.D. dissertation, Washington University, St. Louis, Mo., 1970). For a detailed discussion of the question of Eckart's influence on Hitler, see Rose, *Die Thule-Gesellschaft*, pp. 108–20.

22. The limited extent of Hitler's personal contact with Karl Haushofer may be deduced from Hans-Adolf Jacobsen, *Karl Haushofer: Leben und Werk*, vol. 1 (Schriften des Bundesarchivs 24/1) (Boppard am Rhein: Boldt, 1979), pp. 224–58. However, by the mid-1920s Hitler was certainly acquainted with the writings of Haushofer and his geopolitical school; see Woodruff D. Smith, *The Ideological Origins of Nazi Imperialism* (New York: Oxford University Press, 1986), pp. 240, 305.

23. Louis Pauwels, *Gurdjieff* (Douglas, Isle of Man: Times Press, 1964), pp. 62–65. First edition published under the title *Monsieur Gurdjieff* (Paris: Editions du Seuil, 1954).

24. Jacobsen, *Karl Haushofer*, pp. 86–89, 467.

25. Pauwels and Bergier, *The Morning of the Magicians*, p. 193. The deathbed quotation is wholly unattributed and first appears in this source. It has been regularly repeated in the "Nazi Mysteries" literature.

26. Pauwels and Bergier, *The Morning of the Magicians*, pp. 195–98 (quoted passage, p. 198).

27. Johannes Hering, "Beiträge zur Geschichte der Thule-Gesellschaft," typescript dated 21 June 1939, Bundesarchiv, Koblenz, NS26/865.

28. Bronder, *Bevor Hitler kam*, pp. 234–44.

29. Robert Charroux, *Legacy of the Gods* (London: Sphere, 1979), pp. 116–19, 123f, 176f, 178–97. First published as *Le livre des secrets trahis* (Paris: Laffont, 1965). Charroux's other titles that repeat many of these themes include *One Hundred Thousand Years of Man's Unknown History* (London: Sphere, 1981) [first published as *Histoire inconnue des hommes depuis cent mille ans* (Paris: Laffont, 1963)]; *Masters of the World* (London: Sphere, 1979) [first published as *Le livre des maîtres de monde* (Paris: Laffont, 1967)]; *The Mysterious Unknown* (London: Neville Spearman, 1972) [first published as *Le livre du mystérieux inconnu* (Paris: Laffont, 1969)]; *Lost Worlds: Scientific Secrets of the Ancients* (London: Souvenir, 1973) [first published as *Le livre des mondes oubliés* (Paris: Laffont, 1971)]; *The Mysterious Past* (London: Futura, 1974) [first published as *Le livre du passé mystérieux* (Paris: Laffont, 1973)].

30. Trevor Ravenscroft's military career and the doubtful nature of his contact with Walter Johannes Stein are critically examined in Ken Anderson, *Hitler and the Occult*

(New York: Prometheus Books, 1995), pp. 85–97 and Alan Baker, *Invisible Eagle: The History of Nazi Occultism* (London: Virgin, 2000), pp. 125–30, 132–39.

31. Walter Johannes Stein, *Weltgeschichte im Lichte des Heiligen Gral: Das Neunte Jahrhundert* (Stuttgart: Orient-Occident Verlag, 1928), pp. 6–8, 381–94. This book has been published in English language as *The Ninth Century: World History in the Light of the Holy Grail*, translated by Irene Groves (London: Temple Lodge Press, 1991).

32. Ravenscroft, *The Spear of Destiny*, pp. 47–55.

33. Ravenscroft, *The Spear of Destiny*, pp. 57–88.

34. For Hitler's knowledge of Wagner operas at Linz and Vienna, see August Kubizek, *Young Hitler: The Story of Our Friendship*, 2d ed. (Maidstone, U.K.: George Mann, 1973), pp. 138–44. For Hitler's statements relating to his Parsifal-religion, see Joachim Fest, *Hitler* (London: Weidenfeld and Nicolson, 1974), p. 499, and Hermann Rauschning, *Hitler Speaks*, pp. 227–28.

35. Ravenscroft, *The Spear of Destiny*, pp. 25–31. Cf. Alan Bullock, *Hitler: A Study in Tyranny*, 2d ed. (Harmondsworth, U.K.: Penguin, 1962), pp. 35f.

36. Stein's biographer knows nothing of a personal acquaintance between Hitler and his subject in Vienna. Johannes Tautz, *Walter Johannes Stein: A Biography* (London: Temple Lodge Press, 1990). See also Goodrick-Clarke, *The Occult Roots of Nazism*, pp. 223–24.

37. Ravenscroft, *The Spear of Destiny*, pp. 88, 167–70, 186.

38. Ravenscroft, *The Spear of Destiny*, p. 230.

39. Ravenscroft, *The Spear of Destiny*, pp. 253–59.

40. Ravenscroft, *The Spear of Destiny*, pp. 103–105.

41. Francis King, *Satan and Swastika* (St. Albans, U.K.: Mayflower, 1976), pp. 12–13, 108–9; Dusty Sklar, *Gods and Beasts: The Nazis and the Occult* (New York: Thomas Y. Crowell, 1977), pp. 23f, 47, 56f, 63.

42. Howard A. Buechner and Wilhelm Bernhart, *Adolf Hitler and the Secrets of the Holy Lance* (Metairie, La.: Thunderbird Press, 1988); *Hitler's Ashes: Seeds of a New Reich* (Metairie, La.: Thunderbird Press, 1989).

43. Pauwels and Bergier, *The Morning of the Magicians*, pp. 203–8. Cf. Hermann Rauschning, *Hitler Speaks*, pp. 243–48.

44. A. de Saint-Loup, *Nouveaux cathares pour Montségur* (Paris: Presses de la Cité, 1967); "Entrevue avec Saint-Loup," *Le Nouveau Planète* (Paris), No. 9 (July 1969). These sources were quoted by Miguel Serrano, *El Cordón Dorado: Hitlerismo Esotérico*, 3d ed. (Bogota: Solar, 1985), p. 242.

45. Jean-Michel Angebert [i.e., Michel Bertrand and Jean Angelini], *Les mystiques du soleil* (Paris: Laffont, 1971); Jean-Michel Angebert, *Hitler et la tradition cathare* (Paris: Laffont, 1971); Jean-Michel Angebert, *The Occult and the Third Reich* (New York: McGraw-Hill, 1971); Howard A. Buechner, *Emerald Cup—Ark of Gold: The Quest of SS Lt Otto Rahn of the Third Reich* (Metairie, La.: Thunderbird Press, 1991).

46. The standard scholarly study of the SS Ahnenerbe is Michael H. Kater, *Das "Ahnenerbe" der SS 1935–1945: Ein Beitrag zur Kulturpolitik des Dritten Reiches* (Stuttgart: Deutscher Verlags-Anstalt, 1974).

47. This expedition was recorded in detail in Ernst Schäfer, *Berge, Buddhas und Bären: Forschung und Jagd in geheimnisvollem Tibet* (Berlin: Paul Parey, 1933).

48. Final Intelligence Report (OI-FIR), No. 32, "The Activities of Dr Ernst Schäfer, Tibet Explorer and Scientist with SS-Sponsored Scientific Institutes," Third Army Interrogation Center, dated 12 February 1946.

49. Numerous color plates and photographs in Ernst Schäfer, *Geheimnis Tibet: Erster Bericht der Deutschen Tibet-Expedition Ernst Schäfer 1938/39* (Munich: F. Bruckmann, 1943).

50. Pauwels and Bergier, *Morning of the Magicians*, p. 207.

51. Bronder, *Bevor Hitler kam*, pp. 243–44.

52. Josef Ackermann, *Heinrich Himmler als Ideologe* (Göttingen: Musterschmidt, 1970), pp. 60–62.

53. Brennan, *Occult Reich*, p. 120; King, *Satan and Swastika*, p. 172; Sklar, *Gods and Beasts*, p. 85; Ravenscroft, *The Spear of Destiny*, p. 311.

54. Karl Hüser, *Wewelsburg 1933–1945: Kult- und Terrorstätte der SS* (Paderborn: Verlag Bonifatius-Druckerei, 1982), pp. 10–11, 20–34.

55. Hüser, *Wewelsburg 1933–1945*, pp. 230–31, 274–75, 292–98.

56. Details of Wewelsburg symbolism and ceremonies in Ravenscroft, *The Spear of Destiny*, pp. 309–11; Brennan, *Occult Reich*, pp. 116f; Francis King, *Satan and Swastika*, pp. 15, 174–76; Dusty Sklar, *Gods and Beasts*, p. 99. These stories actually reflect local oral tradition at Wewelsburg, related by Rupprecht, the castle warden in the 1960s. Heinz Höhne, *The Order of the Death's Head: The Story of Hitler's SS* (London: Pan, 1972), pp. 139–40.

57. James Herbert, *The Spear* (London: New English Library, 1978), pp. 192–94; Duncan Kyle, *Black Camelot* (Glasgow: William Collins, 1978), pp. 216–18.

58. J. H. Brennan, *Occult Reich*, p. 130f.

59. Baker, *Invisible Eagle*, pp. 14–15.

NOTES TO CHAPTER 7

1. The life and works of Herman Wirth are summarized in Michael H. Kater, *Das "Ahnenerbe" der SS 1935–1945: Ein Beitrag zur Kulturpolitik des Dritten Reiches* (Stuttgart: Deutsche Verlags-Anstalt, 1974), pp. 11–16, 41–43.

2. Eberhard Baumann, *Herman Wirth: Verzeichnis der Schriften, Manuscripte und Vorträge* (Toppenstedt, Germany: Uwe Berg, 1994).

3. Claude Schweikhart [i.e., Erich Halik], "Um Krone und Gipfel der Welt," *Mensch und Schicksal* 6, No. 10 (1 August 1952), pp. 3–5.

4. Erich Halik, "Das Phänomen der 'Fliegenden Untertassen,'" *Mensch und Schicksal* 5, No. 19 (15 December 1951), pp. 4–7, No. 20 (1 January 1952) pp. 5–8.

5. Claude Schweikhart, "Verkündigung des Pol-Reiches," *Mensch und Schicksal* 8, No. 7 (15 June 1954), pp. 3–6. Erich Halik, "Keine Invasion aus dem Weltraum!" *Mensch und Schicksal* 8, No. 9 (15 July 1954), pp. 3–5.

6. Erich Halik's references to the "Black Sun" are discussed in Rudolf J. Mund, *Vom*

Mythos der schwarzen Sonne (Das andere Kreuz 2) (Vienna: Author, [1981]), pp. 8–10, 41–43.

7. Hanns Hörbiger and Philipp Fauth, *Glacial-Kosmogonie: Eine neue Entwickelungsgeschichte des Weltalls und des Sonnensystems* (Kaiserslautern, Germany: Hermann Kayser, 1913), esp. chapter 25.

8. For a recent study of Hörbiger's World Ice Theory, see Robert Bowen, *Universal Ice: Science and Ideology in the Nazi State* (London: Belhaven, 1993). Its political reception by the Nazis is also examined, pp. 130–52.

9. Kiß published the research results of his first expedition to the Andes in two articles: "Die Kordillerenkolonien der Atlantiden," *Schlüssel zum Weltgeschehen* (1931), No. 8/9, 256ff, and "Nordische Baukunst in Bolivien?" *Germanien* (May 1933), No. 5, 138ff. The latter journal subsequently became the official organ of the SS Ahnenerbe. Kiß's works in support of Hörbiger include *Die oft verlästerte, von vielen gepriesene, von manchen schon vernichtete, aber zäh und kampfbereit weiterlebende Welt-Eis-Lehre, allen Gelehrten und Ungelehrten . . . nach Hanns Hörbigers Lehre dargestellt* (Leipzig: Koehler und Amelang, 1933), and *Die kosmischen Ursachen der Völkerwanderungen* (Leipzig: Koehler und Amelang, 1934), while he interpreted the ruins at Lake Titicaca in *Das Sonnentor von Tihuanaku und Hörbigers Welteislehre* (Leipzig: Koehler und Amelang, 1937).

10. Edmund Kiß, *Das gläserne Meer: Ein Roman aus Urtagen* (Leipzig: Koehler und Amelang, 1930); *Frühling in Atlantis: Roman aus der Blütezeit des Reiches Atlantis* (Leipzig: Koehler und Amelang, 1933).

11. Edmund Kiß, *Die letzte Königin von Atlantis: Ein Roman aus der Zeit um 12000 vor Christi Geburt* (Leipzig: Koehler und Amelang, 1931); *Die Singschwäne aus Thule* (Leipzig: v. Hase & Koehler, 1939).

12. For details of Kiß's activities in the Ahnenerbe, see Kater, *Das "Ahnenerbe" der SS 1935–1945*, pp. 52, 97, 113, and Rüdiger Sünner, *Schwarze Sonne: Entfesselung und Mißbrauch der Mythen in Nationalsozialismus und rechter Esoterik* (Freiburg: Herder Verlag), pp. 46–47. The adoption of the World Ice Theory by the Ahnenerbe and the Pyrmont Protocol are documented in James Webb, *The Occult Establishment* (La Salle, Ill.: Open Court, 1976), pp. 327–30.

13. *Hitler's Table Talk, 1941–55,* edited by H. R. Trevor-Roper, 2d ed. (London: Weidenfeld and Nicolson, 1973), pp. 249, 324, 445.

14. Rudolf J. Mund, "Begegnung mit Edmund Kiss" (Das andere Kreuz) (Vienna: Author, [1983]).

15. Otto Rahn, *Kreuzzug gegen den Gral* (Freiburg: Urban-Verlag, 1933); *Luzifers Hofgesind: Eine Reise zu Europas guten Geistern* (Leipzig: Schwarzhäupter-Verlag, 1937). The fullest biography of Otto Rahn to date with extensive documentation is Hans-Jürgen Lange, "Der Gralssucher," in *Otto Rahn: Leben und Werk*, edited by Hans-Jürgen Lange (Engerda, Germany: Arun-Verlag, 1995), pp. 17–92. See also Christian Bernadac, *Le Mystère Otto Rahn: Du Catharisme au Nazisme* (Paris: France-Empire, 1978); Walter Birks and R. A. Gilbert, *The Treasure of Montségur: A Study of the Cathar Heresy and the Nature of the Cathar Secret* (Wellingborough, U.K.: Crucible, 1987), pp. 38–40; Nicholas Goodrick-Clarke, *The Occult Roots of Nazism: Secret Aryan Cults and Their Influence on*

Nazi Ideology: The Ariosophists of Austria and Germany 1890–1935, 2d ed. (New York: New York University Press, 1992), pp. 188–89. Howard A. Buechner, *Emerald Cup—Ark of Gold: The Quest of SS Lt. Otto Rahn of the Third Reich* (Metairie, La.: Thunderbird Press, 1991), is a fanciful work in the tradition of the "Nazi Mysteries."

16. For Lanz von Liebenfels and the Ordo Novi Templi, see Wilfried Daim, *Der Mann der Hitler die Ideen gab: Die sektierischen Grundlagen des Nationalsozialismus*, 2d ed. (Vienna: Hermann Böhlau, 1985), and Goodrick-Clarke, *The Occult Roots of Nazism*, esp. pp. 90–122.

17. Rudolf J. Mund, *Jörg Lanz v. Liebenfels und der Neue Templer Orden: Die Esoterik des Christentums* (Stuttgart: Rudolf Arnold Spieth, 1976).

18. Rudolf J. Mund, *Der Rasputin Himmlers: Die Wiligut-Saga* (Vienna: Volkstum-Verlag, 1982). The life and influence of Wiligut is also documented in Goodrick-Clarke, *The Occult Roots of Nazism*, pp. 177–91. Further documentation is offered by Hans-Jürgen Lange, *Weisthor: Karl-Maria Wiligut—Himmlers Rasputin und seine Erben* (Engerda: Arun-Verlag, 1998).

19. Mund, *Vom Mythos der Schwarzen Sonne*, pp. 12–30; Emil Rüdiger, *Die Kraft der zwei Sonnen* (Ingelheim, 1994).

20. For an account of Guido von List and the debt of Armanism to Theosophy, see Goodrick-Clarke, *The Occult Roots of Nazism*, pp. 49–55.

21. Helena Petrovna Blavatsky, *The Secret Doctrine*, 2 vols. (London: Theosophical Publishing Company, 1888), vol. 2, pp. 240–41.

22. Guido List, *Die Rita der Ario-Germanen* (Leipzig and Vienna: E. F. Steinacker, 1908), pp. 9–10; *Die Bilderschrift der Ario-Germanen (Ario-Germanische Hieroglyphik)* (Leipzig and Vienna: E. F. Steinacker, 1910), pp. 44–48.

23. Peryt Shou, *Das Mysterium der Zentralsonne* (Leipzig: Jaeger, 1910), pp. 7, 39; *Deutschlands Zukunft im Gesetz kosmologischer Entwicklung* (Berlin: Pyramidenverlag Dr Schwarz, 1923), pp. 269–76, 292ff.

24. Kurt P. Tauber, *Beyond Eagle and Swastika: German Nationalism since 1945*, 2 vols. (Middletown, Conn.: Wesleyan University Press, 1967), vol. 1, pp. 231, 578, 627f.

25. Wilhelm Landig, *Götzen gegen Thule: Ein Roman voller Wirklichkeiten* (Hanover: Hans Pfeiffer, 1971), pp. 137–38. The novel is admirably summarized and discussed in Joscelyn Godwin, *Arktos: The Polar Myth in Science, Symbolism, and Nazi Survival* (Grand Rapids, Mich.: Phanes, 1993), pp. 63–69.

26. Landig, *Götzen gegen Thule*, pp. 158–65.

27. Landig, *Götzen gegen Thule*, pp. 51–55, 472–75, 543–44.

28. Landig, *Götzen gegen Thule*, pp. 250–61 (p. 259).

29. Landig, *Götzen gegen Thule*, pp. 311–33 (p. 319).

30. Landig, *Götzen gegen Thule*, pp. 169–71.

31. Landig, *Götzen gegen Thule*, pp. 166, 367, 371, 472, 516. Cf. *Wolfszeit um Thule* (Vienna: Volkstum-Verlag, 1980), p. 459.

32. Landig, *Götzen gegen Thule*, pp. 471–72.

33. Landig, *Götzen gegen Thule*, p. 169.

34. Landig, *Götzen gegen Thule*, pp. 140, 516f.

35. Landig, *Götzen gegen Thule*, pp. 619–20.

36. Landig, *Götzen gegen Thule*, pp. 629–31.

37. Landig, *Götzen gegen Thule*, pp. 727–30, 734, 745–48.

38. Landig, *Wolfszeit um Thule*, pp. 40–42.

39. Landig, *Wolfszeit um Thule*, pp. 63–66, 134.

40. Landig, *Wolfszeit um Thule*, pp. 121–38.

41. Landig, *Wolfszeit um Thule*, pp. 167–68, 171–76, 186.

42. Landig, *Wolfszeit um Thule*, pp. 197–219.

43. Landig, *Wolfszeit um Thule*, pp. 354–55.

44. Landig, *Wolfszeit um Thule*, pp. 388–94.

45. Landig, *Wolfszeit um Thule*, pp. 470, 476.

46. Landig, *Rebellen für Thule* (Vienna: Volkstum-Verlag, 1991), p. 509.

47. Landig, *Rebellen für Thule*, pp. 569–70.

48. The ensuing Babylon-Bible debate aroused the Kaiser's strongest interest, whereupon Chamberlain published his own views. Geooffrey G. Field, *Evangelist of Race: The Germanic Vision of Houston Stewart Chamberlain* (New York: Columbia University Press, 1981), pp. 255–56.

49. Wilhelm Landig, *Rebellen für Thule*, pp. 517–27. Landig refers to the pioneering work of Peter Jensen, *Das Gilgamesch Epos* (Strasburg: K. J. Trübner, 1906).

50. Landig, *Wolfszeit um Thule*, pp. 31f, 41.

51. Landig, *Wolfszeit um Thule*, pp. 354–55.

52. Russell McCloud, *Die schwarze Sonne von Tashi Lhunpo* (Vilsbiburg, Germany: Arun-Verlag, 1991), pp. 35, 94.

53. The SS occupation and reconstruction of the Wewelsburg is fully documented in Karl Hüser, *Wewelsburg 1933–1945: Kult- und Terrorstätte der SS* (Paderborn, Germany: Verlag Bonifatius-Druckerei, 1982). Extensive pictorial illustration is provided by Stuart Russell and Jost W. Schneider, *Heinrich Himmlers Burg. Das weltanschauliche Zentrum der SS: Bildchronik der SS-Schule Haus Wewelsburg 1934–1945* (Landshut, Germany: RVG, 1989). Photographs of the sun wheel appear in ibid., pp. 81–82.

54. Dorothee Renner, *Die durchbrochenen Zierscheiben der Merowingerzeit* (Mainz: Röm-German. Zentralmuseum, 1970). Examples of symbols very similar to the Wewelsburg sun wheel occur in *Mannus* 28 (1936), 270; Walther Veeck, *Die Alemannen in Württemberg* (Berlin and Leipzig: DeGruyter, 1931); Hans Reinerth (ed.), *Die Vorgeschichte der deutschen Stämme*, 3 vols. (Berlin: Bibliographisches Institut, 1940), vol. 2, plate 219. References in Rüdiger Sünner, *Schwarze Sonne: Entfesselung und Mißbrauch der Mythen in Nationalsozialismus und rechter Esoterik* (Freiburg: Herder, 1999), pp. 148, 245 (note 426).

55. McCloud, *Die schwarze Sonne von Tashi Lhunpo*, pp. 156–58, 285–99.

56. Norbert Hess, *Die schwarze Sonne von Tashi Lhunpo. Das Drehbuch* (*Schatten der Macht: Polit-Thriller*) (Engerda, Germany: Arun-Verlag, 1995); "An interview with Kadmon (Allerseelen/"Aorta"), *The Nexus*, No. 2 (November 1995), pp. 1–6.

57. *Elemente*, No. 6 (Kassel, 1998), pp. 8, 22; *Sol Invictus: Schriftenreihe des Freundeskreises für Brauchtum und Kultur*, Folge 2, "*Mitternacht*" (*Texte zum Mythenkomplex*

Mitternachstberg—Schwarze Sonne—Lichtbringer) (Ilvesheim, Germany [1997]), back cover, both quoted in Sünner, *Schwarze Sonne*, p. 144.

58. Antony Parkin, "Wewelsburg—Himmler's Black Camelot," *The Flaming Sword*, No. 1 (January 1994), pp. 4–7; badge advertisement, *[The] Nexus*, No. 1 (August 1995), pp. 6–7.

59. *Schwarze Sonne: Mythologische Hintergründe des Nationalsozialismus*, directed by Rüdiger Sünner, produced by Elisabeth Müller Filmproduktion, Düsseldorf, 1996.

NOTES TO CHAPTER 8

1. John and Anne Spencer, *Fifty Years of UFOs: From Distant Sightings to Close Encounters* (London: Boxtree, 1997), pp. 12–17. Kenneth Arnold's original report to the military authorities is published in *UFOs 1947–1997: From Arnold to the Abductees: Fifty Years of Flying Saucers* (London: John Brown, 1997), pp. 28–34. Cf. Kenneth Arnold and Ray Palmer, *The Coming of the Saucers* (Amherst, Wis.: Author, 1952).

2. Spencer, *Fifty Years of UFOs*, pp. 30–31.

3. Desmond Leslie and George Adamski, *Flying Saucers Have Landed* (London: Neville Spearman, 1953).

4. Donald M. McKale, *Hitler: The Survival Myth* (New York: Stein and Day, 1981), pp. 49–58. It seems highly likely that Stalin wanted a "live" Hitler, not only to justify Soviet power in Europe to counter the menace of a Nazi revival, but also to embarrass the Western Allies with the suggestion that Hitler had found sanctuary in their sphere of influence.

5. McKale, *Hitler*, pp. 62–64.

6. McKale, *Hitler*, pp. 137–39.

7. Lee Van Atta, *El Mercurio*, 5 March 1947.

8. Ladislao Szabó, *Hitler esta vivo* (Buenos Aries: El Tabano, 1947), pp. 161–63. The French magazine *Bonjour*, the Montevideo paper *El Dia* and the sensational U.S. magazine *The National Police Gazette* all carried similar stories; McKale, *Hitler*, pp. 138, 222–23, notes 4, 6.

9. "Untertassen—sie fliegen aber doch," *Der Spiegel* (30 March 1950), pp. 33–35.

10. "Fliegende Untertassen—eine deutsche Erfindung," *Die 7 Tage: Illustrierte Wochenschrift aus dem Zeitgeschehen*, No. 26 (27 June 1952), p. 1; "Fliegende Untertasse=Deutsche Flugkreisel?" *Das Ufer: Die Farb-Illustrierte*, No. 18 (1 September 1952).

11. "Erste 'Flugscheibe' flog 1945 in Prag," *Welt am Sonntag* (25 April 1953), pp. 1, 14.

12. Erich Halik, "Keine Invasion aus dem Weltraum!" *Mensch und Schicksal* 8, No. 9 (15 July 1954), pp. 3–5.

13. Edgar Sievers, *Flying Saucers über Südafrika* (Pretoria, South Africa: Sagittarius, 1955), pp. 74–83; "Die UFOs—eine deutsche Erfindung," *Das neue Zeitalter* (5 October 1957); Rudolf Lusar, "Fliegende Untertassen: Eine deutsche Erfindung—von Deutschen erprobt—in West und Ost weiterentwickelt," *Das neue Zeitalter*, No. 9 (1958).

14. Rudolf Lusar, *German Secret Weapons of the Second World War and Their*

Further Development (London: Neville Spearman, 1959), pp. 165–66; also the German edition *Die deutschen Waffen und Geheimwaffen des 2. Weltkrieges und ihre Weiterentwicklung* (Munich: J. F. Lehmann, 1966).

15. Renato Vesco, *Intercept UFO* (New York: Pinnacle, 1974), pp. 134–62. First published as *Intercettateli Senza Sparare* (Milan: E. Mursia, 1968).

16. Vesco, *Intercept UFO*, pp. 90–110. The wartime underground factories are extensively documented in Harald Fäth, *1945—Thüringens Manhattan Projekt: Auf Spurensuche nach der verlorenen V-Waffenfabrik in Deutschlands Untergrund* (Suhl, Germany: CTT-Verlag, 1998), and Ulrich Brenzel, *Hitlers Geheimobjekte in Thüringen* (Suhl, Germany: Heinrich Jung, 1999).

17. Michael X. [Barton], *We Want You: Is Hitler Alive?* (Clarksburg, W.Va.: Saucerian Books, 1969), pp. 10–12, 13–16.

18. Michael X. Barton, *The German Saucer Story* (Los Angeles: Futura Press, 1968), pp. 32–49, 53. Barton received the designs of two Schriever-Habermohl flying disks and the larger Bellonzo-Schriever-Miethe flying disk from a German engineer, Hermann Klaas, who had allegedly tested disk models as early as 1941. The illustrations and captions had already been published in an interview with Hermann Klaas by Jan Holger, "UFOs gibt es nicht! Wohl aber: Flugscheiben am laufenden Band!" *Das neue Zeitalter*, No. 34 (20 August 1966), p. 4.

19. Wilhelm Landig, *Götzen gegen Thule* (Hanover: Hans Pfeiffer, 1971), pp. 110, 114–26, 131–33, 141.

20. Landig, *Götzen gegen Thule*, pp. 190–200.

21. Further biographical details of Ernst Zündel and his several Holocaust denial trials may be found in Michael A. Hoffman II, *The Great Holocaust Trial* (Torrance, Calif.: Institute for Historical Review, 1985); Robert Lenski, *The Holocaust on Trial: The Case of Ernst Zundel* (Decatur, Ala.: Reporter Press, 1989).

22. Erich von Däniken, *Chariots of the Gods? Unsolved Mysteries of the Past* (London: Souvenir, 1969); idem, *Return to the Stars: Evidence for the Impossible* (London: Souvenir, 1970); idem, *The Gold of the Gods* (London: Souvenir, 1973); idem, *In Search of Ancient Gods: My Pictorial Evidence for the Impossible* (London: Souvenir, 1973); W. Raymond Drake, *Spacemen in the Ancient East* (London: Neville Spearman, 1968); idem, *Gods and Spacemen in the Ancient West* (London: Sphere, 1974); idem, *Gods and Spacemen in Ancient Israel* (London: Sphere, 1976); Robert Charroux, *Legacy of the Gods* (London: Sphere, 1979) [first published as *Le livre des secrets trahis* (Paris: Laffont, 1965)]; idem, *Masters of the World* (London: Sphere, 1979) [first published as *Le livre des maîtres de monde* (Paris: Laffont, 1967)]; idem, *The Mysterious Unknown* (London: Neville Spearman, 1972) [first published as *Le livre du mystérieux inconnu* (Paris: Laffont, 1969)]; idem, *Lost Worlds: Scientific Secrets of the Ancients* (London: Souvenir, 1973) [first published as *Le livre des mondes oubliés* (Paris: Laffont, 1971)]; idem, *The Mysterious Past* (London: Futura, 1974) [first published as *Le livre du passé mystériux* (Paris: Laffont, 1973)]. The books of Robert Charroux were also an important source for Miguel Serrano (see chapter 9).

23. John A. Saliba, "Religious Dimensions of UFO Phenomena," and J. Gordon

Melton and George M. Eberhart, "The Flying Saucer Contactee Movement, 1950–1994: A Bibliography," in *The Gods Have Landed: New Religions from Other Worlds*, edited by James R. Lewis (Albany: State University of New York Press, 1995), pp. 15–64, 251–332.

24. Willibald Mattern, *UFOs: Unbekanntes Flugobjekt? Letzte Geheimwaffe des Dritten Reiches* (Toronto: Samisdat, [1974]), pp. 23–25, 43–47; Willibald Mattern and Christof Friedrich [i.e., Ernst Zündel], *UFOs: Nazi Secret Weapon?* (Toronto: Samisdat, [1975]), p. 15, 29, 52–61.

25. Mattern, *UFOs: Unbekanntes Flugobjekt?*, pp. 23–24, 50–51, 82–88; Willibald Mattern and Christof Friedrich, *UFOs: Nazi Secret Weapon?*, pp. 42, 48, 66–76.

26. A full account and photographs of the German Antarctic Expedition of 1938–39 was published by Ernst Hermann, *Deutsche Forscher im Südpolarmeer: Bericht von der Deutschen Antarktischen Expedition 1938–1939* (Berlin: Safari-Verlag, 1941). A reprint of the report is included in Ernst Zündel, *Hitler am Südpol?* (Toronto: Samisdat, [1979]), pp. 66–159. A brief account also appeared in Mattern and Friedrich, *UFOs: Nazi Secret Weapon?*, pp. 87–92.

27. Ernst Zündel, *Hitler am Südpol?* pp. 160–74; a map of Neuschwabenland showing detailed features, pp. 62–63. Numerous illustrations of Nazi flying saucers, including the Schauberger, Schriever and Miethe disks, appear in Mattern and Friedrich, *UFOs: Nazi Secret Weapon?* pp. 116–29.

28. Mattern and Friedrich, *UFOs: Nazi Secret Weapon?* pp. 96.

29. Mattern, *UFOs: Unbekanntes Flugobjekt?* pp. 110–20; Mattern and Friedrich, *UFOs: Nazi Secret Weapon?* pp. 95–100. Lee Van Atta quoted Byrd to the effect that "the United States must take defensive measures against the possibility of invasion by hostile aircraft coming from the polar region." He also spoke of "a future war in which the United States could be attacked by pilots capable of flying from one pole to the other"; *El Mercurio*, 5 March 1947.

30. Mattern, *UFOs: Unbekanntes Flugobjekt?* pp. 148–49.

31. Mattern and Friedrich, *UFOs: Nazi Secret Weapon?* pp. 143–46. Schmidt's alien abduction experience took place in Kearney, Nebraska, in November 1957. Reinhold O. Schmidt, *The Kearney Incident and to the Arctic Circle in a Spacecraft* (Kearney: Author, 1959).

32. Wilhelm Landig, *Wolfszeit um Thule* (Vienna: Volkstum-Verlag, 1980), pp. 21–22, 26–29, 32–33, 37, 42.

33. Landig, *Wolfszeit um Thule*, pp. 51–53.

34. Landig, *Wolfszeit um Thule*, pp. 61–63.

35. Landig, *Wolfszeit um Thule*, pp. 77–80, 93, 173.

36. Landig, *Wolfszeit um Thule*, pp. 167–68, 171–76, 247, 258, 268–70.

37. Landig, *Wolfszeit um Thule*, pp. 168, 187–89.

38. Landig, *Wolfszeit um Thule*, pp. 176, 191–96. The appendix includes detailed maps of Neuschwabenland and also the most detailed technical drawings to date of the V-7 German flying saucer; ibid., pp. 486–93.

39. See, only for example, the comprehensive study by Jacques Vallee, *Anatomy of a Phenomenon* (Chicago: Henry Regnery, 1965), and list of UFO landings in Jacques

Vallee, *Passport to Magonia: On UFOs, Folklore, and Parallel Worlds* (Chicago: Henry Regnery, 1969).

40. Harbinson's inspiration was a one-off newsletter *Brisant* distributed at a scientic exhibition at Hanover. Its articles used material from Zündel's books presented in a more scientific vein. "Neu Schwabenland" and "UFOs kommen nicht aus dem All!" *Brisant*, No. 5 (1978), pp. 6–7, 9–11. The second article identified three principal UFO world flight routes, all emanating from Antarctica, on the basis of a quarter of a million sightings over the preceding thirty years. This article also included the most detailed technical drawing of a German flying saucer yet published, later used by Landig in *Wolfszeit um Thule* (1980), pp. 492–93.

41. W. A. Harbinson, *Genesis* (London: Corgi, 1980), pp. 57–63, 114–19, 183–89, 257–64, 332–38, 395–402, 460–67, 521–27. Harbinson eventually completed a quintet of "Projekt Saucer" novels: *Inception* (1991), *Phoenix* (1995), *Millennium* (1995) and *Resurrection* (1999). He has also published a non-fiction study, *Projekt UFO: The Case for Man-Made Flying Saucers* (London: Boxtree, 1995).

42. D. H. Haarmann, *Geheime Wunderwaffen: Zerrbild zwischen Täuschung und Tatsachen* (Wetter, Germany: Hugin, 1983), pp. 15–30.

43. D. H. Haarmann, *Geheime Wunderwaffen: Und sie fliegen doch!* (Wetter, Germany: Hugin, 1983), pp. 23–29, 46–48.

44. D. H. Haarmann, *Geheime Wunderwaffen: Über den Krieg hinaus!* (Wetter, Germany: Hugin, 1985), pp. 46–57, 63f.

45. O. Bergmann, *Deutsche Flugscheiben und U-Boote überwachen die Weltmeere*, 2 vols. (Wetter, Germany: Hugin, 1988–89), vol. 2, p. 203.

46. Jürgen-Ratthofer and Ralf Ettl, *Das Vril-Projekt* (Ardagger: Michael Dämbock, 1992), pp. 10–11.

47. Jürgen-Ratthofer and Ettl, *Das Vril-Projekt*, pp. 12–13, 16–23.

48. Peter Bahn and Heiner Gehring, *Der Vril-Mythos: Eine geheimnisvolle Energieform in Esoterik, Technik und Therapie* (Düsseldorf: Omega-Verlag, 1997), pp. 91–111. The overlap between Ariosophy and the esoteric "alternative energy" researches of Karl Schappeller and Frenzolf Schmid is documented in the "Totgeschwiegene Forscher" issue of *Ariosophie: Zeitschrift für Geistes- und Wissenschaftsreform* 5, No. 9/10 (1930), pp. 203–13. Schmid also linked the ancient wisdom of Atlantis to futuristic energy. Herbert Reichstein, the publisher of this magazine, was the chief promoter of Ariosophy in the interwar period for Lanz von Liebenfels's group. Nicholas Goodrick-Clarke, *The Occult Roots of Nazism: Secret Aryan Cults and Their Influence on Nazi Ideology: The Ariosophists of Austria and Germany 1890–1935* (New York: New York University Press, 1992), pp. 164–76.

49. Jürgen-Ratthofer and Ettl, *Das Vril-Projekt*, pp. 26, 69. The German scholar Peter Jensen had already identified Taurus and Aldebaran as important reference points in Babylonian cosmology, *Das Gilgamesch Epos* (Strasburg: K. G. Trübner, 1906).

50. Jürgen-Ratthofer and Ettl, *Das Vril-Projekt*, p. 69.

51. Jürgen-Ratthofer and Ettl, *Das Vril-Projekt*, pp. 27–31.

52. These drawings were first published in O. Bergmann, *Deutsche Flugscheiben*

und U-Boote überwachen die Weltmeere, vol. 1, pp. 62–65. The drawings reached a mass audience in Jan van Helsing, *Geheimgesellschaften und ihre Macht im 20. Jahrhundert* (Meppen, Germany: Ewertverlag, 1993), which had sold over 100,000 copies by 1998.

53. Jürgen-Ratthofer and Ettl, *Das Vril-Projekt*, pp. 33–60. The close resemblance between the Haunebu II and Adamski's saucer photograph was also highlighted in van Helsing, *Geheimgesellschaften und ihre Macht*, p. 144.

54. Jürgen-Ratthofer and Ettl, *Das Vril-Projekt*, pp. 79–82.

55. Jürgen-Ratthofer and Ettl, *Das Vril-Projekt*, pp. 85–96, 101–6; Norbert Jürgen-Ratthofer, *Demnächst "Kampf um die Erde"?!* (Vienna: Tempelhof, n.d.), pp. 9–16.

56. *UFO—Das Dritte Reich schlägt zurück?* (video), written by Ralf Ettl and Norbert Jürgen-Ratthofer, produced by Abraxas, Vienna, copyright Tempelhofgesellschaft, Vienna, c. 1990.

57. *UFO—Geheimnisse des Dritten Reichs* (video), written by Ralf Ettl and Norbert Jürgen-Ratthofer, produced by Royal Atlantis Film, Kirchheim, c. 1992.

58. Norbert Jürgen-Ratthofer, *Lichtreiche auf Erden* (Siersheim: Author, [1997], pp. 14f, 28, 36–38. Further publications include *Das Vril-Projekt 2* (Ardagger: Michael Dämbock, 1999), and *Der Z-Plan* (Ardagger: Michael Dämbock, 1999), a four-volume novel about "a struggle with weapons and magic in the light of the Black Sun."

59. Jan van Helsing, *Geheimgesellschaften und ihre Macht im 20. Jahrhundert oder wie man die Welt nicht regiert: Ein Wegweiser durch die Verstrickungen von Logentum mit Hochfinanz und Politik. Trilaterale Kommission, Bilderberger, CFR, UNO* (Meppen, Germany: Ewertverlag, 1993), pp. 118–47.

60. Jan van Helsing, *Unternehmen Aldebaran: Kontakte mit Menschen aus einem anderen Sonnensystem* (Gran Canaria: Ewertverlag, 1997), pp. 12, 39ff, 42f.

61. van Helsing, *Unternehmen Aldebaran*, pp. 272–76.

62. Jim Keith, *Casebook on Alternative 3: UFOs, Secret Societies and World Control* (Lilburn, Ga.: IllumiNet Press, 1994), pp. 148–53.

63. *Introduction to Secret German Flying Discs of World War Two* (Gorman, Calif.: German Research Project, [1997]), p. 28. Besides photocopies of out-of-print books and German journal articles, the German Research Project has published a dossier of foreign-language articles in W. A. Harbinson's *Genesis* bibliography and *The Last Battalion and German Arctic, Antarctic and Andean Bases* (Gorman, Calif.: German Research Project, 1997). See also interview with Henry Stevens: D. Guide, "Saucer Kraut: Inside the German Research Project," *Paranoia: The Conspiracy Reader*, No. 15 (Winter 1996–97), pp. 40–45.

64. Tim Hepple, *At War with Society: The Exclusive Story of a Searchlight Mole Inside Britain's Far Right* (London: Searchlight Magazine, 1993), pp. 1–18.

65. Larry O'Hara and Steve Booth, *At War with the Universe: The British X-Files. How and Why Nazi Thug and State Asset Tim Hepple/Matthews Has Infiltrated Ufology* (London: Notes from the Borderland, 1999), pp. 28–33, 40–50.

66. Tim Matthews, *UFO Revelation: The Secret Technology Exposed?* (London: Cassel, 1999), pp. 15–20, 21–28, 73–81.

67. Carl Gustav Jung, "Flying Saucers: A Modern Myth of Things Seen in the Skies," in *Civilization in Transition*, 2d ed. (London: Routledge and Kegan Paul, 1970), pp. 307–433 (pp. 387, 423f). First published as *Ein moderner Mythus: Von Dingen, die am Himmel gesehen werden* (Zurich and Stuttgart: Rascher, 1958).

68. Caroline Tisdall and Angelo Bozzola, *Futurism* (London: Thames and Hudson, 1977), p. 157. The flying saucer has been described as "the perfect expression of Fascist ideals: a glittering example of Aryan supremacy and aggressive masculinity" in David Sivier, "Gazurmah's Sons: The Psychopathology of the Nazi Saucer Myth," *Magonia*, No. 63 (May 1998), pp. 11–14 (p. 14).

69. Karl-Heinz Bohrer, *Die Ästhetik des Schreckens: Die pessimistische Romantik und Ernst Jüngers Frühwerk* (Munich: Hanser, 1978).

NOTES TO CHAPTER 9

1. Friedrich Paul Heller and Anton Maegerle, *Thule: Vom völkischen Okkultismus bis zur Neuen Rechten* (Stuttgart: Schmetterling Verlag, 1995), pp. 89–92.

2. Biographical details are drawn from the four-volume autobiography. Miguel Serrano, *Memorias de Él y Yo*: vol. 1, *Aparición del "Yo"—Alejamiento de "Él"* (Santiago: La Nueva Edad, 1996); vol. 2, *Adolf Hitler y la Gran Guerra* (Santiago: La Nueva Edad, 1997); vol. 3, *Misión en los Transhimalaya* (Santiago: La Nueva Edad, 1998); vol. 4, *El Regreso* (Santiago: La Nueva Edad, 1999).

3. Miguel Serrano, *Adolf Hitler, el Último Avatāra* (Santiago: La Nueva Edad, [1984]), pp. 24–27.

4. The political history of this period and the background of the Movimento Nacional Socialista in Chile is documented in Robert J. Alexander, *The Tragedy of Chile* (Westport, Conn.: Greenwood Press, 1978).

5. Serrano, *Adolf Hitler*, pp. 29–32, 35–50, 53.

6. Serrano, *Adolf Hitler*, pp. 58–60, 61–65.

7. Serrano, *Adolf Hitler*, pp. 76–79.

8. Serrano, *Adolf Hitler*, pp. 107–8, 111–18, 124–25. The order's secret Himalayan headquarters within Mount Kailas, its leadership of seventy-two Brahmans and an exclusive membership of 201 members suggest the influence of Saint-Yves d'Alveydre, *La Mission de l'Inde en Europe* (1910), which described a secret kingdom of Agartha, ruled over by exalted Brahmans, which was transferred underground at the start of the Kali Yuga around 3200 B.C. Joscelyn Godwin, "Saint-Yves d'Alveydre and the Agarthian Connection," *The Hermetic Journal* 32 (Summer 1986), pp. 24–34, 33 (Autumn 1986), pp. 31–38. Serrano lists four titles by Saint-Yves d'Alveydre, including *La Mission de l'Inde* in the bibliography of *El Cordón Dorado*, p. 242. F. K. received his own initiation in Paris, which again implies a source of his teachings in the French esoteric underground around the Theosophists or René Guénon.

9. Serrano, *Adolf Hitler*, p. 119; Miguel Serrano, *El Cordón Dorado: Hitlerismo Esotérico*, 3d ed. (Bogota: Editorial Solar, 1985), pp. 18, 20, 22, 27.

10. Serrano, *Adolf Hitler*, pp. 149–51.

11. Serrano, *El Cordón Dorado*, pp. 37–40. A veiled reference to the purpose of his Antarctic voyage also appeared in his book, *Ni por Mar ni por Tierra* (Santiago: Nascimento, 1950), p. 88.

12. Serrano, *Adolf Hitler*, pp. 147, 384.

13. Serrano, *The Serpent of Paradise: The Story of an Indian Pilgrimage*, 2d ed. (London: Routledge and Kegan Paul, 1974), passim; *Adolf Hitler*, p. 156.

14. *Nos* contains many cryptic references to his Gnostic cosmology, including the extraterrestrial origin of the "solar" Hyperborean race, the white gods of South America, the Black Sun, and wars between those from different worlds. Miguel Serrano, *Nos: Book of the Resurrection* (London: Routledge and Kegan Paul, 1984), pp. 2–5, 26–27, 60–61.

15. C. G. Jung, *Man and His Symbols* (London: Aldus, 1964), pp. 67–69; C. G. Jung, *Die Psychologie der unbewussten Prozesse* (Zurich: Rascher & Cie, 1917), p. 117. In this latter work, Jung used the term "dominants," before redefining them as "archetypes" in "Instinct and the Unconscious," *British Journal of Psychology* 10 (1919), 15–26.

16. Carl Gustav Jung, "Wotan," *Neue Schweizer Rundschau* 3 (March 1936), pp. 657–69. An English translation is published in *Civilization in Transition* (*The Collected Works of C. G. Jung*, vol. 10), translated by R. F. C. Hull, 2d ed. (London: Routledge and Kegan Paul, 1970), pp. 179–93.

17. Quoted in Serrano, *Adolf Hitler*, pp. 119–23. These Jung interviews on Hitler and the other European dictators were originally published in *The Observer* (London), 18 October 1936; *Hearst's International-Cosmopolitan* (New York), January 1939; and *The Psychologist* (London), May 1939. Slightly edited versions were republished as "The Psychology of Dictatorship," "Diagnosing the Dictators" and "Jung Diagnoses the Dictators," in *C. G. Jung Speaking: Interviews and Encounters*, edited by William McGuire and R. F. C. Hull (London: Thames and Hudson, 1978), pp. 91–93, 115–35, 136–40.

18. Serrano, *El Cordón Dorado*, p. 97f; idem, *Adolf Hitler*, pp. 94–96. However, Richard Noll has controversially argued that the early Jung, influenced by Theosophy, solar mysticism and *völkisch* nationalism, personally encountered the archetypes as Aryan-Mithraic and Gnostic gods in his own unconscious. Richard Noll, *The Aryan Christ: The Secret Life of Carl Gustav Jung* (London: Macmillan, 1997), pp. 120–22, 158–60. The development of Jung's early ideas on the collective unconscious and the archetypes are traced in Richard Noll, *The Jung Cult: Origins of a Charismatic Movement* (Princeton, N.J.: Princeton University Press, 1994), pp. 218–33, 269–73.

19. Serrano, *Adolf Hitler*, pp. 33f, 95, 122–24, 130–32, 232. Serrano paid frequent tribute to Savitri Devi and has twice published an account of her own visit to the Externsteine and ritual death and reawakening in the Tomb Rock. Serrano, *Adolf Hitler*, pp. 481, 497f, 620. He has described her "as the greatest fighter after Adolf Hitler, Rudolf Hess and Josef Goebbels . . . the first to discover the secret and spiritual power behind Hitlerism." He noted her belief in the incompatibility of Nazism and Christianity, predicting that posterity would revere her as a pioneer of Esoteric Hitlerism and "the priestess of Odin." "Miguel Serrano ΣΤΟ ΑΝΤΙΔΟΤΟ," ΤΟ ΑΝΤΙΔΟΤΟ, No. 29, pp. 23–31. Savitri Devi's visit to the Externsteine is also described and illustrated in Miguel Serrano, *La*

Resurrección del Heroe (Santiago: Author, 1986), p. 79. The latter book is dedicated to Savitri Devi with a portrait and verse.

20. Serrano, *Adolf Hitler*, pp. 97, 239, 255.

21. Serrano, *Adolf Hitler*, pp. 182–87, 260, 192, 197f.

22. Serrano, *Adolf Hitler*, p. 256.

23. Serrano, *Adolf Hitler*, pp. 98, 183.

24. Serrano, *Adolf Hitler*, pp. 116, 150, 257.

25. Serrano, *Adolf Hitler*, pp. 197–98.

26. Serrano, *Adolf Hitler*, p. 265.

27. Serrano, *Adolf Hitler*, p. 116.

28. Serrano's account of extraterrestrial visitations of semi-divine ancestors, the Hyperborean race and its settlement of the polar region and subsequent migrations owe a certain debt to French writer Robert Charroux (b. 1909), who had published a number of popular works on these subjects from the early 1960s onwards. In *Le Livre des secrets trahis* (1964) and *Le Livre des maîtres du monde* (1967), Charroux expands on the extraterrestrial origin of the Hyperboreans, their eternal emnity with the Jews, the importance of Venus and the Black Sun. With an evident debt to Louis Pauwels and Jacques Bergier, *Le matin des magiciens* (1960) and Pierre Mariel, *L'Europe païenne du vingtième siècle* (1964), Charroux also speculates on the Thule Society and Nazi initiates. In the bibliography of *El Cordón Dorado*, Serrano lists many books of this "Nazi Mysteries" genre that clearly inspired the Hitler Trilogy during his Swiss exile in the 1970s.

29. Serrano, *Adolf Hitler*, pp. 185–87.

30. Serrano, *El Cordón Dorado*, pp. 53–57, 242. Serrano is strongly influenced by the works of the SS historian Otto Rahn (1904–39), who believed the troubadour and *Minnesang* traditions, the Cathar heresy and legends of the Grail in the Languedoc were a Gnostic religion of Visigothic origin. The Cathars were suppressed by the Catholic church in the Albigensian crusade, culminating in the destruction of their stronghold at Montségur in 1244. Serrano asserts that Rahn searched for the Grail, the Cathar treasure, in the caves of Sabarthés nearby, and that the SS later located it and brought it to Hitler's "Grail Castle" in Berchtesgaden; *Adolf Hitler*, p. 290. Cf. "Entrevue avec Saint-Loup," *Le Nouveau Planète* (Paris), No. 9 (July 1969), cit. in *El Cordón Dorado*, p. 242.

31. Serrano, *El Cordón Dorado*, p. 139.

32. Serrano, *Adolf Hitler*, pp. 92f.

33. Serrano, *El Cordón Dorado*, pp. 128–32; idem, *Adolf Hitler*, p. 88.

34. Serrano, *El Cordón Dorado*, p. 138f; *Adolf Hitler*, pp. 102.

35. Serrano, *El Cordón Dorado*, p. 133.

36. Serrano, *Adolf Hitler*, p. 290.

37. Serrano, *Adolf Hitler*, pp. 309–18.

38. Serrano, *Adolf Hitler*, pp. 291–93, 299–300, 342–49, 382f, 402–4. For his account of pre-Columbian immigration to the Americas, Serrano is indebted to the French anthropologist Jacques de Mahieu, who lived in Argentina. The De Mahieu titles include *Le grand voyage du Dieu-Soleil* (Paris: Lattes, 1971); *L'agonie du Dieu-Soleil: Les Vikings en Amérique du Sud* (Paris: Laffont, 1974); *Les Templiers en Amérique* (Paris: Laffont, 1981).

39. Serrano, *Adolf Hitler*, p. 20; idem, *El Cordón Dorado*, p. 96.

40. Jacques de Mahieu, *Des Sonnengottes grosse Reise: Die Wikinger in Mexiko und Peru 967–1532* (Tübingen: Grabert, 1975), pp. 86–106.

41. Jacques de Mahieu, *Des Sonnengottes heilige Steine: Die Wikinger in Brasilien* (Tübingen: Grabert, 1975), pp. 76–85 and passim.

42. Serrano, *Adolf Hitler*, pp. 305, 308f.

43. Serrano, *Adolf Hitler*, pp. 336–42.

44. Serrano, *Adolf Hitler*, p. 340.

45. The sources, motivation, reception and influence of the *Protocols* have been definitively documented in Norman Cohn, *Warrant for Genocide: The Myth of the Jewish World-Conspiracy and the Protocols of the Elders of Zion* (London: Eyre and Spottiswoode, 1967).

46. Serrano, *Adolf Hitler*, pp. 76–81.

47. Serrano, *El Cordón Dorado*, plates xl–xliv.

48. Serrano, *Adolf Hitler*, p. 82; Norman Cohn, *Warrant for Genocide*, p. 70.

49. Serrano, *Adolf Hitler*, p. 327f.

50. Sir John Retcliffe [i.e., Hermann Goedsche], *Biarritz* (Berlin, 1868), vol. 1, pp. 162–93. Quoted in Miguel Serrano, *Adolf Hitler*, pp. 329–35.

51. Cohn, *Warrant for Genocide*, p. 36.

52. Cohn, *Warrant for Genocide*, pp. 33–40, 269–74.

53. The discovery of the *Protocols'* close similarity to Joly's *Dialogue aux Enfers* was first made in 1921. Cohn, *Warrant for Genocide*, pp. 71–76. Serrano, *Adolf Hitler*, pp. 335–36.

54. Serrano, *Adolf Hitler*, pp. 71–74, 93–96. Serrano's whole philosophy of Hyperborean origin and anti-modernity has many Evolian characteristics. However, he criticized Evola as an old-style traditionalist who wanted to restore degenerate aristocratic elites. At their meeting, Evola denied he was a fascist or Hitlerist, but saw Metternich as a conservative ideal, a far cry from Serrano's cult of Hitler and magical Manichaeism.

55. Serrano, *El Cordón Dorado*, pp. 165–69, 223–24.

56. Serrano, *Adolf Hitler*, p. 95.

57. Serrano, *Adolf Hitler*, p. 238.

58. Serrano, *Adolf Hitler*, pp. 602, 615.

59. Serrano, *Adolf Hitler*, pp. 489–96, 502–3, 536–37, 587; *El Cordón Dorado*, pp. 204–5.

60. Serrano, *Adolf Hitler*, pp. 145–46.

61. Serrano, *Adolf Hitler*, pp. 210, 243, 254, 281.

62. Serrano, *Adolf Hitler*, pp. 200, 238.

63. Serrano, *Adolf Hitler*, pp. 498–503, 604–5.

64. Javier Nicolás, "Miguel Serrano: Una visión mágica del NS," *Cedade* (Barcelona), July–August 1985, pp. 28–33.

65. *La Segunda* (Santiago de Chile), 18 May 1984, pp. 14–15.

66. Miguel Serrano, *Nacionalsocialismo, Unica Solución para los Países de América del Sur* (Santiago: Alfabeta, 1986); 2d ed. (Bogota: Editorial Solar, 1987).

67. "Miguel Serrano ΣΤΟ ΑΝΤΙΔΟΤΟ," ΤΟ ΑΝΤΙΔΟΤΟ, No. 29, pp. 23–31. The ΤΟ ΑΝΤΙΔΟΤΟ interview was reprinted in *The Flaming Sword* (Wellington, New Zealand), No. 3 (August 1994), pp. 5–9. A further interview has been published as "Miguel Serrano: 'Esoteric Hitlerist,'" *The Flaming Sword*, No. 4 (November 1994), pp. 4–8, and No. 5 (February 1995), pp. 4–10. The latter interview was reprinted as a booklet in 1995.

68. Miguel Serrano, *Imitacion de la Verdad: La ciberpolitica. Internet, realidad virtual, telepresencia* (Santiago: Author, 1995).

NOTES TO CHAPTER 10

1. *White Noise: Inside the International Nazi Skinhead Scene*, edited by Nick Lowles and Steve Silver (London: Searchlight, 1998), pp. 1–8.

2. *Searchlight*, No. 144 (June 1987), p. 3; *Searchlight*, No. 151 (January 1988), p. 14; *Searchlight*, No. 152 (February 1988), p. 3.

3. Lyrics from the records Skrewdriver, *Freedom? What Freedom?* (Rock-A-Rama Records: Cologne, [1990]), and Ian Stuart, *Patriotic Ballads II* (Rock-A-Rama Records: Cologne, [1992]).

4. *White Noise*, edited by Nick Lowles and Steve Silver, pp. 28–30.

5. "Shut down the peddlers of hate," *Searchlight*, No. 256 (October 1996), pp. 7–18 (p. 10).

6. *Searchlight*, No. 256 (October 1996), p. 13.

7. Quoted in *Der Spiegel*, 6 April 1992, p. 29.

8. Christopher T. Husbands, "Militant Neo-Nazism in the Federal Republic of Germany in the 1990s," in *The Far Right in Western and Eastern Europe*, edited by Luciano Cheles, Ronnie Ferguson and Michalina Vaughan, 2d ed. (London and New York: Longman, 1995), pp. 327–53 (pp. 343–45).

9. Bundesamt für Verfassungsschutz, *Annual Reports 1991, 1992, 1993*, quoted in Husbands, "Militant Neo-Nazism," p. 331.

10. Husbands, "Militant Neo-Nazism," pp. 329, 343.

11. "'Die Seele des Volkes verbogen,'" *Der Spiegel*, 30 November 1992, pp. 14–25.

12. "Bestie aus deutschem Blut" [Die Nazi-Kids: Was Kinder in den Terror treibt], *Der Spiegel*, 7 December 1992, pp. 22–33.

13. *Searchlight*, No. 152 (February 1988), p. 5; *Searchlight*, No. 189 (March 1991), pp. 13–14.

14. *Freedom Videos*, List No. 9, [1996], pp. 16–17.

15. *Searchlight*, No. 256 (October 1996), p. 12.

16. *Searchlight*, No. 256 (October 1996), p. 12.

17. *Freedom Videos*, p. 16.

18. *Young Nazi Killers: The Rising Skinhead Danger* (Anti-Defamation League Special Report, 1993), pp. 1, 3.

19. "An Interview with George Eric Hawthorne," *The Nexus*, No. 3 (March 1996), pp. 2–7; George Eric Hawthorne, "Reasons for Hope," *Resistance*, No. 7 (Summer 1996), p. 4.

20. Thomas Jackson, "What Is Racism?" and Robert Thompson, "Genocide against the White Race," *Resistance*, No. 5 (Fall 1995), pp. 6–8, 42–44; David Duke, "Racial Realities: My India Odyssey," *Resistance*, No. 5 (Fall 1995), pp. 20–24; Sleipner, "Spotlight on Sweden," *Resistance*, No. 2 (Summer 1994), p. 22; Frank Silva, "Hail the Order," *Resistance*, No. 7 (Summer 1996), pp. 34–37.

21. George Eric Hawthorne, "A Cultural Imperative," *Resistance*, No. 5 (Fall 1995), p. 4; "RAHOWA: resurrecting the spirit of ancient Europe," *Resistance*, No. 5 (Fall 1995), pp. 26–27, 36.

22. Joseph Carl, "Jack London: An American Racialist," *Resistance*, No. 6 (Spring 1996), pp. 20–24; Ron McVan, "Charles A. Lindbergh: Making of a Hero," *Resistance*, No. 7 (Summer 1996), pp. 42–46; Kees van Rijn, "The Story of a Waffen SS Soldier," *Resistance*, No. 7 (Summer 1996), pp. 24–32.

23. "A People without Vision," *Resistance*, No. 2 (Summer 1994), p. 27.

24. Friedrich Nietzsche, *Twilight of the Idols* and *The Anti-Christ*, edited by R. J. Hollingdale (Harmondsworth, U.K.: Penguin, 1968), pp. 115–87.

25. Ragnar Redbeard's identity remains a mystery to this day. However, one editor has suggested that he was the New Zealand poet and radical politician, Arthur Desmond (1842?–1927?), who later lived in Sydney, London and Chicago. S. E. Parker, "Ragnar Redbeard and the Right of Might," in Ragnar Redbeard, *Might Is Right; or The survival of the fittest* (Port Townsend, Wash.: Loompanics, 1984), pp. i–vi.

26. Redbeard, *Might Is Right*, pp. 22f.

27. Aaron Garland, "RAHOWA: Heeding the Call of a Cultural Imperative," *Ohm Clock Magazine*, No. 4 (Spring 1996), pp. 4–8.

28. Redbeard, "The Logic of To-Day," *Might Is Right*, pp. 150–52.

29. Gavin Baddeley, *Lucifer Rising: Sin, Devil Worship and Rock 'n' Roll* (London: Plexus, 1999), pp. 123–26.

30. Baddeley, *Lucifer Rising*, pp. 191–93.

31. Hofding Warge and Wiking Herske, "A Blaze in the Northern Sky," *The Heretic*, No. 10 (October 1994), pp. 1–3. For further background on Varg Víkernes and Burzum, see Kadmon, *Oskorei*, *Aorta*, No. 20 (1995). The story of Víkernes, Euronymous and the black metal scene in Norway is documented in detail by Michael Moynihan and Didrik Søderlind, *Lords of Chaos: The Bloody Rise of the Satanic Metal Underground* (Venice, Calif.: Feral House, 1998).

32. Vargr Víkurnes Lárusson, "Draupnir (Odhinn's Ring)," "Wotan Mit Uns," "The Quintessence," "Hamingja," and "Seidhr ok Galdr," *Filosofem* 1, Nos. 1–4 (1994), pp. 3, 4, 6–7, 8, 9.

33. Moynihan and Søderlind, *Lords of Chaos*, pp. 157–59, 162–66.

34. "Spear of Longinus—Interview," *Key of Alocer*, No. 4, pp. 4–8; Wulf Grimwald, "Satanism and Nazism," *Key of Alocer*, No. 4, pp. 34–36; David Myatt, "The Harmony of National-Socialism" and "What Is Aryan?" *Key of Alocer*, No. 6, pp. 10–11, 16–17; Scorpius, "Magik against Democracy," *Key of Alocer*, No. 6, pp. 14–15; "The Dutch SS," *Trumpeter of Evil*, No. 1 (1996), pp. [11–13].

35. Stephen O. Malley, "Nordic Darkness . . . ," *Resistance*, No. 5 (Fall 1995), pp. 28–30.

36. "The Thousand Swords of Graveland," *Resistance*, No. 7 (Summer 1996), pp. 52–55.

37. The background of the murder and the inspiration of the band Absurd are documented in Liane von Billerbeck and Frank Nordhausen, *Satanskinder: Der Mordfall Sandro B.* (Berlin: Ch. Links Verlag, 1994). See also the chapter "Furor Teutonicus" and the Möbus interview in Moynihan and Søderlind, *Lords of Chaos*, pp. 241–66.

38. Devin Burghart and Justin Massa, "Nazi Black Metal Leader Arrested in the US," *Searchlight*, No. 304 (October 2000), pp. 12–13.

39. "Black Circle," *Searchlight*, No. 288 (June 1999), pp. 14–15.

40. "Antihuman: Misanthropy Records," *Searchlight*, No. 288 (June 1999), pp. 16–17.

41. Kadmon, *Blood Axis*, *Aorta*, No. 19 (1995), pp. [21–26]; "Blood Axis: An interview with Michael Moynihan," *The Heretic*, No. 10 (October 1994), pp. 21–26.

42. *Siege: The Collected Writings of James Mason*, edited and introduced by Michael M. Jenkins [i.e., Moynihan] (Denver: Storm Books, 1992), passim, especially chapter 1 (pp. 1–80).

43. Michael Moynihan, "Charles Manson," *Seconds*, No. 32 (1995), pp. 64–74.

44. Michael Moynihan, "Aurora: Where Light Becomes Darkness and Evil Is Good: An Esoteric Inquiry into Hermann Hesse's *Demian*, Gnosticism, Fascism, and the Indo-European World-View," *Filosofem* 1, Nos. 1–4 (1994), pp. 18–22, since reprinted in *Ohm Clock*, No. 4 (Spring 1996), pp. 16–18; idem, "Dionysos-Dithyramben: The Faustian Spirit of Fascism from Oswald Spengler to Oswald Mosley," *Filofosem* 1, Nos. 1–4 (1994), pp. 40–47; idem, "Of Wolves and Death: An Investigation of the Wolf's Hook," *Filosofem* 2, Nos. 1–4 (1995), pp. 31–35.

45. For a detailed examination of both *Lords of Chaos* and Michael Moynihan, see Kevin Coogan, "How 'Black' is Black Metal? Michael Moynihan, *Lords of Chaos* and the 'Countercultural Fascist' Underground," *Hit List*, Vol. 1, No. 1 (February/March 1999), pp. 32–49, and the interview with Michael Moynihan in ibid., pp. 50–53. See also an exchange between Feral House publisher Adam Parfrey and Kevin Coogan in *Hit List*, Vol. 1, No. 3 (June/July 1999), pp. 5–7. For Moynihan's reaction to Coogan's article, see his interview, "Michael Moynihan: From Abraxas to Nietzsche," *Eye*, No. 23 (September/October 1999), pp. 27–35. Coogan's response appears in *Hit List*, Vol. 1, No. 4 (September/October 1999), pp. 10–12. For an article distancing Michael Moynihan from neo-Nazism, see Zach Dundas, "Lord of Chaos," *Williamett Week*, Vol. 26, No. 41 (16 August 2000), pp. 24–32.

46. The *Aorta* tract series (1994–95) comprises the following titles: No. 1, *Lucifer Rising*; No. 2, *Konnersreuth*; No. 3, *Calanda*; No. 4, *Anubis* (Joseph Beuys); No. 5, *Rudolf Schwarzkogler*; No. 6, *Karl Maria Wiligut*; No. 7, *Katharsis* (Otto Rahn); No. 8, *Castel del Monte*; No. 9, *Corneliu Codreanu*; No. 10, *The Blue Light* (Leni Riefenstahl); No. 11, *Montségur*; No. 12, *Medicine of Metals* (Z'ev); No. 13, *Storm Songs* (the magical war of English witches in August 1940); No. 14, *Blood Lamp* (the pagan cult in Munich around

1900); No. 15, *Leonora Carrington*; No. 16, *Angizia*; No. 17, *Fidus* (the theosophic and ariosophic painter and temple artist); No. 18, *Mithras*; No. 19, *Blood Axis*; No. 20, *Oskorei* (Vargr Víkernes). The *Ahnstern* series (1996–) includes No. 1, *Viktor Schauberger*; No. 2, *Lucifer Rising II*; No. 3, *Baptism of Fire* (Ernst Jünger); No. 4, *Hidden World*; No. 5, *Heathen Homeland*; No. 7, *Field of Force*; No. 8, *Feathered Dreams*; No. 9, *The Flying Disks of Joseph Andreas Epp*.

47. Review of "Walked in Line/Ernting," *The Flaming Sword*, No. 3 (August 1994), p. 19; the booklet accompanying the CD, *The Gospel of Inhumanity*, features a photograph of Marienkamp-Szt. Balázs, Lanz's ONT temple in Hungary; Storm flyer.

48. Reports in *The Times*, 22 April 1999, and *The Daily Telegraph*, 22 April 1999; "A Clique within a Clique, Obsessed with Guns, Death and Hitler," *The Guardian*, 22 April 1999, p. 3. See also Niall Ferguson, "The Birthday Boys," *Sunday Telegraph Review*, 25 April 1999, pp. 1–2.

49. Reports in *Independent on Sunday*, 25 February 1996, p. 3, and *Daily Mail*, 27 February 1996, pp. 1, 6; John Mullin and Martin Walker, "Deadliest of Friends," *The Guardian*, Part 2, 26 February 1996, pp. 1–2; *Searchlight*, No. 250 (April 1996), p. 3. The C18 obituary appeared in *Putsch* (March 1996).

50. Quoted in *National Vanguard Books Catalog*, No. 19 (June 2000), p. 65.

51. Devin Burghart and Justin Massa, "Nazi Black Metal Leader Arrested in the US," *Searchlight*, No. 304 (October 2000), pp. 12–13.

NOTES TO CHAPTER 11

1. The most complete biography to date of Aleister Crowley is John Symonds, *The King of the Shadow Realm: Aleister Crowley: His Life and Magic* (London: Duckworth, 1989). A briefer but reliable study is Francis King, *The Magical World of Aleister Crowley* (London: Weidenfeld and Nicolson, 1977).

2. James Webb, *The Occult Establishment* (La Salle, Ill.: Open Court, 1976), pp. 494–96.

3. Gerald Suster, *Hitler and the Age of Horus* (New York: St. Martin's Press, 1981).

4. Two biographies of Anton Szandor LaVey provide details of his varied career and a stylized account of the Church of Satan. Burton H. Wolfe, *The Devil's Avenger: A Biography of Anton Szandor LaVey* (New York: Pyramid, 1974), and Blanche Barton, *The Secret Life of a Satanist: The Authorized Biography of Anton LaVey* (Los Angeles: Feral House, 1990). For the best scholarly history of the Church of Satan, see Massimo Introvigne, *Il cappello del mago: I nuovi movimenti magici dallo spiritismo al satanismo* (Carnago: Sugarco Edizioni, 1990), pp. 386–94, and *Indagine sul satanismo: Satanisti e antisatanisti dal Seicento ai nostri giorni* (Milan: Arnoldo Mondadori, 1994), pp. 265–91.

5. Anton Szandor LaVey, *The Satanic Bible* (New York: Avon Books, 1969), pp. 25–35.

6. Anton Szandor LaVey, *The Satanic Rituals* (New York: Avon Books, 1972), pp. 106–30.

7. Introvigne, *Indagine sul satanismo*, pp. 311–20.

8. Anton Long [i.e., David Myatt], *Diablerie: Revelations of a Satanist* (Shrewsbury, U.K.: Thormynd Press, 1991), [pp. 8–9].

9. David Myatt, *Cosmic Reich: The Life and Thoughts of David Myatt* (Paraparaumu Beach, New Zealand: Renaissance Press, 1995), p. 1.

10. Long, *Diablerie*, [p. 10].

11. "David Myatt and the Occult-Fascist Axis," *Searchlight*, No. 241 (July 1995), pp. 6–7.

12. Long, *Diablerie*, [pp. 16f, 27].

13. "An Interview with Christos Beest," *The Heretic*, No. 8 (April 1994), pp. 11–18 (p. 11).

14. ONA, "Satanism, Blasphemy and the Black Mass" (1974), reprinted in *The Heretic*, No. 9 (July 1994), pp. 25–27.

15. "Diabolic Etymology" in *Hostia: Secret Teachings of the O.N.A.*, 3 vols. (Shrewsbury, U.K.: Thormynd Press, 1992), vol. 1, p. 29.

16. "Satanism—The Sinister Shadow, Revealed" and "A Gift for the Prince—A Guide to Human Sacrifice," in *Hostia*, vol. 1, pp. 14–16 and 51–52; "Satanism, Sacrifice and Crime: The Satanic Truth" and "Guidelines for the Testing of Opfers," in *Hysteron Proteron: The Inner Teachings of the O.N.A.* (Shrewsbury, U.K.: Thormynd Press, 1992), pp. 9–11, 14–15.

17. Stephen Brown [i.e., David Myatt], *The Satanic Letters of Stephen Brown* (Shrewsbury, U.K.: Thormynd Press, 1992), pp. 11–17.

18. "The Seven-Fold Way: A Comprehensive Guide," in *Hostia*, vol. 1, pp. 7–9.

19. "Hangster's Gate," in *Hostia*, vol. 1, pp. 76–77, and "Black Rhadley," in *Fenrir 4*, No. 1 (July 1996), p. 3.

20. "Aeons and Their Associated Civilizations," in *Hostia*, vol. 1, pp. 106–7.

21. "Aeonics and Heresy" and "The Nazarene/Magian Ethos," in *Hostia*, vol. 1, 111–12, 113–15.

22. David Myatt, *Vindex: The Destiny of the West* (Reedy, W.Va.: Liberty Bell Publications, 1984), pp. 10–12.

23. Myatt, *Vindex*, pp. 17–18; "Aeonic Magick—General Notes," "Aeonics: Secret Tradition I" and "Aeonics: Secret Tradition II," in *Hostia*, vol. 1, pp. 107–8, 118–22, 109–10.

24. "Aeonics: Secret Tradition II," in *Hostia*, vol. 1, p. 110; "The Nazarene/Magian Ethos," in ibid., vol. 1, p. 114.

25. "An Interview with David Myatt," in *Cosmic Reich: The Life and Thoughts of David Myatt*, pp. 1–9 (p. 3).

26. For biographical details, see Long, *Diablerie*. A sanitized account is given in David Myatt, "A Political Re-awakening," *Spearhead*, No. 307 (September 1994), pp. 12–14.

27. *Searchlight*, No. 104 (February 1984), pp. 4–5, and No. 106 (April 1984), p. 6.

28. The titles of the series are as follows:

   I *National-Socialism: Principles and Ideals* (Shrewsbury, 1993)
   II *The Truth about National-Socialism and Adolf Hitler* (Shrewsbury, 1994)

III *Honour, Loyalty and Duty: an Introduction to National-Socialism* (Shrewsbury, 1994)

IV *The Nobility of National-Socialism* (Shrewsbury, 1994)

V *The Wisdom of National-Socialism* (Shrewsbury, 1994)

VI *The Galactic Empire: National-Socialism and the Conquest of the Final Frontier* (Shrewsbury, 1994)

VII *The Numinosity of National-Socialism* (Hereford, 1995)

VIII *The Enlightenment of National-Socialism* (Hereford, 1995)

IX *The Religion of National-Socialism* (Hereford, 1995)

X *The Divine Revelation of Adolf Hitler* (Hereford, 1995)

XI *The Revolutionary Holy War of National-Socialism*

XII *National-Socialism, Morality and Justice*

XIII *The Aryan Warrior: Brief Guidelines for the National-Socialist Revolutionary*

XIV *Vision of a Future Golden Age: National-Socialism and the Importance of Honour*

XV *Future Reich: National-Socialism, Order and the Triumph of Individual Will*

29. David Myatt, "The Galactic Empire and the Triumph of National-Socialism," in *Cosmic Reich: The Life and Thoughts of David Myatt*, pp. 20–24. David Myatt, "The Galactic Empire," in *The Black Order: An Introduction for Prospective Members* (Paraparaumu Beach, New Zealand: Renaissance Press, 1995), pp. 34–35.

30. *The National-Socialist*, No. 2 (March–April 1995), pp. 1–8, No. 5 (August–September 1995), pp. 1–4.

31. *The National-Socialist*, No. 17 (9 November 1996), p. 2.

32. "Reichsfolk—Toward a New Elite," leaflet (York, U.K.: Reichsfolk, 1996).

33. *Das Reich*, No. 3 (November 1996), pp. 2, 5–7.

34. "Britain in 1995: Watershed on the Far Right," *Searchlight*, No. 241 (July 1995), pp. 2–4, and "David Myatt and the Occult-Fascist Axis," ibid., pp. 6–7.

35. *Western Magick and the Way of the Warrior: An Introduction to The Fraternity of the Jarls of Bælder* (Reading, U.K.: Fraternity Bælder, 1991, 1993).

36. Stephen B. Cox, *Spartanus: Sports Warrior Ethos of the New Aeon* (Reading: Coxland Press, 1995), pp. 15–16.

37. "The European Library: A Complete Inventory and Guidance Notes," No. 6 (Autumn Equinox 1994).

38. "An Interview with Christian Bouchet," *The Nexus*, No. 6 (November 1996), pp. 1–6.

39. *Sinistra Vivendi* (Paraparaumu Beach, New Zealand: Realist Publications, 1995), pp. 1–7.

40. *The Black Order: An Introduction for Prospective Members* (Paraparaumu Beach, New Zealand: Renaissance Press, 1995), pp. 1–3; "Black Order: Strategy and Tactics," *The Flaming Sword*, No. 1 (January 1994), p. 14; [Kerry Raymond Bolton], *Black Axis: Satanism and Fascism* (Paraparaumu Beach, New Zealand: Renaissance Press, 1995), pp. ii–iii. Lodge news in *The Flaming Sword*, No. 3 (August 1994), pp. 21–22; No. 4 (November 1994), pp. 10–11; No. 5 (February 1995), pp. 25–26; No. 6 (May 1995), pp. 6–7.

41. Kerry Raymond Bolton, "The Foundations of the Twenty-First Century," *Filosofem* 2 (1995), pp. 40–44.

42. [Kerry Raymond Bolton], *Realpolitik: A Satanic Political Science Primer* (Paraparaumu Beach, New Zealand: Realist Publications, 1994), pp. 1–14. A further polemic against "libertarian," individualist Satanism appears in [Kerry Raymond Bolton], *Black Axis: Satanism and Fascism*, pp. 6–20.

43. "Third Way and Third World against the New World Order," *The Nexus*, No. 11 (February 1998), pp. 13–15.

44. "National Revolutionary Faction: An Interview with Troy Southgate," *The Nexus*, No. 13 (August 1998), pp. 13–19.

45. "Stalin: A Perspective from the Summit of Realpolitik," *The Nexus*, No. 15 (February 1999), pp. 1–4.

46. "Return of the Ksatriya: India Challenges the New World Order," *The Nexus*, No. 13 (August 1998), pp. 1–2; "Malaysia Defies Usurers," *The Nexus*, No. 14 (November 1998), pp. 1–2; "Lessons from Kossovo," *The Nexus*, No. 18 (November 1999), pp. 7–8.

47. Peter Georgacarakos, "Paganism: An Aryan Science," *Crossing the Abyss*, No. 3 (Autumn Equinox 1997), pp. 27–32; idem, "The Valknut as Psychogenesis," *Crossing the Abyss*, No. 4 (Summer 1998), pp. 32–37.

NOTES TO CHAPTER 12

1. Kevin Flynn and Gary Gerhardt, *The Silent Brotherhood: The Chilling Inside Story of America's Violent Anti-Government Militia Movement*, 2d ed. (New York: Penguin, 1995), pp. 77–78.

2. Quoted in *Evening Standard* (London), 20 March 1998, p. 25.

3. Betty Dobratz and Stephanie L. Shanks-Meile, *"White Power, White Pride!": The White Separatist Movement in the United States* (New York: Twayne Publishers, 1997), p. 81.

4. Michael Barkun, *Religion and the Racist Right: The Origins of the Christian Identity Movement*, rev. ed. (Chapel Hill: University of North Carolina Press, 1997), pp. 6–11.

5. Barkun, *Religion and the Racist Right*, pp. 29–40.

6. John Wilson, *Lectures on Our Israelitish Origin*, 5th ed. (London: James Nisbet, 1876), pp. 111, 189, 368.

7. Barkun, *Religion and the Racist Right*, pp. 38, 126–27.

8. Barkun, *Religion and the Racist Right*, pp. 49–54.

9. Lothrop Stoddard, "The Pedigree of Judah," *Forum* 75 (March 1926), 324–25, 329–31.

10. Michael Barkun, *Religion and the Racist Right*, pp. 140–42, 128–30.

11. H. Ben Judah [pseud.], *When?: A Prophetical Novel of the Very Near Future* (Vancouver: British Israel Association of Greater Vancouver, 1944), pp. 77, 88, quoted in Michael Barkun, *Religion and the Racist Right*, p. 134.

12. C. F. Parker, *A Short History of Esau-Edom in Jewry*, 2d ed. (London: Covenant

Publishing Company, 1949), pp. 77, 88, quoted in Barkun, *Religion and the Racist Right*, p. 135.

13. Barkun, *Religion and the Racist Right*, p. 135.

14. Barkun, *Religion and the Racist Right*, p. 146.

15. Barkun, *Religion and the Racist Right*, pp. 159–70.

16. H. Ben Judah [pseud.], *When?: A Prophetical Novel of the Very Near Future* (Vancouver: British Israel Association of Greater Vancouver, 1944), pp. 69–71, 73–74.

17. Conrad Gaard, *Spotlight on the Great Conspiracy* (Steilacoon: Wash.: Destiny of America Foundation, n.d.), pp. 1, 4.

18. William Potter Gale, "The Faith of Our Fathers" (January 1974), p. 2, quoted in Michael Barkun, *Religion and the Racist Right*, pp. 181–82.

19. Wesley Swift, *Testimony of Tradition and the Origin of Races* (Hollywood, Calif.: New Christian Crusade Church, n.d.), pp. 9–10, 13, 19, 25, 29 and "Who Are the Jews," *Christian Vanguard* No. 64 (April 1977), pp. 9–10, quoted in Michael Barkun, *Religion and the Racist Right*, pp. 183–84.

20. Revelation 17:4–5.

21. Wesley Swift, "With Violence Shall Babylon Be Cast Down," *Christian Vanguard* No. 86 (February 1979), pp. 5–6, quoted in Michael Barkun, *Religion and the Racist Right*, p. 185.

22. Butler is quoted in James Aho, *The Politics of Righteousness: Idaho Christian Patriotism* (Seattle: University of Washington Press, 1990), p. 55.

23. Kevin Flynn and Gary Gerhardt, *The Silent Brotherhood*, pp. 65–67.

24. Frederick J. Simonelli, *American Fuehrer: George Lincoln Rockwell and the American Nazi Party* (Urbana and Chicago: University of Illinois Press, 1999), pp. 116–17, 120.

25. Robert G. Butler, "This is *Aryan Nations*" (Hayden Lake, Idaho: Church of Jesus Christ Christian, [1980s]).

26. Richard G. Butler, "Twelve Foundation Stones to Establish a State for Our Aryan Racial Nation" (Hayden Lake, Idaho: Aryan Nations [1980s]) and "Aryan Nations Theopolitical Platform" (Hayden Lake, Idaho: Aryan Nations [1980s]).

27. Michael Barkun, *Religion and the Racist Right*, pp. 213–17.

28. Bernard Comparet, "Russia in Bible Prophecy," *Christian Vanguard* No. 123 (March 1982), quoted in Michael Barkun, *Religion and the Racist Right*, pp. 108–10.

29. Kevin Flynn and Gary Gerhardt, *The Silent Brotherhood* offers an extensive narrative account of The Order, its members and operations.

30. Michael Barkun, *Religion and the Racist Right*, pp. 228–33.

31. Kevin Flynn and Gary Gerhardt, *The Silent Brotherhood*, pp. 422–23.

32. Jeffrey Kaplan, *Radical Religion in America: Millenarian Movements from the Far Right to the Children of Noah* (Syracuse: Syracuse University Press, 1997), pp. 62–63; Kevin Flynn and Gary Gerhardt, *The Silent Brotherhood*, pp. 429–30.

33. Jack B. Moore, *Skinheads Shaved for Battle: A Cultural History of American Skinheads* (Bowling Green: Bowling Green State University Popular Press, 1993), p. 104.

34. Associated Press report by Nicholas K. Geranios, Spokane, 24 October 2000.

35. "The Church of the Creator: Creed of Hate" (New York: Anti-Defamation League, 1993); Leonard Zeskind, "Heart of Whiteness," *Searchlight*, No. 290 (August 1999), pp. 6–7.

36. Ben Klassen, *Against the Evil Tide: An Autobiography* (Otto, N.C.: Church of the Creator, 1991), pp. 4f, 13f, 24–32, 42–59, 96–98, 147–59.

37. Klassen, *Against the Evil Tide*, pp. 293–94.

38. Klassen, *Against the Evil Tide*, pp. 295–99, 305–7, 323–39, 362–68.

39. Klassen, *Against the Evil Tide*, pp. 376–78.

40. *Fort Lauderdale News*, 18 November 1970, quoted in *The Klassen Letters Volume One, 1969–1976* (Otto, N.C.: Church of the Creator, 1988), p. 34.

41. "Nationalist White Party: Our Creed: Fourteen Points," *The Klassen Letters Volume One, 1969–1976*, pp. 35–41 (pp. 36–37).

42. Letters to General P.A. Del Valle dated 13 and 26 April 1971, *The Klassen Letters Volume One, 1969–1976*, pp. 61–66 (p. 66); Ben Klassen, *Against the Evil Tide*, pp. 392–97.

43. Letters to Eleanor Kramer dated 16 June and 5 August 1971, *The Klassen Letters Volume One, 1969–1976*, pp. 68–73; Ben Klassen, *Against the Evil Tide*, pp. 408–9.

44. Ben Klassen, *Nature's Eternal Religion* (Niceville, Fla.: Church of the Creator, 1973), pp. 4–38.

45. Klassen, *Nature's Eternal Religion*, pp. 42–48, 94–95.

46. Klassen, *Nature's Eternal Religion*, p. 277; cf. *The Klassen Letters Volume One, 1969–1976*, p. 202.

47. Klassen, *Nature's Eternal Religion*, pp. 50, 296–302.

48. Klassen, *Trials, Tribulations and Triumphs* (Niceville, Fla.: Church of the Creator, 1993), pp. 226–33.

49. Klassen, *Rahowa! This Planet is All Ours* (Otto, N.C.: Church of the Creator, 1987).

50. J. Lanz-Liebenfels, *Theozoologie oder die Kunde von den Sodoms-Äfflingen und dem Götterelektron* (Vienna: Moderner Verlag, [1905]), pp. 158f, quoted in Nicholas Goodrick-Clarke, *The Occult Roots of Nazism: Secret Aryan Cults and Their Influence on Nazi Ideology* (New York: New York University Press, 1992), pp. 97–98.

51. Matt Hale, "The Growing Mayhem of Decadent America," *The Struggle*, No. 26; "The Insane Teaching of 'Equality,'" *The Struggle*, No. 56; "Reclaiming our White Culture," *The Struggle*, No. 64.

52. Jeffrey Kaplan, "Right-Wing Violence in North America," in *Terror from the Extreme Right*, edited by Tore Bjørgo (London: Frank Cass, 1995), pp. 44–95; Jeffrey Kaplan, *Radical Religion in America: Millenarian Movements from the Far Right to the Children of Noah* (Syracuse, New York: Syracuse University Press, 1997), pp. 1–10, 32–42, 46–68; Jeffrey Kaplan, "Religiosity and the Radical Right: Towards the Creation of a New Ethnic Identity," in *Nation and Race: The Developing Euro-American Racist Subculture*, edited by Jeffrey Kaplan and Tore Bjørgo (Boston, Mass: Northeastern University Press, 1998), pp. 102–25.

NOTES TO CHAPTER 13

1. Nicholas Goodrick-Clarke, *The Occult Roots of Nazism: Secret Aryan Cults and Their Influence on Nazi Ideology: The Ariosophists of Austria and Germany, 1890–1935* (New York: New York University Press, 1992), pp. 39, 49f, 129–30.

2. Alfred Müller, *Die neugermanischen Religionsbildungen der Gegenwart: Ihr Werden und Wesen* (Bonn: Ludwig Röhrscheid, 1934), pp. 20–25. Two earlier surveys of German neopaganism in the Weimar era are Alfons Steiger, *Der neudeutsche Heide im Kampf gegen Christen und Juden* (Berlin: Verlag der "Germania," 1924), and Erhard Schlund, *Neugermanisches Heidentum im heutigen Deutschland* (Munich: Franz A. Pfeiffer, 1924).

3. A full bibliography of *völkisch* writers on neo-Germanic religion is provided in Armin Mohler, *Die konservative Revolution in Deutschland 1918–1932: Ein Handbuch* (Darmstadt: Wissenschaftliche Buchgesellschaft, 1972), pp. 375–88.

4. Müller, *Die neugermanischen Religionsbildungen der Gegenwart*, pp. 49–51.

5. Carl Gustav Jung, "Wotan," *Neue Schweizer Rundschau* 3 (March 1936), pp. 657–69. An English-language version of the article is published in *Civilization in Transition* (*The Collected Works of C. G. Jung*, vol. 10), translated by R. F. C. Hull, 2d ed. (London: Routledge and Kegan Paul, 1970), pp. 179–93.

6. Mattias Gardell, *Gods of the Blood: Race, Ethnicity and the Pagan Revival* (Durham, N.C.: Duke University Press, forthcoming). The majority of ensuing references to works by Else Christensen, A. Rud Mills, Wyatt Kaldenberg and Jost Turner are drawn from the chapter, "Wolf Age Pagans: The Odinist Call of Aryan Revolutionary Paganism," in Gardell.

7. A. Rud Mills, *The Call of Our Ancient Nordic Religion* (Melbourne: Author, 1957), pp. 3f.

8. Wyatt Kaldenberg, "A Short History of Odinism in the English Speaking World," *Pagan Revival*, No. 41 (1998), pp. 19–20.

9. Ulick Varange [i.e., Francis Parker Yockey], *Imperium: The Philosophy of History and Politics*, 3d ed. (Torrance, Calif.: Noontide Press, 1983), pp. 12, 305f.

10. Varange, *Imperium*, p. 378.

11. Varange, *Imperium*, p. 404.

12. Varange, *Imperium*, pp. 418–28.

13. Varange, *Imperium*, pp. 535–39.

14. Varange, *Imperium*, pp. 365f.

15. Christensen's debt to Yockey is evident from several articles: "Our View of History," *The Odinist*, No. 10 (December 1973), p. 1; "The Structure of History," *The Odinist*, No. 11 (March 1974), p. 1; and "More Yockey," *The Odinist*, No. 12 (June 1974), p. 1. Mills's inspiration was documented in "The Wisdom of A. Rud Mills," *The Odinist*, No. 65 (1982), p. 1.

16. Varange, *Imperium*, p. 373; Else Christensen, "Odinism—Religion of the New Age," *The Odinist*, No. 92 (1985).

17. Else Christensen, "Odinism—Religion of Relevance," *The Odinist*, No. 82 (1984).

18. Christensen, "Odinism—Religion of Relevance."

19. Else Christensen, "The Communitarian Imperative," *The Odinist*, No. 68 (1982).

20. Else Christensen, "Neo Tribalism," *The Odinist*, No. 43 (1979).

21. Else Christensen, "Racial Consciousness," *The Odinist*, No. 83 (1984).

22. Jeffrey Kaplan, *Radical Religion in America: Millenarian Movements from the Far Right to the Children of Noah* (Syracuse, N.Y.: Syracuse University Press, 1997), pp. 17–21.

23. Wyatt Kaldenberg, "A Short History of Odinism in the English Speaking World," *Pagan Revival*, No. 41 (1998), pp. 19–20.

24. Wyatt Kaldenberg, "Aryan Green Man Arise," *WAR* (June 1995).

25. Wyatt Kaldenberg, "Beyond Love and Hate," *WAR* (December 1998).

26. Wyatt Kaldenberg, undated letter to Brother Jerimy, *Pagan Revival*, No. 42 (1999), pp. 33–34.

27. Wyatt Kaldenberg, "Karmic Justice: A Pagan View of the Holocaust," *WAR* (March 1996).

28. Wyatt Kaldenberg, undated letter to Brother Gary, *Pagan Revival*, No. 41 (1998), pp. 47–48.

29. Wyatt Kaldenberg, undated letter to Brother Allen, *Pagan Revival*, No. 42 (1999), p. 45.

30. Wyatt Kaldenberg, undated letter to Brother D, *Pagan Revival*, No. 43 (2000), pp. 12–14.

31. T. Jost, "About the Author," *Aryan Kriya: The Science of Accelerated Evolution* (N. San Juan, Calif.: Author, 1995).

32. Jost, "Aryan Destiny: Back to the Land," undated e-text distributed by the National Socialist Kindred, quoted in Jeffrey Kaplan and Leonard Weinberg, *The Emergence of a Euro-American Radical Right* (New Brunswick, N.J.: Rutgers University Press, 1998), pp. 154–56.

33. "Folk and Fatherland: The Only Doctrine of National Socialism" (N. San Juan, Calif.: National Socialist Kindred, n.d.).

34. Jost, *The Essentials of Mein Kampf* (Volksberg, Calif.: National Socialist Kindred, 1988), quoted in Kaplan and Weinberg, *The Emergence of a Euro-American Radical Right*, p. 157.

35. Jost, "ARYAN DESTINY: Why Hitler Had to Be Overcome," National Socialist Kindred pamphlet, 1989, and "Love: An Eternal law of Nature and first Tenet of National Socialism," undated National Socialist Kindred flyer.

36. Jost, *Aryan Kriya: The Science of Accelerated Evolution* (N. San Juan, Calif.: Author), p. 17f.

37. Jost, *Aryan Kriya: The Science of Accelerated Evolution* (N. San Juan, Calif.: Author), p. 27f.

38. Jost, *Aryan Kriya: The Science of Accelerated Evolution* (N. San Juan, Calif.: Author), p. 13.

39. Jost, *Aryan Kriya: Guidelines for Aryan Kriya Training* (N. San Juan, Calif.: National Socialist Kindred, n.d.).

40. Jost, *Aryan Kriya: The Science of Accelerated Evolution*, pp. 8, 10.

41. Jost, *Purification of Body and Mind* (N. San Juan, Calif.: National Socialist Kindred, 1995), p. 13.

42. Jost, *Asana Kriya* (N. San Juan, Calif.: National Socialist Kindred, 1995), p. 1ff.

43. Jost, *Kundalini Pranayama Kriya* (N. San Juan, Calif.: National Socialist Kindred, 1995), p. 4.

44. Jost, *Kundalini Pranayama Kriya*, p. 10.

45. Kaplan and Weinberg, *The Emergence of a Euro-American Radical Right*, p. 158.

46. David Lane, "Auto-Biographical Portrait of the Life of David Lane and the 14 Word Motto," in *Deceived, Damned & Defiant: The Revolutionary Writings of David Lane* (St. Maries, Idaho: 14 Word Press, 1999), pp. 7–15.

47. Kevin Flynn and Gary Gerhardt, *The Silent Brotherhood: The Chilling Inside Story of America's Violent Anti-Government Militia Movement*, 2d ed. (New York: Penguin, 1995), pp. 116, 178, 258–59.

48. Flynn and Gerhardt, *The Silent Brotherhood*, p. 466.

49. David Lane, "Statement to the World by the Holy Order of the Bruder Schweigen," *Calling Our Nation*, No. 53 (1987), pp. 11–12, quoted in Michael Barkun, *Religion and the Racist Right: The Origins of the Christian Identity Movement*, rev. ed. (Chapel Hill, N.C.: University of North Carolina Press, 1997), p. 231.

50. David Lane, "88 Precepts," in *Deceived, Damned & Defiant*, pp. 83–99 [Precepts 14, 21, 22, 24] (p. 88).

51. David Lane, "Mystery Religions and the Seven Seals," in *Deceived, Damned & Defiant*, pp. 51–82.

52. David Lane, "White Genocide Manifesto," in *Deceived, Damned & Defiant*, pp. 1–6.

53. Colin Jordan, "Introduction," in Lane, *Deceived, Damned & Defiant*, pp. xvii–xxii.

54. Lane, "88 Precepts," p. 87.

55. David Lane, "Revolution by Number 14," in *Deceived, Damned & Defiant*, pp. 29–50 (pp. 30, 37f).

56. David Lane, "Now or Never," *Focus Fourteen* article reprinted in *Deceived, Damned & Defiant*, pp. 213–20 (p. 220).

57. Lane, "Revolution by Number 14," p. 46.

58. David Lane, "Race to Extinction," *Focus Fourteen* article reprinted in *Deceived, Damned & Defiant*, pp. 359–63 (p. 363).

59. Lane, "Mystery Religions and the Seven Seals," in *Deceived, Damned & Defiant*, pp. 51–82 (pp. 81–82).

60. Ron McVan, *Creed of Iron: Wotansvolk Wisdom* (St. Maries, Idaho: 14 Word Press, 1997), p. 20.

61. McVan, *Creed of Iron*, p. 29.

62. McVan, *Creed of Iron*, pp. 52–55.

63. Jung, "Wotan," pp. 179–93.

64. Letter of Carl Gustav Jung to Miguel Serrano, dated 14 September 1960, in

Miguel Serrano, *C. G. Jung and Hermann Hesse: A Record of Two Friendships*, translated by Frank MacShane (London: Routledge and Kegan Paul, 1966), p. 85.

65. Richard Noll, *The Jung Cult: Origins of a Charismatic Movement* (Princeton, N.J.: Princeton University Press, 1994), pp. 92–108; Richard Noll, *The Aryan Christ: The Secret Life of Carl Gustav Jung* (London: Macmillan, 1997), pp. 114–19, 125–33.

66. Noll, *The Aryan Christ*, pp. 141–43.

67. McVan, *Creed of Iron*, pp. 34–37.

68. McVan, *Creed of Iron*, pp. 154–67.

69. McVan, *Temple of Wotan: Holy Book of the Aryan Tribes* (St. Maries, Idaho: 14 Word Press, 2000), pp. xv, 174–78.

70. McVan, *Creed of Iron*, pp. 168–72 (p. 172).

NOTES TO CHAPTER 14

1. The Patriot/militia movement is extensively documented in Richard Abanes, *American Militias: Rebellion, Racism & Religion* (Downers Grove, Ill.: InterVarsity Press, 1996).

2. Quoted in Ed Vulliamy, "Cults 2: Militias," *The Observer Magazine* (London), 21 May 1995, pp. 20–24 (p. 22).

3. Linda Thompson's background is described in Richard Abanes, *American Militias*, pp. 120–22.

4. Jim Keith, *Black Helicopters over America: Strikeforce for the New World Order* (Lilburn, Ga.: IllumiNet Press, 1994); Jim Keith, *Black Helicopters II: The Endgame Strategy* (Lilburn, Ga.: IllumiNet Press, 1998).

5. Jim Keith, *OKBomb! Conspiracy and Cover-up* (Lilburn, Ga.: IllumiNet Press, 1996), pp. 189–202. For the full account of McVeigh's ideological motivation, see Lou Michel and Dan Herbeck, *American Terrorist: Timothy McVeigh and the Oklahoma City Bombing* (New York: HarperCollins, 2001).

6. For the life, works and influence of Nesta Webster, see Richard Gilman, *Behind World Revolution: The Strange Career of Nesta H. Webster* (Ann Arbor, Mich.: Insights Books, 1982). Mrs. Webster's books *World Revolution* (1921) and *Secret Societies and Subversive Movements* (1924) exercised a major influence on the John Birch Society.

7. J. M. Roberts, *The Mythology of the Secret Societies* (London: Martin Secker and Warburg, 1972), pp. 118–30.

8. Roberts, *The Mythology of the Secret Societies*, pp. 118–30.

9. The modern mythology of the Illuminati in America from the late eighteenth century to modern conspiracy theories is traced in Seymour Martin Lipset and Earl Raab, *The Politics of Unreason: Right-Wing Extremism in America 1790–1970* (London: Heinemann, 1971), pp. 35–38, 77–78, 135–36, 161, 180–82, 252–57, 279–82. A more recent study of the mythology is Neal Wilgus, *The Illuminoids: Secret Societies and Political Paranoia* (Santa Fe, N.M.: Sun Publishing Company, 1978).

10. Conspiracy-theory magazines abound in the United States. Sample titles include *The National Reporter* (Washington, D.C.), *Full Disclosure* (Ann Arbor, Michigan),

Critique: A Journal of Conspiracies and Metaphysics (Santa Rosa, California), *Covert Action Information Bulletin* (Washington, D.C.) and *The Conspiracy Tracker* (Paterson, New Jersey). Many others are devoted to revelations about the assassinations and deaths of public figures such as John F. Kennedy and Marilyn Monroe.

11. William Cooper, *Behold a Pale Horse* (Sedona, Ariz.: Light Technology, 1991), pp. 6–27.

12. Cooper, *Behold a Pale Horse*, p. 27.

13. Cooper, *Behold a Pale Horse*, p. 39.

14. Cooper, *Behold a Pale Horse*, p. 37.

15. Cooper, *Behold a Pale Horse*, p. 80. William Cooper's speculations are derived from such underground conspiracy classics as William Bramley, *The Gods of Eden* (San Jose, Calif.: Dahlin Family Press, 1989); William Guy Carr, *Pawns in the Game* (Palmdale, Calif.: Omni Publications, n.d.); Arkon Daraul, *A History of Secret Societies* (New York: Citadel Press, 1961); A. Ralph Epperson, *The New World Order* (Tucson, Ariz.: Publius Press, 1990).

16. Cooper, *Behold a Pale Horse*, pp. 84–85, 92.

17. Cooper, *Behold a Pale Horse*, pp. 92–94.

18. Cooper, *Behold a Pale Horse*, pp. 110–15.

19. Cooper, *Behold a Pale Horse*, pp. 128–50.

20. Cooper, *Behold a Pale Horse*, pp. 165–76.

21. Cooper, *Behold a Pale Horse*, pp. 115–17.

22. Cooper, *Behold a Pale Horse*, pp. 196–214, 220–35.

23. Ed Vulliamy, "Cults 2: Militias," p. 22. The UFO and secret government mythologies surrounding Area 51 are documented in Phil Patton, *Travels in Dreamland: The Secret History of Area 51* (London: Orion, 1997); revised edition as *Dreamland: Travels Inside the Secret World of Roswell and Area 51* (New York: Villard, 1998); and David Darlington, *The Dreamland Chronicles: The Legends of Area 51—America's Most Secret Military Base* (London: Little, Brown, 1998).

24. Cooper, *Behold a Pale Horse*, p. 73.

25. Samuel L. Blumenfeld, "Waco . . . the untold story," *Nexus* 2, No. 20 (June–July 1994), pp. 16–19; review, ibid., p. 65.

26. Linda Thompson, "F.E.M.A.," *Nexus* 2, No. 18 (February–March 1994), p. 16.

27. The unlikely career claims of Mark Koernke are examined in Abanes, *American Militias*, pp. 118–20.

28. Mark Koernke, "Towards the New World Order: America's Secret Police Force," *Nexus* 2, No. 18 (February–March 1994), pp. 11–15, 64–65.

29. Matthew Kalman and John Murray, "Icke and the Nazis," *Open Eye*, No. 3 (1995), p. 7.

30. David Icke, *The Robots' Rebellion: The Story of the Spiritual Renaissance* (Bath, U.K.: Gateway Books, 1994), pp. 195–235.

31. Icke, *The Robots' Rebellion*, p. 233.

32. Matthew Kalman and John Murray, "New-age Nazism," *New Statesman and Society*, 23 June 1995, pp. 18–20.

33. "The Australian Connection," *Searchlight*, No. 165 (March 1989), p. 3.

34. Jan van Helsing's book and their success in Germany and Austria are documented at length in Edvard Gugenberger, Franko Petri and Roman Schweidlenka, *Weltverschwörungstheorien: Die neue Gefahr von rechts* (Vienna: Franz Deuticke, 1998), Chapters Eight, Nine and Ten.

35. Jan van Helsing, *Geheimgesellschaften und ihre Macht im 20. Jahrhundert oder wie man die Welt nicht regiert: Ein Wegweiser durch die Verstrickungen von Logentum mit Hochfinanz und Politik. Trilaterale Kommission, Bilderberger, CFR, UNO* (Meppen, Germany: Ewertverlag, 1993), pp. 36, 43–49.

36. van Helsing, *Geheimgesellschaften und ihre Macht*, pp. 49, 51–57, 65–66.

37. van Helsing, *Geheimgesellschaften und ihre Macht*, pp. 91–95, 98–102.

38. van Helsing, *Geheimgesellschaften und ihre Macht*, pp. 104–10.

39. van Helsing, *Geheimgesellschaften und ihre Macht*, pp. 109, 115–17, 118–47.

40. Jan van Helsing, *Geheimgesellschaften 2. Interview mit Jan van Helsing: Die Verbindungen der Geheimregierung mit dem Dritten Weltkrieg, dem Schwarzen Adel, dem Club of Rome, AIDS, UFOs, Kaspar Hauser, der reichsdeutschen Dritten Macht, dem Galileo-Projekt, dem Montauk-Projekt, dem Jesus-Projekt, dem Anti-Christ u.v.m.* (Gran Canaria: Ewertverlag, 1995), pp. 87–95.

41. van Helsing, *Geheimgesellschaften und ihre Macht*, pp. 153, 155–56.

42. van Helsing, *Geheimgesellschaften 2*, pp. 80–86.

43. van Helsing, *Geheimgesellschaften und ihre Macht*, p. 170.

44. van Helsing, *Geheimgesellschaften 2*, pp. 101–15.

45. van Helsing, *Geheimgesellschaften 2*, pp. 124–35.

46. van Helsing, *Geheimgesellschaften 2*, pp. 142–54.

47. van Helsing, *Geheimgesellschaften 2*, pp. 164–73; van Helsing, *Geheimgesellschaften und ihre Macht*, p. 243.

48. van Helsing, *Geheimgesellschaften 2*, pp. 173–88. His response on the AIDS question is a verbatim translation of Cooper, *Behold a Pale Horse*, pp. 165–74.

49. van Helsing, *Geheimgesellschaften 2*, pp. 257–302. The MAJESTIC-12 report (pp. 265–302) is taken from Cooper, *Behold a Pale Horse*, pp. 196–235.

50. van Helsing, *Geheimgesellschaften 2*, pp. 232–50.

51. van Helsing, *Geheimgesellschaften 2*, pp. 250–54.

52. Charles Berlitz and William Moore, *The Philadelphia Experiment: Project Invisibility* (London: Souvenir Press, 1979), traces this fable to dubious correspondence from one Carlos Miguel Allende to Dr. Morris Ketchum Jessup in 1955–56.

53. Brad Steiger with Alfred Bielek and Sherry Hanson Steiger, *The Philadelphia Experiment and Other UFO Conspiracies* (New Brunswick, N.J.: Inner Light Publications, 1990).

54. Preston B. Nichols with Peter Moon, *The Montauk Project: Experiments in Time* (New York: Sky Books, 1992); Preston B. Nichols and Peter Moon, *Montauk Revisited: Adventures in Synchronicity* (New York: Sky Books, 1994); Preston B. Nichols and Peter Moon, *Pyramids of Montauk: Explorations in Consciousness* (New York: Sky Books, 1995).

55. Jan van Helsing, *Geheimgesellschaften 2*, pp. 307–20. Peter Moon, *The Black Sun: Montauk's Nazi-Tibetan Connection* (New York: Sky Books, 1997), pp. 91–96.

56. Don Gamalo and Jan van Helsing, *Der Fall Ewert/Van Helsing: Die Beschlagnahme. Dokumentation eines Ermittlungverfahrens* (Gran Canaria: Ewertverlag, 1997). Eduard Gugenberger, Franko Petri and Roman Schweidlenka, *Weltverschörungstheorien: Die neue Gefahr von rechts* (Vienna: Franz Deuticke Verlag, 1998), pp. 198–206.

NOTES TO THE CONCLUSION

1. Christian Joppke, *Immigration and the Nation-State: The United States, Germany, and Great Britain* (Oxford: Oxford University Press, 1999), pp. 150–53.

2. Jared Taylor, *Paved with Good Intentions: The Failure of Race Relations in Contemporary America* (New York: Carroll and Graf, 1992), pp. 34–44, 217–40.

3. Joppke, *Immigration and the Nation-State*, pp. 25–28.

4. Lothrop Stoddard, *The Rising Tide of Color against White World-Supremacy* (London: Chapman and Hall, 1923), pp. 251–55.

5. Peter Brimelow, *Alien Nation: Common Sense about America' Immigration Disaster* (New York: HarperPerennial, 1996), pp. 48–49.

6. Brimelow, *Alien Nation*, p. 219.

7. *The Future of Multi-Ethnic Britain: The Parekh Report of the Commission on the Future of Multi-Ethnic Britain*, established by The Runnymede Trust (London: Profile, 2000), p. 38.

Acknowledgments

The preparation of such an extensive study of the extreme right underground has been a journey of exploration often far removed from the clearly marked highways of university library catalogs and mainstream academic literature. I wish first to express my gratititude to Joscelyn Godwin, Richard Drake, Roger Eatwell, Hans Thomas Hakl, Karl Hüser, Mike Jay, Jeffery Kaplan, and Rüdiger Sünner, all of whom have offered helpful indications and valuable encouragement as I pursued my investigations. I should also like to acknowledge a special debt of thanks to Kevin Coogan. We have corresponded and discussed these topics with great profit since the early 1980s, and he was also kind enough to read and comment extensively on the earlier chapters of this book in manuscript.

In my chapter on Nordic racial paganism in modern America, I am indebted to Mattias Gardell, who has generously allowed me to make use of a chapter in his forthcoming work, *Gods of the Blood: Race, Ethnicity and the Pagan Revival*, to be published by Duke University Press.

Ultimately, my thanks are due to the individuals who have shared their own political beliefs and made materials available to me. These include Colin Jordan, Matt Koehl, William Pierce, Jim Saleam, Ernst Zündel, the late Wilhelm Landig, the late Willibald Mattern, Gerhard Petak (Kadmon), Michael Moynihan, Kerry Raymond Bolton, David Myatt, Katja Lane, Ron McVan, and Miguel Serrano. I also recall the hospitality and kindness of the late Rudolf Mund quite some years ago in Vienna.

I am grateful to Lorraine Woods for her assistance in preparing the section of photographic plates. Finally, I owe thanks to the librarians and staffs of the British Library, London; the Bodleian Library, Oxford; and the Wiener Library, London.

Index

357

About the Author

NICHOLAS GOODRICK-CLARKE is the author of several books on the Western esoteric tradition and ideology, including *Hitler's Priestess* and *The Occult Roots of Nazism: Secret Aryan Cults and Their Influence on Nazi Ideology*, which the *Times Literary Supplement* dubbed "an intriguing study of apocalyptic fantasies." It has remained in print since its publication in 1985 and has been translated into eight languages.

Dr. Goodrick-Clarke has been associated with the University of Oxford since 1975 and is now a full-time author and historian. He lives in a farmhouse on the Berkshire Downs in southern England.